Introduction to Corporate Finance

5 EDITION

Introduction to Corporate Finance

ALEX FRINO

AMELIA HILL

ZHIAN CHEN

5 EDITION

PEARSON

Pearson Australia
(a division of Pearson Australia Group Pty Ltd)
707 Collins Street, Melbourne, Victoria 3008
PO Box 23360, Melbourne, Victoria 8012
www.pearson.com.au

Acquisitions Editor: Karen Hutchings/Simone Bella
Senior Project Editor: Rebecca Pomponio
Development Editor: Katie Pittard
Editorial Coordinator: Aida Reyes/Germaine Silva
Production Controller: Rochelle Deighton
Copy Editor: Laura Davies
Proofreader: Ron Buck
Copyright and Pictures Editor: Lisa Woodland
Indexer: Olive Grove Indexing
Cover and internal design by designBite
Cover photograph from Shutterstock
Typeset by Midland Typesetters, Australia
Printed in Australia by the SOS Print + Media Group

National Library of Australia Cataloguing-in-publication entry

Author: Frino Alex.
Title: Introduction to corporate finance / Alex Frino, Amelia Hill, Zhian Chen.
Edition: 5th ed.

ISBN: 9781442542488 (pbk.)

Notes: Includes bibliographical references.
Subjects: Corporations – Finance.
Other Authors/Contributors: Chen, Zhian. Hill, Amelia.

Dewey Number 658.15

Pearson Australia Group Pty Ltd   ABN 40 004 245 943

Brief Contents

Contents

Foreword

It is my pleasure to welcome you to the fifth edition of *Introduction to Corporate Finance*. That a new edition is required so soon after the 2009 revision reflects the popularity of the book and rapid developments in corporate finance and Australian capital markets.

This book provides an excellent introduction to the basic principles of corporate finance through the derivations of the most important models and theories and straightforward explanations of each of them. I am attracted to the authors' application of models and theories to Australian corporate experience. The new chapter on working capital policies demonstrates the value loss to shareholders where a failure to adopt a sound working capital policy leads to insolvency and the forced sale of assets at a deep discount. In the risk management chapter, the authors have applied analytical modelling to hedging to illustrate the benefit or detriment of a program. While these policies are both known to and adopted by prudent boards, directors seldom appreciate the theoretical principles underpinning them.

Most Australian companies now operate in a global marketplace. Increasingly they are expanding their operations and seeking investment opportunities throughout the world. Irrespective of whether they operate in the financial services, resources or the service sector, they require graduates with a strong understanding of the principles of corporate finance.

Our business educators have also attracted cohorts of students from China and other parts of Asia to their institutions. It is important that Australian business schools provide high quality teaching to their students. This book is an important contribution to the delivery of that teaching and learning.

The authors of this book are distinguished researchers, teachers and practitioners. They combine a deep understanding of the workings of the Australian financial markets with outstanding theoretical and practical knowledge, and experience in Australia and other jurisdictions of corporate finance.

It has been a privilege to write the foreword to this highly regarded work.

I have learnt from reading it and hope that you will have a similar experience.

H Kevin McCann AM
Chairman
Macquarie Group Limited
Origin Energy Limited
Sydney, Australia
May 2012

Preface

This book began as a series of lecture notes and transcribed tapes that were edited for use by students. A large variety of sources were used in developing the original lecture material, which was then combined with knowledge drawn from our experience in industry to produce this book. Well-known overseas and Australian authors have written many corporate finance texts. The obvious question is: why do we need another? A problem with many of the existing texts is that they do not stick to one of the most important principles in practice: the KIS principle, Keep It Simple. Many texts are just too difficult and confusing. Feedback from thousands of students we have taught over the years has confirmed this. Some so-called introductory texts were in fact originally written for higher-level postgraduates. Others suffer from the rewrite bug, with earlier editions being better than later editions where authors have added complications, caveats, extensions and digressions. These changes tend to confuse and quite often distract students from the main issues at the start of their finance education.

Corporate finance is primarily about valuing companies. This book sets out a traditional model of valuation. It relies on the discounted cash flow approach combined with the capital asset pricing model. While this particular alternative has its problems, it is often used in industry. Indeed, one of the wealthiest and most successful investors of all time, Warren Buffett, uses a version of this approach to identify mispriced securities and continues to make winning investment decisions. Nonetheless, many other valuation techniques are used in industry. Unfortunately, most of them are chosen for expediency, and lack a sound theoretical base. For this reason, we do not discuss these techniques in detail.

A number of significant changes accompany the fifth edition of this book.

Consistent with the previous editions, we have attempted to avoid the rewrite bug. The main changes introduced to the new edition are as follows. First, the trading of shares on the Australian Securities Exchange (ASX) has undergone substantial transformation. Specifically, the ASX has introduced a completely new electronic trading system. Consequently, the chapter that describes how shares are traded (Chapter 9) has been completely re-written. Secondly, this book is full of current examples and statistics in an attempt to bring finance to life. Consequently, considerable effort has been expended in reworking all the practical examples and statistics in each chapter to bring them up to date. Thirdly, over 50 problems have been added to the end-of chapter questions to enable instructors to test the knowledge of students with new questions. Finally, a completely new chapter which discusses working capital management has been included. This chapter is motivated by the Global Financial Crisis which unearthed poor working capital management processes of major corporations.

We trust that you will enjoy learning and teaching from the fifth edition of our book.

Alex Frino
Amelia Hill
Zhian Chen

Acknowledgments

This book could not have been completed without the help of many people. We thank in particular Mike Aitken, Henk Berkman, Tim Brailsford, Rob Elstone, Les Hosking, Michael McKenzie, Bob Officer, Peter Swan and Terry Walter for helpful comments and suggestions on this and earlier editions of the book. We would also like to thank previous co-authors who helped update earlier editions, including Tony Cusak, Carole Comerton-Forde, Simone Kelly and Kent Wilson. Thanks also go to the staff at Pearson Australia, especially our editorial team Karen Hutchings, Simone Bella and Katie Pittard and the production team, led by Rebecca Pomponio, for their hard work and perseverance during the development and production of this edition.

Finally, we would also like to thank Julianne Bartels, Francesca Frino, David Gallagher, Elvis Jarnecic, David Forde, Agota Visnyei, Craig Mellare, Kate McCawe, Melissa Mendez, Vito Mollica, Angela Murphy, Kate Neuss, Ian Randall, Rizwan Rahman, Ken Swiss, Danika Wright, Paul Yeo, Darryl Young, Hui Zheng, Nick Hearn, Daniel Maroney and all our students over the years.

Our thanks also goes to the Technical Editor, John Gallacher as well as the following reviewers:

- Sarah Carrington, Deakin University
- Sisira Colombage, Monash University
- Mark Doolan, Queensland University of Technology
- Kym Fraser, University of South Australia
- Michael Gangemi, RMIT
- Shamlee Hasheem, Deakin University
- Peter Phillips, University Southern Queensland
- Lalith Seelanatha, Victoria University of Technology
- Bulend Terzioglu, Australian Catholic University
- Kathy Walsh, University of Sydney

HOW TO USE THIS BOOK

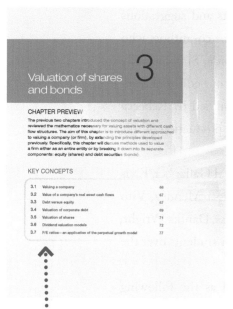

Key concepts Before you begin reading the chapter read the list of key concepts, which introduces the big-picture view of the chapter. Each key concept serves as the heading for a major section of the chapter.

Concept checks When you have finished reading a section, check your understanding by answering the concept check questions. If you can answer them (see *MyFinanceLab* to check your work), you are ready to move on.

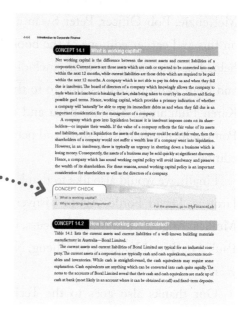

Practitioner's POV These features have been revised by finance practitioner Amelia Hill. Amelia was named one of Australia's Top 20 Equity Capital Markets Advisers by the East Coles survey in 2011, and one of Australia's Top 20 Investment Bankers in 2009. This feature will ensure that the business perspective is a dominant theme of your learning process.

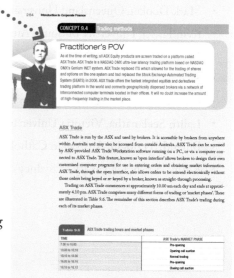

Key terms Definitions of key finance terms are provided in the margin close to the relevant text.

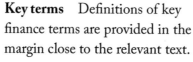

Finance Extra! To add immediacy and relevance to the discussion, 'Finance Extra!' boxes are provided throughout the text, highlighting real-life applications of the principles discussed.

Graded end-of-chapter problems End-of-chapter questions and problems are graded from *basic* to *intermediate* to *challenging* to enable you to build mastery and confidence as you work through them.

Case studies End-of-chapter case studies bring together the core concepts covered in the chapter, and provide you with practical questions to consider to help develop your critical thinking skills.

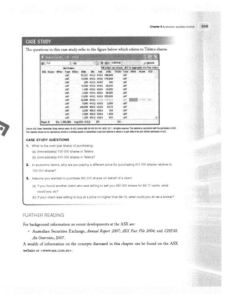

MyFinanceLab

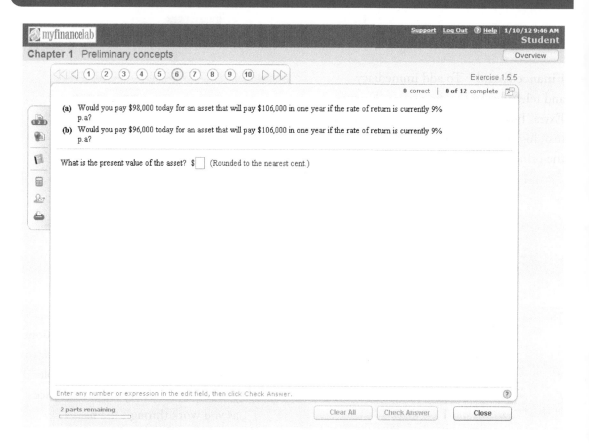

www.pearson.com.au/myfinancelab

MyFinanceLab is a fully integrated homework and tutorial system which solves one of the biggest teaching dilemmas in finance courses: students learn better when they practise by doing homework problems, but grading complex multi-part problems is time-consuming for the instructor. MyFinanceLab offers problems online, algorithmically generates values for extra practice, gives partial credit for sections of the questions students do get right and includes an online Gradebook.

The Frino MyFinanceLab content is authored by Tony Martin, lecturer in finance at La Trobe University. Tony holds a BSc in Computer Science from Monash University and an MFin from RMIT University. He has worked for many years on the development of online testing and the provision of online educational resources. His teaching focus is on introductory finance and financial institutions, and his research interests include equity markets, technical analysis and the use of genetic algorithms in the creation of trading strategies. Tony has authored a number of MyFinanceLabs for Pearson, including MyFinanceLab to accompany Berk and DeMarzo's

Fundamentals of Corporate Finance and MyFinanceLab to accompany Petty *Financial Management: Principles and Applications*.

Registering for MyFinanceLab with an access card

If your textbook came bundled with a MyFinanceLab access code, refer to the card for registration instructions.

Purchasing access

If your textbook did not come bundled with a MyFinanceLab access code, you can purchase an access code at **www.pearson.com.au/myfinancelab**.

Lecturer access

To organise a demonstration, training and/or access to MyFinanceLab, please contact your education consultant. If you are unsure of your consultant's details, please go to **www.pearson.com.au/customer-service/find-an-education-consultant**.

For the instructor

INSTRUCTOR'S MANUAL

This comprehensive teaching resource contains three key elements for each chapter:

1. A chapter orientation, which offers a simple statement of the author's intent for the chapter.
2. A chapter outline for easy reference to key issues.
3. Answers to all end-of-chapter questions in the text.

COMPUTERISED TEST BANK

Each chapter contains a substantial number of true–false, multiple-choice, short-answer, essay and matching questions. All questions have solutions, and the multiple-choice questions have been graded according to levels of difficulty.

POWERPOINT® SLIDES

To facilitate classroom presentation, a full set of PowerPoint® slides is available. The slides have been completely revised and updated.

About the authors

Alex Frino

Alex Frino is Professor in the School of Business at the University of Sydney and the Chief Executive Officer of the Capital Markets Cooperative Research Centre Limited. He holds an MPhil from Cambridge University and a PhD from the University of Sydney. Dr Frino has published over 100 articles in leading scholarly and professional finance journals including *Journal of Finance*, *Journal of Banking and Finance* and *Journal of Portfolio Management*. He has been the recipient of the prestigious Fulbright Senior Scholar Award, and has also held visiting appointments at the Commodity Futures Trading Commission in the USA and Australian Securities Exchange. He currently serves on the Disciplinary Tribunal of the Australian Securities Exchange.

Amelia Hill

Amelia Hill is a Managing Director at Moelis & Company. She holds a PhD and BEc (Hons) from the University of Sydney and received the University Medal in Finance. She is the author of several articles in leading scholarly journals including the *Journal of Banking and Finance*. Dr Hill specialises in capital markets and has advised on numerous initial public offerings, secondary offerings and private capital raisings for public and private companies. In 2011 she was named by the East Coles survey as one of Australia's Top 20 Equity Capital Markets Advisers and in 2009 as one of Australia's Top 20 Investment Bankers.

Zhian Chen

Zhian Chen is a senior lecturer in finance at the University of New South Wales. He holds a PhD from the University of New South Wales and an MComm from the University of Sydney. His teaching focus is introductory finance, and his research speciality is corporate finance and corporate governance.

Preliminary concepts

1

CHAPTER PREVIEW

This chapter aims to introduce the reader to the preliminary concepts
that need to be understood prior to embarking on the study of corporate
finance. The corporate financial objective—maximising the value of the
company and thereby shareholder wealth—is discussed within the context
of introducing financial assets and capital markets.

KEY CONCEPTS

CONCEPT 1.1   The corporate objective and corporate financial decisions

This book deals with corporate finance, which is concerned with the process of corporate financial decision making. Corporate financial decisions are made by managers in the context of meeting the corporate objective, which may be stated as follows: 'Maximise the value of the company.'

It can be demonstrated that this is the same as 'Maximise shareholder wealth.'

At first glance, there may be some people who feel a little uneasy with this objective. To them, although they concede it appears to be a financially reasonable goal for companies, it seems to be, well, a bit socially inequitable. 'Maximise shareholder wealth' might conjure up visions of the 1980s-style excesses and the turbulence of recent corporate revelations such as the Babcock and Brown[1] collapse—an attitude of 'greed is good' and 'the rich get richer'. In reality, however, the corporate objective is nowhere near as insidious as this. Rather, it is a simple application of one of the basic principles of economics—make optimal use of scarce resources. The scarce resources that are used by the company are, primarily, capital and labour. To ensure optimal benefit to an economy, it is imperative that companies apply these resources in the most efficient manner possible. When this is done, the corporate objective is met—optimal use of resources ensures that the value of the company, and the wealth of shareholders, is maximised. This idea is further discussed in Concept 1.4.

Corporate managers face certain choices, requiring decisions to be made, on their way to meeting the corporate objective. The decisions are summarised below, and are explained in more detail later in the chapter.

1. The *investment decision* relates to the manner in which funds raised in capital markets are employed in productive activities. The objective of such investment is to generate future cash flows, thus providing a 'return' to investors. The investment decision is typically dealt with under the heading 'capital budgeting' or, alternatively, 'project evaluation' (Chapters 4 and 5).

2. The *financing decision* relates to the mix of funding obtained from capital markets, in terms of proportional holdings of equity and debt. This decision is typically addressed via an examination of 'capital structure' (Chapter 12).

3. The *dividend decision* relates to the form in which returns generated by the firm are passed on to equity holders. This decision is addressed in detail under 'dividend policy' (Chapter 11).

Look closely at these corporate financial decisions. It is clear that another description of the role of corporate finance is that it deals with the acquisition and use of cash by companies. In acquiring cash (the financing decision), the company has the primary objective of using it to acquire real assets (the investment decision). In turn, real assets are put to productive use to generate future cash flows. These future cash flows can then be used to provide a return to shareholders (the dividend decision).

CONCEPT CHECK

1. What is the objective of the firm from a financial management perspective?
2. What are the three key decisions facing corporate financial managers? Are these decisions interrelated or independent?

For the answers, go to MyFinanceLab

CONCEPT 1.2   Financial assets and capital markets

At this point, the concept of an 'asset' deserves further attention. In its broadest sense, the term 'asset' encompasses all kinds of property, both tangible and intangible (e.g. a legal right can be an asset). Real assets are those that can be put to productive use to generate returns. Machinery and equipment are good examples of real assets. However, in corporate finance we focus on financial assets.

A financial asset is a claim to a series of cash flows against some economic unit. This means that a 'sentimental asset', such as your grandmother's picture of you—something that may be quite valuable to your grandmother—is not a financial asset, because it does not produce cash flows. Only something that produces cash flows, or that you can sell to produce a cash flow in the future, is a financial asset. A bank account is an example of a financial asset. Some people might not think of a bank account as an asset, but it is. It entitles the holder to cash flows— some interest in the future, plus the amount initially deposited into the account. It is also a claim against the bank. Hereafter, a reference to an 'asset' will be taken to mean a financial asset.

This book is primarily concerned with the valuation of assets—in particular, shares and bonds. Shares are a claim against a company. Two types of cash flows emanate from shares: dividends and sales proceeds. Dividends are generated while the shares are held. Then, when the shares are eventually sold, a further cash flow is generated—the share (sale) price. The difference between the sales proceeds and the amount paid for the share (the purchase price) is a capital gain or loss. This is discussed in more detail in Concept 1.6.

A bond is also a claim against an economic entity. In Australia, the main issuer of bonds is the government. The cash flows that stem from bonds are interest payments and a principal repayment on maturity.

A **capital market** is the medium for the issue and exchange of assets. The 'big four' banks are probably the best known elements of the Australian capital market. They are the ANZ Bank, Commonwealth Bank of Australia, National Australia Bank and Westpac. The traditional role of these banks has been to hold deposits on behalf of customers, and to lend funds for purposes such as purchasing real estate, expanding a business, buying a car and so on. These days, however, banks are involved in a lot more than just the borrowing and lending of money. For example, some

Capital market
The medium for the issue and exchange of assets.

of them operate stockbroking businesses. That is, they trade shares in Australian (and sometimes overseas) companies. Others are also money-market dealers, involved in trading bonds. These activities also form part of the capital market.

ASX
Australian Securities
Exchange Limited.

Another well-known element of the Australian capital market is the **Australian Securities Exchange** (ASX). The ASX essentially constitutes the 'meeting place' for buyers and sellers of shares. Until October 1990, one of the meeting places was a trading floor located at 20 Bond Street, Sydney. However, buyers and sellers of shares no longer physically meet on trading floors. The market is now electronic, and transactions in shares are executed using a network of computers.

The Australian government bond market is another important element of the Australian capital market. Again, there is no physical trading floor where traders meet to buy and sell bonds. The bond market is an 'over-the-counter' market. For practical purposes, this means that transactions are typically arranged by telephone.[2] The bond market is also known as a 'dealer' market. Dealers are traders who are in the business of buying and selling bonds on their own account. An investor who wants to buy a bond would normally phone a bond broker, who in turn will usually phone a dealer to organise the transaction. Dealers typically post their quotes on electronic bulletin boards, operated by information vendors such as Reuters and Bloomberg.

At a conceptual level, the capital market is the place where individuals exchange current consumption for future consumption. For example, when you buy shares, you are forgoing current consumption and supplying the capital market with cash in the hope that in the future you will get your cash back plus a bit more (a return). It is likely that when you liquidate your shareholding in the future, you will be doing it to generate cash for consumption.

CONCEPT CHECK

3. What distinguishes 'financial' assets from other types of assets?
4. Is a bond a real asset or a financial asset?

For the answers, go to MyFinanceLab

CONCEPT 1.3   The flow of funds and the corporate capital market

Another way of conceptualising the nature of the capital market is to examine the flow of funds in the economy. Figure 1.1 illustrates that the flow of funds begins with investors. Investors make consumption and investment decisions. That is, they decide whether, and to what extent, they are willing to trade their present consumption for future consumption. If they decide to forgo present consumption, they may put their money in the bank or buy shares, thereby placing their cash into the capital market. Once cash is channelled into the capital market, it will flow to com-

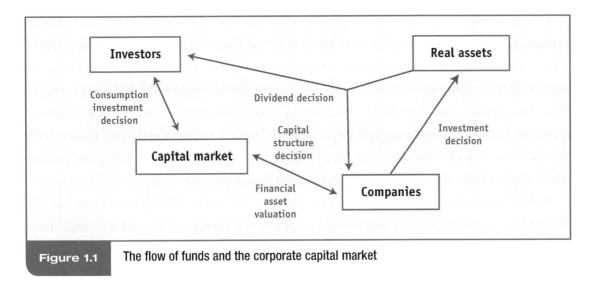

Figure 1.1   The flow of funds and the corporate capital market

panies. The financing decision is associated with this flow of funds from the capital market to companies. Associated with the financing decision is the capital structure decision, which refers to the segment of the capital market where funding is acquired by companies—the debt market or the equity market. Individual companies will normally acquire funding through the sale of financial assets. They can sell debt-type assets such as bonds, or equity-type assets such as shares. Either way, the amount of funding that a company can raise is dictated by the value of the assets sold in the capital market.

Once a company acquires funds, it will generally purchase real (productive) assets—the investment decision. In making investment decisions, companies will analyse the potential return on possible projects. This process is referred to as 'capital budgeting'. The real assets acquired by the firm generate cash flows, which can then be used to do one of three things: they can be paid to shareholders, paid to bondholders or invested back into the assets of the company to fund internally further business opportunities. The third corporate financial decision, the dividend decision, becomes relevant here as the company decides on the level of dividends to be paid out (relative to retention of cash flows).

CONCEPT 1.4   Maximising the wealth of corporate owners

The key corporate objective requires that a company should make decisions that increase the wealth of its owners. Alternatively, this can be expressed as: the company makes decisions that increase the value of the firm. The two are synonymous, because the owners hold the value of a firm, and every time the directors of a company make a good decision, whereby its securities increase in value, the owners of these securities become wealthier.

Owner wealth is measured by the 'market capitalisation' of securities. For shares, market capitalisation is simply the total market value of all the shares of a company on issue. This is a direct measure of the total wealth of shareholders that is invested in the company. Calculating shareholder wealth is therefore relatively straightforward. Consider the following example: News Corporation, one of the largest media companies in the world, is run by the well-known (formerly Australian!) media baron Rupert Murdoch. Table 1.1 illustrates the two main securities issued by News Corporation that were trading on the ASX in 2010, including the price at which the securities were trading on Wednesday, 30 June 2010.

News Corporation is one of the largest companies listed on the ASX. It is also listed on the NASDAQ. News Corporation underwent a corporate restructure and became a United States company in November 2004, but was for many years one of the most successful international Australian companies. Table 1.1 illustrates that in June 2010, News Corporation had 1824.12 million Class A shares on issue, trading at $14.38, and 798.52 million Class B shares trading at $16.75.[3] The product of the number of shares on issue and the last sales price gives the market capitalisation of each security type. For example, the market capitalisation of Class A shares was $26.23 billion, while the market capitalisation of Class B shares was $13.38 billion. News Corporation was therefore worth $39.61 billion in total. The assumption underlying this book is that, ultimately, Rupert Murdoch is trying to increase this value every time he makes a decision. There are a number of incentives and mechanisms in place that encourage the directors of a company to make decisions that maximise the wealth of owners.

Regulators such as the **Australian Securities and Investments Commission** (ASIC) are among these mechanisms. Two important roles of ASIC are to prevent corporate crime and to protect investors. Both of these roles are consistent with the maximisation of owners' wealth. It is unlikely, however, that the existence of ASIC will provide an airtight guarantee that directors of a company will pursue the interests of shareholders. Take, for example, the charges against Storm Financial Limited, a financial advisory firm based in Townsville owned by Emmanuel and Julie Cassimatis. Storm advised many of their clients to take out margin loans (against their houses) to invest in their investment fund. This is akin to investing in the stock market on borrowed money. These clients

ASIC
The Australian Securities and Investments Commission enforces the company and financial services law. It regulates Australian companies, financial markets, financial services organisations and professionals who deal and advise in investments, superannuation, insurance, deposit taking and credit.

Table 1.1	Major News Corp. securities traded on the Australian Securities Exchange 30 June 2010			
SECURITY	ASX STOCK CODE	NO. ISSUED (M)	LAST SALE PRICE ($)	MARKET CAPITALISATION ($B)
Class A common stock	NWSLV	1824.12	14.38	26.23
Class B common stock	NWS	798.52	16.75	13.38
Total				39.61

Source: Thompson Reuters.

eventually suffered large losses as a result of falling stock and property prices. Storm Financial went into administration in January 2009. It was alleged that Storm Financial had deliberately misrepresented the risk of their margin lending practices, especially to clients who were unsophisticated investors (e.g. the elderly). In November 2010, ASIC decided to pursue civil proceedings against Storm Financial and related parties such as banks seeking compensation for Storm's investors. At this stage, it is unclear how much compensation Storm's clients would receive (if any).

Remuneration packages are another way in which the owners of a company can promote decision-making by a company that maximises owner wealth. That is, directors' salaries can be packaged such that every time the value of a company increases, the wealth of the directors also increases. A common and 'approximate' way of doing this is to pay bonuses to directors on the basis of the company's earnings performance. However, two possible problems are associated with this approach. First, it is well known that 'creative accounting' practices reduce the validity of earnings figures as indicators of corporate performance. Second, while earnings performance can influence the market capitalisation of companies, it is certainly not the sole (or even main) influence, which suggests that tying director remuneration to earnings is different from tying remuneration to the market capitalisation of a company.

Directors often hold shares in the companies that they run. This practice increases the likelihood that a director will attempt to maximise the wealth of shareholders, because the director's wealth will increase simultaneously! News Corporation is a good example of a company with such a mechanism in place. Through his family company, Rupert Murdoch owned, as at mid-2010, approximately $6 billion worth of shares in News Corporation. It is highly likely that Rupert Murdoch is very interested in making decisions that result in a News Corporation share price increase, because every time the price of its shares increases by 1%, his own wealth increases by about $60 million.

The market for corporate control (i.e. the takeover market) may also promote the maximisation of shareholder wealth. You may have heard of corporate raiders. They form part of the market for corporate control. One strategy of corporate raiders is to look for companies that are being managed badly. The idea is that if management is running a company inefficiently, the company's share price will be depressed. Corporate raiders aim to take over such companies by purchasing a majority shareholding, then use their acquired voting power partly or completely to replace the existing management. This is known as a 'hostile' takeover—'hostile' in terms of what happens to the existing management. In theory, the new (or upgraded) management team operates the business more efficiently (and therefore profitably), resulting in shareholder gains. The threat of job loss associated with hostile corporate raids therefore provides an incentive to management to pursue the objective of maximisation of share value—that is, shareholder wealth. This mechanism is sometimes referred to as the 'discipline of the capital market'.

FINANCE EXTRA!

CEO pays shoot up in FY 2010-11: CBA, Coles, BHP heads leading

LUMPED together the pay checks collected by the top executives of BHP Billiton, Commonwealth Bank of Australia (CBA) and Coles for financial year 2010-2011 alone and you'll get more than $43 million, which is more than enough for an average Australian to last a lifetime.

As reported by the Australian Council of Superannuation Investors earlier this month, the country's high-flying CEOs enjoyed salary spikes of more than 130 percent over the past 10 years, with an average chief executive from any of the blue chip firms said to have taken home a median pay of $2.79 million in 2010 alone.

Such jaw-dropping executive remunerations were issued by leading companies amidst suggestions that many sectors of domestic economy were struggling, which were reflected by Australian workers average income of about $66,000 each year while given only some 52 percent pay hike over the past decade.

As many companies flagged weak business environment, shareholders, the council report showed, only collected returns of 31 percent, leaving puzzling indicators on how the hefty payments could have been realised against a general backdrop of economic uncertainties, the council said.

From the annual company reports provided by the Australian Securities Exchange (ASX), CBA chief Ralph Norris secured the top position as the country's highest paid CEO as his company revealed that he had a pay slip totalling to $16.2 million in the past financial year.

Coming close was Coles boss Ian McLeod, who amassed a total pay package of $15.6 million last year, which according to Coles parent company, Wesfarmers, was mostly comprised of more than $11 million in numerous form of bonuses.

McLeod, Wesfarmers said, was rewarded for his chief role in turning around the misfortunes of the grocery chain, which on August posted sales increase of more than $32 billion and anchored on its 21 percent improvement on full-year earnings.

The Australian reported on Friday that judging by his declared year-round remuneration, McLeod earned much more in a single day what an average Australian had to toil for a year.

By comparison, McLeod bested the take home pay of BHP chief executive Marius Kloppers, who runs Australia's largest business operations and the world's biggest mining firm, and that of his own boss, Wesfarmers managing director Richard Goyder.

Kloppers, according to BHP's report this week, was paid a total of $11.6 million in financial year 2010-2011 that covered his base salary, cash bonuses and incentives while Goyder's role as Wesfarmers chief only earned him $6.9 million in the same period, which reflected a slide of 13 percent from his previous annual pay.

Source: International Business Times, September 23, 2011, http://au.ibtimes.com/articles/218681/20110923/ceo-pays-shoot-up-in-fy-2010-11-cba-coles-bhp-lead-the-way.htm.

Another mechanism that encourages management of a company to increase owner wealth is shareholder voting power. For example, a group of shareholders who are dissatisfied with the manner in which a company is run may decide to sack the management. Such a 'group' of shareholders typically does not refer to individual investors. While an ASX survey of shareholders in 2008 suggests that approximately 41% of Australian adults own shares, individuals rarely own a significant proportion of any one company. It is well known that the real controllers of companies are institutional investors such as AMP and Colonial (see Chapter 9). These institutions typically hold large portions of companies' shares, and therefore control them. If institutions become dissatisfied with the way in which a company is run, they can combine their voting power and sack existing management.

Despite the fact that a number of mechanisms may be in place to promote the maximisation of owner wealth, there is always the presence of the principal–agent problem. Since the managers of a company (the agents) have control over the funds of shareholders (the principals), there is always a danger that they may not act in the best interests of shareholders. This is because they might prefer to take actions that enhance their own personal position, even if such actions are against shareholders' best interests. Accordingly, the mechanisms that are discussed here may not always be adequate to guarantee that the interests of owners of the firm will be pursued.

CONCEPT CHECK

5. How does market capitalisation relate to owners' wealth?
6. Are the interests of the managers of a company necessarily aligned with increasing shareholders' wealth?
7. What mechanisms are used to align the interests of managers with the interests of the shareholders?

For the answers, go to MyFinanceLab

CONCEPT 1.5   Asset valuation

One of the most important concepts in corporate finance is *value*—in particular, the value of assets. Consider a simple asset that guarantees the holder a cash flow of $105 in one year's time, while at the same time the National Australia Bank (NAB) is offering a 5% p.a. rate of return on a basic passbook account. How much would you be willing to pay for this asset? Figure 1.2 uses a time line to illustrate this problem.

Would you be willing to pay $105 for this asset? The answer to this question should be no! Why? Because if you put $105 in the bank now, in one year's time you would end up with more money than $105. In fact, you would end up with $110.25 (= $105 × 1.05). Hence, you would

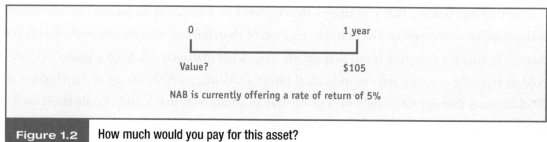

Figure 1.2   How much would you pay for this asset?

not pay $105 for the asset because you would not be maximising your own personal wealth. (Note the use of wealth maximisation here at the individual, rather than corporate, level.) So, at $105 this asset is overpriced. This example also demonstrates that $105 in one year's time is not equal to $105 today. The idea that $1 in the future is not equivalent to $1 today is related to the **time value of money**, which is derived from the fact that interest can be earned on an alternative investment opportunity (the bank account). The interest rate that you get from the bank is the opportunity cost of buying the asset or the **opportunity cost** of capital. It determines the future cash flow that the investor forgoes when purchasing the asset. Hence, the opportunity cost and time value of money are very important concepts in asset valuation.

Would you pay $97 for this asset? The financially rational answer to this question is a resounding yes! The reason is that the alternative investment of $97 in the bank with a 5% return would bring less than $105 in one year's time (actually, $101.85, i.e. $97 × 1.05). Hence, if you were able to purchase the asset for $97, you would be maximising your own personal wealth.

What is the maximum amount that you would pay for the asset? Or alternatively, what value do you place on the asset? It is easy to show that $100 is an appropriate price to pay for this asset. This is because if you pay $100 for the asset, you equalise the rate of return you get from this asset and your opportunity cost. Another way of thinking about this is: if you pay $100 for this asset, you have priced it in such a way that you generate a rate of return on the asset equal to your opportunity cost of capital. Alternatively, your terminal wealth (in one year) from purchasing the asset is the same as what you acquire from investing your money in the alternative opportunity (bank account): $105. This price that you are willing to pay for the asset is sometimes called its **intrinsic value**. The intrinsic value of an asset is determined by: (1) the future cash flow expected from the asset, and (2) the opportunity cost of capital. These two inputs are the only two pieces of information required to value an asset properly.

In valuing the simple asset described above, you were implicitly determining the amount you would have to invest in the bank account, at the bank's prevailing deposit rate, in order to generate a future cash flow (terminal wealth from bank account) equivalent to the asset's promised future

Time value of money
The simple concept that a dollar now is worth more than a dollar in the future, even after adjusting for inflation, because a dollar now can earn interest or other appreciation until the time the dollar in the future would be received.

Opportunity cost
The return an investment or resource could have provided in its best alternative use.

Intrinsic value
The amount that you are willing to pay for an asset, as opposed to its market price.

cash flow (terminal wealth from asset). Put another way, you were finding the value of PV that makes the following expression true:

$$\$105 = PV(1 + 0.05)$$

or more generally:

$$FV = PV(1 + r) \qquad \textbf{(1.1)}$$

where *PV* is the amount that needs to be invested in the bank account at the deposit rate of interest *r* to generate a future cash flow of *FV*. *PV* is also known as the **present value** of the future cash flow *FV*, and *r* is the opportunity cost. Rearranging equation 1.1 gives a general expression for the value of a single cash flow received in one period's time:

Present value
The current value of one or more future cash payments, discounted at some appropriate interest rate.

$$PV = \frac{FV}{1 + r} \qquad \textbf{(1.2)}$$

Equation 1.2 conveys the essence of the value of an asset. It is the future cash flow divided by, or discounted by, (1 + *r*). Equation 1.2 also conveys the notion that $1 today is worth *more* than $1 in the future, because of the time value of money. Furthermore, the time value of money is determined by *r*, the opportunity cost of capital. The rate *r* has a number of different names in the corporate finance literature. In addition to the opportunity cost of capital, it is variously known as the discount rate, hurdle rate or required rate of return.

CONCEPT CHECK

8. Can an individual be indifferent to receiving a dollar now or a dollar one year from now? Explain.
9. If the best interest rate I could receive in the market was 10%, would I prefer $100 now or a guaranteed $110 in one year's time?

For the answers, go to MyFinanceLab

Fisher's Separation Theorem

The concepts covered in the foregoing explanations and examples are formally linked in Fisher's Separation Theorem. In bringing together these concepts, Fisher's Separation Theorem provides a single decision rule for a firm's investment decisions. This decision rule is that management's role is to maximise the present value of the firm's investments in productive assets. The benefit of the theorem is that it is one decision rule that management can follow to aid in optimally allocating the firm's resources among the competing interests of a multitude of shareholders. Fisher argued in 1930 that the firm's investment decision is independent of the preference of the owner and the firm's financing decision. The investment rule is to invest until the return on the marginal dollar invested equals the cost of funds—that is, maximise net present value. Fisher used the concepts of present value, indifference curves and the production possibilities curve to develop a theory that has important implications for the three decisions identified as those facing the corporate manager—the investment decision, the financing decision and the dividend decision.

The implications of Fisher's Separation Theorem are that all investors will agree on the firm's policy to maximise net present value, as it will allow them, as individuals, to achieve their highest level of consumption. It further implies that there is one market interest rate that determines the optimal investment decision for the firm. In modern finance it is recognised that firms operate in differing risk classes, so the market interest rate of Fisher's theorem is interpreted as the market rate for a given level of risk. The theorem also implies that firm value is not affected by the type of security used to finance projects, nor is firm value affected by dividends. If the firm increases dividends, it can replace those funds by borrowing at the market interest rate.

Fisher's theory needs several concepts to provide the building blocks for the development and understanding of a theory of a firm's investment. The first building block is the concept of the indifference of an individual to certain combinations of consumption now and consumption later. The second building block is the concept of capital markets where individuals can borrow and lend at the market rate of interest. The final building block is the recognition that firms have a range of investment opportunities called their production possibilities. Each of these concepts has intuitive appeal.

People, if rational, will always prefer more of something to less of it. However, they will experience diminishing satisfaction from additional consumption. For example, ice-cream lovers enjoy greatly that first spoon of ice-cream. However, the fiftieth spoonful will provide much less satisfaction. So, although investors will always prefer more to less, they experience less satisfaction for every additional unit of good they consume today. Without the ability to borrow and lend, individuals are restricted to consuming now what they earn in the current period and consuming later what they earn in later periods. The limitation on one's satisfaction is that you cannot consume more than you earn. However, modern life dictates that our consumption needs are at odds with our income-earning patterns. Typically, young people have high current consumption needs because they wish to buy a house, educate their children and acquire those assets (stereo, car, washing machine, refrigerator, etc.) that are expected from our standard of living. The older members of the workforce have typically fewer current consumption needs (having paid off the house and educated the children) but higher future consumption needs (in terms of providing for their retirement). The existence of capital markets enables us to adjust our income and consumption patterns to suit our needs. Those who need to spend more now and less later can borrow the money they need—for example, through a housing loan for their house—and use future income to repay the loan. Those with high future consumption needs can invest their excess current income at the market rate of interest and have more consumption later.

However, while capital markets enable individuals to trade off between consumption now and consumption later, the amount one can consume is limited by the income in the present period. The level of consumption in all periods can be increased if we can earn more. This is the role of the company. Because of their aggregation of capital and labour, firms have investment opportunities that give returns higher than those available to the individual investor. Let us consider a firm with $1 million in capital to invest in video game production. The first investment of $100 000 may produce a video game that returns, say, 50%. The second $100 000 invested may also provide a new video game but one with a return of 40%. As the market gets saturated with the firm's games and those of its competitors, the return from each new investment in new video games is less than the previous investment. In economic terms, this is known as the law of diminishing marginal returns.

What is evident is that if investors place their money with a firm that is earning superior returns compared with investing at the market rate of interest, they will earn much higher income later. The present value of this income, less their investment, measures the increase in wealth achieved by investing in firms that offer a return that is higher than the rate of interest prevailing in the capital markets. That is, as long as the firm can earn a rate of return that is higher than the market rate, the investors will be better off allowing the firm to invest in projects that increase their wealth—those that have a higher present value than the amount invested. This will be the case with all investment opportunities that earn more than the market rate of interest. Because they have more future income through future payouts from the firm, the investors have higher wealth now. Individuals who have higher consumption needs now can borrow more against their higher future returns. Individuals with higher future consumption needs relative to now can invest their surplus funds now and gain more future return. As a result, all investors will be better off if the firm invests in projects with higher returns than those available in capital markets.

Firms now have a decision rule that says they should invest in projects that have a return equal to or higher than the market rate of interest. Regardless of whether the investors want consumption now or later, they will benefit from the firm following this decision rule. This frees the managers of the firm from having to consider the consumption preferences of its owners. They will behave in the best interests of their investors if they invest in projects with a return higher than the market rate of interest.

CONCEPT CHECK

10. How can managers make investment decisions without considering the consumption needs of their shareholders?

11. How does the existence of a capital market allow individuals to trade off between present and future consumption?

For the answers, go to MyFinanceLab

CONCEPT 1.6   Rate of return on securities

The importance of the opportunity cost in valuing assets underscores the importance of rates of return more generally. Rates of return is the language of the corporate finance industry. The rate of return on an asset can be defined as the gain from an asset (economic profit), divided by the cost of acquiring the asset (the cost of the investment, or invested capital). More formally:

$$\text{Rate of return} = \frac{\text{net gain from asset}}{\text{invested capital}} \tag{1.3}$$

Assume that a share is bought at the start of a day or the opening of trading, and then sold at the end of the day or at the close of trading. The rate of return on the share can be expressed as:

$$\text{Rate of return on share} = \frac{(\text{closing price} - \text{opening price}) + \text{dividend}}{\text{opening price}} \tag{1.4}$$

The part of the numerator in brackets is the capital gain from holding the share over the day. If you are fortunate enough to be holding the share on the day it pays a dividend, you must also add the dividend to the capital gain in order to calculate the net gain from holding the share.[4] The opening price of the share is the amount that it was purchased for, or the invested capital.

An example will help to illustrate the calculation of rates of return on shares. On Monday, 4 January 2010, BHP Billiton, the largest mining company in the world and one of the largest companies listed on the ASX, opened for trading at a price of $42.75 and closed at a price of $43.08. On the same day, the All Ordinaries Index (colloquially called 'All Ords'), which is an index that tracks the average price movement of the top 500 ASX-listed companies, opened at 4877.7 points and closed at 4889.8 points.

For the purpose of calculating daily returns for BHP Billiton and the All Ordinaries Index, assume that both were purchased at the opening price and sold in the afternoon at the closing price.[5] Applying Equation 1.4 to BHP Billiton, we find:

$$\text{Rate of return on BHP Billiton} = \frac{(\$43.08 - \$42.75)}{\$42.75} = 0.007719, \text{ or approx } 0.77\%$$

Hence the rate of return earned on BHP Billiton shares was 0.77% on 4 January 2010. Similarly, the return on the market can be calculated using the opening and closing values of the All Ordinaries Index, as follows:

$$\text{Rate of return on All Ordinaries Index} = \frac{(4889.8 - 4877.7)}{4877.7} = 0.002481, \text{ or approx. } 0.25\%$$

Hence the rate of return on the Australian share market was 0.25% on 4 January 2010.

Practitioner's POV

Stockbrokers and fund managers often evaluate the share price performance of shares by comparing the rate of return on the shares with the rate of return on the market index. If the return on the shares exceeds the return on the market index (on a risk-adjusted basis), the shares have outperformed the market. If the return on the shares is less than the return on the market, the shareholding has underperformed. The most common indices used by practitioners in Australia to evaluate the performance of shares are the S&P/ASX 200 Index, the S&P/ASX 300 Index, and the All Ordinaries Index. Accumulation versions of these indices (commonly called 'total return indices') are also available and take into account returns from dividend income.

CONCEPT CHECK

12. What are the two types of gain one can get from holding a share?
13. How do you calculate the rate of return on a share?

For the answers, go to MyFinanceLab

CONCEPT 1.7   The 'markets' section of the financial press

The performance of different shares on any day can be ascertained by examining the markets section of *The Australian Financial Review*, in conjunction with the share price indices. Figure 1.3 is an extract of the markets section on 22 September 2010.

The markets section lists all shares that are traded on the ASX, together with a host of market and other information for each share. Take, for example, News Corporation. The row containing 'News Corp b voting' provides market information for certain News Corporation shares on Tuesday, 21 September 2010 (the day prior to the publication date of the newspaper). The ASX code column indicates that the stock code under which News Corp b shares trade on the ASX is 'NWS'. The most critical information is contained in the 'Last sale' column, indicating the last traded price of each share. For example, the last trade in NWS on 21 September 2010 was at $16.49. The previous closing price of the share can be ascertained by examining the +/– column, which reports the change in the price of the shares since the close on the previous trading day. For NWS the change in the price was +12 cents on the day illustrated, suggesting that it traded for $16.37 at the close of trading on 20 September 2010 (which was the previous *trading* day).

Other important information columns are the 'Buy' ('Sell') quotes. These columns report the highest price that a bidder for shares was willing to pay (the lowest price at which a seller of shares was willing to sell) at the close of trading. For example, at the close of trade there was a

52 WEEK HIGH	52 WEEK LOW	DAY'S HIGH	DAY'S LOW	ASX CODE	COMPANY NAME	LAST SALE	+ OR -	VOL 100'S	QUOTES BUY	QUOTES SELL	DPS ¢	DIV YLD %	EPS ¢	P/E RATIO X
.223	.109	.195	.195	MUE	Multiplex European unt......	.195	-	1592	.195	.20	1.87	9.59	16.25	1.2
1.40	.001	-	-	MAFCB	Multiplex Prime Ppty ctg....	1.40	-	-	1.50	-	-	-	46.36	3.0
.01	.002	-	-	MSI	Multistack Intl........................	.003	-	-	.003	.007	-	-	-.15	-
.75	.30	-	-	MCH	Murchison Hldgs.................	.345	-	-	.345	.45	-	-	3.04	11.3
.14	.075	-	-	MNF	My Net Fone..........................	.14	-	-	.125	.14	.75	5.36	3.76	3.7
4.02	2.86	4.02	3.97	MYR	Myer Hldgs............................	3.99	+1	43228	3.99	4.00	- f	-	-	-
3.75	2.60	3.20	3.16	MYS	MyState...................................	3.17	+1	96	3.17	3.20	22.50 f	7.10	27.46	11.5
.49	.35	.42	.415	NAM	Namoi Cotton ccu................	.415	-.5	281	.405	.415	2.50	6.02	4.70	8.8
.80	.44	.80	.68	NAN	Nanosonics...........................	.795	+12.5	15694	.78	.795	-	-	-3.90	-
32.37	22.23	26.07	25.65	NAB	National Aust Bank..............	25.76	-10	48277	25.75	25.80	147.00 f	5.71	199.30	12.9
1.60	1.15	1.25	1.25	NCI	National Can Ind..................	1.25	-	6	1.26	1.59	5.00 f	4.00	7.60	16.4
2.14	1.09	-	-	NHR	National Hire Grp	1.15	-	-	1.17	1.30	-	-	3.89	29.6
.044	.005	-	-	NLG	National Leisure...................	.009	-	-	.009	.011	-	-	-.77	-
5.56	3.34	4.25	4.18	NVT	Navitas	4.21	-4	1892	4.18	4.21	18.80 f	4.47	18.80	22.4
.88	.175	.275	.26	NMS	Neptune Marine	.265	-1	23846	.26	.27	-	-	.20	132.5
.67	.04	.08	.08	NMSO	opt dec10.............................	.08	-.5	540	.08	.085	-	-	-	-
.52	.12	.23	.22	NTC	NetComm..............................	.225	+.5	294	.22	.225	1.00	4.44	1.58	14.2
.054	.016	.019	.017	NEU	Neuren Pharma.....................	.017	-	1538	.017	.019	-	-	.03	56.7
.048	.024	.028	.028	NDL	NeuroDiscovery.....................	.028	+.1	413	.028	.03	-	-	-2.98	-
1.96	1.75	-	-	NHH	Newhaven Hotels.................	1.89	-	-	1.90	2.50	6.00 f	3.17	6.60	28.6
20.18	14.81	16.71	16.48	NWS	News Corp b voting..............	16.49	+12	15822	16.49	16.50	13.90	.84	113.81	14.5
17.56	12.55	14.90	14.76	NWSLV	a nonvote..............................	14.78	+30	24231	14.74	14.78	13.90	.94	-	-
.008	.003	.004	.003	NWT	NewSat...................................	.004	-	50070	.003	.004	-	-	-	-
.475	.055	.083	.078	NBS	Nexbis...................................	.081	+.1	6034	.08	.081	-	-	-10.90	-
1.45	1.13	1.235	1.22	NHF	NIB Hldgs...............................	1.225	-	1606	1.215	1.23	7.00 f	5.71	12.40	9.9
1.75	1.10	1.50	1.48	NCK	Nick Scali..............................	1.50	-2	135	1.50	1.52	9.00 f	6.00	13.90	10.8
1.175	.098	.17	.165	NOD	Nomad Bldg Solutions	.17	+.5	15094	.165	.175	2.50	14.71	-46.10	-
1.50	.96	1.23	1.21	NBL	Noni B....................................	1.22	+1	127	1.21	1.24	9.00 f	7.38	12.10	10.1
1.15	.547	1.15	1.12	NFK	Norfolk Grp............................	1.15	-	744	1.12	1.15	-	-	12.95	8.9

Figure 1.3   The market section of The Australian Financial Review, 22 September 2010

Source: Fairfax Media Publications Pty Limited.

bidder in the market for NWS willing to pay $16.49 per share. Similarly, the lowest-priced seller at the close of trade was willing to accept $16.50. A trade would not have taken place at the close of trade unless a buyer arrived in the market who was willing to pay $16.50, or a seller arrived willing to trade at $16.49. Another reason that the buy and sell quotes are important is that they determine the loss on an immediate round-trip (i.e. buy and then sell) transaction. Someone who purchased NWS shares at the close of trading and then immediately resold them would have lost one cent per share. The difference between the buy and sell quote is known as the **bid–ask spread** and can be thought of as a cost of trading shares.

Bid–ask spread
The difference between the best selling price and the best buying price.

The 52-week high and low columns report the highest and lowest price, respectively, at which each share traded during the previous 12 months. This information can give the reader an indication of the price volatility of each share. For example, the price of NWS ranged from $14.81 to $20.18 during the year, indicating that it was quite volatile in the past 52 weeks. The adjacent columns to the 52-week highs and lows are the daily highs and lows. Here NWS ranged from $16.48 to $16.71 on 21 September 2010, indicating a high degree of intraday price volatility.

Another important piece of market information is the volume column, which indicates the number of shares that were traded during the day. This gives the reader an impression of how actively traded (or 'liquid') the share is. For example, NWS traded more than 1.5 million shares and can be considered highly liquid. In comparison, Nick Scali, a furniture retailer, traded approximately 13 500 shares.

The performance of each share is often evaluated against the market, or a market index. Although many indices are reported, market commentators usually focus on the All Ordinaries Index. Figure 1.4 reports the share price indices section of *The Australian Financial Review* on 22 September 2010. It indicates that on 21 September 2010, the All Ordinaries closed at 4664.9 points, which represented a 0.26% decrease from the previous trading day.

The Internet adds a fast and easy companion to the information sources provided in newspapers and financial magazines. The ASX website <www.asx.com.au> provides access to all the information provided in the financial press, together with a glossary of financial terms. Other sites, such as Yahoo!7 Finance <http://au.finance.yahoo.com>, also provide a source of information on the current prices of various listed securities and the various share price indices. Yahoo!7 provides a price history of traded shares, as well as a history of dividend payments. A wealth of information is available through the various search engines (e.g. <www.google.com>). Searching

		Share Price Index						Accumulation Index		
Code	Description	Sep 20	Sep 21	Var +/-	Day %	Wk %	Mth %	YTD %	Sep 20	Sep 21	YTD %
XAO	All Ordinaries	4677.1	4664.9	-12.2	-0.26	-0.09	4.55	-4.46	33320.6	33234.3	-1.38
XAF	All Australian 50	4604.8	4590.0	-14.8	-0.32	-0.21	3.69	-5.61	33290.2	33182.7	-2.27
XAT	All Australian 200	4631.6	4617.9	-13.7	-0.30	-0.18	4.24	-5.20	33433.3	33334.5	-1.99
XTL	S&P/ASX 20	2788.2	2778.4	-9.8	-0.35	-0.17	3.90	-5.80	39476.9	39338.6	-2.34
XFL	S&P/ASX 50	4617.2	4602.7	-14.5	-0.31	-0.21	3.68	-5.66	33358.7	33253.9	-2.35
XTO	S&P/ASX 100	3773.6	3764.0	-9.6	-0.25	-0.19	3.94	-5.61	8269.0	8248.2	-2.37
XJO	S&P/ASX 200	4631.3	4617.5	-13.8	-0.30	-0.19	4.21	-5.20	33400.9	33301.8	-2.01
XKO	S&P/ASX 300	4630.5	4617.2	-13.3	-0.29	-0.16	4.34	-5.16	33329.8	33234.1	-2.01
XMD	S&P/ASX Midcap 50	4223.9	4233.7	9.8	0.23	-0.00	5.99	-5.11	9688.6	9710.9	-2.36
XSO	S&P/ASX Small Ords	2632.0	2615.0	-17.0	-0.65	0.13	8.59	-0.39	5882.5	5845.6	1.63
XDJ	Consumer Discretionary	1565.6	1568.3	2.6	0.17	0.71	5.83	-4.19	10122.6	10141.2	-1.33
XSJ	Consumer Staples	8210.8	8175.4	-35.4	-0.43	-0.36	4.70	4.69	56984.9	56739.0	8.62
XEJ	Energy	15115.0	15081.3	-33.7	-0.22	0.87	0.79	-6.44	98575.1	98355.8	-4.28
XFJ	Financials	4481.4	4471.8	-9.6	-0.21	-0.35	4.61	-6.91	36409.5	36331.3	-3.17
XXJ	Financials x-A-REIT	5180.6	5163.7	-16.9	-0.33	-0.36	5.05	-7.91	40355.6	40224.0	-4.32
XHJ	Health Care	8087.9	8049.1	-38.7	-0.48	-1.05	1.98	-8.04	46869.0	46644.3	-5.45
XNJ	Industrials	3718.3	3723.7	5.4	0.15	1.25	7.34	-7.03	27200.5	27239.7	-4.51
XIJ	Info Technology	597.4	599.4	2.0	0.33	1.38	2.74	-10.90	3512.8	3524.4	-8.19
XMJ	Materials	12474.4	12425.0	-49.4	-0.40	-0.41	5.22	-2.76	78900.4	78591.3	-0.92
XPJ	A-REIT	883.2	886.6	3.4	0.38	-0.31	2.36	-1.20	20005.9	20082.2	3.34
XTJ	Telecommunications	954.2	937.2	-17.0	-1.78	-2.23	-7.38	-20.26	8903.2	8744.6	-12.60
XUJ	Utilities	4475.1	4471.0	-4.1	-0.09	1.18	6.01	3.30	38322.3	38287.4	8.37
XMM	Metals & Mining	4485.6	4467.6	-18.0	-0.40	-0.19	6.08	-1.50	5856.6	5833.3	0.27
XGD	Gold	7887.8	7774.9	-112.9	-1.43	3.88	17.60	32.75	8923.1	8795.4	33.17
XJR	Resources	5258.5	5239.8	-18.7	-0.36	0.02	4.43	-3.37	25667.4	25576.8	-1.47

Figure 1.4 The share price indices section of The Australian Financial Review, 22 September 2010

Source: Fairfax Media Publications Pty Limited.

for a particular term coupled with the word 'definition' or 'glossary' provides access to the multitude of financial glossaries now available on the Internet. Most Australian companies also provide websites with a range of downloadable material that can be accessed via the ASX site.

Practitioner's POV

Information is the lifeblood of financial markets. Stockbrokers and fund managers obtain information relating to stock market activity from information vendors. The most common vendors are Bloomberg, IRESS and Reuters. These companies typically provide computer screens attached to an electronic feed that continually update share prices, quotes, volumes, etc. during the day as trading occurs in the marketplace. If you were thinking of subscribing, a Bloomberg terminal costs around $1500 a month, or $18 000 a year!

CONCEPT CHECK

14. Financial information sources contain various measures of the activities in the market, market highs and lows, daily closing price and buy and sell quotes. Which measure is the best indicator of the market value of a firm's shares?
15. If you wished to compare the performance of a share with some general measure of performance, what would you use?

For the answers, go to MyFinanceLab

CONCEPT 1.8   An overview of this book

Armed with the key concepts listed at the start of this chapter, it is now possible to study corporate finance. The rest of this book is mainly concerned with asset valuation and the investment decisions of a company.

In this chapter, it was argued that the value of an asset is the present value of its future cash flows. However, the calculation of the value of assets that produce multiple cash flows was not discussed. Chapter 2 reviews the basic mathematics for dealing with such assets. Chapter 3 takes this basic framework and applies it to valuing shares, bonds and entire companies. Chapters 4 and 5 extend this to the valuation of real assets in the context of investment evaluation or project selection by a company.

The importance of the opportunity cost or discount rate in valuing assets was also underscored in this chapter. Chapters 6 and 7 develop and discuss a very important model of the discount rate—the capital asset pricing model. How this model can be applied to determining the opportunity cost of capital for a company is explained in Chapter 8. The model is useful for valuing companies, as well as their real assets.

The last six chapters are essentially concerned with elements of the financing decision. The ASX is an important element of the equity capital market. The meaning of the numbers reported in *The Australian Financial Review* and other financial press is best appreciated by understanding the nature of the market that produces them.

Hence, Chapters 9 and 10 are dedicated to describing the operation of the ASX, and the pricing efficiency of the market. Chapters 11 and 12 focus on two other important aspects of the finance decision: dividend policy and capital structure policy, respectively. Chapter 13 discusses one of the most important practical issues associated with the financing decision: risk management. Risk management refers to the use of complex financial instruments, called options and futures, to control the risk associated with currency and interest rate fluctuations. Finally, Chapter 14 covers working capital: the management of short-term assets and liabilities.

Student Learning Centre

My FinanceLab ■ To test your mastery of the content covered in this chapter and to create your own personalised study plan, go to MyFinanceLab: www.pearson.com.au/myfinancelab

CONCEPT CHECKLIST

In this chapter the following concepts were discussed:

➤ The main objective underlying corporate financial decisions

➤ The nature of financial assets

➤ The flow of funds through the capital market and its relationship to corporate finance

➤ Why directors maximise the wealth of corporate owners

➤ How to value an asset paying a single cash flow

➤ How to calculate the rate of return from holding assets

➤ How to read some of the information contained in the financial press such as *The Australian Financial Review*

SELF-TEST QUESTIONS

1. The cash flows generated from the real assets of the firm can be used for what three purposes?

2. What is the maximum amount a rational investor would be willing to pay for an asset that guarantees the holder a cash flow of $560 in one year's time, while at the same time the rate of return on similar assets is 12%?

Self-test answers

1. (a) Paid to shareholders as dividends.

   (b) Paid to debt holders.

   (c) Invested back into the assets of the company to internally fund further business opportunities.

2. Using Equation 1.2:

   $$PV = \frac{FV}{1 + r}$$

   $$PV = \frac{560}{1.12}$$

   The maximum a rational investor would pay is $500.

DISCUSSION QUESTIONS

1. What is an opportunity cost? Why is it such an important concept in finance?

2. The text refers to three types of financial decision—the investment decision, the financing decision and the dividend decision. Describe each in detail, and explain how these decisions relate to the corporate objective. Categorise each of the following decisions in terms of whether it is an investment, financing or dividend decision, and explain why it is in that category.

   (a) Javelin Pharmaceutical Ltd purchases all of the shares in O'Hara Ltd.

   (b) Tabcorp Holdings Ltd buys new poker machines for its business.

   (c) Brushwood Ltd hopes to raise $53 million in an equity issue of ordinary shares and will use the funds to repay its long-term debt.

   (d) Devastation Games Ltd purchases the copyright for a new video game.

   (e) News Corporation declares a dividend of 20 cents per share.

   (f) Brushwood Ltd pays $5 million to repurchase 1% of the shares held by its current shareholders.

   (g) Creek Ltd announces the raising of $50 million in bonds in the USA.

   (h) Charles Grogin sells shares to finance his new online wine cellar.

3. On what basis is the corporate objective of 'maximising shareholder wealth' justified? How does this corporate objective affect corporate financial decision making?

4. 'Maximising the value of the firm to its shareholders is consistent with the firm exercising considerable social responsibility.' Discuss.

5. What is the difference between a real asset and a financial asset? Give an example of each.

6. What is a capital market? Give examples of Australian capital markets, and state the main participants in these markets.

7. How do capital markets allow consumers to meet their present and future consumption needs?

8. You wish to buy a new laptop. However, your cash is insufficient for this purchase. How can capital markets assist you in this case?

9. How does maximising the price of a firm's share equate to maximising shareholder wealth?

10. What is a bond? What are the cash flows that are received by bondholders?

11. You were told by the management of XYZ Limited that the company's goals are to maximise the company's assets. Is this inconsistent with maximising shareholder wealth?

12. Discuss some of the institutional mechanisms that exist in Australia for ensuring that financial managers act in the best interests of the company owners.

13. It has been said that the objective of a firm is to look after the interests of the owners of the firm—the ordinary shareholders. However, firms are run by managers (directors) who are often not owners (shareholders). Surely, then, managers would be more interested in looking after their own interests rather than those of some faceless crowd. True or false? Explain. Are the interests of the two groups necessarily incompatible?

14. Managers of companies face an impossible task because they cannot really increase the wealth of each and every shareholder. Because there are thousands of shareholders, it is impossible to find projects that allow the manager to meet the investment and consumption needs of every shareholder. As a consequence, managers should follow the rule that they should invest in projects that provide them with the best satisfaction and not consider the needs of investors. Do you agree? What investment rules should managers follow and why?

15. What is meant by 'the market for corporate control'? How does this market contribute to the efficiency of capital markets overall?

16. A security exists that promises to pay $300 in one year's time. If the market rate of interest is 20% p.a. and the security is for sale for $200, what would you do and why? Ultimately, what would you expect to happen?

17. How does investing in projects that have a rate of return equal to or greater than the market rate of interest maximise shareholders' wealth?

PRACTICAL QUESTIONS

1. Your current part-time job pays $500 per week. Another similar job requiring similar effort pays $550 per week. You are thinking of quitting your current job to take up the higher paying job. What is the opportunity cost of doing so?   **BASIC**

2. Refer to Table 1.1 in the chapter. Assume that one week earlier (i.e. 23 June 2010), prices of News Corp.'s major securities were: **BASIC**

Security	ASX stock code	Last sale price ($)
Class B common stock	NWS	15.38
Class A common stock	NWSLV	17.75

What is News Corp.'s market capitalisation as at 23 June 2010?

3. If you placed $5000 in a bank for one year, how much would you have accumulated in one year if the rate of return was 6.75%?   **BASIC**

4. What is the rate of return on an asset that will pay $104 000 in one year if it is priced at $97 000 today?   **BASIC**

5. What is the rate of return on an asset priced at $4695 today that will pay $5000 in one year?   **BASIC**

6. You bought an ounce of gold last year for $1300 and sell it today for $1400. What is your rate of return?   **BASIC**

BASIC

7. How much would you receive in one year if you invested in an asset priced at $8000 today, with a rate of return of 5.25%?

BASIC

8. How much would you have to invest today to accumulate $20 000 in one year if the current rate of return is 9.8%?

INTERMEDIATE

9. If you were able to obtain a rate of return of 6.5% by placing funds in a bank for one year, how much would you be willing to pay for an alternative asset that promises to return $18 000 in one year?

INTERMEDIATE

10. (a) Would you pay $100 000 today for an asset that will pay $105 000 in one year if the rate of return is currently 6% p.a? Explain your answer.

    (b) Would you pay $98 000 today for an asset that will pay $105 000 in one year if the rate of return is currently 6% p.a? Explain your answer.

INTERMEDIATE

11. (a) What is the rate of return on the All Ordinaries Index if its opening value is 4030.3 points and its closing value is 4096.6 points?

    (b) What is the rate of return on the All Ordinaries Index if its opening value is 4041.5 points and its closing value is 4033.3 points?

INTERMEDIATE

12. If you purchased National Australia Bank shares in the morning at $28.78 and sold them at the end of the day at $28.93, what rate of return would you have realised?

INTERMEDIATE

13. A company is expected to produce one (and only one) cash flow of $44 million in one year. If the appropriate interest rate is 10% p.a., what is the value of the company? If there are one million shares on issue, what should its share price be?

INTERMEDIATE

14. A firm has identified the following six potential projects. Each project requires an investment of $100 and will return (without risk) the following amounts:

    Project A $124
    Project B $106
    Project C $112
    Project D $118
    Project E $108
    Project F $110

    (a) If the firm has $500 to invest, which projects (if any) should it select?

    (b) If the firm has $500 to invest and the opportunity to lend to or borrow from the capital market at 10% p.a., what investments should it make?

    (c) If the firm has $500 to invest and the opportunity to lend to or borrow from the capital market at 5% p.a., what investments should it make?

CHALLENGING

15. Refer back to Figure 1.3. Using the information provided for Neuren Pharmaceuticals Ltd and National Australia Bank, work out:

    (a) which stock is more liquid

    (b) which stock is more volatile

    (c) which stock is more expensive to trade (in terms of the bid–ask spread).

CHALLENGING

16. Refer back to Figures 1.3 and 1.4:

    (a) What is the rate of return on Neuren Pharmaceuticals Ltd and National Australia Bank, and what is the price volatility of the shares over the year?

(b) What is the return on the All Ordinaries Index?

(c) Have the shares outperformed or underperformed the index? Do you think you can provide an explanation for this?

17. (a) Write an equation which enables you to calculate the price (P_t) of a cash flow to be received in one year's time (F_t) when the interest rate is r.

    (b) Rearrange the equation to make r the subject of the formula.

    (c) Explain what happens to returns as the future cash flow increases.

    (d) Explain what happens to returns as the price you pay for the asset increases.

CHALLENGING

18. A financial asset is expected to return $400 000 exactly one year from today. It is expected to return another $400 000 exactly two years from today. If the opportunity cost of capital for one year is 10%:

    (a) Calculate the value of the cash flow to be received in year 1 today.

    (b) Calculate the value of the cash flow to be received in year 2 today.

    (c) What is the (total) value of the asset today?

CHALLENGING

19. Refer to the table below.

CHALLENGING

Company	JB Hi-Fi Limited (JBH)	Rio Tinto Limited (RIO)
Chief Executive Officer	Richard Uechtritz	Tom Albanese
Cash remuneration 2006	$1 217 631	$1 741 000
Cash remuneration 2007	$1 631 757	$2 771 000
Share price 31 Dec 2006	$6.55	$74.79
Share price 31 Dec 2007	$15.60	$133.95

Source: JB Hi-Fi 2007 Annual Report, Rio Tinto Limited 2007 Annual Report and Yahoo7! Finance.

(a) Calculate the return on JB Hi-Fi shares and Rio Tinto Shares.

(b) Calculate the percentage change in the cash remuneration of Richard Uechtritz and Tom Albanese.

(c) Which company has a cash remuneration policy which is more likely to align the interests of the CEO with that of the companies' shareholders?

(d) What other types of remuneration may the CEOs of JB Hi-Fi and Rio Tinto receive that would align their interests with those of shareholders?

CASE STUDY

The questions in this case study refer to the information in the table below.

Commonwealth Bank (CBA) CEO—Ralph Norris	2009	2010
Cash remuneration (fixed)	$3 253 551	$3 128 875
Incentive remuneration (options, variable)	$1 936 546	$6 415 735
Share price (30 June)	$39.00	$48.64
Number of shares on issue (million)	1554	1644
Dividends per share (cents)	228	290
Operating cash flow ($m)	$1476	$3445

CASE STUDY QUESTIONS

1. Calculate the market capitalisation of CBA in the two years.

2. Assume the net operating cash flow increases by 6% p.a., and that the relevant interest rate or discount rate is 14%. Based on 2010 figures, calculate the present value of your cash flow forecast for 2011. What portion of the market capitalisation does this represent?

3. Calculate the return on shares for the year ended 30 June 2010.

4. Calculate the percentage change in the cash and incentive remuneration of Ralph Norris from 2009 to 2010.

5. Will the cash remuneration policy alone align the interests of the CEO with those of the company's shareholders?

6. What other types of remuneration policies may be in place to align the incentives of the CEO with those of shareholders?

FURTHER READING

For a review of research examining the objective of corporate financial decision making see:

- Garvey, G. T. and Swan, P. L. (1994), 'The economics of corporate governance: Beyond the Marshallian firm', *Journal of Corporate Finance*, vol. I, 139–74.

For a comprehensive discussion of almost all the financial information contained in *The Australian Financial Review* see:

- Dunstan, B. (1992), *Understanding Finance with The Australian Financial Review*, Financial Review Library, Sydney.

NOTES

1. Babcock & Brown (BNB) was an Australian investment bank that specialised in structured products, and was worth $9.1 billion at its peak. It was started by James Babcock and George Brown in 1977, and in 2004 it was listed on the Australian Stock Exchange. After a tightening of the credit market during the Global Financial Crisis, BNB found it increasingly difficult to refinance its short-term debt obligations, and went into voluntary administration in March 2009.

2. The term 'over-the-counter' comes from the days when an investor wishing to purchase or sell bonds would go into a bank and negotiate the trade over the (bank) counter.

3. At this stage, it is not important to understand the difference between class A and class B stock, which are actually shares issued by American companies such as News Corporation. The main point is that News Corporation had two different types of shares on issue, and the sum of the market value of these two different types of shares make up the value of the company's equity.

4. There are only two days in the year when a share can pay a dividend—the days that it pays the interim and final dividends. Hence, there are only two days in the year when this whole formula is relevant. Most of the time you can ignore the dividend variable and just take the difference between the closing price and the opening price in calculating the rate of return on the share.

5. If you calculate a weekly rate of return, what you implicitly assume is that you buy at the start of the week and sell at the end of the week. If you calculate a monthly return, you assume that you buy at the start of the month and sell at the end of the month and so on.

2

A review of financial mathematics

CHAPTER PREVIEW

The objective of this chapter is to review the basic mathematics used in valuing assets. The principles underlying each asset valuation were introduced and demonstrated in the previous chapter, where their role in the valuation of an asset that produced a single cash flow over one period with a single-period interest rate was examined. This chapter reviews the basic mathematics required to value an asset with multiple cash flows occurring in the future.

KEY CONCEPTS

CONCEPT 2.1   The aim of financial mathematics

The broad aim of financial mathematics is to convert single or multiple cash flows that will be received at different points in time to one number. This number is the value of all of an asset's cash flows, as at a given point in time.[1] It enables direct comparison of assets that provide different cash flow payoffs, which is important for two reasons. First, it provides the basis for a rational choice between different assets. This is because the cash flows of all assets under consideration are stated in 'like' terms (i.e. at the same point in time). Second, this number determines the maximum price that an investor should be willing to pay for an asset. That is, it represents the 'intrinsic value' of an asset.

To re-illustrate the concept of the time value of money, let us begin with the time lines in Figure 2.1. In this figure, asset 1 provides a cash flow of $100 in five years' time, whereas asset 2 will return $100 in three years' time.

A NOTE ON TIME LINES

Time lines are used throughout this and subsequent chapters to illustrate cash flows associated with different assets and opportunities. They are particularly useful for complex cash flow situations (e.g. deferred annuities and equivalent annuities, discussed later in this chapter). Time lines often help to clarify, both to the reader and to the user, the nature of the problem, the assumptions underlying the problem or the interpretation of the problem. The use of time lines is important and recommended when attempting any financial mathematics problems.

Would you rather own asset 1 or asset 2? The rational answer to this question is that you would rather own asset 2. This is because the intrinsic value of asset 2 is greater, because of the time value of money. That is, an amount received sooner rather than later is more valuable, *ceteris paribus*.

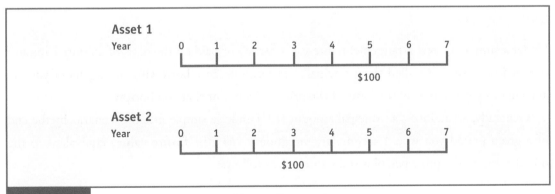

| **Figure 2.1** | Which of these assets would you rather own? |

What if you had a desire to consume in year 5 and not year 3? Would you still rather own asset 2? The answer is again yes, because if you owned asset 2 you would still be better off. Specifically, you could reinvest the $100 received at the end of year 3 and accumulate more than $100 by year 5.

Now, what if you had a desire to consume in year 2? Would you still prefer to own asset 2? The answer is once again yes, because you could borrow the desired amount for year 2 consumption from the bank and use the $100 cash flow at the end of year 3 as repayment for this loan. Effectively, this means you could borrow more than if you used a year 5 cash flow of $100 as repayment.

In a developed economy, people are compensated if they defer their consumption to later, and charged if they wish to consume more now than their income allows. This compensation or charge is called 'interest' and is usually expressed as a percentage, per period, of the money borrowed (when we wish to consume more now) or the money invested (the consumption we defer until later periods). In this text, the symbol r is used to represent the interest rate, although any symbol would serve the purpose. Chapter 1 discussed Fisher's insight into how the capital markets allow companies and consumers to match their consumption needs and income flows, with the interest rate being a key component of Fisher's Separation Theorem.

CONCEPT CHECK

1. What are the aims of financial mathematics?
2. Would a rational person prefer to receive $100 in one year's time or $100 in five years' time?

For the answers, go to MyFinanceLab

CONCEPT 2.2   Interest rate arrangements

Simple interest

Under a simple interest arrangement, interest is earned or paid on the basis of an initial amount invested or borrowed, called the 'principal'. For example, in a borrowing arrangement you are agreeing to pay interest on the basis of the principal amount that you borrow.

Generally, if you invest a principal amount (PV) under a simple interest scenario, by the end of a given period you would accumulate an amount (FV, the **future value**) equivalent to the initial amount, the principal, plus some interest, as follows:

Future value
The value at some point in the future of a present amount of money invested at some interest rate.

$$FV = PV + interest$$

By definition, the interest is calculated as a fraction of the principal (PV) under simple interest. In fact, it is the product of the interest rate (r) and the PV. Hence, the above equation can be expressed as follows:

$$FV = PV + PVr$$

Factoring out PV yields:

$$FV = PV(1 + r) \tag{2.1}$$

where:

FV = the accumulated (future) value

PV = the initial amount invested or borrowed

r = the simple interest rate over the entire period

Since r is the simple interest rate over the entire investment or borrowing period, if the interest rate is expressed on a per annum basis, it is necessary to convert this to an interest rate over the full investment or borrowing period. Example 2.1 clarifies the application of Equation 2.1 above.

EXAMPLE 2.1

Simple interest

QUESTION

A credit union pays 5% p.a. simple interest. If $1000 is invested today, how much will the account accrue in four years?

ANSWER

$$FV = PV(1 + r)$$
$$r = \text{4-year interest rate} = 0.05 \times 4 = 0.20$$

Hence:

$$FV = 1000(1 + 0.20) = 1200$$

An amount of $1200 will accrue in the account in four years.

If simple interest is applied to periods of less than one year, the interest rate r is apportioned over the number of days the interest rate is applied:

$$1 + (r \times dtm/365)$$

where dtm is the days to maturity of the loan or investment, and 365 represents the number of days in a calendar year.

Practitioner's POV

There is one point that needs to be made about the material in this chapter. While the mathematics is indeed frequently used in practice, there are a large number of electronic calculators and computer software packages that can be used to do the calculations. A Hewlett-Packard 12C financial calculator has all the formulae covered in this chapter built into it. Common spreadsheet packages such as Microsoft Excel also have built-in financial functions.

Compound interest

As is the case with simple interest, under a compound interest scenario interest is earned or paid on the principal. The difference is that, at the end of each compounding period, the amount of interest earned or accrued is calculated and added to the balance of the principal. This new balance is used to calculate the next period's interest. The distinguishing feature of compound interest is that interest is earned (or paid) on interest that has accrued in previous periods.

To illustrate the concept of compound interest and derive an expression for the accumulated value under this type of arrangement, consider an amount of cash, PV, that you invest at a compound interest rate, r. The accumulated value of your investment at the end of the first year (FV_1) will be:

$$FV_1 = PV(1 + r)$$

Under a compound interest scenario, in the second year this entire amount, $PV(1 + r)$, will be reinvested at the prevailing interest rate (r) and will accumulate to:

$$FV_2 = PV(1 + r)(1 + r) = PV(1 + r)^2$$

Repeating the logic for the third year yields:

$$FV_3 = PV(1 + r)^2(1 + r) = PV(1 + r)^3$$

A clear pattern is now emerging. The exponent attached to the $(1 + r)$ term is equivalent to the year for which we wish to calculate the accumulated value. Hence, in year n the following amount would have accrued (and for simplicity dropping the n subscript on FV):

$$FV = PV(1 + r)^n \tag{2.2}$$

where:

FV = the accumulated amount in period n

PV = the initial amount invested

r = the interest rate per period

n = the number of periods

It is important to ensure that the same compounding period underlies the interest rate (r) and the number of periods over which the amount (PV) is invested (n). Hence, if r is the interest rate per year (or per annum), n must be expressed in years. Alternatively, if r is the interest rate per month, n must be expressed in months, and so on. Example 2.2 illustrates an application of Equation 2.2.

EXAMPLE 2.2

Compound interest

QUESTION

A credit union pays 5% p.a. interest compounded annually. If $1000 is invested today, how much will the account accrue in four years?

ANSWER

$FV = PV \times (1 + r)^n$

Hence:

$FV = 1000 \times (1 + 0.05)^4 = \$1216$

An amount of $1216 will accrue in the account in four years.

Comparing different financing arrangements

Where interest rates are subject to compounding, they are commonly quoted as either **nominal interest rates** or **effective interest rates**. The distinction between these two ways of quoting an interest rate is due solely to the differences in the number of compounding periods per annum. When nominal interest rates are quoted, it is normal to include the number of compounding periods per annum—for example, 10% p.a. compounded semi-annually. The convention for interpreting this nominal rate is to divide the nominal rate by the number of compounding periods per year to get the rate per period. Thus, a nominal rate of 10% p.a. compounded semi-annually is equivalent to 5% per half-year (0.10/2).

If the nominal rate is r_{nom}% p.a. compounded m times per year, the effective interest rate is:

$$\text{Effective rate} = \left(1 + \frac{r_{nom}}{m}\right)^m - 1 \tag{2.3}$$

Nominal interest rate
Quoted annual interest rate that is adjusted to match the frequency of payments or compounding by taking a proportion of the quoted nominal rate to obtain the actual interest rate per period. It does not take into account that interest is reinvested and that interest is earned on both principal and reinvested interest.

Effective interest rate
Interest rate that accounts for the true amount of interest that is earned on both reinvested interest and principal earned over a year. It is the interest rate which, compounded annually, is equivalent to a given nominal interest rate.

FINANCE EXTRA!

Borrowers fixed on low rates and discounts loans

DEMAND for fixed rate loans doubled over the past year, peaking in November and reaching its highest level since April 2008, national loan approval data from Mortgage Choice has revealed.

This type of loan accounted for 20% of all new loan approvals during November, up on the six-month average of 16%, the 12-month average of 14% and this period last year when only 11% of new loans were fixed rate loans.

Ongoing discount rate home loans rose marginally, from 43% to 45% of home loans among new borrowers in November – and well ahead of the 12-month average of 33%.

Company spokesperson Belinda Williamson said, 'When comparing our November loan approval data to one year ago, it is evident fixed rate loans have become far more popular.'·

'There has been a lot of rate movement in fixed rate loans in recent weeks and months. We've seen some fixed rate loan products almost a whole percentage point lower than lenders' variable rates.

'Demand for ongoing discount loans has risen steadily, with this type of loan representing 45% of all home loans in November, compared with 43% six months ago and 33% a year earlier.

'Snapping up relatively low fixed rates and attractive variable rate discounts, borrowers are certainly making the most of lenders' pricing war as they battle each other for business.'

Variable rate home loans accounted for 80% of all loan approvals this month, on par with the previous month and lower than the 12-month average of 86%.

Standard variable loan demand rose to 17% of approvals in November from 15% in October, below the 12-month average of 24%. Demand for basic variable loans fell to 14% in November from 16% in October, down on the 12-month average of 21%, and interest in line of credit loans and introductory rate loans fell slightly to 4% and 1% respectively.

Source: Mortgage Choice press release, 05 December, 2011. Accessed 10 January 2012.

where:

r_{nom} = the nominal rate

m = the number of compounding periods underlying the nominal rate

We can interpret this formula as the value of $1 after one year, invested at a nominal interest rate of r_{nom}% compounded m times per year, less the original $1. The effective interest rate will be greater than the nominal rate for compounding periods of less than one year (e.g. quarterly compounding). The nominal rate is equal to the effective interest rate if, and only if, there is one compounding period per annum—that is, if interest is charged on an annual basis.

The concept of an effective rate of interest is very useful in comparing different interest rate arrangements. For example:

- comparing nominal compound interest rates with different underlying compounding periods
- comparing compound interest rates with simple interest rates.

Suppose that a credit union offers you a five-year loan at 6% p.a. compounded annually, or 5.95% p.a. compounded quarterly. Which rate is cheaper? This question can be answered by comparing the effective rate of 5.95% p.a. compounded quarterly with 6% p.a. As there is only one compounding period for the 6% p.a. option, the effective rate is the same as the nominal rate. The effective rate for the quarterly compounding option is given by:

$$\text{Effective rate} = \left(1 + \frac{0.0595}{4}\right)^4 - 1 = 0.0608, \text{ or } 6.08\% \text{ p.a.}$$

Hence, 6.08% p.a. compounded annually, is the same as 5.95% p.a. compounded quarterly. Therefore, a loan at 6% p.a. compounded annually is preferred to 5.95% p.a. compounded quarterly. Comparison of nominal interest with effective interest is useful in evaluating financing alternatives. Example 2.3 provides a comparison of nominal interest with effective interest rates on credit cards, while Example 2.4 addresses the different way a housing loan may be quoted.

Practitioner's POV

Simple, nominal and effective interest rates are used commonly in day-to-day business. While changes to the Consumer Credit Acts require interest rates to be quoted at the nominal annual rate (sometimes referred to as the annual percentage rate, or APR), some finance companies and banks calculate an interest rate on lease or hire-purchase agreements using simple interest (also called the 'flat rate'). Simple interest is also used for bills of exchange. When borrowing from a credit union, obtaining a home loan or an overdraft, or using credit card facilities, the quoted rate is normally a nominal rate. When investing in a fixed certificate of deposit or other liquid security with a financial institution, the rate quoted is often the effective rate of interest.

EXAMPLE 2.3

Effective interest rates

QUESTION

What is the effective interest rate (per annum compounded annually) on the outstanding balance on a credit card if the nominal rate quoted on the card is 15.75% p.a. compounded daily?

ANSWER

The number of compounding periods in one year is 365. Interest on any outstanding balance is calculated daily and added to the amount outstanding. The formula for calculating the effective rate is:

$$\text{Effective rate} = \left(1 + \frac{r_{nom}}{m}\right)^m - 1$$

where:

r_{nom} = the nominal rate (15.75%)

m = the number of compounding periods (365)

$$\text{Effective rate} = \left(1 + \frac{0.1575}{365}\right)^{365} - 1 = 0.1705, \text{ or } 17.05\% \text{ per annum compounded annually.}$$

There is a difference of more than 1% between the nominal rate quoted on credit cards and the effective rate when compounding is daily.

EXAMPLE 2.4

Comparing interest rates

QUESTION

Is a loan which charges interest at 14% per annum compounded monthly cheaper than a loan with a 14.75% interest rate with annual compounding? Would you prefer a loan with a 14.5% interest rate with semi-annual compounding?

ANSWER

We need to recognise that these are nominal rates with different compounding frequencies and are not directly comparable. We must convert them to a single, consistent format in the form of effective annual interest rates.

Nominal rate		Effective rate
14.75% p.a. with annual compounding		14.75%
14% p.a. with monthly compounding	$= (1 + r_{nom}/m)^m - 1 = (1 + 0.14/12)^{12} - 1$	14.93%
14.5% p.a. with semi-annual compounding	$= (1 + r_{nom}/m)^m - 1 = (1 + 0.145/2)^2 - 1$	15.03%

The 14% p.a. rate loan with monthly compounding is not cheaper than the 14.75% p.a. rate loan with annual compounding, although it is cheaper than the 14.5% p.a. loan with semi-annual compounding.

Example 2.5 illustrates an investment problem where the interest rates on deposits are much lower than interest rates charged in the loan example, Example 2.4. With low interest rates, the number of compounding periods does not make a significant difference to the effective rate. The 6.85% quarterly compounding rate pays only three cents extra per $100 than does the 7% annual rate.

EXAMPLE 2.5

Comparing investment rates

QUESTION

Two banks are offering different deposit rates on fixed deposits. Is 7.00% p.a. compounded annually a better investment than a deposit attracting 6.85% p.a. with quarterly compounding?

ANSWER

Again, to compare the rates we need to recognise that these are nominal rates and are not directly comparable. We need to express them in a single, consistent format using effective interest rates before we can compare them.

Nominal rate	Number of compounding periods	Formula	Effective interest rate
6.85%	Quarterly	$[(1 + 0.0685/4)^4] - 1$	7.03%
7.00%	Annual	$[(1 + 0.07/1)^1] - 1$	7.00%

The 6.85% p.a. with quarterly compounding is the best investment, giving an effective rate of 7.03% per annum compounded annually, despite the fact that the other stated rate appears higher (7% p.a. compounded annually).

In addition to moving from nominal to effective rates, we can compare simple interest with compound interest. Suppose that a bank offers you a fixed-term deposit at 5% p.a. compounded annually for four years, or 6% simple interest for four years. Which deal is better? There are many financial advisers who make a living out of solving these types of problems for their clients. One way of answering this question is to convert the compound interest rate into an *equivalent simple interest rate*.

The equivalent simple interest rate converts any compound interest rate into its simple interest rate equivalent. Such rates can be used validly to compare different interest rate arrangements. In order to calculate the equivalent simple interest rate, you need to find the simple interest rate that generates a future accumulated value equal to the accumulated value generated by the compound interest arrangement, as follows:

$$\$1 \times (1+ \text{simple interest rate} \times t) = \$1 \times (1 + \text{compound interest rate}_m)^{mt}$$

where m is the compounding frequency per year and t is the number of years over which the amount is invested. Both the left-hand side and the right-hand side of the equation give an estimate of the accumulated value of $1 under different interest rate arrangements. Making the simple interest rate the subject of the above equation yields:

$$\text{Simple interest rate} \times t = (1+ \text{compound interest rate}_m)^{mt} - 1 \qquad \textbf{(2.4)}$$

where:

$$\text{simple interest rate} = \text{effective simple interest rate}$$

$$m = \text{the compounding interval}$$

$$\text{compound interest rate}_m = \text{interest rate with compounding frequency } m$$

$$(\text{also calculated as } [r_{nom}/m] \text{ in Equation 2.4})$$

Alternatively, the compound interest rate can be estimated from the simple interest rate by rearranging Equation 2.4 as follows:

$$\text{Compound interest} = \sqrt[mt]{[1 + (\text{simple interest} \times t)]} - 1 \qquad \textbf{(2.5)}$$

Example 2.6 provides a worked example to illustrate how a compound interest rate can be converted into an equivalent simple interest rate.

EXAMPLE 2.6

Comparing simple and compound rates of interest

QUESTION

A credit union pays interest at 5% p.a. compounded annually. If $1000 is invested for five years, what is the equivalent simple interest rate that the amount will earn?

ANSWER

Effective simple interest rate $\times t = (1 + \text{compound interest rate}_m)^{mt} - 1$

Effective interest rate $= (1 + 0.05)^5 - 1 = 28\%$ over 5 years, or 5.6% p.a. (i.e. 28/5 = 5.6)

Hence, the simple interest rate that is *equivalent* to a compound rate of 5% p.a. compounded annually is 5.6%.

Continuous compounding

Continuous compounding is the theoretical case where interest is calculated at every single point in time and added to the balance. Another way of thinking about continuous compounding is that the compounding period is infinitely small. While you would be hard-pressed to find a bank that pays continuously compounded interest, the concept is used quite extensively in many finance applications and for many security valuation models. Appendix 2.1 derives the following expression for the accumulated value (FV) of an amount (PV) invested at a continuously compounded rate of interest:

$$FV = PVe^{rt} \qquad \textbf{(2.6)}$$

where:

$FV =$

$PV =$ the cash flow invested or borrowed

$r =$ the continuously compounded rate of return

$t =$ time over which the cash flow is invested/borrowed

$e =$ the base of natural logarithms (a constant), $\doteqdot 2.718$

Equation 2.6 is useful for calculating the implied continuously compounded rate of return on an investment. Example 2.7 illustrates an application of Equation 2.6.

EXAMPLE 2.7

Continuous compounding return

QUESTION

On Monday, 6 December 2010, Lend Lease Corporation (LLC) opened for trading at a price of $7.67, and on the Friday of the same week, it closed at a price of $8.07. If you bought LLC shares at the open price on Monday, and sold them at the closing price on Friday, what is the continuously compounded rate of return you earned in the 5-day holding period?

ANSWER

$$FV = PVe^{rt}$$
$$8.07 = 7.67e^{rt}$$

Rearranging the above equations gives:

$$r = \ln(8.07/7.67)/5$$
$$= 1.02\%$$

Hence, the continuously compounded rate of return on LLC is 1.02% per day, or 2.21% over the 5 days.

Continuous compounding is an important concept in pricing options and other derivatives. Options are financial contracts that give the holders the right, but not the obligation, to buy or sell an asset at a specified price and date. Options also have extensive application in managing risk (see Chapter 13).

CONCEPT CHECK

3. Name the three ways of quoting an interest rate.
4. What is the difference between a compounding interest rate and a nominal interest rate?
5. What is an effective interest rate?
6. When compounding occurs more than once per year, will the annual effective interest rate be higher or lower than the nominal rate?

For the answers, go to MyFinanceLab

CONCEPT 2.3   Present value of a single amount

The concept of present value was introduced in the previous chapter. The present value of a single cash flow can be defined as the present worth of a payment to be received in the future, taking into account the time value of money. For example, how much is $1, to be received in four years, worth today? The amount that $1 in the future is worth today is the amount that you would have to invest in order to generate that $1 in the future. This is one way of looking at the concept of present value. Equation 2.2 (described earlier) gives the accumulated amount of an investment of *PV*, under an interest rate *r*, over *n* years:

$$FV = PV(1 + r)^n$$

If we make *PV* the subject:

$$PV = \frac{FV}{(1 + r)^n} \text{ or, alternatively, } PV = FV(1 + r)^{-n} \tag{2.7}$$

where:

    FV = the future cash flow to be received

    PV = the present value of the future cash flow

    r = the compound interest rate on an alternative comparable investment

    n = the number of periods before *FV* is received

Present value
The current value of one or more future cash payments, discounted at some appropriate interest rate.

PV is the **present value** because it is the amount that needs to be invested at a rate *r* over *n* periods in order to generate the future cash flow (*FV*). Equation 2.7 enables the conversion of a future cash flow into an equivalent current cash flow. It is the most basic building block used to value assets. Example 2.8 illustrates the application of this equation.

EXAMPLE 2.8

Present value of a single sum to be received in the future
QUESTION
You are offered an asset that pays $1500 in five years. Currently, an investment opportunity of similar risk is available to you, paying interest at 5% p.a. compounded annually. What is the (present) value of the asset?
ANSWER

$PV = FV(1 + r)^{-n}$
$PV = 1500(1 + 0.05)^{-5}$
    = $1175

The *PV* of the asset is $1175.

This example illustrates that receiving $1175 today is equivalent to receiving $1500 in five years' time, given an interest rate of 5% p.a. over the five years. Accordingly, an investor should be indifferent to the choice of either of the two cash flows, which means that $1175 is the appropriate price to pay for the asset today.

CONCEPT 2.4   Present value and future value of multiple amounts

The approach for valuing a single cash flow can also be applied to a stream of cash flows. Consider the time line with cash flows in Figure 2.2. It is assumed that at the end of year 1,

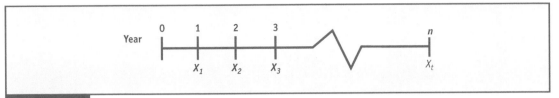

| Figure 2.2 | Time line for a stream of cash flows |

cash flows to the value X_1 are received. In year 2 the cash flows received are X_2 to time n where X_t are received.

To find the present value of this cash flow stream, each period's cash flow must be discounted at the interest rate r and then added together. The general formula for the present value of this multiple cash flow stream is:

$$PV = \sum_{t=1}^{n} \frac{X_t}{(1 + r)^t} \text{ or } PV = \sum_{t=1}^{n} X_t(1 + r)^{-t}$$ **(2.8)**

where:

> PV = the present value of the future multiple cash flows
>
> X_t = cash flow received in period t
>
> r = the compound interest rate on an alternative comparable investment
>
> t = the number of periods before X_t is received
>
> n = the number of periods over which cash flows are received

This is the essence of how assets are valued. Indeed, it will be demonstrated later that the only difference between this example and the valuation of more complicated assets, such as bonds and shares, is the structure of the cash flows. Example 2.9 is an example of the present value of a stream of unequal cash flows.

EXAMPLE 2.9

Present value of an asset paying multiple cash flows in the future

QUESTION

You are offered an investment that promises a stream of cash flows. The cash flows are $1000 in the first year, $2000 in the second year, $3000 in the third year and $500 in the fourth year. Currently, an investment opportunity of similar risk is available to you, paying interest at 10% p.a. compounded annually. What is the maximum you would be prepared to pay for the asset?

ANSWER

The first step is to establish a time-line diagram to determine the nature of the cash flows and to formulate the problem clearly.

Interest rate 10%

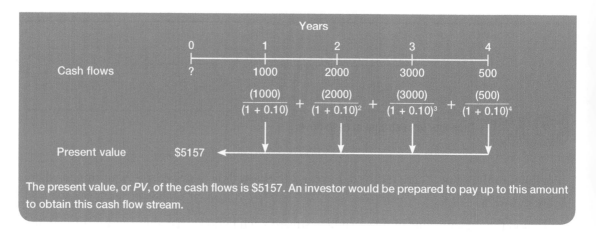

The individual cash flows in Example 2.9 are discounted to the present and then they are added together to find the present value of the entire stream. The present value of the cash flows, $5157, is equivalent to the cash flow stream. This concept of equivalence is important in understanding what 'present value' means. In terms of Example 2.9, it means that if we invest $5157 at 10% interest we can create the equivalent cash flow stream, as shown in the shaded area below.

Year	1	2	3	4
Investment at beginning	$5157	$4673	$3140	$454
Interest at 10%	$516	$467	$314	$45
Balance	$5673	$5140	$3454	$500
Less withdrawal	$1000	$2000	$3000	$500
Balance at end of year	$4673	$3140	$454	$0

The table shows that if we invest $5157 at the beginning of the first year, it earns $516 in interest for the first year, giving a total investment balance of $5673. Withdrawing $1000 leaves $4673 for the second year, on which we again earn interest and are able to withdraw the $2000 promised in year 2 in Example 2.9. We continue to withdraw from our fund $3000 in year 3 and the final $500 in year 4. The fund has no money left after the fourth withdrawal. We have demonstrated that we have created the same cash flow stream provided by our investment opportunity. At an interest rate of 10%, $5157 is equivalent to a cash flow stream that promised $1000 in year 1, $2000 in year 2, $3000 in year 3 and $500 in year 4. We now have a powerful tool that enables us to evaluate promised cash flow streams in the future by comparing their present values.

Of course, it is also possible to find the future value (FV) of a stream of cash flows. The general formula for future values of a multiple cash flow stream is:

$$FV = \sum_{t=1}^{n} X_t(1 + r)^t \qquad \textbf{(2.9)}$$

where:

FV = the future value of a multiple stream of cash flows

X_t = cash flow received in period t

r = the compound interest rate on an alternative comparable investment

t = the number of periods before X_t is received

The future value is the sum of the individual cash flows compounded forward. Example 2.10 illustrates the future value of a multiple cash flow stream using the same data as Example 2.9.

EXAMPLE 2.10

Future value of multiple cash flows

QUESTION

Assume you own an investment that promises a stream of cash flows. The cash flows are $1000 in the first year, $2000 in the second year, $3000 in the third year and $500 in the fourth year. Currently, an investment opportunity of similar risk is available to you, paying interest at 10% p.a. compounded annually. How much will you have accumulated at the end of five years?

ANSWER

The first step is to establish a time-line diagram to determine the nature of the cash flows and to formulate the problem clearly.

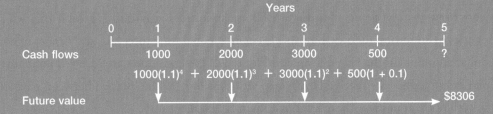

Years

| 0 | 1 | 2 | 3 | 4 | 5 |

Cash flows   1000   2000   3000   500   ?

$1000(1.1)^4 + 2000(1.1)^3 + 3000(1.1)^2 + 500(1 + 0.1)$

Future value $8306

Each of the cash flows is compounded forward to the end of year 5 to give a future value of $8306.

CONCEPT CHECK

7. How would you define present value?

8. How are present and future values dependent on interest rates?

9. What are two ways of estimating the present value of a cash flow stream that contains multiple cash flows of unequal value?

10. How would you estimate the future value of a cash flow stream?

For the answers, go to MyFinanceLab

CONCEPT 2.5   Annuities

Annuities are a special case of multiple cash flows. An annuity is a series of cash flows of equal size that occur at regular time intervals extending into the future. A good example of an annuity is a constant superannuation payment made to retirees on a monthly basis throughout the remainder of their lives. Other examples are rentals paid in arrears (or in advance) and interest payments on a bond. Figure 2.3 provides examples of cash flow patterns that are annuities.

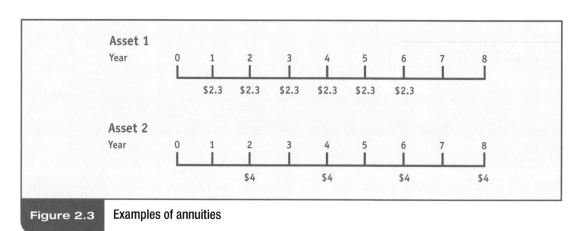

Figure 2.3   Examples of annuities

Ordinary annuity
A series of cash flows of equal size which occur regularly with an equal time period between each subsequent cash flow extending into the future, with the first cash flow occurring at the end of the first period.

Annuity due
An annuity in which the first cash flow is to occur immediately—that is, on the valuation date.

Deferred annuity
Annuity where the cash flows are deferred for one or more periods. That is, the first cash flow is to occur after a time period that exceeds the time period between each subsequent cash flow.

The cash flows (assets) depicted in Figure 2.3 are annuities because they exhibit the two key characteristics of annuities: their cash flows (1) occur at equal time intervals, and (2) are of equal size or dollar amounts. In the first example in Figure 2.3 the cash flows are received annually; in the second example they are received every two years. As long as the interval between payments is constant, they are annuities. There are three main types of annuity:

- **ordinary annuity**: where cash flows occur at the end of each period and, hence, the first cash flow occurs at the end of the first year
- **annuity due**: where cash flows occur at the beginning of each period and, hence, the first cash flow occurs immediately
- **deferred annuity**: where the first cash flow in an annuity is delayed by x periods.

Future value

A four-year ordinary annuity paying $100 cash flows would look like this:

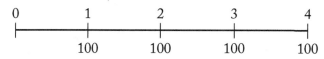

The future values of the four payments of this annuity can be calculated by compounding each cash flow forward to the fourth year and adding them together, as illustrated in Example 2.11.

EXAMPLE 2.11

Accumulated value of an ordinary annuity

QUESTION

If you receive $100 at the end of each year for four years, and invest these cash flows at 5% p.a. compounded annually, what is the future or accumulated value of this annuity?

ANSWER

FV_1	$100(1 + r)^3$	$100 × 1.1576	$115.76
FV_2	$100(1 + r)^2$	$100 × 1.1025	$110.25
FV_3	$100(1 + r)$	$100 × 1.05	$105
FV_4	$100	$100	$100
		Total	$431.01

The $100 received in year 4 is not compounded because it is already expressed in year 4 dollars. Hence, an amount of $431.01 will accrue after four years.

Because of the special nature of the cash flows in an annuity, the complexity of compounding individual cash flows forward can be simplified by using an annuity formula. Consider the following annuity:

Appendix 2.2 derives the following expression for the accumulated value of an annuity of $A that lasts for n periods:

$$FV = A\left[\frac{(1 + r)^n - 1}{r}\right]$$ **(2.10)**

where:

FV = the accumulated or future value of the annuity

A = the cash flow in dollars received/paid under the annuity

n = the number of cash flows that form the annuity

r = the compound interest rate per period

This is the equation for the future value of an *ordinary annuity*. There are two key characteristics of ordinary annuities that underlie this expression and are depicted in the time line above. They are: (1) there is no cash flow at time zero, and (2) there is a cash flow at time n. Time n is the date at which we calculate the accumulated value. In some respects, this makes the cash flow structure unusual. For example, a logical savings plan would normally begin with an immediate cash flow, and would be paid out one period after the last cash flow. Hence, care must be taken in applying Equation 2.10 and ensuring that the payments that the equation is applied to match the payments underlying the equation.

Example 2.12 illustrates the calculation of the accumulated value of an annuity using this equation.

EXAMPLE 2.12

Accumulated value of an ordinary annuity

QUESTION

At the end of each year, you place $500 in an account that earns 5% interest p.a. compounded annually. How much will be in the account at the end of five years?

ANSWER

Using Equation 2.10:

$$FV = A \left[\frac{(1 + r)^n - 1}{r} \right]$$

$$FV = 500 \left[\frac{(1 + 0.05)^5 - 1}{0.05} \right] = \$2763$$

Alternatively, using the table in Appendix 2.5:

The future value of $1 per period for five periods at an interest rate of 5% = $5.526.

Hence, the future value of $500 per year for five years at an interest rate of 5% is:

$$FV = 500 \times 5.526 = \$2763$$

The account will accumulate to $2763 at the end of five years.

As demonstrated, problems such as that in Example 2.12 can be solved using one of two methods. First, the ordinary annuity formula (Equation 2.10) can be applied. Alternatively, a table that describes the accumulated value of an annuity of $1 per period for a variety of different periods and interest rates, such as that contained in Appendix 2.5, may be used.

Present value

Just as the future value of an annuity may be calculated either from the compounding of individual cash flows or by applying a simplified formula, so the present value of an annuity may be found by discounting the individual cash flows or by applying a simplified formula. In the future-value illustration in Example 2.11, a four-year annuity paying $100 cash flows was considered, as follows:

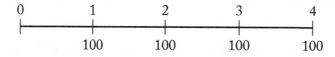

The present values of the four components of this annuity can be calculated by discounting each cash flow to the present and adding them together. This is illustrated in Example 2.13.

EXAMPLE 2.13

Present value of an ordinary annuity

QUESTION

If you receive $100 at the end of each year for four years, what is the value of these cash flows if the current rate of interest is 5% p.a. compounded annually?

ANSWER

PV_1	$100 \times (1 + r)^{-1}$	$\dfrac{\$100}{1.05}$	$95.24
PV_2	$100 \times (1 + r)^{-2}$	$\dfrac{\$100}{(1.1025)}$	$90.70
PV_3	$100 \times (1 + r)^{-3}$	$\dfrac{\$100}{(1.1576)}$	$86.39
PV_4	$100 \times (1 + r)^{-4}$	$\dfrac{\$100}{(1.2155)}$	$82.27
		Total	$354.60

The value of the cash flows (today) is $354.60.

The present value can also be calculated using a simplified formula derived in Appendix 2.3. This formula is based on an ordinary annuity with cash flows of the following general form:

The present value of an annuity of $A that occurs for n years is:

$$PV = A\left[\frac{1 - (1 + r)^{-n}}{r}\right] \qquad (2.11)$$

where:

- PV = the present value of the annuity
- A = the cash flow received/paid under the annuity
- n = the number of cash flows that form the annuity
- r = the compound interest rate per period

Applying that formula to the annuity of $100 per year for four years in Example 2.13 gives:

$$PV = 100\left[\frac{1 - (1 + 0.05)^{-4}}{0.05}\right] = \$354.60$$

Once again, the two key characteristics of the annuity that underlie this expression are: (1) there is no cash flow at time zero, and (2) there is a cash flow at the end of year n. Hence, Equation 2.11 relates to an ordinary annuity. Example 2.14 applies Equation 2.11 to value an ordinary annuity.

EXAMPLE 2.14

Present value of an annuity

QUESTION

What is the present value of a security that pays you $1.40 per half-year for 15 years, if the current interest rate is equivalent to 6.09% p.a. compounded annually?

ANSWER

The first step is to match the interest rate to the payment period. That is, payments are made half-yearly so we must convert the annual interest rate into a six-monthly interest rate.

$$(1 + r_6)^2 = (1 + 0.0609) \therefore r_6 = 0.03, \text{ or } 3\%$$

This means that 3% compounded every six months is equivalent to 6.09% compounded annually. We now use the six-monthly interest rate in Equation 2.11.

$$PV = 1.4 \left[\frac{1 - (1 + 0.03)^{-30}}{0.03} \right] = \$27.44$$

Alternatively, using the table in Appendix 2.6:

Present value of $1 per period for 30 periods at 3% is $19.60. Accordingly, the *PV* of $1.40 per period for 30 periods at 3% is: $19.60 × 1.40 = $27.44.

Thus, the value of the share is approximately $27.44.

Again, this example demonstrates that problems such as those described above can be solved in one of two ways. As before, the first method is to apply the ordinary annuity formula (Equation 2.11). Alternatively, a table that describes the present value of an annuity of $1 per period for a variety of different periods and interest rates, such as that contained in Appendix 2.6, may be used.

Synchronisation of interest rate compounding period and period between cash flows

A complicating issue in Example 2.14 was the non-synchronisation of the cash flows and the interest rate. The interest rate was an annually compounded rate, while the cash flows occurred every six months. In these circumstances, it is necessary to ensure that the compounding interval associated with the interest rate is synchronised with the cash flow intervals. The equivalent simple interest relationship derived earlier (Equation 2.4) is typically used to make any necessary conversions.

Annuity due

To date, an assumption has been made that the first cash flow in a series occurs at the end of the first year. However, there are many situations where the stream of payments starts immediately. This is the case for many financing arrangements (such as lease payments) and for most rental agreements where rental payments are made in advance. When annuity payments occur at the *beginning* of each period, this is called an 'annuity due'. The value of an annuity due is similar to that of an ordinary annuity, with the exception that the payments can be thought of as a single payment today (at time 0) plus an ordinary annuity of $n - 1$ payments, as shown below.

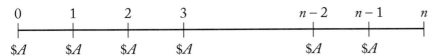

With an annuity due, the cash flows occur one period earlier than the cash flows for an ordinary annuity. The present value can be represented as follows:

$$PV = A + A \left[\frac{1 - (1 + r)^{-(n-1)}}{r} \right]$$ **(2.12)**

Equation 2.12 shows that the present value of an annuity due has two components, the cash flows received or paid initially and the present value of an annuity of $A for $n - 1$ periods. Example 2.15 applies Equation 2.12 to value an annuity due.

EXAMPLE 2.15

Present value of an annuity due

QUESTION

What is the present value of a $1000 annuity that pays five regular payments when the interest rate is 10% p.a. with the first payment due immediately?

ANSWER

The above cash flow is equivalent to an amount of $1000 now plus an ordinary annuity of four payments of $1000.

$$PV = 1000 + 1000 \left[\frac{1 - (1 + 0.10)^{-(5-1)}}{0.10} \right]$$

$$= 1000 + 1000 \times 3.170$$

$$= \$4170$$

Alternatively, using the table in Appendix 2.6:

Present value of $1 per period for four periods (5 years less 1) at 10% is $3.170. Accordingly, the *PV* of $1000 per period for four periods at 10% is: $3.170 × 1000 = $3170. Add to this the $1000 received immediately and the present value of the five payments is $4170.

Deferred annuities

A slightly more complex annuity is a *deferred annuity*, which is an ordinary annuity that does not begin in one period's time, but at a later date. Figure 2.4 illustrates two examples of deferred annuities. Asset 1 is an *ordinary* annuity which begins in three years (first cash flow is in four years), while Asset 2 is an *ordinary* annuity which begins in two years.

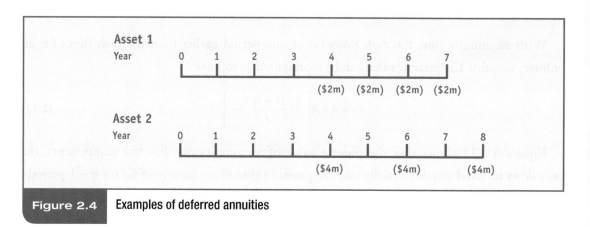

| **Figure 2.4** | **Examples of deferred annuities** |

With a deferred annuity, the cash flows are deferred for one or more periods. The present value can be calculated as follows:

$$PV = \left[A \times \frac{[1 - (1 + r)^{-n}]}{r} \right] / (1 + r)^{x-1} \tag{2.13}$$

Equation 2.13 shows the present value as having two components. The term in the large brackets is the present value of an ordinary annuity of n payments. The second term gives the present value of the single lump sum calculated from the first term, discounted back $x - 1$ periods, where x is the number of periods before the first cash flow occurs.

Another way of thinking about how deferred annuities are valued is that there are two steps involved.

1. Calculate the present value of the deferred annuity at the beginning of the period before it commences.

2. Then calculate the present value of step (1) back to time 0.

Example 2.16 illustrates the calculation of the present value of a deferred annuity.

EXAMPLE 2.16

Present value of a deferred annuity

QUESTION

What is the present value of an asset that commences paying cash flows of $2 million in two years' time for four years, when the interest rate is 5%?

ANSWER

Note that an ordinary annuity would commence in one year's time, so the above series of cash flows is the equivalent of an ordinary annuity deferred for one year.

Step 1 Present value of $2 million payments at start of year 2 (= end of year 1). The annuity formula discounts the four payments back to the beginning of the second period.

$$PV = A \times \left[\frac{1 - (1 + r)^{-n}}{r} \right]$$

$$PV_2 = \$2m \times \left[\frac{1 - (1 + 0.05)^{-4}}{0.05} \right] = \$7.09m$$

Step 2 Calculate the present value of this lump-sum cash flow occurring at the end of period 1 back to time 0 (i.e. one period earlier). In this example, $x = 2$, so $x - 1 = 1$, giving the number of periods that the *PV* from step 1 needs to be discounted back to the present value at time 0:

$$PV = FV/(1 + r)^n$$

$$PV = \$7.09/1.05 = \$6.75m$$

Hence, the present value of the deferred annuity is $6.75 million.

Equivalent annuity

The formula for the present value of an annuity is useful not only for valuation problems such as those examined above, but also for converting a cash flow or series of cash flows into an *equivalent annuity*. This is an annuity that has the same present value as another series of cash flows. In other words, the present value of an equivalent annuity (which can be determined using Equation 2.11) is equal to the present value of another cash flow or series of cash flows. Converting cash flow(s) into an equivalent annuity involves two steps.

1. Calculate the present value of the cash flows you wish to convert into an equivalent annuity.
2. Determine the annuity whose present value is equal to the cash flows calculated in step (1).

The equivalent annuity technique can be used to evaluate problems such as the one depicted in Figure 2.5. This figure depicts two machines that can be employed to perform the same job but differ in their cash flow requirements. Machine 1 requires a cash outflow of $7 million every five years, with the first payment being due at the end of the first year, while machine 2 requires

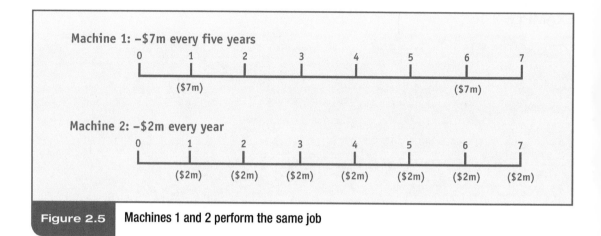

Figure 2.5   Machines 1 and 2 perform the same job

a cash outlay of $2 million every year starting with the first payment also occurring at the end of the first year. The problem arises: which of the machines would a company prefer to operate continuously?

We can solve this problem by comparing the equivalent annual cash flows of operating each machine. In this case, we can convert machine 1's $7 million payment every five years into an **equivalent annual cost**. The optimal choice of preferred machine is the one with the lower equivalent annual cost. Example 2.17 provides an illustration of the application of the concept of an equivalent annuity.

Figure 2.6 illustrates the effect of converting the cash flow associated with machine 1 into an equivalent annual cash flow, as calculated in Example 2.17 assuming a discount rate of 5% p.a. Once converted to a comparable base, it is straightforward to determine which of the machines is preferable. As depicted in Figure 2.6, machine 1 is clearly preferred since it has a lower equivalent annual operating cost.

Equivalent annual cost
Involves converting the net present value of a series of cash flows into an annual cash flow of an annuity that has the same life as the project.

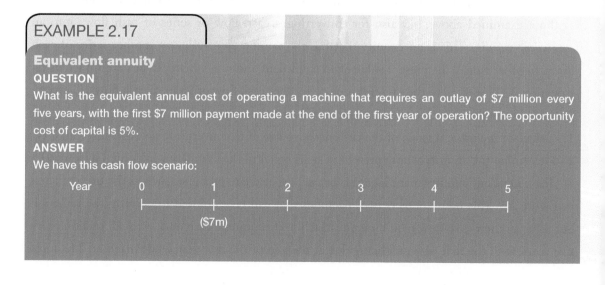

EXAMPLE 2.17

Equivalent annuity
QUESTION
What is the equivalent annual cost of operating a machine that requires an outlay of $7 million every five years, with the first $7 million payment made at the end of the first year of operation? The opportunity cost of capital is 5%.
ANSWER
We have this cash flow scenario:

We want to know the value of x in the following, if x's present value is equal to the above:

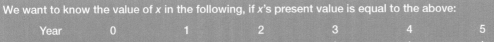

Year   0   1   2   3   4   5

($x)   ($x)   ($x)   ($x)   ($x)

Step 1 Calculate the present value of the cash payments made in operating machine 1 (in this example, it is only one cash flow of $7 million occurring at the end of period 1):

$PV = FV/(1 + r)^n$ (*PV* of one payment, compound interest)

$PV = 7/(1 + 0.05)^1 = 6.67$

Step 2 Determine the ordinary annuity over five years with a present value of $6.67 million:

$$PV = A \frac{[1 - (1 + r)^{-n}]}{r}$$

(*PV* of an ordinary annuity of *A.*)

$$6.67 = A \frac{[1 - (1 + 0.05)^{-5}]}{0.05}$$

$6.67 = A \times 4.329$

$A = \$1.54$

Hence, $7 million every five years is equivalent to $1.54 million per year.

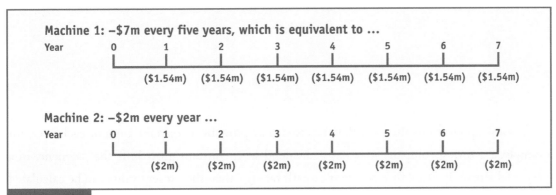

Machine 1: –$7m every five years, which is equivalent to ...

Year   0   1   2   3   4   5   6   7

($1.54m)   ($1.54m)   ($1.54m)   ($1.54m)   ($1.54m)   ($1.54m)   ($1.54m)

Machine 2: –$2m every year ...

Year   0   1   2   3   4   5   6   7

($2m)   ($2m)   ($2m)   ($2m)   ($2m)   ($2m)   ($2m)

Figure 2.6   Equivalent annual annuity for machines 1 and 2

Perpetuities

A perpetuity is a special type of annuity. It is a **perpetual annuity**; that is, a perpetuity is an annuity that continues indefinitely. An example of a perpetuity is a share that pays a constant dividend each year. Appendix 2.4 derives the following expression for the present value of a perpetuity:

Perpetual annuity
An annuity that is expected to continue forever. Also known as a perpetuity.

$$PV = \frac{A}{r} \qquad\qquad (2.14)$$

where

A = the constant cash flow

r = the interest rate

Example 2.18 illustrates the application of Equation 2.14.

EXAMPLE 2.18

Present value of a perpetuity

QUESTION

On 14 April 2010, AMP Limited (AMP), a prominent Australian insurance and wealth management company, paid a final dividend of 16 cents per share. At the same time, interest rate on the 10-year Australian bonds was 5.63% p.a. (10-year bonds pay interest every 6 months). Assume: (1) you are going to buy AMP shares and hold them forever; (2) AMP is expected to pay this dividend every 6 months forever; and (3) the 10-year bond rate is appropriate to valuing AMP shares. What is the maximum price you are willing to pay for a share of AMP?

ANSWER

As the market rate of interest is 5.63% p.a. nominal, we divide by two to get the six monthly compounding rate of 2.815%.

$$PV = \frac{A}{r}$$

$$PV = \frac{0.16}{0.02815}$$

$$PV = 5.68$$

Hence, if dividends are perpetual (and do not grow), the fair value of AMP shares is $5.68.

In some applications the cash flow received may grow by a constant amount each year; for example, a growing company may pay a dividend with constant growth. If the payments in a perpetual stream increase by a constant growth rate (g), then the present value can be calculated as follows:

$$PV = \frac{A_1}{r - g} \qquad \textbf{(2.15)}$$

where A_1 is the cash flow to be paid at the *end* of the first year.

The application and derivation of this equation are discussed in Chapter 3.

CONCEPT CHECK

11. What is an annuity?

12. Describe the three basic types of annuity.

13. Explain the two ways used to calculate the present value of an ordinary annuity.

14. What is an equivalent annuity?

15. What is the value of a perpetuity?

For the answers, go to MyFinanceLab

Student Learning Centre

MyFinanceLab ■ To test your mastery of the content covered in this chapter and to create your own personalised study plan, go to MyFinanceLab: www.pearson.com.au/myfinancelab

CONCEPT CHECKLIST

In this chapter the following concepts were discussed:

➤ Simple, compound, effective and continuously compounded interest rates

➤ Accumulated values and present values of single amounts under different interest rate arrangements

➤ Accumulated values and present values of annuities

➤ Annuities due

➤ Deferred annuities

➤ Equivalent annuities

➤ Perpetuities

SELF-TEST QUESTIONS

Comparing present values of alternative forms of cash flow

You have just won a lottery. In keeping with its advertised flexibility, Lotteries Corp. is offering you three alternatives.

1. You may take a lump sum of $1.3 million, payable immediately.

2. You may receive instalments of $400 000 every six months (payable in advance) for two years.

3. You may receive $100 000 p.a. forever. Evaluate the three alternatives, assuming that the best return you can get is a nominal interest rate of 7% p.a.

Self-test answers

1. Option 1: The present value of $1.3 million is $1.3 million.

2. Option 2: The present value of the six-monthly payments can be found from the formula for the present value of an annuity due (the first payment commences immediately). As the market rate

of interest is 7% nominal, we divide by two to get the six-monthly compounding rate of 3.5%. The present value is calculated as follows:

$$PV = A + A\left[\frac{1 - (1 + r)^{-(n-1)}}{r}\right]$$

$$PV = 0.4m + 0.4m\left[\frac{1 - (1 + 0.035)^{-3}}{0.035}\right]$$

$$PV = \$1.52m$$

3. Option 3: The present value of $100 000 forever can be found from the formula for a perpetuity:

$$PV = \frac{A}{r}$$

$$PV = \frac{0.1m}{0.07}$$

$$PV = \$1.43m$$

The optimal choice is to choose option 2 and receive four payments of $400 000 over the next two years, payable in advance, as it provides the largest present value of $1.52 million.

DISCUSSION QUESTIONS

1. What is meant by the 'intrinsic value' of an asset? What action would you take if you observed an asset that was selling at less than its intrinsic value?

2. Can an individual be indifferent to receiving a dollar now or a dollar one year from now? Explain.

3. Consider Figure 2.1 in the chapter. If you did not wish to spend the extra $100 until year 5, does this mean that the asset paying $100 in year 5 is preferred to the asset that pays $100 in year 3? Why or why not?

4. If you were given the choice of borrowing at an interest rate of 10% p.a. simple interest or 9.2% p.a. compounded monthly, which should you choose? Why?

5. Government pensions in Australia are typically paid fortnightly to those who are of a retirement age (i.e. aged 65 or over). While you can value these pension payments by treating them as annuities, what assumptions are you implicitly making? What difficulties are you expected to encounter when you attempt to calculate a present value?

PRACTICAL QUESTIONS

BASIC

1. Find the simple interest earned on $900 at 4.5% from 1 April to 16 May (both inclusive).

BASIC

2. Would you rather have a savings account that pays 6% interest compounded semi-annually or one that pays 6% compounded monthly? Why?

BASIC

3. You're a financial advisor working for the Golden Eggs Financial Advisory Limited. You come across a particular security that pays $10 000 in four years' time. Currently, an investment opportunity of similar risk is available to you, paying an interest of 6% p.a. compounded annually. What is the fair value (present value) of this security?

4. What is the present value of $121 received in two years if the nominal interest rates were:

   (a) 6% with annual compounding?

   (b) 6% with semi-annual compounding?

   (c) 6% with monthly compounding?

   BASIC

5. How long will it take for $100 to accumulate to $200 at 8% p.a. compound interest?

   BASIC

6. An investment cost $150 and pays $200 in two years. What is the effective annual compound interest rate? What is the nominal rate if the investment is compounded monthly?

   INTERMEDIATE

7. 'Mad Dog' McNamara wishes to accumulate $9500 at the end of three years. How much does he need to deposit now if the interest rate is:

   (a) 10% p.a. compounded annually?

   (b) 8% p.a. compounded annually?

   (c) 8% p.a. compounded monthly?

   Can you explain why the amounts differ in each case?

   INTERMEDIATE

8. What is the present value of a cash flow of $10 000 to be received in five years given an interest rate of 6% p.a. over five years (a) compounded annually, (b) compounded monthly and (c) continuously compounded?

   INTERMEDIATE

9. What is the present value of $50 000 due in 15 years if the interest rate is 14% p.a. compounded semi-annually?

   INTERMEDIATE

10. An antique vase your grandfather bought 25 years ago for $5000 has now appreciated in value to $16 000. Do you consider this to be a large gain? What if you were told that the average interest rate over the 25 years was 5% p.a.?

    INTERMEDIATE

11. The price of a Beatles recording made during their historic first visit to Australia has tripled in value in the past 40 years. Since you could have earned 3% p.a. in a savings account over the same period, was your investment in the recording (a) a terrific success, (b) okay or (c) a disaster? At what interest rate would you be indifferent to these investments?

    INTERMEDIATE

12. An investment repays $40 000 in five years and a further $60 000 in 10 years. If the interest rate over the period of the investment is 12% p.a. compounded monthly, what is the investment's present value?

    INTERMEDIATE

13. If, in Queston 12, the interest rate for the first five years had been 12% p.a. compounded monthly but had increased to 15% p.a. compounding semi-annually, what would the investment's present value be?

    INTERMEDIATE

14. An investor is earning $15 000 this year but expects to be earning $60 000 next year. What is the maximum amount that the investor can consume today if the interest rate is 10%? If the investor decides to consume zero this year, how much could they consume next year?

    INTERMEDIATE

15. You wish to place $1000 in a bank account for five years, at an interest rate of 7% p.a. How much would you accumulate after five years assuming (a) simple interest and (b) compound interest? Explain the difference between (a) and (b).

    INTERMEDIATE

16. You have $10 000 to invest for one year and the following choices are offered by the banks in your area:

    (a) 6% p.a. compounded annually

    (b) 5.8% p.a. compounded quarterly

    (c) 5.65% p.a. compounded continuously

    Which of the alternatives would you choose? Why?

    INTERMEDIATE

INTERMEDIATE

17. You have fallen seriously ill, and would not be able to work for the next two years. Fortunately, your insurance company has agreed to pay you $2000 a month for the next two years, with the first payment in one month's time. If the current interest rate is 6.17% p.a. compounded annually, what is the present value of this stream in cash flows (to the nearest dollar)?

INTERMEDIATE

18. Your grandmother has a debt that she may repay by paying $5000 now or $10 000 in four years' time. If the interest rate is 14% p.a. compounded monthly, would you advise her to repay the debt now or in four years?

INTERMEDIATE

19. If you borrowed $10 000 from a bank for five years at an interest rate of 10% p.a. compounded quarterly, how much would you owe the bank when the loan matures?

INTERMEDIATE

20. What is the continuously compounded return equivalent of a return of 10% p.a. compounded annually? Explain the difference between the two.

INTERMEDIATE

21. If you purchased NAB shares for $28.95 and later sold them for $29.60, what continuously compounded rate of return have you realised?

INTERMEDIATE

22. An investor can buy a government bond for $45 000 that will pay $50 000 in a year.
(a) What is the rate of return on this bond?
(b) If the interest rate is 9% p.a. compounded annually, what is the present value of the bond?
(c) What is the net present value of the bond?
(d) Should the investor buy the bond?
(e) If the market interest rate rises to 12% p.a., should the investor buy the bond?

INTERMEDIATE

23. Consider Figure 2.3 in the chapter. Given the cash flow structure of asset 1—that is, $2.3 million per year from years 1 to 6—answer the following, assuming an interest rate of 10% p.a. compounded annually.
(a) What is the accumulated (future) value of this asset?
(b) What is the present value of this asset?
Now assume that the interest rate of 10% p.a. is compounded monthly.
(c) What is the accumulated (future) value of this asset?
(d) What is the present value of this asset?

INTERMEDIATE

24. A four-year security is selling today for $25 000. The applicable interest rate is 8% p.a. and the security offers an equal annual cash flow at the end of each year. What cash flow would the purchaser of this security receive each year?

INTERMEDIATE

25. You wish to borrow $20 000 for five years, and your bank will charge interest at 10% p.a. compounded annually.
(a) If you were to repay the loan in equal annual instalments, what annual payment would you be making for the next five years?
(b) If you were to repay the loan in equal monthly instalments, what monthly payment would you be making for the next five years?

CHALLENGING

26. Your sister has just graduated from university and has begun employment with an investment bank. She intends to retire in 30 years from now and would like to be able to withdraw $30 000 per year from her savings for a period of 20 years after retirement. She expects to earn 9% annually on her savings. Assuming end-of-year cash flows, what equal annual amount must your sister save during her 30 years of employment in order to be able to withdraw the desired annual amount during the 20 years of retirement?

27. (a) You have the opportunity to purchase security Y that will pay $2000 per year forever. At an interest rate of 8% p.a., what is this security worth?

    (b) An alternative security, Z, will pay $2000 per year for the next 20 years. Assuming the same interest rate compounded annually, what is this security worth?

    (c) explain the difference between the values of securities Y and Z.

28. Your company is deciding between two investment choices: one that pays $100 per year in perpetuity, and another that pays $100 per year for 100 years. The current market interest rate for investments of similar risk is at 10% p.a. What is the present value of these two investments? Why are they so similar?

29. You work at Rest Assured Insurance Co. and have just received a claim from an individual involved in a work-related accident. The claim has a value of $200 000. It is the company's policy to provide multiple payment options with various maturities. The claimant may choose to cash out the claim now, or cash out with monthly payments over a span of three, five or ten years. If the current market interest rate is 6% p.a. (compounded monthly), what should be the monthly payments in each case?

30. You are a private equity firm that invests in brand-new and high-risk projects. You are considering investing in a new tollway. The tollway will take five years to build and require $1 billion in outlays in each of those five years. The tollway is expected to produce revenue of $1 billion in years 6 and 7, and then $2 billion per year in perpetuity from year 8 onwards. What is the value of the investment if the interest rate is 10% p.a. compounded annually?

31. You have just bought a mine with a proven gold reserve. You have two sets of machinery which you can use to extract and process the gold in the mine. The first requires an outlay of $1.5 million every three years, with the first payment to be made in one year's time. The second set of machinery requires an outlay of $5 million every seven years, also with the first payment to be made in one year's time. Which set of machinery is cheaper to operate, if the interest rate is 10% p.a. compounded annually?

32. Mr Thought has just had a son, and wants to send him to a private school. School fees from kindergarten to Year 6 are expected to total $15 000, while those from Year 7 to Year 12 are expected to total $20 000. Mr Thought's son is due to start school when he is five years old.

    How much money must Mr Thought set aside now if fixed-term deposit rates from five to 10 years are currently 5% p.a. compounded annually, and from 10 to 20 years are currently 6% p.a. compounded annually? There is a penalty of 3% for withdrawal of funds from a fixed-term deposit before maturity.

33. Today is your 30th birthday. Given the recent changes in the tax law relating to retirement, the earliest you can retire is your 60th birthday. Your employer contributions to your superannuation are $2500 p.a. on each birthday, starting immediately. You estimate that you will need $60 000 per annum to live on from your 61st birthday to your 90th birthday (inclusive). You estimate that you can earn 12% p.a. between now and your 90th birthday.

    (a) Can you afford to retire on your 60th birthday? Demonstrate your answer with calculations.

    (b) Given your savings plan, how much can you expect to receive as income each year when you retire—that is, from your 61st to your 90th birthday?

34. A close friend who is financially naive is trying to compare two loan contracts. Your friend wishes to borrow $15 000 over the next five years and make monthly payments.

CHALLENGING (×8)

Loan 1

South West Bank is offering a loan at 10% p.a. (monthly compounding) over five years.

(a) What are the monthly payments on this loan?

(b) What is the effective annual rate?

Loan 2

Local Credit Company has told your friend that the monthly payments he will make are $311.20. However, Local Credit Company has not revealed the interest rate it used to calculate this payment. Local Credit Company did state that all loans are calculated using monthly compounding. What is the annual nominal interest rate on this loan?

(a) What is the effective annual rate?

(b) Which loan should your friend choose, and why?

CHALLENGING

35. The current interest rate on two-year Australian Treasury bonds is 5.5% nominal with interest paid every six months. Your bank account offers a two-year fixed-term deposit of 5% p.a. compounded six monthly, and a bank account which pays interest of 3% p.a. compounded six monthly and which is expected to pay interest at this rate for the foreseeable future. Should you invest your money in Treasury bonds or the fixed-term deposit? (Careful)

CASE STUDY

The questions in this case study refer to the information in the table below. The table provides information for Commonwealth Bank of Australia (CBA), a stock listed on the Australian Securities Exchange.

Company	Commonwealth Bank of Australia (CBA)
Share price 30 Jun 2009	$39.00
Share price 30 Jun 2010	$48.64
Operating cash flow 2010 ($m)	3445
Issued shares (million)	1644

Source: CBA 2010 Annual Report.

CASE STUDY QUESTIONS

1. What is the simple rate of return on CBA shares for the year ended 30 June 2010?

2. What is the six-monthly compound rate of return on CBA shares for the year ended 30 June 2010?

3. What is the continuously compounded rate of return on CBA shares for the year ended 30 June 2010?

4. Assume you invest $1000 at the beginning of the year and the money earns the same rate of return as CBA shares over 2010. How much would you have by the end of the year?

5. Assume that the discount rate is 7% and the operating cash flow of CBA remains at the current level for the next 15 years, and then increases by 20% and remains at that level forever. What would be the value of CBA's shares?

6. Assume that the discount rate is 7% and the operating cash flow of CBA grows at 2.5% a year forever. What would be the value of CBA's shares?

7. Using the market capitalisation of CBA as at 30 June 2010, what annuity over 30 years is equivalent in value assuming a discount rate of 7%?

FURTHER READING

For further discussion and numerous worked examples on the mathematics discussed in this chapter, refer to:

- Knox, D. M., Zima, P. and Brown, R. L. (1999), *Mathematics of Finance*, 2nd edn, McGraw-Hill, Sydney.

NOTE

1. Typically, this point in time will be today, or time 0. Therefore, it is common to use financial mathematics to determine the present value (*PV*) of assets.

Appendix 2.1

DERIVATION OF FUTURE VALUE OF A SINGLE CASH FLOW UNDER CONTINUOUSLY COMPOUNDED RATES OF RETURN

The expression for the future value of a single amount (PV) under discrete compounding is:

$$FV = PV(1 + \frac{r}{m})^{mt} \qquad \textbf{(A2.1.1)}$$

where m is the compounding frequency (daily, monthly, quarterly, etc.), r is the annual rate of return under the compounding arrangement, and FV is the future cash flow to be received in t years' time. Multiplying mt by $\frac{r}{r}$ and rearranging yields:

$$FV = PV[(1 + \frac{r}{m})^{m/r}]^{rt}$$

Setting $m/r = a$ yields:

$$FV = PV[(1 + \frac{1}{a})^{a}]^{rt} \qquad \textbf{(A2.1.2)}$$

But, by definition:

$$lim^{a \to \infty}\left(1 + \frac{1}{a}\right)^{a} = 2.71828 = e \text{ (the base of natural logarithms)}$$

Hence, Equation A2.1.2 reduces to:

$$FV = PVe^{rt} \qquad \textbf{(A2.1.3)}$$

where r is the continuously compounded rate of return, and t is the length of time over which PV is invested.

APPENDIX 2.2

DERIVATION OF FUTURE VALUE OF AN ANNUITY

Take the following annuity:

Year	0	1	2	3		$n - 2$	$n - 1$	n
		$1	$1	$1		$1	$1	$1

The future value or accumulated value (FV) of the $1 amounts by year n is the sum of their individual future values. Starting with the $1 in year n and working back yields the following:

$$FV = 1 + 1(1 + r) + 1(1 + r)^{2} \ldots + 1(1 + r)^{n-2} + 1(1 + r)^{n} - 1 \qquad \textbf{(A2.2.1)}$$

Multiplying both sides of Equation A2.2.1 by $(1 + r)$ yields:

$$FV(1 + r) = 1(1 + r) + 1(1 + r)^2 + 1(1 + r)^3 \ldots + 1(1 + r)^{n-1} + 1(1 + r)^n \tag{A2.2.2}$$

Subtracting Equation A2.2.1 from Equation A2.2.2 yields:

$$FV(1 + r) - FV = (1 + r)^n - 1 \tag{A2.2.3}$$

Finally, rearranging Equation A2.2.3 to make FV the subject of the formula yields:

$$FV = \frac{(1 + r)^n - 1}{r}$$

This is the future value of $1 per year for n years invested at an interest rate of $r\%$. Multiplying this amount by A yields the future value of $$A$ per year.

APPENDIX 2.3

DERIVATION OF PRESENT VALUE OF AN ANNUITY

Take the following annuity:

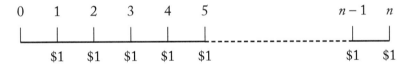

Year   0   1   2   3   4   5 $n - 1$ n

         \$1   \$1   \$1   \$1   \$1   \$1   \$1

The present value (PV) of these amounts is the sum of the present value of each individual \$1 discounted by an appropriate factor as follows:

$$PV = \frac{1}{(1 + r)} + \frac{1}{(1 + r)^2} \ldots + \frac{1}{(1 + r)^{n-1}} + \frac{1}{(1 + r)^n} \tag{A2.3.1}$$

Multiplying both sides of Equation A2.3.1 by $(1 + r)$ yields:

$$PV(1 + r) = 1 + \frac{1}{(1 + r)} \ldots + \frac{1}{(1 + r)^{n-2}} + \frac{1}{(1 + r)^{n-1}} \tag{A2.3.2}$$

Subtracting Equation A2.3.1 from Equation A2.3.2 yields:

$$PV(1 + r) - PV = 1 - (1 + r)^{-n} \tag{A2.3.3}$$

Finally, rearranging Equation A2.3.3 to make PV the subject of the formula yields:

$$PV = \frac{1 - (1 + r)^{-n}}{r}$$

This is the present value of \$1 per year for n years invested at an interest rate of $r\%$. Multiplying this amount by A yields the present value of $$A$ per year.

APPENDIX 2.4

DERIVATION OF PRESENT VALUE OF A PERPETUITY

Recall that the present value of an ordinary annuity is given by:

$$PV = A \times \frac{1 - \frac{1}{(1 + r)^n}}{r}$$

(A2.4.1)

(see Appendix 2.3)

Since a perpetuity is simply the case where $n \rightarrow \infty$, and as n becomes very large $\frac{1}{(1 + r)^n}$ approaches 0, then in the limit Equation A2.4.1 reduces to:

$$PV = \frac{A}{r}$$

which is the present value of a perpetuity A.

APPENDIX 2.5

FUTURE VALUE OF ORDINARY ANNUITY OF $1 = $\dfrac{(1 + r)^n - 1}{r}$

Interest rate (r) / Period (n)	0.5%	1.0%	1.5%	2.0%	2.5%	3.0%	3.5%	4.0%	4.5%	5.0%	5.5%	6.0%	6.5%	7.0%	7.5%	8.0%	8.5%	9.0%	9.5%	10.0%
1	1.000	1.000	1.000	1.000	1.000	1.000	1.000	1.000	1.000	1.000	1.000	1.000	1.000	1.000	1.000	1.000	1.000	1.000	1.000	1.000
2	2.005	2.010	2.015	2.020	2.025	2.030	2.035	2.040	2.045	2.050	2.055	2.060	2.065	2.070	2.075	2.080	2.085	2.090	2.095	2.100
3	3.015	3.030	3.045	3.060	3.076	3.091	3.106	3.122	3.137	3.153	3.168	3.184	3.199	3.215	3.231	3.246	3.262	3.278	3.294	3.310
4	4.030	4.060	4.091	4.122	4.153	4.184	4.215	4.246	4.278	4.310	4.342	4.375	4.407	4.440	4.473	4.506	4.540	4.573	4.607	4.641
5	5.050	5.101	5.152	5.204	5.256	5.309	5.362	5.416	5.471	5.526	5.581	5.637	5.694	5.751	5.808	5.867	5.925	5.985	6.045	6.105
6	6.076	6.152	6.230	6.308	6.388	6.468	6.550	6.633	6.717	6.802	6.888	6.975	7.064	7.153	7.244	7.336	7.429	7.523	7.619	7.716
7	7.106	7.214	7.323	7.434	7.547	7.662	7.779	7.898	8.019	8.142	8.267	8.394	8.523	8.654	8.787	8.923	9.060	9.200	9.343	9.487
8	8.141	8.286	8.433	8.583	8.736	8.892	9.052	9.214	9.380	9.549	9.722	9.897	10.077	10.260	10.446	10.637	10.831	11.028	11.230	11.436
9	9.182	9.369	9.559	9.755	9.955	10.159	10.368	10.583	10.802	11.027	11.256	11.491	11.732	11.978	12.230	12.488	12.751	13.021	13.297	13.579
10	10.228	10.462	10.703	10.950	11.203	11.464	11.731	12.006	12.288	12.578	12.875	13.181	13.494	13.816	14.147	14.487	14.835	15.193	15.560	15.937
11	11.279	11.567	11.863	12.169	12.483	12.808	13.142	13.486	13.841	14.207	14.583	14.972	15.372	15.784	16.208	16.645	17.096	17.560	18.039	18.531
12	12.336	12.683	13.041	13.412	13.796	14.192	14.602	15.026	15.464	15.917	16.386	16.870	17.371	17.888	18.424	18.977	19.549	20.141	20.752	21.384
13	13.397	13.809	14.237	14.680	15.140	15.618	16.113	16.627	17.160	17.713	18.287	18.882	19.500	20.141	20.806	21.495	22.211	22.953	23.724	24.523
14	14.464	14.947	15.450	15.974	16.519	17.086	17.677	18.292	18.932	19.599	20.293	21.015	21.767	22.550	23.366	24.215	25.099	26.019	26.977	27.975
15	15.537	16.097	16.682	17.293	17.932	18.599	19.296	20.024	20.784	21.579	22.409	23.276	24.182	25.129	26.118	27.152	28.232	29.361	30.540	31.772
16	16.614	17.258	17.932	18.639	19.380	20.157	20.971	21.825	22.719	23.657	24.641	25.673	26.754	27.888	29.077	30.324	31.632	33.003	34.442	35.950
17	17.697	18.430	19.201	20.012	20.865	21.762	22.705	23.698	24.742	25.840	26.996	28.213	29.493	30.840	32.258	33.750	35.321	36.974	38.714	40.545
18	18.786	19.615	20.489	21.412	22.386	23.414	24.500	25.645	26.855	28.132	29.481	30.906	32.410	33.999	35.677	37.450	39.323	41.301	43.391	45.599
19	19.880	20.811	21.797	22.841	23.946	25.117	26.357	27.671	29.064	30.539	32.103	33.760	35.517	37.379	39.353	41.446	43.665	46.018	48.513	51.159
20	20.979	22.019	23.124	24.297	25.545	26.870	28.280	29.778	31.371	33.066	34.868	36.786	38.825	40.995	43.305	45.762	48.377	51.160	54.122	57.275
21	22.084	23.239	24.471	25.783	27.183	28.676	30.269	31.969	33.783	35.719	37.786	39.993	42.349	44.865	47.553	50.423	53.489	56.765	60.264	64.002
22	23.194	24.472	25.838	27.299	28.863	30.537	32.329	34.248	36.303	38.505	40.864	43.392	46.102	49.006	52.119	55.457	59.036	62.873	66.989	71.403
23	24.310	25.716	27.225	28.845	30.584	32.453	34.460	36.618	38.937	41.430	44.112	46.996	50.098	53.436	57.028	60.893	65.054	69.532	74.353	79.543
24	25.432	26.973	28.634	30.422	32.349	34.426	36.667	39.083	41.689	44.502	47.538	50.816	54.355	58.177	62.305	66.765	71.583	76.790	82.416	88.497
25	26.559	28.243	30.063	32.030	34.158	36.459	38.950	41.646	44.565	47.727	51.153	54.865	58.888	63.249	67.978	73.106	78.668	84.701	91.246	98.347
26	27.692	29.526	31.514	33.671	36.012	38.553	41.313	44.312	47.571	51.113	54.966	59.156	63.715	68.676	74.076	79.954	86.355	93.324	100.914	109.182
27	28.830	30.821	32.987	35.344	37.912	40.710	43.759	47.084	50.711	54.669	58.989	63.706	68.857	74.484	80.632	87.351	94.695	102.723	111.501	121.100
28	29.975	32.129	34.481	37.051	39.860	42.931	46.291	49.968	53.993	58.403	63.234	68.528	74.333	80.698	87.679	95.339	103.744	112.968	123.094	134.210
29	31.124	33.450	35.999	38.792	41.856	45.219	48.911	52.966	57.423	62.323	67.711	73.640	80.164	87.347	95.255	103.966	113.562	124.135	135.788	148.631
30	32.280	34.785	37.539	40.568	43.903	47.575	51.623	56.085	61.007	66.439	72.435	79.058	86.375	94.461	103.399	113.283	124.215	136.308	149.688	164.494

APPENDIX 2.6

PRESENT VALUE OF ORDINARY ANNUITY OF $1 = $\dfrac{1 - (1 + r)^{-n}}{r}$

Interest rate (r) Period (n)	0.5%	1.0%	1.5%	2.0%	2.5%	3.0%	3.5%	4.0%	4.5%	5.0%	5.5%	6.0%	6.5%	7.0%	7.5%	8.0%	8.5%	9.0%	9.5%	10.0%
1	0.995	0.990	0.985	0.980	0.976	0.971	0.966	0.962	0.957	0.952	0.948	0.943	0.939	0.935	0.930	0.926	0.922	0.917	0.913	0.909
2	1.985	1.970	1.956	1.942	1.927	1.913	1.900	1.886	1.873	1.859	1.846	1.833	1.821	1.808	1.796	1.783	1.771	1.759	1.747	1.736
3	2.970	2.941	2.912	2.884	2.856	2.829	2.802	2.775	2.749	2.723	2.698	2.673	2.648	2.624	2.601	2.577	2.554	2.531	2.509	2.487
4	3.950	3.902	3.854	3.808	3.762	3.717	3.673	3.630	3.588	3.546	3.505	3.465	3.426	3.387	3.349	3.312	3.276	3.240	3.204	3.170
5	4.926	4.853	4.783	4.713	4.646	4.580	4.515	4.452	4.390	4.329	4.270	4.212	4.156	4.100	4.046	3.993	3.941	3.890	3.840	3.791
6	5.896	5.795	5.697	5.601	5.508	5.417	5.329	5.242	5.158	5.076	4.996	4.917	4.841	4.767	4.694	4.623	4.554	4.486	4.420	4.355
7	6.862	6.728	6.598	6.472	6.349	6.230	6.115	6.002	5.893	5.786	5.683	5.582	5.485	5.389	5.297	5.206	5.119	5.033	4.950	4.868
8	7.823	7.652	7.486	7.325	7.170	7.020	6.874	6.733	6.596	6.463	6.335	6.210	6.089	5.971	5.857	5.747	5.639	5.535	5.433	5.335
9	8.779	8.566	8.361	8.162	7.971	7.786	7.608	7.435	7.269	7.108	6.952	6.802	6.656	6.515	6.379	6.247	6.119	5.995	5.875	5.759
10	9.730	9.471	9.222	8.983	8.752	8.530	8.317	8.111	7.913	7.722	7.538	7.360	7.189	7.024	6.864	6.710	6.561	6.418	6.279	6.145
11	10.677	10.368	10.071	9.787	9.514	9.253	9.002	8.760	8.529	8.306	8.093	7.887	7.689	7.499	7.315	7.139	6.969	6.805	6.647	6.495
12	11.619	11.255	10.908	10.575	10.258	9.954	9.663	9.385	9.119	8.863	8.619	8.384	8.159	7.943	7.735	7.536	7.345	7.161	6.984	6.814
13	12.556	12.134	11.732	11.348	10.983	10.635	10.303	9.986	9.683	9.394	9.117	8.853	8.600	8.358	8.126	7.904	7.691	7.487	7.291	7.103
14	13.489	13.004	12.543	12.106	11.691	11.296	10.921	10.563	10.223	9.899	9.590	9.295	9.014	8.745	8.489	8.244	8.010	7.786	7.572	7.367
15	14.417	13.865	13.343	12.849	12.381	11.938	11.517	11.118	10.740	10.380	10.038	9.712	9.403	9.108	8.827	8.559	8.304	8.061	7.828	7.606
16	15.340	14.718	14.131	13.578	13.055	12.561	12.094	11.652	11.234	10.838	10.462	10.106	9.768	9.447	9.142	8.851	8.575	8.313	8.062	7.824
17	16.259	15.562	14.908	14.292	13.712	13.166	12.651	12.166	11.707	11.274	10.865	10.477	10.111	9.763	9.434	9.122	8.825	8.544	8.276	8.022
18	17.173	16.398	15.673	14.992	14.353	13.754	13.190	12.659	12.160	11.690	11.246	10.828	10.432	10.059	9.706	9.372	9.055	8.756	8.471	8.201
19	18.082	17.226	16.426	15.678	14.979	14.324	13.710	13.134	12.593	12.085	11.608	11.158	10.735	10.336	9.959	9.604	9.268	8.950	8.650	8.365
20	18.987	18.046	17.169	16.351	15.589	14.877	14.212	13.590	13.008	12.462	11.950	11.470	11.019	10.594	10.194	9.818	9.463	9.129	8.812	8.514
21	19.888	18.857	17.900	17.011	16.185	15.415	14.698	14.029	13.405	12.821	12.275	11.764	11.285	10.836	10.413	10.017	9.644	9.292	8.961	8.649
22	20.784	19.660	18.621	17.658	16.765	15.937	15.167	14.451	13.784	13.163	12.583	12.042	11.535	11.061	10.617	10.201	9.810	9.442	9.097	8.772
23	21.676	20.456	19.331	18.292	17.332	16.444	15.620	14.857	14.148	13.489	12.875	12.303	11.770	11.272	10.807	10.371	9.963	9.580	9.221	8.883
24	22.563	21.243	20.030	18.914	17.885	16.936	16.058	15.247	14.495	13.799	13.152	12.550	11.991	11.469	10.983	10.529	10.104	9.707	9.334	8.985
25	23.446	22.023	20.720	19.523	18.424	17.413	16.482	15.622	14.828	14.094	13.414	12.783	12.198	11.654	11.147	10.675	10.234	9.823	9.438	9.077
26	24.324	22.795	21.399	20.121	18.951	17.877	16.890	15.983	15.147	14.375	13.662	13.003	12.392	11.826	11.299	10.810	10.354	9.929	9.532	9.161
27	25.198	23.560	22.068	20.707	19.464	18.327	17.285	16.330	15.451	14.643	13.898	13.211	12.575	11.987	11.441	10.935	10.465	10.027	9.618	9.237
28	26.068	24.316	22.727	21.281	19.965	18.764	17.667	16.663	15.743	14.898	14.121	13.406	12.746	12.137	11.573	11.051	10.566	10.116	9.697	9.307
29	26.933	25.066	23.376	21.844	20.454	19.188	18.036	16.984	16.022	15.141	14.333	13.591	12.907	12.278	11.696	11.158	10.660	10.198	9.769	9.370
30	27.794	25.808	24.016	22.396	20.930	19.600	18.392	17.292	16.289	15.372	14.534	13.765	13.059	12.409	11.810	11.258	10.747	10.274	9.835	9.427

Valuation of shares and bonds

3

CHAPTER PREVIEW

The previous two chapters introduced the concept of valuation and reviewed the mathematics necessary for valuing assets with different cash flow structures. The aim of this chapter is to introduce different approaches to valuing a company (or firm), by extending the principles developed previously. Specifically, this chapter will discuss methods used to value a firm either as an entire entity or by breaking it down into its separate components: equity (shares) and debt securities (bonds).

KEY CONCEPTS

CONCEPT 3.1   Valuing a company

Previously it was demonstrated that the value of an asset is a function of two factors: the cash flows generated by the asset, and the appropriate discount rate applied to these cash flows. This principle also applies when valuing firms.[1] Broadly speaking, a firm can be valued in two different ways. The first approach involves calculating the present value of the cash flows generated by the firm's real (productive) assets, to generate a valuation for the firm in its entirety. The other approach involves calculating the present value of the firm's individual securities (i.e. its equity and debt securities), and then simply adding these together. These ideas are discussed in more detail below. Theoretically, the calculated value of the firm must be the same. The reason is that, regardless of which method is used, the same set of cash flows is being valued. A diagram can be used to explain this concept.

Figure 3.1 illustrates that the cash flows generated by a firm's real assets ultimately flow through to the shareholders and debt holders of the firm as dividends and interest, respectively. In the case of debt holders, there is also a repayment of principal. Obviously, calculating the present value of cash flows generated by a firm's real assets after subtracting the cost of maintaining them (reinvestment costs, or capital expenditure) is the same as calculating the value of cash flows flowing to shareholders and debt holders. Hence, the value of a company (V) is equivalent to the value of debt (D) plus the value of equity (E), as follows:

$$V = D + E \qquad \textbf{(3.1)}$$

where:

V = the present value of cash flows generated by the firm

D = the present value of cash flows generated by debt securities

E = the value of cash flows generated by equity securities

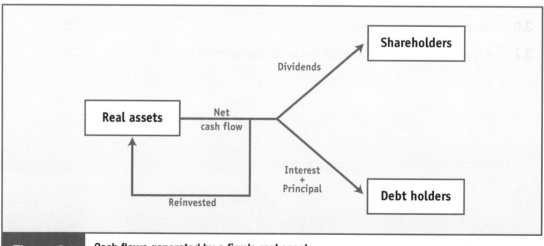

| **Figure 3.1** | Cash flows generated by a firm's real assets |

Practitioner's POV

Equity research analysts work for stockbroking firms. Analysts produce forecasts of the earnings and cash flows of listed companies and then use these numbers to carry out valuations using some or all of the techniques discussed in this chapter. If an analyst believes that a share is trading at a price less than, greater than, or roughly equal to its value, they will issue a buy, sell or hold recommendation, respectively, to their clients (typically fund managers). Investment bankers carry out valuations for clients (typically companies), advising on a fair price to pay for another company in a takeover, or a fair price at which to issue shares in a float.

CONCEPT 3.2   Value of a company's real asset cash flows

As stated above, one valuation approach proceeds on the basis that the value of a firm is given by the present value of its net cash flows from real assets, after reinvestment costs, otherwise known as its *free cash flows*. If it can be assumed that a firm has an infinite life, the value of the firm (V) is given by the following equation:

$$V = \sum_{t=1}^{\infty} \frac{F_t}{(1 + r)^t}$$ **(3.2)**

where:

F_t = free cash flow generated by the company in period t

r = required rate of return (i.e. appropriate discount rate for the company)

The calculation of free cash flows to be used in valuing a company (F_t) will be discussed in Chapter 8, while determination of the appropriate discount rate will dominate the discussion in Chapters 6 to 8.

CONCEPT 3.3   Debt versus equity

The alternative approach to valuing a firm involves breaking it down into its separate funding components—that is, the **equity** and **debt** securities that are on issue. The portion of debt and equity used to finance a company is known as the firm's *capital structure*. The value of the firm is then determined by calculating the present value of each capital structure component, and adding these together.

Before discussing this valuation approach in detail, it is appropriate to examine further the nature of securities that make up a firm's capital structure. In practice, although components are typically classified as either debt or equity (i.e. shares), an enormous variety of debt, equity and

Equity
A security which typically (a) pays a variable rate of return (dividends), (b) has an indefinite life, and (c) in the event of insolvency of a company, entitles owners to the residual proceeds from sale of the assets of the business after all other creditors have been paid.

Debt
A security which typically (a) pays a contractually fixed rate of return (interest), (b) has a finite life, and (c) in the event of default on payment of interest, the owners have first call on the assets of the issuer.

hybrid securities[2] are currently available in capital markets. However, for exposition purposes, the remainder of this chapter proceeds on the basis of a simplified (debt and equity only) capital structure.

There are fundamental differences between debt and equity that give rise to alternative approaches to their valuation. These differences mainly revolve around (1) the nature of cash flows paid by the security, (2) the life of the security and (3) the right to claim against the assets of the company in case of insolvency. These features are summarised in Table 3.1.

The first distinction is that debt and equity differ in terms of the returns that are paid to their holders. The return on debt—interest—is usually contractually fixed for the life of the security, and is stipulated in the debt contract, known as the trust deed. In contrast, the return on equity—dividends—is usually decided semi-annually and can vary at the discretion of management.

The lives of the securities also differ. Debt essentially represents the borrowing of funds for a fixed period of time. At the end of the life of the debt security, it is typically redeemed at its face value, which is also stated in the debt contract. The face value of the debt is the nominal amount of principal borrowed by the company. In contrast, once shares are issued they are rarely bought back by the company. Accordingly, an investor who desires to redeem an investment in shares for cash cannot do so by going to the company. Rather, the investor will sell the shares to another investor on a stock exchange.

Finally, the entitlement to repayment of the amount invested in the company in the event of insolvency and liquidation also differs for debt holders and equity holders. Debt holders generally have first claim against the assets of a company, while equity holders have a right to the residual cash from selling those assets after all others have been repaid money owed. However, in the case of debt holders, even this does not mean that redemption of their investment is guaranteed. An infamous example of this in Australia is the case of Bond Corporation, which in the 1980s was run by the well-known former 'entrepreneur' Alan Bond. Bond Corporation went into liquidation with billions of dollars in debt in 1992, and because of the significant shortfall in assets relative to debt, the company's debt holders (mainly banks) received less than one cent for each dollar that they were owed.

Table 3.1	Characterisation of debt and equity	
Characteristic	**Debt**	**Equity**
Return	Fixed (interest)	Variable (dividend)
Life	Fixed (redeemed)	Indefinite
Security (claim)	First	Residual

1. Broadly speaking, what are the two different approaches to valuing a firm?
2. What are the main characteristics that distinguish the return on debt securities from the return on equity securities?

For the answers, go to MyFinanceLab

CONCEPT 3.4 Valuation of corporate debt

For the purposes of illustration, this section focuses on a specific type of debt: bonds. A bond may be defined as a contract between the issuer and the investor (borrower and lender, respectively) stipulating the issuer's obligation to make specified payments to the investor on specified future dates.

As is the case with other financial assets, the valuation of bonds is based on the present-value principles outlined in previous chapters. Consequently, the key variables are the (timing of) cash flows and yield. The cash flows associated with holding a bond are the periodic interest payments which are determined by the interest rate attaching to the bond (or **coupon rate**), and repayment of the principal amount (**face value**) upon maturity of the bond.

The yield on a bond is its cost of debt, r_d. This can be thought of as the rate of return currently required to induce investors to hold the firm's debt. Whereas the coupon rate is set by the company when debt is issued and hence does not change throughout the life of the debt, the yield is determined by the market, and therefore can vary through time. Therefore, it is the discount rate that equates a series of cash inflows (the bond's interest and principal repayment) with the current price of the bond. An important point to note is that the only time the yield on a bond is the same as its coupon rate is when the bond is trading at its face (or 'par') value.

The formula for valuing a bond (and debt securities generally) can be stated as follows:

$$D = \sum_{t=1}^{n} \frac{F_t}{(1+r_d)^t} + \frac{B}{(1+r_d)^n}$$ **(3.3)**

This formula implies that the value of a bond (D) given (1) a cost of debt capital, r_d, (2) a remaining life of n, (3) interest payments (or coupon) of F and (4) a face value of B is calculated by taking the present value of the interest payments plus the present value of the face value.

Since the interest cash flows paid by the debt (F) are an annuity, and the value of an annuity (Equation 2.7) was derived in the last chapter, then the present value of the interest payment is:

$$PV_F = F \frac{1 - (1+r_d)^{-n}}{r_d}$$

and the value of a debt security whose interest payments can be expressed as an annuity is given by substituting the above equation into Equation 3.4:

Coupon rate
The interest paid on bonds as a percentage of the face value of the bonds.

Face value
The lump sum paid by a bond to its owner at the end of the life of the bond.

$$D = F\frac{1 - (1 + r_d)^{-n}}{r_d} + \frac{B}{(1 + r_d)^n} \qquad\qquad \textbf{(3.4)}$$

The example below illustrates the application of Equation 3.4. Note that the interest paid by bonds in dollars is obtained by multiplying the coupon rate by the face value of the securities.

EXAMPLE 3.1

The present value of a debt security

QUESTION

Brookfield Multiplex is a property fund manager. On 23 November 2009, it listed on the ASX 650 000 secured bonds carrying a coupon of 8.79% p.a., with interest paid quarterly, at a face value of $100 and maturing on 23 November 2012. Assuming that the bonds were issued at a yield set 2.63% higher than the 10-year Australian Government bond yield (which was running at 5.47% p.a. in November 2009, compounded semi-annually), what was the total value of the bonds issued by Brookfield Multiplex?

ANSWER

Interest payment = coupon rate × face value = 0.0879/4 × $100 = $2.20 every quarter, and there are 12 quarterly periods.

The yield is 8.10% p.a. compounded semi-annually, so the effective quarterly yield is $(1 + 0.081/2)^{1/2} = 2.0\%$. The present value of the interest payment is:

$$F\left[\frac{1 - (1 + r_d)^{-n}}{r_d}\right] = 2.20 \times \left[\frac{1 - (1 + 0.02)^{-12}}{0.02}\right] = \$23.27$$

The present value of the face value of the bond, to be repaid in 12 quarters is:

$$100/(1.02)^{12} = \$78.85$$

Hence the market value of one Brookfield Multiplex bond is $23.27 + $78.85 = $102.12. The total value of all bonds is therefore $102.12 × 650 000 = $66 378 000.

Forecasting the cash flows involved in valuing the debt of a company is relatively straightforward as it is stipulated in the contract between debt holders and the company. The tricky part in the valuation of debt is deciding on the appropriate cost of debt to apply. In practice, analysts normally apply a premium to the current 10-year Australian Government bond rate, usually one or two points, depending on their assessment of the risk of default by the company.

CONCEPT CHECK

3. What are the cash flows that are to be discounted in valuing bonds?
4. What is the appropriate discount factor to be applied in valuing bonds?
5. Why does the yield change through time but the coupon rate does not?

For the answers, go to MyFinanceLab

CONCEPT 3.5   Valuation of shares

As is the case with other financial assets, including debt, equity securities are valued by calculating the present value of the cash flows generated, which are (1) dividends and (2) the share price. The latter is realised only when the shares are sold in the market—that is, on the stock exchange.

At first glance there may appear to be some circularity involved in valuing equity securities. This is because an investor values shares simply by calculating the present value of the dividends that will be received over the life of the shareholding, then adding the present value of the shares at the expected date of termination of their shareholding. That is, a share's current value is determined in part by its future value. However, it is this circularity which implies that the value of equity reduces to the value of all future dividends. This is because in valuing the shares in the future, the next investor will calculate the present value of the dividends that they expect to receive over the life of the shareholding, plus the future value of the shares. If you repeat this line of reasoning, it becomes evident that the value of the shares to the first purchaser of the shares is the sum of the present value of the dividends that all subsequent investors will receive over the life of their shareholding. This is formally proven in Appendix 3.1. Hence, the value of equity is given by the present value of all future dividends that the company is expected to pay:

$$E = \sum_{t=1}^{\infty} \frac{d_t}{(1 + r_e)^t} \tag{3.5}$$

where:

E = the value of equity

d_t = the dividend paid in period t

r_e = the cost of equity

Although Equation 3.5 is mathematically elegant, it is also, unfortunately, not particularly useful. The equation suggests that, compared with debt, equity is difficult to value because (1) equity cash flows (dividends) are unstable and unpredictable and (2) the life of equity is indefinite. In order to make the valuation problem tractable, analysts typically make assumptions about the character of future dividends to be paid by the company. This can then be used to turn Equation 3.5 into something that can be used to calculate the value of equity. The next section considers two examples of what can broadly be referred to as dividend valuation models.

CONCEPT CHECK

6. Why is it appropriate that expected future dividends are discounted to obtain the current value of a share?

For the answers, go to MyFinanceLab

CONCEPT 3.6   Dividend valuation models

Constant-dividend model

One commonly made simplifying assumption is that companies pay a *constant* dividend year after year. Thus, the present value of future dividends is a perpetuity, for which an expression was developed in Chapter 2. It is the perpetual cash flow divided by the appropriate discount rate. Hence, the value of a constant-dividend-paying share is given by:

$$P_t = \frac{d}{r_e}$$ (3.6)

where:

P_t = current value of share

d = (constant) dividend per period

r_e = the required return on the share

Realistically, while companies that pay a constant dividend are somewhat rare, they do exist. Example 3.2 illustrates the application of Equation 3.6 to a company that has paid reasonably constant dividends in recent years, Telstra Corporation Limited. Note that the focus of this example is different from simply applying the formula to determine the value of the shares—since both the share price and the constant dividend amount are known, the discount rate (cost of equity) can be implied using the formula.

The solution generated by the application of the model to Telstra in Example 3.2 is plausible, given the 10-year government bond rate in August 2010 was around 5.11% p.a. This suggests that Telstra shareholders required a premium of around 8.03% over the 10-year bond rate at the time.

Practitioner's POV

Analysts rarely rely on dividend discount models to produce valuations of shares and generate recommendations. The more common approach is to calculate the value of a company's free cash flows (i.e. value the entire business) and then subtract the book value of net debt (interest-bearing debt less cash) to arrive at a value for equity. Despite this, calculations based on dividend discount models are sometimes used to support a valuation based on a company's entire free cash flow.

EXAMPLE 3.2

Applying the constant-dividend model

QUESTION

Telstra Corporation Limited (TLS) is the largest provider of telecommunications services in Australia and closed for trading on 23 August 2010 at $2.77. The cash dividend by Telstra in the previous year (including tax credits[3]) was 36.4 cents per share. If it was believed that Telstra would continue paying the same dividend each year, what discount rate is being applied by the investors of Telstra?

ANSWER

$$P_0 = \frac{d_0}{r_e}$$

$$2.77 = \frac{0.364}{r_e}$$

$$r_e = 13.14\%$$

Hence the implied required rate of return on Telstra's stock is 13.14%.

Constant-dividend growth model

An obvious limitation of the constant-dividend model is the unrealistic assumption regarding constant dividends paid by a company. A more plausible assumption to make regarding the behaviour of the dividends of a company is that they grow at a steady rate. As will be discussed in Chapter 11, directors of a company generally prefer paying dividends that grow steadily. In this section a model is developed for pricing equity securities under the constant-growth assumption.

Consider the dividend stream in Figure 3.2, which grows perpetually at a rate g, where the first dividend is paid at the end of the first year and is equivalent to $d_0(1 + g)$.

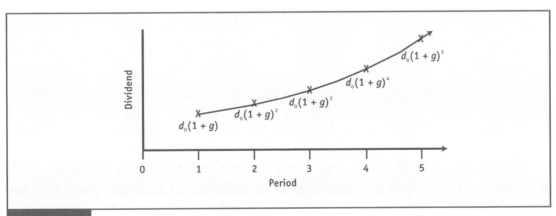

| **Figure 3.2** | Dividend stream with constant growth |

Appendix 3.2 derives an expression for valuing a perpetually growing dividend stream as depicted in Figure 3.2:

$$P_t = \frac{d_1}{r_e - g}$$
(3.7)

where:

$d_1 = d_0(1 + g) =$ the dividend at the end of the first period

$r_e =$ the equity cost of capital

$g =$ the constant growth rate in dividends

There are two critical features of this formula that need to be understood in order to apply it correctly. First, the model does not take into account any dividend that has just been paid or is about to be paid (i.e. d_0, dividend at time 0). Second, the derivation of the model in Appendix 3.2 assumes that the equity cost of capital must be greater than the dividend growth rate (i.e. $r_e > g$). In fact, if this condition does not hold, the value of the share is negative according to the model, which of course does not make any sense. Example 3.3 illustrates an application of the model.

EXAMPLE 3.3

Applying the perpetually growing dividend model

QUESTION

TPG Telecom Limited (TPM), a smaller provider of telecommunication services, closed for trading at $1.63 on 23 August 2010. TPG Telecom paid a total divided of around 3.9 cents per share in the previous year. Assuming that the required rate of return on Telstra (13.14%) is appropriate for valuing TPG, what perpetual dividend growth rate is being used by the market to price TPG's shares?

ANSWER

$$P_0 = \frac{d_0(1 + g)}{r_e - g}$$

Rearranging this, we obtain:

$$g = \frac{P_0 \times r_e - d_0}{P_0 + d_0}$$

$$g = \frac{1.63 \times 0.1314 - 0.039}{1.63 + 0.039} = 10.49\%$$

Hence, the implied perpetual dividend growth rate for TPG Telecom is approximately 10.49%.

This example implies that if the model used is correct, and the discount rate being applied is correct, then the market is expecting dividend growth of around 10.49%. In practice, the key question relates to whether or not the estimated rate of growth is reasonable.

Note that the model can be applied even where the growth of a company is not expected to be constant and smooth. However, in these circumstances it is necessary to convert the 'lumpy' forecast dividend growth of a company into an equivalent perpetually growing one.

Estimating the growth rate, *g*

Estimating a company's growth rate, *g*, is a key issue in the application of the perpetual growth model. One approach that is sometimes used is outlined in this section. For exposition purposes, ANZ Banking Group Limited is used. ANZ bank is one of the 'big four' banks in Australia and is one of the largest companies listed on the ASX by market capitalisation. In order to depict the dividend growth process for ANZ, a number of items of information were extracted from its annual report for the year ended 30 September 2009. ANZ had earnings per share (EPS) of 131 cents (i.e. $1.31), paid a dividend per share (DPS) of 102 cents (i.e. $1.02) and had return on (book) equity of about 10.3%. Figure 3.3 shows how these crucial numbers can combine to generate future earnings growth for ANZ, assuming it remains constant.

According to this model, dividend growth is derived from the earnings of a company. As noted, in 2009 the EPS of ANZ was 131 cents. The EPS can be thought of as the profit generated for each share on issue. When ANZ generated this profit, management had to decide how to use it. Management could choose to pay it out to the shareholders as a dividend, retain it in the company to fund future operations, or employ a combination of the two (pay part as a dividend and retain part for reinvestment). In 2009, ANZ management decided on the latter option, and paid out 102 cents per share, or 78% of EPS, as a dividend. The proportion of EPS paid out as dividends is called the 'payout ratio'. These earnings paid out as dividends represent lost funds to the company, and cannot be used to generate future profits. In the case of ANZ, since 78% of EPS was paid out as dividends, management must have retained 22% of EPS, or 29 cents per share. The proportion of funding that is retained by the company is sometimes called the 'plough back ratio', because implicitly the company is going to reinvest or 'plough back' these funds into its future operations. In turn, the funding reinvested in the company is expected to

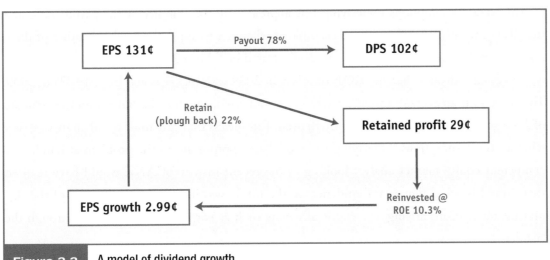

Figure 3.3   A model of dividend growth

be returned (eventually) to shareholders, along with an additional return. The question arises: how much more? Well, in this case the rate of return on equity (ROE, or r_e) is 10.3%. This is an estimate of the return that ANZ generates for every dollar of equity invested in its business. Hence, 2.99 cents (29 cents $\times$ 10.3%) is the incremental return expected to be generated by ANZ on the reinvested income. This return essentially joins the base EPS generated in the next year (assuming things keep going as they are), and so the cycle continues.

The model described above can be more rigorously stated as follows. First, it assumes a constant dividend payout ratio and a constant return on equity. Given these assumptions, dividend growth will be equal to the product of retained funds and the return on retained funds, as follows:

$$\text{Dividend growth} = \text{funding retained} \times \text{return on funding retained}$$

However, since the portion of retained funds is equivalent to 1 less the payout ratio (which is equivalent to the plough back ratio), then:

$$\text{Funding retained} = \text{plough back ratio} = (1 - \text{payout ratio})$$

And since the return on funding retained is equal to the ROE:

$$\text{Return on funding retained} = \text{ROE}$$

then the dividend growth rate (g) can be expressed as follows:

$$g = (1 - \text{payout ratio}) \times \text{ROE} \tag{3.8}$$

Example 3.4 provides an illustration of the application of the model in Equation 3.8 to ANZ. The example suggests that the future earnings and dividend growth of ANZ is expected to be 2.3% p.a.

The crucial assumptions underlying this approach are the stability of the payout ratio and the ROE. However, ANZ is a good example of when *not* to apply the model! Neither of these assumptions held over the past 10 years, as illustrated in Table 3.2.

Table 3.2 indicates that the ROE of ANZ in 2009 was 10.3%, down from 19.3% in 2000. This represents an average annual growth of around 6.4%, which is different from the estimate of 2.3% generated by the model of growth used. This means that care must be taken in assessing whether the assumptions underlying the model are appropriate to the problem at hand. Any competent equity market analyst looking at the recent history of ANZ would have realised that using historical figures for guidance on the future was inappropriate, because of the significant fluctuations arising as a result of events such as corporate restructuring through the last decade.

EXAMPLE 3.4

Estimating perpetual dividend growth

QUESTION

In the year ending on 30 September 2009, ANZ Banking Group (ANZ) generated EPS of 131 cents per share, paid a dividend of 102 cents per share, and its return on (book) equity is 10.3%. Assuming that the ROE and the payout ratio of ANZ are stable, what is its expected perpetual growth rate on earnings and dividends?

ANSWER

Payout ratio = 102/131 = 0.7786

$g = (1 - \text{payout ratio}) \times ROE$

$g = (1 - 0.7786) \times 0.103 = 0.0228$

Hence, the expected perpetual growth rate in ANZ's EPS and DPS is approximately 2.3%.

Table 3.2 Stability of ANZ's return on equity, dividend payout ratio, and their effects on growth estimates, 2000–2009

Year	2009	2008	2007	2006	2005	2004	2003	2002	2001	2000	Avg
Earnings per share (cents)	131.0	170.4	224.1	200.0	169.5	153.1	142.4	141.4	112.7	102.5	154.7
Dividends per share (cents)	102.0	136.0	136.0	125.0	110.0	101.0	95.0	85.0	73.0	64.0	102.7
Dividend payout ratio	0.78	0.80	0.61	0.63	0.65	0.66	0.67	0.60	0.65	0.62	0.67
Return on equity (%)	10.3	14.5	20.9	20.7	18.3	19.1	20.6	21.6	20.2	19.3	18.6
Computed growth (%)	2.3	2.9	8.2	7.8	6.4	6.5	6.9	8.6	7.1	7.2	6.4

Source: ANZ Banking Group Limited, *2000–2009 Annual Reports.*

CONCEPT CHECK

7. Why is the constant-dividend model unlikely to be commonly used in practice?
8. What is the relevance of the 'payout ratio' in dividend growth valuation models?

For the answers, go to MyFinanceLab

CONCEPT 3.7   P/E ratios—an application of the perpetual growth model

Without doubt, the industry standard for attempting to determine whether a company is overpriced or underpriced is the P/E ratio, or **price–earnings ratio**. The P/E ratio is simply the price of a company divided by its EPS. Analysts sometimes compare the P/E ratios of similar companies to ascertain whether one is overpriced or underpriced by the market relative to another. Take, for example, the P/E ratios of ANZ and the Commonwealth Bank of Australia (CBA) at the end of their reporting seasons from 2006–2009, presented in Table 3.3. These figures have been extracted from ANZ's and CBA's annual reports.

Given that ANZ and CBA are both banks, and both are listed in the 10 largest stocks on the ASX, it is reasonable to assume that they (and their P/E ratios) are comparable. However,

Price–earnings (P/E) ratio
The price of a share divided by its earnings per share.

FINANCE EXTRA!

Tax threatens Twiggy's fortune

ANDREW FORREST'S mantle as one of Australia's richest men is under threat as new figures show the government's proposed resource rent tax could strip a third of earnings from his company, Fortescue Metals.

Goldman Sachs JBWere has updated its initial estimate of the effect of the 40 per cent tax and its prognosis is dire for some of Australia's largest miners.

Goldman predicts that West Australian iron-ore producer Fortescue will suffer a 33 per cent fall by 2018 on an earnings-per-share basis, with a valuation impact of about 29 per cent.

'Fortescue has a greater impact for its earnings and valuations and its impact from spiking prices than BHP Billiton as Fortescue has all its operations in Australia, all its exposure to high-margin iron ore and unlike BHP Billiton has no petroleum exposure, which is already subject to the petroleum resource rent tax,' Goldman said.

'Our estimates of the impact of the new tax have generally increased (i.e. more negative) for net present values and earnings in the longer term as we have factored in more details.'

Adrian Prendergast, Fortescue analyst at EL & C Baillieu, said he expected an earnings-per-share effect of about 26 per cent over the same period.

'While Fortescue's short-term growth plan is quite secure, medium to longer term it is increasingly brought into question given the growth that they are expected to go through,' he said.

The Goldman analysis forecasts that the earnings-per-share effect on Rio Tinto in 2018 will be 18 per cent and on BHP 14 per cent. BHP's net present value would be cut by 13 per cent and could be further reduced by 8 per cent if it did not proceed with the $22 billion Olympic Dam expansion.

BHP said yesterday its Yeelirrie project in WA was under review in light of the tax, while its boss, Marius Kloppers, has said the expansion of Olympic Dam will be 'very difficult' to start.

Goldman says it expects the new tax will have a valuation effect on the resource sector and cause a de-rating.

'We believe there will be severe additional negative impacts from this proposed tax other than NPV [net present value] and earnings impacts,' it said.

'These include management time and focus, motivation of future management, tax implications of contractor versus owner-operator, the need to spread sovereign risk, the loss of trust and the implications for large high-risk capital expenditure, and the potential for new projects to be delayed or cancelled.'

Resource stocks fell again on the sharemarket, with BHP, Rio and Fortescue falling by a greater percentage than the wider market. Fortescue was the most affected of the three, down 22¢, or 5 per cent, to $4.16. Rio fell $1.70, or 2.5 per cent, to $67.10 while BHP fell 87¢, or 2.2 per cent, to $38.13.

Source: Mathew Murphy, *Sydney Morning Herald*, 12 May 2010. Fairfax Media Publications Pty Limited.

Table 3.3	P/E ratios for ANZ and CBA, 2006–2009					
	ANZ			CBA		
	EPS	PRICE	P/E RATIO	EPS	PRICE	P/E RATIO
2009	131.0	24.39	18.62	328.5	39.00	11.87
2008	170.4	18.75	11.00	363.0	40.17	11.07
2007	224.1	29.7	13.25	344.7	55.25	16.03
2006	200.0	26.86	13.43	308.2	44.41	14.41

Table 3.3 indicates that this has not been the case in the past four years. The divergent figures in the table illustrate that, if historical EPS numbers are used, a comparison of the P/E ratios of two companies would suggest that shareholders were paying too much for one of the shares and/or the other was relatively underpriced by the market. For example, such an interpretation of the 2009 P/E ratios of ANZ and CBA would hold that CBA shares were relatively underpriced (i.e. CBA investors were paying too little for the shares) and/or ANZ was relatively overpriced by the market (i.e. ANZ investors were paying too much for their shares). In these circumstances, the question arises: are the differences in the P/E ratios economically justifiable? The basic models developed in this chapter can assist us in answering this question. Consider the following possible interpretation of P/E ratios.

Starting with the constant-dividend growth model (Equation 3.7) (note that Equation 3.7 has been written with slightly different notation in this example):

$$P_t = \frac{d_{t+1}}{r_e - g}$$

and dividing both sides of the model by next year's EPS_{t+1}, yields:

$$\frac{P_t}{EPS_{t+1}} = \frac{d_{t+1}}{r_e - g} \times \frac{1}{EPS_{t+1}}$$

But $\frac{d_{t+1}}{EPS_{t+1}}$ is the dividend payout ratio (ρ), hence:

$$\frac{P_t}{EPS_{t+1}} = \frac{\rho}{r_e - g}$$

Note that the P/E ratio used above is known as the **prospective P/E ratio**, because the current share price is divided by the one-year-ahead forecast (not historical) EPS, EPS_{t+1}. This P/E ratio is far more commonly used in practice. The model demonstrates that the prospective P/E ratio is:

- positively related to the payout ratio
- negatively related to the cost of equity
- positively related to the dividend growth rate.

Prospective P/E ratio The price of shares divided by its forecast earnings per share.

Hence, it is possible that the P/E ratios of ANZ and CBA differ due to differences in these factors across the two companies.

Practitioner's POV

P/E ratios are by far the most popular basis used by analysts to identify mispriced shares. Analysts divide the current price of shares by their forecasts of the following year's EPS, or their forecasts of the EPS in two years' time. This P/E ratio is then typically compared against the P/E ratio of other shares in the same industry to assess whether the share is overpriced (P/E ratio is too high) or underpriced (P/E ratio is too low). The factors above (mainly earnings growth and discount rate/risk) are then used to assess whether a share with a P/E ratio quite different from its industry is likely to be fairly priced.

Student Learning Centre

MyFinanceLab ■ To test your mastery of the content covered in this chapter and to create your own personalised study plan, go to MyFinanceLab: www.pearson.com.au/myfinancelab

CONCEPT CHECKLIST

In this chapter the following concepts were discussed:

➤ The value of a company
➤ Differences between debt and equity
➤ The valuation of debt securities
➤ The valuation of equity, and various dividend valuation models
➤ The interpretation of P/E ratios

SELF-TEST QUESTIONS

1. Using the information provided in Example 3.1, answer the following.
    (a) If the coupon payments were annual rather than quarterly, what would be the market value of the Brookfield Multiplex bonds?
    (b) If the coupon rate was 6% p.a. (with quarterly payments), what would be the market value of the Brookfield Multiplex bonds?
2. Using the information provided in Table 3.3, answer the following.
    (a) If ANZ's share price as at 30 September 2009 was $23.58, what would its P/E ratio be at that time?
    (b) What would this P/E ratio imply about the market price of ANZ shares relative to CBA earnings as at 30 September 2009?

Self-test answers

1. Following Example 3.1:

   (a) Since the yield is 8.10% p.a. compounded semi-annually, the annual yield is $(1 + 0.081/2)^2 - 1 = 8.3\%$ per annum compounded annually. The present value of the interest payments is:

   $$F\frac{1-(1+r_d)^{-n}}{r_d} = \$8.79 \times \left[\frac{1-(1+0.083)^{-3}}{0.083}\right] = \$22.53$$

   The present value of the face value of the bond, to be repaid in three periods, is:

   $100/(1.083)^3 = \$78.73$

   Hence, the market value of one Brookfield Multiplex bond is $22.53 + $78.73 = $101.26.

   (b) Interest payment = coupon rate × face value = 0.06/4 × $100 = $1.50 every quarter, and there are 12 quarterly periods.

   The yield is 8.10% p.a. compounded semi-annually, so the effective quarterly yield is

   $(1+0.081/2)^{1/2} = 2.0\%$

   The present value of the interest payment is therefore:

   $$\$1.50 \times \left[\frac{1-(1+0.02)^{-12}}{0.02}\right] = \$15.86$$

   The present value of the face value of the bond, to be repaid in 12 quarters is:

   $100/(1.02)^{12} = \$78.85$

   Hence the market value of one Brookfield Multiplex bond is $15.86 + $78.85 = $94.71.

2. Based on Table 3.3:

   (a) P/E ratio = 23.58/1.31 = 18.

   (b) This P/E ratio implies that investors in ANZ shares are willing to pay around 18 times current earnings to purchase a share. This compares with investors in CBA shares who are willing to pay about 11 times current earnings to purchase a share. Thus, ANZ shares appear to be relatively overpriced compared with CBA shares.

DISCUSSION QUESTIONS

1. Refer to Figure 3.1 in the chapter. Explain how a company generates cash flows, and describe the subsequent flows of these funds.

2. What are 'free cash flows'? How can they be used to value a company?

3. Compare and contrast the basic components of a firm's capital structure—debt and equity. Why is the required rate of return on a firm's equity capital typically higher than that for the firm's debt?

4. How do you value a company using 'free cash flows' when a company currently has negative cash flows? Can these negative cash flows persist in the long run?

5. What are the factors that result in equity capital being more difficult to value than debt capital? What practical techniques are typically used to overcome these difficulties?

6. What is the coupon rate on a debt security? What is its relevance to the valuation of the security?

7. Debt instruments typically have a fixed and predetermined life. However, this is not the case with

equity. For example, few companies have lasted in excess of 200 years. How greatly does this affect the valuation of equity securities?

8. We know that equity securities (shares) can be valued by calculating the present value of future cash flows: dividends and future share price. How can this valuation approach be effective given the apparent circularity of the calculation—that is, using the future share price to determine the current share price?

9. Outline some of the features of the alternative equity valuation models that were presented in this chapter. Are the assumptions underlying the models reasonable? Are the input variables able to be estimated accurately in practice? What are the practical implications if the answer to the preceding two questions is no?

10. What would be the effect on the price of bonds of (1) an unexpected rise in interest rates and (2) an unexpected fall in interest rates? Would these interest rate changes have a similar effect on the price of shares? Explain.

11. In practice, we observe that different stocks have different P/E ratios. Why do you think this happens? What is the relationship between P/E ratios, earnings growth rates, company dividend payout ratios and the required rate of return on shares?

12. Provide an economic interpretation of what a firm's cost of debt, r_d, represents. (That is, what is the 'return' that this cost of debt provides?)

13. Perform the same analysis as in Question 12 in respect of a firm's cost of equity, r_e.

14. What is the basis for using P/E ratios as a rough indication of the value of a company? What is the risk associated with this approach?

15. What is the justification for the use of a 'prospective' P/E ratio in assessing the value of a share?

PRACTICAL QUESTIONS

BASIC
1. A 10-year government bond with a face value of $1 million dollars has a coupon rate of 6% with coupons paid semi-annually. If the current market interest rate is also 6% (compounded semi-annually), what is the price of the bond? Can you comment on this?

BASIC
2. An 8% Commonwealth government Treasury bond has five years to maturity. Given that the bond pays interest semi-annually and an interest payment has just been made, what is the current value of the bond if the market interest rate is 11% p.a. and the face value of the bond is $100 000?

BASIC
3. Calculate the market price of a 12% 10-year bond of $100 000 face value to be issued today, given a current yield on 10-year bonds of 7.6% p.a.

BASIC
4. What is the price of a one-year zero-coupon bond with a face value of $1 million if the annual interest rate is (a) 6%, (b) 8%, (c) 10% and (d) 12%? Sketch a rough graph of your results. What general relationship between price and interest rates is being demonstrated?

BASIC
5. Two Treasury bonds have a face value of $100 000 and pay coupons at the rate of 10% p.a. semi-annually. Bond P has four years to maturity and bond Q has eight years to maturity.
   (a) If the current interest rate is 7.5% p.a., what are the prices of the two bonds?
   (b) If the interest rate rises to 12% p.a., what are the prices of the two bonds?

6. Consider the following two bonds that pay coupons annually.

BASIC

Coupon rate	Time to maturity	Price per $100 face value
8%	1 year	$93.91
12%	10 years	$84.94

   (a) Calculate the yield to maturity of the one-year bond.

   (b) Assume that interest rates at all maturities increase by 1%. Calculate the market price of each bond at the new interest rates.

7. Suppose that you are considering investing in a debt security that promises to pay 7.5% p.a. semi-annually in arrears for six years. What is the value of this security if its yield is 7% and its face value is $100 000?

BASIC

8. BBB Ltd is a shoe manufacturing business. Its finance manager expects earnings of $0.75 per share at the end of this year and has forecast that these earnings will grow at a rate of 4% p.a. in perpetuity. The company's historical dividend payout ratio has been constant at 60% of EPS, and is expected to remain at that level. At what price should BBB Ltd shares be trading if the required return on equity is 12% p.a.?

INTERMEDIATE

9. What is the implied rate of growth in earnings on a stock with the following characteristics?

INTERMEDIATE

   • Current share price is $9.09.

   • EPS in the next period is forecast at $2 per share.

   • Dividend payout ratio is 50%.

   • Cost of equity is 15%.

10. You wish to value a company that paid a dividend of $1.23 per share yesterday. Furthermore, you are aware that five years ago the company paid a dividend of $0.80 and in the interim years the dividend paid has grown at a constant rate.

INTERMEDIATE

   (a) What has the annual growth rate in dividends been during the past five years?

   (b) If dividends are expected to grow at the same annual growth rate for the foreseeable future, what is the maximum price that you would be willing to pay for a share in the company if you require a return on equity of 15% p.a.?

11. Determine the expected share price of the following companies using the dividend growth model. Assume that a cost of equity of 10% is applicable.

INTERMEDIATE

   (a) ABC Ltd has current earnings of $4 per share. It does not reinvest any of its funds and therefore is not expected to show any earnings growth in the foreseeable future.

   (b) DEF Ltd is a fast-growing company with current earnings of 90 cents per share. These earnings have been growing at a rate of 6% p.a., but only 30% of earnings are paid out as a dividend.

   (c) GHI Ltd has current earnings of $1 per share and a dividend payout ratio of 50%. It is expected that earnings will grow at the rate of 6% p.a. for the next three years and then level off (i.e. revert to zero growth).

12. A stock has just paid a dividend of 50 cents per share. The dividend is expected to grow at a rate of 6% p.a. for the next 20 years, after which it will level off. If the discount rate of shares of similar risk is 9% p.a., what is the value of the shares?

INTERMEDIATE

13. You are the CEO of Glowing Future Ltd. Your company's 5-year bonds are currently trading with a yield to maturity of 9% p.a. compounded semi-annually. The bond's coupon rate is 7% p.a., with semi-annual interest payments. You have just heard of distressing rumours that Moody's will soon downgrade the rating of your bonds from Aaa to Baa, which will result in a 3% p.a. increase in the discount rate. What is the expected change in the price of Glowing Future's bonds?

14. You hold 8% bonds in a company which have a face value of $100 and 10 years to maturity. The bonds pay a coupon every six months. The yield on bonds of companies with similar risk is currently 1% above the Australian 10-year government bond rate of 5.5%. You are offered the option of converting each bond you hold into shares which are expected to pay a dividend of $1.307 per share in the next half-year, and these are expected to grow at approximately 2.5% every half-year. If shares in businesses of similar risk are currently trading at a discount rate of 9% p.a. nominal, should you accept the option?

15. Two stocks—ABC Ltd and XYZ Ltd—operate in the same industry, and you reason that their dividend growth rates and discount rates are similar. ABC Ltd has a share price of $5, is forecast to pay a dividend of 20 cents per share next year and has a dividend payout ratio of 60%. In contrast, XYZ Ltd has a share price of $8.50, is forecast to pay a dividend of 17 cents per share next year and has a dividend payout ratio of 50%. What is the implied dividend growth rate and implied discount rate of the two stocks?

16. What is the market value of 10% debentures redeemable in 10.25 years at a face value of $1m, when similar securities are yielding 5%? The debentures pay interest quarterly and the last coupon payment has just occurred.

17. L Ltd is a beer brewing company that last traded for $6.00 and last paid a DPS of 38 cents. Its dividend has been stable the last two years, and it is expected to remain constant over time. F Ltd is also a beer brewing company that last traded at $4.53 and last paid a dividend of 26.8 cents per share (cps). What is the implied future dividend growth rate of F Ltd if L Ltd's discount rate is applicable?

18. Below is the data for two banking stocks:

	A Ltd	B Ltd
DPS	25 cps	18 cps
EPS	56 cps	36 cps
Profitability		
ROE	15%	9.5%
Share price	$4.70	$4.77

Is B Ltd underpriced or overpriced by the market relative to A Ltd?

19. Refer back to Tables 3.2 and 3.3. Given the data in these tables and the following data for NAB:

	DPS	EPS
2007	136c	224.1c
2006	125c	200.0c
2005	110c	169.5c

(a) Provide three hypothetical reasons why the P/E ratio of NAB differs from the P/E ratio of ANZ in the most recent year.

(b) Given the data in the tables, which of the three reasons is the likely explanation for the difference in P/E ratios?

CASE STUDY

The questions in this case study refer to the information in the table below. The table provides information for Commonwealth Bank of Australia (CBA) for years ending 30 June.

Commonwealth Bank (CBA)	2009	2010
Share price (30 June)	$39.00	$48.64
Dividend per share (cents)	228	290
Dividend per share (inc. tax credits)	325.7	414.3
Earnings per share (cents)	305.6	395.5
Return on equity (%)	15.8	18.7

Source: CBA 2010 Annual Report

CASE STUDY QUESTIONS

1. If the DPS of CBA was to remain at 2010 levels indefinitely into the future, estimate the discount rate of CBA. If the risk free rate on 30 June 2010 was 4.5%, and there is almost no risk in CBA defaulting, is this discount rate reasonable?

2. If the DPS of CBA grew at 2.5% p.a. (approximately in line with inflation), estimate the discount rate of CBA. Is the number realistic?

3. Forecast the dividend growth rate of CBA based on the data provided for 2009. How does this figure compare with the actual growth rate in dividends of CBA between 2009 and 2010? Use the forecast dividend growth rate of CBA to estimate its discount rate. Is it realistic?

4. Forecast the growth rate in EPS of CBA in 2010 using the EPS, DPS and return on equity figures provided. Use this to forecast the EPS in 2011, and calculate the prospective P/E ratio. Repeat this exercise for 2009. Provide three reasons why the prospective P/E ratio of CBA may have changed.

5. Australian 10-year Commonwealth government bonds were yielding 5.3% p.a. on 30 June 2010, and had a coupon rate of 8%. What is the face value of a Commonwealth government bond that you would accept for one CBA share as at 30 June 2010?

FURTHER READING

For a review of research examining the objective of corporate financial decision making see:

- Lonergan, W. (2003), *The Valuation of Businesses, Shares and Other Equity*, 4th edn, Allen & Unwin, Sydney, NSW.

NOTES

1. It is important to realise that we distinguish between the value of an asset and its price. The price of an asset is the amount of cash for which the asset trades in the marketplace (e.g. on the stock exchange). This chapter is concerned with the valuation of a company, not its price. Although the two are related, it is possible to find companies that trade at various times at a price higher or lower than their intrinsic value.
2. Hybrid securities are so named because they comprise both equity-like and debt-like features. Common examples of hybrid securities are preference shares and convertible notes. Equity, debt and hybrid securities are discussed in more detail in Chapter 12.
3. In Australia, a dividend imputation system of corporate taxation has been in operation since 1 July 1987. Among other outcomes, this system results in dividends being paid with tax credits attached. Since these tax credits are of value to Australian shareholders (they reduce the tax paid), they are typically included in the value of dividends paid. The dividend system is explained in detail in Chapter 8.

PROOF THAT THE VALUE OF A SHARE IS EQUAL TO THE PRESENT VALUE OF FUTURE DIVIDENDS

Assume that an investor who purchases a share at time t holds it for one period and then sells it at time $t + 1$. The following represents the return achieved by the investor who pays P_t for the share, receives a dividend of d_t over a holding period and sells the share for P_{t+1}:

$$r_e = \frac{d_t + (P_{t+1} - P_t)}{P_t} \tag{A3.1.1}$$

Rearranging Equation A3.1.1 to isolate the price, P_t, that the investor will pay in order to achieve a particular return r_e (or required return) yields:

$$P_t = \frac{d_t + P_{t+1}}{1 + r_e} = \frac{d_t}{1 + r_e} + \frac{P_{t+1}}{1 + r_e} \tag{A3.1.2}$$

Hence, the price that the investor is willing to pay now can be interpreted as the present value of the dividend to be paid during the period over which the share is held, plus the present value of the share at the end of the holding period.

However, using Equation A3.1.2, the price at which a new investor is willing to buy the share at the end of the first year (and, hence, the price at which the current investor is able to sell the share) is given by the following:

$$P_{t+1} = \frac{d_{t+1} + P_{t+2}}{1 + r_e} \tag{A3.1.3}$$

Substituting Equation A3.1.3 into Equation A3.1.2 yields:

$$P_t = \frac{d_t}{1 + r_e} + \frac{\dfrac{d_{t+1} + P_{t+2}}{1 + r_e}}{1 + r_e} = \frac{d_t}{1 + r_e} + \frac{d_{t+1}}{(1 + r_e)^2} + \frac{P_{t+2}}{(1 + r_e)^2}$$

Equation A3.1.3 gives the present value of the dividends paid at the end of both the first and second years, plus the present value of the share at the end of the second year.

Repeating this reasoning to infinity yields:

$$P_t = \frac{d_t}{1 + r_e} + \frac{d_{t+1}}{(1 + r_e)^2} + \frac{d_{t+2}}{(1 + r_e)^3} \cdots \frac{d_\infty}{(1 + r_e)^\infty}$$

Thus, the value of a share is given by the present value of all future dividends paid in relation to the share.

APPENDIX 3.2

DERIVATION OF PRESENT VALUE OF A PERPETUALLY GROWING DIVIDEND STREAM

Consider the existence of a stream of dividends that begins at time 0 at d_0, and grows perpetually at a rate g. Ignoring time 0, the dividend stream can be represented as follows.

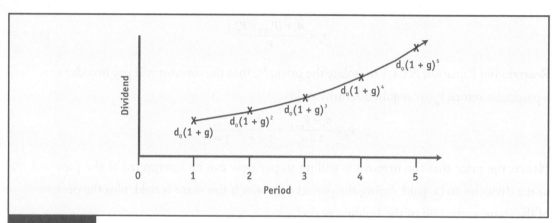

Figure A3.2.1 Dividend stream with constant growth

The present value (PV) of these amounts is the sum of the present value of each individual dividend discounted by an appropriate factor r_e (required return on equity) as follows:

$$PV = \frac{d_0(1+g)}{(1+r_e)} + \frac{d_0(1+g)^2}{(1+r_e)^2} \ldots + \frac{d_0(1+g)^{n-1}}{(1+r_e)^{n-1}} + \frac{d_0(1+g)^n}{(1+r_e)^n} \tag{A3.2.1}$$

Multiplying both sides of Equation A3.2.1 by $\frac{(1+r_e)}{(1+g)}$ yields:

$$PV \frac{(1+r_e)}{(1+g)} = d_0 + \frac{d_0(1+g)}{(1+r_e)} \ldots + \frac{d_0(1+g)^{n-2}}{(1+r_e)^{n-2}} + \frac{d_0(1+g)^{n-1}}{(1+r_e)^{n-1}} \tag{A3.2.2}$$

Subtracting Equation A3.2.1 from Equation A3.2.2 yields:

$$PV \frac{(1+r_e)}{(1+g)} - PV = d_0 - \frac{d_0(1+g)^n}{(1+r_e)^n} \tag{A3.2.3}$$

Since a perpetually growing dividend stream is simply the case where $n \to \infty$, and if we assume that $r_e > g$, then as n becomes very large, $\frac{d_0(1+g)^n}{(1+r_e)^n}$ approaches 0. Hence, in the limit, Equation A3.2.3 reduces to:

$$PV \frac{(1+r_e)}{(1+g)} - PV = d_0 \tag{A3.2.4}$$

Finally, rearranging Equation A3.2.4 to make *PV* the subject of the formula yields:

$$PV = \frac{d_0(1 + g)}{(r_e - g)}$$

This is the present value of a dividend stream which grows at a rate *g*, with the first dividend of $d_0(1 + g)$ occurring at the end of the first year, and where $r_e > g$.

4

Capital budgeting: Basic techniques

CHAPTER PREVIEW

Companies exist as a means of pooling funds of individuals and other economic entities to enable production on a large scale. To this end, companies invest available funds in capital projects, typically involving the purchase of real assets. As explained in Chapter 1, the decision as to which particular projects should be undertaken is known as the investment decision, and the process is known as 'capital budgeting'.

The previous two chapters discussed the discounted cash flow model of valuation and its application to valuing securities, namely debt and equity. This chapter is concerned with the application of the technique to valuing individual projects available to a company in making capital budgeting decisions. Specifically, this chapter aims to compare the discounted cash flow approach with other commonly used capital budgeting techniques.

KEY CONCEPTS

Practitioner's POV

In a 'breakup valuation' an analyst will take all the individual projects (e.g. divisions or product lines) of a company and value them. The sum of the values of the individual projects is equal to the value of the company. Breakup valuations are sometimes used to identify the main contributors to the value of a company or to assess whether a particular project detracts from the value of a company.

Warren Buffett, renowned as one of the most successful investors in the world, religiously applies a discounted cash flow approach when choosing between the various projects available to him. Among the better known wealth-increasing 'projects' that Buffett has chosen over the years are Salomon Inc. (the investment bank), American Express, Coca-Cola and Walt Disney. Testimony to the success that is possible from applying the approach is the increase in the value of the company that he uses to invest in these 'projects', Berkshire Hathaway Inc. The value of Berkshire Hathaway shares increased from a price of a few US dollars in 1965 to $120 450 in 2010! The 'projects' that Buffett evaluates with the techniques discussed in this chapter are entire companies. This type of application is possible because the issues involved in choosing which projects to undertake are practically identical to those involved in choosing companies in which to invest. Hence, the ideas discussed in this chapter are also relevant to valuing entire companies, not just the individual projects or assets making up the company.

FINANCE EXTRA!

Gold shines and mines reopen

DURING the last several years, the price of gold has risen sharply, and at the beginning of May 2011 it reached a historic high of more than US$1500 per ounce. At this high price, many mining projects in Australia have become economically viable, and many miners have reopened their previously abandoned projects. On 31 January 2011, Ivanhoe Australia Ltd, a company listed on the ASX (ASX: IVA), announced that it had approved a $30 million budget for pre-production development at its Kulthor/Osborne operations in Queensland's Cloncurry region. Twenty-seven million dollars will be spent in 2011 to resume production at the Osborne complex, previously operated by the world's largest gold miner, Barrick Gold Corporation. Gold and copper production is expected in the first quarter of 2012. Ivanhoe's decision to reopen the Osborne plant is a capital budgeting decision, and the firm should not only factor the record high precious metals prices but also the price fluctuations and other variations into its investment strategies.

Source: Market release 'Ivanhoe Australia approves $30 million budget for Kulthor/Osborne pre-production development', viewed at <www.ivanhoeaustralia.com> on 31 January 2011.

CONCEPT 4.1   What is capital budgeting?

When a company allocates funds to long-term investment projects, the outlay is made in the expectation of future benefits, in the form of future cash flows. The most common examples of long-term investment projects are the purchase of new or replacement manufacturing plant or equipment. In making the decision to invest in available projects, the key consideration is whether or not the proposal provides an adequate return to investors. In theory, the number of projects that a company can undertake is limited only by the imagination of its managers and, of course, the available cash. The process used by a company to select projects from the set of available projects is called capital budgeting (or, alternatively, project evaluation).

Accordingly, capital budgeting is essentially the process by which a company decides on the optimum use of scarce cash resources. There are three fundamental stages in deciding whether a particular project is acceptable, or in choosing between a number of possible projects. Stage 1 is the forecasting of costs and benefits associated with a project. The most important costs and benefits in this case are the financial ones—that is, the cash inflows and outflows and/ or the revenues and expenses. These two sets of costs and benefits can be different, as will be discussed later in the next chapter. Stage 2 requires the application of an investment evaluation technique to these forecast costs and benefits, to determine whether a particular project is acceptable, or optimal, among a set of available alternatives. In stage 3, a final choice as to the acceptance or rejection of a project is made, on the basis of the (stage 2) quantitative analysis and other qualitative factors. The following section outlines investment evaluation techniques that can be used in the capital budgeting process, after which the role of qualitative factors will be explained.

The four best known investment evaluation techniques will be discussed. Two of the techniques are based on the discounted cash flow (DCF) model:

- net present value
- internal rate of return (IRR).

The two other techniques are *ad hoc* (accounting-based) techniques:

- payback
- (average) accounting rate of return (ARR).

Although these are not the only methods of investment evaluation, they are the most commonly used in practice, and some others are simply variations of these methods. In choosing which method to use, it is useful to have some evaluation criteria to assess the acceptability of the methods. Four general criteria provide a basis for such an assessment.

1. Does the method correctly identify wealth-increasing projects?
2. Does the method correctly rank competing projects?

3. Does the method recognise the timing of the cash flows and their relative magnitude?

4. Can management understand the results?

The first three criteria deal with the objective of maximising wealth and the recognition of the principle that money has a time value. The fourth criterion recognises that senior management needs to be able to understand the results.

CONCEPT CHECK

1. What are the three stages in choosing an acceptable investment project?
2. What criteria should we use in evaluating capital budgeting techniques?
3. What are the four most common project evaluation techniques?

For the answers, go to MyFinanceLab

CONCEPT 4.2   Investment evaluation techniques

The net present value (NPV) technique

The **net present value (NPV)** technique involves the discounting of cash flows to determine the value of a project in present-value terms. Specifically, a project's NPV is calculated by discounting all expected cash inflows and outflows to their present value, using an appropriate discount rate. The positive and negative present values are then netted off against one another, giving the project's NPV. Under this method, it can be determined whether or not the future (cash flow) benefits expected from an investment project justify the project's cost. The decision rule for this approach is to accept all projects with a positive NPV and to reject all projects with a negative NPV.

> **Net present value (NPV)**
> The difference between the present value of a project or investment's benefits and the present value of its costs.

The NPV is effectively a measure of the net change in firm value (and therefore the wealth of the owners of the firm) arising from undertaking a project. The reason for this is simple. To illustrate, consider a project with a (present) value of $110 million that is acquired for $100 million; in this case, the wealth of the acquirer must increase by $10 million. This implies the key decision rule of the NPV method: if the NPV of a project is positive, it should be accepted. Conversely, if a project's NPV is negative, it should be rejected.

Note that if an available project has an NPV of zero, it is a matter of indifference whether the company undertakes the project or pays the available cash back to shareholders. This is because zero NPV indicates that the project yields the same future wealth for shareholders as they could otherwise obtain from reinvesting the cash themselves.[1] This highlights another way of thinking about the NPV technique. That is, NPV implicitly weighs up an opportunity to invest in an asset against the alternative of paying the cash back to investors as a dividend, allowing the investors to reinvest the cash themselves. The NPV technique will indicate that a project is acceptable if the accumulated cash flow (including interest from reinvestment of proceeds) at the end of the life of the project exceeds the terminal cash flow that investors would have generated had they invested the cash spent on the project themselves. To clarify this, consider the following alternatives available to a company with $100 million in surplus cash. Option 1 is to invest $100 million in a project paying $106 million in one year. Option 2 is to pay $100 million in dividends, which shareholders can reinvest at 7%.

In this illustration, it is clear that the company's shareholders are better off if the cash is repaid to them (option 2). Why? Because by receiving $100 million now they will accumulate more cash at the end of the year by accepting the cash dividend and investing it at their opportunity cost of capital, 7%. While option 1 will generate additional cash for shareholders in a year's time ($106 million up from $100 million), it is less than the $107 million that would be generated if they were to invest the $100 million at the reinvestment rate of 7%. In effect, were the company to choose option 1, they would be reducing the future wealth of shareholders by $1 million. In these circumstances, the NPV rule would indicate rejection of option 1 and acceptance of option 2.

Stated formally, the net present value of a project is calculated as follows:

$$NPV = \sum_{t=1}^{n} \frac{F_t}{(1+r)^t} - C_0 \tag{4.1}$$

where:

F_t = cash flow generated by the project in year t

r = the opportunity cost of capital

C_0 = the cost of the project (initial cash flow, if any)

n = the life of the project in years

To explain, this formula means that we sum all cash flows *(F)* expected in future time periods, *t*, discounted by the appropriate discount rate, *r*. This discount rate is the company's cost of capital (or it may be a project-specific cost of capital, as explained in Chapter 6). NPV is generally regarded as the best method of project evaluation, for reasons that will be discussed later.

The simple example below illustrates the mechanics of the NPV technique using the same numbers as above.

EXAMPLE 4.1

The NPV technique

QUESTION

Apply the NPV rule to a project that costs $100 million and yields $106 million in one year when the opportunity cost of capital is 7%.

ANSWER

The present value of the project's cash inflows after year 0 is:

$$\sum_{t=1}^{n} \frac{F_t}{(1+r)^t} = \frac{106m}{1.07} = \$99m$$

The cost of the project is $100 million, so the NPV of the project is:

$$\$99m - \$100m = -\$1m$$

Since the NPV of the project is negative, it should be rejected.

Example 4.1 illustrates clearly that in rejecting the project a company avoids paying more for it than it is worth. It is an undesirable project, as it would decrease the wealth of shareholders by $1 million. A more complex example of the NPV technique follows in Example 4.2.

There are a number of strengths associated with the NPV technique. First, using this technique always ensures the selection of projects that maximise the wealth of shareholders, as it has been specifically designed to make this type of decision. Second, the NPV technique takes into account the time value of money. It does not ignore the fact that $1 in one year's time is worth less than $1 today. Third, the NPV technique considers all cash flows expected to be generated by a project, and hence uses all available information. On the other hand, it is sometimes pointed out that this is a weakness of the NPV technique because it requires extensive forecasts of the costs and benefits of a project, which can be problematic. Forecasting future cash flows is dealt with in detail in the next chapter. As a ranking technique when choosing between competing projects, the NPV approach performs very well. The ranking criterion is simple. More is preferred to less, so projects with the highest NPV are ranked first. The limitation of the NPV technique is that it is difficult for non-finance-trained managers to understand the concept fully. In summary, the NPV technique performs excellently on the first three ranking criteria and moderately on the fourth criterion.

EXAMPLE 4.2

The NPV technique

QUESTION

A company is currently considering whether it should outlay $500 000 for a machine that will have a useful life of five years. The forecast net cash flows from using the machine are $150 000 each year for the next five years, with no residual value at the end. What is the NPV of this project, given an opportunity cost of capital of 10%?

ANSWER

Since the expected cash inflows are a series of equally sized and regularly occurring cash flows, we know from Chapter 2 that they can be valued as an annuity (using Equation 2.11):

$$PV = A \left[\frac{1 - (1+r)^{-n}}{r} \right]$$

The NPV of the project's cash flows is therefore:

$$NPV = -\$500\,000 + \$150\,000 \times \left[\frac{1 - (1+10\%)^{-5}}{10\%}\right]$$

$$= -\$500\,000 + \$568\,618 = \$68\,618$$

Since the NPV of the project is positive, it should be accepted.

An alternative way of representing the same problem is to discount back the future cash flows individually. In this case, the project's cash flows would be represented on a time line and then discounted.

Year	0	1	2	3	4	5
Initial outlay	−500 000					
Annual cash flows		150 000	150 000	150 000	150 000	150 000
Net cash flows	−500 000	150 000	150 000	150 000	150 000	150 000
PVC of NCFs	−500 000	136 364	123 967	112 697	102 452	93 138

Net present value = $68 618

Where a project's cash flows do not follow an annuity pattern, this is the approach that is normally taken. Calculating the NPV can be done manually, as above, with the use of a financial calculator, or by using the NPV function in a spreadsheet package.

Practitioner's POV

Although an NPV approach may very well be best in theory, in practice the problem with using the approach is choosing an appropriate discount rate. This discount rate is often referred to as the 'hurdle rate'. It is quite difficult to come up with a sensible number using some of the techniques that will be discussed later in the book. For this reason, some people still treat DCF valuations with scepticism. However, modern developments in the analysis options available in spreadsheet packages have made the problem far more tractable. In practice, no project is going to be presented to the executive that does not have a present value well in excess of the outlay costs. In addition, the concept of a net present value is more difficult to explain to executives and members of governing boards who have not had finance training. Despite these difficulties, net present value is frequently used in combination with a host of other techniques to add strength to a particular valuation or recommendation.

The internal rate of return (IRR) technique

Internal rate of return (IRR)
The interest rate that sets the net present value of the cash flows equal to zero.

The next technique, the **internal rate of return (IRR)**, is also based on a DCF model, but focuses on the rate of return in the DCF equation rather than the NPV. The IRR is defined as the discount rate that equates the present value of a project's cash inflows with the present value of its cash outflows. This is the equivalent of saying that the IRR is the discount rate at which the

NPV of the project is equal to zero. The IRR is also sometimes referred to as the *internal yield* of a project. Stated formally:

$$0 = \sum_{t=1}^{n} \frac{F_t}{(1 + irr)^t} - C_0 \qquad (4.2)$$

where:

F_t = cash flow generated by the project in year t

C_0 = the cost of the project (initial cash flow, if any)

n = the life of the project in years

irr = the internal rate of return of the project

Equation 4.2 has only one unknown variable—the *irr*. Hence, it is possible to solve the equation for the *irr* using a mathematical technique or by trial and error, as explained below.

The decision rule under the IRR approach is: accept a project if its *irr* is greater than the cost of capital, or reject a project if its *irr* is less than the cost of capital. It is clear from a comparison of Equations 4.1 and 4.2 that the NPV and IRR techniques use the same framework and inputs. Consequently, if properly applied, the two techniques should result in the same accept/reject decision.

Example 4.3 illustrates the application of the IRR technique, using the numbers from Example 4.1.

As illustrated, in making the investment decision a project's IRR is evaluated against a pre-determined 'hurdle' rate (the cost of capital). In this example, if the hurdle rate is set at 7% (as assumed for the NPV method), the project is not acceptable since the calculated IRR is below the hurdle rate.

EXAMPLE 4.3

The IRR technique

QUESTION

Apply the IRR rule to a project that costs $100 million and yields $106 million in one year when the opportunity cost of capital is 7%.

ANSWER

Set up the problem within the IRR framework.

$$0 = \sum_{t=1}^{n} \frac{F_t}{(1 + irr)^t} - C_0$$

$$0 = \sum_{t=1}^{1} \frac{106m}{(1 + irr)^t} - 100m$$

Solving for the *irr*: *irr* = 6%.

Since the IRR of the project is less than the opportunity cost of capital of 7%, it should be rejected.

What are the strengths of the IRR technique? Given that the IRR uses the same structure as the NPV technique, it shares most of the latter's advantages. Furthermore, many financial managers have difficulty understanding what the NPV number actually means, but the IRR is a percentage rate of return that is intuitive to most, and can easily be compared with rates of return on alternative investments, such as bonds, equities and so on. For this reason, in practice the IRR is sometimes favoured over the NPV technique.

Despite this, there are some problems that can be encountered in applying the IRR technique. One common problem with the IRR method is the difficulty associated with its calculation. That is, in most circumstances the IRR of a project can only be found by trial and error. This is because the number of periods (or cash flows) involved in the project determines the power of the equation that needs to be solved to calculate the IRR. Take, for example, the project in Example 4.4.

EXAMPLE 4.4

The IRR can sometimes only be solved by trial and error

Year	0	1	2	3	4	5
Net cash flows	−2000	−1000	2000	2000	−1000	4000

To find the IRR, solve the following equation:

$$0 = -2000 + \frac{-1000}{(1 + irr)} + \frac{2000}{(1 + irr)^2} + \frac{2000}{(1 + irr)^3} + \frac{-1000}{(1 + irr)^4} + \frac{4000}{(1 + irr)^5}$$

To solve this problem requires a trial-and-error approach. You first choose a discount rate that you feel may be close to the IRR and find the NPV of the cash flow stream. If the answer is negative, the discount rate is too high. If it is positive, the discount rate is too low. By narrowing down the difference between the two discount rates, we can approach the actual IRR. Solving this equation (by trial and error) gives an IRR of about 31%.

Although closed-form solutions to equations with lower powers exist (e.g. quadratics and polynomials to the third root), the equation depicted in Example 4.4 can only be solved by trial and error.[2] How was this IRR of 31% calculated? A common technique used for solving by trial and error is known as **interpolation**. This technique is further explained and demonstrated below.

Interpolation

Method of solving by trial and error the internal yield of a project.

We know that the IRR is, by definition, the discount rate at which the NPV of a project's cash flows is equal to zero. Since zero is a number that lies between a positive number and a negative number, it follows that the IRR must lie between two discount rates: one that results in a positive NPV when discounting the project's cash flows, and the other resulting in a negative NPV. This is where the trial-and-error aspect of the calculation comes in: we need to 'guess' a starting point to perform the interpolation. Using Example 4.4, assume that we first guess a discount rate of 30%. Applying this discount rate to the project's cash flows results in an NPV of $51.72. Since this is a positive NPV, we know that 30% is below the project's IRR (i.e. the rate that gives a zero NPV must be higher than a rate that gives a positive NPV). So now we guess a higher rate, say 35%. This rate produces an NPV of −$239.48.

Now we know that the IRR lies between 30% and 35%. Specifically, the IRR is at least 30%, plus some proportion of the difference between 30% and 35% (i.e. 5%). The interpolation calculation proceeds on this basis, as follows:

$$IRR = 30\% + [51.72/(51.72 + 239.48)] \times 5\% = 30.9\% \approx 31\%$$

Fortunately, most financial calculators and spreadsheet programs can perform this calculation in a few seconds, since they have inbuilt functions to solve for IRR. The IRR function in spreadsheet packages uses the same interpolation procedure as that illustrated above, which is why it requires the analyst to enter a first guess for the function to work.

We have discussed the difficulty associated with calculating the IRR. The second problem with the IRR technique is that the nature of the rule must be modified depending on whether the project under evaluation is an **investing project** (a capital investment) or a **financing project** (e.g. borrowing money from a bank). In the case of an investment, a company will accept a project with a high rate of return. With a financing project, the company is looking for the cheapest source of finance—that is, the lowest interest rate. Hence, the decision rule for a project must be modified to take into account whether it is an investing project or a financing project. The complication caused by financing projects is demonstrated in Example 4.5.

Investing project
A project involving a capital investment where the decision rule is to accept the project with the highest positive net present value.

Financing project
A project that involves borrowing money from a financial institution like a bank, where the decision rule is to accept the lowest cost of finance.

EXAMPLE 4.5

Applying the IRR rule to investing and finance projects

Investing project:

Year	0	1	IRR
Project A	−100	130	30%
Project B	−100	140	40%

Decision: Choose project with highest IRR (B).

Financing project:

Year	0	1	IRR
Project A	100	−130	30%
Project B	100	−140	40%

Decision: Choose project with lowest IRR (A).

Example 4.5 demonstrates the application of the IRR to a clear investing project and a clear financing project. In such circumstances it is very simple to modify and apply the IRR rule. However, in practice there are often projects with both positive and negative future cash flows (net inflows and outflows), and it can be difficult to determine whether they are investing or financing projects.

A further problem with the IRR technique, also associated with projects having both positive and negative future cash flows, is that in some circumstances multiple internal rates of return can exist. Consider Example 4.6.

4.6 EXAMPLE

Multiple rates of return

Year	0	1	2
Net cash flows	−100	230	−132

IRR calculation:

$$0 = -100 + \frac{230}{(1 + irr)} + \frac{-132}{(1 + irr)^2}$$

Solving for the *irr*:

$$irr = 10\% \text{ or } 20\%$$

An easy way to illustrate the relationship between IRR and NPV techniques is to plot the path of the NPVs for a range of discount rates. On the graph, the discount rate is on the *x*-axis and the NPV is on the *y*-axis. The curve is the NPV profile of the project. When the NPV profile crosses the *x*-axis, it is the NPV of the project at zero discount rate. While the NPV of the project is zero, the NPV profile cuts through the *x*-axis and it is the IRR of the project.

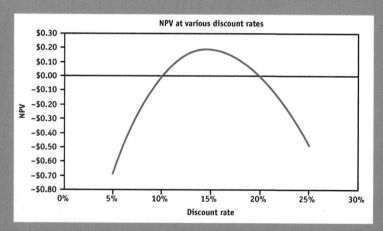

The cash flows for this type of project typify the general form of projects in the mining industry, where remediation to the environment is required as a condition of mining leases.

If the cost of capital for Example 4.6 were, say, 15%, based only on the IRR technique, it is unclear whether the project should be undertaken. Once again, an application of the NPV technique would resolve this problem.

When evaluating independent projects, the NPV technique and the IRR technique usually provide a consistent conclusion if there is a single IRR. For independent projects, the decision making would not have any impact on the decision making of the other projects, which means the firm decides to accept or reject each project, and it can accept one or more projects or it can reject all of them. In the case of mutually exclusive projects, owing to limited available resources or limited capital, by accepting one project the firm has to reject the other projects. An example of mutually exclusive projects is as follows. A firm has a piece of land and it is deciding whether to build an office block or a warehouse on the land. Obviously, it cannot undertake both projects on the same piece of land at the same time. Therefore, these two projects are mutually exclusive. Or, to take another example: a firm has a fixed budget of $2 million for this year and is considering two projects. One requires $1.5 million and the other requires $1 million. Obviously, only one project can be undertaken this year, so these two projects are also mutually exclusive. When evaluating mutually exclusive projects by using the NPV technique, a firm should choose the project that provides the highest NPV. However, the IRR technique indicates that the project with the highest IRR is the best. These two techniques may provide different answers for capital budgeting decision making, and the reason for this often relates to the differences between the size and timing of the cash flows.

Therefore, another problem with the IRR technique arises from the fact that a rate of return does not take into consideration the size of a project when evaluating mutually exclusive projects. This is sometimes referred to as the 'problem of scale'. Example 4.7 highlights the difficulty that this causes.

EXAMPLE 4.7

The IRR does not take into account the size of projects

Year	0	1	IRR
Small project	−1	1.5	50%
Large project	−100	110	10%

Which project is better if the opportunity cost of capital is 5%?

The problem with the IRR decision in Example 4.7 can be highlighted by considering what would happen if a company had $100 million to spend. That part of the $100 million not spent by the company would be returned to shareholders, who would invest the cash at the opportunity cost of capital of 5%. This results in the large project being the better option, even though it has the lower IRR. Why? Because if the company took on the small project it would generate $1.5 million, and the remaining (unspent) $99 million would be returned to shareholders and rein-vested at 5%, accumulating to about $104 million (99 × 1.05) at the end of the year. Hence, the total wealth of shareholders at the end of the year from this strategy would be around $105.5 million, clearly lower than the total wealth generated from investing in the large project ($110 million). As such, incorrect investment decisions could be made when applying the IRR rule, because it ignores the size of projects.

Even for projects of the same size, because of the timing of the cash flows, the NPV and IRR methods may still provide different conclusions. The best way to compare the differences between using NPV and IRR methods when evaluating mutually exclusive projects is to use the NPV profile. This shows the NPVs of the projects at different discount rates. Example 4.8 illustrates the problem of using the IRR technique in considering mutually exclusive projects of the same size.

EXAMPLE 4.8

Mutually exclusive projects of the same size under NPV and IRR rules

Year	0	1	2	3	4
Project *L*	−1000	100	300	400	600
Project *E*	−1000	500	400	300	100

Assuming project *L* and project *E* are mutually exclusive, which project is better if the opportunity cost of capital is 5%?

Which project is better if the opportunity cost of capital is 10%?

The IRR for project *L* is 11.79%, and the IRR for project *E* is 14.49%. If only based on the IRR, the one with the higher IRR, which is project *E*, should be chosen whatever the opportunity cost of capital is. However, it may be incorrect. In order to see the reason, the NPVs of these two projects for different opportunity costs of capital are as follows.

Discount rate (%)	NPV (project *L*)	NPV (project *E*)
0	400.00	300.00
5	206.50	180.42
10	49.18	78.82
15	−80.14	−8.33
20	−187.50	−83.72

When using the NPV method, the capital budget decision would be based on the opportunity cost of capital.

If the opportunity cost of capital is 5%:

$$NPV_L = 206.50 > NPV_E = 180.42$$

So, accept project L.
If the opportunity cost of capital is 10%:

$$NPV_L = 49.18 < NPV_E = 78.82$$

So, accept project E.

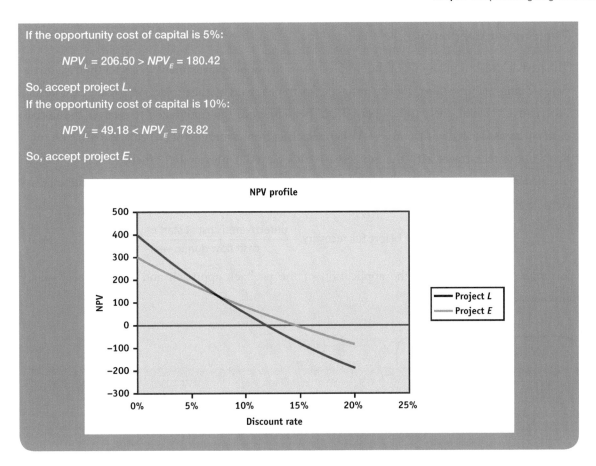

The inconsistency between NPV and IRR methods for mutually exclusive projects can be further illustrated by drawing the NPV profiles of the two projects in Example 4.8. The NPV profiles of the two projects cross at 7.17%, and this rate is known as the crossover rate. At the crossover rate, the NPVs of the two projects are exactly the same. Project L has a higher NPV at a lower discount rate, while project E has a higher NPV when the discount rate is higher than the crossover rate. Project L's cash flows occur at the later period relative to project E, so its NPV is more sensitive to the change in discount rate. The NPV profile of project L is also steeper than that of project E.

So, what is the verdict on the IRR technique? While in theory it supposedly leads to the same investment decision as the NPV technique, the IRR method clearly has some problems that the NPV approach avoids. Although it does incorporate the concept of the time value of money, it does not provide a direct measure of the increase in wealth that a project may provide. Nor does it rank projects in terms of the capacity to increase wealth. However, it is easy for management to understand. Because it meets fewer of our criteria than the NPV technique, the best solution is to apply the NPV approach.

For completeness, two common alternative evaluation techniques are explained, both of which are considered inferior to the DCF-based techniques outlined above.

The payback technique

The payback technique is one of the simplest ways to evaluate investments. This method involves determining the time taken for the initial outlay to be repaid by the project's expected cash flows. Alternatively stated, the payback period can be defined as the time taken to recover the initial cash outlay associated with a project. When selecting from a number of projects, the decision rule is to choose the project with the shortest payback period. Unfortunately, there is little guidance on what an appropriate payback period for a single project should be and, hence, it is difficult to determine whether a project should be accepted or not. The payback is given by:

$$\text{Payback} = \text{year before full recovery} + \frac{\text{unrecovered cost at start of year}}{\text{cash flow during year}} \qquad \textbf{(4.3)}$$

Example 4.9 demonstrates the application of the payback approach and highlights possible problems.

EXAMPLE 4.9

The payback approach—some problems?

Year	0	1	2	3	4	5	6	Payback
Project A	−1000	100	200	800	100	100	100	
Cumulative NCF		−900	−700	100	200	300	400	2.875 years
Project B	−1000	800	150	0	200	100	100	
Cumulative NCF		−200	− 50	−50	150	250	350	3.250 years
Project C	−1000	100	150	250	450	500	6000	
Cumulative NCF		−900	−750	−500	−50	450	6450	4.100 years

For project A, the initial outlay is −$1000, and the cash flows are $100 in the first year, $200 in the second and $800 in the third. The cumulative net cash flows are −$900 at the end of the first year, −$700 at the end of the second year and $100 at the end of the third year. At the end of the third year, the sign of the cumulative net cash flow has changed from negative to positive, which means the cumulative cash inflows have recovered the initial outlay. Therefore, the payback occurred during the third year. If we assume the year 3 cash inflow, $800, is earned evenly during year 3, then the payback period is as follows:

$$\text{Payback}_A = \text{year before full recovery} + \frac{\text{unrecovered cost at start of year}}{\text{cash flow during year}}$$

$$\text{Payback} = 2 + \frac{700}{800} = 2.875 \text{ years}$$

When applying the same procedure to projects B and C, we find $\text{Payback}_B = 3.25$ years and $\text{Payback}_C = 4.1$ years.

In Example 4.9, project *A* has the shortest payback period, and hence would be chosen under a naive application of the payback rule. However, it may be a poor decision when compared with projects *B* and *C*. The fallacy of the payback method can be easily illustrated. If a company invested in project *B*, the proceeds acquired in the early period could be reinvested at current interest rates. Therefore, the main problem with the payback technique is that it ignores the time value of money. It treats one dollar received today in the same way as one dollar received in one year's time, or in any other period. This can result in inferior decisions that do not maximise the wealth of shareholders, as illustrated by comparing projects *A* and *B* above.

Now consider project *C* relative to project *A*. Under the payback method, project *C* would also be considered as inferior relative to project *A*. Project *C* also costs $1000, but the payback technique fails to take into account the large cash flow ($6000) that stems from project *C* in the sixth year. If project *A* or project *B*'s cash flow was reinvested at a high interest rate of 20%, neither project would generate as much terminal wealth for its owners as would project *C*. The problem illustrated here is that the payback technique ignores cash flows beyond the minimum payback period. That is, it does not take into account all the information relevant to project selection. Hence, the cash flow beyond the fifth year for project *C* is ignored and the project would be rejected by strict application of the payback rule. It is clear that the NPV technique is superior to the payback technique because it takes into account all future cash flows in evaluating projects.

A variation of the normal payback, the discounted payback period, is similar to the normal payback period except that the cash flows are discounted to present value. Therefore, the discounted payback period can be defined as the time taken to recover the initial cash outlay associated with a project from discounted cash flows. Example 4.10 illustrates the calculation procedure of the discounted payback period. Instead of cumulating the net cash flows as in the normal payback, the discounted net cash flows are cumulated. When the sign of the cumulative DCFs changes from negative to positive, it indicates the year before full recovery. The fractional part is the unrecovered cost at the start of the year in present value divided by the cash flow during the year in the present value.

The payback technique is often favoured in practice because it is simple to calculate and to interpret. However, the problems associated with it far outweigh any benefits. The illustrations in example 4.10, while obviously exaggerated, clearly illustrate two basic shortcomings of the technique. The message is that, in more subtle cash flow circumstances, application of the payback technique can inadvertently result in poor capital budgeting decisions. Other disadvantages of the payback method are that it does not indicate the effects of the project on wealth, it does not recognise the time value of money, it cannot rank projects that have the same payback period and it does not recognise the cash flows beyond the payback period. Since the NPV approach overcomes these problems, it should be favoured in making capital budgeting decisions. At the very least, it should be applied alongside the payback approach, and any significant differences in the decisions arrived at by either technique should be examined closely.

EXAMPLE 4.10

The discounted payback approach—some problems?

Year	0	1	2	3	4	5	6	Discount payback
Project A	−1000	100	200	800	100	100	100	
Discount NCF (at 10%)	−1000	91	165	601	68	62	56	
Cumulative discount NCF		−909	−744	−143	−74	−12	44	5.219 years
Project B	−1000	800	150	0	200	100	100	
Discount NCF (at 10%)	−1000	727	124	0	137	62	56	
Cumulative discount NCF		−273	−149	−149	−12	50	106	4.196 years
Project C	−1000	100	150	250	450	500	5000	
Discount NCF (at 10%)	−1000	91	124	188	307	310	6000	
Cumulative discount NCF		−909	−785	−597	−290	21	6021	4.934 years

The average accounting rate of return (ARR) technique

Accounting rate of return (ARR)
A measure of profitability calculated by dividing the average annual net profit from an asset by the average amount invested in the asset.

The final investment evaluation approach to be discussed in this chapter is the average **accounting rate of return (ARR)** technique. The ARR is the percentage return on invested physical capital. It is based on accounting income and historical cost asset figures generated by the accountant of a company. More formally, the ARR is given by:

$$\text{ARR} = \frac{\text{average income}}{\text{average invested capital}} \tag{4.4}$$

Under this evaluation method, the decision benchmark is to compare the calculated ARR with a predetermined ARR target, or 'cut-off', rate. However, as is the case with the payback technique, there is little guidance on what an appropriate target rate should be. This again poses problems as to whether or not a project should be accepted.

There are essentially four stages in calculating the ARR. First, the average income after tax over the life of the project is estimated. This average income is calculated as the earnings before depreciation, interest and tax (EBDIT), less depreciation and tax. Second, the average net investment (after depreciation) over the life of the project is estimated. Third, the ARR is calculated using these estimates of average income and average invested capital as in Equation 4.4. Finally, if the ARR is greater than the target return, the project should be accepted. Example 4.11 provides an illustration of the application of the ARR technique.

EXAMPLE 4.11

The average ARR technique

QUESTION

Calculate the average ARR for a two-year project which involves a machine costing $100 million, and which is expected to yield EBDIT of $53 million and $65 million in years 1 and 2, respectively. For tax purposes, the machine can be depreciated on a straight-line basis. The current corporate tax rate is 30%.

ANSWER

Calculate the average net income that the project can be expected to generate.

Year	1	2
EBDIT	53	65
Less		
Depreciation	50	50
Taxable income	3	15
Tax (30%)	1	5
Net income	2	10

Average net income = (2 + 10)/2 = 6

Calculate the average investment:

Year	0	1	2
Machine cost	100	100	100
Less			
Accum. depreciation	0	50	100
Investment	100	50	0

Average investment = (100 + 50 + 0)/3 = 50

Calculate the ARR:

ARR = 6/50 = 12%

The average ARR of the project is 12%.

The problems with the ARR technique can be explained with reference to Example 4.11. First, the average ARR relies on revenues, expenses and investment numbers that are the product of accounting standards, and do not necessarily bear any relationship to actual cash flows. Let us assume for a moment that the project required an upfront payment of $100 million for the machinery, as compared with an alternative that required payment at the end of the life of the project. In this case, the ARR of the two projects would still be the same because 'accrual' accounting practices charge the cost of the machinery over its life. The ARR does not discriminate between the projects, when clearly the project requiring later payment would be preferable, because of the time value of money.

Another problem with the ARR is that it ignores the time value of money. This is severely limiting. In the project described in Example 4.11, a smaller EBDIT (a close cousin of operating cash flows) is generated in the first year ($53 million) than in the second year ($65 million). The

ARR of a project identical to the one depicted, except that it generates an EBDIT of $65 million in the first year and $53 million in the second year, would also be 12%. Hence, the technique is not able to discriminate between the two projects, when clearly the latter project is preferable because of time-value-of-money considerations. This is another weakness of the technique.

One final problem with the ARR technique was mentioned earlier: what is an acceptable target ARR? In the context of Example 4.11, how do we determine if 12% is a sufficiently large return for the project? Unlike the cost of capital concept underlying the NPV technique, there is little theoretical or other guidance on setting an appropriate target ARR. Again, this creates problems when using the technique to determine whether a project will enhance or detract from the wealth of the owners of a company.

In summary, the ARR fails almost all of our criteria for assessing a project evaluation technique. It does not indicate an increase in wealth; it does not recognise the time value of money; and it is not capable of discriminating between projects with the same ARR but differing wealth implications. However, because it is expressed as a percentage, it is easy for management to understand even if its meaning is unclear.

Which technique is used in practice?

There have been a number of different surveys of capital budgeting practices in Australia, including studies by McMahon (1981),[3] Freeman and Hobbes (1991),[4] Kester et al. (1999),[5] and more recently Truong et al. (2008).[6] The key results of these surveys are depicted in Table 4.1.

A number of interesting findings emerge from the surveys conducted. First, each of the totals of the different responses exceeds 100%. This is because most of the companies in the survey used more than one technique in making capital budgeting decisions. Second, these companies used all of the techniques reviewed in this chapter. For example, usage varies from 73% for the ARR technique to 96% for the NPV technique in the Kester et al. survey. Third, the techniques relying on DCF (i.e. the IRR and NPV techniques) emerge as the most popular across the three surveys. The survey results also indicate that these techniques have become more prevalent in recent times. The increase in the popularity of the payback method is worth noting. There are two possible explanations for its increase in popularity. First, it may be used as a capital rationing tool. That is, when projects are equally attractive under the present-value techniques, the one that returns the invested funds in the earliest time is ranked higher. The second reason is that, under strict assumptions, the payback approach does substitute for a present-value approach. Where the cash flows have an annuity in perpetuity pattern, the payback method equates to the inverse of the IRR. Thus, it provides a good rule of thumb when capital availability is restricted.[7]

Table 4.1

METHOD	McMAHON (1981)	FREEMAN AND HOBBES (1991)	KESTER ET AL. (1999)	TRUONG ET AL. (2008)
Payback	53%	44%	93%	91%
ARR	49%	33%	73%	57%
IRR	66%	72%	96%	80%
NPV	55%	75%	96%	94%

CONCEPT CHECK

4. Which capital budgeting techniques belong to the DCF family?
5. Which capital budgeting technique is the preferred one? Why is it preferred?
6. Why are the non-DCF techniques popular in practice?

For the answers, go to MyFinanceLab

CONCEPT 4.3   The role of qualitative factors

The foregoing analysis focused solely on the role of quantitative factors in capital budgeting. In practice, however, qualitative factors also play an important role in capital budgeting. An example may help to clarify the nature of this role. Consider BHP's decision in 1997 to shut down the steel mill that it operated in Newcastle. This was one of the most newsworthy capital budgeting decisions ever made in Australia, mainly because of the size of BHP and the large number of people it employed. It is likely that this decision was made after BHP's financial officers carried out a valuation of the Newcastle mill—probably applying the NPV or IRR technique—and decided that the value of continued operations was negative. However, this financial analysis would undoubtedly have been only one of the factors considered by management in its final decision to close down the site. The negative value of the business would have been weighed against a number of qualitative factors, including the likelihood of possible adverse political consequences and the impact on workforce morale at BHP's other sites. While it would have been very difficult for BHP's financial officers to include such effects in their calculations, they would nevertheless have been important factors to consider for the future successful operation of BHP.

Student Learning Centre

My Finance Lab ■ To test your mastery of the content covered in this chapter and to create your own personalised study plan, go to MyFinanceLab: www.pearson.com.au/myfinancelab

CONCEPT CHECKLIST

In this chapter the following concepts were discussed:

➤ The nature of capital budgeting

➤ Commonly used capital budgeting techniques, and their strengths and weaknesses, including:

— NPV

— IRR

— payback

— average ARR

➤ The techniques used in practice

➤ The role of qualitative factors in capital budgeting

SELF-TEST QUESTIONS

Acme Ltd, a scrap-metal dealer, is considering the acquisition of a 'Roadrunner' metal compactor at a cost of $25 000. The compactor is estimated to have zero value at the end of its five-year life. It will return the following annual after tax net cash flow and net income adjusted for depreciation and tax:

Year	After tax net cash flow	Net income
	$	$
1	6 000	1 000
2	10 000	5 000
3	12 000	7 000
4	15 000	10 000
5	7 000	2 000

Tax-allowable depreciation is 20% of the initial cost per annum. The required rate of return is 10% p.a.

(a) Calculate the project's payback period. If Acme's maximum payback period is three years, should the project be accepted?

(b) Calculate the project's discounted payback period. If Acme's maximum discounted payback period is three years, should the project be accepted?

(c) Calculate the project's accounting rate of return, using the initial outlay. If Acme's target accounting rate of return is 25%, should the project be accepted?

Calculate the project's NPV. Should the project be accepted?

Self-test answer

(a) Payback calculation

$$\text{Payback} = \text{year before full recovery} + \frac{\text{unrecovered cost at start of year}}{\text{cash flow during year}}$$

Year	0	1	2	3	4	5
Net cash flow	−25 000	6 000	10 000	12 000	15 000	7 000
Cumulative NCF		−19 000	−9 000	3 000	18 000	25 000

$$\text{Payback} = 2 + \frac{9000}{12\,000} = 2.75 \text{ years}$$

Hence, payback is 2.75 years so the project is acceptable.

(b) Discounted payback calculation

Year	0	1	2	3	4	5
Net cash flow	−25 000	6 000	10 000	12 000	15 000	7 000
Discounted NCF at 10%	−25 000	5 455	8 264	9 016	10 245	4 346
Cumulative discounted NCF		−19 545	−11 281	−2 265	7 980	12 326

$$\text{Payback} = 3 + \frac{2265}{10\,245} = 3.22 \text{ years}$$

Hence, discounted payback is 3.22 years, so the project should be rejected.

(c) Accounting rate of return:

$$\text{ARR} = \frac{\text{average income (excluding adjustment for depreciation)}}{\text{average invested capital (excluding adjustment for depreciation)}}$$

Average income = (1000 + 5000 + 7000 + 10 000 + 2000)/5 = 25 000/5 = 5000

Average invested capital = (25 000 + 20 000 + 15 000 + 10 000 + 5000 + 0)/6

= 75 000/6 = 12 500

$$\text{ARR} = \frac{5000}{12\,500} = 0.40, \text{ or } 40\%$$

Accept the project, as ARR of 40% is greater than target ARR of 25%.

(d) $\text{NPV} = -25\,000 + \dfrac{6000}{(1+10\%)^1} + \dfrac{10\,000}{(1+10\%)^2} + \dfrac{12\,000}{(1+10\%)^3} + \dfrac{15\,000}{(1+10\%)^4} + \dfrac{7000}{(1+10\%)^5} = \$12\,326.44$

The project has a positive NPV; therefore it should be accepted.

DISCUSSION QUESTIONS

1. What criteria should one use in evaluating the usefulness of various capital budgeting techniques?

2. Discuss the strengths and weaknesses of the four most commonly used capital budgeting techniques. Which of the techniques is considered the best? Why?

3. What are the decision rules with using the net present value technique? Would shareholders be better off if their firm rejected a project with negative NPV?

4. True or false? If the net present value of a project is positive, the internal rate of return must be less than the required rate of return.

5. True or false? Two projects with the same internal rates of return will have the same net present values.

6. How would you respond to a financial manager whose justification for using the payback technique as the basis for making capital budgeting decisions was 'It is a good indication of a project's risk'?

7. If an investment project has a discounted payback period less than the project's life, what can you say about the NPV of the project? Explain.

8. You are working with a medium-sized Australian manufacturing company, ZZ Pty Ltd (ZZ), in their finance division. Your boss, Bill, asks you to assist him in the evaluation of a capital project—the acquisition of manufacturing equipment. Bill, who is also ZZ's accountant (having been an accountant for over 30 years), advises you that the established company policy in relation to project evaluation is to calculate both payback period and IRR, and make a decision with regard to both of the measures.

   Comment on the merits of the company's current capital budgeting procedures. Is the calculation of payback period a complete waste of time? What might be the justification for performing this calculation along with a DCF method?

9. When analysing mutually exclusive projects what are the two basic conditions that can cause NPV profiles to cross and thus conflicts to arise between using the net present value and internal rate of return techniques?

PRACTICAL QUESTIONS

BASIC

1. Consider a project with the following cash flows:

Year	0	1	2	3	4	5
Cash flow	−120	30	35	40	50	55

   (a) If the opportunity cost of capital is 10%, should the project be accepted?
   (b) If the opportunity cost of capital is 15%, should the project be accepted?
   (c) If the opportunity cost of capital is 20%, should the project be accepted?

BASIC

2. You are considering a project with an initial outlay of $350 000 and EBDIT of $11 000 in years 1–2 and $130 000 in years 3–4, respectively. For tax purposes, the machine can be depreciated on a straight-line basis till its book value of zero at the end of year four. The current corporate tax rate is 30%. What is the project's average accounting rate of return?

3. Calculate the payback period, ARR, IRR and NPV (at 12%) for two proposed four-year projects, B1 and B2, the cash flows (EBDIT) for which are as follows:

BASIC

Year	0	1	2	3	4
B1	−60 000	9 000	10 000	25 000	30 000
B2	−60 000	30 000	25 000	10 000	9 000

(Assume that straight-line depreciation is applicable and that there is no income tax.)

Why are the NPV and IRR of project B2 superior to project B1?

4. Consider the following projects:

BASIC

Year	0	1	2	3	4	5
Project A	−1 000	1 000				
Project B	−6 000	1 000	1 000	4 000	1 000	1 000
Project C	−10 000	1 000	2 000	3 000	4 000	5 000

(a) If the cost of capital is 8%, which of the projects have a positive NPV?

(b) Calculate the payback period and the discounted payback period for each project.

(c) Which of the projects would a firm using the payback method accept if its policy were to accept all projects with a payback period of three years or less?

(d) What is the internal rate of return on project A? What is it on project B?

(e) If you could choose only one of these three projects (they are mutually exclusive), which one would you choose? Why?

5. You are evaluating two capital projects, X and Y, only one of which can be implemented. At 6% discount rate, the net present values of the two projects are exactly the same. The projects actually have the following IRR and NPV (calculated at the firm's cost of capital).

INTERMEDIATE

	Project X	Project Y
IRR	21.22%	15.91%
NPV	$442.00	$552.95

(a) Within what range of values does the firm's cost of capital lie?

(b) What characteristics of the cash flows associated with these two projects might give rise to this type of relationship between the IRR and the NPV?

(c) Which project should be chosen?

INTERMEDIATE

6. Consider a project with the following cash flows:

Year	0	1	2	3	4
Net cash flows	1000	−300	−500	−150	−200

(a) Draw the NPV profile for this project.

(b) What is the IRR of this project?

(c) At what discount rates should you accept this project?

(d) What is the decision rule as using IRR technique here?

INTERMEDIATE

7. Consider a project with the following cash flows:

Year	0	1	2	3
Net cash flows	−4000	5000	4380	−5544

(a) Draw the NPV profile for this project.

(b) What is the IRR of this project?

(c) At what discount rates should you accept this project?

INTERMEDIATE

8. You are evaluating two capital projects, X and Y, only one of which can be implemented (they are mutually exclusive). The projects have the following cash flows:

Year	0	1	2	3	4
Project X	−2700	1400	1100	800	200
Project Y	−2700	300	800	1100	1600

(a) What is the crossover rate for these two projects?

(b) Which project should be chosen if the cost of capital is 5%?

(c) Which project should be chosen if the cost of capital is 10%?

INTERMEDIATE

9. You are evaluating two mutually exclusive projects, project X and project Y. The cost of capital is 10%, and the projected cash flows of these two projects are as follows:

Year	0	1	2	3	4	5
Project X	−3000	1200	1500	450	600	1200
Project Y	−4500	1797	1200	1800	1050	1200

(a) Based on the NPV technique, which project should be accepted?

(b) Based on the IRR technique, which project should be accepted?

(c) Draw the NPV profiles of these two projects, and discuss why the NPV and IRR techniques provide different conclusions.

10. A project has the following cash flows:

Year	0	1	2	3	4
Net cash flows	?	1500	2500	3000	1500

The discounted payback period is 2.5 years and the cost of capital is 11%. What is the NPV of this project?

11. You are evaluating two pieces of equipment for the company, a truck and an overhead pulley system. A truck has a low initial cost but high annual operating costs, and an overhead pulley system costs more but has lower operating costs. The cost of capital is 10%, and the equipment's expected net costs are as follows:

Year	0	1	2	3	4	5
Truck	−110 000	−82 000	−82 000	−82 000	−82 000	−82 000
Pulley	−240 000	−49 000	−50 000	−50 000	−50 000	−50 000

(a) What is the present value of costs of each piece of equipment? Which equipment should be chosen?

(b) If the cost of capital is 7%, which equipment should be chosen?

12. You are evaluating two mutually exclusive projects, X and Y. The cost of capital is 12% and the expected cash flows of the two projects are as follows:

Year	0	1	2	3	4	5
Project X	−1200	250	290	460	470	510
Project Y	−1200	320	500	450	270	260

What is the payback period of the better project?

13. You are evaluating a project with an IRR of 12%. The cost of capital is 10% and expected cash flows of the project are as follows:

Year	0	1	2	3	4
Net cash flows	?	200	250	300	350

What is the NPV of the project?

14. Your firm only accepts projects providing an IRR of more than 15%. You are evaluating an eight-year project that requires $74 515 in initial investment and provides $15 000 in annual net cash inflows.

(a) What is the IRR of the project? Is it acceptable?

(b) Assuming the annual net cash inflows continue to be $15 000, how many additional years would the flows continue in order to make the project acceptable (to have an IRR of 15%)?

(c) With the given project life (eight years) and initial investment, what are the minimum annual net cash inflows that will make the project acceptable?

CHALLENGING

15. You are evaluating a project that requires an initial investment of $350 000, and which will provide a net cash inflow of $30 000 during the first year. The net cash inflow is projected to grow at 8% p.a. constantly forever. Assuming the cost of capital is 15%:

(a) Is this project acceptable?

(b) If you are uncertain about the projected 8% growth rate, at what constant growth rate will the company just break even?

WebEx

Take a look at the website of an Australian listed company, such as BHP Billiton (www.bhpbilliton. com), and download the most recent annual report. What do you think of the firm's strategic investment plan? What was the size of capital investment of the firm and what major investments did the firm make during the last financial year? Do you think these investments are able to increase shareholders' value?

Excel questions

1. Consider a project with the following cash flows:

Year	0	1	2	3	4	5
Net cash flows	−9000	2000	4050	5000	1000	1500

(a) What is the internal rate of return of this project?

(b) If the cost of capital is 10%, should you accept this project?

(c) If the cost of capital is 15%, should you accept this project?

(d) What is the NPV of the project if the cost of capital is 10%? 15%?

2. You are evaluating two mutually exclusive projects, A and B. The projects have the following cash flows:

Year	0	1	2	3	4	5
Project A	−4500	2000	1800	1500	500	750
Project B	−4500	500	750	1500	1900	2500

(a) Draw the NPV profiles for project A and project B.

(b) What are the IRRs of these two projects?

(c) What is the crossover rate for these two projects?

CASE STUDY

Lez Foxwell has been operating a small transportation company for 25 years. The business has boomed in recent years, and Lez decided to invest another $300 000 to expand his business. There are two proposed mutually exclusive projects, and their cash flows are as follows.

Year	0	1	2	3	4	5
Project A	–300 000	50 000	50 000	50 000	150 000	430 000
Project B	–300 000	200 000	100 000	100 000	100 000	100 000

Although Lez only has limited formal business training, he feels that project *B* is better since he can get his initial invested money back in two years' time. He also wants to get some advice from his son David, who will soon graduate with an undergraduate degree in commerce. For Lez's small business, the cost of capital is 10%. David would like to provide some information about the capital budgeting to Lez by addressing the following questions.

CASE STUDY QUESTIONS

1. What is capital budgeting? Why is it important for the firm?

2. What is the payback period? What are the payback periods for both projects?

3. What is the discounted payback period? What are the discounted payback periods for both projects?

4. What are the weaknesses of using the payback period to choose the project? Does the payback period technique have any usage?

5. What is the net present value? What is the NPV for each project? Based on the NPV technique, which project should be accepted?

6. What is the internal rate of return? What is the IRR for each project? Based on the IRR technique, which project should be accepted?

7. What is the net present value for each project if the cost of capital of Lez's small business is 15%? In this case, which project should be accepted?

8. What is the IRR for each project if the cost of capital of Lez's small business is 15%? In this case, which project should be accepted?

9. Draw NPV profiles for both projects. At what discount rate do the NPV profiles cross?

10. Using the NPV profiles explain why sometimes there is conflict between the NPV and IRR techniques.

FURTHER READING

For a discussion of the use of the discounted cash flow approach to valuing entire companies by the most successful fund manager ever see:

- Hagstrom, R. (1995), *The Warren Buffett Way*, Wiley, New York.

NOTES

1. This assumes that the shareholders can obtain a rate of return of r, the cost of capital used as the project's discount rate. This is explained in detail in Chapter 6.
2. You may recall from high-school algebra that the root of a quadratic equation of the form:

$$0 = a + bx + cx^2$$

is given by the following:

$$x = \frac{x = -b \pm \sqrt{b^2 - 4ac}}{2a}$$

3. McMahon, R. G. (1981), 'The determination and use of investment hurdle rates in capital budgeting: A survey of Australian practice', *Accounting and Finance*, vol. 21(1), 15–25.
4. Freeman, M. and Hobbes, G. (1991), 'Capital budgeting: Theory and practice', *Australian Accountant*, September, 36–41.
5. Kester, G. W., Chang, R. P., Echanis, E. S., Haikal, S., Isa, M. M., Skully, M. T., Tsui, K. and Wang, C. (1999), 'Capital budgeting practices in the Asia–Pacific region: Australia, Hong Kong, Indonesia, Malaysia, Philippines, and Singapore', *Financial Practice and Education*, Spring/Summer, 7–15.
6. Truong, G., Partington, G., Peat, M. (2008), 'Cost-of-capital and capital-budgeting practice in Australia', *Australian Journal of Management*, vol. 33(1), 95–121.
7. In theory, there should be no capital rationing. A firm that has a new wonder drug that prolongs life would have no trouble in finding the capital for development. If firms have a high NPV project, it is likely that they will be able to raise the capital they need. However, sometimes firms behave as if the pool of investment funds is limited and impose self-restrictions on funds available for capital projects.

5

Capital budgeting: Further issues

CHAPTER PREVIEW

The basic techniques of capital budgeting were covered in the last chapter. Given a project's expected cash flows, it is easy to calculate its NPV, IRR, payback, discounted payback and ARR. However, in reality, financial managers of the company have to use information collected from different sources to estimate a project's cash flows. Furthermore, the risk levels of different projects will vary, and there are uncertainties involved with estimating cash flows. In this chapter we first develop procedures for estimating cash flows associated with capital budgeting projects. We then describe some techniques for considering the project's risk. Finally, we discuss some special cases in capital budgeting.

KEY CONCEPTS

CONCEPT 5.1   Issues in estimating cash flows

Cash flow estimation is the most important, and also the most difficult, procedure in capital budgeting. In this section we examine a number of issues in estimating cash flows which are discounted in discounted cash flow models, and the impact of taxation and inflation on the NPV calculation.

Practitioner's POV

Accounting numbers need to be used very carefully in valuations. Subtle differences in accounting techniques across companies in the same industry, or changes in accounting techniques used by a company, can have significant effects on valuations. Some analysts often adjust items such as depreciation to assess whether these items are affecting a valuation.

What to include in cash flows

The processes of calculating a project's NPV seem simple on the surface: take the cash flows generated by the project and discount them at an appropriate cost of capital. In practice, of course, it is not always so straightforward, since complications can arise in estimating both cash flows and the appropriate cost of capital. Issues relating to the latter are dealt with in detail in Chapter 6. Here we discuss a number of complicating issues relating to the cash flows to be discounted. Specifically, in calculating net cash flows, the following rules apply:

- Use cash flows, not accounting income.
- Ignore sunk costs.
- Include opportunity costs.
- Include side effects.
- Include working capital.
- Include taxation.
- Ignore finance charges (interest and loan repayments).

Free cash flows
The cash flows available for distribution to the owners of a company. They are equal to the operating cash flows after capital expenditure and taxes.

Use free cash flows, not accounting income

The net cash flow to be discounted in an NPV calculation is the 'free' cash flow generated by a project. It is important to understand that **free cash flows** are quite different from accounting income.

$$\text{Free cash flow} = \frac{\text{After-tax incremental earnings} + \text{Depreciation}}{- \text{Capital expenditure} - \text{net working capital}} \qquad (5.1)$$

Cash flows represent actual flows of cash to and from the real assets underlying a project. In contrast, accounting income is based on arbitrary revenue and expense recognition rules that are set out in accounting standards. One of the most important differences between accounting income and free cash flows is the treatment of capital expenditure on fixed assets such as plant and machinery. In calculating accounting income, this cost is usually expensed (depreciated) over the life of the asset. In calculating net cash flow, it is necessary to pinpoint precisely the time at which the cash is to be paid for the asset, and bring it into calculations at that point. (In most cases, this is the project's initial, time 0, cash outflow.) Example 5.1 uses the facts from Example 4.11, and illustrates the large potential difference between accounting income and net cash flow.

The nature of accounting practices is such that income is smoothed over time. Typically, the time value of money is ignored. In the case of depreciation, the cost of a capital asset is spread over future years. In Example 5.1 an NPV calculation based on the accounting numbers and a cost of capital of 10% would incorrectly imply that the NPV of the project is $10.08 million, even though the actual NPV of the project based on free cash flows is −$3.14 million.[1] The result of this is that an accounting income approach would lead to acceptance of a project that in fact reduces the wealth of the owner when the time value of money is taken into account.

EXAMPLE 5.1

Free cash flows and accounting income

QUESTION

Calculate the accounting income and free cash flow for a two-year project involving a machine that costs $100 million. The project is expected to yield EBDIT of $53 million and $65 million in years 1 and 2, respectively, and the machine is depreciated for tax and accounting purposes on a straight-line basis. The current corporate tax rate is 30%.

ANSWER

Calculate the net income generated by the project.

Year	1	2
EBDIT	53	65
Less		
Depreciation	50	50
Taxable income	3	15
Less		
*Tax (30%)	0.9	4.5
Net income	2.1	10.5

Calculate the free cash flows generated by the project.

Year	0	1	2
EBDIT		53	65
Capital outlay	−100		
Tax (30%)	0	−0.9	−4.5
Free cash flow	−100	52.1	60.5

*Tax in year 1 is calculated as 30% (53 − 100/2). Year 2 tax is calculated in the same way.

Ignore sunk costs

Sunk costs

Unavoidable cash flows, or cash flows that have been incurred in the past, which are irrelevant in project evaluation.

Sunk costs are unavoidable cash flows, or cash flows that have been incurred in the past. Accordingly, they are irrelevant in evaluating a prospective project, even though they may have been incurred as a direct result of evaluating the project. The reason that they are irrelevant is that the cost has been (or will be) incurred regardless of whether or not the project goes ahead.

Generally, the effect of including sunk costs is that the NPV of the project will be underestimated, introducing a bias towards the rejection of value-enhancing projects. Example 5.2 provides an illustration of the effects of incorrect inclusion of a sunk cost in the NPV calculation.

EXAMPLE 5.2

Possible consequences of incorrectly including sunk costs in making an investment decision

A fee of $10 000 is paid to a marketing company for assessing the market (a market feasibility study) for a potential project that costs $125 000 and is expected to yield net cash flows of $75 000 in each of the following two years. The discount rate is 10%.

If the sunk cost (market feasibility study) is *incorrectly* included, the NPV is:

$$-135\,000 + \frac{75\,000}{(1 + 10\%)^1} + \frac{75\,000}{(1 + 10\%)^2} = -4835$$

Accordingly, the company would reject the project.

If the sunk cost (market feasibility study) is *correctly* ignored, the NPV is:

$$-125\,000 + \frac{75\,000}{(1 + 10\%)^1} + \frac{75\,000}{(1 + 10\%)^2} = 5165$$

Accordingly, the company would accept the project.

In this example the company has already incurred the cost associated with the market feasibility study. Regardless of whether or not it subsequently undertakes the project, the wealth of the owners of the company (investors) has been reduced by $10 000, so the cost of the market feasibility study is not relevant to the decision to undertake the project. Quite clearly, although investors spent $10 000 in commissioning the market feasibility study, by subsequently implementing the project they would not compound this loss, but would in fact recuperate $5165 of the lost wealth.

Include opportunity costs

If a company uses a resource in a project that could otherwise be put to some productive use, then the dollar value of that alternative use—that is, the **opportunity cost** of using the resource— must be included as a cash outflow in calculating the NPV of the project. In effect, the value of the opportunity cost is 'consumed' in undertaking the project. A good example of an opportunity cost is the value of a vacant building that is currently owned by a firm if the building is used for a new project. The value of the building must be included as a cash outflow because using the building is analogous to the company liquidating (selling) the building at its current value, then buying it back (i.e. incurring a negative cash flow) for use in the project. In essence, the company is using the cash equivalent of the value of the building in the project. Example 5.3 helps to clarify the treatment of opportunity costs.

Opportunity cost
The return an investment or resource could have provided in its best alternative use.

> ### EXAMPLE 5.3
>
> **Possible consequences of incorrectly excluding opportunity costs in making an investment decision**
>
> A company owns machinery that it can lease for $3 million per year. It decides to use the machinery in a proposed project that yields $20 million in each of the following two years and requires a further outlay of $30 million. The opportunity cost of capital is 10%.
>
> If the opportunity cost (lease of machinery) is *incorrectly* excluded, the NPV is:
>
> $$-30 + \frac{20}{(1 + 10\%)^1} + \frac{20}{(1 + 10\%)^2} = \$4.7m$$
>
> Accordingly, the company would accept the project.
>
> If the opportunity cost (lease of machinery) is *correctly* included, the NPV is:
>
> $$-30 + \frac{17}{(1 + 10\%)^1} + \frac{17}{(1 + 10\%)^2} = -\$0.5m$$
>
> Accordingly, the company would reject the project.

In this example the company is better off leasing out the machinery than using it for the proposed project. This demonstrates that the omission of opportunity costs from the calculation of a project's NPV results in an overestimation of the NPV. This is hardly surprising, as the cash value of resources used in a project is excluded from the calculation. The omission of opportunity costs can lead to the acceptance of projects that decrease the wealth of investors. Unfortunately, sometimes opportunity costs can be a little subtle and, therefore, difficult to identify and value. Hence, care needs to be taken in an NPV calculation to determine whether there are any opportunity costs associated with the project under consideration.

Include side effects

Side effect
A positive or negative cash flow that relates to other aspects of a company's business as a result of implementing a project.

In the context of capital budgeting, a **side effect** is a positive or negative cash flow that relates to other aspects of a company's business as a result of implementing a project. For example, in August 2009, fast food giant McDonald's introduced a new Angus beef burger range in its 800 outlets across Australia. Presumably, the release of the new premium burger range would reduce the sales of other McDonald's burgers. This is a good example of a negative side effect, and hopefully the financial officer of McDonald's included estimates of this negative side effect in evaluating the new burger range. Example 5.4 provides another illustration of a side effect and the impact of excluding such effects on the NPV calculation.

It also demonstrates that the omission of side effects can result in an incorrect investment decision. To re-state, it is important to consider all possible by-products or side effects associated with taking on a project and to factor them into the NPV calculation as positive or negative cash flows.

EXAMPLE 5.4

Possible consequences of incorrectly excluding side effects in making an investment decision

A company has recently constructed a copper smelter at a cost of $400 million. It is expected to yield $33.5 million next year in revenue, growing at 2% p.a. thereafter. Demand for copper is expected to remain high and the smelter is expected to run at full capacity for the foreseeable future. This will also generate chemical wastes, which will cost $2 million per year to dispose of. The opportunity cost of capital is 10%. Note that the cash inflow is expected every year, so it is a (growing) perpetuity, as discussed in Chapter 2. Accordingly, Equation 2.15 can be applied to obtain the present value of future cash flows. That is:

$$PV = \frac{A_1}{r - g}$$

If the side effect (disposal costs) is *incorrectly* excluded, the NPV is:

$$-400 + \frac{33.5}{(10\% - 2\%)} = \$18.75m$$

Accordingly, the company would accept the project.
If the side effect (disposal costs) is *correctly* included, the NPV is:

$$-400 + \frac{33.5}{(10\% - 2\%)} + \frac{-2}{10\%} = -\$1.25m$$

Accordingly, the company would reject the project.

Include net working capital

Net working capital
Consists of all current assets needed for a project to run smoothly, minus any current liabilities.

The commencement of any major project requires an investment in **net working capital**. Net working capital consists of inventory, cash, accounts receivable and any other current assets needed for the project to operate smoothly, less any current liabilities, including accounts payable and accruals. Before a project can begin, inventories of raw materials must be purchased, the firm must set aside sufficient cash to be able to pay the monthly wages and creditors, and the firm must set aside funds to cover accounts receivable. At the same time, those current assets can be partially financed by interest-free current liabilities, such as accounts payable provided by suppliers. The firm generally still needs to invest the difference between current assets and current liabilities, and this cash investment in net working capital is as significant and necessary as expenditure on plant and equipment. In capital budgeting, the general practice is to assume that the net working capital needs are constant throughout the project's life. At the end of the project, all inventories will be sold, all accounts receivable will be collected, cash held for meeting the needs of the project will be available for other uses, and all accounts payable will be paid. As a consequence, net working capital is shown as an initial outflow at the commencement of the project and an inflow in the final year. Example 5.5 gives an illustration of the need to provide for net working capital when evaluating a project. In this example, a beverage company plans to introduce a new 1.5 litre bottle of cola.

EXAMPLE 5.5

The need to include net working capital when calculating cash flows

A soft-drink manufacturer currently markets a number of cola and carbonated fruit drinks throughout Australia and Southeast Asia. Market research suggests that a demand exists for a 1.5 litre soft drink to supplement their existing 1 litre and 2 litre products. The company expects to outlay $280 000 for new bottling equipment, $123 733 for plastic 1.5 litre bottles, $35 000 for the marketing launch and $60 000 in net working capital. The equipment has a useful life of four years and has no expected salvage value at the end. The company uses straight-line depreciation. The annual cash inflows and cash outflows are shown in the table below. The cost of capital for the company is 16%. After four years there will be no market for this bottle size as consumers will be looking for something new.

Note that the net working capital is treated as a cash outflow at the beginning of the project and as a cash inflow in the final year of the project (year 4). You should also note that the 'lost sales' represent the reduction in sales of the 1 litre and 2 litre products that result from introducing the 1.5 litre product. The incremental costs for the project should also include the reduction in costs that accrue to the company because these sales are not being made.

Year	0	1	2	3	4
Production equipment	−280 000				
Plastic bottles	−123 733				
Marketing	−35 000				
Working capital	−60 000				60 000
New sales		1 000 000	1 300 000	1 600 000	2 200 000
Lost sales		−400 000	−50 000	−50 000	−50 000
Net sales		600 000	1 250 000	1 550 000	2 150 000
Incremental costs		−460 000	−966 500	−1 235 000	−1 793 000
Net cash flows	−498 733	140 000	283 500	315 000	417 000

$$-498\,733 + \frac{140\,000}{(1 + 16\%)^1} + \frac{283\,500}{(1 + 16\%)^2} + \frac{315\,000}{(1 + 16\%)^3} + \frac{417\,000}{(1 + 16\%)^4} = \$264\,756$$

The project's NPV is positive and it should be accepted. Through interpolation, the internal rate of return can be assessed at 36.5%. At nearly double that of the market rate of interest, the project is an attractive investment.

Company tax

Taxation represents a cash outflow and needs to be deducted from operating cash flows in order to determine free cash flows.[2] There are three sets of tax that are relevant to evaluating capital projects: goods and services tax, (corporate) income tax and capital gains tax. The goods and services tax (GST) is a supply-side tax where the end-user of a service is taxed at 10%. The Australian Taxation Office (ATO) levies income tax in Australia on the difference between **assessable income** (revenues) and **allowable deductions** (expenses) at the company tax rate, which was 30% at the time of writing. Capital gains tax is levied at the company tax rate on the gain in the value of the capital assets of a company, once they are sold.

Assessable income
Income according to ordinary concepts, such as salary and wages, rent dividends, interest and annuities.

Allowable deductions
Expenses that are incurred in gaining assessable income.

While it is beyond the scope of this text to provide a detailed description of taxable revenues and allowable deductions, it is important to focus on a couple of items that almost always have an impact on NPV calculations. First, it should be made clear that the GST can be ignored in most capital budgeting situations. Firms pay GST on their inputs to production and, in most cases, collect GST from their customers on behalf of the government. GST paid on inputs such as materials, consulting and other expenses (excluding wages and interest on loans) is deducted from the amount of GST collected from customers, and the balance is paid to the government. Therefore, GST has no direct impact on the cash outflows and will affect inflows indirectly via its effect on demand. The exception to this is the banking and finance industry. There is no GST levied on financial transactions and as such the financial institutions are defined as the end-users under the GST legislation. They will pay GST on their cash purchases of goods and services from external parties, but they will not receive a credit back from the government. When dealing with large companies, only financial institutions need include the GST component in their cash payments for external goods and services.

Capital gains tax is levied at the corporate tax rate on the increase in the value of a taxable capital asset once it is sold. Unlike individuals, companies are given no concessions in calculating capital gains tax for any investments after September 1999. Both corporate tax and capital gains tax are treated as regular cash outflows in calculating the (after company tax) free cash flows.

For the calculation of income tax, most 'allowable deductions' are the incremental cash expenses incurred in the running of the business, but there are some that do not represent actual cash flows (e.g. depreciation). Although non-cash expenses do not form part of the free cash flow estimates, their impact must still be taken into account in project evaluation since they reduce the amount of tax that must be paid by a company. They are commonly called 'tax shields'.

The NPV rule does not change when performing project evaluation on an after-tax basis. That is, free cash flows after tax must be discounted at an after-company-tax rate of return. It is important to apply a required rate of return that is consistent with the cash flows being discounted. (Similarly, if the analysis were to be performed on a before-tax basis, a before-tax rate of return would be used. Using cash flows and returns estimated on the same basis is known as the 'consistency principle'.) Example 5.6 expands on Example 5.5 to show the detail of the income and expenses used to calculate corporate tax. It illustrates how tax is incorporated into an NPV calculation.

Example 5.6 illustrates a number of basic features of the impact of tax on NPV calculations. First, the incremental taxable profit is calculated. Because the firm loses sales as a result of introducing the new product, it also incurs fewer costs in those product areas. Tax attributable to the profits on the 1 litre and 2 litre drinks will be reduced by the net loss of margin but will be increased for the new product.

EXAMPLE 5.6

Detailed estimation of taxation and the calculation of NPV

Profit calculation

Year	0	1	2	3	4
Sales		1 000 000	1 300 000	1 600 000	2 200 000
Lost sales		–400 000	–50 000	–50 000	–50 000
Net sales		600 000	1 250 000	1 550 000	2 150 000
Incremental prod. costs		480 000	830 000	1 070 000	1 600 000
Incremental delivery		40 000	40 000	50 000	60 000
Incremental marketing		20 000	25 000	35 000	40 000
Incremental advertising		15 000	20 000	25 000	30 000
Saving—lost sales		–125 000	–40 000	–50 000	–60 000
Depreciation		70 000	70 000	70 000	70 000
Additional net costs		500 000	945 000	1 200 000	1 740 000
Incremental taxable profit		100 000	305 000	350 000	410 000
Tax at 30%		30 000	91 500	105 000	123 000
Net profit after tax		70 000	213 500	245 000	287 000

(continued)

Cash flows calculation					
Year	**0**	**1**	**2**	**3**	**4**
Production equipment	–280 000				
Plastic bottles	–123 733				
Marketing	–35 000				
Working capital	–60 000				60 000
Incremental earnings before tax		100 000	305 000	350 000	410 000
Plus Depreciation		70 000	70 000	70 000	70 000
Free cash flows before tax	–498 733	170 000	375 000	420 000	540 000
Less Tax		–30 000	–91 500	–105 000	–123 000
Free cash flow	–$498 733	$140 000	$283 500	$315 000	$417 000

Calculate the NPV of the project:

$$-498\,733 + \frac{140\,000}{(1+16\%)^1} + \frac{283\,500}{(1+16\%)^2} + \frac{315\,000}{(1+16\%)^3} + \frac{417\,000}{(1+16\%)^4} = \$264\,756$$

The project NPV is positive and the same as that of the previous example; however here we specifically show the calculation of the taxation expense. The net effect on tax is a payment of $30 000 in tax for the first year rising to $123 000 in the fourth year.

Notes

Generally, the free cash flows of a project are from the following three areas:
- initial outlay: capital expenditure of the project plus any increases in net working capital
- operating cash flows over the project's economic life;

    operating cash flow = after-tax incremental earnings + depreciation

- terminal cash flows: cash flows which occur at the end of a project other than the operating cash flows, e.g. after-tax salvage value of fixed assets and recovery of net working capital.

The free cash flows of a project in each year are determined as the sum of the cash flows in each of the areas above.

Second, the tax outlay is assumed to occur in the year in which the tax is calculated. This is not the case in all jurisdictions but is a reasonable assumption in Australia, where corporate tax is paid quarterly in advance. Third, the after-corporate-tax rate of return is applied to free cash flows after corporate tax, for consistency. The model used to calculate the required rate of return is discussed in Chapter 6 and is used as an appropriate after-corporate-tax rate of return. Finally, depreciation has the effect of lowering the taxable income of the company by $70 000 p.a. ($280 000/4), thereby lowering the amount of tax payable by the company by $21 000. This is the depreciation tax shield.[3] The product of the size of the allowable deduction and the corporate tax rate (which in this case is $70 000 × 30%) gives the tax shield. Because straight-line depreciation is used, the tax shield is constant throughout the project. However, equipment can be depreciated at an accelerated rate (1.5 times the straight-line rate). In this case the accelerated rate would be 0.375 (0.25 × 1.5), giving a deduction of $105 000 and a tax shield of $31 500 in the first year of operation. While this method results in the same overall tax shield ($84 000 in total), accelerated methods are preferred because of the time value of money. That is, it would be preferable to receive a tax saving of $31 500 in year 1 than the $21 000 provided by straight-line depreciation. The present value of the cash flow savings from using the accelerated method as shown in Example 5.7 is $2234, using the firm's cost of capital of 16%.

EXAMPLE 5.7

Tax shield—accelerated depreciation

Year	0	1	2	3	4
Accelerated depreciation		−105 000	−65 625	−41 016	−68 359
New tax shield		−31 500	−19 688	−12 305	−20 508
*Tax shield under straight line		21 000	21 000	21 000	21 000
Tax saving		10 500	−1 313	−8 695	−492

Calculate PV of tax saving:

$$\frac{10\,500}{(1 + 16\%)^1} + \frac{-1313}{(1 + 16\%)^2} + \frac{-8695}{(1 + 16\%)^3} + \frac{-492}{(1 + 16\%)^4} = \$2234$$

*Tax shield under straight-line depreciation method is calculated as $70 000 × 0.3.

The disposal of depreciable assets may give rise to taxable gains or losses on disposal. This will occur when the **residual value**, otherwise known as the selling price of the asset, is different from the recorded book value of the asset. The recorded book value of the asset is the original cost of the asset less accumulated depreciation, as demonstrated in Example 5.8.

Residual value
Disposal value of a project's assets, less any dismantling and removal costs associated with the project's termination.

Finance charges

What is also evident from the cash flows shown in Example 5.6 is that interest expenses and loan repayments are excluded from the free cash flow calculation. The reason for this is simple. We wish to know if the project is value-increasing before we determine how we are to finance it. That is, we wish to know if the project achieves the market rate of return for a given level of risk.

In Example 5.9 a company is considering a project that requires an outlay of $1200 and returns $400 p.a. for four years. If the required rate of return is 15%, then the net present value of the project is −$58.01 and the project should be rejected. If we include the finance option, we get a different answer. Assume that the company borrows half of the funds needed at 5%. The second row in Example 5.9 shows that the repayments over four years would be $169 p.a. (using the annuity formula from Chapter 2). The third row shows the net cash flows that now have a positive NPV of $59.50 and an IRR of 20%. The bottom half of the example shows the same conditions but with all the money borrowed at 5%. The NPV is now $177.01 with an infinite IRR. As the example shows, the NPV can always be made positive if you borrow at less than the project's IRR. However, the market rate of return for a project of this nature is 15% and the project's NPV is negative at that discount rate. We should always assess the project using the market rate of return for the given level of risk before we determine the financing mix. The effect of financing (interest paid) is captured in the discount rate in the weighted average cost of capital (discussed in Chapter 8) and hence is not included in the cash flows, as this would be double counting.

EXAMPLE 5.8

Calculation of loss on sale of a depreciable asset

To illustrate the effects of gains or losses on the disposal of assets, assume the same cash flows and taxation conditions as per Example 5.6. However, the new production equipment will not only accommodate the new 1.5 litre bottles but will also make the machine that filled the 750 mL bottles redundant. Assume this machine had an original cost of $150 000 and an expected life of 10 years. Its current book value is $60 000. The 750 mL machine can now be retired and sold for $25 000. The yearly depreciation is $15 000. The scrapping of the old machine has three cash flow effects.

1. An inflow occurs in year 0 equal to $25 000.
2. There is a tax saving in year 0 equal to the loss on the sale of the machine. This loss is equal to the book value minus the salvage value or selling price.

Cost	$150 000
Less Accumulated depreciation (15 000 × 6 years)	90 000
Closing book value	60 000
Less Sale price	25 000
Book loss	35 000

The tax saving is $35 000 × 30% = $10 500.

3. There is an increase in taxation over the next four years as the annual depreciation of $15 000 will not be allowed. Increased tax equals $15 000 × 30% = $4500 for four years.

Year	0	1	2	3	4
Free cash flows as per Example 5.6	−498 733	140 000	283 500	315 000	417 000
Selling price	25 000				
Increase in tax	10 500	−4 500	−4 500	−4 500	−4 500
Net cash flow	−463 233	135 500	279 000	310 500	412 500

Calculate the NPV of the project:

$$-463\,233 + \frac{135\,500}{(1 + 16\%)^1} + \frac{279\,000}{(1 + 16\%)^2} + \frac{310\,500}{(1 + 16\%)^3} + \frac{412\,500}{(1 + 16\%)^4} = \$287\,664$$

The project's NPV is positive and has increased from $264 756 to $287 664.

EXAMPLE 5.9

Estimating perpetual dividend growth

Year	0	1	2	3	4
PV at 15% is –$58.01	–$1200	400	400	400	400
Borrow half at 5%	–$600	169	169	169	169
Net cash flow with a PV of $59.50	–$600	$231	$231	$231	$231
IRR	20%				
Present value	–$1200	400	400	400	400
Borrow all at 5%	–$1200	338	338	338	338
Net cash flow with a PV of $177.01	$0.00	$62	$62	$62	$62
IRR	∞				

This section has demonstrated that there are many rules to remember when considering inclusions and exclusions in forecasting cash flows. This may seem confusing at first but, in fact, the task requires the application of only one key principle: include in the analysis all (and only) cash flows, or cash flow equivalents, that would arise as a result of implementing the project. In other words, only the direct consequences of undertaking the project should be included. These cash flows are called incremental cash flows. The basic question we can ask is: 'Will this cash flow still occur if we accept the project?' If the answer is 'yes', we should include this cash flow in our analysis. If the answer is 'no', we should exclude it. If the answer is 'partially yes', we should only include that part of the cash flow related to the project.

Inflation

As will be shown, inflation too can have an impact on capital budgeting, as it has the effect of reducing the purchasing power of future cash flows. Consider Example 5.10.

EXAMPLE 5.10

The effect of inflation on rates of return

Consider $100 that can be invested at 10% for one year when inflation is expected to be 6% for the year and hamburgers currently cost $1. What is the increase in the number of hamburgers that can be bought (the real rate of return) if their price rises in line with inflation?

The number of hamburgers that can be purchased today:

$$\frac{\$100}{\$1} = 100$$

The price of hamburgers in one year:

$$\$1 \times (1 + 6\%) = \$1.06$$

The amount of cash available in one year (invested at 10%):

$100 × (1 + 10%) = $110

Hence, the number of hamburgers that can be purchased in one year:

$\dfrac{\$110}{\$1.06} = 103.8$

The percentage increase in the number of hamburgers that can be bought in one year (which equates to the real rate of return on a 10% investment rate with 6% inflation):

$\dfrac{103.8}{100} - 1 = 3.8\%$

The real rate of return is 3.8%.

One important point to note from this is that the real rate of return is not simply the arithmetic difference between the inflation rate (6%) and the nominal rate of return (10%), but something less. In fact, the real rate of return can be calculated using the following equation, known as the Fisher effect (or the Fisher relation):

$$(1 + r_n) = (1 + r_r)(1 + \rho) \tag{5.2}$$

where:

r_n = the nominal rate of return

r_r = the real rate of return

ρ = the inflation rate

The Fisher effect is a useful expression in NPV calculations because it can be used to convert nominal interest rates to real interest rates, or vice versa. As discussed earlier in the case of before- or after-tax estimates, when calculating a project's NPV it is very important to ensure that the discount rate and the cash flows are based on consistent estimates (in the case of inflation, levels of purchasing power). That is, application of the consistency principle remains paramount, where actual or nominal cash flows are discounted using a nominal rate of return, and real cash flows are discounted at a real rate of return. If calculated correctly, the NPV will always be the same using either approach and will be expressed in terms of current purchasing power. This is demonstrated in Example 5.11.

Example 5.11 illustrates quite clearly that, regardless of whether real interest rates and cash flows or nominal interest rates and cash flows are used, the NPV must be the same. This is because the NPV is the increase in net wealth in terms of current purchasing power.

EXAMPLE 5.11

Capital budgeting and inflation

A project costs $1000 and is expected to return a (nominal) cash flow of $1200 in two years' time. The nominal required rate of return is 10% p.a. and the expected inflation rate is 6% p.a. Should the project be taken on?

Calculate the NPV using the actual (nominal) cash flows and nominal rate of return.

$$\frac{\$1200}{(1 + 10\%)^2} - \$1000 = -\$8.3$$

Or, the NPV can be calculated by converting the nominal cash flow to a real cash flow and the nominal rate of return to a real rate of return. Or, the NPV can be calculated by converting the nominal cash flow to a real cash flow and the nominal rate of return to a real rate of return.

The real rate of return is:

$$(1 + r_n) = (1 + r_r)(1 + \rho)$$
$$(1 + 10\%) = (1 + r_r)(1 + 6\%)$$
$$r_r = 0.0377 = 3.77\%$$

The future cash flow expressed in terms of current purchasing power is:

$$\frac{\$1200}{(1 + 6\%)^2} = \$1068$$

The NPV based on real cash flows and the real rate of return is:

$$\frac{\$1068}{(1 + 3.77\%)^2} - \$1000 = -\$8.3$$

Either way, the NPV of the project is –$8.3 and the project should be rejected.

Practitioner's POV

In practice, many firms conduct post-auditing as an important process of the capital budgeting. The operating divisions are required to report how an undertaken project is operating regularly. The post-auditing allows managers to decide how and why differences between estimated and actual outcomes occur, and allows managers to learn from their mistakes and improve their operational efficiency and forecasting skills.

CONCEPT CHECK

1. Should companies use cash flow or accounting income in project NPV calculation? Why?
2. What are sunk costs and opportunity costs, and how do they affect the project's cash flows?
3. What is a side effect? Give an example of a positive side effect.
4. What are the two approaches to account for inflation in capital budgeting?
5. What are the incremental cash flows in cash flow forecasting?
6. Why should we exclude finance charges in the free cash flow calculation?

For the answers, go to MyFinanceLab

FINANCE EXTRA!

Westfield Sydney flagship project

THE WESTFIELD Group, a company listed on ASX (ASX: WDC), is one of the world's largest retail property groups. In October 2010, six months ahead of schedule, the Group officially opened the first stage of the $3.26 billion flagship project in the heart of Sydney's central business district with 130 new retail shops and restaurants and a 30 000 square metre office building. The whole project is due for completion in early 2012 with a 25-storey office tower and a further 120 new stores.

The Group commenced the redevelopment project in 2008 with an anticipated internal rate of return around 8%. Even though very few global developers had progressed with major projects during the global financial crisis, the project has been paying off. The project will generate more than $600 million a year in sales for the Group. Upon completion, the project development profit is expected to be approximately $780 million.

Sources: Westfield Group website, <www.westfield.com>; Westfield Group 2008, 2009 and 2010 annual reports; Carolyn Cummins, 'Westfield to reap Pitt Street windfall', *The Sydney Morning Herald*, 29 October 2010.

CONCEPT 5.2   Risk analysis in capital budgeting

We have discussed how to estimate cash flows in the capital budgeting, but those projected cash flows will not occur with certainty. There are several techniques which can provide some ideas of the risk level of a project, and this risk level is directly related to the uncertainty of the project's cash flow. In Example 5.6 above, the net cash flows are determined by several different variables, such as sales of the new 1.5 litre cola, loss of sales of existing 1 litre and 2 litre products, incremental product costs, etc. However, the actual sales of the new 1.5 litre cola will probably be higher or lower than the projected value, and the actual lost sales of existing products will also be different from the projected figure. The distribution of each variable and the correlations between each of them determine the distribution of the cash flows, the distribution of the project's NPV and the risk level of the project. This section discusses three techniques used to assess the risk level of the project: sensitivity analysis, scenario analysis and simulation (Monte Carlo) analysis.

Sensitivity analysis

Sensitivity analysis measures the impact on NPV by changing only one variable of the project while holding all other variables constant. In a sensitivity analysis, one variable of the project

---

Sensitivity analysis
Analysis that measures the impact on NPV by changing only one variable of the project while holding all other variables constant.

is changed by several percentage points below or above the expected value, while all the other variables are held at the expected values. New NPVs are calculated by using these values. The new NPVs indicate how sensitive the project's NPV is to changes in each variable. Example 5.12 illustrates a sensitivity analysis using the numbers from Example 5.6.

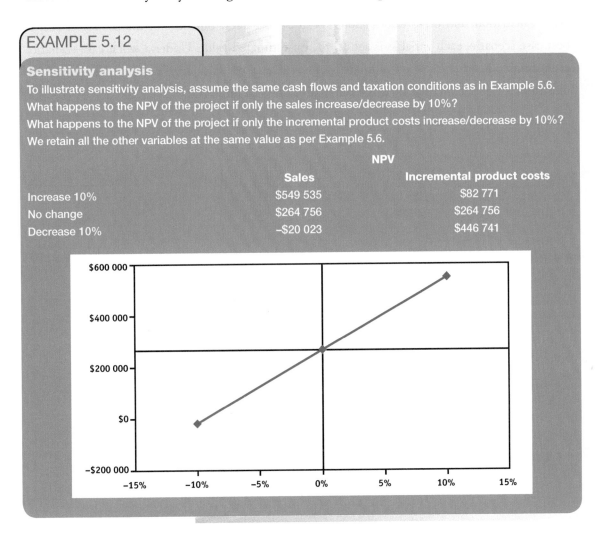

EXAMPLE 5.12

Sensitivity analysis

To illustrate sensitivity analysis, assume the same cash flows and taxation conditions as in Example 5.6.
What happens to the NPV of the project if only the sales increase/decrease by 10%?
What happens to the NPV of the project if only the incremental product costs increase/decrease by 10%?
We retain all the other variables at the same value as per Example 5.6.

	NPV	
	Sales	Incremental product costs
Increase 10%	$549 535	$82 771
No change	$264 756	$264 756
Decrease 10%	–$20 023	$446 741

Example 5.12 shows that the NPV of the project is more sensitive to the changes in sales of the new products than to the changes in incremental product costs. In fact, even though the incremental product costs increase by 10%, the NPV is still positive. The results of the sensitivity analysis can also be illustrated graphically. In the graph which appears in Example 5.12, the percentage change of the variable is on the x-axis, and the NPV is on the y-axis. The line indicates the sensitivity of the NPV to changes in the sales of the new products. The steeper the line, the more sensitive the NPV is to a change in this variable. We should normally pay more attention to estimating those sensitive variables in order to reduce the forecasting error in capital budgeting.

Scenario analysis

Scenario analysis
Analysis that measures the impact on NPV by changing several variables of the project at the same time and normally includes a base case scenario, a best case scenario and a worst case scenario.

Scenario analysis measures the impact on NPV by changing several variables of the project at the same time. Normally, it includes a base case scenario, a best case scenario and a worst case scenario. Under a base case scenario, the expected values of a project's aspects are used in the NPV calculation, and these values should be the most likely outcome of the project. Under a best case scenario, each variable is set at its best estimated value. Under a worst case scenario, each variable is set at its worst estimated value, such as low sales, high cost, etc. Example 5.13 illustrates a scenario analysis by using the figures from Example 5.6.

EXAMPLE 5.13

Scenario analysis

To illustrate scenario analysis, assume the same cash flows and taxation conditions as in Example 5.6. Supposing that the projections for all the following variables are accurate to within ± 10%, what are the best case and worst case NPVs of the project?

Aspects	Best case	Base case	Worst case
Sales	Increase 10%		Decrease 10%
Lost sales	Decrease 10%		Increase 10%
Incremental prod. costs	Decrease 10%		Increase 10%
Incremental delivery	Decrease 10%		Increase 10%
Incremental marketing	Decrease 10%		Increase 10%
Incremental advertising	Decrease 10%		Increase 10%
Saving—lost sales	Increase 10%		Decrease 10%
Production equipment	Decrease 10%		Increase 10%
Plastic bottles	Decrease 10%		Increase 10%
Marketing	Decrease 10%		Increase 10%
Working capital	Decrease 10%		Increase 10%
NPV	$836 210	$264 756	–$306 699

If the project is highly successful the NPV of the project will be $836 210. On the other hand, if the project goes badly the NPV will be –$306 699. The difference between worst NPV and best NPV provides some ideas regarding the risk level of the project. If even under the worst case scenario, the project still provides a positive NPV, we can be fairly confident in undertaking the project. However, worst case and best case scenarios are improbable, because both make an extreme assumption.

Simulation analysis
(also called Monte Carlo analysis)
Analysis that the NPV distribution is simulated by randomly choosing the values of different variables of the project based on the assumption of mathematical distribution of these variables.

Simulation (Monte Carlo) analysis

In **simulation analysis (also called Monte Carlo analysis),** the values of different variables of the projects are chosen randomly based on the assumption of mathematical distribution of these variables. As a result, one NPV is calculated each time. By doing this repeatedly, a large number of NPVs are obtained, and the distribution of the NPV can be seen at the end. The NPV distribution would provide considerable information regarding the project's NPV, such as its mean, standard deviation and the probability of resulting negative NPVs. Obviously, in order to do simulation analysis, computer assistance is essential.

CONCEPT CHECK

7. Briefly describe how to use the techniques of sensitivity, scenario and simulation analyses to estimate project risk.
8. Why should we usually pay more attention to estimating those sensitive variables in capital budgeting?

For the answers, go to MyFinanceLab

CONCEPT 5.3　Some special cases in capital budgeting

Projects with unequal lives

There are many situations where a company must decide between two mutually exclusive projects that both have a positive present value but have different lives. If you were able to undertake one project and still choose the other, there would be no problem. If both projects have positive NPVs, you would undertake both. However, where undertaking one project excludes the other, the analysis can become more complex. When two projects have different lifetimes, the standard NPV analysis may not always give the correct answer. Consider Example 5.14.

Conventional analysis would have us choose crop *B*, as it has the higher NPV. However, crop *B* has a higher NPV because it has an additional year of cash flows.

If crop *A* is chosen, we could replant the crop at the end of year 2 and gain another two-year income. Over the four-year period, crop *A* would have a higher present value ($340), but again it would have an extra year of income, which would distort the comparison. We could continue to replicate both the crops until we have a common life. This would occur if we repeated crop *A* three times, giving it a six-year life, and crop *B* twice, also giving it a life of six years. While this is a reasonable approach for projects with short lives, such a comparison between present values becomes difficult if the lives are, say, 11 years and 13 years, respectively. It would take a 143-year replication period for the two projects to have the same life span for cash flows.

However, the flexibility of the present-value analysis provides a simpler method of analysis. Just as we can convert a series of cash flows into a present value, so we can also convert a present value into a future cash flow stream using the annuity formula. When we apply the concept of an annuity to the net present value for crop *A*, we get an equivalent annual value of $115 per year. That is, planting crop A is equivalent to receiving zero at the beginning and $115 p.a. for years 1 and 2. For crop B, the equivalent annual value is $101 p.a. Planting crop *A* gives a greater equivalent annual value than does crop *B*. All other things being equal, we would prefer crop *A* to crop *B*.

EXAMPLE 5.14

Analysis problems when evaluating projects with unequal lives

Consider a pastoral company that must decide which crop to plant in a given field. Both crops cost the same with initial planting costs of $100. Crop A has a lifetime of two years and returns net cash flows of $184 in the first year and $161 in the second year. After this time, the crop must be ploughed in and a new one planted. At a discount rate of 10%, it has an NPV of $200. A second crop, B, is also being considered. It has a three-year lifetime and produces net cash flows of $170, $136 and $111 in years 1, 2 and 3, respectively. The net present value of crop B is $250.

Crop A

Year	0	1	2	3
Cash flow	−100	184	161	
NPV	$200.33			

Annual equivalent value estimate:

$$\$200 = A \left[\frac{1 - (1 + r)^{-n}}{r} \right]$$

$$A = \frac{200}{\left[\dfrac{1 - (1 + r)^{-n}}{r} \right]} = \frac{200}{\left[\dfrac{1 - (1 + 0.1)^{-2}}{0.1} \right]} = \$115$$

Year	0	1	2	3
Equivalent annual value of crop A		115	115	

Crop B

Year	0	1	2	3
Cash flow	−100	170	136	111
NPV	$250.34			

Annual equivalent value estimate:

$$\$250 = A \left[\frac{1 - (1 + r)^{-n}}{r} \right]$$

$$A = \frac{250}{\left[\dfrac{1 - (1 + r)^{-n}}{r} \right]} = \frac{250}{\left[\dfrac{1 - (1 + 0.1)^{-3}}{0.1} \right]} = \$101$$

Year	0	1	2	3
Equivalent annual value of crop B		101	101	101

The assumption in this analysis is that whichever project is selected it will be replaced by another with a similar cash flow pattern—that is, the projects repeat. Conventional NPV analysis holds that we should accept the project with the greater NPV. However, when projects have different lives this will not be a correct analysis as the projects repeat.

The most common application of the annual equivalence approach is to evaluate machine or vehicle replacements. In these cases, we calculate the equivalent annual costs of each competing machine and choose the one with the lowest equivalent annual cost. One exercise close to every executive's heart is deciding what the optimum time is to replace the company vehicle—one year, two years, three years, etc. In solving this type of problem, each holding period is treated as a separate, mutually exclusive project. Trading a car in after one year is a project with a one-year life. Trading a car in after five years is a project with a five-year life. The approach is to calculate the equivalent annual cost of each option and then compare these costs.

In some situations, the firm may decide to abandon the project. Or, the firm can decide when to invest in the project. These are the options available to the company in capital budgeting. The firm may use the decision tree technique to decide the timing of their investment.

Real option value consideration in capital budgeting

In capital budgeting, financial managers should also consider the real options of the project, which may dramatically change its value. These real options embedded in the project enable financial managers to alter the size and timing of the project's cash flows. One example of these real options is the abandonment option, which allows managers to abandon or terminate an unsuccessful project before its planned life. This option would minimise the expected losses from projects that have turned out badly. Another example is determining when to start a project. In this case, there is a timing option attached to the project, and the company may find it worthwhile to wait for some time in order to collect more information before undertaking the project. Example 5.15 illustrates a project with an embedded timing option.

EXAMPLE 5.15

Timing option consideration in capital budgeting

QUESTION

A company is considering a five-year project which requires a $10 million initial investment. However, the cash inflows of the project will depend on the market conditions. If the market conditions were good, the project would generate $5 million cash inflows each year for five years. If the market conditions were bad, the project would generate only $2 million cash inflows each year. There is a 50% chance that the market will be good, and a 50% chance that it will go badly. One option is for the company to wait for an additional year so as to collect more information regarding the market conditions. After one year's time, the company will be able to determine whether the market conditions are good or bad. The required rate of return of the project is 10%. What is the expected NPV of the project if the company undertakes the project now? What is the expected NPV of the project if the company waits for another year?

ANSWER

A **decision tree** is very useful in answering this kind of question. A decision tree is a diagram illustrating the different possible outcomes that may result from a particular situation or decision. Each possible outcome is shown as a branch of the decision tree. The probability of each outcome is also used so that the NPV from a particular situation or decision can be estimated, taking into account the likelihood of that particular set of circumstances occurring. The expected NPV for the project can then be estimated taking into account all the possible outcomes.

If the company undertakes the project now, the figures are as follows:[4]

Year	0	1	2	3	4	5	6	NPV	Probability	NPV × Probability
Market good		5	5	5	5	5		8.95	50%	4.48
		−10								
Market bad		2	2	2	2	2		−2.42	50%	−1.21
								Expected NPV		3.27

If the market is good, the NPV of the project will be $8.95 million. On the other hand, if the market is bad, the NPV of the project will be –$2.42 million. The expected NPV of the project is the weighted average of the NPVs of the two possible outcomes, and the weight is the probability of each outcome. Therefore, if the company undertakes the project now, the expected NPV is $3.27 million. The positive expected NPV indicates that the company should undertake this project, even though there is a 50% chance that it will produce a negative NPV.

If the company undertakes the project in one year's time, the figures are as follows:

Year	0	1	2	3	4	5	6	NPV	Probability	NPV × Probability
Market good		−10	5	5	5	5	5	8.14	50%	4.07
Market bad		0	0	0	0	0	0	0	50%	0
								Expected NPV		4.07

If the company waits for another year it can see what the market conditions are. If the market conditions were good, then the company would undertake the project; if the conditions were bad, the company would reject the project. If the company rejects the project, no investment is made and the NPV will be zero. If the company undertakes the project in one year's time, the NPV will be $8.14 million.[5] Therefore, if the company waits for another year to make sure the market conditions are good, the expected NPV of the project is $4.07 million. Therefore, in deciding whether to invest in the project right now or wait another year before making the decision, the results suggest that the company should wait for another year since waiting would provide a higher NPV.

Decision tree
A diagram that illustrates the different possible outcomes that may result from a particular situation or decision.

CONCEPT CHECK

9. Why may the standard NPV analysis not provide the correct answer in evaluating mutually exclusive projects with different lives? And, what is the annual equivalence approach?

10. Give some examples of real options in projects.

For the answers, go to MyFinanceLab

Student Learning Centre

My FinanceLab ■ To test your mastery of the content covered in this chapter and to create your own personalised study plan, go to MyFinanceLab: www.pearson.com.au/myfinancelab

CONCEPT CHECKLIST

In this chapter the following concepts were discussed:

➤ Issues in estimating cash flows, including what to incorporate in cash flow calculations:
- use cash flows, not accounting income
- ignore sunk costs
- include opportunity costs
- include side effects
- include working capital
- include taxation
- exclude financing charges
- the effect of taxation
- the effect of inflation

➤ Risk analysis in capital budgeting
- sensitivity analysis
- scenario analysis
- simulation (Monte Carlo) analysis

➤ Some special cases in capital budgeting
- issues for projects with unequal lives
- issues for projects with real options

SELF-TEST QUESTIONS

Your company is considering introducing a new type of industrial electric motor and has collected the following information about the proposed product. (Note: You may not need to use all of this information; use only what is relevant.)

The project has an anticipated economic life of four years.

It would cost the company $20 million to purchase a new product line to manufacture the new motor. The new product line will be depreciated on a straight-line basis to zero over four years (i.e. the company's depreciation expense will be $5 million in each of the first four years). The company anticipates that the product line will last for four years, at which time it can be sold at a market price of $1 million.

The company has spent $500 000 on market research, the results of which indicate that it will be able to sell these new motors for $20 000 per unit, with 1000 units sold each year. The variable costs would be $11 000 per unit. Your company's fixed costs would also rise by $1 million each year. The new motor is expected to reduce the sales of the company's existing products by $2 million a year, but the costs of these existing products would also reduce by $1 million a year because these sales are not being made.

During the operating life of the project, conditions are expected to remain stable, which means there is no other change in unit sales, sales price and costs.

If the company goes ahead with the proposed product, it will have an effect on the company's net operating working capital. The company will need to purchase $500 000 worth of inventory, and at the same time accounts payable will increase by $100 000. After the project is completed, the net operating working capital will be fully recovered.

The company's interest expense each year will be $100 000.

The company's tax rate is 30%. The project's after-tax required rate of return is 10%.

What is the net present value of the proposed project?

Self-test answer

In year 0:

- The company purchases the machine line, and cash outflows are –$20 million.
- The company also needs to invest in working capital, which is the difference between inventory and accounts payable, $500 000 – $100 000 = $400 000. This is a cash outflow at year 0, and the company will recover that investment in working capital at the end of the project. The $400 000 cash inflow occurs at the end of year 4.
- The $500 000 that the company has spent on market research is a sunk cost, and as such is irrelevant to the current decision making.

During the life of the project:

- Cash flows are the incremental taxable profit plus depreciation, then less tax.
- The lost sales of the existing products and the corresponding reduced costs should both be considered in the estimation.
- The interest expense should not be included in the cash flow estimation, since it has already been considered in the discount rate.

At the end of the project:

- Recovery of the working capital, $400 000, should be included.
- The market price of the product line is $1 million, and its book value is zero (fully depreciated). The company needs to pay 30% capital gains tax on the $1 million capital gain. Therefore, the after-tax market value of the product line is $700 000.

Profit calculation (unit: $1000):

Year	0	1	2	3	4
Sales		20 000	20 000	20 000	20 000
Lost sales		-2 000	-2 000	-2 000	-2 000
Net sales		18 000	18 000	18 000	18 000
Variable costs		11 000	11 000	11 000	11 000
Fixed costs		1 000	1 000	1 000	1 000
Saving—lost sales		-1 000	-1 000	-1 000	-1 000
Depreciation		5 000	5 000	5 000	5 000
Net costs		16 000	16 000	16 000	16 000
Incremental taxable profit		2 000	2 000	2 000	2 000
Tax at 30%		600	600	600	600
Net profit after tax		1 400	1 400	1 400	1 400

Cash flows calculation (unit: $1000):

Year	0	1	2	3	4
Product line	-20 000				700
Working capital	-400				400
Incremental taxable profit		2 000	2 000	2 000	2 000
Plus Depreciation		5 000	5 000	5 000	5 000
Free cash flows before tax	-20 400	7 000	7 000	7 000	8 100
Less Tax		600	600	600	600
Free cash flows	-20 400	6 400	6 400	6 400	7 500

$$NPV = -20\,400 + \frac{6400}{(1 + 10\%)^1} + \frac{6400}{(1 + 10\%)^2} + \frac{6400}{(1 + 10\%)^3} + \frac{7500}{(1 + 10\%)^4}$$

$$= \$638.45$$

Therefore, the company should accept this project.

DISCUSSION QUESTIONS

1. Discuss the various types of cash flows and related items that should be included in the NPV calculation for capital budgeting purposes, and then outline those that should be excluded. What is the rationale for including some items while excluding others?

2. 'When evaluating a project, only cash flows should be considered. Since depreciation is a non-cash expense, there is no need for the financial managers to know the depreciation method when estimating cash flows.' Comment on this statement.

3. 'When evaluating a project, only cash flows should be considered. Since interest expenses are cash expenses, the financial managers should include interest expenses in the capital budgeting decision-making process.' Comment on this statement.

4. What is the essential difference between sensitivity analysis and scenario analysis?

5. Why can't the NPVs of unequal-life, mutually exclusive projects be compared? Which method should we use instead?

6. What are real options? What are they used for?

7. What is a decision tree? When and how should it be used?

8. What is the abandon option? Explain what happens if we ignore this option in capital budgeting.

PRACTICAL QUESTIONS

BASIC

1. A company is considering investing in a new, improved widget-producing machine. The machine will cost $95 000 and is expected to generate the following series of net cash flows (stated in real terms).

Year	1	2	3	4	5
Net cash flows	12 000	23 000	20 000	34 000	28 000

The company currently uses a nominal discount rate of 10% for capital budgeting purposes. If inflation is expected to be 4% p.a. for the next five years, should the company buy the new widget-producing machine?

BASIC

2. A company is considering a project to enter a new line of business. The new business will require the company to purchase a new machine that will cost $930 000. These costs will be depreciated on a straight-line basis to zero over three years. At the end of three years the company will get out of the business and will sell the machine at a market value of $70 000. Working capital of $50 000 will be required from the outset, which will be fully recovered at the end of year 3. The project is expected to generate $1.6 million in sales each year. The operating costs, excluding depreciation, are expected to be $1.15 million per year.

The company tax rate is 30%, and the project's required rate of return is 12%. What is the net present value of the project?

BASIC

3. Two competing project proposals, 1 and 2, are currently under consideration for the manufacture of a new product line. Information for each of the projects is as follows, with cash flows stated in nominal terms.

Project	1	2
Estimated life	3 years	5 years
Initial outlay	$200 000	$600 000
Annual after-tax cash flows	$175 000	$245 000

(a) Assume that projects 1 and 2 are of average risk to the firm, and the firm's cost of capital is 5.5%, stated in real terms. If long-term inflation is expected to be 4.25% p.a., calculate the net present value of each project.

(b) Advise which project should be implemented. Briefly explain the method that you have employed in making this decision.

4. You are employed as a consultant to a hospital that is considering expenditure on some expensive medical equipment, which costs $100 000. The hospital estimates that the incremental cash flows associated with purchasing the equipment, before any taxes, will be as follows:

BASIC

Year	1	2	3	4	5
Cash flow	25 000	25 000	25 000	40 000	50 000

The applicable tax rate is 30%. The equipment can be depreciated for tax purposes at 25% of original cost over four years. The hospital requires an after-tax rate of return of 10% p.a. Calculate the after-tax cash flows and determine whether the equipment should be purchased.

5. Your company is considering whether to drill for oil on a piece of land it already owns. The company estimates that it would require an initial investment of $5 million to start the project. The expected free cash flows will be $2 million each year for the next five years. However, they could be much higher or lower, depending on market conditions. If your company waits for another year to drill, there is a 50% chance that market conditions will be good. In this case, the expected free cash flow will be $3 million a year for the next five years. There is also a 50% chance that market conditions will be bad, in which case the expected free cash flow will be only $1 million a year for the next five years. If your company waits for one year, the initial investment will remain at $5 million, and the company will have the option of drilling or not drilling, depending on the market conditions. If the required rate of return of your company is 10%, should it drill now, or wait for another year?

BASIC

6. Your company is considering the development of a new product. In evaluating the proposed project, your company has collected the following information.

INTERMEDIATE

*   The company estimates that the project will last for five years.
*   The company will need to purchase new machinery that has an upfront cost of $300 million. The machinery will be depreciated on a straight-line basis to zero over five years. At the end of the project the machinery can be sold at an estimated market price of $50 million.
*   Production of the new product will take place in a recently vacated facility that the company owns. Otherwise, the facility can be leased to collect $5 million in rent per year for the company.
*   The project will require a $50 million investment in inventory, and the company expects that its accounts payable will rise by $10 million as well. At the end of the project, the working capital will have been completely recovered.
*   The company estimates that sales of the new product will be $195 million in each of the next five years.
*   The operating costs, excluding depreciation, are expected to be $100 million each year.
*   The company tax rate is 30%, and the project's required rate of return is 10%.

What is the net present value of the project?

7. Your company is considering buying a new machine to improve its production efficiency. The new machine costs $500 000, which will result in $105 000 in annual before-tax cost savings. The new machine can be used for five years, and it will be depreciated on a straight-line basis to zero over five years. At the end of year 5 the new machine can be sold at a market price of $90 000. If it installs the new machine, your company will also need to increase inventory by $15 000. The company tax rate is 30%, and your company's required rate of return is 15%. Should your company buy and install the new machine?

8. Sprowl Limited is considering two projects. Each requires an immediate cash outlay: $10 000 for project A, $9000 for project B. Project A has a life of four years, and project B has a life of five years; neither will have any salvage value at the end of its life. For tax purposes, each would be depreciated by the straight-line method: project A at 30% and project B at 24%. The company's tax rate is 30%, and its required rate of return after tax is 11%. Net cash flows before taxes have been projected as follows:

Year	1	2	3	4	5
Project A	$3200	$3200	$4000	$4100	
Project B	$4000	$4000	$1900	$1800	$1800

(a) Calculate the net cash flows after tax for each project. (Assume that Sprowl Limited has a substantial taxable income, so where a project has a negative taxable income in a particular year, this will give rise to a tax saving by the firm.)

(b) Calculate the payback for each investment.

(c) Calculate the average accounting rate of return for each investment.

(d) Calculate the net present value for each investment.

(e) Should Sprowl Limited adopt project A, project B, both or neither? Why?

9. A company is considering two mutually exclusive competing projects, A and B, each requiring an upfront outlay of $1 million. The expected future cash flows associated with each of the projects ($'000, stated in nominal terms), along with the annual expected inflation rates, are as follows:

Year	1	2	3	4
Project A	400	250	600	300
Project B	0	100	800	950
Inflation	5%	5%	4%	3%

The company's real cost of capital is 10%. Calculate the net present value of the projects and advise the company of the appropriate capital investment decision.

10. Your company is interested in developing a new communication device. The project requires an initial investment cost of $300 million and will last for five years. The project's subsequent cash flows critically depend on whether the device becomes the industry standard. There is a 50% chance that this will occur, in which case the project's expected cash flows will be $150 million at the end of each of the next five years. There is also a 50% chance that the device will not become the industry standard, in which case the project's expected cash flows will be $35 million at the end of each of the next five years. The project's required rate of return is 15%.

Assume that after receiving the first year's cash flows your company will know if the device has become the industry standard. If your company is able to abandon the project at that time, all the fixed assets related to the project can be sold to generate a further $130 million in after-tax cash flows for the company. Assume that the abandon option does not affect the project's required rate of return.

(a) What is the project's expected net present value if there is no abandon option?

(b) What is the project's expected net present value if the company can abandon the project after one year?

(c) What is the estimated value of this abandon option?

11. Your company is interested in investing in a new project. If it undertakes the project now, the expected net present value of the project is $50 000. Rather than making the investment now, your company can wait one year and pay $10 000 now to hire a consultant to collect additional information regarding the project. There is a 50% chance that the additional information would be positive, in which case the expected NPV of the project one year from now (not including the cost of consulting) will be $130 000. There is also a 50% chance that the additional information will be negative, in which case the expected NPV of the project one year from now will be –$30 000. If your company chooses to wait a year, it has the option of investing or not investing in the project after receiving the additional information about the project. If the required return of the project is 12%, should your company hire the consultant to collect additional information or just undertake the project now? **INTERMEDIATE**

12. Your company is considering a project to supply 1500 containers per year to a shipping company for the next four years. It will cost your company $5 million to install the equipment necessary to start production, and this cost will be depreciated on a straight-line basis to zero over four years. At the end of year 4, the equipment will have a market value of $950 000. The fixed production costs will be $1.1 million per year, and the variable costs should be $1000 per container. Your company also needs to invest $800 000 in working capital initially, which can be fully recovered at the end of year 4. If the company tax rate is 30% and your company's required rate of return on this project is 12%, what is the lowest bid price you can submit? **CHALLENGING**

13. Your company is considering buying a new machine to improve its production efficiency. The new machine costs $660 000, and it can be used for six years. It will be depreciated on a straight-line basis to zero over six years. At the end of year 6 the new machine can be sold at a market price of $85 000. If installing the new machine, your company also needs to invest $35 000 in initial working capital. The company tax rate is 30%, and the required rate of return is 14%. What is the minimum annual before-tax saving this new machine should achieve? **CHALLENGING**

14. At the beginning of 2012, James Finnegan is evaluating the introduction of a photocopier–printer that costs $15 000 and has an economic life of four years. The market price for used printers and the net cash receipts, at the end of each year, are as follows: **CHALLENGING**

	Market price	Net receipts
2012	$11 000	$7 000
2013	$5 500	$6 000
2014	$3 500	$5 000
2015	0	$4 000

Assuming a discount rate of 15%, what is the optimal replacement period? (Note that the firm does not consider buying a used printer.)

CHALLENGING

15. The Titanic Shipbuilding Company is bidding on a contract to build an unsinkable ocean liner.

Estimates of the project are as follows. The ship will take three years to build. It will generate total revenue of $30 million paid, in equal instalments of $10 million, over the next three years. (Payments will be received at the end of each year.) The project will require immediate establishment of a new shipyard at a cost of $4 million. The capital cost of the new yard can be depreciated at 20% p.a. straight line. The yard can be sold in three years for an estimated $3 million in the real dollar term.

While working capital of $1 million will be required from the outset, no additional allocation need be made to working capital, regardless of any escalation in other costs due to inflation. Working capital is also assumed to be fully recovered in real term at the end of year three. Wages and other operating costs are estimated at $7 million for the first year and are forecast to rise at the rate of inflation (10% p.a.) thereafter. These costs can be treated as though they occur at the end of each year.

The real after-tax rate of return (adjusted for risk) required by Titanic's management is 5%. Tax is payable at the rate of 30%.

(a) Set out the cash flows of the project in nominal dollars, and calculate the net present value of the project.

(b) Set out the cash flows of the project in real dollars, and calculate the net present value of the project.

(c) Is the project worth doing?

WebEX

Economic value added (EVA) has been increasingly used to measure company performance. Search the Internet to find out more about the EVA, and the difference between EVA and discounted cash flow techniques. Search the Internet to find out which Australian companies are using EVA to measure their performance.

Excel questions

1. Your company is considering the development of a new product. In evaluating the proposed project your company's CFO has collected the following information:
   • The company estimates that the project will last for 10 years.

- The company will need to purchase a new product line that has an upfront cost of $230 million. The machinery will be depreciated on a straight-line basis to zero over 10 years. At the end of the project the product line can be sold at an estimated market price of $24 million.

- Production of the new product will take place in a recently vacated facility that the company owns. Otherwise, the facility can be leased out to collect $5.5 million in rent per year for the company.

- The project will require a $44 million investment in inventory, and the company expects that its accounts payable will rise by $7 million as well. At the end of the project, the working capital will have been completely recovered.

- The company estimates that sales of the new product will be $200 million for the first year, and the sales will grow at 7% each year later.

- The fixed operating costs, excluding depreciation, are expected to be $22 million each year, and the variable operating costs, excluding depreciation, are expected to be 65% of the sales each year.

- The company tax rate is 30%, and the project's required rate of return is 12%.

What is the net present value of the project?

2. Your company needs to choose between two machines, A and B, which perform exactly the same operations but have different lives of four and seven years, respectively. The two machines have the following costs:

Year	0	1	2	3	4	5	6	7
Machine A	50 000	33 600	33 600	33 600	33 600			
Machine B	89 000	28 400	28 400	28 400	28 400	28 400	28 400	28 400

(a) Assume that both machines are of average risk to the firm and the firm's cost of capital is 12%. Which machine would your firm choose?

(b) If the firm's cost of capital were 18%, which machine would your firm choose?

CASE STUDY

Your friend Jennifer Connolly has operated a family restaurant for several years, and she is considering opening another one using a place she owns already. Jennifer asks you to help her in evaluating the proposed project. You are also provided with the following information:

(a) Jennifer plans to operate the restaurant for 10 years.

(b) Jennifer will need to spend $200 000 to decorate the restaurant and purchase some equipment. The costs of decoration and equipment will be depreciated on a straight-line basis to zero over 10 years. At the end, the equipment can be sold at an estimated market price of $50 000.

(c) The new restaurant will be in a place that Jennifer owns. Otherwise, the place can be leased out to collect $40 000 in rent per year.

(d) The new restaurant will require a $30 000 investment in inventory, and Jennifer expects that her accounts payable will rise by $10 000 as well. At the end, the working capital will have been completely recovered.

(e) Jennifer estimates that 15 000 customers will visit her new restaurant each year and on average each customer will spend $20 which is almost identical to those of her current restaurant.

(f) The fixed operating costs, excluding depreciation, are expected to be $100 000 each year, and the variable operating costs, excluding depreciation, are expected to be 25% of the sales each year.

(g) Jennifer had paid $5000 to a consultant to collect information for her.

(h) Jennifer is negotiating with the bank to borrow half of the decoration expenses, and the commercial lending rate of the bank is 7.2% p.a.

(i) Jennifer also assumes that the new restaurant will decrease sales of her current restaurant by $20 000 per year.

(j) The tax rate is 30%, and the project's required rate of return is 12%.

After getting this information, you evaluate the proposed project by addressing the following questions.

CASE STUDY QUESTIONS

1. Why should cash flow instead of accounting profit be used in capital budgeting?

2. What kinds of cash flow should be included in capital budgeting analysis? Use the project to demonstrate.

3. Should Jennifer undertake the project and open the new restaurant? Why?

4. What is a sensitivity analysis? What happens to the NPV of the project if only one key variable increases/decreases by 10%? Use the following variables to demonstrate the number of customers, fixed operating costs and variable operating costs.

5. Assume that Jennifer is comfortable about the estimates of all the variables except the number of customers and the average spending of each customer. If the new restaurant becomes popular, the number of customers would be 20 000 and the average spending of each customer would be $25. On the other hand, if the new restaurant becomes unpopular, the number of customers would be 10 000 and the average spending of each customer would be $15. In either case, the variable operating costs, excluding depreciation, are expected to be 25% of the sales. What is the NPV under the best case, and what is the NPV under the worst case?

FURTHER READING

For a book which includes advanced techniques in evaluating capital budgeting projects see:

- Dayananda, D., Irons, R., Harrison, S., Herbohn, J. and Rowland, P. (2002), *Capital Budgeting: Financial Appraisal of Investment Projects*, Cambridge University Press, New York.

For a discussion of using real options in capital budgeting see:

- Trigeorgis, L. (1996), *Real Options: Managerial Flexibility and Strategy in Resource Allocation*, MIT Press, Cambridge, Mass.

NOTES

1. NPV(accounting) = $2/(1 + 10\%) + 10/(1 + 10\%)^2 = \$10.08$m
   NPV(free cash flows) = $-100 + 52/(1 + 10\%) + 60/(1 + 10\%)^2 = -\$3.14$m.
2. While in theory it is possible to work with before-tax cash flows and before-tax discount rates, in practice this is rarely done since cash inflows are subject to taxation.
3. If the company were unable to claim a deduction for the depreciation expense, the amount of tax payable on operating income would have been $170m 30\% = \$51$m. The effect of the depreciation tax shield is to reduce the tax liability to \$30m p.a., a saving of \$21m (= depreciation expense 30\%).
4. If the market is good, NPV = $-10 + 5 \dfrac{(1 - 1/(1 + 10\%)^5)}{10\%} = \$8.95$m. If the market is bad,

   NPV = $-10 + 2 \dfrac{(1 - 1/(1 + 10\%)^5)}{10\%} = -\$2.42$m.
5. If the company undertakes the project after waiting for another year to make sure the market is good,

   NPV = $[-10 + 5 \dfrac{(1 - 1/(1 + 10\%)^5)}{10\%}]/(1 + 10\%) = \$8.14$m.

6

Risk and return

CHAPTER PREVIEW

Chapter 1 introduced the concept of valuation using the example of a simple asset that is *guaranteed* to return $105 in one year's time. It showed that if the prevailing interest rate on a comparable investment, which also *guarantees* a rate of return, is 5%, it is straightforward to value the first asset at $100. The question addressed in this chapter is: what if there is some chance that the asset will not return $105 in one year? That is, what if the future $105 payoff involves some element of *risk*? Intuitively, the answer to this question is that an investor would pay less than $100 for the asset. Hence, the investor would require the asset to generate a higher rate of return (relative to the guaranteed 5% on the alternative asset) before being willing to buy the asset. More formally, the investor adds an extra rate of return, called the *risk premium*, over the guaranteed, or *risk-free*, rate as follows:

$$\text{Required rate of return \% = risk-free rate \% + risk premium \%} \tag{6.1}$$

Rearranging Equation 6.1 yields:

$$\text{Risk premium \% = required rate of return \% − risk-free rate \%} \tag{6.2}$$

Accordingly, the risk premium is the portion of return required by an investor on a risky security over and above the risk-free rate of return.

This chapter and the next deal with the quantification of this risk premium. This chapter discusses a number of concepts required to understand properly the nature of risk and return and the risk premium. Most importantly, this chapter provides the framework necessary for understanding the formal model of the risk premium introduced in Chapter 7—the capital asset pricing model (CAPM).

KEY CONCEPTS

CONCEPT 6.1   Historical rates of return on Australian securities

A good starting point for understanding the rates of return required by investors in Australian securities is to examine the historical rates of return on well-known securities with different levels of **risk**. Presumably, if investors are pricing these securities properly, and do not *system-atically* under- or overstate future cash returns, then the actual rate of return should bear some resemblance to the required rate of return. However, since the future rarely produces what is expected, considerable volatility, or 'noise', tends to exist in observed historical rates of return. In this section, historical returns on three sets of securities are examined: **bank-accepted bills**, 10-year government bonds and shares in listed Australian companies (hereafter referred to as 'stocks'). Government bonds are long-term, government-backed debt securities, whereas stocks are risky securities in the sense that no element of their return is guaranteed. Accordingly, government securities lie close to one end of the risk spectrum (riskless) because their return is essentially guaranteed, whereas stocks tend to lie closer to the other end of this spectrum (very risky).

> **Risk**
> The extent to which the return of a security is expected to vary from its expected return.

> **Bank-accepted bill**
> A bill of exchange (commercial bill) of which the acceptor is a bank. See also *commercial bill*.

Bank-accepted bills (BABs) are short-term debt securities effectively guaranteed by banks (see Chapter 12). They typically have a term to maturity of up to 180 days. They are referred to as 'zero-coupon' securities because they do not offer an interim return in the form of a coupon (interest payment). Rather, they return one lump sum on maturity, equivalent to their face value. Investors purchase these securities at a discount to face value, and the amount of the discount represents the return on the investment. Currently, BABs have a minimum face value of $5000. Hence, using the simple DCF (discounted cash flow) approach, the value of one BAB is:

$$V = \frac{5000}{1 + i \times \dfrac{t}{365}} \qquad \text{(6.3)}$$

where:

V = current value of a bank-accepted bill

t = the time to maturity in days

i = yield p.a.

Since BABs are effectively guaranteed by banks, their return is generally considered to be close to riskless. An investor who holds these securities to maturity is virtually guaranteed to earn the yield at which the notes are issued. The only risk faced by investors is inflation risk, as the purchasing power of the face value of the securities is not guaranteed and depends on inflation.

Practitioner's POV

Not all government-issued debt is risk free, as the current European sovereign debt crisis is testament to. From late 2009, fears of a European sovereign debt crisis developed among investors concerned about rising government debt levels and downgrades of the government debt of certain European states. Despite various rescue packages, at the time of writing there remained continued speculation of Greek sovereign default and little progress in other affected countries such as Italy and Spain. In early 2012, European leaders were continuing to engage in negotiations on a lasting solution to the crisis, in the face of a worsening economic outlook.

Ten-year bonds are long-term government debt securities. The example and discussion of Commonwealth government bonds in this section has been simplified. For a detailed discussion of the quotation and trading of bonds in Australia, refer to Appendix 6.3 at the end of this chapter. One example of a 10-year bond is a bond issued with a minimum face value of $1000 and a coupon rate of 12% p.a. They pay interest every six months, and hence the coupon on the bonds is $60. Since the interest payments on 10-year bonds represent an annuity,[1] their value is given by applying a formula analogous to Equation 3.4 in Chapter 3. For 10-year bonds with a coupon rate of 12%, the F variable (coupon amount) will be $60, and the t variable (number of periods) will be 20 when they are first issued. The specific formula for valuing these 10-year bonds is therefore:

$$V = \frac{60\left[1 - \left(\frac{1}{1+i}\right)^t\right]}{i} + \frac{1000}{(1+i)^t} \tag{6.4}$$

where:

V = current value of 10-year bonds

t = time to maturity in years × 2

i = annual yield on bonds p.a. ÷ 2

As explained in Chapter 3, the first half of Equation 6.4 is the present value of the six-monthly interest payments paid by the bonds, while the second half gives the present value of the face value—which is the amount in dollars to be paid back at maturity. As the time to maturity decreases, the number of half-yearly periods (initially a maximum of 20) declines.

While 10-year bonds are located on the same end of the risk spectrum as BABs, they are slightly more risky. In addition to inflation risk, they also face interest rate risk. This latter risk is associated with the change in value of the bond that arises as a result of a market interest rate change. (For example, in Equation 6.4, a change in the i variable will result in a change in the bond's market value.) Table 6.1 reports that between 2000 and 2009 the government adjusted official interest rates 31 times. Therefore, history indicates that it is very likely that the life of a 10-year bond will straddle many more interest rate changes, which can affect the rate of return achievable by investors that have shorter investment horizons than the time remaining to maturity. The reason for this is that 10-year bonds guarantee a rate of return only to investors who hold them to maturity. Investors seeking to exit from their holdings prior to maturity must sell them at a market price that is influenced by fluctuations in market bond yields, as illustrated by Equation 6.4.

Whereas the rate of return on government bonds and BABs is known at the time of purchase and is in some sense guaranteed, shares do not share either of these features. Investors in shares participate directly in the business risk of a company, because they are entitled to residual cash flows after obligations relating to debt have been paid. As noted in Chapter 1, the average return generated by investing in the share market is measured by share indices. Traditionally, the best known share market index in Australia has been the **All Ordinaries Index**, which provides a measure of the average movement in the price of shares on the Australian Securities Exchange (ASX). The 'All Ords', as it is more commonly known, is similar to the Hang Seng in Hong Kong, the FTSE 100 in the United Kingdom and the S&P 500 and Dow Jones indices in the USA.

All Ordinaries Index
An index of approximately 500 of the largest Australian companies. The companies are weighted in the index according to their size in terms of market capitalisation.

In April 2000 the ASX responded to changing market conditions and requirements and, in a joint initiative with Standard & Poor's (S&P), introduced a range of new indices. The All Ordinaries Index was retained, but it was amended to cover a group (or portfolio) of 500 securities, based on market capitalisation, up from 251 securities. At the time, the 500 securities in the All Ords represented about 97.7% of the market capitalisation of all Australian shares listed on the ASX. Three new indices were also introduced, as follows:

- the S&P/ASX 100, covering the top 100 securities listed on the ASX (by market capitalisation) and representing approximately 74% of ASX market capitalisation
- the **S&P/ASX 200**, covering the top 200 securities listed on the ASX (by market capitalisation) and representing approximately 80% of ASX market capitalisation
- the S&P/ASX 300, covering the top 300 securities listed on the ASX (by market capitalisation) and representing approximately 81% of ASX market capitalisation.

S&P/ASX 200 Index
An index of approximately 200 of the largest Australian companies. The S&P/ASX 200 Index is recognised as the main benchmark for the Australian equity market.

Table 6.1	Changes in official interest rates, 2000–2009	

DATE	CHANGE	NEW RATE
2 Dec 09	0.25	3.75
4 Nov 09	0.25	3.50
7 Oct 09	0.25	3.25
8 Apr 09	−0.25	3.00
4 Feb 09	−1.00	3.25
3 Dec 08	−1.00	4.25
5 Nov 08	−0.75	5.25
8 Oct 08	−1.00	6.00
3 Sep 08	−0.25	7.00
5 Mar 08	0.25	7.25
6 Feb 08	0.25	7.00
7 Nov 07	0.25	6.75
8 Aug 07	0.25	6.50
8 Nov 06	0.25	6.25
2 Aug 06	0.25	6.00
3 May 06	0.25	5.75
2 Mar 05	0.25	5.50
3 Dec 03	0.25	5.25
5 Nov 03	0.25	5.00
5 Jun 02	0.25	4.75
8 May 02	0.25	4.50
5 Dec 01	−0.25	4.25
3 Oct 01	−0.25	4.50
5 Sep 01	−0.25	4.75
4 Apr 01	−0.50	5.00
7 Mar 01	−0.25	5.50
7 Feb 01	−0.50	5.75
2 Aug 00	0.25	6.25
3 May 00	0.25	6.00
5 Apr 00	0.25	5.75
2 Feb 00	0.50	5.50

Source: Reserve Bank of Australia. Reproduced with permission.

Since the introduction of the new indices, the most commonly quoted indices are the S&P/ASX 200 and the All Ords. Not surprisingly, given their shared compositions, movements in the two indices are highly correlated, as illustrated by a plot of monthly index values since the introduction of the new indices, shown by Figure 6.1. This chapter will continue to use the

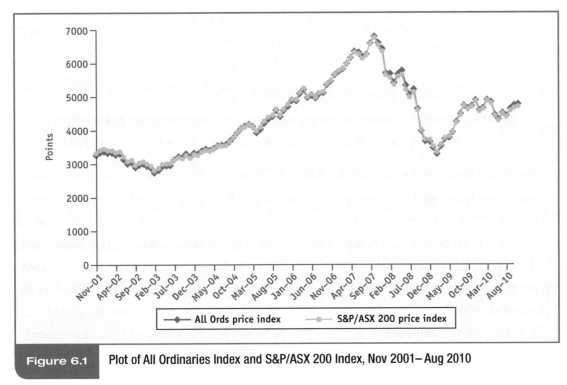

| **Figure 6.1** | Plot of All Ordinaries Index and S&P/ASX 200 Index, Nov 2001– Aug 2010 |

Source: www.yahoo.com.au

All Ords in illustrations and examples, but note that the principles covered extend to the other ASX indices.

The All Ords, the S&P/ASX 200 and other S&P/ASX indices are calculated by Standard & Poor's Index Services each day (in fact, each 30 seconds) using the following formula:

$$I_t = I_{t-1} \times \frac{\text{market capitalisation}_t}{\text{market capitalisation}_{t-1}} \qquad \textbf{(6.5)}$$

where:

$$I_t = \text{index at the end of interval } t$$

$$\text{market capitalisation}_t = \text{market capitalisation of securities in the index at the end of interval } t$$

The All Ords traces the change in the aggregate market capitalisation of the securities in the index. For example, a 10% rise in the market capitalisation of these securities will be reflected in a 10% rise in the value of the index. The index number itself is expressed in *points* and does not directly measure any physical quantity.

One of the limitations of the All Ords and other simple 'price' indices is that they do not fully reflect the change in the wealth of shareholders, because they ignore dividends paid to holders of shares. An alternative to the All Ordinaries Index, the All Ordinaries Accumulation Index (AOAI), captures this element of shares returns. The AOAI is calculated daily using the following formula:

$$AOAI_t = I_{t-1} \times \frac{\text{market capitalisation}_t + \text{dividends}_t}{\text{market capitalisation}_{t-1}}$$

(6.6)

where:

$AOAI_t$ = index at the end of interval t

market capitalisation$_t$ = market capitalisation of securities in the index at the end of interval t

dividends$_t$ = value of dividends paid by securities in the index during interval t

Accumulation index
Takes into account both capital appreciation and dividend income when measuring the market return.

The ASX commenced reporting the AOAI in December 1979, and it was the benchmark **accumulation index** until the introduction of the new indices in April 2000. Since that time, the S&P/ASX 200 Accumulation Index has become the preferred benchmark accumulation index.

The table in Appendix 6.1 provides a time series of yearly BAB yields, 10-year bond yields, the Consumer Price Index (CPI) and the AOAI from December 1979 to December 2009. Figure 6.2 depicts the annual rate of return on each of these three groups of securities over the period, along with the CPI, which represents changes in the inflation level over the period.

A number of important trends are illustrated by Figure 6.2. First, interest rates have generally been declining over the past three decades. Whereas 90-day BABs and 10-year bonds traded at yields in the 10–20% range for most of the 1980s, in the 1990s and beyond they tended to trade in the 5–10% range, and in recent years in particular have been at or below the lower end of that

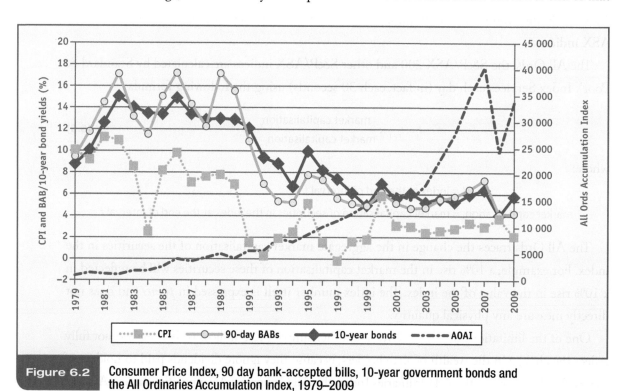

Figure 6.2   Consumer Price Index, 90 day bank-accepted bills, 10-year government bonds and the All Ordinaries Accumulation Index, 1979–2009

Source: Reserve Bank of Australia

range. Not surprisingly, this decline is also apparent in the trend in inflation, which declined from a peak of 11.3% in 1981 to a negligible level by 2009 (2.1% p.a.). The stock market indices demonstrate that 'in its major swings the market has never failed, following a fall, to rise above the previous high point[2], or in the case of the recent Global Financial Crisis, a healthy recovery'. Hence, historically at least, the market has not failed to provide investors with a reward for bearing risk. But is the return higher than that on bonds and BABs?

Table 6.2 reports the mean returns on each of the three groups of securities depicted above in the last quarter of a century (calculations appear in Appendix 6.1). Consistent with the argument that BABs are the least risky security, they have offered the lowest average rate of return historically in both nominal (9.09%) and real terms (4.28%).[3] The additional risk implicit in 10-year government bonds and shares has been rewarded by slightly higher average rates of return of 4.43% and 9.95%, respectively, in real terms. The last column shows the 'risk premium' on 10-year bonds and shares in the AOAI, relative to BABs (simply the difference between the two). It implies that the stock **market risk premium** is in the order of 5–6% p.a. in real terms. This result is consistent with the findings of a long-term study (covering 1882 to 1987) of bond and share returns in Australia, by Officer (1989).[4]

Market risk premium
The extra expected return over the risk-free rate demanded by investors to compensate them for investing in the market portfolio because of the higher risk assets.

If these numbers were accepted at face value, the discount rate that should be used to price the average stock market security is the sum of the current 90-day BAB yield plus 5.67%. (This assumes that inflation remains at a negligible level.[5]) For example, in December 2009 the yield on 90-day BABs was approximately 4.21%, which implied an expected return on the stock market of 9.88% at the time.

Table 6.2	The average nominal and real rate of return on selected Australian securities, 1980–2009		
	AVERAGE ANNUAL RATE OF RETURN (NOMINAL) %	AVERAGE ANNUAL RATE OF RETURN (REAL) %	AVERAGE REAL RISK PREMIUM (RELATIVE TO BANK-ACCEPTED BILLS) %
90-day bank-accepted bills (BABs)	9.09	4.28	
10-year government bonds	9.20	4.43	0.15
All Ordinaries Accumulation Index	14.95	9.95	5.67

CONCEPT CHECK

1. Why are 10-year bonds more exposed to interest rate risk than 90-day bank-accepted bills?

2. What is the difference between a price index and an accumulation index?

For the answers, go to MyFinanceLab

Practitioner's POV

A broad market share price index, such as the All Ordinaries, is frequently used in analysis as a valuation reference point. However, the way it is used often implies that the risk–return coordinates of the index have the fixedness of the North Star. In practice, the risk–return characteristics of an index may well change over time. One reason for this is that significant shifts can occur in the basic mix of the different types of shares that make up the index. For example, industries with different risks to the average risk of stocks may become more represented in the index.

CONCEPT 6.2   Measuring risk from investing in single securities

The risk of a security is the extent to which payoffs on the security are expected to vary from their expected value. Hence, the variability in returns on the AOAI, depicted in Figure 6.3, indicates the historical (total) risk of investing in Australian shares. Figure 6.4 illustrates the same data using a frequency histogram. The degree to which returns are spread out (dispersion) in Figure 6.4 is also indicative of the risk of investing in Australian securities.

A natural way of measuring the expected dispersion in returns of an investment (representing total risk) is by calculating the standard deviation of returns, $\sigma(\tilde{r})$, on a security, as follows:

$$\sigma(\tilde{r}) = \sqrt{E(\tilde{r} - \bar{r})^2} \qquad (6.7)$$

where:

E = expected outcome

$\tilde{r}$ = random return on the security

$\bar{r}$ = expected return on the security

The standard deviation of returns is an appropriate measure of the risk of an investment because, statistically, standard deviation measures the extent to which a random variable (in this case, the returns on a security) is expected to differ from its expected value.

Calculating the riskiness of a security using a historical time series of returns

The standard deviation of returns can be calculated from a historical time series of returns if two simple assumptions are made: (1) the random process that generated returns in the past is also the process that will generate returns in the future; and (2) an observed set of historical returns represents a random draw from an underlying distribution of returns. Given these assumptions, the standard deviation can be calculated as follows:

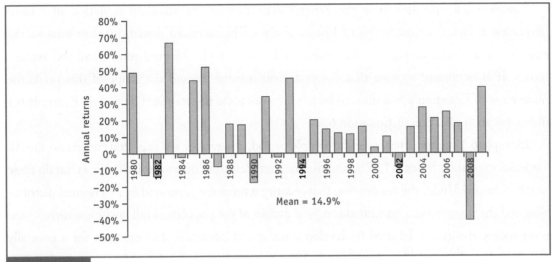

Figure 6.3   The variability of returns on the All Ordinaries Accumulation Index, 1980–2009

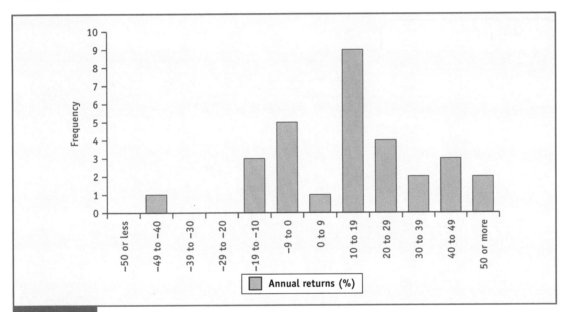

Figure 6.4   The distribution of returns on the All Ordinaries Accumulation Index, 1980–2009

$$\sigma(\tilde{r}) = \sqrt{\frac{\sum_{t=1}^{n}(r_t - \overline{r})^2}{n - 1}} \qquad (6.8)$$

where:

r_t = the observed return during interval t

$\overline{r}$ = the mean (expected) return on the security

n = the number of available observations

Equation 6.8 operationalises the general definition of the standard deviation of returns (Equation 6.7) for a time series of historical data. The standard deviation of returns in the equation is a special average of the difference between each observed return and the average return. It is important to note that, for statistical reasons beyond the scope of this book, the numerator of Equation 6.8 is divided by $n - 1$ to calculate the standard deviation. Example 6.1 illustrates an application of Equation 6.8.

Example 6.1 suggests that, over the sample period, the average (or expected) return on the All Ords Accumulation Index is 12.7%, and the standard deviation of returns is 30.8%. What do these numbers imply? Under the assumption that security returns are generated from a normal distribution, and the sample mean generated is representative of the population (all possible returns), then econometric theory can be used to develop some useful inferences. For example, for a normally distributed random variable, approximately 68% of possible outcomes lie within plus or minus one standard deviation of the mean of the random variable.[6] This is illustrated in Figure 6.5.

EXAMPLE 6.1

Estimating the standard deviation of security returns from a historical time series of data

QUESTION

Calculate the standard deviation of returns on the AOAI from 2005 to 2009.

Year	Return (%)
2005	21.1
2006	25.0
2007	18.0
2008	−40.4
2009	39.6

ANSWER

Calculate the mean return ($\bar{r}$).

$$r = \frac{\sum_{t=1}^{n} r_t}{n}$$

$$= (21.1 + 25.0 + 18.0 - 40.4 + 39.6)/5$$

$$= 12.66\%$$

Calculate the variance of returns.

$$\sigma = \frac{\sum_{t=1}^{n} (r_t - \bar{r})^2}{n - 1}$$

$$= [(21.1 - 12.66)^2 + (25.0 - 12.66)^2 + (18 - 12.66)^2 + (-40.4 - 12.66)^2 + (39.6 - 12.66)^2]/4$$

$$= 948.3 \text{ squared } \%$$

Hence, the standard deviation of returns is 30.8% ($\sqrt{948.3}$).

Figure 6.5 illustrates that the boundaries of returns that are within plus or minus one standard deviation of the mean return on the AOAI (12.7%) are −18.1% and 43.5%, respectively. Hence, if this is the distribution from which returns on the market are drawn, there is a 68% chance that future returns on the market will lie between −18.1% and 43.5%. The importance of the standard deviation of returns is that it assists in estimating the range of future possible outcomes. It follows that the higher the standard deviation of returns, the higher the range of possible outcomes, and hence the more risk that is associated with stock market investment.

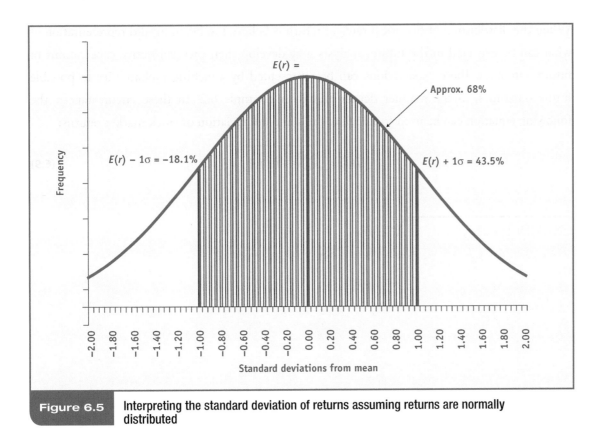

| Figure 6.5 | Interpreting the standard deviation of returns assuming returns are normally distributed |

A caveat

Example 6.1 implies that it is possible to determine the riskiness of an investment (the standard deviation of returns) by examining historical returns. This is based on the assumption that the distribution from which stock market returns are generated is constant over time. Table 6.3 shows the results of calculating the standard deviation of returns on the AOAI after dividing the 30-year period since its inception into three equal sub-periods. Quite clearly, the riskiness of the investment depends on the period over which the standard deviation of returns is calculated. This is an indication of the danger associated with using past or historical rates of return to measure the riskiness of a future investment. However, if risk were predictable, it wouldn't be risk—would it?

Table 6.3	The standard deviation of returns on the All Ordinaries Accumulation Index for selected years between 1980 and 2009

YEARS	STANDARD DEVIATION
1980–1989	30.1%
1990–1999	18.9%
2000–2009	22.4%

Calculating the riskiness of a security using a subjective probability distribution

When the distribution of historical rates of return is believed to be an invalid representation of what can be expected in the future, analysts may develop their own subjective expectations of future outcomes. These expectations can be represented by attaching probabilities to possible future outcomes, in the manner demonstrated in Example 6.2. In these circumstances, the following equation can be used to calculate the standard deviation of stock market returns:

$$\sigma(\tilde{r}) = \sqrt{\sum_{i=1}^{n} (r_i - \overline{r})^2 \times P_i} \qquad \text{(6.9)}$$

EXAMPLE 6.2

Estimating the standard deviation of security returns from a probability distribution of returns

QUESTION

An analyst predicts the following return possibilities on the AOAI next year.

Return	Midpoint	Probability
Less than 0% to –25%	–12.5%	1/5
0% to 25%	12.5%	3/5
More than 25% to 35%	30%	1/5

Calculate the expected return and standard deviation of returns.

ANSWER

Calculate the expected return.

$$E(r) = \sum_{t=1}^{n} r_i P_i$$
$$= (-12.5 \times 1/5) + (12.5 \times 3/5) + (30 \times 1/5)$$
$$= 11.0\%$$

Calculate the variance of returns.

$$\sigma^2(\tilde{r}) = \sum_{i=1}^{n} (r_i - \overline{r})^2 P_i$$
$$= [(-12.5 - 11)^2 \times 1/5] + [(12.5 - 11)^2 \times 3/5] + [(30 - 11)^2 \times 1/5]$$
$$= 184.0 \text{ squared } \%$$

Hence, the standard deviation of returns is 13.6% ($\sqrt{184.0}$).

where:

r_i = return outcome i

$\bar{r}$ = the expected return on the security = $\sum_{t=1}^{n} r_i P_i$

P_i = the probability of return i occurring

n = the number of possible return outcomes

Equation 6.9 operationalises the general definition of the standard deviation of returns (Equation 6.7) for a discrete probability distribution of returns. The equation takes the sum of the difference between each possible return and the expected return, and weights them by the probability of the return occurring. Example 6.2 illustrates the application of Equation 6.9.

The interpretation of the expected return and standard deviation of returns is analogous to the previous example. For example, the analyst's forecasts imply that there is a 68% probability that the return generated by the AOAI will lie between 24.6% and −2.6% (i.e. 11.0 ± 13.6%).

Practitioner's POV

In building a probability distribution of future returns for a stock, perhaps a practical starting point is to look at the distribution of the stock's forecast earnings, cash flows or dividends. One way of doing this is to perform an analysis of the current set of stockbroker analyst forecasts for these variables. Some professional fund managers have established sophisticated systems for the capture and analysis of forecast data sent to them directly by brokers via the Internet. Alternatively, commercial services provide a compilation of broker forecasts. I/B/E/S is a source of consensus forecasts of earnings and dividends. It is delivered online and although US based, includes comprehensive Australian stock coverage. This service is available on a subscription basis, but at a cost that probably precludes most private investors.

CONCEPT CHECK

3. What is investment risk?
4. How can the risk associated with investing in a stock be measured?
5. What limitations are there with using historical stock return data to quantify risk and how can it be overcome?

For the answers, go to MyFinanceLab

CONCEPT 6.3   The risk of portfolios

To this point only single assets have been dealt with. Specifically, we have been looking at measures of return and risk relating to investing in an asset. We now extend this analysis to examine the effect of holding a number of assets together.

A 'portfolio' is the name for a *group* of assets held by an investor. It is advantageous for investors to hold portfolios of stocks, since it enables a reduction in their investment risk. In order to understand how holding a number of stocks together reduces overall investment risk, consider Table 6.4. This table demonstrates the effect of investing in two stocks that are in the top 100 (by market capitalisation) on the ASX—News Corp. (NWS) and Newcrest Mining (NCM). These two stocks are in unrelated industries. NWS is in the media sector, while NCM is in the mining sector. Table 6.4 traces the value of an investment of $100 in NWS (about 6.8 shares) and $100 in NCM (about 36.6 shares) for the financial year that ended 30 June 2010. (For the purposes of the illustration, we have ignored dividends.) Panel B of Table 6.4 indicates that by the start of July 2010, the value of the portfolio would have been $269.97 (i.e. a gain of about 35% over the year). Panel C describes the monthly return on the investment in each of the stocks, as well as the portfolio. The last column in Panel C depicts the standard deviation of monthly returns on the investment in NWS, in NCM and in the two stocks combined. Whereas the standard deviation of returns on an investment in NWS and NCM was 7.73% and 11.59%, respectively, the standard deviation of monthly returns on the entire portfolio was less at 6.51%. Why?

To understand why the risk of the portfolio is smaller than the risk of the individual investment in NWS or NCM, consider Figure 6.6, which is a graphical plot of the data in Panel C of Table 6.4.

Figure 6.6 graphically demonstrates that, in any month, the returns on the individual investment in NWS and NCM were considerably more volatile than the returns on the portfolio. That is, the returns on the portfolio were smoother through time, or the portfolio was less risky. The reason is evident in the diagram. Poor returns on one stock are offset by stronger returns on the other. For example, the negative return on NWS in October 2009 was partly offset by the positive return on NCM in that month. Conversely, the negative return on NCM in December 2009 was partly offset by the positive return on NWS.

The process described above suggests that the extent to which the returns on the portfolio are 'smoothed' is dictated by the degree to which returns on the two stocks move together. Figure 6.6 demonstrates that the prices of NWS and NCM do not move in tandem—that is, they are not positively related. In fact, their returns are negatively related. It is this very feature that allows *offsetting* of returns to take place and the elimination of risk. Figure 6.7 plots the returns on NWS against the returns on NCM. The broken line best fits the relationship between returns on the two stocks, and demonstrates that there is a negative association between returns on NWS and returns on NCM.

| Table 6.4 | The effect of holding portfolios on investment risk |

	JUL 09	AUG 09	SEP 09	OCT 09	NOV 09	DEC 09	JAN 10	FEB 10	MAR 10	APR 10	MAY 10	JUN 10	JUL 10	STD. DEV.
Panel A: Stock Prices of News Corp. Limited (NWS) and Newcrest Mining Limited (NCM)														
NWS	14.63	15.08	16.02	15.29	15.06	17.83	16.44	17.53	18.5	19.44	18.23	16.83	16.4	
NCM	2.73	2.73	2.76	3	3.56	3.25	2.74	2.64	3.01	3.79	3.96	4.29	4.31	
Panel B: Value of $100 investment in NWS (6.835 shares) and $100 investment in NCM (36.630 shares) made on 1 July 2009														
NWS	100.00	103.07	109.50	104.51	102.94	121.87	112.37	119.82	126.45	132.87	124.60	115.03	112.09	
NCM	100.00	100.00	101.10	109.89	130.40	119.05	100.37	96.70	110.26	138.83	145.05	157.14	157.88	
Portfolio	200.00	203.07	210.60	214.40	233.34	240.92	212.73	216.52	236.70	271.70	269.66	272.18	269.97	
Panel C: Return on portfolios (%)														
NWS		3.08%	6.23%	−4.56%	−1.50%	18.39%	−7.80%	6.63%	5.53%	5.08%	−6.22%	−7.68%	−2.55%	7.73%
NCM		0.00%	1.10%	8.70%	18.67%	−8.71%	−15.69%	−3.65%	14.02%	25.91%	4.49%	8.33%	0.47%	11.59%
Portfolio		1.54%	3.70%	1.81%	8.83%	3.25%	−11.70%	1.78%	9.32%	14.78%	−0.75%	0.93%	−0.81%	6.51%

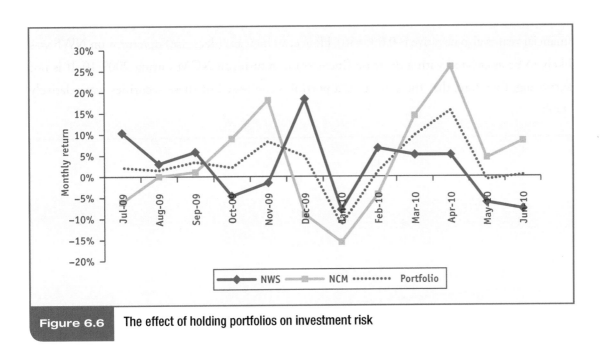

| Figure 6.6 | The effect of holding portfolios on investment risk |

A raw measure of the degree of association between two variables is the 'covariance'. The covariance of returns between two securities (σ_{ij}) can be calculated as follows (from a time series of historical returns):

$$\sigma_{ij} = \frac{\sum_{t=1}^{n} (r_{i,t} - \overline{r}_i)(r_{j,t} - \overline{r}_j)}{n-1} \tag{6.10}$$

where:

r_{it} = the return on security i during interval t

r_{jt} = the return on security j during interval t

$\bar{r}_i$ = expected return on security i

$\bar{r}_j$ = expected return on security j

n = the number of observations

Negative covariance implies that an increase in returns on asset i is associated with a decrease in returns on asset j, while a decrease in returns on asset i is associated with an increase in returns on asset j. Hence, if the covariance is negative, the returns on two securities are negatively correlated. If the covariance is positive, the returns on two securities are positively correlated (i.e. expected to move in the same direction). Example 6.3 illustrates the calculation of the covariance of returns between two securities.

Example 6.3 illustrates that the covariance of returns between NWS and NCM was negative (–0.010) for the last four calendar months of 2009, implying that their returns were negatively correlated. Figure 6.7 shows that the covariance of returns using the *entire* sample for the 2009/10 financial year is also negative (–0.000656). Hence, an increase (decrease) in returns on NWS was likely to be associated with a decrease (increase) in returns on NCM during 2009/10. It is not surprising, therefore, that the return on a portfolio composed of these securities was relatively stable.

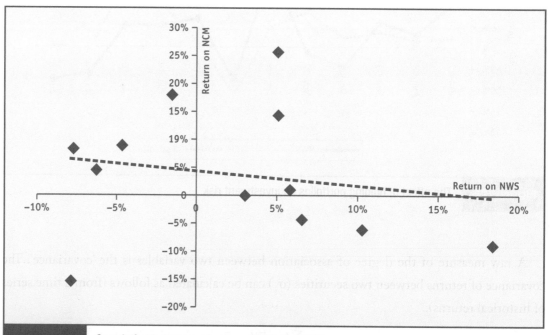

Figure 6.7   Correlation between returns on NWS and NCM

EXAMPLE 6.3

Calculating the covariance of returns between two stocks

QUESTION

Calculate the covariance of monthly returns on NWS and NCM for the last four months of 2009.

2009	Return on NWS	Return on NCM
Sep	0.0623	0.0110
Oct	−0.0456	0.0870
Nov	−0.0150	0.1867
Dec	0.1839	−0.0871

ANSWER

Call NWS security i, and NCM security j.

Calculate the mean return on NWS and NCM.

$$E(r) = \frac{\sum_{t=1}^{n} r_t}{n}$$

$E(r_i)$ = (0.0623 − 0.0456 − 0.0150 + 0.1839)/4 = 0.0464 (i.e. 4.64% per month)

$E(r_j)$ = (0.0110 + 0.0870 + 0.1867 − 0.0871)/4 = 0.0494 (i.e. 4.94% per month)

Calculate the sample covariance.

$$\sigma_{ij} = \frac{\sum_{t=1}^{n} (r_{it} - \bar{r}_i)(r_{jt} - \bar{r}_j)}{n-1}$$

= [(0.0623 − 0.0464) × (0.0110 − 0.0494) + (−0.0456 − 0.0464) × (0.0870 − 0.0494) +
(−0.0150 − 0.0464) × (0.1867 − 0.0494) + (0.1839 − 0.0464) × (−0.0871 − 0.0494)]/3

= −0.010

Hence, the covariance of returns between NWS and NCM is −0.010 for the period.

The effect of combining two stocks with returns that are positively related—that is, with positive covariance—is depicted in Figure 6.8. The figure describes the returns on a $100 investment in BHP Billiton (BHP), a $100 investment in Rio Tinto (RIO) and a $200 investment in a portfolio comprising both BHP and RIO, on a month-by-month basis during the 2009/10 financial year. Both stocks are in the top 10 listed securities on the ASX (by market capitalisation), and are the two largest Australian mining stocks. Hence, their returns are expected to be influenced by the same factors. The covariance of monthly returns on BHP and RIO was 0.004, evidence that their returns were positively correlated in 2009/10. Not surprisingly, then, there is little observed offsetting of returns to smooth the variability of returns on the portfolio. The standard deviation of returns on BHP, RIO and the portfolio was 5.68%, 7.66% and 6.53%, respectively, in 2009/10. Hence, there is only a little reduction in risk from combining these stocks in a portfolio.

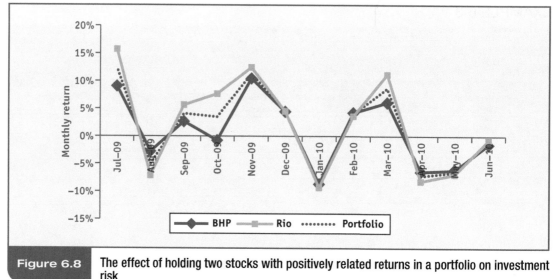

| **Figure 6.8** | The effect of holding two stocks with positively related returns in a portfolio on investment risk |

An alternative, and closely related, measure of the degree of association between two securities is the **correlation coefficient**. This is typically denoted by ρ_{ij} and can be calculated as follows.

$$\rho_{ij} = \sigma_{ij}/(\sigma_i\sigma_j) \tag{6.11}$$

Correlation coefficient
A coefficient whose value lies between +1 and −1 which indicates the direction and strength of the relationship between two variables.

where:

σ_{ij} = the covariance between returns on securities i and j

σ_i = the standard deviation of returns on security i

σ_j = the standard deviation of returns on security j

It is clear from Equation 6.11 that the correlation coefficient is calculated by modifying the covariance measure. Specifically, it takes the covariance between two securities and divides (or *standardises*) it by the product of the two securities' standard deviations. The effect of this standardisation is that the correlation coefficient measure will always lie between +1 and −1. This is useful because it gives a more readily interpretable measure of the degree of association between two securities. To illustrate, again consider the stocks in the previous examples, NWS and NCM. We know that the standard deviations of these stocks are 7.73% and 11.59%, respectively, and the covariance has been calculated at −0.000656.

Example 6.4 illustrates that the correlation of returns between NWS and NCM is negative, implying (like covariance) that an increase (decrease) in returns on NWS was likely to be associated with a decrease (increase) in returns on NCM. The usefulness of the correlation coefficient is that it is a more intuitive measure than the covariance. That is, the covariance of −0.000656 doesn't really tell us anything about the strength of the association between returns on the two securities, other than that the relationship is negative. On the other hand, the correlation coefficient indicates the strength of the association between the two securities.

EXAMPLE 6.4

Calculating the correlation coefficient between two stocks

QUESTION

Calculate the correlation coefficient for NWS and NCM for the 2009/10 financial year, given that the standard deviation of returns on the two stocks was 7.73% and 11.59%, respectively, while the covariance of returns between the two stocks is –0.000656.

ANSWER

Call NWS security i, and NCM security j. Applying Equation 6.11:

$$\rho_{ij} = \sigma_{ij}/(\sigma_i\sigma_j) = -0.000656/(0.0773 \times 0.1159) = -0.073$$

Hence, the correlation coefficient between NWS and NCM is –0.073.

At the extremes, securities for which $\rho = 1$ are said to be perfectly **positively correlated**, meaning that returns on the securities vary in a directly uniform manner. Those for which $\rho = -1$ are **perfectly negatively correlated**, meaning that changes in returns on the securities are inversely proportional. In practice, the vast majority of correlation coefficients lie within the extremes of +1 and –1. A correlation coefficient of 0 indicates that there is no association between the returns on two securities. A correlation coefficient of –0.073 indicates that there is a weak negative relationship between the returns of NWS and NCM.

Perfectly positively (negatively) correlated Two variables with a correlation coefficient of +1 (–1). This implies that an increase in the value of one variable results in a certain increase (decrease) in the value of another variable.

CONCEPT 6.4   Calculating the risk of portfolios

The previous section demonstrates that the risk of a portfolio is related to the standard deviation of returns on stocks in a portfolio, and the degree of correlation—measured by covariance—between returns on shares in the portfolio. But how exactly do these two variables combine to determine the total risk of a portfolio? The following equation can be used to calculate the variance of returns (σ_p^2) on a portfolio.

$$\sigma_p^2 = \sum_{i=1}^{n} \sum_{j=1}^{n} x_i x_j \sigma_{ij} \tag{6.12}$$

where:

x_i, x_j = proportion of the portfolio invested in security i or j

σ_{ij} = variance of security i if $i = j$, or the covariance of returns on securities i and j if $i \neq j$

Appendix 6.2 describes the process of expanding out Equation 6.12. In Example 6.5, the application of the formula is illustrated for a two-security portfolio utilising the case in Table 6.4 above.

EXAMPLE 6.5

Calculating the standard deviation of returns on a portfolio of securities

QUESTION

Calculate the risk of a $1 million portfolio, comprising $0.5 million in NWS and $0.5 million in NCM. The standard deviation of returns on NWS and NCM is 7.73% and 11.59%, respectively, and the covariance of returns on the stocks is –0.000656.

ANSWER

Labelling NWS security 1 and NCM security 2:

$$\sigma_p^2 = x_1^2\sigma_1^2 + x_2^2\sigma_2^2 + 2\,x_1 x_2 \sigma_{12} \text{ (see Appendix 6.2)}$$
$$\sigma_p^2 = (0.5^2 \times 0.0773^2) + (0.5^2 \times 0.1159^2) + (2 \times 0.5 \times 0.5 \times -0.000656)$$
$$= 0.004524$$

Therefore, the standard deviation of returns expected on the portfolio is about 6.73% (i.e. $\sqrt{0.004524}$ = 0.0673).

CONCEPT CHECK

6. What is the benefit of combining assets with low or negative correlation in a portfolio?

7. What specific elements contribute to the risk of a portfolio?

For the answers, go to MyFinanceLab

CONCEPT 6.5   Components of risk

It is clear at this stage that the risk of investing in a single security can be reduced by combining the security with others in a portfolio. But does this mean that (in the limit) all risk can be eliminated? The answer to this question is 'no!'. In the limit, if all available securities are held in a portfolio (2192 were listed on the ASX as at 30 June 2010), the change in the value of the portfolio will be the same as the movements in the *market* as a whole.

Figure 6.9 plots the monthly share price return for 10 well-known and large Australian companies during the 2009/10 financial year, which have been drawn from different industry sectors.[7] The returns on a portfolio that is equally weighted in each of the stocks and the returns on the All Ordinaries Index (AOI) are also depicted. Figure 6.9 demonstrates that if a large number of securities are held in a portfolio, there is considerable offsetting of returns. Despite this, the returns on the portfolio demonstrate considerable volatility. Quite clearly, the returns on the portfolio are quite similar to the returns on the AOI, which reflects broad (market-wide) movements.

Figure 6.9 can be used to understand the components of the total price variability, or *total* risk, associated with a security. The first element of risk relates to events that affect individual securities alone. This element of risk is commonly referred to as **unsystematic (or diversifiable) risk,** because it does not influence all securities and can be diversified away. Unsystematic risk relates to price movements that are caused by an event that influences a single company alone. One example of price volatility associated with the unsystematic risk of a security is the price movement in Qantas Airways Limited (QAN) on the afternoon of 4 November 2010. The price volatility experienced by Qantas and the All Ordinaries Index on this day is depicted in Figure 6.10. The diagram clearly illustrates a 1.7% fall in the price of QAN over a one-and-a-quarter hour period extending from 2:00 pm to 3:15 pm. This price volatility was unrelated to broad market movements. Over the same period, the All Ordinaries Index remained comparatively flat. The cause of the price volatility was a mid-air engine failure in one of its newer Airbus A380 passenger jets. The rest of the market was uninfluenced by the announcement because the information that caused the price fall was specific to Qantas. Share price movements associated with news announcements are discussed in detail in Chapter 10.

The second element of total risk is related to macroeconomic events that affect the prices of all securities and are reflected in broad market movements. This is commonly referred to as **systematic (or non-diversifiable) risk,** because it is common to all securities and cannot be diversified away. Systematic risk is driven by broad economic conditions. A good example of systematic risk

Unsystematic risk (or diversifiable risk)
The movement in the price of a security which results from an event specific to the security. Unsystematic risk can be eliminated by combining a security in a large portfolio.

Systematic risk (or non-diversifiable risk)
The movement in the price of a security which is driven by broad market-related factors. The systematic risk of a security is measured by beta, which measures the relationship between movements in the price of the security and movements in the market as a whole.

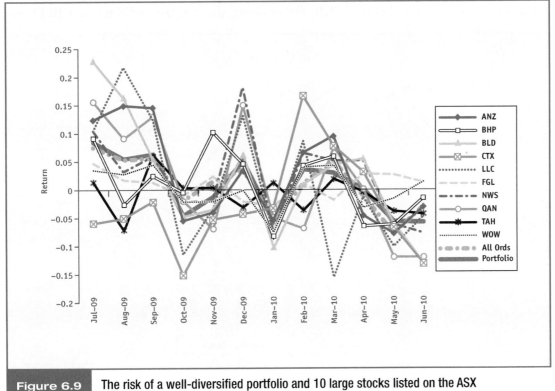

Figure 6.9   The risk of a well-diversified portfolio and 10 large stocks listed on the ASX

is the price movement caused by the Asian currency crisis that occurred in October 1997. Many companies in Australia are engaged in contracts with companies in Asian nations. The currency crisis that occurred in October 1997 saw the value of currencies of many Southeast Asian nations decline by 30–50% (relative to the US dollar), which influenced the viability of many Asian companies. The expected impact of the currency crisis on Australian companies resulted in a major reassessment of value for almost all shares listed on the ASX in October 1997. Hence, it was unlikely that investors would have held a portfolio in October 1997 that diversified away this element of share price risk. An analogous situation occurred in January 2010 (see Figure 6.9), when the return on almost all shares and the market declined relative to the previous month.

One of the implications of this analysis is that a well-diversified portfolio faces market risk alone. Taking this argument one step further, it must follow that the market risk of a portfolio is determined by the market risk of securities included in the portfolio. Hence, the extent to which a security responds to changes in broad economic conditions must dictate the degree of price variability experienced by a well-diversified portfolio. Holding securities in a portfolio that are not sensitive to broad market or economic movements will reduce the variability of returns on the portfolio, whereas holding securities that are broadly exposed to market movements will increase the risk of a portfolio comprising these securities. Figure 6.9 makes it quite clear that some Australian securities were more influenced than others by the broad change in market conditions experienced in January 2010. For example, the diagram indicates that BLD was

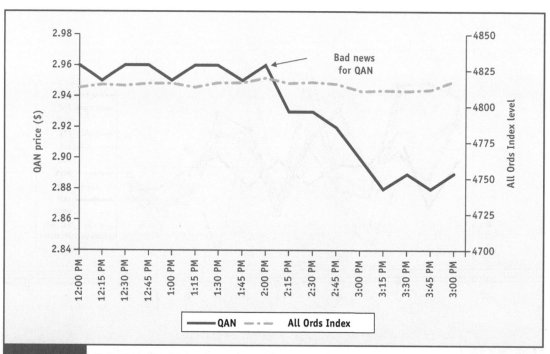

Figure 6.10   Unsystematic share price movement

influenced to a greater extent than was TAH. This is evident in the degree of price movement that occurred in these stocks in that month. (BLD experienced the largest fall in returns in January 2010, while TAH experienced a small increase in returns.) Hence, holding securities (or a greater portion of securities) such as BLD in a portfolio would have greatly increased the price variability experienced by the portfolio.

CONCEPT 6.6   Measurement of the components of total risk

The previous section demonstrated that when shares are combined into diversified portfolios investors face systematic or market risk alone. Intuitively, then, in pricing portfolios of securities or the individual securities making up the portfolio, investors need be concerned only with market risk. But how exactly can market risk be measured?

One way that market risk can be measured is by assessing, in a statistical sense, how sensitive the movement in a share is to a movement in the market. If we take the equation for a straight line:

$$Y = \alpha + \beta X \qquad\qquad (6.13)$$

where:

   Y = the dependent variable

   α = the intercept coefficient (Y intercept)

   β = the slope coefficient (slope of the line)

   X = the independent variable

and substitute in the return on a share (r_i) for Y, the return on the market (r_m) for X yields:

$$r_i = \alpha + \beta r_m \qquad\qquad (6.14)$$

where:

   r_i = return on share i

   α = the intercept coefficient (Y intercept)

   β = the slope coefficient (slope of the line)

   r_m = return on the market

Equation 6.14 is known as the 'market model'. Clearly, β measures the degree of exposure of the individual share i to market risk, because it measures the relationship between broad market movements and share i's price movements. The interpretation of β is set out in Table 6.5. Detail relating to the actual calculation of β is left to the next chapter.

Hence, a value of β of less than 1 suggests that, if the market moves by 10% in response to a broad economic event, the price of the share is expected to change by less than 10%. Conversely, a β of greater than 1 suggests that a market movement of 10% will be associated with a share price change of more than 10%. Finally, if β is equal to 1, the share carries the same level of risk as the market.

Table 6.5	Interpretation of β

IF	INTERPRETATION
β = 1	Share as risky as market
β > 1	Share more risky than market
β < 1	Share less risky than market

CONCEPT CHECK

8. What is the difference between total risk, unsystematic risk and systematic risk?
9. What is the impact of portfolio diversification on these respective risk elements?

For the answers, go to MyFinanceLab

Student Learning Centre

MyFinanceLab ■ To test your mastery of the content covered in this chapter and to create your own personalised study plan, go to MyFinanceLab: www.pearson.com.au/myfinancelab

CONCEPT CHECKLIST

In this chapter the following concepts were discussed:

➤ The riskiness and average historical rate of return on 90-day bank-accepted bills, 10-year government bonds, the All Ordinaries Index and the All Ordinaries Accumulation Index

➤ Calculation of total risk (standard deviation of returns) for individual securities using:
    – a historical time series of returns
    – a probability distribution

➤ The total risk of a portfolio, including:
    – the role of diversification in reducing portfolio risk
    – the effect of security return covariance on portfolio risk
    – the calculation of portfolio risk (standard deviation of returns)

➤ Components of total risk, including:
    – unsystematic risk
    – systematic risk and β

SELF-TEST QUESTIONS

The estimated returns on two shares, A and B, are given in the table below for each of three possible economic states, along with their estimated probability of occurring.

	Probability (%)	Return (%) on A	Return (%) on B
Good	30	16	2
Average	50	5	8
Bad	20	−5	10

(a) Calculate the expected return and standard deviation of returns for each share.

(b) Calculate the correlation coefficient between the shares.

(c) Calculate the risk of a portfolio consisting of equal proportions of each share.

Self-test answer

(a) Expected returns: $E(R_A) = (0.3 \times 16\%) + (0.5 \times 5\%) + (0.2 \times -5\%) = 6.3\%$

$E(R_B) = (0.3 \times 2\%) + (0.5 \times 8\%) + (0.2 \times 10\%) = 6.6\%$

Variance of returns: $\sigma_A^2 = [0.3 \times (16\% - 6.3\%)^2] + [0.5 \times (5\% - 6.3\%)^2] +$

$[0.2 \times (-5\% - 6.3\%)^2] = 54.61$ squared %

$\sigma_B^2 = [0.3 \times (2\% - 6.6\%)^2] + [0.5 \times (8\% - 6.6\%)^2] +$

$[0.2 \times (10\% - 6.6\%)^2] = 9.64$ squared %

Standard deviation of returns: $\sigma_A = \sqrt{54.61\%} = 7.4\%$ or 0.074

$\sigma_B = \sqrt{9.64\%} = 3.1\%$ or 0.031

(b) First calculate the covariance:

$= [0.3 \times (16\% - 6.3\%) \times (2\% - 6.6\%)] + [0.5 \times (5\% - 6.3\%) \times (8\% - 6.6\%)] + [0.2 \times (-5\% - 6.3\%) \times$ $(10\% - 6.6\%)] = -21.98$ squared % or −0.0022

Now calculate the correlation coefficient: $-21.98/(7.4 \times 3.1) = -0.96$

(c) Risk of a portfolio comprising 50% invested in each share. First, labelling A security i, and B security j:

$\sigma_p^2 = x_A^2 \sigma_A^2 + x_B^2 \sigma_B^2 + 2x_A x_A \sigma_{AB}$

$\sigma_p^2 = (0.5^2 \times 0.074^2) + (0.5^2 \times 0.031^2) + (2 \times 0.5 \times 0.5 \times -0.0022)$

$= 0.000\ 509$

Therefore, the standard deviation of returns expected on the portfolio is about 2.26% (= $\sqrt{0.000\ 509}$).

DISCUSSION QUESTIONS

1. If there is some risk attaching to the cash flow expected from investing in an asset, what does this imply about the rate of return required by an investor before investing in the asset?

2. Outline the key differences between zero-coupon bonds and coupon-paying bonds. Which type of bond's price is more sensitive to interest rate changes?

3. True or false? The price of a five-year, 10% p.a. coupon-paying bond is greater than its face value; therefore, the bond's yield to maturity is greater than 10% p.a.

4. What does a share index measure? Why is this of use to investors?

5. Why does the ASX recognise and report different share indices (e.g. the S&P/ASX 100, 200 and 300 indices)? What differential information is conveyed by these indices?

6. What is the advantage of an accumulation index, such as the S&P/ASX 200 Accumulation Index or the All Ordinaries Accumulation Index, over the better known S&P/ASX 200 or All Ordinaries indices?

7. Why is it useful to calculate the standard deviation of expected returns on a security? What is the main practical reality that limits the usefulness of this calculation?

8. What is a portfolio? How can investors reduce investment risk by constructing an investment portfolio?

9. Give an intuitive explanation as to why investors cannot reduce investment risk by constructing an investment portfolio comprising perfectly positively correlated assets.

10. The diagram presented in Figure 6.6 indicates that the variability of investment returns can be reduced by combining negatively correlated assets in a portfolio. What drives this outcome?

11. True or false? When considering adding an asset to a large, diversified portfolio, only the asset's standard deviation need be considered.

12. Explain both the covariance and the correlation between two securities. What is the difference between the two? When is one of the measures preferable to the other?

13. The total risk of an individual stock comprises both systematic and unsystematic risk. Explain these two risk components and describe how each is affected by increasing the number of stocks in a portfolio.

14. How does unsystematic risk arise? Will investors be compensated for bearing this risk? Explain.

15. What are some of the potential systematic risks faced by investors? Discuss by drawing on your knowledge of recent events in the financial markets. Why are these risks difficult to diversify away?

16. The current market risk (standard deviation of the All Ords Index) is 15%. Someone is offering to sell you a portfolio of stocks that supposedly has a standard deviation of 10%. Is this possible? What about a portfolio of bonds?

17. Refer to Table 6.2 in the chapter, which implies that there was an average real risk premium (relative to BABs) of 5.67% on the All Ordinaries Accumulation Index over the period 1980–2009.
    (a) What does 'real' refer to in this context?
    (b) Discuss some of the factors that result in this (equity) risk premium.
    (c) What is the implication of this risk premium on forecasting future expected returns on the Australian share market?

PRACTICAL QUESTIONS

BASIC
1. What is the market price of a $100 000 face value 10-year bond with six years remaining to maturity, issued at a coupon rate of 6.25%, with coupons paid (a) annually and (b) semi-annually?

BASIC
2. What is the current price of a 90-day BAB issued 11 days ago (i.e. with 80 days to maturity), given a market yield of 6.4% p.a.?

3. A BAB has a face value of $1 million, a yield of 5.5% and 90 days to maturity. Assuming that the yield does not change, what is its price (a) today, (b) in 30 days' time and (c) in 75 days' time? Explain your results. **BASIC**

4. There are two states in the economy: good and bad with equal probability of occurrence. You have the choice of two investments. One earns you $5 from a $100 investment irrespective of economic conditions. The second investment earns you $10 in the good state, but nothing in the bad state. Calculate the expected return and standard deviation of returns on these two investments. Which investment would you prefer and why? **BASIC**

5. Your younger siblings have decided to set up a lemonade stand tomorrow to fund their Christmas consumption. The total initial investment required for this venture is $100. The weather report suggested a 60% probability of a sunny day, 25% probability of a cloudy day, and a 15% probability of rain. If it's a sunny day, your siblings expect to make $50. However, if it's cloudy or rainy, they expect to make $10 and $2 respectively. As a university finance student, you are asked by your siblings to calculate the expected return and standard deviation of this lemonade venture. **BASIC**

6. The following table details an analyst's prediction of the probabilities of different states of the market over the next year, along with the forecast returns on security A in each different market state. Calculate the expected return and standard deviation of returns on security A. **BASIC**

State	Probability	Return
Very good	0.1	31%
Good	0.3	13%
Average	0.4	12%
Bad	0.2	–9%

7. The following table shows the probabilities of all possible economic conditions next year, along with the associated returns on a security under each market condition. **BASIC**

	Probability	Return
Boom	0.2	16.0%
Moderate	0.5	9.0%
Recession	0.3	2.0%

Calculate the expected return and standard deviation of returns on the security.

8. You form a portfolio by investing $5000 in each of securities A and B. Security A has a standard deviation of returns equal to 15%, whereas security B's standard deviation of returns is 10%. If the returns on A and B are uncorrelated, what is the standard deviation of your portfolio? **INTERMEDIATE**

9. Assets Alpha and Beta have the following estimated returns in the three possible states of the market.

	State of the market		
	1	**2**	**3**
Return on Alpha	12%	3%	−20%
Return on Beta	4%	2%	−5%
Probability of state occurring	0.5	0.4	0.1

(a) Calculate the expected returns of assets Alpha and Beta.

(b) Calculate the variance and standard deviation of assets Alpha and Beta.

(c) Calculate the covariance and correlation coefficient between assets Alpha and Beta.

10. Similar to Question 6 above, the following table details an analyst's prediction of the probabilities of different states of the market over the next year, along with forecast returns on security B in each different market state.

State	Probability	Return
Very good	0.1	15%
Good	0.3	18%
Average	0.4	10%
Bad	0.2	3%

Calculate:

(a) the expected return and standard deviation of returns on security B

(b) the covariance of returns between securities A (from Question 6) and B

(c) the correlation coefficient for securities A and B.

11. Consider shares in two companies, X and Y, as follows:

	$E(R_i)$	σ_i
Share X	10%	20%
Share Y	30%	50%

The correlation between X and Y (i.e. ρ_{XY}) = 0.4

(a) What is the expected return and standard deviation of returns on a portfolio comprising 25% invested in share X and 75% invested in share Y?

(b) Recalculate the portfolio's expected return and standard deviation assuming equal weights in X and Y.

12. Using the following stock price data for BHP:

August 2007	38.42
September 2007	44.55
October 2007	46.10
November 2007	42.98

(a) Calculate the standard deviation of returns on BHP.

(b) Assuming that the returns in these months are a random draw from a normal distribution generating the returns on BHP, provide an interpretation of the risk from investing in BHP.

(c) Do you realistically believe that the standard deviation of returns you have calculated is a reasonable estimate of the risk of investing in BHP?

13. Use the following share price data for BHP Billiton Limited (BHP) and Rio Tinto Limited (RIO) to answer these questions.

	RIO	BHP
August 2007	93.52	38.42
September 2007	108.22	44.55
October 2007	110	46.1
November 2007	145.19	42.98

(a) Calculate the standard deviation of returns on BHP and RIO.

(b) Calculate the covariance and correlation coefficient between BHP and RIO.

(c) Calculate the variance of an equally weighted portfolio composed of the shares.

14. On 15 June 2007 an Australian Commonwealth government bond with a coupon rate of 5.75% maturing in June 2011 was trading at a yield of 6.87%. How much must be paid to purchase the bond?

15. Suppose that 10-year government bonds with a face value of $1 million and coupon rate of 6% p.a. (interest paid semi-annually) is currently trading at par. What would happen if the market interest rate increases to 6.5% p.a. (compounded semi-annually)? Is this consistent with the notion that government securities are typically risk-free?

FURTHER READING

For a book which includes Windows-based graphics software and allows you to plot stock returns and observe directly the effects of portfolio diversification see:

- O'Brien, J. and Srivastava, S. (1995), *Investments: A Visual Approach*, South-Western College Publishing, USA.
- For information on the calculation of the ASX indices and stocks included in these indices see: <www.asx.com.au>.

For information on the interpretation of yields on Australian bonds refer to:

- Reserve Bank of Australia, Price and Yield Formulae used by the Reserve Bank of Australia, Reserve Bank of Australia.

NOTES

1. See equation 2.11.
2. S. Salsbury and K. Sweeney (1988), *The Bull, the Bear and the Kangaroo*, Allen & Unwin, Sydney.
3. The nominal returns have been converted to real returns using the Fisher Relation discussed in Chapter 4 (see equation 4.4).
4. R. R. Officer (1989), 'Rates of return to shares, bond yields and inflation rates: An historical perspective', in R. Ball, P. Brown, F. J. Finn and R. R. Officer (eds), *Share Markets and Portfolio Theory*, 2nd edn, University of Queensland Press, Brisbane.
5. Of course, these numbers need to be interpreted with a grain of salt as they are based on a short period of time (30 years). For historical averages generated over a longer period of time, see T. Taylor (1998), 'Australia stands out in long-term real stock market returns', ASX Perspective, 2nd Quarter.
6. See D. Gujarati (2003), *Essentials of Econometrics*, 4th edn, McGraw-Hill, New York, Appendix A, 888.
7. The codes, name and respective sectors of the stocks are ANZ (ANZ Banking Group/Banks), BHP (BHP Billiton/Materials), BLD (Boral/Materials), CTX (Caltex/Energy), LLC (Lend Lease Corporation/Real Estate), FGL (Foster's Group/Food Beverage and Tobacco), NWS (News Corp./Media), QAN (QANTAS/Transportation), TAH (Tabcorp/Consumer Services), and WOW (Woolworths/Food and Staples Retailing).

APPENDIX 6.1

RATES OF RETURN ON VARIOUS AUSTRALIAN SECURITIES, 1979–2009

	Raw numbers					Raw returns (%)				Real return (%)			
				All Ordinaries				All Ordinaries				All Ordinaries	
Year	90-day bank-accepted bills % p.a.	10-year bonds % p.a.	CPI (%)	Index Points	Accumulation Index Points	90-day bank-accepted bills % p.a.	10-year bonds % p.a.	Index Points	Accumulation Index Points	90-day bank-accepted bills % p.a.	10-year bonds % p.a.	Index Points	Accumulation Index Points
1979	9.51	8.8	10.1	500	1000	9.510	8.800						
1980	11.78	10.1	9.2	713.5	1488.6	11.780	10.100	42.700	48.860	2.36	0.82	30.68	36.32
1981	14.50	12.6	11.3	595.5	1296	14.500	12.600	−16.538	−12.938	2.88	1.17	−25.01	−21.78
1982	17.12	15.0	11.0	485.4	1116.3	17.120	15.000	−18.489	−13.866	5.51	3.60	−26.57	−22.40
1983	13.17	14.0	8.6	775.3	1862	13.170	14.000	59.724	66.801	4.21	4.97	47.08	53.59
1984	11.50	13.5	2.6	726.1	1820	11.500	13.500	−6.346	−2.256	8.67	10.62	−8.72	−4.73
1985	15.04	13.4	8.2	1003.8	2621.9	15.040	13.400	38.245	44.060	6.32	4.81	27.77	33.14
1986	17.19	14.9	9.8	1473.2	3991	17.190	14.900	46.762	52.218	6.73	4.64	33.66	38.63
1987	14.33	13.4	7.1	1318.9	3677.5	14.330	13.400	−10.474	−7.855	6.75	5.88	−16.41	−13.96
1988	12.29	12.9	7.6	1487.2	4334.9	12.290	12.900	12.761	17.876	4.36	4.93	4.80	9.55
1989	17.21	13.0	7.8	1649.8	5089.2	17.210	13.000	10.933	17.401	8.73	4.82	2.91	8.91
1990	15.57	12.9	6.9	1279.8	4197.7	15.570	12.900	−22.427	−17.517	8.11	5.61	−27.43	−22.84
1991	10.91	12.1	1.5	1651.4	5634.9	10.910	12.100	29.036	34.238	9.27	10.44	27.13	32.25
1992	6.93	9.4	0.3	1549.9	5504.6	6.930	9.400	−6.146	−2.312	6.61	9.07	−6.43	−2.60
1993	5.34	8.9	1.9	2173.6	8001.6	5.340	8.900	40.241	45.362	3.38	6.87	37.63	42.65
1994	5.19	6.7	2.5	1912.7	7307.8	5.190	6.700	−12.003	−8.671	2.62	4.10	−14.15	−10.90
1995	7.78	10.0	5.1	2203	8783.1	7.780	10.000	15.177	20.188	2.55	4.66	9.59	14.36
1996	7.36	8.2	1.5	2424.6	10065.2	7.360	8.200	10.059	14.597	5.77	6.60	8.43	12.90
1997	5.58	7.4	−0.2	2558.9	11296	5.580	7.400	5.539	12.228	5.79	7.62	5.75	12.45
1998	5.10	6.1	1.6	2813.4	12610.1	5.100	6.100	9.946	11.633	3.44	4.43	8.21	9.88
1999	4.89	5.0	1.8	3152.5	14640.1	4.890	5.000	12.053	16.098	3.04	3.14	10.07	14.05
2000	6.09	7.0	5.8	3206.2	15166.6	6.090	7.000	1.703	3.596	0.27	1.13	−3.87	−2.08
2001	5.22	5.5	3.1	3416.6	16701.8	5.220	5.500	6.562	10.122	2.06	2.33	3.36	6.81
2002	4.68	6.0	3.0	2991.7	15351.3	4.680	6.000	−12.436	−8.086	1.63	2.91	−14.99	−10.76
2003	4.79	5.2	2.4	3293.8	17786.7	4.790	5.200	10.098	15.864	2.33	2.73	7.52	13.15
2004	5.47	5.6	2.6	4045.3	22690.1	5.470	5.600	22.816	27.568	2.80	2.92	19.70	24.34
2005	5.63	5.2	2.8	4708.8	27474.9	5.630	5.200	16.402	21.088	2.75	2.33	13.23	17.79
2006	6.39	5.9	3.3	5644.3	34334.2	6.390	5.890	19.867	24.966	2.99	2.51	16.04	20.97
2007	7.29	6.3	3.0	6421	40498.4	7.290	6.330	13.761	17.954	4.17	3.23	10.45	14.52
2008	4.08	4.0	3.7	3659.3	24143.2	4.080	3.990	−43.010	−40.385	0.37	0.28	−45.04	−42.51
2009	4.21	5.7	2.1	4882.7	33698.6	4.210	5.730	33.433	39.578	2.07	3.56	30.69	36.71
									Average	4.28	4.43	5.54	9.95

Sources: Reserve Bank of Australia, Bulletin, various issues, and Bloomberg.

APPENDIX 6.2

EXPANDING OUT THE EXPRESSION FOR THE VARIANCE OF A TWO-SECURITY PORTFOLIO

For a two-security portfolio, Equation 6.12 can be written as follows:

$$\sigma_p^2 = \sum_{i=1}^{2} \sum_{j=1}^{2} x_i x_j \sigma_{ij} \qquad \text{(A6.2.1)}$$

The double summation signs can be expanded out one at a time. The summation notation (Σ) simply means: create n new elements; wherever you see an i in the first element, replace it with a 1 and wherever you see an i in the second element replace it with a 2. Hence, after expanding Equation A6.2.1 for the first summation sign:

$$\sigma_p^2 = \sum_{j=1}^{2} x_1 x_j \sigma_{1j} + \sum_{j=1}^{2} x_2 x_j \sigma_{2j} \qquad \text{(A6.2.2)}$$

The process can be repeated for each of the remaining summation signs. Hence, two new elements are created for each of the summation signs, as follows:

$$\sigma_p^2 = x_1 x_1 \sigma_{11} + x_1 x_2 \sigma_{12} + x_2 x_1 \sigma_{21} + x_2 x_2 \sigma_{22} \qquad \text{(A6.2.3)}$$

The above can be simplified as follows (making use of the fact that σ_{ij} = variance of security i if $i = j$, or the covariance of returns on securities i and j if $i \neq j$):

$$\sigma_p^2 = x_1^2 \sigma_1^2 + x_2^2 \sigma_2^2 + 2 x_1 x_2 \sigma_{12} \qquad \text{(A6.2.4)}$$

which is an equation that can be applied to calculating the standard deviation of returns on a two-security portfolio.

Expanding out Equation 6.12 for the variance of a portfolio comprising three or more securities is analogous to the two-security case.

APPENDIX 6.3

A DESCRIPTION OF TREASURY BONDS AND BOND MARKETS IN AUSTRALIA

Treasury bonds are debt securities issued by the Australian government. They are generally issued by the government through a tender process. Table A6.3.1 lists the Treasury bond tenders that took place in November and December 2010.

The table illustrates that the federal government has many tenders each month, and issues Treasury bonds with 2 years to 18 years to maturity. Treasury bonds pay interest every six months, on the 15th day of the month. One of the months in which bonds pay interest coincides with the maturity month. Hence, bonds with a maturity of February pay interest in February and again six months later in July. Those maturing in June pay interest in June and December, and so on.

Figure A6.3.1 illustrates the buying and selling prices quoted by different bond dealers on an electronic page on Bloomberg.[1] The page depicts the dealer quotes for the Australian Commonwealth government bond with a 6.75 per cent coupon rate and maturing in November 2006 (ACGB 6¾ 11/06).[2] The Bloomberg page illustrates that the buying and selling prices are quoted in yields in the 'Bid Yield/Ask Yield' column. For example, Deutsche Bank Group (a bond dealer) is willing to buy the bonds at a yield of 5.328 and sell them at a yield of 5.308. In order to convert these yields to a dollar value, a bond pricing formula is needed. This is discussed in the next section.

Table A6.3.1 Treasury bond tenders, November and December 2010

TENDER DATE	TENDER NUMBER	YIELD (%)	MATURITY DATE	AMOUNT ALLOTTED ($ MILLIONS)
8 Dec 2010	419	5.5	21 Jan 2018	650
3 Dec 2010	418	4.75	15 Nov 2012	700
1 Dec 2010	417	4.50	15 April 2020	500
26 Nov 2010	416	5.50	15 Dec 2013	700
24 Nov 2010	415	5.50	21 Jan 2018	800
19 Nov 2010	414	4.50	21 Oct 2014	700
17 Nov 2010	413	4.50	15 Apr 2020	500
12 Nov 2010	412	4.75	15 Jun 2016	700
10 Nov 2010	411	5.75	15 July 2022	500
5 Nov 2010	410	4.50	21 Oct 2014	700
3 Nov 2010	409	4.50	15 Apr 2020	500

Source: Reproduced with permission of the Reserve Bank of Australia.

A summary of trading in Treasury bonds for each day is reported in *The Australian Financial Review*. For example, Figure A6.3.2 illustrates the Treasury section of *The Australian Financial Review* on 8 March 2012. It sets out the results of tenders of various types of Treasury bonds. At the bottom of the section is the average yield at which the bonds were quoted across dealers at 4.30 pm (e.g. as in the Bloomberg page). The yields of all of the bonds underlying the bond basket are reported in the exhibit. For example, at 4.30 pm on 15 March 2004, the bonds maturing in November 2006, October 2007 and August 2008 were quoted at average yields of 4.99, 5.095 and 5.175 per cent, respectively. While the maturities of these bonds are approximately 7 years, 9 years and 11 years, respectively, their yields are reasonably similar and differ by a maximum of 18.5 basis points (or 0.185 of 1 per cent).

TREASURY

TREASURY BOND TENDER
Results of Tender Number 516 – 7 March, 2012

Series Offered: 5.25% 15 March 2019. Amount offered $700 min. Take-up by RBA:–. Amount allotted $700 min. Weighted average issue yield: 3.8459%. The range of yields accepted: 3.840–3.850 (%). Amount allotted at the highest accepted yield as a percentage of the amount bid at that yield: 58%. Average ratio: 2.10.

TREASURY INDEXED BOND TENDER
Results of Tender Number 67– 22 November, 2011

Series Offered: 2.50% 20 September 2030. Amount offered $100 min. Take-up by RBA:–. Amount allotted $100 min. Weighted average bid: 1.8454%. Worst bid–Best bid: 1.945–1.805 (%) Number of bids allocated in full: 6. Coverage ratio: 3.07.

Series Offered: Amount offered. Take-up by RBA:. Amount allotTed. Weighted average bid: %. World bid–Best bid:–(%). Number of bids allocated in full:. Coverage ratio:.

TREASURY NOTE TENDER
Results of Tender Number 05/12–1 March, 2012

Maturity date	Allocated ($m)	Yield (%)	Yield Range (%)
24 February 2012	1000	4.0656	4.000–4.150
9 March 2012	1000	4.0332	3.950–4.100
27 April 2012	1000	4.1976	4.170–4.220
11 May 2012	1000	4.2308	4.170–4.250
8 June 2012	1000	4.2162	4.140–4.250

TREASURY INDEXED BONDS

Aug 2015	1.075	Aug 2020	1.145	Sep 2025	1.315	Sep 2030	1.480

Figure A6.3.2   **Treasury section of The Australian Financial Review, 8 March 2012**

Source: The Australian Financial Review, 8 March 2012

Quotes and values

When market participants offer bonds for sale in Australia, they do not typically quote the sales price in dollars but in yield points.[3] In order to convert the quoted yields of bonds into a dollar value which represents the price of the contract, the following Reserve Bank of Australia (RBA) bond formula needs to be applied:[4]

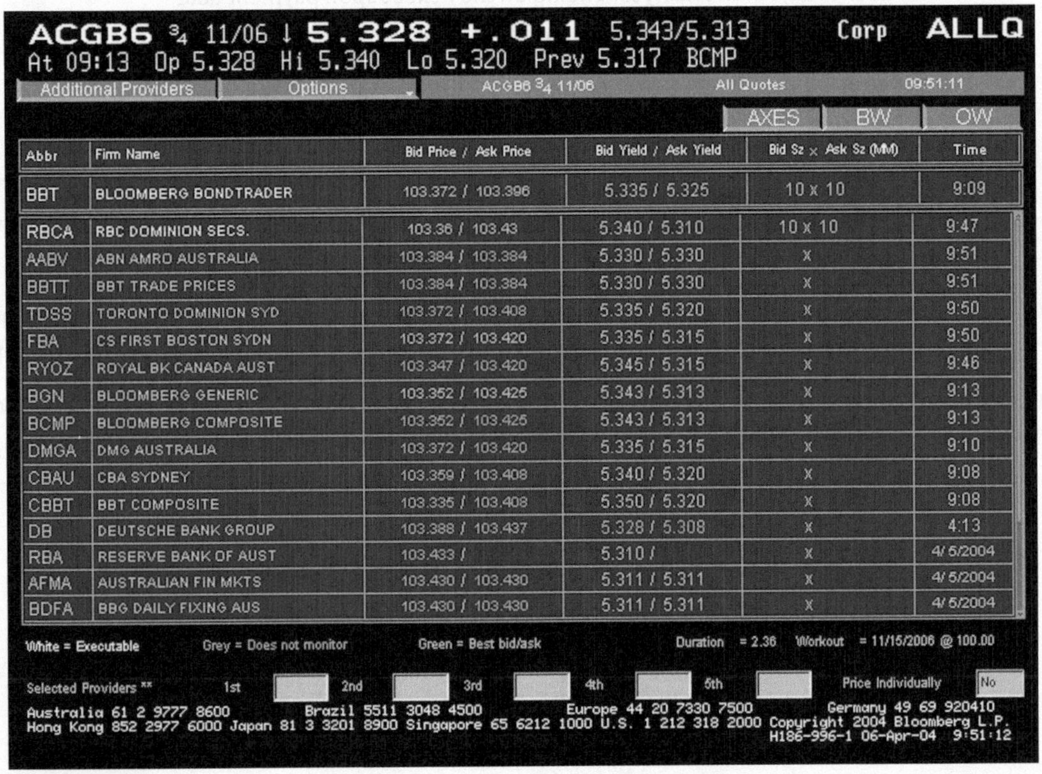
ACGB6 ¾ 11/06 ↓ 5.328 +.011 5.343/5.313 Corp ALLQ
At 09:13 Op 5.328 Hi 5.340 Lo 5.320 Prev 5.317 BCMP
Additional Providers | Options | ACGB6 ¾ 11/06 | All Quotes | 09:51:11
AXES | BW | OW

Abbr	Firm Name	Bid Price / Ask Price	Bid Yield / Ask Yield	Bid Sz x Ask Sz (MM)	Time
BBT	BLOOMBERG BONDTRADER	103.372 / 103.396	5.335 / 5.325	10 x 10	9:09
RBCA	RBC DOMINION SECS.	103.36 / 103.43	5.340 / 5.310	10 x 10	9:47
AABV	ABN AMRO AUSTRALIA	103.384 / 103.384	5.330 / 5.330	x	9:51
BBTT	BBT TRADE PRICES	103.384 / 103.384	5.330 / 5.330	x	9:51
TDSS	TORONTO DOMINION SYD	103.372 / 103.408	5.335 / 5.320	x	9:50
FBA	CS FIRST BOSTON SYDN	103.372 / 103.420	5.335 / 5.315	x	9:50
RYOZ	ROYAL BK CANADA AUST	103.347 / 103.420	5.345 / 5.315	x	9:46
BGN	BLOOMBERG GENERIC	103.352 / 103.425	5.343 / 5.313	x	9:13
BCMP	BLOOMBERG COMPOSITE	103.352 / 103.425	5.343 / 5.313	x	9:13
DMGA	DMG AUSTRALIA	103.372 / 103.420	5.335 / 5.315	x	9:10
CBAU	CBA SYDNEY	103.359 / 103.408	5.340 / 5.320	x	9:08
CBBT	BBT COMPOSITE	103.335 / 103.408	5.350 / 5.320	x	9:08
DB	DEUTSCHE BANK GROUP	103.388 / 103.437	5.328 / 5.308	x	4:13
RBA	RESERVE BANK OF AUST	103.433 /	5.310 /	x	4/5/2004
AFMA	AUSTRALIAN FIN MKTS	103.430 / 103.430	5.311 / 5.311	x	4/5/2004
BDFA	BBG DAILY FIXING AUS	103.430 / 103.430	5.311 / 5.311	x	4/5/2004

White = Executable Grey = Does not monitor Green = Best bid/ask Duration = 2.36 Workout = 11/15/2006 @ 100.00
Selected Providers ** 1st 2nd 3rd 4th 5th Price Individually No
Australia 61 2 9777 8600 Brazil 5511 3048 4500 Europe 44 20 7330 7500 Germany 49 69 920410
Hong Kong 852 2977 6000 Japan 81 3 3201 8900 Singapore 65 6212 1000 U.S. 1 212 318 2000 Copyright 2004 Bloomberg L.P.
H186-996-1 06-Apr-04 9:51:12

Figure A6.3.1 Bond quotes on Bloomberg screen at 9.51 am on 6 April 2004

Source:

$$P = V^{f/d}(g(1 + a_n) + 100V^n) \tag{A6.3.1}$$

where:

i = quoted yield ÷ 2

$$V = \frac{1}{1 + i}$$

$$a_n = \frac{1 - V^n}{i} = V + V^2 + \dots V^n$$

f = number of days until the next coupon payment

d = number of days in the half-year ending on the next coupon payment date

g = half-yearly coupon payment per $100 of face value

n = half-years from the next coupon payment until maturity

Equation A6.3.1 gives the price of the bond for every $100 of face value. It is nothing more than an equation which gives the present value of the annuity composed of the coupon payments until maturity (the first term in brackets), plus the present value of the face value of the bonds (the second term in brackets). The term outside the brackets is merely an adjustment to the present value of the coupon and face value brought about because there is generally something less than one full compounding period remaining until the first coupon payment. Example A6.3.1 provides an illustration of the calculation of the value of bonds.

EXAMPLE A6.3.1

Application of RBA bond pricing formula

On 15 March 2004, a 6.75 per cent Treasury bond maturing in November 2006 is trading at a yield of 4.990 per cent. How much must be paid in order to purchase the bond?

Given that the yield is 0.0499, then:

i = 0.0499 ÷ 2 = 0.024 95 per 6 months

$$v = \frac{1}{1 + i} = \frac{1}{1 + 0.024\ 95} = 0.9757$$

The bond matures in November, and hence the coupon payments for the bond occur on the 15th day of November, and then six months later in May. Given that the current date is 15 March 2004, the next coupon payment will occur on 15 May 2004. Since the maturity date is 15 November 2006, the number of full half-year periods from the next coupon payment until maturity (n) is 5. Hence:

$$a_n = \frac{1 - v^n}{i} = \frac{1 - 0.9757^5}{0.024\ 95} = 4.6465$$

Since the six-monthly coupon rate is 3.375 per cent (6.75 ÷ 2), the coupon per $100 of face value ($g$) is $3.375. Since the current date is 15 March 2004, and the next coupon payment is on 15 May 2004, the number of days until the next coupon payment (f) is 61.

Since the current date is 15 March 2004, the start of the current half-year period was 15 November 2003 and the number of days in the half-year ending on the next coupon payment date (d) is 182.

We now have the values for each of the elements in the bond valuation formula, and can make a substitution to get the value of the bond:

$$= V^{f/d}(g(1 + a_n) + 100V^n)$$
$$= 0.9757^{61/182} \times [3.375 \times (1 + 4.6465) + 100 \times 0.9757^5]$$
$$= \$106.60 \text{ per } \$100 \text{ of face value}$$

Level of trading activity

Table A6.3.2 provides data on the level of trading activity in Commonwealth government securities in Australia in recent years.

The table reveals an interesting trend. The level of trading activity in Commonwealth government bonds has increased sharply since 2008/09. In fact, trading activity has increased by roughly 130 per cent from 2008/09 to 2010/11.

Table A6.3.2 Turnover in Commonwealth government securities ($ millions)

	COMMONWEALTH GOVERNMENT BONDS
2006/07	320 761
2007/08	284 681
2008/09	299 261
2009/10	452 481
2010/11	689 834

Source: Australian Financial markets Association, <www.afma.com.au>.

Trading mechanism

There is an active secondary market in Commonwealth government securities. Unlike shares, which trade on an organised exchange, trading in Commonwealth government securities is off-exchange in a market known as the over-the-counter (OTC) market. The main participants in the OTC market are dealers. Dealers are banks that buy and sell securities on their own account. Table A6.3.3 lists the major dealers in Commonwealth government bonds. Dealers trade securities with their own clients—for example, major fund managers who want to buy or sell bonds. Dealers also trade with each other in the so-called *inter-dealer market*. For example, a trade between ABN AMRO and CS First Boston in 10-year government bonds is referred to as a trade in the inter-dealer market.

Transactions require dealers and other buyers and sellers to communicate their desires to trade. There are a number of mechanisms through which this takes place in bond markets. Dealers post quotes with information vendors. The two main information vendors are Bloomberg and Reuters. Figure A6.3.1 earlier provided an illustration of the quotes posted by dealers on Bloomberg. If a market participant wants to trade against these quotes (which are not guaranteed), they must call the dealer who is posting the quotes in order to effect a transaction. Alternatively, a market participant can phone dealers directly looking for the best price and then consummate a trade.

Another mechanism through which dealers execute transactions in the inter-dealer market is electronic inter-dealer trading systems operated by commercial companies.[6] The one main such systems in Australia is operated by ICAP Limited which is listed on the London Stock Exchange. Australian Commonwealth government bonds are listed on ICAP electronic trading systems, and allow dealers to place buy and sell orders and to execute trades automatically against each other. Most of the dealers listed in Table A6.3.3 have access to ICAP.

Chapter 3 introduced corporate bonds, which are bonds issued by companies. The corporate bond market, including quoting and trading conventions, is virtually identical to the Treasury bond market.

Source: Appendix 6.3 is taken from Frino, A. and Jarnecic, E. (2005), *Introduction to Futures and Options Markets in Australia*, Pearson Education Australia.

Table A6.3.3	Major dealers in Commonwealth government debt markets		
1	ABN AMRO Australia	6	National Australia Bank
2	Commonwealth Bank of Australia	7	RBC Dominion Securities
3	CS First Boston Australia	8	Toronto Dominion
4	Deutsche Bank	9	UBS Capital Markets
5	Macquarie Bank	10	Westpac Banking Corporation

Source: Sydney Futures Exchange Bulletin, 35/03.

NOTES

1. Bloomberg are an information vendor. They electronically collect information from various market participants and disseminate this information to the market.
2. The page also includes various averages of quotes on the day depicted (e.g. Bloomberg Generic and Bloomberg Composite), as well as averages relating to trading on the previous day (e.g. Reserve Bank of Australia, Australian Financial Markets and BBG Daily Fixings Australia). Bloomberg Bond Trader is a trading system operated by Bloomberg which allows banks and fund managers to trade bonds with each other. The two best quotes from the trading system are also depicted in Exhibit A6.3.1.
3. This is in contrast to US markets, where bond prices are actually quoted in dollars, not yield points.
4. See Reserve Bank of Australia, 'Pricing formulae for Commonwealth government securities', Operational Note, <www.rba.gov.au/mkt-operations/tech-notes/pricing-formulae.html>.
5. A dedicated website was set up to administer the review at <http://debtreview.treasury.gov.au/content/home.asp>.
6. Much like the Australian Securities Exchange operates ASX.

7

Capital asset pricing model

CHAPTER PREVIEW

The previous chapter introduced the notion of portfolios and provided some insight into the impact of forming portfolios on investment risk and return. This chapter builds on these basic concepts, and reviews the well-developed theory of portfolio selection first set out by an eminent scholar, Professor Harry Markowitz, in the early 1950s.[1] Markowitz's basic theory of portfolio choice is important for two reasons. First, his ideas form the basis for the model of the 'risk premium' that is discussed in this chapter—the *capital asset pricing model* (CAPM). Second, the principles developed by Professor Markowitz are widely applied in practice. For example, major fund managers such as BlackRock, Colonial First State, AMP and others apply these principles when investing cash provided by superannuation and other funds.

This chapter discusses a number of concepts that are related to selecting portfolios and are fundamental to understanding the CAPM. The chapter then proceeds to set out the specifics of the CAPM, and discusses the rationale underlying the model. The final two sections of the chapter examine two issues relevant to applying the CAPM.

KEY CONCEPTS

CONCEPT 7.1   Rational portfolio choice

The distribution of security returns

Underlying the theory of rational portfolio selection is the assumption that an investor focuses on the expected return and standard deviation of returns on shares (representing risk) in deciding which shares to include in a portfolio. This assumption is valid if these two parameters completely describe the range of possible investment outcomes—that is, possible returns.

Econometric theory suggests that the expected value and standard deviation of a normally distributed random variable are the only two parameters that need to be known in order to describe completely the probability of an outcome.[2] Hence, if returns on assets are normally distributed, then expected future return outcomes are completely described by their expected value and standard deviation. But are returns on assets normally distributed?

The bar chart in panel A of Figure 7.1 plots the distribution of **daily returns** on BHP Billiton (BHP) for the 2010 calendar year. The daily mean return and standard deviation of returns on BHP in that year were 0.0298% and 1.4346%, respectively. Also plotted is a line representing a theoretical normal distribution, with a mean of 0.0298 and standard deviation of 1.4346. The figure suggests that the distribution of daily returns on BHP appears *roughly* to approximate a normal distribution.

Daily returns
The return on a security measured over a trading day.

Panel B of Figure 7.1 plots the distribution of daily returns for Wesfarmers (WES) (bars), and a theoretical normal distribution with the same mean and standard deviation as WES (line). Again, the figure suggests that the distribution of returns on individual shares is crudely described by a normal distribution. Is this true of the market as a whole?

Figure 7.2 plots the distribution of monthly share returns on the All Ordinaries Index for the 20-year period ended 2010. Again, the distribution of returns on the market as a whole is crudely normal, although there does appear to be a little skewness. This recent evidence is consistent with findings presented in previous academic research.[3] The implication of this evidence is that there is some crude justification for focusing on the expected return and standard deviation of returns on shares in selecting a portfolio.

Possible portfolios—two stocks

The return and risk possibilities that can be achieved by combining stocks into portfolios are called **feasible portfolios**. The set of feasible portfolios can best be understood by examining some historical data for two stocks. Table 7.1 sets out the average daily return and the standard deviation of daily returns for BHP and WES during 2010. The covariance of daily returns for BHP and WES is also given. Note that this covariance is positive, which suggests that on a day-by-day basis the returns on these two stocks tended to move together.

Feasible portfolios (opportunity set)
All the possible portfolios (which provide different risk and return outcomes) that can be constructed from a given set of securities.

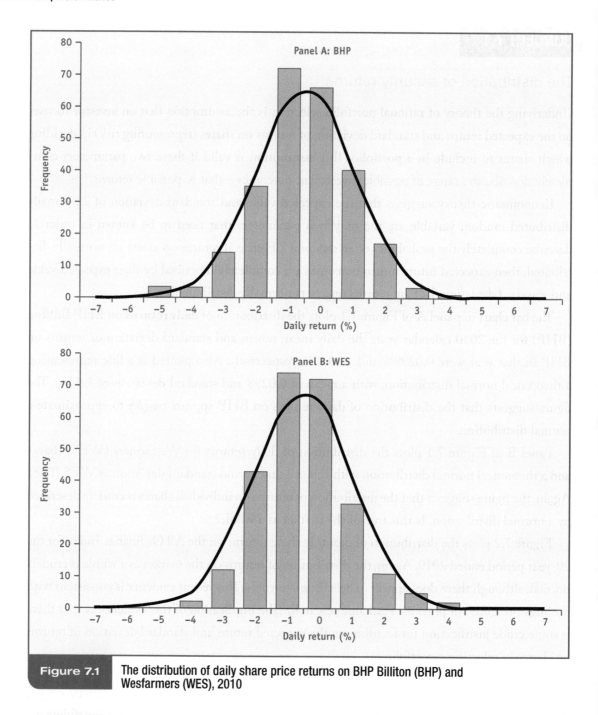

| Figure 7.1 | The distribution of daily share price returns on BHP Billiton (BHP) and Wesfarmers (WES), 2010 |

| Table 7.1 | Daily return–risk characteristics for BHP and WES, 2010 |

	BHP	WES
Mean (%)	0.0298	0.0186
Standard deviation (%)	1.4346	1.3733
Covariance with BHP		0.000096

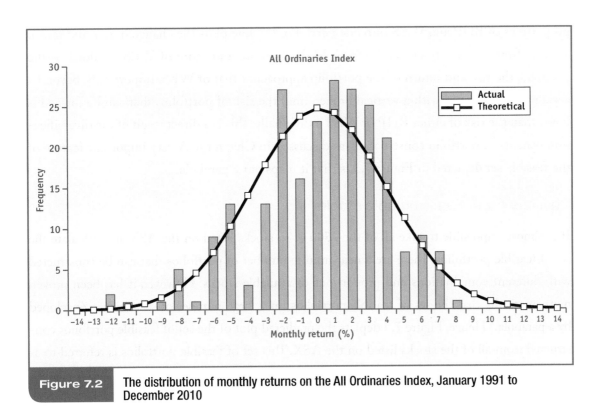

Figure 7.2   The distribution of monthly returns on the All Ordinaries Index, January 1991 to December 2010

The information provided in Table 7.1 can be used to calculate the return and risk levels that could have been achieved by combining different proportions of BHP and WES in a portfolio in 2010. Assuming portfolios in which only positive weights (proportions) are held in each security, consider the effect of varying the weights held in each security by 5% at a time. The resulting portfolios are set out in Table 7.2. The mean return and standard deviation of returns for each of the 21 portfolios depicted in Table 7.2 have been calculated using the formula developed in Appendix 6.2 (and illustrated in Example 6.5) and the information given in Table 7.1 above.

To interpret Table 7.2, note that portfolio 1 relates to a portfolio invested 100% in BHP and 0% in WES. Not surprisingly, the daily mean and the standard deviation of returns on the portfolio are equivalent to those of BHP. The table also sets out the mean return and the standard deviation of returns on a number of other portfolios comprising combinations of BHP and WES. For example, a portfolio composed of equal weightings of BHP and WES (i.e. 50% of the portfolio is invested in each stock) would have yielded a mean daily return of 0.0236% and a standard deviation of returns of 1.209%.

Figure 7.3 plots the final two columns of Table 7.2—that is, the mean return and the standard deviation of returns. The curve depicts the set of feasible portfolios, or, more specifically, the actual levels of risk and return that could have been achieved in 2010 by combining different proportions of BHP and WES into one portfolio. The line plots the change in risk and return starting from an investment of 100% in BHP. As more and more of WES is added to the portfolio, the risk and return of the portfolio approaches that of WES. Importantly, beyond a certain point (marked with a vertical broken line) the risk of portfolios that can be formed is lower than the risk of either BHP or WES individually. This is a direct result of the diversification benefits of portfolio construction, as discussed in Chapter 6. A very important feature of the feasible set depicted in Figure 7.3 is that it maps out a parabola.

Possible portfolios—multiple stocks

It is almost impossible to take all of the 2500 or so stocks listed on the ASX and calculate the set of feasible portfolios. There are a near infinite number of portfolios that can be constructed with different combinations and proportions of available stocks. However, it has been proven mathematically that the set of feasible portfolios for a large number of securities is enveloped by a parabola.[4] Hence, Figure 7.4 depicts the predicted plot of the set of feasible portfolios constructed from all of the stocks listed on the ASX. This set of feasible portfolios is referred to as the opportunity set of risky portfolios. Each point on and within the *opportunity set* represents a possible level of risk and return that an investor can achieve, by holding the portfolio (or individual share) represented by that point.

Choosing the optimum portfolio

Faced with effectively an infinite number of possible portfolios from which to choose, the question arises as to which portfolio is optimum or 'rational'. The theory that provides an answer to this question is based on the idea that investors desire to maximise their returns for a level of risk they are willing to accept.[5] There are two important concepts that arise from this idea, and these concepts underpin rational portfolio choice. They are **minimum variance portfolios** and **efficient portfolios**. A minimum variance portfolio is the subset of feasible portfolios that offers the lowest level of risk for each level of return. Minimum variance portfolios are represented by the perimeter of the opportunity set, as represented by portfolios corresponding to the unbroken curve in Figure 7.5.

Portfolio *A* depicted in Figure 7.5 is one of the minimum variance portfolios because it offers the lowest risk (relative to other portfolios inside the opportunity set) for the level of return marked by the dotted line. Note also that the portfolio with the lowest possible level of risk attainable lies at the opportunity set's left-most point, represented in Figure 7.5 by portfolio *G*. This portfolio is the **global minimum variance portfolio**.

Markowitz (1952) extends the analysis to identify a set of portfolios that a rational investor would choose, called the 'efficient set'. Efficient portfolios are a subset of minimum variance

Minimum variance portfolios
A subset of feasible portfolios. The set of feasible portfolios which provide minimum risk for each level of return.

Efficient portfolios
A subset of minimum variance portfolios. The set of minimum variance portfolios which maximise return at each level of risk.

Global minimum variance portfolio
The portfolio among the feasible set which provides the lowest level of risk.

Table 7.2	Possible return and risk levels that could have been achieved by combining different portions of BHP and WES, 2010			
PORTFOLIO NUMBER	**PROPORTION OF PORTFOLIO IN**		**STANDARD DEVIATION (%)**	**MEAN DAILY PORTFOLIO RETURN (%)**
	BHP	**WES**		
1	1	0	1.435	0.0298
2	0.95	0.05	1.398	0.0292
3	0.9	0.1	1.363	0.0287
4	0.85	0.15	1.332	0.0281
5	0.8	0.2	1.304	0.0275
6	0.75	0.25	1.279	0.0270
7	0.7	0.3	1.258	0.0264
8	0.65	0.35	1.240	0.0259
9	0.6	0.4	1.226	0.0253
10	0.55	0.45	1.216	0.0248
11	0.5	0.5	1.211	0.0242
12	0.45	0.55	1.209	0.0236
13	0.4	0.6	1.212	0.0231
14	0.35	0.65	1.219	0.0225
15	0.3	0.7	1.230	0.0220
16	0.25	0.75	1.245	0.0214
17	0.2	0.8	1.264	0.0209
18	0.15	0.85	1.286	0.0203
19	0.1	0.9	1.312	0.0198
20	0.05	0.95	1.341	0.0192
21	0	1	1.373	0.0186

portfolios, and are the set of minimum variance portfolios offering the highest return for each level of risk. The efficient set is effectively the top half of the minimum variance set, starting from the global minimum variance portfolio. The efficient set is sometimes referred to as the **efficient frontier**. Figure 7.6 illustrates the set of efficient portfolios.

Efficient frontier
The line on a chart mapping risk and return which maps out the efficient portfolios.

Portfolio *B* depicted in Figure 7.6 is one of the efficient portfolios, because (1) it is a minimum variance portfolio (together with portfolio *A*) and (2) it offers the highest level of return at the risk level it achieves (in contrast to portfolio *A*). Rational investors would choose portfolio *B* over portfolio *A* because, for the given level of risk, the (efficient) portfolio provides the highest expected rate of return.

Assuming that investors are rational, in the sense that they desire to maximise their return for any given level of risk borne, only portfolios lying on the efficient set would be considered for investment. The specific portfolio chosen from the efficient set by a given investor will depend on

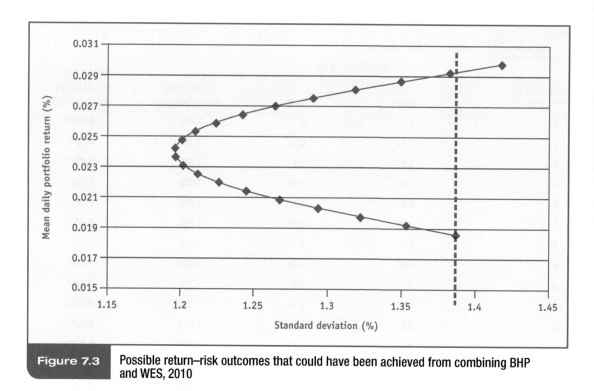

Figure 7.3 Possible return–risk outcomes that could have been achieved from combining BHP and WES, 2010

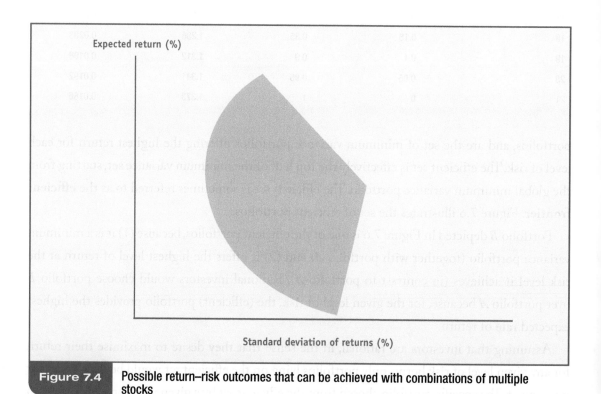

Figure 7.4 Possible return–risk outcomes that can be achieved with combinations of multiple stocks

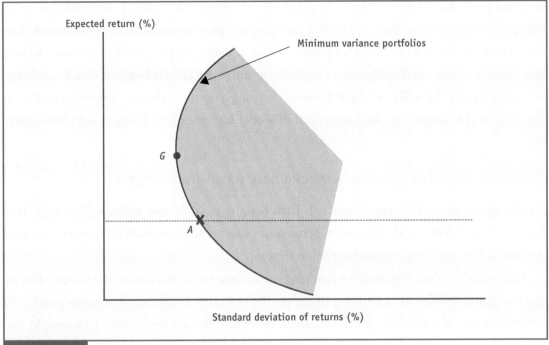

Figure 7.5   Minimum variance portfolios

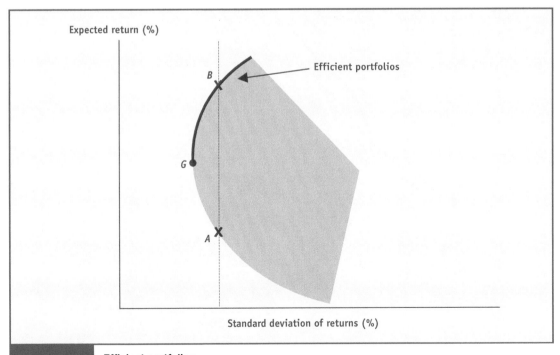

Figure 7.6   Efficient portfolios

their risk preferences. That is, the degree of risk that the investor is willing to bear will determine the appropriate portfolio they choose. For example, an investor who is more averse to risk than most others would tend to choose a portfolio that lies close to the global minimum variance portfolio. At this end of the efficient set, expected returns are relatively low, as is risk. The willingness to bear more risk will result in an investor choosing a portfolio that is represented further to the right on the efficient set, since such portfolios offer higher expected returns but carry greater risk.

Optimum portfolios—multiple stocks plus a risk-free asset

To this point, assets that carry zero risk have been ignored in the analysis. It is clear that Figures 7.4 to 7.6 omit risk-free assets, because not one point (or portfolio) represents a return that is risk free (i.e. has a standard deviation of zero).

Markowitz's analysis continues by assuming the existence of a risk-free asset. He notes that by combining the risk-free asset with any of the portfolios in the efficient set it becomes possible to construct a new set of feasible portfolios. These new portfolios are represented by a straight line between each point on the efficient set and the risk-free asset.[6] Examples of such portfolios are depicted in Figure 7.7, where point r_f represents the risk (zero) and return of the risk-free asset. Only one set of the new feasible portfolios is optimal. This set of portfolios is described by the line that originates from the point representing the risk-free asset and is at a tangent to the old efficient

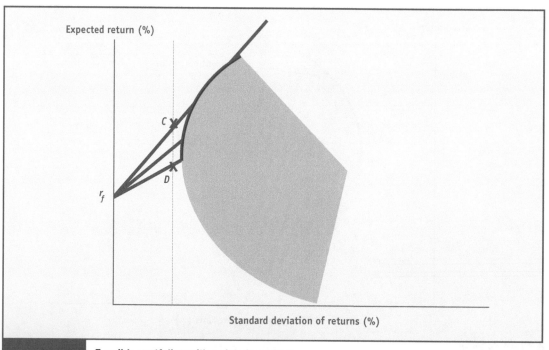

Figure 7.7   **Feasible portfolios with a risk-free asset**

set. The reason that this set of portfolios is optimal is because each portfolio in the set generates a higher level of return for each level of risk. To illustrate, consider portfolios C and D in Figure 7.7. Portfolio C dominates D because it offers a higher rate of return for the same level of risk.

Figure 7.8 depicts the new efficient set with a risk-free asset. This is the straight line that includes point M (the point of tangency) on the old efficient set and r_f. The set of portfolios depicted by this line is optimal—that is, a rational investor would choose them because they maximise returns at each given level of risk.

Accordingly, all investors would hold a portfolio comprising some proportion of the risk-free asset and some proportion of portfolio M. While rational investors would choose a portfolio on the efficient set, the specific portfolio that they would choose is again dictated by their risk preferences. That is, their decision will be based on the level of standard deviation of returns (risk) that they are willing to accept, to achieve a given expected return.

What is portfolio M? Portfolio M is an 'equilibrium' outcome. Since all available stocks must be held by someone at any point in time, portfolio M is a theoretical portfolio that contains *all available stocks*. In other words, it is the **market portfolio**—a portfolio that contains all shares

Market portfolio
A portfolio made up of every single security in the market held in proportion to its market capitalisation relative to the value of the market as a whole.

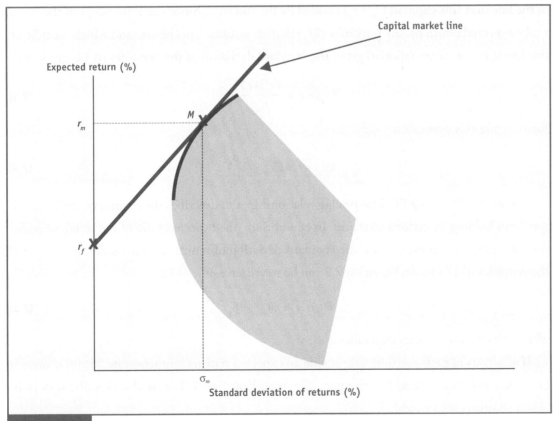

Figure 7.8   Efficient set with a risk-free asset (capital market line)

that are available to investors. Portfolio theory is based on the assumption that all investors hold some proportion of their investment in the market portfolio.

> ## CONCEPT CHECK
>
> 1. What are 'feasible portfolios'? How are they constructed?
> 2. What effect does the existence of a risk-free asset have on the efficient frontier of risky portfolios?
>
> For the answers, go to MyFinanceLab

CONCEPT 7.2   The capital asset pricing model (CAPM)

The logic underlying the CAPM

Capital asset pricing model (CAPM)
A model for determining the risk premium on a security. The CAPM implies that the risk premium is a linear function of the market risk of a security. Also known as the Sharpe Lintner and Black model after the researchers who developed the model.

Capital market line (CML)
The efficient portfolio in the presence of risky securities and a risk-free security. On a risk-return chart, it is represented by the line that goes through the coordinates representing the risk-free rate and the market portfolio.

The efficient set with a risk-free asset (depicted in Figure 7.8) is otherwise known as the **capital market line (CML)**. Note that both the risk-free asset (r_f) and the market portfolio (which has a return r_m and a standard deviation σ_m) lie on the CML.

Turning to the portion of the line between r_f and M, the slope of the line is given by the rise of the line over this segment ($r_m - r_f$) divided by the run (σ_m). Since the Y-intercept of the line is r_f, the expected return on any portfolio $E(r_p)$ that an investor can choose (and which must lie on this line if investors are rational) given the standard deviation of the portfolio (σ_p) is given by:[7]

$$E(r_p) = r_f + \frac{E(r_m - r_f)}{\sigma_m} \sigma_p \tag{7.1}$$

Rearranging this expression yields:

$$E(r_p) = r_f + E(r_m - r_f)\frac{\sigma_p}{\sigma_m} \tag{7.2}$$

Equation 7.2 is an equilibrium pricing relationship, and describes the return *expected* by investors from holding a portfolio of shares. In equilibrium, the expected ratio of the standard deviation of returns on a portfolio and the standard deviation of returns on the market is the beta of the portfolio (β_p).[8] Hence, Equation 7.2 can be rewritten as:

$$E(r_p) = r_f + E(r_m - r_f)\beta_p \tag{7.3}$$

where $E(\cdot)$ denotes an expected outcome.

If all shares in each portfolio (p) provide an expected return commensurate with the amount of market risk that they add to the portfolio, then Equation 7.3 must also describe how individual securities are priced:[9]

$$E(r_i) = r_f + E(r_m - r_f)\,\beta_i \tag{7.4}$$

where:

$E(r_i)$ = the expected return on security i

r_f = the risk-free rate of return

$E(r_m)$ = the expected return on the market

β_i = the beta of security i

Equation 7.4 is the CAPM. It can be used to determine the expected return on any security. It is consistent with the notion that the price (or expected return) of a security is determined by its market risk. The reason why investors are concerned only with market risk in pricing shares is that rational investors hold a portion of the market portfolio, a well-diversified portfolio, and the risk of a well-diversified portfolio is market risk. Hence, the only portion of the risk of a share faced by an investor is its market risk. For a more rigorous derivation of the CAPM, refer to Appendix 7.1.

Another way of thinking about the CAPM

A casual examination of Equation 7.4 suggests that the CAPM implies that the return on a security is the sum of the risk-free rate and a **risk premium**:

$$E(r_i) = r_f + \text{risk premium} \tag{7.5}$$

Since investors hold assets in portfolios (market portfolios), the only portion of risk that they take into consideration in pricing assets is market risk. The quantity of market risk attributable to an asset is given by its β_i. For each unit of market risk faced by the investor in holding the security, the investor expects to be remunerated by a market rate of return over and above the risk-free rate $(r_m - r_f)$. This is the price of risk. Hence, the risk premium is the product of the quantity of market risk and the price of market risk faced by the investor:

$$\text{risk premium} = \text{quantity of risk} \times \text{price of risk} = \beta^i \times E(r_m - r_f) \tag{7.6}$$

Note that substituting Equation 7.6 into Equation 7.5 yields the CAPM (Equation 7.4).

The security market line

The CAPM can be graphically represented by a relationship known as the **security market line (SML)**. In equilibrium, all risky securities should be priced according to their market, or systematic, risk (measured by beta) such that their expected returns plot on the SML. Figure 7.9 provides an illustration.

When the risk-free rate and expected return on the market have been estimated, the expected return for each individual security can be specifically stated as a function of its beta. For example,

> **Risk premium**
> The return over and above the risk-free rate that a security is expected to generate given its risk.

> **Security market line (SML)**
> The capital asset pricing model (CAPM). Represented by a straight line which plots the expected return on a security against the beta of the security.

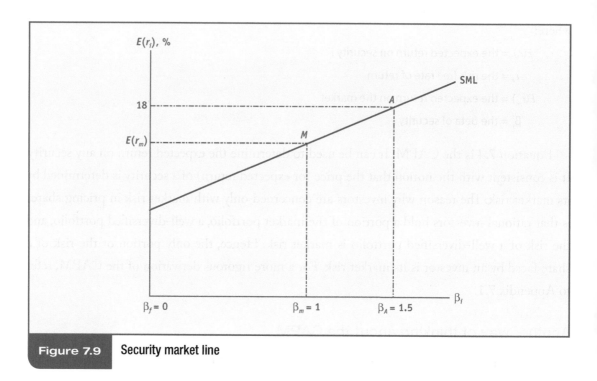

Figure 7.9   Security market line

if we observed r_f = 6% and estimated $E(r_m)$ = 14%, the SML would be stated as $E(r_i)$ = 6 + 8β_i. In these circumstances, a security with a beta of 1.5 (security A) would therefore yield an expected return of 18%, and would plot on the SML at point A in Figure 7.9.

What happens when the observed rate of return of a security differs from that predicted by the CAPM? Take, for example, security A, which is expected to plot at point A in Figure 7.9. Given the observed SML and its beta estimated at 1.5, what are the implications of observing a return on security A of, say, 16%? This situation is depicted in Figure 7.10: we can see that point A does not plot on the SML, but below it. In terms of the CAPM, this security is not priced in equilibrium. However, in circumstances such as this, this disequilibrium will be only temporary.

Specifically, the disequilibrium depicted in Figure 7.10 is that security A is currently over-priced—that is, it is generating a return below that expected by investors commensurate with its market risk, as measured by its beta of 1.5. In these circumstances, investors are not being fully compensated for the risk that they are bearing, and would therefore have an incentive to sell security A and invest in other securities that provide an appropriate return for their level of market risk. This selling pressure would have the effect of pushing down the price of security A (thereby increasing its expected return). The question then arises: at what point would this selling of security A cease? It would cease when the price of security A is reduced to the level at which its observed return equates to 18% (i.e. that required by investors given security A's level of market risk).

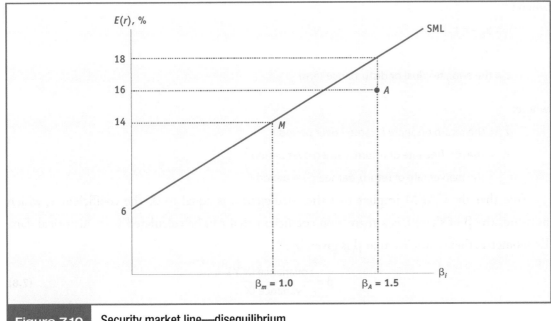

Figure 7.10   Security market line—disequilibrium

CONCEPT CHECK

3. What relationship is represented by the capital market line (CML)?
4. What relationship is represented by the security market line (SML)?

For the answers, go to MyFinanceLab

CONCEPT 7.3   Estimation of beta (β_i)

An examination of the CAPM reveals that, in order to apply the model to determine the expected return (or discount rate) of a share, estimates are required of (1) the risk-free rate (r_f), (2) the expected return on the market over and above the risk-free rate $E(r_m - r_f)$, and (3) β_i (the share's beta). While the risk-free rate is usually a directly observable figure, estimating the expected return on the market over and above the risk-free rate will be discussed in Chapter 8. This section outlines the procedure for estimating the beta of a share using historical data.

Since β is the expected relationship between returns on a share and returns on the market, the beta of a share can be estimated by quantifying the historical relationship between price movements on the share and price movements on the market as a whole. For the purposes of estimating the CAPM from historical data, its equation, Equation 7.4, can be rewritten in the following general form that students of econometrics would be familiar with:

$$Y_t = a + bX_t + \varepsilon_t \tag{7.7}$$

where:

$$Y_t = (r_{i,t} - r_{f,t})$$
$$X_t = (r_{m,t} - r_{f,t})$$

ε_t = the error, residual or disturbance term.

where:

$r_{i,t}$ = the return on share i, earned over period t

$r_{f,t}$ = the risk-free rate of return, earned over period t

$r_{m,t}$ = the market rate of return, earned over period t

Note that the CAPM implies that the coefficient a is equal to 0. The coefficient b, which measures the β of share i, is a regression coefficient that can be calculated from historical data. Econometric theory implies that β is given by:[10]

$$\beta = \frac{\text{covariance } (X_t, Y_t)}{\text{variance } (X_t)} \tag{7.8}$$

Hence, beta is given by the covariance of 'excess' returns on the share and 'excess' returns on the market, divided by the variance of 'excess' returns on the market. Note that 'excess' returns are those above, or in excess of, the risk-free rate. Accordingly, the excess return on the market over period t is $(r_{m,t} - r_{f,t})$ and the excess return on share i over period t is $(r_{i,t} - r_{f,t})$.

The first step in calculating the beta of a security is to collect historical data and calculate a sequence of excess returns on a share and excess returns on the market. This is illustrated in Example 7.1 using monthly share price data for Wesfarmers (WES), the All Ordinaries Accumulation Index and 10-year bond yields.[11]

It is important to realise that since 10-year bond yields are expressed on an annual basis they must be converted to a monthly rate of return (roughly, by simply dividing the yield by 12). Furthermore, the return on Wesfarmers in any month must include the dividend paid (if any), as follows:

$$r_{i,t} = \frac{P_t - P_{t-1} + d_t}{P_{t-1}} \tag{7.9}$$

where P_t is the price of the share at the end of month t, and d_t is the dividend paid during month t (if any). The return on the market is simply the percentage change in the index:

$$r_{m,t} = \frac{I_t - I_{t-1}}{I_{t-1}} \tag{7.10}$$

where I_t is the index level at the end of month t.

Once the monthly excess returns on the share and market have been calculated by subtracting the bond yield from share and market returns, the covariance of the excess returns on the share and market can be calculated using the following expression:

$$\sum_{t=1}^{n} \frac{[(r_{i,t} - r_{f,t}) - E(r_i - r_t)] \times [(r_{m,t} - r_{f,t}) - E(r_m - r_t)]}{n - 1}$$ **(7.11)**

where n is the number of observations used to estimate beta.

As stated and illustrated above, beta is the ratio of the covariance between excess share returns and excess market returns to the variance of excess market returns. Example 7.1 calculates the historical beta of Wesfarmers at 0.93. To clarify further the nature of the beta figure, consider the 'characteristic line' between two variables. The characteristic line for a share is the line that best fits the relationship between excess returns on the share and excess returns on the market. The slope of the characteristic line is the beta of the share. Figure 7.11 plots Wesfarmer's characteristic line.

EXAMPLE 7.1

Calculating the beta of a security*

QUESTION

Using the following monthly data, calculate the beta (β) of Wesfarmers for 2010:

Month end t	Share price ($) P	All Ordinaries Accumulation Index (points) I	10-year bond yield (%) r_t(p.a.)	Dividend paid per share (cents) d_t	Ex-dividend date
December 2009	31.27	33698.602	5.47		
January 2010	27.51	31727.352	5.56		
February 2010	31.13	32304.449	5.48	55	23 Feb 10
March 2010	31.79	34188.092	5.62		
April 2010	29.29	33785.445	5.80		
May 2010	29.10	31228.615	5.48		
June 2010	28.65	30415.156	5.33		
July 2010	31.09	31701.608	5.15		
August 2010	31.96	31475.951	4.97	70	24 Aug 10
September 2010	32.89	33055.927	5.00		
October 2010	33.14	33773.519	5.09		
November 2010	31.46	33538.085	5.38		
December 2010	32.00	34812.763	5.56		

ANSWER

Calculate the monthly returns on the stock (Wesfarmers), the stock market (AOAI) and 10-year bonds.

Month end t	Stock return $(r_{i,t})$	Index return $(r_{m,t})$	Monthly bond return $(r_{f,t})$	Excess stock return (Y)	Excess index return (X)
January 2010	–0.1202	–0.0585	0.0046	–0.1249	–0.0631
February 2010	0.1516	0.0182	0.0046	0.1470	0.0136
March 2010	0.0212	0.0583	0.0047	0.0165	0.0536
April 2010	–0.0786	–0.0118	0.0048	–0.0835	–0.0166
May 2010	–0.0065	–0.0757	0.0046	–0.0111	–0.0802
June 2010	–0.0155	–0.0260	0.0044	–0.0199	–0.0305
July 2010	0.0852	0.0423	0.0043	0.0809	0.0380
August 2010	0.0505	–0.0071	0.0041	0.0464	–0.0113
September 2010	0.0291	0.0502	0.0042	0.0249	0.0460
October 2010	0.0076	0.0217	0.0042	0.0034	0.0175
November 2010	–0.0507	–0.0070	0.0045	–0.0552	–0.0115
December 2010	0.0172	0.0380	0.0046	0.0125	0.0334
Calculation	$\dfrac{P_t - P_{t-1} + d_t}{P_{t-1}}$	$\dfrac{I_t - I_{t-1}}{I_{t-1}}$	$\dfrac{r_t(\text{p.a.})}{12}$	$r_{i,t} - r_{ft}$	$r_{m,t} - r_{ft}$

*Readers who are attempting to replicate the calculations in the tables above beware! All figures have been calculated using Microsoft Excel. Hence, while all figures calculated are reported to four decimal places, in fact all the decimal places are used in calculations and hence do not include any rounding error at any point.

Calculate the monthly excess returns and mean monthly excess returns on the stock and market, the variance of returns on the market and the covariance of returns on the market.

	Excess stock return (Y)	Excess index return (X)	Covariance calculation		
			Variation in excess stock return (Y-E[Y])	Variation in excess index return (X-E[X])	Product of variation in excess return (Y-E[Y])• (X–E[X])
January 2010	–0.1249	–0.0631	–0.1280	–0.0622	0.00796
February 2010	0.1470	0.0136	0.1439	0.0145	0.00209
March 2010	0.0165	0.0536	0.0134	0.0545	0.00073
April 2010	–0.0835	–0.0166	–0.0866	–0.0157	0.00136
May 2010	–0.0111	–0.0802	–0.0141	–0.0793	0.00112
June 2010	–0.0199	–0.0305	–0.0230	–0.0296	0.00068
July 2010	0.0809	0.0380	0.0778	0.0389	0.00303
August 2010	0.0464	–0.0113	0.0433	–0.0103	–0.00045

(continued)

	Excess stock return (Y)	Excess index return (X)	Covariance calculation		
			Variation in excess stock return (Y-E[Y])	Variation in excess index return (X-E[X])	Product of variation in excess return (Y-E[Y])• (X-E[X])
September 2010	0.0249	0.0460	0.0218	0.0469	0.00103
October 2010	0.0034	0.0175	0.0003	0.0184	0.00000
November 2010	−0.0552	−0.0115	−0.0583	−0.0105	0.00061
December 2010	0.0125	0.0334	0.0094	0.0343	0.00032
Mean	0.0031	−0.0009		Total	0.01849
Variance		0.001811		Covariance	0.001681

$$\beta = \frac{\text{covariance } (r_i - r_f, r_m - r_f)}{\text{variance } (r_m - r_f)} = \frac{0.001681}{0.001811} = 0.93$$

Hence, the beta of Wesfarmers is 0.93.

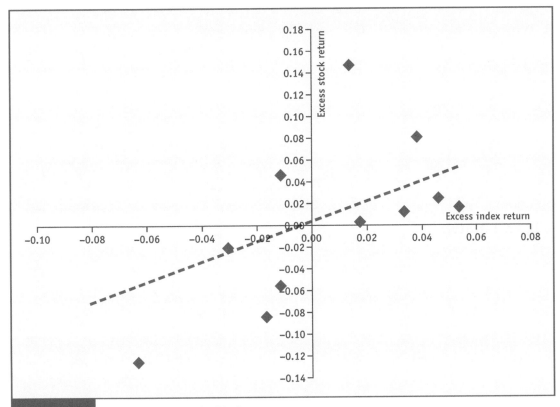

Figure 7.11   Characteristic line for Wesfarmers

Practitioner's POV

There are many arbitrary decisions that need to be made in order to calculate beta, including the choice of a market index and risk-free rate, the time period over which to estimate beta (one year, five years and so on) and the frequency of the data (daily, weekly or monthly returns). There are also a number of very technical statistical problems and a large number of generally imperfect solutions available to solve these problems. The choice made by an analyst on any of these issues can result in, at times, wildly different estimates of beta. Good analysts always apply a reality check to any numbers calculated from historical data. Analysts will often start with the market beta of 1, and, in light of the type of business a company is involved in, decide whether they expect its beta to be greater or less than 1. This expectation is then used to test any beta calculated. If, as sometimes happens, the beta estimated from historical data is an unrealistic number, an analyst will apply their professional judgment and adjust the estimated beta to a realistic level.

CONCEPT CHECK

5. What are 'excess returns'? Why are they used in the calculation of the beta of a share?
6. What market data are required in order to estimate a share's beta?

For the answers, go to MyFinanceLab

FINANCE EXTRA!

Mix and match

A little taste of everything will ensure you don't miss out on market gains, writes Debra Cleveland.

WHETHER you are a new investor or already own shares, it's important to think about the big picture. Just as shares form only part of your overall investment portfolio, you need to use diversification strategies in your stock picks.

Being invested in a range of companies and sectors will leave you less exposed to volatility in the sharemarket.

When you invest in the sharemarket, explains a market strategist at CMC Markets, Ric Spooner, you're taking on two different types of risk: market risk, meaning you're exposed to general falls in share prices; and industry or company-specific risk, whereby you lose if an industry or company in which you invest underperforms. In the most extreme case, Spooner says, the company may go broke. Diversification can help limit your exposure to industry or company risk.

When starting out, Spooner suggests establishing your profile as an investor.

'A good starting place is to think clearly about what you want to achieve with share investments and how much risk is appropriate for you to take,' he says.

'The answer to these questions will allow you to make some sensible rules about how much you should invest and what type of investments you make. Having made these rules, it is important to stick to them unless your circumstances change.'

For example, younger investors who want shares as a long-term investment to fund their retirement may have more of their holdings directed towards companies with better growth prospects. These include large mining companies, which feed profits back into future development. But those already retired will need income, so they may have more invested in companies that distribute profits via dividends.

Companies yielding high dividends are important to investors across the board, says the head of research at education and research specialist Australian Stock Report, Geoff Saffer. Often the focus is just on good share price growth but consistently high dividends offer not only good income but also the chance to reinvest in the business. Financial stocks tend to be high-yielding, Saffer adds.

Your next question may be how much to invest

and that, of course, depends on your finances. Don't buy too small, Saffer says.

'As much as it is important to diversify, investors should avoid "overdiversification",' he says. 'Don't spread your money so thinly that you can't get any bang for your buck. In theory you can buy as little as $500 worth of shares but it's hard to make money on such a small amount. Anything from $2500 to $3000 is more sensible. On a $500 purchase, if you pay $30 brokerage to buy the stock and $30 to sell, the stock would need to go up by 12 per cent just for you to break even.'

As a guide, Spooner says, owning seven to 20 shares across different industries will offer reasonable diversification. A suggestion is to invest across four separate categories: resources (mining and energy), financials (banks and insurance), defensive industrials (food and staples, health-care, utilities) and cyclical industrials (consumer discretionary, media, property, industrials).

'Because you can never be sure of what will happen in the economy, you should never have less than 10 per cent or more than 35 per cent of your portfolio in any one sector,' Spooner says. 'However, you may adjust your exposure within these bands depending on your investment themes.'

Last, keep a watching brief on your shares and the proportion of your equities portfolio that each makes up. If there are huge gains in a few companies, this means they will be 'overweight' in your portfolio and you will need to adjust it—either by selling some stocks or buoying up other parts of the portfolio with more share buys to balance things out.

Source: Debra Cleveland, *The Sydney Morning Herald*, 30 May 2010. © Fairfax Media Publications Pty Limited.

CONCEPT 7.4   Does the CAPM work?

A casual inspection of the CAPM equation suggests that it implies at least two things.

1. There is a positive relationship between share returns and beta.[12]

2. Beta is the only factor that explains share returns.

Professor Eugene Fama of the University of Chicago has carried out two of the best known studies that test these two implications of the CAPM. In an early study, using data from the New York Stock Exchange (NYSE) over a period prior to 1969, Professor Fama documented the existence of a positive relationship between beta and average share returns.[13] In a subsequent, controversial paper that hit the headlines of the financial papers in the year it was published (1992),[14] Fama's conclusion had changed—he demonstrated that there does not seem to be an obvious relationship between beta and returns, but rather there appears to be a strong negative relationship between share returns and the market capitalisation of securities.[15] In this section, the details of this second paper are discussed, given its apparent significance.

The 1992 paper by Fama, co-written with his colleague Ken French, carried out a series of informal tests and formal tests, each of which produced similar conclusions. The data used in the tests were a monthly price series for shares trading on the NYSE, the American Stock Exchange and NASDAQ markets in the USA over the years 1963 to 1990. Hence, a very large and broad data set was used. In the informal tests reported in the paper, the following steps were carried out in order to determine whether there was a positive relationship between beta and share returns:

1. For June of each year, the beta for each share was estimated using share price data from two to five years beforehand.

2. Shares were ranked on the basis of the betas calculated, and divided into 10 equally sized portfolios.

3. The average beta and average monthly returns on each portfolio were then calculated.

4. The process was repeated for each year, and the average return over all years was calculated for each portfolio.

The four steps were then repeated, except that shares were ranked on the basis of their market capitalisation ('size') rather than their beta. The findings of the study are encapsulated in Figure 7.12.

The first prediction of the CAPM implies that the average return on portfolios containing shares with smaller betas (say, portfolio 1) should be lower than average returns on portfolios with larger betas (say, portfolio 10), and that the average return should increase from portfolio 1 to portfolio 10. However, we can see that the results in Panel *A* of Figure 7.12 are inconsistent with this prediction. There is no obvious relationship between average returns and betas.

The second prediction of the CAPM implies that there should be *no relation* between the size

Practitioner's POV

Despite its apparent shortcomings, the CAPM is indeed widely used in practice. The CAPM can be used, together with an estimate of the expected or required return on the market as a whole, to estimate the required return of a company and value its free cash flows. Stockbrokers often use it in this way to value companies and determine whether they are underpriced or overpriced by the market, and produce buy or sell recommendations accordingly. Investment banks also often use the CAPM in a similar way to value companies about to be offered to the public (i.e. in a float) or to determine the fair value of a company involved in a takeover bid.

of shares and their average return. Panel B of Figure 7.12 appears to provide evidence that contradicts this prediction. The average return on shares in portfolio 10 (the largest) is smaller than the average return on shares in portfolio 1 (the smallest). Further, there is a general tendency for share returns to rise from portfolio 10 to portfolio 1.

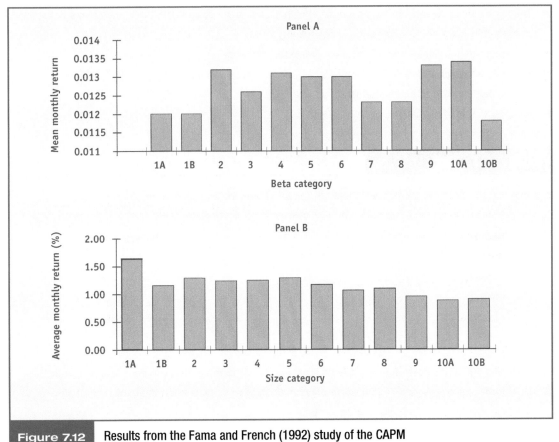

Figure 7.12   **Results from the Fama and French (1992) study of the CAPM**

Source: Constructed from Table 11 in E. F. Fama and K. R. French (1992), 'The cross section of expected stock returns', *Journal of Finance*, vol. 48, 427–65.

In general, the study implies that the CAPM is a poor representation of historical returns. However, there is a large body of literature that questions these findings.[16] This literature is left to the interested reader. The practical implications of these findings are straightforward. In applying the CAPM, the reader should be aware that there are problems with its validity.

Student Learning Centre

MyFinanceLab ■ To test your mastery of the content covered in this chapter and to create your own personalised study plan, go to MyFinanceLab: www.pearson.com.au/myfinancelab

CONCEPT CHECKLIST

In this chapter the following concepts were discussed:

➤ The distribution of share returns
➤ The risk–return outcomes or feasible portfolios that can be constructed by combining two stocks, many stocks, and stocks and bonds in portfolios
➤ The optimum or efficient portfolios rational investors choose
➤ The logic underlying the CAPM
➤ How to calculate beta from historical data
➤ Important tests of the CAPM

SELF-TEST QUESTIONS

Assume that the CAPM is correct and the following securities are available to you.

Security	Beta	Expected return
Share P	0.6	
Share Q	0.7	
Market		14.0%
Risk free		5.5%

You have $50 000 of your own funds available for investment. Suppose that you decide to sell (short) $25 000 worth of share P and $75 000 worth of share Q and invest all funds in the market portfolio.

(a) Calculate the beta and expected return on your portfolio.

(b) Comment on the riskiness of your strategy. If the return on the market portfolio fell by 20%, what would be the expected impact on your portfolio?

Self-test answer

Background: Short selling is the strategy of selling an asset that you don't yet own. Since you don't own the asset, you will need to obtain the asset by a certain date, for delivery to the buyer under the short-sale contract. The proceeds from the **short sale** are typically not provided in cash. Rather, the funds are credited to an account held with the broker and may be used to purchase other securities.

Short sale
The sale of shares that are not currently owned by the investor. This typically requires that the investor borrows the shares.

(a) Portfolio beta is a weighted average of the betas of the individual securities in the portfolio—that is,

$\beta_p = \Sigma\, w_i\beta_i$.

Portfolio weights must always (by definition) add to 1, where 1 represents 100% of the funds available for investment (and all individual asset weights are proportionate to this amount). Note that the beta of the market portfolio is 1.

Accordingly, $w_p = -0.5 \left(\dfrac{-25\,000}{50\,000}\right)$, $w_Q = -1.5 \left(\dfrac{-75\,000}{50\,000}\right)$ and $w_m = 3.0$

(since $-0.5 + -1.5 + 3 = 1$), so $\beta_p = (-0.5 \times 0.6) + (-1.5 \times 0.7) + (3.0 \times 1) = 1.65$.

Now, treating the portfolio as a single risky asset, and applying CAPM:

$E(R_p) = 5.5 + 1.65 \times (14 - 5.5) = 19.525\%$.

(b) This would be considered as a riskier than average strategy, even though all available funds are invested in the market portfolio (which is, by definition, of average risk). This is because the strategy of short selling brings with it two fixed obligations: (1) the requirement to purchase the sold securities within a specified time-frame, and (2) the interest payable on the borrowed share. These obligations are certain, while the return on holding the market portfolio is only expected, and therefore risky. Furthermore, the two shares that are sold short, P and Q, can be regarded as 'defensive' shares (i.e. less than average risk), since they each have a beta of less than 1. Selling defensive shares to invest in the market portfolio gives an overall risk that is greater than that of the market portfolio itself, due to the gearing, or leveraging, effect, which is reflected in the portfolio's beta of 1.65.

Should the return on the market portfolio fall by 20%, the effect on this portfolio would be magnified due to the beta of the portfolio. Therefore, the return on the portfolio would be expected to fall by 20% $\times 1.65 = 33\%$.

DISCUSSION QUESTIONS

1. What is the importance of the assumption that security returns are normally distributed? Based on the evidence presented in this chapter, does it appear that returns on Australian equities are normally distributed?

2. Explain why the risk of a (feasible) portfolio of two shares can be less than the individual risk of each of those shares individually.

3. Provide an interpretation of Figures 7.4 and 7.5 in the chapter. Theoretically, what do they represent in the context of the Australian share market?

4. The parabola-shaped opportunity set of portfolios represents all possible risky asset investment combinations in an economy, which could amount to billions of portfolios. Under Markowitz's portfolio theory, how does an investor choose the appropriate one in which to invest?

5. Under Markowitz's portfolio theory, how do investors maximise their utility if (1) only risky securities exist (i.e. there is no risk-free security), or (2) there is a risk-free security in existence, with which investors can lend and borrow?

6. What is the market portfolio? Why is it a key concept in portfolio theory?

7. What is the capital market line (CML)? What does its existence imply in relation to rational portfolio investment?

8. Provide an intuitive explanation of the slope of the CML.

9. Why are investors focused on market risk only when applying the CAPM to price-risky securities?

10. Outline some of the practical uses of the CAPM in Australian markets.

11. What is the security market line (SML)? What does portfolio theory predict will happen when disequilibrium of the SML is observed?

12. If everyone in the market is risk neutral, that is, they only care about expected returns and not risk, what would the slope of the SML be? Is this likely? Under what conditions would you expect a negatively sloped SML? How likely is this?

13. Define beta and discuss how it might be estimated in practice.

14. Consider a SML with the equation $E(r) = y + z\beta$. If the expected return of a stock is w, which is less than y, what can you say about the beta of this stock?

15. In the context of the CAPM, what would be the implication if a share had a negative beta?

16. Given that many of the authoritative empirical studies seem to provide evidence that the CAPM does not work very well in practice, why is it still routinely used?

17. In relation to the CAPM, indicate for each of the following statements whether it is true or false and explain why.

    (a) Investors do not differ in their attitudes towards risk.

    (b) In equilibrium, all risky assets are priced such that their expected return lies on the SML.

    (c) If a share's expected return is 4% and the expected return on the market portfolio is 15%, the share's beta must be negative.

    (d) Two securities with the same expected returns can have different betas.

    (e) Two securities with the same standard deviations can have different betas.

    (f) Two securities that have the same correlation coefficients with the market portfolio will have the same betas.

    (g) The return on a share with a beta of zero is expected to vary directly with the return on the market portfolio.

    (h) The equation for the SML when the expected return on the market is 15% and the risk-free rate is 6% is $r_j = 9 + 6\beta_j$.

    (i) A security lying above the SML is currently overpriced.

PRACTICAL QUESTIONS

1. The following table provides information in respect of two securities, A and B.

BASIC

	A	B
Mean expected return, % p.a.	12.5	16.0
Standard deviation, % p.a.	23.0	30.0
Covariance A, B		−0.00021

(a) Use this information to construct a set of feasible portfolios in which only positive weights in A and B are held (i.e. no short selling occurs), by starting with a portfolio comprising 100% in A (0% in B) and varying the weights held in each security by 10% at a time.

(b) Now plot the set of feasible portfolios in (a). Interpret the resulting diagram.

2. The following table provides standard deviations and correlation coefficients relating to two risky securities, J and K, and the market portfolio. Use this information to estimate the beta and expected returns on securities J and K, assuming an expected return on the market portfolio of 13% and a risk-free return of 4.5%.

BASIC

Security	Standard deviation	Correlation with J	Correlation with K
Asset J	0.09		0.75
Asset K	0.20	0.75	
Market portfolio	0.16	0.66	0.25

3. The following probability distributions relating to returns on an individual security and the market portfolio are given.

BASIC

State	Probability	Return on security (%)	Return on the market (%)
Boom	0.10	32	25
Good	0.15	22	18
Average	0.30	10	14
Poor	0.25	3	6
Crash	0.20	−15	−5

Calculate the following:

(a) the expected return and standard deviation of returns for both the security and the market portfolio

(b) the beta of both the security and the market portfolio

(c) the current risk-free rate of return.

BASIC

4. The following table provides information in respect of three securities.

Security	X	Y	Z
Mean return, % p.a.	15	15	25
Standard deviation, % p.a.	20	20	20

(a) Note that each of the securities has the same standard deviation of returns but Z has a different expected return. Assuming that these assets are priced in accordance with the CAPM, how can this situation persist?

(b) What, if anything, can you say about the beta of security Z relative to securities X and Y? Explain your answer.

BASIC

5. The following diagram depicts the SML estimated at $E(r_i) = 5 + 5\beta_i$, along with three securities, X, Y and Z, plotted by their returns observed in the market.

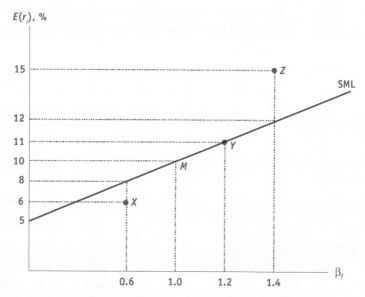

(a) What situation does this diagram depict?

(b) What does portfolio theory predict will happen in these circumstances?

(c) How could you make a profit by trading in these securities, assuming that you can trade immediately and that the adjustment predicted by portfolio theory does not take place for two weeks?

BASIC

6. Using the CAPM, you find that the expected annual return of stock XYZ is 15%. If the current price of XYZ is $100 per share, what is the expected price in one year's time? Stock ABC has an expected return of 25%. If the risk-free rate is 5%, and the market risk premium is 10%, what is the beta of XYZ and ABC?

BASIC

7. Draw an efficient frontier and locate the minimum variance portfolio and the market portfolio. In the absence of a risk-free asset, highlight the range of possible investment choices. How does your analysis change with the introduction of a risk-free asset? Does it make you better off as an investor?

8. Suppose there are two stocks in the market. Stock X has a beta of 0.5 while stock Y has a beta if 1.5. If the risk-free rate is 6% and the market risk premium is 8%, what proportion do you need to invest in X and Y to achieve overall portfolio returns of 16%? What is the beta of your portfolio?

9. Assume that a particular equities market contains only three (risky) equity securities and a risk-free asset, details of which are as follows.

Security	Market capitalisation ($)	Expected return (%)	Standard deviation (%)
1	1 600 000	11	20
2	3 800 000	9	12
3	7 600 000	15	30
Risk free	n.a.	10.4	0

(a) If an investor in this market was seeking to replicate the market portfolio, what percentage of total investment outlays should be held in each of securities 1, 2 and 3?

(b) What is the standard deviation of returns on this market portfolio, given correlation coefficients between the securities as follows: 1 and 2: 0.45; 1 and 3: 0.66; 2 and 3: –0.2.

(c) Specify an efficient portfolio (i.e. one comprising the market portfolio and the risk-free security) that provides an expected return of 17% p.a. What is the standard deviation of this portfolio?

10. Data for FHZ Ltd and the market index are as follows.

Date	Share price	Accumulation index
30 June	22.78	1065.0
30 September	24.40	1160.0
30 December	22.08	1022.0
30 March	23.67	1114.0

If the risk-free rate over the period is running at 6.5% p.a., what is the beta of the share?

11. ABC Ltd and XYZ Ltd operate in different industries. You feel that the dividend growth rate of share XYZ Ltd is twice the size of the dividend growth rate of share ABC Ltd. You are given the following information.

	Share price	Forecast dividend next year	Beta
ABC Ltd	4.40	55 cps	1.5
XYZ Ltd	7.50	82.5 cps	2.0

If the risk-free rate is running at 5% p.a., what is the expected market return and dividend growth rate of the two shares?

12. Rework Example 7.1 in the chapter to determine the beta of another Australian mining stock, Fortescue Metals Group (FMG), for 2010. FMG's month end share prices for 2010 are contained in the following table. What is FMG's beta if it paid no dividends during 2010? What if a dividend of 10 cents per share was paid during February?

12/09	01/10	02/10	03/10	04/10	05/10	06/10	07/10	08/10	09/10	10/10	11/10	12/10
4.44	4.53	4.65	4.9	4.58	4.04	4.12	4.29	4.68	5.21	6.25	6.32	6.54

What can you conclude about the two companies in comparing their betas?

13. You want to construct a portfolio out of two shares—RIO and ORI. The standard deviation of returns on ORI is 2.18%, for RIO it is 2.33%, and the correlation coefficient describing the relationship between returns on the two securities is 0.327. You are risk averse and want to minimise your investment risk. What portion of the portfolio needs to be invested in each security to build the portfolio? What is the risk associated with the portfolio? (Hint: You will need to use some calculus to solve this problem.)

CASE STUDY

Below is the end of month closing price for two securities. One is Rio Tinto Group (RIO), one of the largest stocks listed on the Australian Securities Exchange, and the other is the SPDR S&P/ASX 200 Fund (STW) which is a company which does nothing more than invest in the stocks in the S&P/ASX 200 Index, and the investment in each stock is proportionate to their market capitalisation (i.e. more is invested in larger stocks). Essentially, by buying a share in STW, you are buying a small portion of the portfolio that underlies the S&P/ASX 200 Index. Consequently, your investment performance should be very close to the market index.

	RIO	STW
December 2009	74.89	45.59
January 2010	68.00	42.80
February 2010	70.50	43.65
March 2010	78.40	46.25
April 2010	72.10	45.51
May 2010	67.14	42.18
June 2010	66.66	40.40
July 2010	70.61	42.12
August 2010	70.09	41.65
September 2010	76.77	43.58
October 2010	82.69	44.25
November 2010	82.21	43.81
December 2010	85.47	44.60

CASE STUDY QUESTIONS

1. What is the average return and standard deviation of returns on RIO and STW?

2. Calculate the covariance between returns on RIO and returns on STW.

3. Calculate and plot the portfolio standard deviation and average returns of a portfolio with the following weight in RIO (and the balance in STW):
   (a) 10%
   (b) 25%
   (c) 50%
   (d) 75%
   (e) 90%

4. Approximate, by examining the chart in (3) the minimum variance portfolio.

5. Recognising that the returns on STW are in fact the returns on the market, write down the equation for the capital market line given that the current 10-year bond rate is approximately 5.5%.

6. Based on your answer to (2) and (3), what is the beta of RIO? Interpret the beta.

FURTHER READING

For a more advanced treatment of the derivation of the CAPM, refer to Chapters 6 and 7 of the following text:

- Copeland, T. E., Weston, J. F. and Shastri, K. (2004), *Financial Theory and Corporate Policy*, International Edition, 4th Edition, Pearson, U.K.

For a discussion of the many small issues associated with calculating beta from historical data see:

- Brailsford, T., Faff, R. and Oliver, B. (1997), *Research Design Issues in the Estimation of Beta*, McGraw-Hill, Sydney.

For further details on testing the CAPM, refer to the informal tests in:

- Fama, E. F. and French, K. R. (1992), 'The cross section of expected stock returns', *Journal of Finance*, vol. 48, 427–65.

NOTES

1. H. Markowitz (1952), 'Theory of portfolio selection', *Journal of Finance*, vol. 7, 77–91.
2. See, for example, D. Gujarati (1999), *Essentials of Econometrics*, 2nd edn, McGraw-Hill, New York.
3. Earlier evidence relating to the distribution of Australian share returns is presented by W. L. Beedles (1986), 'Asymmetry in Australian equity returns', *Australian Journal of Management*, vol. II.
4. R. Merton (1972), 'An analytic derivation of the efficient portfolio frontier', *Journal of Financial and Quantitative Analysis*, vol. 7.
5. The theory of portfolio selection does not suggest that there is only one optimum portfolio. The actual portfolio selected by an investor is dictated by the level of risk that they are willing to accept. What the theory does explain is how an investor identifies the portfolio that maximises the return given the level of risk the investor is willing to accept.

6. It is possible to prove mathematically that the change in returns relative to a change in the standard deviation of returns for a portfolio made up of the risk-free asset and any other (risky) portfolio is a constant (results in a line as depicted in Figure 7.7). The intuition behind this proof is that the standard deviation of returns on the risk-free asset is 0, and hence the risk of the new portfolio is merely a proportion of the market (risky) portfolio.

7. Recall that the equation of a line is given by $Y = a + bX$, where in this case Y is the expected return on a portfolio (r_p), a is the Y-intercept (r_f), b is the slope of the line $(\frac{r_m - r_f}{\sigma_m})$ and X is the risk of the portfolio (σ_p).

8. It is important to realise that β_p is a portion of the market portfolio (a well-diversified portfolio) and, hence, the risk of the portfolio, σ_p, is expected to be a portion of the total market risk, σ_m.

9. For a proof of Equation 7.4, refer to Appendix 7.1.

10. See D. Gujarati (1999), *Essentials of Econometrics*, 2nd edn, McGraw-Hill, New York.

11. Readers beware! The appropriate risk-free rate and market index to use is not a simple issue. Here, we use the All Ordinaries Accumulation Index and 10-year bond yields (1) for expositional purposes, and (2) because they are commonly used in the industry. The frequency (i.e. monthly, weekly, daily, etc.) of data that should be used to calculate beta is also an issue. Again, monthly data are used here for expositional purposes only. For a discussion of these and other issues involved in calculating beta, see T. Brailsford, R. Faff and B. Oliver (1997), *Research Design Issues in the Estimation of Beta*, McGraw-Hill, Sydney.

12. Of course this assumes that $E(r_m - r_f)$ is positive. If this were not the case, it would imply that investors expect returns smaller than the risk-free rate from investing in the (highly risky) stock market—which is not rational.

13. E. F. Fama and J. D. MacBeth (1973), 'Risk, return and equilibrium: Empirical tests', *Journal of Political Economy*, vol. 81, 607–36.

14. See, for example, *Financial Times*, June 1992.

15. E. F. Fama and K. R. French (1992), 'The cross section of expected stock returns', *Journal of Finance*, vol. 48, 427–65.

16. See, for example, F. Black (1993), 'Beta and return', *Journal of Portfolio Management*, vol. 20.

APPENDIX 7.1

DERIVATION OF THE CAPITAL ASSET PRICING MODEL[1]

It has already been argued that, if the market portfolio is efficient, the capital market line (which describes the expected return on portfolios made up of the market portfolio and the risk-free asset) is given by the following equation:[2]

$$r_p = r_f + \frac{r_m - r_f}{\sigma_m} \sigma_p \tag{7.1}$$

Note that $(r_m - r_f)/\sigma_m$ is the slope of the capital market line.

Now consider a portfolio made up of the proportion a of security i and $(1 - a)$ of the market portfolio. The expected return on the portfolio (r_p) and standard deviation of returns on the portfolio (σ_p) are given by the following equations:[3]

$$r_p = a\,r_i + (1 - a)\,r_m \tag{A7.1.1}$$

$$\sigma_p = [a^2\sigma_i^2 + (1 - a)^2\sigma_m^2 + 2a(1 - a)\sigma_{im}]^{\frac{1}{2}} \tag{A7.1.2}$$

The risk–return trade-off for a portfolio made up of various levels of security i and security m can be calculated using these two equations, and is depicted in the following diagram.

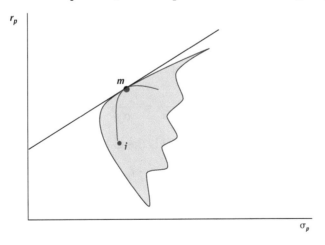

Thus, the slope of the line mapping out combinations of i and m can be found by differentiating Equation A7.1.1 and Equation A7.1.2 with respect to a, and taking the ratio of the two. First, taking the derivatives of Equations A7.1.1 and A7.1.2 yields:[4]

$$\frac{\partial r_p}{\partial a} = r_i - r_m$$

and

$$\frac{\partial \sigma_p}{\partial a} = \frac{1}{2} \times [2a\sigma_i^2 - 2\sigma_m^2 + 2a\sigma_m^2 + 2\sigma_{im} - 4a\sigma_{im}] \times$$

$$[a^2\sigma_i^2 + (1-a)^2\sigma_m^2 + 2a(1-a)\sigma_{im}]^{-1/2}$$

Next, taking the ratio of these two derivatives yields:

$$\frac{\dfrac{\partial(r_p)}{\partial a}}{\dfrac{\partial(\sigma_p)}{\partial a}} = \frac{r_i - r_m}{\dfrac{1}{2} \times [2a\sigma_i^2 - 2\sigma_m^2 + 2a\sigma_m^2 + 2\sigma_{im} - 4a\sigma_{im}] \times [a^2\sigma_i^2 + (1-a)^2\sigma_m^2 + 2a(1-a)\sigma_{im}]^{-1/2}} \qquad \text{(A7.1.3)}$$

One of the important pieces of intuition underlying the derivation of the CAPM is that the market portfolio already contains 100% of security i. Hence, a must represent overinvestment (the amount greater than 100% invested) or underinvestment (the amount less than 100% invested) in security i. That is, a must represent excess supply and excess demand for security i. However, in equilibrium, excess supply and demand must be equal to 0. This in turn implies that at point m (which describes equilibrium) in the diagram, $a = 0$. Hence, to calculate the slope of the trade-off between risk and return in equilibrium we evaluate Equation A7.1.3 at $a = 0$ to yield the following:

$$\frac{\dfrac{\partial(r_p)}{\partial a}}{\dfrac{\partial(\sigma_p)}{\partial a}} = \frac{r_i - r_m}{(\sigma_{im} - \sigma_m^2)/\sigma_m} \qquad \text{(A7.1.4)}$$

There is one final piece of intuition needed to derive the CAPM. Equation A7.1.4 describes the slope of the portfolio containing i and the market portfolio at point m. However, this is an equilibrium point and in equilibrium all portfolios are priced along the capital market line. Hence, Equation A7.1.4 must be equal to the slope of the capital market line (in Equation 7.1 above):

$$\frac{r_i - r_m}{(\sigma_{im} - \sigma_m^2)/\sigma_m} = \frac{r_m - r_f}{\sigma_m}$$

Finally, making r_i the subject of the formula yields the CAPM (Equation 7.4):

$$r_i = r_f + \beta_i(r_m - r_f)$$

where:

$$\beta_i = \frac{\sigma_{im}}{\sigma_m^2}$$

NOTES

1. The derivation in this appendix closely follows Copeland, Weston and Shastri (2004).
2. In this appendix the expectations operator $E(\cdot)$ has been dropped for convenience. Every expression for return in this appendix, however, is the expected return. Hence, r_i is $E(r_i)$, $r_p = E(r_p)$, $r_m = E(r_m)$ and indeed $r_f = E(r_f) = r_f$ because the risk-free rate is known with certainty.
3. This is the expected return and standard deviation of returns of a 'two-asset' portfolio, one 'asset' being i and the other 'asset' being the market portfolio.
4. The calculus is a little involved. The derivative of the equation for the standard deviation requires an application of the chain rule.

Company cost of capital 8

CHAPTER PREVIEW

The valuation of entire companies is a very important activity, and one that is carried out by many market participants. Investment bankers undertake corporate valuations to advise their corporate clients of the appropriate price at which to issue shares, or a 'fair' price to pay for buying (taking over) another company. Stockbrokers calculate the value of companies in advising investors on whether they appear to be overpriced (and should be sold) or underpriced (and should be bought) on the stock market. Fund managers also value companies in seeking to determine whether there are overpriced or underpriced stocks in the market.

In Chapter 3, it was demonstrated that there are two ways of valuing an entire company. First, the value of equity and debt can be estimated separately, by calculating the present value of dividends and the present value of interest and debt repayments. The sum of these two values represents the value of the company. Alternatively, we can estimate the value of the firm in one step, by calculating the present value of total cash flows after capital expenditure (i.e. free cash flows). It was argued that these two techniques should produce the same result because free cash flows are eventually distributed to equity holders and debt holders in the form of dividends or interest/principal payments.[1] In this chapter many of the ideas developed in previous chapters are brought together to demonstrate more specifically how to value an entire Australian company. Much of the analysis will focus on a simplified—debt and equity only—capital structure.

As with any asset, the value of a company is a function of (1) the return required by the providers of capital (or the company discount rate), and (2) the company's future cash flows. The return required by the providers of capital is known as the *company cost of capital*. Given that the providers of capital are debt holders and equity holders, the company cost of capital must be some combination of the cost of debt capital and the cost of equity capital.

The three broad steps in the valuation of a company are (1) estimation of the company cost of capital before or after company tax, (2) preparation of cash flow forecasts, and (3) discounting cash flows at the appropriate company cost of capital (before or after tax). In discussing the valuation of a company, this chapter is structured as a discussion of each of these steps.

KEY CONCEPTS

CONCEPT 8.1   The company cost of capital

In Chapter 3 the following expression for the value of a company was presented (Equation 3.2):

$$V = \sum_{t=1}^{\infty} \frac{F_t}{(1 + r)^t}$$

where F_t is the net cash flows after tax generated by the company for its owners (both shareholders and debt holders) and r is the company cost of capital. It is this latter r variable that is the focus of the majority of this chapter.

Company cost of capital
The return required by the providers of capital. See also *weighted average cost of capital (WACC)*.

To illustrate how the **company cost of capital** is determined, consider the information in Table 8.1, relating to the shareholders and debt holders of a company. The shareholders have invested $2 million and have an opportunity cost of 15%.[2] This implies that they require the company to generate a return of at least $0.3 million per year. In contrast, the debt holders of the company have invested $8 million, and charge interest at a rate of 10% p.a. This implies that they require the company to generate a return of at least $0.8 million per year. Hence, the total invested capital is $10 million, and the total return required by the owners of the company is $1.1 million, or 11%. This rate is the company cost of capital.

There are a number of observations that can be made in relation to the company cost of capital using the above example. First, the company cost of capital is a combination of the equity

Table 8.1	What is the company cost of capital?		
Capital	Amount	Annual cost	Annual cost
equity	$2 million	15%	$0.3 million
Debt	$8 million	10%	$0.8 million
Total	$10 million	?	$1.1 million

cost of capital and the debt cost of capital. Second, as a direct result of this, the company cost of capital lies between the cost of equity capital and the cost of debt capital. This implies that the company cost of capital is a special average of the debt and equity cost of capital. It is in fact a weighted average of the cost of debt and equity capital, and hence is commonly referred to as the **weighted average cost of capital** (or simply WACC).

Weighted average cost of capital (WACC)
A weighted average of the returns required by different classes of security holders—used as a required rate for capital investment.

The WACC

The WACC of a company funded by debt and equity capital can be calculated using the following expression:

$$WACC = \left(r_d \times \frac{D}{D+E}\right) + \left(r_e \times \frac{E}{D+E}\right)$$ **(8.1)**[3]

where:

r_d = the cost of debt capital

r_e = the cost of equity capital

D = the value of debt used by the company

E = the value of equity used by the company

That is, the WACC is the sum of the product of the cost of debt and the proportion of debt capital invested and the product of the cost of equity and the proportion of equity invested in the company. Example 8.1 illustrates the calculation of the WACC of a company using the figures in Table 8.1.

EXAMPLE 8.1

Calculating the weighted average cost of capital (WACC) of a company

QUESTION

The debt holders and equity holders of a company have invested $8 million and $2 million in a company, respectively. The debt holders of the company charge an interest rate of 10% p.a., while the equity holders require a return of 15% on their investment. What is the company cost of capital?

(continued)

ANSWER

Calculate the proportion of debt invested in (or used by) the company.

$$\frac{D}{D+E} = \frac{8}{8+2} = 0.80$$

Calculate the proportion of equity invested in (or used by) the company.

$$\frac{E}{D+E} = \frac{2}{8+2} = 0.20$$

Calculate the WACC.

$$WACC = \left(r_d \times \frac{D}{D+E}\right) + \left(r_e \times \frac{E}{D+E}\right)$$

$$WACC = (0.10 \times 0.80) + (0.15 \times 0.20)$$

Hence, the company cost of capital is 11% p.a.

The foregoing implies that, in order to be able to estimate the company cost of capital, it is necessary to estimate the proportion of debt and equity used by a company, and the costs of debt and equity capital.[4] The next sections discuss the estimation of the respective costs of debt and equity.

CONCEPT CHECK

1. How does the cost of capital relate to the value of the firm?
2. What are the two components of the cost of capital?
3. How is the weighted average cost of capital calculated?

For the answers, go to MyFinanceLab

CONCEPT 8.2   The cost of debt capital

The concept

In Chapter 3 the following expression for the value of a debt security, whose cash flows in the form of interest (i.e. coupon) can be characterised as an annuity, was derived (Equation 3.3):

$$D = \sum_{t=1}^{n} \frac{F}{(1+r_d)^t} + \frac{B}{(1+r_d)^n}$$

where:

D = the market value of the debt

n = the time to maturity of the debt

F = the interest paid (in dollars) on the debt

B = the face value of the debt (in dollars)

r_d = the discount rate

The cost of the debt is the discount rate (r_d) in the equation above. It is the return built into the cash flows of the debt security by the purchasers of the debt. Stated in another way, it is the discount rate that makes the present value of the debt's future cash flows equal to its market value.

Estimating the cost of debt

In theory, if the traded value of debt (its price) were substituted into Equation 3.3, together with the face value of debt and interest payments, the only unknown in the equation would be the cost of debt. Hence, it would be possible to *imply* the cost of debt applied by the market. Unfortunately, the problem with this theory is its practical applicability. The cash flows paid by a debt security are usually stated in the debt contract of the security and, hence, are fairly easy to obtain. However, the debt used by Australian companies is rarely publicly traded, which means that the current price of the debt cannot usually be observed.[5] Hence, an approach that implies the current cost of debt is generally impractical in the Australian debt market.

Many alternative approaches are used by analysts to develop estimates of the cost of debt capital. Some assume that corporate debt is risk free, and apply government bond yields such as the 10-year bond yield as an estimate of the corporate cost of debt. However, since it can be logically assumed that corporate debt is indeed risky, the problem with this approach is that it may understate the cost of debt and, hence, the corporate cost of capital. In order to avoid this problem, some analysts add 100 to 200 basis points (1–2%) to the 10-year bond yield and use this figure as an estimate of the cost of debt for large Australian companies.[6] This represents an attempt to add some sort of risk premium to current bond rates, but it is a rather crude approach.

Another method that can be used to estimate the cost of debt involves taking the book value of debt together with interest payments reported in the financial statements of companies. The following expression is then applied:

$$r_d = \frac{\text{net interest}}{\text{average net debt}} \tag{8.2}$$

where:

net interest = interest paid less interest received

average net debt = reported book value of debt less cash

In essence, this approach assumes that the net debt observed in the financial statements of a company is equivalent to its market value, and that this level of debt will be held in perpetuity.[7] While such an approach provides only a crude approximation of the borrowing cost of a company, this approximation is sufficient for valuation of companies with stable or insignificant levels of debt. A refinement of this approach is to use Equation 8.2 to estimate the risk premium on the debt of a company, and then to add the risk premium to the current risk-free rate to obtain the estimate of the company's current cost of debt. This is illustrated in Example 8.2.

Note that industry convention is to use net debt rather than total debt in valuing companies. The reason for this is that the difference between debt and cash represents the 'true' debt position of the company, because at any instant in time the cash could be used to reduce the debt. For reasons of consistency, since cash earns interest (while debt accrues interest), it is necessary to reduce the interest paid by the interest received to provide an estimate of the 'true' interest charge.

Where the capital structure of the company is very simple, the interest rates reported in the notes to the financial statements of the company can be used to develop a risk premium and then used to calculate the current cost of debt analogously to Example 8.2. More sophisticated approaches for estimating the cost of debt also exist; however, a discussion of such approaches is beyond the scope of this book.[8]

EXAMPLE 8.2

Estimating the cost of debt

QUESTION

Below are extracts from the balance sheet and Note 2 to the financial statements of Tabcorp Holdings Limited, which have been obtained from its *Annual and Financial Reports 2010*.

As at 30 June 2009 and 30 June 2010, 10-year bond yields stood at 5.52% and 5.10%, respectively. Use this information to estimate Tabcorp Holdings Limited's risk premium on its debt and the current cost of debt as at 30 June 2010.

Extract from balance sheet for Tabcorp Holdings Limited as at 30 June 2010

	2010 $M	2009 $M
Current assets		
Cash and cash equivalents	261.9	291.4
Receivables	80.5	70.5
Inventories	13.8	14.3
Derivative financial instruments	–	6.1
Other	24.9	20.9
Total current assets	381.1	403.2
Non-current assets		
Property, plant and equipment	1762.9	1566.3
Intangible assets—licences	652.6	688.1
Intangible assets—other	3627.5	3641.8

Other receivables	8.1	2.3
Derivative financial instruments	2.8	13.3
Other	22.7	24.4
Total non-current assets	6076.6	5936.2
TOTAL ASSETS	6457.7	6339.4
Current liabilities		
Payables	510.3	492.2
Interest-bearing liabilities	175.0	–
Current tax liabilities	46.8	56.5
Provisions	76.4	88.8
Derivative financial instruments	22.0	35.2
Other	15.5	24.3
Total current liabilities	846.0	697.0
Non-current liabilities		
Interest-bearing liabilities	1816.8	2040.9
Deferred tax liabilities	273.4	273.8
Provisions	10.6	11.3
Derivative financial instruments	53.9	35.5
Other	2.3	4.1
Total non-current liabilities	2157.0	2365.6
TOTAL LIABILITIES	3003.0	3062.6
NET ASSETS	3454.7	3276.8
Equity		
Issued capital	3733.9	3670.7
Accumulated losses	−310.0	−416.5
Reserves	30.8	22.6
TOTAL EQUITY	3454.7	3276.8

Extract from Note 2 to financial statements from Tabcorp Holdings Limited as at 30 June 2010

	2010 $M	2009 $M
2. Revenue and expenses		
(a) Other income		
Net gain on disposal of non-current assets	1.6	0.3
Net foreign exchange loss	−0.2	−3.2
	1.4	−2.9
(b) Depreciation and amortisation		
Depreciation		
– buildings	17.4	14.9

	2010 $M	2009 $M
– leasehold improvements	13.9	12.9
– plant and equipment	95.2	79.4
	126.5	107.2
Amortisation		
– Victorian wagering and gaming licences	26.5	26.5
– NSW wagering licence	3.6	3.7
– Star City and Treasury casino licences	3.1	3.2
– Queensland Keno licence	2.3	2.4
– Star City casino concessions	2.9	0.2
– software	36.6	32.4
– rental in advance	0.3	0.3
– other	1.8	1.3
	77.1	70.0
	203.6	177.2
(c) Employment costs include:		
– defined benefit plan expense	0.1	0.3
– defined contribution plan expense	41.2	39.1
– share based payments expense	3.2	2.7
	44.5	42.1
(d) Operating lease rentals		
Minimum lease payments	31.1	30.4
(e) Other expenses include:		
Cost of sales	76.0	74.5
(f) Finance income		
Interest revenue	6.8	6.9
Unwinding of discount on other receivables	0.3	0.2
	7.1	7.1
(g) Finance costs		
Interest costs	151.5	158.9
Capitalised interest	–3.6	–0.5
Other finance costs	5.3	2.1
Unwinding of discount on provisions	7.7	8.4
Net(gain)/loss on fair value hedges	0.4	–8.6
Net loss on cash flow hedges	–	0.1
	161.3	160.4

Source: Tabcorp Holdings Limited Annual & Financial Reports 2010.

ANSWER

Using the information from Note 2:

Net interest$_{2010}$ = 151.5 – 6.8 = 144.7 million

where interest paid represents borrowing costs reported in Note 2 of Tabcorp Holdings Limited's financial statements.

Using information from the statement of financial position:

Net debt = interest bearing debt – cash

Net debt$_{2009}$ = 0 + 2040.9 – 291.4 = 1749.5 million

Net debt$_{2010}$ = 175 + 1816.8 – 261.9 = 1729.9 million

Average net debt = (1749.5 + 1729.9)/2 = 1739.7 million

(Note that an examination of the entire financial statements indicates that none of the other items in the balance sheet appear to be interest bearing. The amounts in the above calculation represent current and non-current interest-bearing liabilities and cash assets.)

Hence, the cost of debt for Tabcorp Holdings Limited over the 2010 financial year can be calculated as follows:

$r_{d,2010}$ = net interest/average net debt = 144.7/1739.7 = 8.32%

The average 10-year bond yield over the 2010 financial year was:

Average 10-year bond yield$_{2010}$ = (5.52 + 5.10)/2 = 5.31%

The risk premium of Tabcorp Holdings Limited is approximately 3.01% (8.32% – 5.31%) or 301 basis points. Add this premium to the current 10-year bond yield to estimate the current cost of debt of Tabcorp Holdings Limited:

r_d = 3.01% + 5.10% = 8.11%

Hence, the current cost of debt of Tabcorp Holdings Limited is approximately 8.11% p.a.

Practitioner's POV

There are many professional agencies around the world that assess the creditworthiness or riskiness of debt issued by companies and develop so-called 'debt ratings'. Examples of such agencies include Standard & Poor's and Moody's. The rating of debt can be used by an analyst to adjust government bond yields upwards to develop an appropriate cost of debt for a company. Interestingly, following the global financial crisis of 2008–2010, we now live in an economic environment characterised by low inflation rates and, consequently, low interest rates. As well, interest rates are less volatile than they have been historically. As a result, estimating the cost of debt is less of an issue than it has been.

CONCEPT CHECK

4. How does the cost of debt capital relate to the value of a debt security?
5. How do analysts estimate the cost of non-traded debt?
6. What is meant by the 'true' debt position of a company?

For the answers, go to MyFinanceLab

CONCEPT 8.3   The cost of equity capital

The cost of equity is the minimum rate of return required on an investment in the shares of a company by its shareholders, given their risk. Since real assets determine the actual return on shares generated by a company, the risk of the cash flows generated by shares is derived from the business risk of the company issuing those shares. Theory aside, there are two general ways of generating an estimate of the required return on shares. First, the required return can be implied from the share price and fundamentals of the company (or a company in the same line of business). Second, the capital asset pricing model (CAPM) can be used to estimate the required return. Each of these methods will be discussed in turn.

Estimating the cost of equity

IMPLYING THE COST OF EQUITY

Recall that in Chapter 3 it was proven that the value of a company's shares is given by the present value of future dividends, as follows (Equation 3.5):

$$P = \sum_{t=1}^{\infty} \frac{d_t}{(1 + r_e)^t}$$

where:

   P = the current price of shares

   d_t = the dividend paid in year t

   r_e = the required return on shares

Since the price of a company can be observed in the sharemarket, if the dividends of a company can be forecast, the required return on shares, r_e, can be implied using Equation 3.5. Example 8.3 illustrates how the required return on a company's shares can be implied from current share prices and forecast dividends.

Example 8.3 assumes that Tabcorp Holdings Limited's dividend will grow constantly and hence Gordon's growth model developed earlier in Chapter 3 is applied. Clearly, the cost of equity implied for Tabcorp Holdings Limited is plausible. At 7.8%, it is approximately 2.6% higher than the 10-year bond rate (as at 3 June 2011) (a proxy for the risk-free rate of return).

However, there are at least two reasons why this estimate of the required return on Tabcorp Holdings Limited might be flawed. First, Tabcorp Holdings Limited might be over- or under-priced by the stock market, and therefore this implied cost of capital might be under- or over-estimated. Second, the assumption that Tabcorp Holdings Limited pays a constantly growing dividend might be inappropriate. The first problem is difficult to overcome, but the second problem may be overcome by assuming other (perhaps more reasonable) rates of dividend growth, and implying the required rate of return using the constant-dividend growth model given by Equation 3.7 in Chapter 3.

EXAMPLE 8.3

Implying the cost of equity

QUESTION

On Friday 3 June 2011 the following information was available for Tabcorp Holdings Limited from <www.yahoo.com>:

> Forecast growth for the next year is 1.4%
> Dividend for the year ended 3 June 2011 is 49 cents per share
> Share price is $7.72

What is the cost of equity for Tabcorp Holdings Ltd?

ANSWER

Assuming that the forecast dividend growth is an accurate estimate of the perpetual dividend growth, then Gordon's growth model can be used to imply the cost of equity as follows:

$$P = \frac{d_1}{r - g}$$

$$7.72 = \frac{0.49 \times (1 + 0.014)}{r - 0.014} = \frac{0.4969}{r - 0.014}$$

$$7.72 \, (r - 0.014) = 0.4969$$

$$r - 0.014 = \frac{0.4969}{7.72}$$

$$r = 0.078$$

Hence, Tabcorp Holdings Limited's cost of equity is approximately 7.84% p.a.

USING THE CAPM TO ESTIMATE THE COST OF EQUITY

An alternative method of estimating the cost of equity capital is the CAPM, derived in Chapter 7 as follows (Equation 7.4):

$$E(r_i) = r_f + E(r_m - r_f)\beta_i$$

where:

$E(r_i)$ = required return on the equity of stock i

$E(r_m - r_f)$ = expected return on the market over and above the risk-free rate

r_f = risk-free rate

β_i = beta of stock i

Since the expected return in the CAPM refers to returns on equity, the CAPM can be used to estimate the expected or required return on a share. Such an estimate requires the following:

1. Estimate the beta of the share using historical data.

2. Determine the current risk-free rate.

3. Determine the expected market risk premium.

4. Substitute 1 to 3 into the CAPM equation to estimate the cost of equity.

Example 8.4 illustrates the application of the CAPM to estimating the cost of equity for Tabcorp Holdings Limited.

EXAMPLE 8.4

Estimating the cost of equity using the CAPM

QUESTION

Using one year of daily data to June 2011, the beta of Tabcorp Holdings Limited is estimated at approximately 1.46. The yield on 10-year bonds as at 3 June 2011 is 5.24%. It is believed that the long-run real average return on the market in excess of the 10-year bond rate, totalling 5.3% p.a., provides a reasonable estimate of the market risk premium. What is the cost of equity capital of Tabcorp Holdings Limited?

ANSWER

Using the CAPM:

$$E(r_i) = r_f + E(r_m - r_f)\beta_i$$
$$E(r_i) = 0.0524 + (0.053 \times 1.46)$$
$$E(r_i) = 0.1298$$

Hence, Tabcorp Holdings Limited's cost of equity is approximately 12.98%.

Step 1 above was discussed at the end of the previous chapter, and steps 2 and 4 are relatively straightforward. However, step 3—estimation of the market risk premium—can pose significant problems in applying the CAPM. A number of different approaches have been developed to solve this problem. There are numerous complex issues associated with estimating the market risk premium, so a thorough treatment of the topic is beyond the scope of this text. However, a brief overview of three different approaches is provided in the remainder of this section.

HISTORICAL AVERAGE RETURNS ON THE STOCK MARKET

To this point, examples and illustrations in this book have relied on estimates of the market risk premium based on *long-term* average returns on equities in excess of bond rates.[9] There are a number of assumptions underlying this approach, including (1) that realised returns are equivalent to returns expected by market participants for bearing risk in the future, and (2) that the market risk premium is constant over time. Unfortunately, both of these assumptions may be untenable, especially the latter and, hence, alternative approaches have been developed.[10]

IMPLIED FROM SHARE PRICES AND ANALYSTS' FORECASTS

The market risk premium can also be implied using analysts' forecasts of earnings and dividends.[11] This approach uses a rearrangement of the constant-dividend growth model (see Equation 3.7) as a framework for implying required returns:

$$r_{e,i} = \frac{d_{1,t}}{P_{i,t}} + g_i$$

where:

$r_{e,i}$ = the equity cost of capital for stock i

d_1 = the one-year-ahead forecast dividend for stock i

g_i = the constant growth rate for stock i

$P_{i,t}$ = the current price of stock i

The following procedure can be used to produce estimates of the market risk premium at a point in time.

1. For each firm in the market index, estimate r_{ei} as follows. Use the constant-dividend growth model above and:
   (a) average year-on-year growth in analysts' forecast earnings as estimates of g_i
   (b) dividend forecasts as estimates of d_{1i}
   (c) share price data for $P_{i,t}$[12]
2. An estimate of the required rate of return on the market is developed by calculating a market capitalisation weighted average of $r_{e,i}$ across stocks.
3. The market risk premium is then calculated by subtracting the bond yield from the estimated required return on the market.

While this approach avoids the assumptions that the market risk premium is constant, the estimate of the risk premium is accurate only *if* analysts' forecasts of dividends and earnings are accurate—a big if!

ESTIMATE THE RELATIONSHIP BETWEEN STOCK MARKET VOLATILITY AND STOCK MARKET RETURNS

Another method of estimating the market risk premium takes into account the fact that market risk as a whole and, hence, the expected return on the market, may be changing.[13] The approach estimates the relationship between market volatility (i.e. market risk) and excess stock market returns (returns on the market less the risk-free rate). The parameter relating price volatility to excess stock returns is called the *reward-to-risk ratio*. Hence, the approach requires the estimation of b in the following model:[14]

$$r_{m,t} - r_{f,t} = a + b\sigma^2(t)$$

where:

$r_{m,t}$ = the market return over period t

$r_{f,t}$ = the risk-free rate of return over period t

b = 'reward-to-risk ratio' (risk aversion parameter)

$\sigma^2(t)$ = stock market return volatility (i.e. variance of stock market returns) over period t

Once the parameter b is estimated in a similar fashion to beta using regression analysis and historical data, an estimate of the current market risk premium is the product of the estimated b and current stock return volatility.

Practitioner's POV

In the past decade, people working in the markets have significantly changed their views on the size of the market risk premium. In the early 1990s many stockbrokers and fund managers were using a risk premium in the order of 5–6% in valuing stocks. Then in the early 2000s risk premiums of 3-4% became more common. More recently, and in the wake of the Global Financial Crisis, many have gone back to 5-6 %. The market risk premium is not an immutable quantity.

CONCEPT CHECK

7. What is the cost of equity?
8. What two methods are commonly used to estimate the cost of equity?
9. When using the CAPM, how does one estimate the risk premium?

For the answers, go to MyFinanceLab

CONCEPT 8.4   Taxation and the company cost of capital

To this point, taxation has been ignored in calculating the company cost of capital. Implicitly, the statement of cost of capital represented by Equation 8.1 has been derived under a 'no taxes' assumption. Similarly, the costs of debt and equity included in this calculation have not been adjusted for the existence of tax. In practice, of course, taxation is a fact of life and therefore should be incorporated in the analysis.

Before discussing the approaches to incorporating taxation into the cost of capital, the Australian corporate taxation system is reviewed.[15]

Company taxation in Australia and the impact on shareholders

On 1 July 1987 the Australian government introduced a new method of taxing company profits in Australia known as the 'imputation' system of taxation. Prior to 1987 the tax system in place was known as a 'classical' taxation system. The classical system remains in operation in a number of other countries, including the USA. Under a classical tax system, corporate profits are effectively taxed twice. Companies pay company tax on their net income, at the company tax rate. Next, when the after-tax income is distributed to shareholders as dividends, shareholders also pay income tax on these (net) dividends, at the personal tax rate. Accordingly, every dollar of corporate income is effectively taxed twice: once at the company level, and then again in the hands of shareholders.

The imputation system of taxation was introduced to overcome this effective double taxation. Under this system, taxation at the company level is similar to that under the classical system. That is, net company income is still subject to corporate income tax, and dividends are paid from after-tax income. However, attaching to such dividends is a tax credit known as a 'franking credit', which shareholders can use to reduce their own personal income tax liability. The franking credit is equal to the corporate tax paid on the income from which the dividend has been paid to the shareholder. Hence, under the imputation system of tax, corporate income distributed as dividends is effectively taxed only once—in the hands of the shareholder, at the shareholder's marginal tax rate (as explained below). In economic terms, franking credits essentially represent tax that has been prepaid by the company on behalf of shareholders.

The mechanics of calculating corporate tax and personal income tax on company profits is relatively straightforward. At the corporate level, tax is levied at a flat (constant) rate on **taxable income**. The corporate tax rates that have been in effect since the imputation system was introduced are set out in Table 8.2. As noted in earlier chapters, the current corporate tax rate is 30% of taxable corporate income.

Taxable income
Assessable income less deductible expenses.

Under the Corporations law, companies can distribute profits after tax as dividends, together with franking credits equivalent to the amount of company tax paid. The shareholder is then charged income tax on the sum of the cash dividend paid and the franking credit, at their personal income tax rate.[16] The personal income tax rates applicable to the financial year ended 30 June 2011 are set out in Table 8.3.

Be aware that, unlike the flat rate of tax that is applicable to companies, individuals are subject to graduated, or marginal, tax rates on different levels of income.[17] This is best explained by way of an example. Consider an individual who has a taxable income of $50 000 for the year ended 30 June 2011. This individual will pay no tax on the first $6000 of income (the tax-free threshold), then pays tax at a rate of 15% on the next $31 000 (i.e. $37 000 − $6000), totalling $4650.

The final $13 000 of income (i.e. $50 000 – $37 000) is then taxed at 30%. Adding the resultant tax of $3900 to the previous total of $4650 gives total tax payable of $8550 on the taxable income of $50 000.

Note that this tax of $8550 represents an *average* tax rate of 17.1% on $50 000 income. Due to the graduated scale of personal tax rates, the average tax rate for an individual taxpayer will always be below the marginal tax rate. The latter is the rate applicable to the income bracket in which the individual's current taxable income lies, and can be thought of as the rate at which the next dollar of income received will be taxed. In contrast, for companies there is no graduated tax scale, so the average rate is equal to the marginal rate which is equal to the corporate tax rate.

Example 8.5 illustrates the mechanics of calculating corporate and personal income tax on company profits and dividends under the imputation and classical systems of tax.

This example demonstrates that the effect of the imputation system is that corporate income is effectively taxed in the hands of the shareholder receiving a dividend. This is because the company effectively prepays the tax on the dividend income, for which the shareholder subsequently receives a tax credit. This implies that the return to shareholders after company tax is dictated by their marginal tax rate. To reinforce this concept, Example 8.6 uses the same information as above, but assumes that the recipient shareholder is subject to a marginal tax rate of 15%.

Table 8.2	Australian company tax rates since the introduction of imputation on 1 July 1987
Effective from (date)	**Australian corporate tax rate (%)[18]**
1 July 1987	49
1 July 1988	39
1 July 1993	33
1 July 1995	36
1 July 2000	34
1 July 2001	30

Table 8.3	Australian personal income tax rates for the financial year ended 30 June 2011
Income bracket ($)	**Marginal tax rate (%)**
0–6000	Nil
6001–37 000	15
37 001–80 000	30
80 001–180 000	37
Above 180 000	45

Source: Australian Taxation Office. © Commonwealth of Australia

EXAMPLE 8.5

How is $1 of corporate income taxed under the classical and imputation systems of tax?

QUESTION

Assume that a company generates $1 of income and that 100% of after-tax company income is paid out as a dividend to a shareholder currently subject to a marginal tax rate of 45%. What after-company-and-personal-tax income will the shareholder receive under (1) a classical tax system, and (2) an imputation tax system?

ANSWER

	Classical tax system	Imputation tax system
At the corporate level:		
Net income	$1.00	$1.00
Company tax	0.30[1]	0.30[1]
Cash dividend	0.70	0.70
At the shareholder level:		
Taxable income	0.70[2]	1.00[3]
Personal tax liability	0.32[4]	0.45[4]
Franking credit	n.a.	0.30[5]
Tax paid	0.32	0.15
Dividend after income tax	0.38[6]	0.55[6]

Notes to calculations

1. Corporate tax rate × net income = 0.30% × $1.
2. Taxable income under the classical tax system is the dividend distributed by the company, $0.70.
3. Taxable income under the imputation tax system is the sum of the cash dividend distributed by the company, $0.70, and the imputation credit equal to tax paid by the company, $0.30. (The total can also be calculated as $0.70/(1 − 0.30).)
4. Personal tax liability is the product of the shareholder's marginal tax rate (45%) and taxable income.
5. The franking credit distributed is equal to the corporate tax paid on the income distributed by the company ($0.30), leaving the shareholder with a net tax liability of $0.15.
6. Dividend income after tax is equal to the cash dividend received less net personal tax paid. Under the classical system, this is equal to $0.70 − 0.32 = $0.38. Under the imputation system, this is equal to $0.70 (cash dividend) − 0.15 = $0.55.

Example 8.6 again demonstrates that corporate income is effectively taxed in the hands of the shareholder, at the shareholder's marginal tax rate. However, where the shareholder is subject to a marginal tax rate that is lower than the corporate tax rate, the franking credit that attaches to the dividend is greater than the tax payable on the grossed-up dividend. Where the shareholder has tax payable on other income, the excess franking credit can be offset against other tax payable. The excess franking credit may give rise to a refund if the shareholder does not have any tax payable on other income. In Example 8.6, up to 15 cents of the total tax credit (30 cents) distributed by the company could give rise to a cash refund if there were insufficient other tax payable to utilise the credit fully.

EXAMPLE 8.6

How is $1 of corporate income taxed under the classical and imputation systems of tax?

QUESTION

Assume that a company generates $1 of income and that 100% of after-tax company income is paid out as a dividend to a shareholder currently subject to a marginal tax rate of 15%. What after-company-and-personal-tax income will the shareholder receive under (1) a classical tax system, and (2) an imputation tax system?

ANSWER

	Classical tax system	Imputation tax system
At the corporate level:		
Net income	$1.00	$1.00
Company tax	0.30	0.30
Cash dividend	0.70	0.70
At the shareholder level:		
Taxable income	0.70	1.00
Personal tax liability	0.11[1]	0.15[1]
Franking credit	n.a.	0.30
Tax paid	0.11	−0.15[2]
Dividend after income tax	0.59[3]	0.85[3]

Notes to calculations

1. Personal tax liability is the product of the shareholder's marginal tax rate (15%) and taxable income.
2. The franking credit distributed is equal to the corporate tax paid on the income distributed by the company ($0.30), only $0.15 of which is required to offset the tax liability on the dividend, leaving the shareholder with a net (imputation) tax credit of $0.15. This credit can be used to offset tax on other income or can give rise to a tax refund (negative tax payment) if no income tax is payable on other income.
3. Dividend income after tax is equal to the cash dividend received less net personal tax paid. Under the classical system, this is equal to $0.70 – 0.11 = $0.59. Under the imputation system, the dividend income after tax is equal to the cash dividend received plus the credit or cash refund of 15 cents ($0.70 + 0.15 = $0.85).

Company taxation in Australia and the impact on shareholder returns

In some circumstances only a portion—say γ—of the franking credit can be used by an investor, depending on their tax rate and other taxable income. For example, overseas investors such as

US residents cannot use their franking credits and hence $\gamma = 0$. Hence, the return on a share that pays a fully franked dividend before personal income tax can be stated as follows:

$$r_t' = (p_t - p_{t-1} + d_t + \gamma.f_t)/p_{t-1} \qquad \text{(8.3)}$$

where:

r_t' = after-company-tax-but-before-personal-tax rate of return

p_t = price of the share in period t

d_t = cash dividend paid per share

f_t = dollar amount of tax (or 'franking') credits per share distributed at time t

γ = portion of the franking credit that will be used to reduce personal tax

Since the cash return on a share (see Equation 1.4 in Chapter 1) is:

$$r_t = (p_t - p_{t-1} + d_t)/p_{t-1} \qquad \text{(8.4)}$$

hence Equation 8.3 can be re-written as:

$$r_t' = r_t + \tau \qquad \text{(8.5)}$$

where:

$$\tau = \gamma.f_t/p_{t-1}$$

This implies that the return on an equity investment under the imputation system of tax is equivalent to the cash return (capital gain plus cash dividend) plus the value of franking credits relative to the price of the shares (τ). Example 8.7 illustrates the calculation of the return from holding a share under the imputation system of tax. This example demonstrates that in February 2011 the per-share return to the shareholders of Tabcorp Holdings Limited comprised a capital gain of 69 cents, a cash dividend of 24 cents and a franking credit of 10.29 cents. In circumstances where a shareholder is not able to use the full value of the franking credit to offset other tax payable, the franking credit will result in a cash refund.

EXAMPLE 8.7

Return after corporate tax but before personal tax on shares, under the imputation system of tax

QUESTION

On 8 February 2011 Tabcorp Holdings Limited paid a dividend of 24 cents per share that was fully franked. If Tabcorp Holdings Limited's share price at the beginning of February 2011 was $6.95 and had increased to $7.61 by the end of February, what is the gross return after company tax but before personal tax for a shareholder on the top marginal tax rate?

ANSWER

Since the dividend paid by Tabcorp Holdings Limited is after corporate tax, the grossed-up value of the dividend (i.e. including the franking credit) is:

$$0.24/0.70 = 0.3429 = d_t + f_t$$

Hence:

$$f_t = 0.3429 - 0.24 = 0.1029$$

Given a personal tax rate of 45%, the shareholder will use the full value of imputation credits; hence, $\gamma = 1$. Thus:

$$r_t' = (p_t - p_{t-1} + d_t + \gamma.f_t)/p_{t-1}$$
$$= (7.61 - 6.95 + 0.24 + [1 \times 0.1029])/6.95 = 0.1443 \text{ or } 14.43\%$$

Hence, the return (before personal tax) on Tabcorp Holdings Limited over the month of February 2011 is a gain of 14.43%.

Practitioner's POV

The value of imputation credits differs across investors. For some, such as offshore investors, they are worthless. For other investors, they hold some value depending on the tax rate the investors face. Some analysts ignore imputation considerations in a valuation exercise and, as a result, implicitly ignore the value of imputation credits. These analysts then separately value a company after taking into account imputation under a number of different assumptions. This type of sensitivity analysis can be used by clients to assess the value of the company to them depending on the value they place on imputation credits. It also brings out the sensitivity of the calculated value of a company to assumptions about the value of imputation credits.

Incorporating the effect of taxation into the company cost of capital

The WACC needs to be adjusted to reflect the effect of tax. Such adjustment is, to an extent, dependent on the taxation system that is in operation—that is, classical or imputation. This can be a complex issue and, in particular, the consensus on the appropriate approach to be used for incorporating tax in the calculation of the cost of capital in Australia under an imputation tax system is far from resolved in the academic literature, as well as in practice. In this chapter, the approach developed by Officer (1994) is described. This approach involves two elements: (1) deriving an expression for WACC that is consistent with the measurement of cash flows under evaluation, since cash flows can be stated on either a before-company-tax basis or an after-company-tax basis; and (2) adjusting the CAPM to obtain a tax-adjusted cost of equity capital under imputation.

THE CLASSICAL SYSTEM

Under both the classical and the dividend imputation taxation systems there is an asymmetric (tax) treatment of the payments to fund providers—debt holders and equity holders. That is, interest payments give rise to a tax deduction, while paying dividends has no effect on the taxable income of the company. This asymmetry is what leads to *the requirement for an adjustment to the WACC which is dependent on the manner in which cash flows are stated (i.e. before or after tax)*. A further adjustment is required under a dividend imputation system, because, as discussed above, some (or all) of the corporate tax paid effectively becomes a prepayment or withholding of personal tax.

Starting with the *classical* tax system, if we need to discount forecast cash flows that are estimated on a *before-tax* basis, the appropriate WACC to use is:

$$WACC = r_d(D/V) + (r_e/[1 - t_c])(E/V) \tag{8.6}$$

where:

t_c = the corporate tax rate

The intuition behind this measure is that it adjusts the components of the cost of capital for their differing tax treatments. Specifically, it grosses up the cost of equity (r_e)—effectively already stated on an after-tax basis since no tax applies to payments to equity holders—to be on an equal footing with the tax deductible r_d. To reiterate, this WACC is to be used with *before-tax* cash flows under a *classical taxation* system.

Alternatively, cash flows to be discounted may be stated in after-tax terms. In these terms, the cash flows can be thought of as before-tax cash flows multiplied by $(1 - t_c)$. In these circumstances, we can convert the before-tax WACC to an after-tax measure, WACC′, by multiplying through by $(1 - t_c)$, to give:

$$WACC' = (r_d[1 - t_c])(D/V) + r_e(E/V) \tag{8.7}$$

This statement of WACC effectively offsets the implicit 'understatement' of *after-tax* cash flows by adjusting WACC to reflect the tax deductibility of interest payments. To reiterate, this WACC is to be used with *after-tax* cash flows under a *classical taxation* system.

THE IMPUTATION SYSTEM

Under a dividend *imputation* system, the adjustments required to account for tax in the WACC proceed on a similar basis to those above in relation to the classical system. However, there is an additional complication under the imputation system, arising from the fact that under this system the company tax collected is a mixture of both company tax and personal tax, referred to earlier as γ.

Officer (1994) develops alternative statements of WACC under a dividend imputation system, based on different definitions of before- and after-tax cash flows.

For discounting *before-tax* cash flows, the before-tax WACC under an imputation system is:

$$WACC = r_d(D/V) + [r_e/(1 - t_c[1 - \gamma])](E/V) \tag{8.8}$$

Although Equation 8.8 looks very cumbersome, a close examination reveals that it is actually quite similar to the classical before-tax WACC, Equation 8.6. In fact, the only difference is that t_c is replaced by what is known as the 'true' company tax rate, $t_c(1 - \gamma)$. For example, if shareholders were not able to utilise the franking credits paid by a company, then $\gamma = 0$ and $t_c(1 - \gamma) = t_c$, and Equation 8.8 is the same as Equation 8.6. The measure of WACC represented by Equation 8.8 is for use with *before-tax* cash flows under an *imputation taxation* system.

For after-tax cash flows, again stated as before-tax cash flows multiplied by $(1 - T)$, the WACC under imputation is defined by Officer[19] as:

$$r_i = r_E \times \frac{(1 - T)}{(1 - T[1 - \gamma])} \times \frac{E}{V} + r_D \times (1 - T) \times \frac{D}{V} \tag{8.9}$$

where:

  r_i = company cost of capital after corporate tax

  r_E = expected return on equity before tax

  r_D = expected return on debt before tax

  D = market value of debt

  E = market value of equity

  V = market value of the firm $(D + E)$

  T = effective rate of company tax on the cash flows of the company

  γ = proportion of franking credits valued by the shareholders of the company

Note that T is the *effective* corporate tax rate, which is not necessarily equivalent to the actual corporate tax rate. The effective tax rate is the rate applied to *free cash flows after interest* and yields the corporate tax paid by the company. This is to be contrasted to the corporate tax rate, which is the rate applied to the *taxable income* of a company to determine the corporate tax paid by the company.

The formulation above, while initially quite daunting, is intuitive, since the required return on equity is reduced as the proportion of franking credits that can be used by shareholders rises. That is, the factor $\frac{(1 - T)}{(1 - T[1 - \gamma])}$ rises as γ falls. To see this, note that if γ is 0, then $\frac{(1 - T)}{(1 - T[1 - \gamma])}$ is equal to 1. However, if $\gamma = 1$, then $\frac{(1 - T)}{(1 - T[1 - \gamma])}$ is equal to $(1 - T)$ and hence only a portion of r_E enters into the calculation of the WACC. This reflects the notion that the more of a franking credit that can be used by a shareholder, the lower the required return after tax. Example 8.8

illustrates the application of Equation 8.9 to calculate the company cost of capital for Tabcorp Holdings Limited.

You may be wondering at this stage how you estimate the required return on equity after company tax but before personal tax which is required to calculate the company cost of capital. This is discussed in the next section.

EXAMPLE 8.8

Estimating the weighted average cost of capital under an imputation system of tax

QUESTION

As at 3 June 2011, you obtain the following information for Tabcorp Holdings Limited.

The estimated required return on equity after company tax but before personal tax is 15.5%.

The estimated cost of debt is 8.11%.

Net debt as at 30 June 2010 is $1729.9 million

The number of shares on issue is 688 million.

The share price of Tabcorp Holdings Limited is $7.72

Estimate the company cost of capital which can be applied to free cash flows that have had the full rate of effective corporate tax applied to them.

ANSWER

1. Assume that the effective tax rate on gross free cash flows is the current corporate tax rate (30%).[20]
2. Market value of equity = shares on issue × share price = 688m × $7.72 = $5311.36m.
3. Market value of the firm = $E + D$ = $5311.36m + $1729.9m = $7041.26m.
4. Calculate WACC.

$$r_i = r_E \times \frac{(1 - T)}{(1 - T[1 - \gamma])} \times \frac{E}{V} + r_D \times (1 - T) \times \frac{D}{V}$$

$$r_i = 0.155 \times \frac{(1 - 0.3)}{(1 - 0.30[1 - 1])} \times \frac{5311.36}{7041.26} + 0.0811 \times (1 - 0.3) \times \frac{1729.9}{7041.26}$$

$$r_i = 0.155 \times 0.70 \times 0.7543 + 0.0811 \times 0.70 \times 0.2457 = 0.0958$$

Hence Tabcorp Holdings Limited's cost of capital is approximately 9.58% p.a.

CAPM under an imputation system of tax

Under the Australian imputation system of tax, Officer (1994) points out that, in order for the parameters of the CAPM to be properly estimated, the value of franking credits must be included in the calculation of returns both on the stock and on the market overall. In these circumstances, the CAPM needs to be redefined as follows[21]:

$$r_{j,t}' = r_{f,t} + E[(r_{m,t} + \tau_{m,t}) - r_{f,t}] \times \beta_j \qquad \textbf{(8.10)}$$

where:

$r_{j,t}'$ = expected return on share j before personal tax in period t, including value of franking credits that are used

$r_{f,t}$ = risk-free rate of return over period t

$r_{m,t}$ = return on the market over period t

$\tau_{m,t}$ = value of franking credits paid on stocks in the market index over period t

β_j = beta of share j

E = expected value

The value of franking credits paid out by shares in the market is difficult to estimate with any reliability, and is likely to vary considerably over time and across stocks.[22] For this reason, there is no market index published in Australia that includes the value of franking credits paid on shares in the market. Appendix 8.1 demonstrates one crude method of producing an 'Adjusted' All Ordinaries Accumulation Index from the All Ordinaries Index and the All Ordinaries Accumulation Index. The Adjusted All Ordinaries Accumulation Index assumes that the dividends paid by all shares in the index are fully franked at the applicable corporate tax rate (and $\gamma = 1$). While this is an improvement over the All Ordinaries Accumulation Index, which completely ignores the value of franking credits, it is not entirely consistent with the formulation in Officer (1994). Furthermore, note that (1) not all shares pay franked dividends, and (2) shares that pay franked dividends do not necessarily issue franking credits at the full corporate tax rate.

The method described in Appendix 8.1 can be used to convert any accumulation index which does not take into account franking credits into one which does. Such an index, together with share price data, dividend and franking credit data for a share can be used to calculate returns on an index and returns on a share which take into account franking credits. In turn, these returns can be used to calculate a beta for a share taking into account franking credits using the process outlined in the previous chapter.

Example 8.9 uses the formulation of the CAPM under an imputation tax system (Equation 8.6) to provide an estimate of the beta of Tabcorp Holdings Limited, taking into account dividend imputation.

EXAMPLE 8.9

Calculating the beta of a security assuming that imputation credits are fully valued

QUESTION

Using the following data, if Tabcorp Holdings Limited dividends are fully franked at the current corporate tax rate, calculate the beta (β) of Tabcorp Holdings Limited if all shareholders of Tabcorp Holdings Limited are able to utilise fully (and hence fully value) imputation credits.

Date	Tabcorp share price	Adjusted All Ordinaries Accumulation Index (points)	10-year bond yield (%)	Ex-dividend date	Dividend paid per share (cents)
Jun 10	6.33	30660.6	5.095		
Jul 10	6.86	31958.3	5.20		
Aug 10	6.39	31841.9	4.77	10 Aug 10	0.25
Sep 10	7.00	33516.1	4.96		
Oct 10	7.38	34256.6	5.21		
Nov 10	7.10	34092.3	5.41		
Dec 10	7.11	35410.7	5.51		
Jan 11	6.95	35434.8	5.49		
Feb 11	7.61	36314.7	5.47	8 Feb 11	0.24
Mar 11	7.49	36633.2	5.45		
Apr 11	7.63	36426.3	5.40		
May 11	7.81	35796.1	5.21		
Jun 11*	7.72	34951.9	5.24		

*For June 2011 we use the price as at 3 June 2011. Month end prices for all other dates.

ANSWER

Calculate the monthly returns on the stock (Tabcorp Holdings Limited), the stock market (Adjusted All Ordinaries Accumulation Index) and 10-year bonds.

Date	Stock return (r_{it}')	Index return (r_{mt}')	Monthly bond return $(r_{f,t}')$	Excess stock return (Y)	Excess index return (X)
Jul 10	0.0837	0.0423	0.0043	0.0794	0.0380
Aug 10	−0.0165	−0.0036	0.0040	−0.0204	−0.0076
Sep 10	0.0955	0.0526	0.0041	0.0913	0.0484
Oct 10	0.0543	0.0221	0.0043	0.0499	0.0178
Nov 10	−0.0379	−0.0048	0.0045	−0.0424	−0.0093
Dec 10	0.0014	0.0387	0.0046	−0.0032	0.0341
Jan 11	−0.0225	0.0007	0.0046	−0.0271	−0.0039
Feb 11	0.1443	0.0248	0.0046	0.1397	0.0203
Mar 11	−0.0158	0.0088	0.0045	−0.0203	0.0042
Apr 11	0.0187	−0.0056	0.0045	0.0142	−0.0101
May 11	0.0236	−0.0173	0.0043	0.0192	−0.0216
Jun 11	−0.0115	−0.0236	0.0044	−0.0159	−0.0280
Calculation	$\frac{S_t - S_{t-1} + d_t/(1-0.30)}{S_{t-1}}$	$\frac{I_t - I_{t-1}}{I_{t-1}}$	$\frac{r_f(\text{p.a.})}{12}$	$r_{it}' - r_{f,t}$	$r_{mt}' - r_{f,t}$

Calculate the monthly excess returns and mean monthly excess returns on the stock and market, variance of returns on the market and covariance of returns on the market.

Date	Excess stock return (Y)	Excess index return (X)	Covariance calculation		
			Variation in excess stock return $(Y - \bar{Y})$	Variation in excess index return $(X - \bar{X})$	Product of variation in excess returns $(Y - \bar{Y}) \times (X - \bar{X})$
Jul 10	0.0794	0.0380	0.0574	0.0311	0.0018
Aug 10	−0.0204	−0.0076	−0.0425	−0.0145	0.0006
Sep 10	0.0913	0.0484	0.0693	0.0416	0.0029
Oct 10	0.0499	0.0178	0.0279	0.0109	0.0003
Nov 10	−0.0424	−0.0093	−0.0645	0.0162	0.0010
Dec 10	−0.0032	0.0341	−0.0252	0.0272	−0.0007
Jan 11	−0.0271	−0.0039	−0.0491	0.0107	0.0005
Feb 11	0.1397	0.0203	0.1177	0.0134	0.0016
Mar 11	−0.0203	0.0042	−0.0424	−0.0026	0.0001
Apr 11	0.0142	−0.0101	−0.0079	−0.0170	0.0001
May 11	0.0192	−0.0216	−0.0028	−0.0285	0.0001
Jun 11	−0.0159	−0.0280	−0.0379	−0.0348	0.0013
Mean	0.0220	0.0069		Sum	0.009693
Variance		0.000604		Convariance	0.000881

Hence, the beta of Tabcorp Holdings Limited taking into account the imputation system of tax is 1.46.

Using this technique, the beta of Tabcorp Holdings Limited is estimated at 1.46. This beta estimate, combined with an expected market risk premium consistent with the definition of returns (that market participants use the full value of franking credits), can be used to calculate Tabcorp Holdings Limited's cost of equity capital under imputation. The Adjusted All Ordinaries Accumulation Index outlined in Appendix 8.1 can be applied to produce such an estimate. The real return on the market over the 31 years to December 2010, assuming that all stocks paid out fully franked dividends, is 11.38% or approximately 7% higher than the 10-year bond rate, see Appendix 8.2—this is an estimate of the market risk premium.

This beta estimate, together with an estimate of the market risk premium which takes into account franking credits and a 'guestimate' of γ, can be used as the basis for estimating the cost of equity capital for a company that takes into account franking credits using Equation 8.10.[23] This is illustrated in Example 8.10.

EXAMPLE 8.10

Estimating the required return under imputation using the CAPM

QUESTION

Using one year of monthly data for Tabcorp Holdings Limited and an All Ordinaries Accumulation Index which has been adjusted for franking credits, you estimate the beta for Tabcorp Holdings Limited at 1.46. The yield on 10-year bonds as at 3 June 2011 is 5.24%. It is believed that the long-run *real* average return on the market over and above the 10-year bond rate, including franking credits of 7.01% p.a., provides a reasonable estimate of the market risk premium. What is the cost of equity capital of Tabcorp Holdings Limited after company tax but before personal tax?

ANSWER

$$r_t' = r_{f,t} + E[(r_{m,t} + \tau_{m,t}) - r_{f,t}] \times \beta_j \qquad (8.10)$$

$$= 0.0524 + (0.0701 \times 1.46)$$

$$= 0.1547$$

Hence, Tabcorp Holdings Limited's cost of equity after company tax is 15.47 % p.a.

CONCEPT CHECK

10. How does the 'imputation' system of taxation differ from the 'classical' system of taxation?

11. What is a fully franked dividend?

12. Should financial managers focus on after-corporate-tax or after-personal-tax returns?

13. What is the formula for the WACC under the classical system of taxation?

14. What is the formula for the WACC under the imputation system of taxation?

For the answers, go to MyFinanceLab

CONCEPT 8.5   Australian corporate financial reporting and calculating free cash flows in valuing a company

Figure 8.1 illustrates that the cash flows of a company after reinvestment costs (capital expenditure) are distributed to the government, shareholders and debt holders of the company. The value of a company is determined by the cash flows distributable to its shareholders and debt holders—these are the free cash flows after tax. Hence, in a valuation exercise, the free cash flows need to be forecast and discounted at the company cost of capital. Furthermore, the form of the WACC in Equation 8.9 requires the calculation of free cash flows before tax, and application of the full rate of corporate tax.

The cash flow statement in the 2010 financial reports of Tabcorp Holdings Limited is reproduced as Table 8.4. This statement was produced in accordance with Australian accounting standards, which promote the reporting of historical cash flows in a similar form across Australian

FINANCE EXTRA!

Relief over dividend imputation

INVESTMENT experts have expressed relief that Treasurer Wayne Swan has ruled out exploring changes to dividend imputation at the government's October tax summit.

Russell Investments chief investment strategist Andrew Pease said dividend imputation should remain because it prevented sharemarket investors from being taxed twice and to remove it would be a tax injustice.

'Imputation is one the best things about our tax system and it encourages companies to payout higher dividends,' Mr Pease said.

He added that imputation was also one of the main reasons why Australian shares had outperformed fixed income over the course of the past decade.

A discussion paper published last week, outlining the proposed topics of the tax summit, stated the government had no intention of removing the benefits of imputation, where savers receiving a dividend also received a credit for tax paid by the company.

Critics have complained that generous tax breaks such as dividend imputation— otherwise known as franking credits—had inflated returns, encouraged risk-taking and exposed the local economy to the vagaries of international capital markets.

But Mr Pease said he had never understood such arguments and challenged critics to explain why the revenue a company earned should be taxed at a higher rate in the hands of the investor.

'If I am an investor in a company, I will pay my personal tax but I also want to get back the tax that the company has paid on my behalf,' he said.

UBS Wealth Management head of investments George Boubouras said that, while governments needed to review certain arrangements, at this stage dividend imputation worked 'wonderfully well' and had done so since being introduced in 1987.

The 2009 Australian Tax Forum chaired by Ken Henry recognised that there had been a global trend away from dividend imputation and questioned whether alternative tax relief should be discussed.

Mr Pease said that, despite Australia being one of the few countries to provide dividend imputation, local investors and companies were better off as a result.

'It is good for companies because it makes it cheaper for them to raise finance by issuing shares, otherwise investors would have to take the double taxation into account.

'And it certainly gives local investors an advantage,' Mr Pease said.

Mr Boubouras said that, generally, imputation contributed about 1.25 per cent per year to a typical large-cap equity portfolio.

The Treasurer has said the October summit would consider a number of changes.

These would include lowering the corporate tax rate, new concessions for equity finance, and streamlined depreciation rules.

Source: Bianca Hartge-Hazelman, *The Australian Financial Review*, 1 August 2011. © Fairfax Media Publications Pty Limited.

companies. These cash flows usually form the basis for forecasting future cash flows for the purpose of valuing companies. As demonstrated in Table 8.4, the cash flow statement is broken up into three distinct sections, all of which describe the generation or distribution of cash flows as demonstrated in Figure 8.1. The 'cash flows from operating activities' section describes cash flows generated from the real assets of the company ('Net cash receipts in the course of operations', 'payments to suppliers, service providers and employees' and other forms of income received such as 'interest revenue'). It also describes how those cash flows are distributed to debt holders in the form of interest and other 'finance costs paid' and to the government in the form of 'income tax paid'. The 'cash flows from investing activities' section sets out the capital expenditure of the company, while the 'cash flows from financing activities' sets out other distributions to debt holders and shareholders. Hence, in terms of calculating free cash flows, the first and second sections are the most important.

Example 8.11 illustrates the calculation of free cash flows before company tax for Tabcorp Holdings Limited using the information provided in its cash flow statement. Hence, the cash flows generated by Tabcorp Holdings Limited's basic business were $618.5 million before company tax in the year ended 30 June 2010.

If it were possible to forecast the growth rate of this free cash flow, then a cost of capital calculated according to Equation 8.8 could be used to discount these cash flows and estimate the value of Tabcorp Holdings Limited's basic business. Alternatively, the forecast cash flows could be multiplied by $1 - T$ (where T is the effective company tax rate on the cash flows of the company) and then discounted at a company cost of capital given by Equation 8.9. Example 8.12 shows how cash flow forecasts and WACC are brought together to calculate the value of the company.

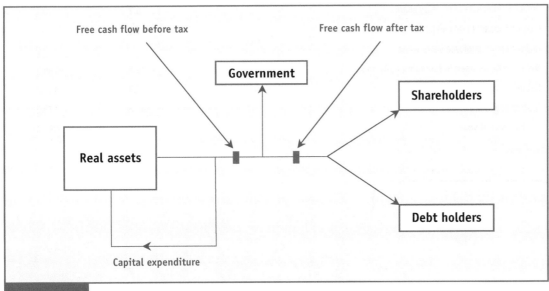

Figure 8.1   **The generation and distribution of free cash flows**

| Table 8.4 | The statement of cash flows of an Australian company |

STATEMENT OF CASH FLOWS (FOR THE YEAR ENDED 30 JUNE 2010)

	2010 $M	2009 $M
Cash flows from operating activities		
Net cash receipts in the course of operations	4280.2	4258.5
Payments to suppliers, service providers and employees	−2213.6	−2192.0
Payment of government levies, betting taxes and GST	−1038.0	−1020.7
Interest revenue received	6.6	7.1
Finance costs paid	−155.0	−171.4
Income tax paid	−179.0	−209.0
Net cash flows from operating activities	701.2	672.5
Cash flows from investing activities		
Payment for property, plant and equipment and intangibles	−408.1	−256.5
Proceeds from sale of property, plant and equipment and intangibles	2.7	1.7
Loans advanced to customers	−4.7	–
Net cash flows used in investing activities	−410.1	−254.8
Cash flows from financing activities		
Proceeds from debt raising	–	434.5
Proceeds from issue of shares	–	387.0
Net repayments of borrowings	−15.0	−770.3
Payment of transaction costs for share issue	–	7.8
Dividends paid	−303.4	−341.0
Payments for on-market share buy back	−1.9	−2.2
Proceeds from sale of Treasury shares	0.7	0.1
Loans advanced to related party	−1.0	–
Repayment of employee share loans	–	0.2
Net cash flows used in financing activities	−320.6	−299.5
Net increase/(decrease) in cash held	−29.5	118.2
Cash at beginning of year	291.4	173.2
Cash at end of year	261.9	291.4

Source: Tabcorp Holdings Limited Annual Report 2010.

EXAMPLE 8.11

The calculation of free cash flows for Tabcorp Holdings Limited for the year ended 30 june 2010

QUESTION

Using the cash flow statement of Tabcorp Holdings Limited for the year ended 30 June 2010, estimate its free cash flows before tax using only regular or recurring relevant cash flows.

ANSWER

		$ million
Cash receipts from operations		4280.2
Less Payments to suppliers, service providers and employees and payments of government levies, betting taxes and GST	2 213.6 + 1 038.0 =	3251.6
Net capital expenditure		405.4
Free cash flows before tax		623.2

Hence, the free cash flows (before tax) available for distribution to the owners of Tabcorp Holdings Limited (i.e. both debt holders and equity holders) = $623.2 million. The example demonstrates that there are only three pieces of information that are relevant for the calculation of free cash flows—operating cash receipts, operating cash payments and capital expenditure. All other items, such as interest received and paid and items relating to financing activities, describe the distribution of cash flows and are irrelevant to valuing the firm.

EXAMPLE 8.12

Estimating the value of the firm, and the value of equity

QUESTION

As at 3 June 2011 you obtain the following information for Tabcorp Holdings Limited.

The estimated *real* company cost of capital under an imputation system of tax to be applied to cash flows after tax is 6.64% p.a. (assuming the effective tax rate is 30%).

The free cash flows before tax for the year ended 30 June 2010 are $623.2 million.

The number of shares on issue is 688 million.

The net debt reported in its balance sheet is $1729.9 million. Federal Treasury is forecasting *real* economic growth of approximately 3.75% p.a. between 30 June 2010 and 30 June 2013.

The forecast inflation rate between 30 June 2010 and 30 June 2013 is approximately 3.0% p.a.

Assuming that the free cash flows of Tabcorp Holdings Limited are sustainable and are expected to grow perpetually at the current forecast real economic growth rate, estimate the value of each share.

ANSWER

(1) Free cash flows after tax, applying full corporate tax rate ($m)

$$F_t = 623.2 \times (1 - 0.30) = 436.2$$

(2) Value of the firm using the constant dividend growth model.

$$V = \frac{F_t(1 + g)}{WACC - g} = \frac{436.2(1 + 0.0375)}{0.0664 - 0.0375} = \$15\ 659.4$$

(3) Value of equity = value of firm − net book value of debt

$$= 15\ 649.4 - 1729.9 = 13\ 929.5$$

(4) Value of each share = value of equity/issued shares

$$= 13\ 929.5/688 = \$20.25$$

Hence, the value of Tabcorp Holdings Limited shares (if free cash flows before tax grow in line with current forecasts of economic growth!) is estimated at $20.25.

CONCEPT CHECK

15. What are free cash flows?

16. What are the three categories of cash flows shown in a company's statement of cash flows?

17. What role do free cash flows play in a company valuation?

For the answers, go to MyFinanceLab

Student Learning Centre

My Finance Lab ■ To test your mastery of the content covered in this chapter and to create your own personalised study plan, go to MyFinanceLab: www.pearson.com.au/myfinancelab

CONCEPT CHECKLIST

In this chapter the following concepts were discussed:

➤ The company cost of capital

➤ The cost of debt capital

➤ The cost of equity capital

➤ Company tax and its impact on the cost of capital

➤ Australian corporate financial reporting and the calculation of free cash flows in valuing a company

SELF-TEST QUESTION

The Noel Corporation, the provider of Christmas cheer, has decided to use the weighted average cost of capital (WACC) to discount the after-tax cash flows associated with project evaluation. You have been given the task of determining the after-tax WACC of the firm. You are informed that the Noel Corporation uses the following securities to fund its operations.

- Debentures with a face value of $400 000 that will mature in five years' time and offer a coupon that is paid half-yearly. The coupon rate for these debentures is 8% p.a. The current market yield for these debentures is 6% p.a., calculated half-yearly.

- A zero coupon bond with a face value of $100 000, the current market value of which is $92 000. Assume that interest is calculated on the bond on a yearly basis. The bond will mature in three years.

- Five hundred thousand (500 000) ordinary shares, which recently paid a dividend of 20 cents. Dividends are expected to grow at 5% p.a. The beta of the Noel Corporation is 1.2, the risk-free rate is currently 3% p.a. and the expected return on the market is 12% p.a.

- Two hundred thousand (200 000) preference shares, which pay a dividend of $1. Each preference share is trading at a market price of $8.

Noel Corporation's tax rate is 30% p.a.

(a) What is the after-tax WACC of the Noel Corporation?

(b) When is it appropriate to use the WACC you have estimated?

Self-test answer

Market value of debentures

$$FV = -400\ 000, n = 5 \times 2 = 10, i = 6\%/2 = 3\%, PMT = -16\ 000$$

$$PV = 16\ 000 \left[\frac{1 - (1.03)^{-10}}{0.03} \right] + \frac{400\ 000}{1.03^{10}}$$

$$= (16\ 000 \times 8.5302) + 297\ 637.57 = 136\ 483.20 + 297\ 637.57$$

Present value = $434 121

Annual market interest rate on debentures

$$i_e = \left(1 + \frac{j}{m}\right)^m - 1 = \left(1 + \frac{0.06}{2}\right)^2 - 1 = 0.0609$$

After-tax cost of debentures

$6.09(1 - t_c) = 6.09(0.70) = 4.26\%$

Zero-coupon bond

Cost of zero-coupon bond

$$FV = -100\ 000, PV = 92\ 000.00, PMT = 0, n = 3, i = ?$$

$$92\ 000 = \frac{100\ 000}{(1 + r)^3}$$

$$(1 + r)^3 = \frac{100\ 000}{92\ 000}$$

$$(1 + r)^3 = 1.087$$

$$(1 + r) = 1.087^{\frac{1}{3}}$$

$$1 + r = 1.028$$

$$r = 0.0282 \text{ or } 2.82\%$$

After-tax cost of zero coupon bonds

$2.82(1 - t_c) = 2.8(0.7) = 1.97\%$

Equity

$$E(R_{sc}) = R_f + \beta_{sc}(E[R_m] - R_f) = 3 + 1.2(12 - 3) = 13.8\%$$

Market value of equity

$$P_0(SC) = \frac{0.20(1 + 0.05)}{0.138 - 0.05} = \frac{0.21}{0.088} = \$2.386 \text{ per share}$$

Market value of equity = $2.386 × 500 000 = 1 193 182

Preference shares

$$P_0 = \frac{D}{r}$$

$$8 = \frac{1}{r} \therefore r = \frac{1}{8} = 0.1250 \text{ or } 12.50\%$$

Market value of preference shares

$8 \times 200\ 000 = \$1\ 600\ 000$

Calculation of WACC

	Market value	Cost after tax	Weight	Weighted cost
Equity	1 193 182	13.80%	0.3595	4.96%
Preference	1 600 000	12.50%	0.4820	6.03%
Debentures	434 121	4.26%	0.1308	0.56%
Zero coupon	92 000	1.97%	0.0277	0.05%
TOTAL	3 319 303			11.60%

DISCUSSION QUESTIONS

1. What is a company's cost of capital used for? Broadly speaking, how is it calculated?

2. Discuss some of the alternative approaches used for estimating the cost of debt component of the company cost of capital. What are the practical limitations relating to each approach? Which approach do you think is the most appropriate in practice?

3. What are the assumptions underlying the use of a dividend growth model for the estimation of a company's cost of equity?

4. Compare and contrast the two different models that can be used for estimating a company's cost of equity capital—the dividend growth model and the CAPM. Which model is preferred? Why?

5. Why is an estimate of the market risk premium useful in calculating a company's cost of capital? How is this premium determined in practice?

6. Compare and contrast the essential features of the alternative systems of corporate taxation— classical and dividend imputation.

7. What is a franking credit? How does it affect the after-tax returns of a shareholder?

8. Explain why the average tax rate is lower than the marginal tax rate for individual taxpayers in Australia, whereas the two rates are equal for companies.

9. What does the dividend imputation system of taxation imply about 'true' corporate tax? What is the impact of this on the calculation of a company's cost of capital?

10. Outline the alternative measures of adjusting WACC for the effect of the dividend imputation system of taxation.

11. What does γ represent in the context of taxation under a dividend imputation system of taxation? How might it be estimated in practice?

PRACTICAL QUESTIONS

1. Consider a company that has the following values: BASIC

Cost of equity	17.6%
Cost of debt	9.5%
Book value of equity	$1 700 000
Book value of debt	$500 000
Market value of equity	$2 319 000
Market value of debt	$541 650

    What is this company's WACC, assuming no taxes?

2. A shareholder who is currently subject to a marginal tax rate of 34% receives a dividend of $2000.   BASIC
    Determine the after-tax return to the shareholder, assuming (a) a classical tax system and
    (b) a dividend imputation system (assume that the dividend is fully franked and the company tax
    rate is 30%).

3. Calculate the WACC of AOI Ltd, using the following information.   INTERMEDIATE

    Statement of financial performance extract

    Liabilities

10% debentures ($100 par)	$10 000 000

    Shareholders' funds

Paid-up capital—ordinary shares ($1 par)	$25 000 000
12% preference shares ($10 par)	$5 000 000

    Additional information

    *   The ordinary shares are currently trading at $4.20 per share.
    *   Commonwealth government bonds trade at 5%.
    *   The return on the market portfolio is 13.5%.
    *   AOI's beta is 1.25.
    *   Its debentures are priced at $96.50 and its preference shares are trading at par.
    *   The current return on AOI debentures is 2% above the government bond rate.
    *   No company or personal taxes are levied.
    *   The existing capital structure is unlikely to change.

4. Scrumptious Cookies, a national baking franchise, has decided to professionalise its project   INTERMEDIATE
    evaluation. Previously, franchise locations had been selected on an *ad hoc* basis, with mixed results.
    The managing director has decided that net-present-value analysis is the best method. You have been
    given the task of determining the WACC of the firm. You are told that the firm has used the following
    securities to finance its operations.

    *   Four hundred thousand (400 000) ordinary shares, issued at a par value of $1.50. The beta of
        Scrumptious Cookies is 1.5, the risk-free rate is currently 4% p.a. and the expected return on the
        market is 10% p.a. Scrumptious Cookies is expected to pay a dividend of 10 cents per share next
        year, and has an expected growth rate of 8% p.a.
    *   An overdraft of $300 000. The current interest rate on the overdraft is 9.5% p.a., with interest
        calculated on a monthly basis.

- Debentures with four years to maturity. The debentures offer a coupon of 8% p.a., paid half-yearly. (The coupon is calculated on the face value.) The face value of the debentures is $300 000, and the current market interest rate for these securities is 10% p.a., calculated half-yearly.

- A zero-coupon bond with a face value of $150 000, the current market value of which is $73 790.06. Assume that interest is calculated on the bond on a quarterly basis. The bond will mature in six years' time.

If Scrumptious Cookies pays tax at 33% p.a., what is its WACC (after tax)? (Show all your workings.)

INTERMEDIATE

5. Refer back to Examples 8.8 and 8.9. Using the information in Appendix 8.2 to develop an estimate of the market risk premium, and assuming a long-term forecast inflation rate of 3%, estimate the WACC of Tabcorp Holdings Limited that would be used to discount (a) its before-company-tax free cash flows, and (b) its free cash flows after they have been multiplied by $1 - T$ (where T is the effective company tax rate charged to cash flows).

INTERMEDIATE

6. Refer back to Example 8.12. Using the cost of capital calculated in the previous practical question, if the cash receipts and payments from operations of Tabcorp Holdings Limited are all from its basic business, and its cash receipts are expected to grow in line with the forecast long-term nominal economic growth rate of 6% p.a., and the remaining cash flows are expected to grow in line with the long-term forecast inflation rate of 3% p.a, what is the total value of Tabcorp Holdings Limited's basic business?

CHALLENGING

7. (a) Calculate the company cost of capital (or WACC) of Kangas Ltd, a company that commenced operations many years ago. Relevant details relating to the company include the following.

   Extract from statement of financial performance

   Liabilities

Debentures ($100 par, 12.5% coupon—annual)	$4 000 000
Preference shares ($3 par, 7% cumulative)	1 500 000

   Owners' equity

Ordinary shares ($0.50 par)	$7 500 000
Retained earnings	2 500 000

   Additional information

   - An interest payment in relation to the debentures has just been made, and they mature three years from today. The market rate of interest on the debentures is 15%. (Use this to calculate the market value of the debt.)

   - The preference shares are trading on the market at $3.00, and a dividend of 21 cents per share has just been paid.

   - Forecasts in relation to market returns are as follows: expected risk-free rate of return = 6.5%; expected return on the market portfolio = 16.0%; and the systematic risk of Kangas ordinary shares is the same as the market portfolio's systematic risk. These shares are trading on the market at $0.63 each.

   (b) In practice, why would management wish to calculate a company's WACC? That is, what does it represent?

   (c) Briefly describe the circumstances under which it would be appropriate for Kangas management to use the WACC calculated in part (a) for project evaluation. Under what specific circumstances would it be inappropriate to use this WACC?

8. Recalculate the company cost of capital for the company in Question 1, assuming:

(a) a classical tax system applies and cash flows are stated in after-tax terms.

(b) a dividend imputation system applies and cash flows are before tax.

(c) a dividend imputation system applies and cash flows are after tax.

Assume 30% company tax rate.

9. You believe that a company's shares are overpriced by up to 20%. You are given the following information about the company.

- Its beta base on the CAPM including imputation is 1.0, the market risk premium is 7% after company tax but before personal tax and the risk-free rate of return is running at 6%.
- The cost of debt is 9%, and the company's net debt is $1675 million.
- It has 423 million shares on issue.
- The effective company tax rate is approximately 30%.
- The company's net operating cash flows before tax are currently $712 million, and its capital expenditure is approximately $100 million. All cash flows are expected to grow at a rate of around 3% perpetually.
- Investors in the company are able to utilise fully franking credits.

(a) If the current share price of the company were $14, and you were to use this price to calculate the WACC of the company, to what extent would you miscalculate the true WACC of the company?

(b) Using the information given above, calculate the fair market value of the company's equity. (Hint: You don't need to know the share price of the company to answer this question, and you may need to use trial and error to solve for the value of the company.)

10. You are considering investing in XYZ. XYZ is a mining company with operations in Australia. You wish to obtain the value of XYZ after company tax and including the effect of franking credits. Following the release of XYZ's financial reports for the year ending 30 June 2011 XYZ's stock price dropped to $0.80. What is the value of XYZ's stock and based on your valuation is XYZ a good investment?

- The market risk premium including the effect of franking credits is approximately 5% over the long term.
- Dividends are partially franked at 50%.
- The imputation adjusted beta is 1.2. The non-imputation adjusted beta is 1.1.
- The yield on 10-year government bonds is 5.2%.
- Real economic growth is forecast to be 2.5% according to the Federal Treasury.
- Cash receipts from operations for the financial year 2011 was $120 million, payments to employees was $20 million, payments to suppliers was $10 million, net capital expenditure was $20 million and dividends paid for the year was $10 million.
- The estimated cost of debt for XYZ is 7%.
- XYZ has 40 million shareholders.
- XYZ's net debt as at 30 June 2011 is $70 million.
- The corporate tax rate is 30%.

11. Four years ago Company ABC issued $40 million in corporate bonds with a yield and coupon rate of 5.2%. The coupon payments occur twice per year. The current market yield for the corporate bonds

has increased to 8% p.a. Company ABC has viewed this as an opportunity to reduce its debt levels because of the inverse relationship between bond prices and the yield. What is the current market value of the corporate bonds? The latest stock price for ABC is $10.20. Assuming no dilution effects on the stock price how many new shares will have to be issued in order to repay the corporate bonds? The debt to equity ratio prior to the issuance of new shares was 2:1. The total market value of all debt owed by ABC based on the most recent financial report is $100 million. The current market value of equity is $50 million. What is the new debt to equity ratio and does ABC have more debt than it does equity after the issuance of new shares?

FURTHER READING

For a comprehensive treatment of the calculation of the weighted average cost of capital under an imputation system of tax, including further examples, refer to:

- Officer, R. (1994), 'The cost of capital under an imputation system of taxation', *Accounting and Finance*, vol. 34.

For a discussion of three different approaches to estimating the market risk premium see:

- Carleton, W. and Lakonishok, J. (1985), 'Risk and return on equity: The use and misuse of historical estimates', *Financial Analysts Journal*, January–February 1985.
- Harris, R. and Marston, F. (1992), 'Estimating shareholder risk premia using analysts' growth forecasts', *Financial Management*, vol. 21.
- Merton, R. (1980), 'On estimating the expected return on the market', *Journal of Financial Economics*, vol. 8, 323–61.

NOTES

1. Even if the cash flows are reinvested in the near term, if the management of a company are rational such cash flows will be reinvested at a rate of return expected by the providers of the capital (equity holders and debt holders) and will eventually be available for distribution.
2. The determination of the specific opportunity costs of equity holders and debt holders is explained more fully in Concepts 8.2 and 8.3 in this chapter.
3. Equation 8.1 technically relates to one class or form of debt capital and equity capital each. When a company has n forms of capital, the following general expression is used:

$$\text{Weighted average cost of capital} = \sum_{t=1}^{n} r_x \times W_x$$

where:

   x = form of finance of company (e.g. debt or equity)
   r_x = the required return on finance form x
   W_x = proportion of company's total finance made up of x

4. While not commonly appreciated by most market analysts, there is an element of circularity in estimating the WACC from this commonly used expression and then applying it in a discounted cash flow framework to estimate the market value of equity. The reason is that you need to know the market value of equity in order to work out the WACC and yet, if this were known, there would be no need to estimate the WACC. Sophisticated practitioners simultaneously solve for the WACC and the market value of equity.
5. While there are some exceptions, in the cases where debt securities are listed on the Australian Securities Exchange trading in such securities is fairly light.
6. Bond yields in Australia are normally quoted to the second decimal place—for example, 10.29%. For this reason, one basis point refers to 0.01 of 1%, and hence 100 basis points refers to 100×0.01 of 1%, which is 1%.

7. To see this, note that the present value of interest payments made in *perpetuity* is given by:

$$\text{Value of debt} = \frac{\text{net interest}}{r_d}$$

and hence:

$$r_d = \frac{\text{net interest}}{\text{value of debt}}$$

8. A discussion of this issue can be found in Chapter 14 in G. Foster (1986), *Financial Statement Analysis*, Prentice Hall, New York.

9. For a discussion of the issues in applying this approach, see W. Carleton and J. Lakonishok (1985), 'Risk and return on equity: The use and misuse of historical estimates', *Financial Analysts Journal*, January–February 1985.

10. One of the reasons the market risk premium may be varying over time is because expected (and possibly actual) returns on bonds and the sharemarket are a function of inflation. Many historical estimates of the market risk premium ignore inflation. It is relatively straightforward to convert historical nominal returns to real returns using the Fisher relation produced in Chapter 5:
$$R_e^n - 1 = (1 + \rho)(R_e^r - 1)$$
where ρ is the inflation rate, R is a return, e denotes equity, n denotes nominal returns and r denotes real returns.

11. An example of a published US study that applies this approach is R. Harris and F. Marston (1992), 'Estimating shareholder risk premia using analysts' growth forecasts', *Financial Management*, vol. 21.

12. The forecasts for earnings and dividends in Australia can be extracted from IBES. I/B/E/S produces averages of current earnings and dividend forecasts of the analysts of major stockbrokers in Australia.

13. See R. Merton (1980), 'On estimating the expected return on the market', *Journal of Financial Economics*, vol. 8.

14. This equation can be represented as a straight line:
$$Y = a + bX$$
where $Y = r_{m,t} - r_{f,t}$ and $X = \sigma^2(t)$; econometric theory implies that b is a regression parameter which is calculated as follows (refer to Chapter 7):
$$b = \frac{\text{covariance }(X,Y)}{\text{variance }(X)}$$

15. R. Officer (1994), 'The cost of capital under an imputation system of taxation', *Accounting and Finance*, vol. 34.

16. A note on jargon. The sum of franking credits and cash dividends is often referred to as the 'grossed-up' dividends. The franking credit is called 'imputed income' at this point.

17. Personal income tax rates change from year to year. Current rates can be sourced from the Australian Taxation Office website.

18. Tax rates first influence dividends paid out in the calendar year following the financial year in which they first became effective. For example, dividends paid in the 1989/90 financial year were the first to be issued with a tax credit at a 39% rate, first applicable to companies in the year ended 30 June 1989. The reason for this is that dividends are paid from after-tax income.

19. This derivation is reproduced in Appendix 8.1. The authors would like to thank Professor Bob Officer from Melbourne University for private discussions in which he clarified various elements of his approach.

20. One of the main reasons why the rate of tax paid on taxable income will differ from the apparent rate of tax paid on free cash flows is because depreciation differs from capital expenditure. For Tabcorp Holdings Limited in the year in question, depreciation and amortisation for the year totalled $142.3 million, while capital expenditure was $206.1 million. Hence, the assumption that the rate of tax applied to free cash flows will be the same as that applied to taxable income is a very crude approximation at best.

21. Officer (1994), op. cit., 10.

22. For clues on how to imply such values from share price and dividend data, see P. Brown and A. Clarke (1993), 'The ex-dividend day behaviour of Australian share prices before and after dividend imputation', *Australian Journal of Management*, vol. 18.

23. Note that although, in practice, beta estimates which take into account franking credits are unlikely to differ substantially from classical betas, the cost of capital based on the CAPM which takes into account franking credits may differ substantially. The reason for this is the very different market risk premium which may be applied. For example, Appendix 8.2 illustrates that the real market risk premium estimated from historical All Ordinaries Accumulation Index data of approximately 6.3% (10.9 – 4.6) is lower than a similarly estimated market risk premium which takes into account franking credits of approximately 8.5% (13.1 – 4.6).

APPENDIX 8.1

ADJUSTING THE ALL ORDINARIES ACCUMULATION INDEX TO TAKE INTO ACCOUNT FRANKING CREDITS ON DIVIDENDS PAID BY SHARES IN THE INDEX

Calculations required

This appendix demonstrates how to adjust the All Ordinaries Accumulation Index to include the value of franking credits, using the All Ordinaries Index and the All Ordinaries Accumulation Index. One critical assumption made in these adjustments is that all companies in the index pay fully franked dividends at the full corporate tax rate (currently 30%). While this is a questionable assumption, it is nevertheless an improvement on the assumption that companies do not pay franked dividends, which is the assumption that underlies the All Ordinaries Accumulation Index.

Equations 6.5 and 6.6 in Chapter 6 set out the daily updating formulas used by the Australian Securities Exchange to calculate the All Ordinaries Index and the All Ordinaries Accumulation Index, respectively, which can be rearranged to yield the following:

$$\frac{I_t}{I_{t-1}} = \frac{E_t}{E_{t-1}} \tag{A8.1.1}$$

and

$$\frac{I^*_t}{I^*_{t-1}} = \frac{E_t + D_t}{E_{t-1}} \tag{A8.1.2}$$

where:

I_t, I^*_t = index level at the end of interval t

E_t = market capitalisation of securities in the index at the end of interval t

D_t = value of dividends paid by securities in the index during interval t

In order to extract the dividend yield from the two indices, rearrange Equations A8.1.1 and A8.1.2 and take their difference as follows:

$$\frac{I^*_t}{I^*_{t-1}} - \frac{I_t}{I_{t-1}} = \frac{E_t + D_t}{E_{t-1}} - \frac{E_t}{E_{t-1}} = \frac{D_t}{E_{t-1}} \tag{A8.1.3}$$

That is, the difference in the index relatives of the All Ordinaries Index and the All Ordinaries Accumulation Index is the dividend yield.[*]

---

[*] A note on jargon. The ratio of two consecutive prices is called the price relative—that is, $\frac{price_t}{price_{t-1}}$ while the ratio of a dividend to the price of a share is called the dividend yield—that is, $\frac{dividend_t}{price}$.

Next, calculate the value of the grossed-up dividend yield (i.e. the ratio of the sum of the dividend yield and franking credit to the market capitalisation of shares in the index), by dividing both sides of Equation A8.1.3 by 1 less the corporate tax rate t_c (e.g. 0.30):

$$\left[\frac{I^*_t}{I^*_{t-1}} - \frac{I_t}{I_{t-1}}\right] \times \frac{1}{(1-t_c)} = \frac{D_t}{E_{t-1}} \times \frac{1}{(1-t_c)} = \frac{D_t/(1-t_c)}{E_{t-1}} \quad \text{(A8.1.4)}$$

Note, however:

$$\frac{D_t}{(1-t_c)} = D_t + C_t \quad \text{(A8.1.5)}$$

where C_t is the value of the total franking credits distributed with the dividends D_t.

Finally, if the ratio (Equation A8.1.4) above is added to the price relative of the All Ordinaries Index, and 1 is subtracted, this will yield an estimate of the return on an index which takes into account the value of dividends and franking credits. That is, the following calculation is carried out.

$$\frac{I_t}{I_{t-1}} + \left[\frac{I^*_t}{I^*_{t-1}} - \frac{I_t}{I_{t-1}}\right] \times \frac{1}{(1-t_c)} - 1 \quad \text{(A8.1.6)}$$

It is straightforward to prove that Equation A8.1.6 reduces to the return on the market from capital gains, dividends and franking credits, by substituting Equations A8.1.1, A8.1.2, A8.1.4 and A8.1.5 into A8.1.6 above and simplifying:

$$= \frac{E_t}{E_{t-1}} + \frac{D_t + C_t}{E_{t-1}} - \frac{E_{t-1}}{E_{t-1}}$$

$$= \frac{[E_t - E_{t-1}] + [D_t + C_t]}{E_{t-1}}$$

The equation above demonstrates that a calculation along the lines of Equation A8.1.6 is equivalent to calculating the return on the market, which includes the capital gain on shares in the market index $(E_t - E_{t-1})$, plus total cash dividends paid out by shares in the market index (D_t), plus the sum of franking credits (C_t) paid by shares in the market index.

Calculations

Table A8.1.1 demonstrates the calculation of an 'Adjusted All Ordinaries Accumulation Index', which takes into account the value of franking credits paid by shares in the index, using the All Ordinaries Index and the All Ordinaries Accumulation Index. The necessary calculations are derived in the previous section. Note that the calculations in this appendix should be regarded as approximations only, because the updating formulae for the All Ordinaries and All Ordinaries

Accumulation Indices are applied daily. This means that dividends earned are reinvested daily for the accumulation index, while this appendix applies the formulae to annual data (and assumes annual reinvestment of dividends).

Table A8.1.1   The calculation of an Adjusted All Ordinaries Accumulation Index from the reported All Ordinaries Index and the All Ordinaries Accumulation Index, which includes imputation credits in the definition of returns

	All ordinaries		All ordinaries relatives[1]		Dividend yield		Adjusted all ordinaries	
	Index	Accumulation index	Index	Accumulation index	Cash[2]	Plus franking credit[3]	Accumulation return[4]	Accumulation index[5]
Dec 09	4882.7	33698.6						33698.60
Jan 10	4596.9	31727.4	0.9415	0.9415	0.0000	0.0001	−0.0585	31727.95
Feb 10	4651.1	32304.4	1.0118	1.0182	0.0064	0.0091	0.0209	32391.93
Mar 10	4893.1	34188.1	1.0520	1.0583	0.0063	0.0090	0.0610	34367.91
Apr 10	4833.9	33785.4	0.9879	0.9882	0.0003	0.0005	−0.0116	33967.81
May 10	4453.6	31228.6	0.9213	0.9243	0.0030	0.0043	−0.0744	31440.81
Jun 10	4324.8	30415.2	0.9711	0.9740	0.0029	0.0041	−0.0248	30660.61
Jul 10	4507.4	31701.6	1.0422	1.0423	0.0001	0.0001	0.0423	31958.35
Aug 10	4438.8	31476	0.9848	0.9929	0.0081	0.0116	−0.0036	31841.91
Sep 10	4636.9	33055.9	1.0446	1.0502	0.0056	0.0079	0.0526	33516.11
Oct 10	4733.4	33773.5	1.0208	1.0217	0.0009	0.0013	0.0221	34256.59
Nov 10	4676.4	33538.1	0.9880	0.9930	0.0051	0.0072	−0.0048	34092.29
Dec 10	4846.9	34812.8	1.0365	1.0380	0.0015	0.0022	0.0387	35410.67
Jan 11	4850.0	34836.1	1.0006	1.0007	0.0000	0.0000	0.0007	35434.82
Feb 11	4923.6	35600.2	1.0152	1.0219	0.0068	0.0097	0.0248	36314.69
Mar 11	4928.6	35829.6	1.0010	1.0064	0.0054	0.0078	0.0088	36633.18
Apr 11	4899.0	35623.4	0.9940	0.9942	0.0003	0.0004	−0.0056	36426.29
May 11	4788.9	34951.8	0.9775	0.9811	0.0036	0.0052	−0.0173	35796.09
Jun 11	4666.6	34107.0	0.9745	0.9758	0.0014	0.0020	−0.0236	34951.86

NOTES TO TABLE A8.1.1

1. Index relative = $\dfrac{\text{index}}{\text{index}_{t-1}}$

2. Cash dividend yield = $\dfrac{d_t}{AMV_{t-1}}$, where d_t are dividends paid out by shares in the index in month t, and AMV is the aggregate market capitalisation of shares in the index. It is calculated as follows:
   Cash yield = All Ordinaries Accumulation Index relative – All Ordinaries Index relative

3. Cash plus franking credit dividend yield = $\dfrac{d_t + C_t}{AMV_{t-1}}$, where items are as defined in note 2 and C_t is the value of all franking credits paid out by the index assuming they are all fully franked at a 30% tax rate. It is calculated as follows:
   Cash dividend yield/(1 – 0.30)

4. Return on an index which includes franking credits, dividends and capital gains—that is, return on Adjusted Accumulation
   Index = $\dfrac{AMV_t - AMV_{t-1}}{AMV_{t-1}}\dfrac{d_t + C_t}{}$, where items are as defined in notes 2 and 3. It is calculated as follows:
   (Price relative of All Ordinaries Index + cash plus franking credit dividend yield) – 1

5. The All Ordinaries Accumulation Index reflecting the value of franking credits. This is calculated as follows:
   (1 + return on Adjusted All Ordinaries Accumulation Index$_t$) × (Adjusted All Ordinaries Accumulation Index$_{t-1}$)
   Note that the first observation is the actual reported All Ordinaries Accumulation Index.

APPENDIX 8.2

Table A8.2.1 The 31-year average return on an Adjusted All Ordinaries Accumulation Index from 1979 to 2010*

| | RAW NUMBERS | | | | | RAW RETURNS (%) | | | | | REAL RETURNS (%) | | | |
| | | | All Ordinaries | | | | All Ordinaries | | | | | All Ordinaries | | |
Year	10-year bonds % p.a.	CPI (%)	Avg corporate tax	Index points	Accumulation Index points	10-year bonds % p.a.	Index points	Accumulation Index points	Adj Accum Index points	10-year bonds % p.a.	Index points	Accumulation Index points	Adj Accum Index points
1979	8.8	10.1		500	1000	8.800							
1980	10.1	9.2		713.5	1488.6	10.100	42.700	48.860	48.860	0.824	30.678	36.319	36.319
1981	12.6	11.3		595.5	1296	12.600	−16.538	−12.938	−12.938	1.168	−25.012	−21.777	−21.777
1982	15.0	11.0		485.4	1116.3	15.000	−18.489	−13.866	−13.866	3.604	−26.566	−22.402	−22.402
1983	14.0	8.6		775.3	1862	14.000	59.724	66.801	66.801	4.972	47.075	53.592	53.592
1984	13.5	2.6		726.1	1820	13.500	−6.346	−2.256	−2.256	10.624	−8.719	−4.733	−4.733
1985	13.4	8.2		1003.8	2621.9	13.400	38.245	44.060	44.060	4.806	27.768	33.143	33.143
1986	14.9	9.8		1473.2	3991	14.900	46.762	52.218	52.218	4.645	33.663	38.632	38.632
1987	13.4	7.1		1318.9	3677.5	13.400	−10.474	−7.855	−7.855	5.882	−16.409	−13.964	−13.964
1988	12.9	7.6	49%	1487.2	4334.9	12.900	12.761	17.876	22.791	4.926	4.796	9.550	14.118
1989	13.0	7.8	39%	1649.8	5089.2	13.000	10.933	17.401	21.535	4.824	2.907	8.906	12.742
1990	12.9	6.9	39%	1279.8	4197.7	12.900	−22.427	−17.517	−14.379	5.613	−27.434	−22.841	−19.905
1991	12.1	1.5	39%	1651.4	5634.9	12.100	29.036	34.238	37.564	10.443	27.129	32.254	35.531
1992	9.4	0.3	39%	1549.9	5504.6	9.400	−6.146	−2.312	0.139	9.073	−6.427	−2.605	−0.161
1993	8.9	1.9	39%	2173.6	8001.6	8.900	40.241	45.362	48.636	6.869	37.626	42.652	45.865
1994	6.7	2.5	33%	1912.7	7307.8	6.700	−12.003	−8.671	−7.029	4.098	−14.149	−10.898	−9.297
1995	10.0	5.1	33%	2203	8783.1	10.000	15.177	20.188	22.656	4.662	9.588	14.356	16.704
1996	8.2	1.5	36%	2424.6	10065.2	8.200	10.059	14.597	17.150	6.601	8.433	12.904	15.419
1997	7.4	−0.2	36%	2558.9	11296	7.400	5.539	12.228	15.991	7.615	5.751	12.453	16.223

	RAW NUMBERS			All Ordinaries		RAW RETURNS (%)	All Ordinaries			REAL RETURNS (%)	All Ordinaries		
Year	10-year bonds % p.a.	CPI (%)	Avg corporate tax	Index points	Accumulation Index points	10-year bonds % p.a.	Index points	Accumulation Index points	Adj Accum Index points	10-year bonds % p.a.	Index points	Accumulation Index points	Adj Accum Index points
1998	6.1	1.6	36%	2813.4	12610.1	6.100	9.946	11.633	12.583	4.429	8.214	9.875	10.810
1999	5.0	1.8	36%	3152.5	14640.1	5.000	12.053	16.098	18.374	3.143	10.072	14.045	16.281
2000	7.0	5.8	36%	3206.2	15166.6	7.000	1.703	3.596	4.661	1.134	-3.872	-2.083	-1.077
2001	5.5	3.1	34%	3416.6	16701.8	5.500	6.562	10.122	11.956	2.328	3.358	6.811	8.590
2002	6.0	3.0	30%	2991.7	15351.3	6.000	-12.436	-8.086	-6.222	2.913	-14.987	-10.763	-8.953
2003	5.2	2.4	30%	3293.8	17786.7	5.200	10.098	15.864	18.336	2.734	7.518	13.149	15.562
2004	5.6	2.6	30%	4045.3	22690.1	5.600	22.816	27.568	29.604	2.924	19.703	24.335	26.320
2005	5.2	2.8	30%	4708.8	27943.1	5.200	16.402	23.151	26.044	2.335	13.231	19.797	22.611
2006	5.9	3.3	30%	5644.3	34334.2	5.890	19.867	22.872	24.160	2.507	16.038	18.947	20.193
2007	6.3	3.0	30%	6421	40498.4	6.330	13.761	17.954	19.750	3.233	10.447	14.518	16.263
2008	4.0	3.7	30%	3659.3	24143.2	3.990	-43.010	-40.385	-39.260	0.280	-45.044	-42.512	-41.427
2009	5.6	2.1	30%	4882.7	33698.6	5.645	33.433	39.578	42.212	3.472	30.688	36.707	39.287
2010	5.51	2.7	30%	4846.9	34812.8	5.510	-0.733	3.306	5.038	2.736	-3.343	0.590	2.276
									Average	4.368	5.249	9.644	11.380

*This table uses the procedure outlined in Appendix 8.1 to estimate an Adjusted All Ordinaries Accumulation Index. Corporate tax rates used are those in effect in the calendar year in which dividends are paid. Table 8.2 contains the history of corporate taxation rates.

APPENDIX 8.3

A DERIVATION OF THE WACC UNDER AN IMPUTATION SYSTEM OF TAX

This chapter reproduces a derivation of the WACC under an imputation system of tax as per Officer (1994).*

Since free cash flows before tax can be distributed to the government, debt holders or shareholders, then:

$$X_0 = X_G + X_D + X_E \tag{A8.3.1}$$

where:

X_0 = free cash flows (before tax)

X_G = government share of free cash flows (taxation)

X_D = debt holders' share of free cash flows (interest)

X_E = equity holders' share of free cash flows

The actual tax collected from a company is given by:

$$T(X_0 - X_D)$$

where:

T = the effective tax rate

However, part of the company tax paid can be thought of as tax collected on behalf of shareholders. This is the portion of tax paid that is passed on as a tax credit to shareholders and used by them to reduce their own tax bill. The remainder (tax credit not used by shareholders) can be thought of as the actual share of company tax drawn directly from the company (i.e. it does not represent prepaid personal tax). Hence, the value of franking credits used by the shareholders must be removed from the expression above to derive the share of the company tax retained by the government:

$$X_G = T(X_0 - X_D) - \gamma T(X_0 - X_D) = T(X_0 - X_D)(1 - \gamma) \tag{A8.3.2}$$

where:

γ = the portion of the franking credit paid by the company that is used by its shareholders

---

*R. Officer (1994), 'The cost of capital under an imputation system of taxation', *Accounting and Finance*, vol. 34.

Substituting Equation A8.3.2 into Equation A8.3.1:

$$X_0 = T(X_0 - X_D)(1 - \gamma) + X_D + X_E \tag{A8.3.3}$$

Assuming that all cash flows paid by the company are perpetuities, the following definitions can be made:

$$E = \frac{X_E}{r_e} \tag{A8.3.4}$$

$$D = \frac{X_D}{r_D} \tag{A8.3.5}$$

where:

E = value of equity

D = value of debt

V = value of firm

r_D = required return on debt

r_E = required return on equity after company tax but before personal tax

This appendix derives the WACC to be applied to free cash flows after the full rate of tax has been applied. That is:

$$X_0(1 - T)$$

Solving for $X_0(1 - T)$ in Equation A8.3.3 yields:

$$X_0(1 - T) = X_E + X_D(1 - T[1 - \gamma]) - X_0 T\gamma \tag{A8.3.6}$$

The value of the firm is as follows:

$$V = \frac{X_0(1 - T)}{r_i} \tag{A8.3.7}$$

where:

V = value of the firm

r_i = company cost of capital after company tax

Substituting Equations A8.3.4, A8.3.5 and A8.3.7 into Equation A8.3.6 and solving for r_i yields:

$$r_i = r_E \times \frac{(1 - T)}{(1 - T[1 - \gamma])} \times \frac{E}{V} + r_D \times (1 - T) \times \frac{D}{V}$$

which is the WACC after company tax but before personal tax that needs to be applied to the free cash flows that have been fully taxed to calculate the value of the firm.

9

Australian equities market

CHAPTER PREVIEW

Chapters 1 to 8 of this book dealt with the valuation of companies—that is, the estimation of their intrinsic worth. This chapter is concerned with the trading of a company's equity securities. In particular, it considers how the Australian equities market operates and the parties that trade in it. In Australia, the predominant marketplace where shares are traded is the Australian Securities Exchange (ASX).

When companies issue securities directly to the public for the first time, they do so by issuing a prospectus directly to the public. For example, in 1997 the Australian government sold to the public one-third of the publicly owned telecommunications utility Telstra, by forming a company that issued shares in return for cash. The issue of new shares by a company to the public is commonly referred to as the 'primary equity market'. Share markets such as the ASX are known as the 'secondary equity market', since they enable subsequent trading of the issued shares. That is, the secondary market is the place where buyers and sellers (excluding the company, except in the case of on-market buybacks) trade shares. Accordingly, the ASX is the place where, if they so desire, the current shareholders of Telstra can sell (or 'liquidate') their shareholdings. In facilitating the liquidation of shareholdings, the ASX encourages investors to buy (invest) in the primary equity market. This is the most important role of the secondary market. The Telstra issue was the most heavily subscribed share issue in the history of the Australian market. How many people would have purchased shares in Telstra if they thought that it would be difficult to sell them later on? The likely answer is, not many!

This chapter is concerned with the manner in which shares are traded on the ASX. To understand properly how shares are traded, it is necessary to understand the trading protocols, regulations, information, participants and technology of the ASX. These elements, many of which are interrelated, are discussed in this chapter.

KEY CONCEPTS

CONCEPT 9.1   Process of trading shares

Market orders
An order where the client is prepared to buy or sell a given volume of shares at the current best market price. For a buy order the client is prepared to buy at the lowest ask price, and for a sell order the client is willing to receive the highest bid price.

Limit orders
An order which specifies the maximum price at which a client is willing to buy shares or the minimum price at which a client is willing to receive to sell shares.

Counterparty
The party taking the other side of a trade. For example, if the client is a buyer, the counterparty is a seller.

Settlement
The process by which payment is made by the buyer to the seller and shares (ownership) are transferred from the seller to the buyer.

Imagine that you wanted to purchase some shares in Tabcorp Holdings Limited. The first thing you would do is contact a stockbroker (hereafter referred to as simply a 'broker'), since brokers are currently the only parties legally allowed to trade directly on the ASX. After the broker has opened an account for you, in which you have deposited some money, you can commence your purchase of shares.

The first step in purchasing shares is to *place an order* with the broker. Brokers currently allow their clients to place orders with them either over the Internet or by telephone. Broadly speaking, there are two types of orders that can be placed with brokers—**market orders** and **limit orders**. A market order is one that a client places with a broker to buy or sell a certain number (volume) of shares to be executed 'at the current best market price'. That is, the client is willing to purchase at the lowest selling price available on the ASX (if a prospective buyer), or to sell at the highest available buying price (if a seller). A limit order is one that specifies the maximum price at which the client is willing to buy shares, or the minimum price at which the client is willing to sell. Hence, in the case of a limit order the client specifies a desired trade price in addition to the volume to trade.

Once the broker receives an order, they attempt to 'execute' it. Trade execution requires the broker to find a **counterparty**. This means that if the client is a prospective buyer (seller), the broker will attempt to find a seller (buyer). There are two main ways that brokers can attempt to execute a trade. First, they can execute the order on the electronic market operated by the ASX known as ASX Trade. Alternatively, under certain circumstances the trading rules of the ASX allow brokers to trade 'off-market'.[1] That is, brokers can attempt to contact their other clients directly (by telephone) to find a counterparty.

Once a share trade has been executed, clearing and **settlement** takes place. This is the process by which ownership of shares is transferred from seller to buyer, and cash is transferred from the buyer's account to the seller's account.

CONCEPT 9.2   Nature of securities traded

Although the bulk of securities traded on the ASX are shares (or equity securities), a variety of other securities are also traded. These include debt instruments, including corporate and government bonds, hybrid securities, warrants and **exchange-traded funds (ETFs)**. This chapter focuses on equity securities. Figure 9.1 profiles the stocks that are traded on the ASX. Panel A indicates that the number of stocks traded on the ASX has generally exceeded 1000, and in fact has ranged from 1400 in December 2002 to 2077 in January 2011. It should be noted that a small number of stocks are companies that are based overseas and are listed on a foreign exchange as well as the ASX. The number of foreign companies has grown from 37 in 1993 to 88 in 2011. Most of the overseas stocks that trade on the ASX are New Zealand companies—for example, Telecom New Zealand.

Panel B of Figure 9.1 provides an indication of the value of stocks (their market capitalisation) that are traded on the ASX. For example, the market capitalisation of stocks traded on the ASX was $1419.0 billion in December 2010.

Table 9.1 lists the 10 largest Australian stocks traded on the ASX as at 31 December 2010 by market capitalisation. Interestingly, the 'big four' banks—ANZ, Commonwealth, National Australia and Westpac—all feature in the list. Together, the market capitalisation of these stocks totalled $571.1 billion, representing approximately 40.2% of the total market capitalisation of the stocks in the All Ordinaries Index at that time.

> **Exchange-traded fund (ETF)**
> An open-ended listed investment fund that combines some of the characteristics of shares and managed funds.

CONCEPT 9.3   Market participants

The process of trading shares, described in Concept 9.1, highlights the three main participants involved in share trading. The first is the ASX, which provides the facilities for trading, while the Australian Securities and Investments Commission act as a regulatory body. Second are the buying and selling parties, which in the example were an individual (you) and another party, the seller (which could have been another individual, an institution or a fund manager). The final participant is the broker, who provides trade execution and settlement services. In this section, each of these participants is briefly profiled, following an outline of the historical development of the ASX.

The Australian Securities Exchange

Figure 9.2 illustrates the historical development of the ASX. Between 1871 and 1889, six separate stock exchanges were formed in state capitals around Australia. These stock exchanges operated

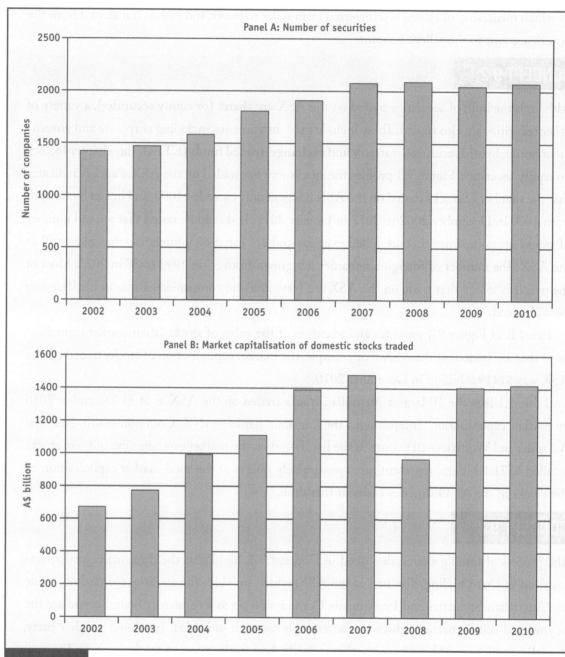

Panel A: Number of securities

Panel B: Market capitalisation of domestic stocks traded

Figure 9.1   Size and growth of trading on ASX (as at December)

independently of one another until 1937, when they formed an association known as the Australian Associated Stock Exchange. Although the exchanges shared information, and in many cases traded the same shares, they continued to operate independently until 1987. On 1 April 1987 the six separate exchanges formally merged and became one entity—the Australian Stock Exchange. In that year an electronic trading system known as the Stock Exchange Automated

Table 9.1	Ten largest Australian securities (by market capitalisation) on the ASX as at 31 December 2010		
STOCK NAME	**STOCK CODE**	**INDUSTRY CODE**	**MARKET CAPITALISATION ($BN)**
BHP Billiton	BHP	Materials	149.70
Commonwealth Bank	CBA	Banks	77.90
Westpac	WBC	Banks	66.20
ANZ	ANZ	Banks	59.20
National Australia Bank	NAB	Banks	51.70
Rio Tinto	RIO	Materials	36.70
Wesfarmers	WES	Food & staples retailing	36.20
Woolworths	WOW	Food & staples retailing	32.50
Telstra	TLS	Telecommunication Services	31.60
Newcrest Mining	NCM	Materials	29.40
Total for top 10			571.10

Source: IRESS Market Technology Limited, <www.iress.com.au>, 31 December 2010.

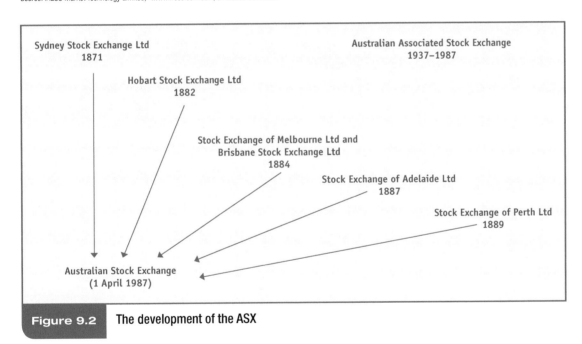

Figure 9.2	The development of the ASX

Trading System (SEATS) was also introduced and had the effect of electronically *consolidating* trading that was previously conducted separately on trading floors around Australia.

The consolidation of trading meant that an order submitted in any location around Australia was visible to all other market participants regardless of their location. For example, an order submitted by a broker located in Sydney was visible to brokers located in Sydney, Brisbane, Melbourne, Perth and so on. In contrast, prior to consolidated trading, an order submitted by a broker on the floor of the Sydney Stock Exchange was visible only to other traders on the

FINANCE EXTRA!

ASX decision is a hard one to swallow

IN AN 873-word statement last week, the Treasurer listed his reasons for rejecting the proposed merger between ASX Ltd and Singapore Exchange (SGX).

I believe that the rejection of the most important proposed merger in Australian capital markets history, which would have created the third-largest equities exchange in the world, worth roughly $12 billion, deserved a little more explanation.

Entitled 'Foreign Investment Decision', the statement contains general remarks about equities markets and what is needed to create a successful merger. But it contains nothing specific and very little explanation of the reasons given.

The so-called 'meat' of the statement (though my guests would stop at McDonald's after dinner if I offered them such meagre pickings) is contained in paragraphs eight and nine of the statement—230 words that apparently explain the precise reasons for rejecting the merger.

Paragraph eight is 94 words long. It states that 'the benefits of the merger are greatly exaggerated' and that to 'diminish Australia's economic and regulatory sovereignty over the ASX could only be justified if there were very substantial benefits for our nation'.

These statements raise more questions than answers. So what exactly are the specific benefits that were exaggerated? How were they quantified? Was there any real hard analysis? How exactly is regulatory sovereignty diminished? How much regulatory sovereignty do we really have over the $400 billion to $500 billion in superannuation savings invested offshore?

Do we really have regulatory sovereignty over transactions involving Australian superannuation funds transacted on the New York or London stock exchanges today? Is the Australian Securities and Investments Commission really completely powerless to regulate these transactions involving precious Australian savings?

The only other paragraph in the statement that 'explains' the reasons for rejecting the merger is paragraph nine, which is a whopping 136 words.

The explanation in this paragraph is that ASIC, the Reserve Bank of Australia and the Treasury provided advice that 'not having full regulatory sovereignty over the ASX-SGX holding company would create risks and supervisory issues, particularly its clearing and settlement functions'. Again, no specifics are given.

But I have a couple more questions.

Why are we, in a regulatory sense, so ill-prepared for a badly needed merger of this nature when they have been going on en masse around the world for more than a decade?

What exactly are the 'risks and supervisory issues'? What exactly are the clearing and settlement issues? What happened to the 'systemic risk' issue that was touted in the papers last week? In any case, how does systemic risk increase when there is more and internationally diversified investor capital behind each transaction following a merger?

Again, more questions than answers.

I want to avoid leaving you with more questions than answers.

Consider some very hard facts. The world's seven largest equities exchanges are Hong Kong Stock Exchange ($US23 billion), Deutsche Börse ($US14 billion), NYSE/Euronext ($US10 billion), SGX ($US6 billion), ASX ($US6 billion), NASDAQ/OMX ($US5 billion), and London Stock Exchange ($US4 billion). The traded value of these companies provides a measure of their so-called 'balance sheets': their ability to buy or merge with another exchange.

To merge with another exchange you need to be large enough to offer an attractive value proposition (a dollar offer) to the shareholders of that exchange. Worth about $US6 billion, the ASX is clearly an exchange that punches above its weight. Precious few exchanges in the world have the balance sheet to make an attractive offer to its shareholders.

Big names such as NASDAQ/OMX and London Stock Exchange are smaller than the ASX and unlikely to be able to mount a bid attractive to ASX shareholders.

Further up the list are Deutsche Börse and NYSE/Euronext, which are in the middle of their own merger bid process and unlikely to be able to 'go it again' for many years.

That leaves the Hong Kong Stock Exchange. It's difficult to see how it could offer a national-interest value proposition more powerful than that of SGX—especially with such little information provided by the statement.

Let me leave you with a few more facts. The ASX is an exchange dominated by domestic companies, and local investor capital is the dominant source of investment in these companies.

For good reasons, the ASX has not focused on increasing its international reach—which requires enormous investment and is therefore uneconomic.

As a result, Australian companies are increasingly listing offshore.

Consider the 31 Australian companies listed on the Toronto Stock Exchange, worth about $30 billion, and turning over some $1.3 billion per month. These companies have gone offshore to raise capital and liquidity because there is insufficient risk capital in Australia to meet their needs.

These are companies such as the effectively previously Australian-domiciled Teranga Gold, which listed in December last year and raised $96 million in Canada and only $26 million in Australia.

The importance of a merger with a partner like SGX—which has built its success on attracting international capital and listings—is that it provides a clear national-interest value proposition: global reach. It enhances the ability of Australian companies to raise capital offshore. Of course, it also increases the possibilities for Australian investors.

So let me return to the original question I posed. The Treasurer has just rejected a merger bid between ASX and one of the very few suitors in the world that can offer a deal attractive to ASX shareholders, and one with a strong national-interest value proposition.

So where does this leave us? With a diminishing national ability to raise capital, a possible alternative suitor nowhere in sight and a poor understanding of what is needed to be a successful suitor.

We are not in a very good place.

Source: Alex Frino, *The Australian Financial Review*, 14 April 2011.

Sydney floor and so on. On 2 October 2006, a new trading system was introduced, known as the Integrated Trading System (ITS), which allowed for the trading of shares and options on one system. Finally, on 3 December 2010, the ASX launched its next generation trading system, ASX Trade, providing the fastest integrated equities and derivatives trading system in the world.

The Australian Securities Exchange, as it is now known, resulted from a merger of the Australian Stock Exchange and the Sydney Futures Exchange in December 2006. Originally, the Australian Stock Exchange was a not-for-profit organisation, run for the benefit of its members (mainly its member brokers). However, in 1998 it took the unprecedented step of 'demutualising' (i.e. issuing shares to its members, thereby becoming a company) and allowing its shares to be traded on its own market. Since 1998 many other exchanges around the world have followed suit, including the Hong Kong and Singapore exchanges.

Figure 9.3 provides a brief profile of the size and growth of the Australian equities market over the 15 years to December 2010. Panel A illustrates the average daily number of trades, and the daily average turnover or value of trading (the amount of cash that changes hands) executed on the ASX. The average value of trading has increased explosively from a daily average of less than $1 billion in 1996 to more than $5 billion per day in 2010 (although there was an intermittent reversal of the trend during the global financial crisis from 2007 to 2009). Similarly, the daily average number of trades executed on the ASX has grown as spectacularly, rising from 20 000 in 1996 to 538 000 in the year ended 31 December 2010. Panel B of Figure 9.3 illustrates the average value of transactions, or the amount of cash that changed hands in each transaction for the period. In 2010, the average trade size was approximately $10 000—quite high. The decrease in trade size since 2007 is due to high-frequency trading. High-frequency trading involves a computer making the trade decision and then executing a trade—no human intervention. High-frequency trading often involves holding an investment position only for very brief periods of time and trading in and out of positions numerous times within a trading day.

Brokers

Brokers are currently the only participants with direct access to trading on the ASX.[2] In practical terms, this means that brokers are the only parties permitted access to ASX Trade. As a result, anyone who wants to purchase shares must do so through a broker, who usually charges a fee, called 'brokerage commission'. This and the other costs of trading are discussed in Chapter 11.

In Australia, brokers are either partnerships or companies. As at 31 July 2011 there were 90 active brokers.[3] The biggest brokers (in terms of total value of trades) are those listed in Table 9.2. Note that the market is very concentrated, with the top 10 brokers representing more than 77% of trading.

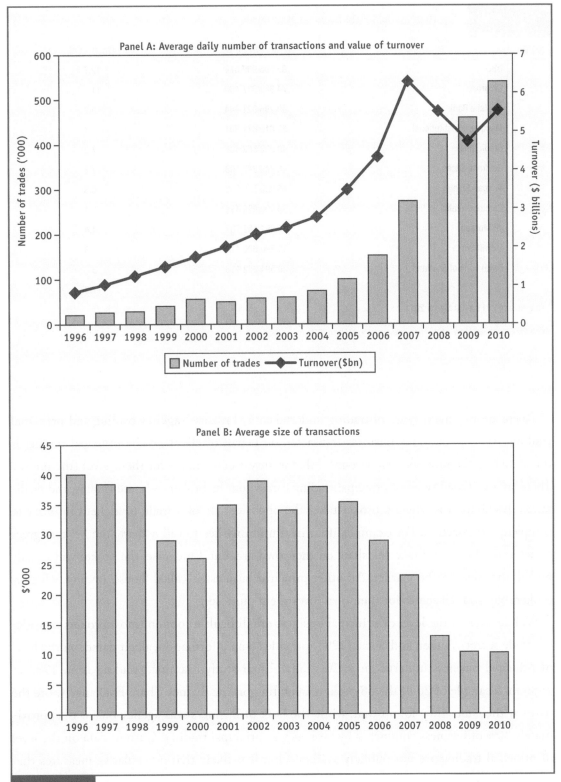

Figure 9.3   A profile of trading on the ASX (all figures are for the year ended December)

Table 9.2	Top 10 brokers in 2011 by value of turnover		
RANK	BROKER	TOTAL VALUE A$	TRADED %
1	UBS	85 996 989 072	12.7
2	Citigroup	74 882 337 450	11
3	Deutshe Bank	59 298 921 444	8.7
4	Macquarie Institutional	53 819 671 801	7.9
5	Credit Suisse	48 932 582 405	7.2
6	Goldman Sachs	48 845 247 103	7.2
7	Morgan Stanley	43 036 568 366	6.3
8	Commonwealth	34 590 896 414	5.1
9	JP Morgan	30 054 162 282	4.4
10	Merrill Lynch	29 290 680 418	4.3
11	Royal Bank of Scotland	20 594 252 113	3
			77.8
Year to date 2011 at 30 March 2011			

Source: IRESS Market Technology Limited, <www.iress.com.au>, 30 March 2011.

Agency trading
A trade which a broker executes on behalf of a client.

Principal trading
A trade which a broker executes on their own behalf.

There are two main types of trading undertaken by brokers—**agency trading** and **principal trading**. Agency trading is business transacted on behalf of clients, while principal trading is transacted on the broker's own account—that is, investments made for themselves (the house). There are two broad types of principal trading carried out by brokers—house trading and facilitation. Facilitation is where a broker takes the opposite side of a trade to a client in order to complete a transaction. For example, if an institution wishes to sell a share, the broker agrees to act as the buyer and take the share on their own account. Of course, the broker will usually on-sell the share in the market. All other principal business is called 'house' trading, whereby brokers buy and sell shares for their own investment purposes.

While data on the level of principal business are difficult to obtain (most brokers consider it a trade secret), Aitken and Swan (1993) provide some information, albeit dated, on the level of principal business undertaken in Australia.[4] Their study examined trading from 1982 to 1986 for a sample of 20 of the 38 brokers operating on the Sydney Share Exchange (note the date) at the time. They found that, while the bulk of business was agency business, approximately 30% of business conducted by brokers was principal trading! Current data on the level of principal trading are not publicly available, but it is likely that deregulative measures that occurred on the ASX in the 1980s and 1990s have resulted in an increase in the amount of principal business.[5]

Practitioner's POV

The broking industry has experienced significant restructuring over the past decade with a large number of mergers and acquisitions involving the top brokers. Despite this, many people argue that the Australian market remains an over-brokered market and that this consolidation will continue. There has also been a systematic increase in the market share of the large global houses such as UBS and Deutsche. Note that there are only two Australian brokers, Macquarie Institutional and Commonwealth, listed among the top 10 brokers.

Fund managers

Fund managers are organisations that invest cash (funds) on behalf of their clients. In Australia, fund managers typically invest superannuation contributions sourced from companies. These types of fund managers are called 'wholesale' managers. The other main group of fund managers are 'retail'—they obtain cash by issuing savings policies or selling 'units' (similar to shares) directly to the public.

Investors in funds essentially own the securities in which the funds invest, and are entitled to income and capital gains generated by these securities. Investors are typically charged investment management fees on a per annum basis, to cover managers' expenses incurred in the investment process, including research, trading costs and client administration. Further expenses levied by managers include buy–sell spreads that are levied on an investor entering into, or exiting from, a fund.

The funds management industry in Australia is dominated by 10 fund managers that between them manage around 57% of the total available funds in Australia. Industry estimates place the amount of funds invested in Australian equities at close to $261 billion as at 30 June 2010.[6] The main Australian fund managers as at 1 January 2010 are set out in Table 9.3. Between them, Commonwealth/Colonial Group, Macquarie Bank Group (the funds management arm of Macquarie Bank, as opposed to the broking arm reported in Table 9.2) and State Street Global Advisors account for nearly one-quarter of the funds under management.

It is important to note that, although there are only 10 major fund managers, each manager allows investors to participate in a number of different funds. The funds are distinguished by the trading strategy offered (e.g. 'active' or 'passive') and the type of securities in which a fund can invest (e.g. equities, bonds, property, Australian or international). The objective of active funds is to outperform the market index, by buying and selling shares in an attempt to realise capital gains arising from movements in share prices. In contrast, the objective of passive funds

Table 9.3	Top 10 fund managers by assets under management as at 1 January 2010	
MANAGER	**TOTAL FUNDS UNDER MANAGEMENT (A$ BILLION)**	**MARKET SHARE (%)**
Commonwealth/Colonial Group	105.1	10
Macquarie Bank Group	79.2	8
State Street Global Advisors	78.9	8
Vanguard Investments Ltd	72.6	7
AMP Group	60.2	6
BlackRock	50.4	5
ING/ANZ Group	46.7	4
BT Financial Group	42.4	4
AXA Australia/AllianceBernstein	34.2	3
PIMCO	27.9	3
Total	597.6	58

AUSTRALIAN SOURCED TOTAL FUNDS UNDER MANAGEMENT CONSOLIDATED ASSETS – 1 JANUARY 2010

Sources: Morningstar, InvestorSupermarket MarketWrap, Data File, Worksheet 2; Austrade. © <www.abs.gov.au/ausstats>.

is to earn returns similar to the market index, which is achieved by adopting a 'buy and hold' strategy. As identified in Chapter 6, in Australia the most commonly followed market index is the S&P/ASX 200 Index.

Table 9.4 documents the different types of shareholders for stocks in the ASX 200 index as at 30 June 2011. The table illustrates that retail investors (people like you or I) own, on average, less

Table 9.4	The types of investors that own shares in companies listed on the Australian Securities Exchange as at June 2011
INVESTOR TYPE	**AVERAGE SHAREHOLDING IN S&P/ASX 200 STOCKS (%)**
Domestic institutions	32.98
Foreign institutions	18.95
Hedge funds	2.34
Domestic brokers	1.44
Foreign brokers	1.15
Employees etc.	7.59
Corporate stakeholders	6.38
Retail shareholders	29.18
Total	100.00

Source: ©2011 Orient Capital Pty Ltd.

than 30 percent of the shares in these stocks. In contrast, Australian and overseas institutional investors (i.e. fund managers) own, on average, half the shares in the top 200 companies.

Individual investors

Individual investors can invest in the share market in one of two broad ways. First, they can invest directly in the market by purchasing shares. Alternatively, they can invest indirectly by purchasing shares through a corporate entity (e.g. through a private company). The ASX conducts an annual survey which reports the level of direct and indirect investment by individuals, whose results are summarised in Table 9.5.

Table 9.5 provides an indication of the amount of direct ownership in shares. In 2010 approximately 43% of all Australian adults owned shares in at least one company. This proportion increased rapidly between 1991 and 2000, before levelling off. The biggest contributors to the growth over those years were the listings of Australian icons such as Telstra and AMP in 1997 and 1998, respectively.

It is interesting to note that, although the proportion of Australians who directly hold shares is quite high, very few of these shareholders are active traders. Of those who sold shares in the 12 months prior to late 2010, half had held them for between one and five years, and 51% of direct shareholders claimed not to have traded in the previous 12 months.[7]

CONCEPT CHECK

1. What role does each of the three major market participants play in the process of share trading?
2. What are the two ways in which individual investors can own shares?

For the answers, go to MyFinanceLab

Table 9.5	Proportion of the Australian adult (over 20 years) population who own shares (%)							
	1991	1994	1997	2000	2002	2004	2006	2010
Direct only	1.4	3.2	8.5	25.1	18	23	22	30
Indirect only	4.5	3.9	13.6	13.1	19	21	8	4
Both direct and indirect	8.8	12.8	11.9	15.5	13	11	16	9
Total	14.7	19.9	34	53.7	50	55	46	43

Source: ASX Share Ownership Study, various years. © ASX Limited ABN 98 008 624 691 (ASX) 2011. All rights reserved. This material is reproduced with the permission of ASX. This material should not be reproduced, stored in a retrieval system or transmitted in any form whether in whole or in part without the prior written permission of ASX.

CONCEPT 9.4   Trading methods

Practitioner's POV

As at the time of writing, all ASX Equity products are screen traded on a platform called ASX Trade. ASX Trade is a NASDAQ OMX ultra-low latency trading platform based on NASDAQ OMX's Genium INET system. ASX Trade replaced ITS which allowed for the trading of shares and options on the one system and had replaced the Stock Exchange Automated Trading System (SEATS) in 2006. ASX Trade offers the fastest integrated equities and derivatives trading platform in the world and connects geographically dispersed brokers via a network of interconnected computer terminals located in their offices. It will no doubt increase the amount of high-frequency trading in the market place.

ASX Trade

ASX Trade is run by the ASX and used by brokers. It is accessible by brokers from anywhere within Australia and may also be accessed from outside Australia. ASX Trade can be accessed by ASX-provided ASX Trade Workstation software running on a PC, or via a computer connected to ASX Trade. This feature, known as 'open interface' allows brokers to design their own customised computer programs for use in entering orders and obtaining market information. ASX Trade, through the open interface, also allows orders to be entered electronically without those orders being keyed or re-keyed by a broker, known as straight-through processing.

Trading on ASX Trade commences at approximately 10.00 am each day and ends at approximately 4.10 pm. ASX Trade comprises many different forms of trading or 'market phases'. These are illustrated in Table 9.6. The remainder of this section describes ASX Trade's trading during each of its market phases.

Table 9.6	ASX Trade trading hours and market phases
TIME	**ASX Trade's MARKET PHASE**
7.00 to 10.00	Pre-opening
10.00 to 10.10	Opening call auction
10.10 to 16.00	Normal trading
16.00 to 16.10	Pre-opening
16.10 to 16.12	Closing call auction

Pre-opening and opening call auction

From 7 o'clock each morning, brokers can enter or amend orders on ASX Trade. However, these orders are not executed until ASX Trade goes into the 'opening' phase for each stock. From 10.00 am, 'batches' of stocks are opened (i.e. not all stocks listed on the ASX open for trading at the same time). The opening time for each stock is determined by the first letter of their stock code, as described in Table 9.7.

Stocks open randomly within ±15 seconds of the opening time given in Table 9.7. At this opening time, all overlapping buy and sell orders are opened at a single price for each stock determined by ASX Trade using a computer algorithm.[8] This algorithm is described and illustrated in Appendix 9.1. After the opening phase has occurred for a share, normal trading begins.

Table 9.7	ASX Trade opening hours for stocks
STOCK CODE	OPENING TIME ± 15 SECONDS
A to B	10.00.00
C to F	10.02.15
G to M	10.04.30
N to R	10.06.45
S to Z	10.09.00

Normal trading

Unlike the opening phase, orders submitted during ASX Trade's normal trading may execute immediately after they are entered. Highest-priced buy orders and lowest-priced sell orders are given priority in executing against incoming sell and buy orders, respectively. If a sell order arrives at a price equal to the best standing (i.e. unexecuted) buy order, a trade will automatically be recognised by ASX Trade (i.e. executed). If two standing buy orders have the same price, the standing order placed first has priority in execution against incoming sell orders. Hence, standing orders are executed by ASX Trade according to a price and time priority rule.

On the ASX Trade Workstation, brokers can view information for many different securities (both shares and derivatives) on one screen. Figure 9.4 provides an example of the Price Information Window on an ASX Trade Workstation. The Price Information window reports a summary of the market for each of the shares including the best or highest limit buy order price (Bid) and best or lowest limit sell order prices (Ask). It also displays the volume available at the best bid and ask prices (BQty and AQty), commonly known as the market 'depth'.

The Price Information window also provides information regarding the instrument being traded including the:

- stock code (ID)
- name of the security (Short Desc)
- instrument session state (ISS), which indicates which of the phases outlined in Table 9.6 are relevant
- status notes (SN), which describe the current status of an instrument (e.g. NR for notice received, TH for trading halt); if there is no status note, the security has no exceptional status and is open for normal trading
- basis of quotation codes (BoQ), which describe how a security is quoted (e.g. XD for ex-dividend, RE for reconstructed); if there is no basis of quotation code displayed alongside a security, the security is trading on a cum basis. (See Chapter 11 for a discussion of ex-dividend and cum-dividend concepts.)

Figure 9.4 illustrates that for Batavia Ltd (Stock ID BTV), the best bid (buying price) is 4.9 cents, and the best ask (selling price) is 5 cents. The corresponding volumes available for the best bid and ask are 750 000 (BQty) and 170 937 (AQty), respectively.

A list of all the unexecuted orders for a particular share can be obtained from the Order Depth window, illustrated in Figure 9.5 for Telstra (TLS). There is a similar page for each stock on ASX Trade.

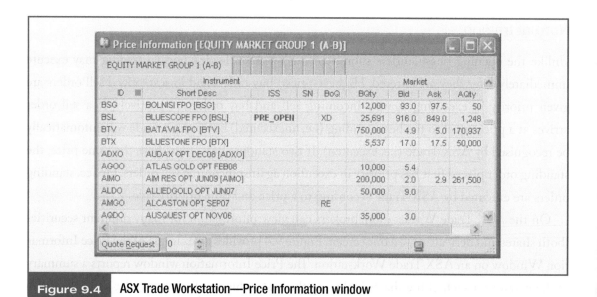

| **Figure 9.4** | **ASX Trade Workstation—Price Information window** |

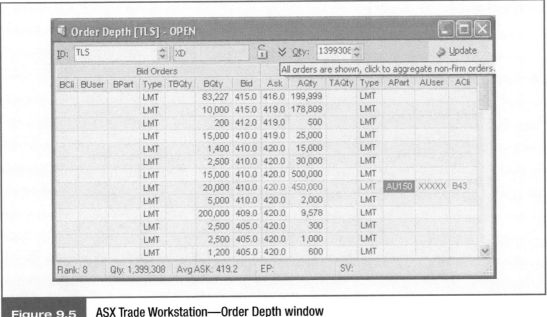

BCli	**BUser**	**BPart**	**Type**	**TBQty**	**BQty**	**Bid**	**Ask**	**AQty**	**TAQty**	**Type**	**APart**	**AUser**	**ACli**

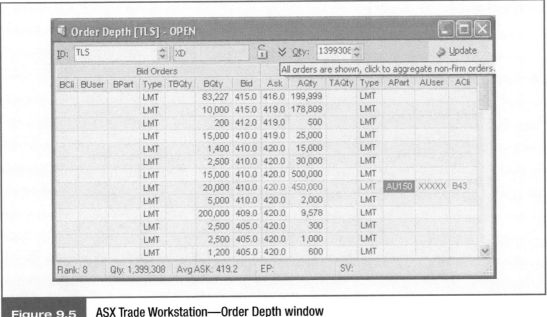

Figure 9.5   ASX Trade Workstation—Order Depth window

The Order Depth window lists the individual orders which make up the depth at each bid and ask price for a single share. Each line in the Order Depth window represents an order placed by a broker. The orders are listed with the highest priority order at the top and lowest priority orders at the bottom. An order with a higher priority will be traded before others. The 'Type' column reports the type of order placed, such as limit order (LMT) or market order (MKT). A limit order is an order with a specified buy or sell price, whereas a market order will execute at the current best bid or ask price, for sell and buy orders respectively. Figure 9.5 illustrates that the volume available at the best ask ($4.16) is 199 999 shares. In contrast, the volume available at the best bid ($4.15) is 93 227 and is composed of two limit orders, one with volume 83 227 and another with volume 10 000. However, the order with BQty 83 277 has higher priority than the order with BQty 10 000, which indicates that the order with 83 227 volume was placed before the one with 10 000 volume and hence has 'time priority'. This stock also has a bid–ask spread of one cent, since the best sell order is priced at $4.16 and best buy order is priced at $4.15.

All the other fields in Figure 9.5 (BCli, BUser, BPart, TBQty, TAQty, APart, AUser, ACli) relate to trading participant and client IDs and references and are only visible to the broker who owns the terminal (and not the entire market).

EXAMPLE 9.1

Order execution during normal trading on ASX trade

QUESTION

If a market order to sell 85 227 shares in Telstra (TLS) is placed at a price of $4.15, and the market is as described in Figure 9.5, describe:

(a) the trades that will occur, and

(b) the effect on sell orders.

ANSWER

Since orders on ASX Trade are executed on a price and then time priority basis, the following trades will result.

Price	Volume	Row
4.15	83 227	1
4.15	2 000	2

As a result, the buy order currently in row one under 'Bid Orders' will disappear from the screen as it has executed, and the volume attached to the buy order on the second row currently will be reduced to 8000, as 2000 shares have executed against the incoming sell order. All other orders will remain as displayed.

Trade history

A list of trades that have occurred during the day for a particular security can also be viewed on an ASX Trade Workstation. Figure 9.6 illustrates a typical trade history window for a fictitious security with a code ZZA, and lists all the executed trades on that day with the latest trade in the bottom row. The trade history of other securities can also be viewed by simply choosing the relevant security code from the drop down list on the top left.

Figure 9.6 illustrates that the trade history window for ZZA reports a number of important trade specific pieces of information. For each trade the quantity traded is displayed in the 'Qty' column, where figures with 'M' indicate millions and 'T' indicates thousands. The price of each trade is also displayed in the 'Prc' column along with the exact date and time (to the nearest second) that the trade executed in the 'Time' column. The 'Part' and 'ClrPart' columns under the Buy and Sell tabs highlight the relevant trading participants and trade clearing participants (derivatives only), respectively, involved in the trade. Here participants refer to brokers and clearing participants refer to clearing houses, which will be discussed in the next section.

Further information is provided such as the trade type (TType), where if a trade is cancelled (when both counterparties have agreed to cancel their side of the trade), the trade line is highlighted in red and the TType is set to **Rev**. The condition code (Cond) reports the manner in which the trade was executed, e.g. **S1XT** for a Special Crossing (refer to the section 'Off market trading' later in this chapter).

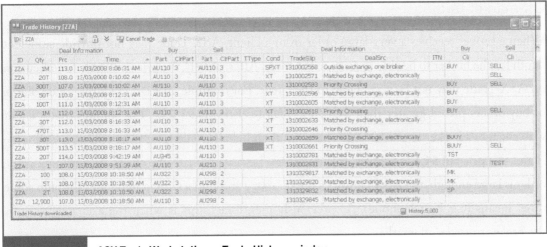

| Figure 9.6 | ASX Trade Workstation—Trade History window |

The Trade History window also reports a unique identifier number assigned by the central system for each trade under 'TradeSlip'. Finally the 'DealScr' column reports the way in which the trade was matched (e.g. electronically, as a trade report, or as a tailor-made combination). The remaining fields are only visible to the broker using the terminal and relate to clients' IDs and references.

The Trade History window reports the most recent trade to be executed (displayed in the bottom row) for the security 'ZZA' which occurred at 10.18.50 am at a price of $1.07, involving trading participants (brokers) AU110 and AU298.

Closing call auction

On 10 February 1997 the ASX began operating what it called a 'Closing Single Price Auction (CSPA)' at the end of normal trading each day. The CSPA is similar to the opening call. It allows brokers to enter new orders, and retains unexecuted orders from normal trading. These orders are not executed until a time chosen randomly between 4.10 and 4.12 pm, when an instantaneous 'opening' occurs and overlapping orders are executed using an algorithm identical to that used to open the market in the morning (for normal trading).

POSTSCRIPT

At the time of writing this book, the ASX had introduced a large number of important new initiatives that would allow brokers new choices in the way they execute trades.

Off-market trading

When a broker receives a very large order from a client, ASX Trade may not provide sufficient depth for the broker to be able to execute the trade. Alternatively, the price available for execution on ASX Trade may not be acceptable to the client. For example, in Figure 9.5 the total volume of buy orders priced greater than $4.12 for TLS (Telstra) is 93 227. This implies that a client who engages a broker to sell 100 000 shares on their behalf would have to be willing to sell some shares at a price of $4.12 or lower. This might not be acceptable to the client. Accordingly, if the order is large enough, the ASX permits a broker to try and find a willing purchaser through some other means (e.g. by telephone). As previously mentioned, this is when the exchange permits the broker to trade 'off-market'.

The conditions under which a broker is permitted to trade off-market are stipulated in the ASX market rules. An order can be executed off-market if it is worth more than $1 million. An order can also be executed off-market if it is part of a *portfolio of orders* from the *same client* (1) that is worth more than $5 million, (2) that involves more than 10 securities, and (3) where

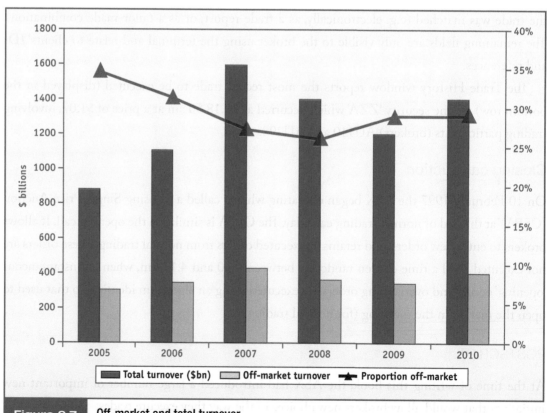

| **Figure 9.7** | **Off-market and total turnover** |

the order in any security is worth more than $200 000. Off-market trades must be disclosed to the market, through ASX Trade, immediately on execution.[9]

Figure 9.7 sets out the size and significance of ASX Trade and off-market trading activity on the ASX. The average value of off-market trades executed on the ASX has increased from approximately $300 billion per annum in 2005 to approximately $600 billion in 2007. While quite high in the early 1990s (above 40%), the proportion of total trading on the ASX executed off-market has been in the range of 27–35% since 2005. This implies that since 2005, 65–73% of trade volume has been executed on ASX Trade (or its forerunners—ITS and SEATS).

In September 2001 the ASX introduced a trial 'New Reporting Regime' (NRR) for large principal facilitated trades. The purpose of this trial was to increase liquidity and efficiency for large trades by providing an environment that supported greater levels of broker facilitation. The trial was designed to reduce the risk taken by principal brokers, allowing them to offer better prices and thereby reducing trading costs for large institutional clients. This was achieved by allowing brokers to delay the publication of principal facilitated trades that met certain size requirements until 9.45 am the following day. The trial operated for approximately 12 months, and during this time 109 trades with a value of $925 million were executed using the NRR.[10] A modified version of the facility became a permanent feature of the market on 30 September 2002 and was renamed 'Facilitated Specified Size Block Special Crossings' (FSSBSC).[11]

Information dissemination procedures

The manner in which companies that trade on the ASX must release information is prescribed in the Listing Rules of the ASX. Section 3.1 of the ASX Listing Rules requires that companies notify the ASX immediately of any information of which they become aware that could have 'a material effect on the price or value of securities of the company'. Section 3.1 goes on to list a large number of information types that fall within this category. Once notified, the ASX follows the procedure depicted in Figure 9.8.

The main content of the information must be provided to the ASX electronically.[12] Once received, ASX then makes a decision as to whether or not the information is market sensitive. If the information is deemed to be market sensitive, a 'trading halt' is *immediately* instituted for a period of 10 minutes (except for takeover initiation announcements, which last 30 minutes) in the stock that is affected by the information (or stocks, if the information relates to a number of companies). During a trading halt, ASX Trade allows new orders to be placed or cancelled, but does not allow overlapping orders to execute. At the end of the trading halt, the market resumes trading after a brief 'opening' phase, which determines the new traded price.[13] Regardless of whether a trading halt is instituted, all information is released as quickly as possible by the ASX ComNews™. This service provides the full text of company announcements in a searchable

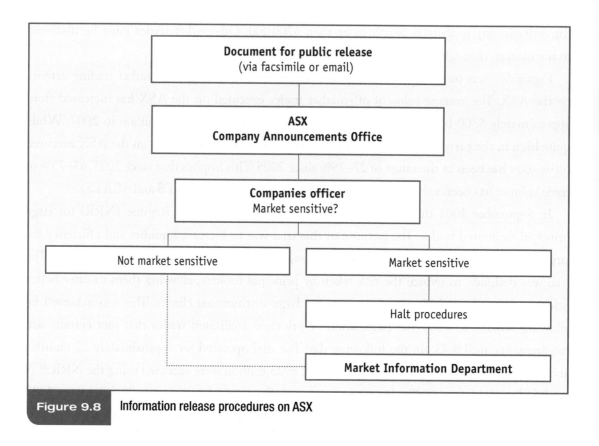

Figure 9.8 Information release procedures on ASX

format.[14] This service is available directly through the ASX (website) or through information vendors, such as IRESS, Reuters and Bloomberg.[15]

Table 9.8 details the types of information released by companies to the ASX. The table demonstrates that announcements are a common occurrence on the ASX. For example, between January 2004 and December 2007 there were over 160 000 information announcements. The table also demonstrates that the most common types of information release are periodic reports (mainly earnings and dividend releases) and progress reports by companies. Together, these two categories of information accounted for almost one quarter of the announcements that occurred in this period.

CONCEPT CHECK

3. What are the two ways in which trades can be executed on the ASX?

4. What are the main trading phases on the ASX

For the answers, go to MyFinanceLab

Table 9.8	ASX information releases by announcement type from January 2004 to December 2007		
Code	**Announcement type**	**Frequency**	**Percentage (%)**
1000	Takeover announcements	3 511	2.09
2000	Security holder details	26 376	15.67
3000	Periodic reports	33 721	20.03
4000	Quarterly activities report	3 207	1.90
5000	Quarterly cash flow report	2 554	1.52
6000	Issued capital	24 481	14.54
7000	Asset acquisition & disposal	4 536	2.69
8000	Notice of meeting	10 338	6.14
9000	Asx announcement	2 880	1.71
10000	Dividend announcement	6 003	3.57
11000	Progress report	28 262	16.79
12000	Company administration	7 218	4.29
13000	Notice of call (contributing shares)	16	0.01
14000	Other	6 487	3.85
15000	Chairman's address	2 678	1.59
16000	Letter to shareholders	2 163	1.28
17000	Asx query	441	0.26
18000	Structured products	1 719	1.02
19000	Commitments test entity quarterly reports	1 758	1.04
	Total	168 349	100.00

CONCEPT 9.5   Settlement procedures

Settlement is the process by which payment is made by the buyer to the seller, and shares (ownership) are delivered from the seller to the buyer. Since February 1999 this process has been completed with a 'T+3 discipline'. This means that delivery versus payment (DvP) occurs exactly three working days after a transaction takes place.

Share certificates, which are paper documents that prove ownership of shares, were used in the settlement process until 1995. Transfer of ownership was achieved by the seller delivering a share certificate to, and the buyer obtaining a share certificate from, their respective brokers. In 1995 the ASX implemented an electronic means of effecting and recording the transfer of ownership, called the **Clearing House Electronic Subregister System (CHESS)**. CHESS is essentially an electronic list of shareholders of ASX-listed companies—that is, it is a shareholder *register*. It is legally recognised as a record of ownership of shares. Accordingly, since the intro-

Clearing House Electronic Subregister System (CHESS)
Provides an electronic record of transfers of share ownership.

duction of CHESS all shareholdings have been 'uncertificated'. This means that shareholders no longer need to hold a paper certificate to prove ownership. Ownership is now established through an electronic entry on CHESS that is updated as transactions occur. CHESS allows DvP to occur at exactly T+3.

While the notion of settling transactions sounds simple the technology and the procedures underlying the process are complex and lengthy.[16] Figure 9.9 provides an overview of the settlement process for a typical transaction. The ASX Settlement Corporation (ASX Settlement), a wholly owned subsidiary of the ASX, executes the settlement process and operates CHESS. The settlement process typically commences with a transaction on ASX Trade, which is notified to CHESS. A number of exchanges of information then take place (electronically) between CHESS and the brokers of the buyer and seller. The net result of this process is an amendment to the electronic register (CHESS) reflecting a change in legal ownership of the shares. Investors are mailed records of their shareholdings (called CHESS holding statements) at the end of the month in which the number of shares that they own changes.

CONCEPT CHECK

5. What happens after a trade has occurred on the ASX?

For the answers, go to MyFinanceLab

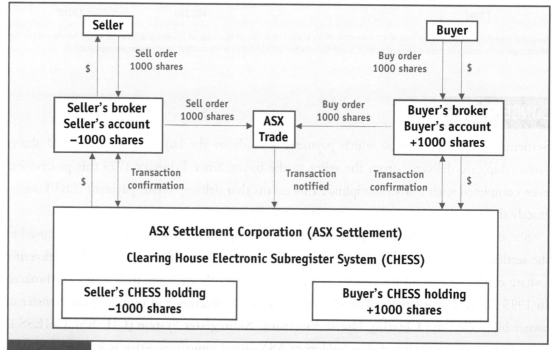

Figure 9.9   Settlement on the ASX of a 1000-share transaction

Student Learning Centre

MyFinanceLab To test your mastery of the content covered in this chapter and to create your own personalised study plan, go to MyFinanceLab: www.pearson.com.au/myfinancelab

CONCEPT CHECKLIST

In this chapter the following concepts were discussed:

➤ The nature of securities trading

➤ The different types of securities traded on the Australian Securities Exchange (ASX)

➤ The parties involved in securities trading, including:

  – the ASX

  – stockbrokers

  – fund managers

  – individual investors

➤ Trading methods on the ASX, including:

  – ASX Trade

  – off-market trading

  – information dissemination procedures

➤ Settlement of transactions

SELF-TEST QUESTIONS

Using the information provided in Figure 9.5, answer the following.

(a) If I wanted to buy 1000 shares in this stock immediately, what price would I have to pay?

(b) What is the maximum number of shares that I could buy at this price?

Self-test answer

If I wanted to buy immediately, I would have to pay the current best selling (ask) price. This is currently $4.16.

(a) The amount of stock currently available for sale at $4.16 is 199 999.

DISCUSSION QUESTIONS

1. (a) Define the terms 'primary' and 'secondary' equity markets.

   (b) How are these markets related to one another and what are their respective roles?

2. (a) What types of orders can investors place with stockbrokers?

   (b) What are the different methods by which brokers can 'execute' orders?

   (c) What happens after an order has been executed by a broker?

3. Describe the three main share market participants, including discussion of their respective rights, obligations and objectives.

4. What is the role of fund managers in Australian equity markets?

5. Discuss the extent to which trading activity on the ASX is 'concentrated'. What issues does this raise for the ASX?

6. Briefly describe the following features of ASX Trade trading on the ASX:

   (a) price and time priority

   (b) the closing single price auction

7. The ASX uses a relatively complex opening process.

   (a) Describe this process.

   (b) Explain the benefits of this process.

8. Is trading on ASX Trade anonymous? Discuss.

9. Transparency refers to the amount of information disclosed to the overall market relating to trading activity. Compare and contrast the transparency of ASX Trade and off-market trading.

10. Identify possible motivations for principal trading by brokers. Be specific, and provide two illustrative examples.

11. Over 40% of Australians own shares directly and/or indirectly.

    (a) What is the difference between direct and indirect investment in the share market?

    (b) Which of these accounts for the majority of share ownership by individual Australians?

    (c) Why do you think this is the case?

12. Market efficiency refers to how quickly a share price reflects new information that arrives in the market. Discuss the impact of ASX information release procedures on the pricing efficiency of shares.

13. In Australia, brokers may execute trades either on- or off-market.

    (a) What requirements must be met for a broker to execute a trade 'off-market'?

    (b) Why do you think that these rules are in place?

14. The ASX Listing Rules require that listed companies disclose to the exchange any information that may have a 'material effect on the price or value of securities of the company'. Under certain circumstances the ASX will halt trading prior to releasing this information to the market.

    (a) Under what circumstances will the ASX halt trading?

    (b) Describe some of the types of information releases that can result in trading halts.

    (c) What is the purpose of implementing trading halts?

    (d) Do you think halts are effective in achieving this objective?

15. Compare and contrast the current system of settlement of share transactions, CHESS, with the previous system.

16. Discuss the need for an ultra-low latency trading platform in recent times (in regards to the proliferation of algorithmic trading).

17. Discuss the advantages/disadvantages of a stock portfolio that held an equal value of shares in each of the top 10 largest securities in Australia (by market capitalisation) as at 31 December 2010 (refer to Table 9.1).

18. Provide four reasons for holding a closing call auction at the end of each trading day on the ASX. What are some other alternatives?

PRACTICAL QUESTIONS

BUY				SELL			
Ln	Bkr	Qty	Price	Price	Qty	Bkr	Ln
A	926	500	635	605	1000	321	A
B	451	500	634	635	500	287	B
C	668	500	634	636	500	386	C
D	878	1000	629	637	518	363	D
E	357	500	628	638	521	671	E

1. Refer to Figure 9.5 in the chapter. This shows that there are a number of buy orders at $4.15. Which order will execute first?   **BASIC**

2. D 298uring the pre-opening phase, you observe the market for a stock as follows.   **INTERMEDIATE**
   (a) Demonstrate how the opening price will be calculated.
   (b) Provide details of the trades that will occur when the market opens.
   (c) What orders will remain in the order book after the open?
   (d) If I wanted to sell 100 shares immediately following the open, what price would I receive?
   (e) What would happen if I entered an order to buy 500 shares at $6.34 immediately after the market opened?

3. Obtain a copy of *The Australian Financial Review*.   **INTERMEDIATE**
   (a) What was the closing value of the S&P/ASX 200 Index?
   (b) What was the worst-performing stock?
   (c) What was the best-performing sector?
   (d) What volume was traded in AMP Ltd?

INTERMEDIATE

4. Obtain a copy of the annual reports of AMP Ltd and National Australia Bank. (These are available on the companies' websites.)

   (a) What proportion of each of these companies is owned by the top 20 shareholders?

   (b) Who is the largest shareholder in each of these companies?

   (c) What similarities do you notice in the list of the top 20 shareholders in each of these companies?

INTERMEDIATE

5. Visit the website of one of the top fund managers listed in Table 9.3. Identify three funds that they offer to retail investors. What are the investment objectives of these funds?

6. (a) Craig James wishes to trade a parcel of 21 800 Commonwealth Bank of Australia shares currently priced at $45.62. Is his broker able to execute this transaction off-market? What if Craig James decides to trade it along with a portfolio of 12 other stocks valued at $4.2 million?

   (b) Refer to Figure 9.5 and calculate the average price received by a trader who submits a market order for the sale of 110 000 TLS shares.

   (c) In financial markets, market impact is the effect that a market participant has when it buys or sells an asset. It is the extent to which the buying or selling moves the price against the buyer or seller, i.e. upward when buying and downward when selling. Refer to Figure 9.5 and provide an indication of the market impact of a market participant who decides to submit a market order for the sale of 110 000 TLS shares.

INTERMEDIATE

7. Refer to Figure 9.5 in the chapter. If a broker entered a market order to sell 120 000 shares, describe the trade(s) that would occur. What is the average price of the trade? What mechanisms are available to the broker to obtain a higher price from selling the shares?

CHALLENGING

8. Obtain a copy of *The Australian Financial Review*. Visit the website <www.tradingroom.com.au>. Compare and contrast the information that is available about trading in the newspaper, on the website and on an ASX Trade screen.

CASE STUDY

The questions in this case study refer to the figure below which relates to Telstra shares.

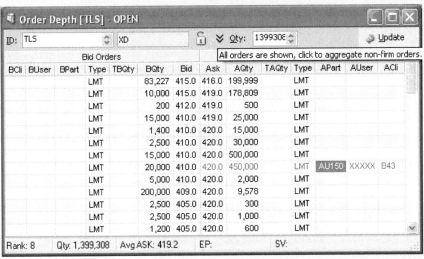

BCli	BUser	BPart	Type	TBQty	BQty	Bid	Ask	AQty	TAQty	Type	APart	AUser	ACli
			LMT		83,227	415.0	416.0	199,999		LMT			
			LMT		10,000	415.0	419.0	178,809		LMT			
			LMT		200	412.0	419.0	500		LMT			
			LMT		15,000	410.0	419.0	25,000		LMT			
			LMT		1,400	410.0	420.0	15,000		LMT			
			LMT		2,500	410.0	420.0	30,000		LMT			
			LMT		15,000	410.0	420.0	500,000		LMT			
			LMT		20,000	410.0	420.0	450,000		LMT	AU150	XXXXX	B43
			LMT		5,000	410.0	420.0	2,000		LMT			
			LMT		200,000	409.0	420.0	9,578		LMT			
			LMT		2,500	405.0	420.0	300		LMT			
			LMT		2,500	405.0	420.0	1,000		LMT			
			LMT		1,200	405.0	420.0	600		LMT			

Rank: 8   Qty: 1,399,308   Avg ASK: 419.2   EP: SV:

CASE STUDY QUESTIONS

1. What is the cost (per share) of purchasing:

    (a) (immediately) 100 000 shares in Telstra

    (b) (immediately) 410 000 shares in Telstra?

2. In economic terms, why are you paying a different price for purchasing 410 000 shares relative to 100 000 shares?

3. Assume you wanted to purchase 450 000 shares on behalf of a client.

    (a) If you found another client who was willing to sell you 450 000 shares for $4.17 cents, what could you do?

    (b) If your client was willing to buy at a price no higher than $4.16, what could you do as a broker?

FURTHER READING

For background information on recent developments at the ASX see:

- Australian Securities Exchange, *Annual Report 2007; ASX Fact File 2004;* and *CHESS: An Overview,* 2007.

A wealth of information on the concepts discussed in this chapter can be found on the ASX website at <www.asx.com.au>.

NOTES

1. For a discussion of the rules governing off-market trading, see Concept 9.4, 'Trading methods'.
2. Historically, access to the market was secured by becoming a member of the ASX. The demutualisation of the ASX in 1998 has meant that this is no longer the case. As stated in the ASX 1998 *Annual Report:* 'Access to the equities market after demutualisation will no longer have membership of the ASX as a requirement, nor a shareholding, but regulatory requirements will remain. Access will be open to any organisation or individual meeting the existing qualifications' (p. 13).
3. ASX website.
4. M. J. Aitken and P. L. Swan (1993), 'Principal and agency trades by brokers are complementary: The welfare effects of deregulating agency trading and banning principal trades', *Accounting and Finance*, vol. 33(2), 19–42.
5. For a discussion of the deregulative measures and their impact on the market, see M. Aitken (1990), 'The Australian securities industry under negotiated brokerage commissions', *Journal of Business Finance and Accounting*, vol. 17(2), 213–45.
6. Australian Bureau of Statistics (ABS).
7. ASX Share Ownership Update, November 2010.
8. Overlapping buy and sell orders are those with prices higher (lower) than the best available selling (buying) price. Hence, a buy order entered before the market opening at a price of $20.00 when there is a seller in the market for $19.95 is an overlapping order. Market participants may enter such orders because, when the market opens, highest-priced buy orders and lowest-priced sell orders have priority in execution.
9. A portfolio executed by a broker, where the broker participates as principal, does not have to be reported to the market until the next morning.
10. *Taking Stock*, ASX Broker Newsletter, September 2002, Edition 7.
11. Further details about the FSSBSC can be found on the ASX website.
12. ASX mandated electronic provision of this information in July 2003.
13. This is the same procedure as the one used to open and close the market described in Concept 9.4.
14. *Taking Stock*, ASX Broker Newsletter, April 2003, Edition 10.
15. ComNews™ replaces the previous company news service provided by the ASX, known as Signal G.
16. For detailed information about the settlement process, refer to ASX (1999), *CHESS: An Overview*, November 1999.

APPENDIX 9.1

THE CALCULATION OF THE OPENING PRICE ON ASX TRADE

This appendix describes the current algorithm used to determine the opening price on ASX Trade.[1] Every morning orders are carried over from the previous trading day, and new orders entered from 7.00 am to the opening time (around 10.00 am) when ASX Trade is in what is known as the 'pre-opening' phase.

During the pre-opening phase new orders can be entered and the price and quantity associated with existing orders can be amended. Price and time priority still applies to orders entered or amended during the pre-opening, although overlapping orders do not execute.[2]

Opening prices for the market are established during the market opening phase. The opening algorithm uses a four-step approach and involves the use of conditional decision rules. If an opening price cannot be determined after the first step, the algorithm progresses to the next step and so on. The decision rules applied are as follows.

The algorithm applies only if there are overlapping orders (i.e. the best bid price is lower than the best ask price). If there are no overlapping orders, there is no call auction and the opening price is set by the first trade during continuous trading.

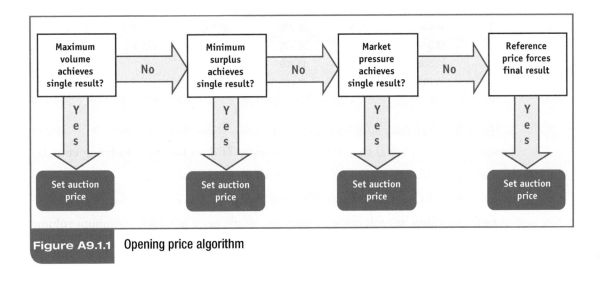

Figure A9.1.1   Opening price algorithm

The simplest way to obtain an understanding of how these principles are applied is through the use of an example.[3] Assume that the market for a given security immediately before the auction is as follows.

BUY				SELL			
Ln	Bkr	Qty	Price	Price	Qty	Bkr	Ln
A	111	4 500	825	818	6 600	666	A
B	222	25T	824	818	5T	777	B
C	333	3 200	824	819	3 600	888	C
D	444	1 900	822	820	17 500	999	D
E	555	49 700	820	823	1 900	111	E
F	666	8T	819	824	16 900	999	F
G	777	16 400	818	825	8 500	888	G
H	888	5 400	815	826	21 650	666	H
I	999	900	814	828	11 420	444	I
J	111	4 575	812	831	290	222	J

To facilitate an understanding of the algorithm, it is best to reorganise the order book to show the cumulative buy and sell quantity available at each price.

Price	Buy quantity	Cumulative buy quantity	Sell quantity	Cumulative sell quantity	Principle 1: Maximum executable volume	Principle 2: Minimum surplus	Principle 3: Market pressure
825	4 500	4 500	8 500	60 000	4 500		
824	28 200	32 700	16 900	51 500	32 700	−18 800	
823	0	32 700	1 900	34 600	32 700	−1 900	−
822	1 900	34 600	0	32 700	32 700	+1 900	+
821	0	34 600	0	32 700	32 700	+1 900	+
820	49 700	84 300	17 500	32 700	32 700	+51 600	
819	8 000	92 300	3 600	15 200	15 200		
818	16 400	108 700	11 600	11 600	11 600		

PRINCIPLE 1: MAXIMUM EXECUTABLE VOLUME

Principle 1 establishes the price(s) that maximises volume. It does this by calculating cumulative quantities at each price and then finding the maximum executable volume based on these cumulative quantities at each price. The maximum executable volume is the smaller of the cumulative buy and sell quantities at each price. If there is a single price at which maximum volume occurs, this is the opening price. If there are multiple prices that maximise volume, principle 2 is applied. In the above example, the maximum executable volume is 32 700. This occurs at all prices between 820 and 824.

PRINCIPLE 2: MINIMUM SURPLUS

Principle 2 establishes the minimum surplus volume that would result at each price as determined in principle 1. The surplus is the difference between the cumulative buy quantity and the cumulative sell quantity at each price. The price that exhibits the minimum surplus becomes the opening price. If more than one price exhibits the minimum surplus, principle 3 is applied. In the example above the minimum surplus is 1900 shares. This occurs at prices between 821 and 823.

PRINCIPLE 3: MARKET PRESSURE

Principle 3 involves identifying whether the market pressure of the potential auction prices exists on the buy or the sell side. A positive (+) sign indicates that there will be buy-side pressure at the end of the auction and a negative (−) sign indicates that there will be sell-side pressure at the end of the auction. If only buy pressure exists at each price exhibiting the minimum surplus, the highest of these prices is chosen as the opening price. If only sell pressure exists at each price, the lowest of these prices is chosen as the opening price. If there is no minimum surplus or both positive and negative signs exist, the process moves to principle 4. In the above example there is both buy- and sell-side pressure.

PRINCIPLE 4: REFERENCE PRICE

Principle 4 establishes possible prices by comparing the range of prices identified in principle 3 with a reference price. The reference price is generally the last matched (automatically executed) traded price.

If the minimum surplus is zero, the lowest and highest prices exhibiting this zero minimum surplus are chosen to compare with the reference price.

If the signs change from negative to positive, the two prices around the change are chosen to compare with the reference price. In the above example, 822 and 823 are compared with the reference price.

If the reference price is above the highest price established under principle 4, the highest price is used as the auction price. If the reference price is below the lowest price established under principle 4, the lowest price is used as the auction price. If the reference price lies between the highest and lowest prices as determined in principle 4, the reference price is used as the auction price.

If a reference price does not exist, the auction price becomes the lowest price as established in principle 4.

In the above example, if the reference price were 822, the price would be set at 822.

At the end of this process, the following trades would occur:

- Broker 111 purchases 4500 securities at $8.22 from broker 666.
- Broker 222 purchases 2100 securities at $8.22 from broker 666.
- Broker 222 purchases 5000 securities at $8.22 from broker 777.
- Broker 222 purchases 3600 securities at $8.22 from broker 888.
- Broker 222 purchases 14 300 securities at $8.22 from broker 999.
- Broker 333 purchases 3200 securities at $8.22 from broker 999.

The order book immediately following the auction would be as follows.

	BUY			SELL			
Ln	Bkr	Qty	Price	Price	Qty	Bkr	Ln
A	444	1 900	822	823	1 900	111	A
B	555	49 700	820	824	16 900	999	B
C	666	8T	819	825	8 500	888	C
D	777	16 400	818	826	21 650	666	D
E	888	5 400	815	828	11 420	444	E
F	999	900	814	831	290	222	F
G	111	4 575	812				

NOTES

1. The procedure was introduced on 18 March 2002, and superseded a procedure that calculated a single price based on the last two overlapping orders in the order book at the time of the open. This algorithm is also used to reopen the market following a trading halt and for the CSPA.

2. Overlapping orders may exist during the pre-opening phase where buy-order prices for a particular security can be higher than sell-order prices.

3. See Chapter 9 or the *ASX Trade Reference Manual* for more information.

The pricing efficiency of capital markets

10

CHAPTER PREVIEW

The previous chapter described the functioning of the Australian Securities Exchange (ASX), and in particular identified the factors that shape the way in which buyers and sellers meet to trade. In trading, investors reach agreement on, or 'form', the prices at which they are willing to transact. Hence, the previous chapter can be thought of as describing the market structure through which price formation takes place on the ASX. This chapter is concerned with the manner in which prices are formed. That is, in this chapter the pricing efficiency of the ASX is examined. This raises an interesting question. What does 'efficiency' mean in the context of securities' pricing?

An initial illustration of the meaning of pricing efficiency can be provided using the discounted cash flow model of value, introduced in Chapter 3. Recall that the value of a security is given by the present value of expected future cash flows discounted at an interest rate reflecting the time value and market risk of those cash flows. Where do future cash flow estimates come from? Market participants use information from various sources to forecast both the expected future cash flows and the market risk of a security. Hence, when new information becomes known to investors (arrives to the market), forecasts of the expected cash flows of a security and/or its market risk will be revised. This in turn can change the value that investors place on securities and, hence, the price at which they are willing to trade. *Market efficiency* specifically relates to informational efficiency, and is concerned with how rapidly security prices reflect or impound new information that arrives to the market. That is, market efficiency refers to how quickly, following the arrival of new information, investors revise their expectations and commence trading a security at a new price.

It is important to realise that this chapter is concerned with a 'theory'— the theory of market efficiency. The *Oxford English Dictionary* defines a theory as a 'scheme or system of ideas or statements held as an explanation or account of a group of facts or phenomena'.[1] This necessarily implies that some of the ideas in the chapter are quite abstract and hypothetical, and seemingly divorced from reality. However, a valid theory is usually supported by tests against the 'real world'. Hence, this chapter will also discuss tests of the theory of market efficiency using data from the ASX.

The chapter begins by outlining the theory itself. First, the term 'market efficiency' is defined, together with an explanation of how markets are kept efficient, followed by a discussion of the different possible levels of market efficiency. The chapter then examines various tests of the efficiency of the ASX. In particular, a review of some relevant research published in academic journals is provided.

KEY CONCEPTS

CONCEPT 10.1 Market efficiency theory

Definition

Efficient market
A market is efficient when prices reflect all available information.

A famous paper written by Professor Eugene Fama from the University of Chicago provides a widely discussed definition of market efficiency and identifies a number of different levels of market efficiency.[2] Fama defines market efficiency (an **efficient market**) as follows: 'I take the market efficiency hypothesis to be the simple statement that security prices fully reflect all available information.'[3]

Fama is always careful to frame his ideas in terms of a 'hypothesis'. A 'hypothesis' is defined in the *Oxford English Dictionary* as a 'supposition or conjecture put forth to account for known facts . . . a provisional supposition from which to draw conclusions that shall be in accordance with known facts, and which serves as a starting point for further investigation by which it may be proved or disproved and the true theory arrived at'.[4] This is exactly what the notion of market efficiency is at this point in time: 'a provisional supposition from which to draw conclusions that . . . serve as a starting point for further investigation by which it may be proved or disproved'. But how are security prices kept efficient?

What keeps security prices efficient?

As stated above, market efficiency is related to information. Figure 10.1 demonstrates the importance of information in securities markets. The illustration depicts a rise in the share price of Tabcorp Holdings Limited on 19 July 2011, from a level of around $3.09 at 2:00 pm to $3.29 at 2:30 pm (a gain of 6.5%), following the announcement that Tabcorp Holdings Limited was to be awarded the new wagering and betting licence by the Victorian government (released at around 2:15 pm). Note that the price of Tabcorp Holdings Limited eased a little during the afternoon but closed the day at $3.26. Hence, it appears that the release provided new information to the investors in Tabcorp Holdings Limited, and this was used to revise (upward) the cash flows forecast for Tabcorp Holdings Limited. This revision resulted in a permanent upward revaluation in the fair value of the operations of Tabcorp Holdings Limited and consequently in its price. It appears that the price of Tabcorp Holdings Limited reflected or impounded the information contained in the earnings release very quickly within approximately 30 minutes of its announcement.

An implication of this is that anyone who accurately predicted the content of the preliminary final report and the impact of this information could have made a profit from this prediction. This person could have bought Tabcorp Holdings Limited shares for $3.09 prior to 2:00 pm and then sold them at $3.29 following the announcement, thereby earning a gross profit of 20 cents per share.

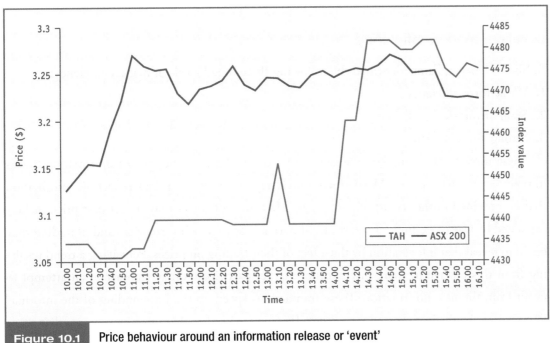

Figure 10.1 Price behaviour around an information release or 'event'

Sources: ASX and Reuters.

Now take the hypothetical case where by 2:05 pm all market players had accurately predicted the content of the information release. Large buying pressure would have occurred in Tabcorp Holdings Limited prior to 2:05 pm, and this would have pushed the price up *before* the release. In such a scenario, when Tabcorp Holdings Limited's licence news was made public the share price would not have changed, because the release contained no new information useful for forecasting the future cash flows of Tabcorp Holdings Limited. In these circumstances, any attempt to trade on the content of the information released would have netted no profit, because the price of Tabcorp Holdings Limited shares would already have reflected or 'impounded' the content of the information release.

The process described above can be used to explain how security prices are kept efficient. More importantly, it can be used to identify who keeps security prices efficient. Security analysts are well-paid individuals who work for large stockbroking firms. They are in the business of analysing and uncovering information related to shares that they follow, and forecasting the future cash flows and share value (fair price) of these shares. They provide this information to their clients, typically fund managers, who may decide to reward them by implementing trades and paying brokerage commissions. The act of trading by fund managers on the basis of the information and analysis provided by analysts has two important consequences. First, it enables the fund managers that trade first to make profits. Second, the trading process causes security prices to reflect the information uncovered by analysts. Hence, it is the activities of security analysts and their clients—fund managers—that cause prices to be efficient.

Levels of market efficiency

In his 1970 paper, Fama identified the following three broad levels of market efficiency:
1. Weak-form efficiency
2. Semi-strong-form efficiency
3. Strong-form efficiency.

These three levels of market efficiency differ on the basis of the type of information that is impounded in share prices. **Weak-form efficiency** occurs when prices reflect all information that is contained in the record of past prices. How current prices may reflect past prices is best explained by way of example. Traders might have access to new information, and in trading they begin to reveal that information by the effect of their trading on prices. Perceiving a trend resulting from this change in share prices, other market participants may transact in an attempt to profit from the new information. These transactions speed up the impounding of the information revealed by the initial price movement. This in turn implies that price movements that occur after the price trend 'information' has been impounded will not necessarily be related to previous price movements (the trend)—that is, price movements are expected to be random.

Weak-form efficiency
Theory that current prices of securities reflect all information that is contained in the record of past prices.

Semi-strong-form efficiency occurs when 'current prices "fully reflect" all publicly available information'.[5] This version of the efficient markets hypothesis has at least two implications. First, for a market to be regarded as efficient at the semi-strong-form level, it must also be weak-form efficient, because historical prices become public immediately after they occur (e.g. refer to the ASX Trade screen on page 289 in the previous chapter). The second implication is that semi-strong-form efficient markets should react immediately to 'public' information. The public information referred to here is any new information that is announced to the market, causing investors to reassess the value of shares and the price that they are willing to pay for them. Hence, for the ASX to be semi-strong-form efficient, prices should react immediately to any new information contained in information announcements, such as those listed in Table 9.8, on their release. As noted in the previous chapter, the most common and significant information releases are dividend and earnings releases.

Semi-strong-form efficiency
Theory that current prices of securities fully reflect all publicly available information.

Strong-form efficiency implies that 'all available information is fully reflected in prices'.[6] This form of efficiency also has two implications. First, a market must be at least semi-strong-form efficient (and, by implication, weak-form efficient) to be strong-form efficient, because publicly available information, of course, forms part of 'all available information'. Second, prices should reflect non-public information (or private information), or information known only to a group (but not all) of market participants.

Strong-form efficiency
Theory that all available information is fully reflected in prices of securities.

A good example of private information is inside information. This is information that is available only to someone in a privileged position in relation to a company, known as an 'insider'. Consider, for example, the director of a company. Company directors are privy to earnings reports before they are released to the public. Prior to their release, earnings reports are inside information. When the earnings figures are eventually released via the process described in the previous chapter, they become publicly available. How can private information be impounded in prices if the market as a whole does not have access to it? In theory, the answer is that transacting by insiders or those with private information can move prices and cause that information to be revealed. There is, however, a practical problem with this mechanism, in that insider trading is illegal in Australia. Section 1043A of the *Corporations Act 2001* prohibits people from trading on or disclosing 'inside information'. Information is deemed to be 'inside information' by section 1042A when: '(a) the information is not generally available; and (b) if the information were generally available, a reasonable person would expect it to have a material effect on the price or value of' a share.

It would seem that inside information is exactly the type of information that is referred to in the strong-form version of the efficient markets hypothesis. For such information to be impounded quickly, it would be necessary for the insider to trade on this information. However, following the above definition of 'inside information', the *Corporations Act* explicitly states that persons in possession of 'insider information' (i.e. insiders) must not: '(a) apply for, acquire or dispose of' securities or 'enter into an agreement to apply for, acquire or dispose of relevant' securities; or '(b) procure another person to apply for, acquire or dispose of relevant' securities.[7]

The Australian legal position relating to insider trading is in line with most other developed economies. However, as will be discussed later in this chapter, the mere existence of such provisions does not mean that such trading activities do not occur!

CONCEPT CHECK

1. What does the term 'efficient markets' mean?
2. What are the three different levels of market efficiency?
3. In the three different levels of market efficiency, what types of information are referred to?

For the answers, go to MyFinanceLab

CONCEPT 10.2   Tests of the efficiency of the Australian Securities Exchange

Is the ASX weak-form efficient?

It was discussed earlier that, if a market is weak-form efficient, price movements should be random and should not exhibit trends. There are at least two possible implications of this prediction. First, prices should follow a pattern known as a 'random walk'. Prices follow a random walk if the current price (P_t) is unrelated to the previous price (P_{t-1}), or if the value linking the two (e.g. ε) is a random number, as follows:

$$P_t = P_{t-1} + \varepsilon \tag{10.1}$$

Practitioner's POV

For many years academics and their students have followed the so-called Chicago School and subscribed to the belief that markets are efficient, which implies that you can't make money out of predicting price patterns using historical price data. However, the most recent breed of trader to have entered the Australian marketplace in the last few years—high frequency traders—do just this. A high frequency trader is a computer that has been connected directly to an exchange trading system (such as ASX Trade), that takes data from the trading system, makes the decision to trade, and then executes the trade without any human intervention. While there are many forms of high frequency trader, a set of them can best be described as 'technical traders' in the sense that based on transaction price movements over very short intervals in time (seconds) they attempt to predict forthcoming price movements over equally short periods of time and trade on this basis. Some of them are trying to detect the execution of a large order which has been broken up into smaller pieces and is being 'pushed' though the marketplace subsequently causing the price of a stock to move in a particular direction over short periods of time (or 'trend'). While it is difficult to estimate exactly how much high frequency trading is going on in Australian markets, some market commentators claim it could be more than 50 percent. Next time you trade, without even knowing it, you may be trading against a machine.

The next implication is that trading rules based on detecting and trading on the basis of price patterns should be unprofitable. A trading rule is an algorithm that is applied to a price sequence and that generates buy and sell signals. The objective is to identify overpriced or underpriced securities, by examining historical price sequences. This is known as 'technical analysis' or 'charting'. These two implications or predictions of the weak-form efficient markets hypothesis can be used to determine whether this form of the efficient markets hypothesis is valid for the ASX. Accordingly, in asking whether or not the ASX is weak-form efficient, we are really posing the question: 'Do share prices on the ASX exhibit trends?'

Figure 10.2 presents two different ways of depicting the price movements of shares traded on the ASX over the period 30 June 1992 to 30 June 2011. Casual observation of panel A in Figure 10.2—depicting the level of the ASX 200 Index—might lead to the conclusion that there appears to be periods when there are broad trends in prices. For example, during the period 30 June 2003 to close to 30 June 2005 (marked A) there was a general tendency for prices to increase. Closer scrutiny indicates that, over shorter time-frames, upward movements in the index generally seem to follow previous upward movements, such as in the area labelled A, and downward movements generally seem to follow previous downward movements, such as in the area labelled B. The implication of either of these perceived patterns occurring regularly is that there should be a very strong positive relationship between price movement on one day and the price movement on the previous day. Now look at panel B of Figure 10.2, which depicts the relationship between one day's (ASX 200) price level movement against the previous day's movement. When depicted in this way there is little evidence of a positive relationship in the movement in index prices from one day to the next. In fact, the diagram in panel B suggests that the relationship between market price movements in adjacent days is a random one. This is consistent with the notion that the ASX is weak-form efficient.

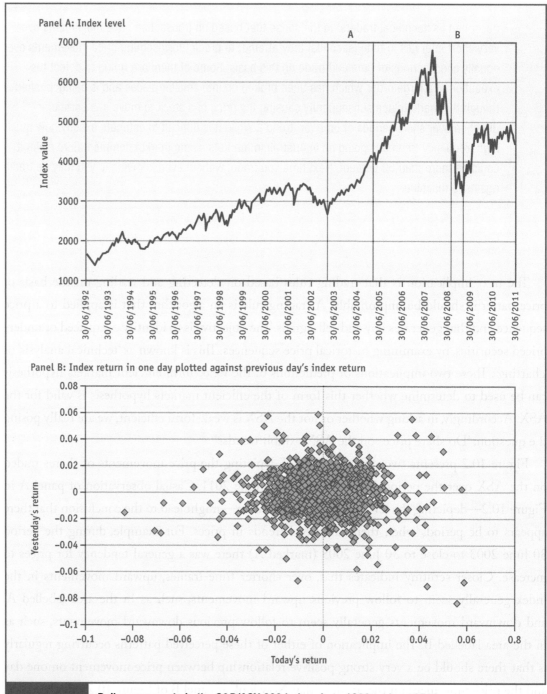

Figure 10.2   Daily movements in the S&P/ASX 200 Index, June 1992 to June 2011

Source: © Australian Stock Exchange Limited ABN 98 008 624 691 (ASX) 2002. All rights reserved. This material is reproduced with the permission of ASX. This material should not be reproduced, stored in a retrieval system or transmitted in any form whether in whole or in part without the prior written permission of ASX. © by Standard & Poor's, A Division of The McGraw-Hill Companies, Inc. Reproduced with permission of Standard & Poor's.

Are mechanical trading rules profitable on the ASX?

The second testable implication of weak-form efficiency is that it should not be possible to make systematic profits from trading rules set up to detect and trade on the basis of price trends. A paper by Ball (1978) represents a rare example of an Australian published study (based on Australian data) in this area.[8] This study attempts to determine whether trading rules can be used to generate profits. While the study is somewhat dated, drawing on share price data from the 1960s and 1970s, it nonetheless represents an authoritative test of whether the ASX is weak-form efficient.

Ball tests whether it is possible to generate profits from a trading strategy known as 'filter rules', where the filter is a percentage value applied to share price movements. The form of filter rule tested by Ball generates a buy signal when the price of a security is observed to rise by a certain (percentage) amount from its previous lowest point. The security is then held, and sold when it is first observed to fall by the same amount from its next lowest point. Alternatively, the security is short-sold if it is first observed to fall, and then purchased back when it is observed to rise.[9] For example, a 10% filter rule is as follows.

1. Buy if the price rises 10% from its previous lowest price.
2. Sell if the price falls 10% from its previous highest price.

Panel A of Figure 10.3 illustrates the application of this filter rule. The figure depicts monthly share price data for BHP from January 1969 to July 1970 (one of the securities and periods studied by Ball). To apply a 10% filter rule to BHP, a trader would commence tracking the price of BHP from January 1969, when BHP shares were trading at $19.33. When it first exhibited a 10% rise (or fall), the share would be bought (or short-sold). In this case, the shares fell in value by 10% by February 1969 and, hence, the trader is assumed to have short-sold the shares at this point for $17.40. The trader would then track the price of BHP until its price rose by at least 10% from its next lowest point. The price continued to fall for a period of time, first rising by a full 10% in December 1969. The trader is assumed to have bought back the shares at this point for $17.00. In this way, shares were purchased for $17.00 and sold for $17.40, yielding a profit of 40 cents to the trader. It is quite clear that, in order for the strategy to be successful, the price of the shares needs to continue moving in the same direction for a period of time (i.e. the market needs to be weak-form *inefficient*). For example, when the price falls and the shares are short-sold, the trader profits from the continuation in the price fall that occurs.

Ball was very diligent in testing these filter rules. He applied a number of different levels of filter (e.g. 5% and 10% filters) and also tried to establish whether the filter rules were actually profitable, or whether they merely appeared to be successful due to sheer luck. In order to do this, he 'paired' each security under analysis with another and strictly applied the buy or sell signals

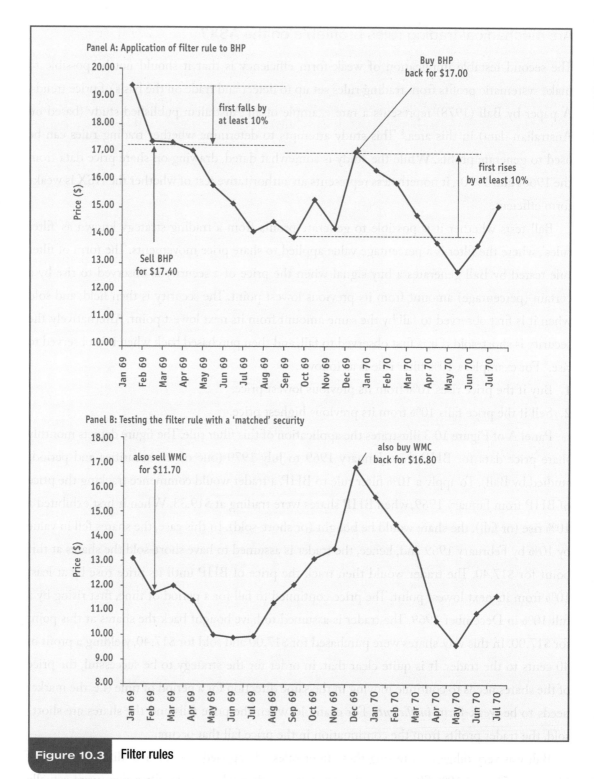

Panel A: Application of filter rule to BHP

Buy BHP
back for $17.00

first falls by
at least 10%

first rises
by at least 10%

Sell BHP
for $17.40

Panel B: Testing the filter rule with a 'matched' security

also sell WMC
for $11.70

also buy WMC
back for $16.80

Figure 10.3   Filter rules

generated to the 'paired' security. This process is demonstrated in panel B of Figure 10.3. For example, if Western Mining Corporation Ltd (WMC) was paired with BHP, when the sell signal was generated for BHP in February 1969, Ball also assumed that WMC shares were short-sold. Similarly, when the buy signal was generated for BHP in December 1969, Ball also assumed that WMC was bought. If the filter rule returned as much profit on trading strategies applied to the 'paired' security as the actual security under analysis, then it was concluded that it was not the filter rule that was profitable but the demon of chance! This is because the strategy underlying the filter rule was not being applied to the 'matched' security, so the trading signals applied should not generate as much profit as the security to which the filter is applied—except by chance.

Ball examined monthly price data for 126 stocks that traded on the Melbourne Stock Exchange from 1958 to 1970. In summary, and in his own words, he found that 'the differences between the filter securities and the average paired security returns are quite small' (p. 12). He went on to conclude that 'filter rules do not appear to have been profitable on the Melbourne Exchange over 1958–1970' (p. 14). The finding that it is not possible to make profits from trading rules relying on price patterns suggests that there aren't any systematic price patterns, or at least there are none of the type being sought. The absence of price patterns is consistent with the notion of weak-form efficiency. Hence, Ball's study is consistent with the notion that the ASX is weak-form efficient. This conclusion is also relevant today. Given the huge electronic trading advances that have occurred since the 1960s and 1970s which have sped up the execution of trades and the reporting of price information, the ASX must be more efficient than it was.

More recently there have been numerous other published studies that have examined technical trading rules in a variety of markets.[10] These studies have unanimously reported that no useful information can be obtained from past prices.

Is the ASX semi-strong-form efficient?

It was pointed out previously that in order for a market to be semi-strong-form efficient, it must first be weak-form efficient. Given the evidence discussed in the previous section, the ASX seems to meet this condition. The next question that arises is: is the ASX semi-strong-form efficient? Given that a semi-strong-form efficient market impounds all publicly available information, share prices should adjust immediately after information announcements to reflect appropriately the new information. A large number of studies have examined how quickly prices of ASX-listed shares react to new information at the time that it is released. Originally, studies of this nature examined share price behaviour in the months surrounding earnings announcements, but later studies moved to finer observation intervals: weekly, daily and eventually intraday (minute-by-minute or trade-by-trade). These studies are implicitly testing whether the ASX is semi-strong-form efficient, implying that prices should react quite rapidly to new information.

Studies of this nature are known as 'event studies', because they examine market pricing behaviour around information announcements, or information 'events'. Event studies examine share price returns generated around the time of different types of information announcements. Since share price movements may be caused by broad market movements as well as any information conveyed by an event, it is necessary to subtract returns caused by broad movements in order to isolate properly the effects of an information release. In doing so, researchers typically calculate so-called **abnormal returns** (AR_t), as follows:

Abnormal return
Excess of actual return over the expected return predicted by an asset pricing model.

$$AR_t = R_t - E(R_t) \tag{10.2}$$

where R_t is the actual return and $E(R_t)$ is the expected return in the interval t.

Practitioner's POV

The sheer volume of information released to the market on any day means that it will take time for prices to adjust to publicly released information. This in turn implies that share prices can be mispriced relative to their 'fundamentals'—that is, their earnings, dividends, debt levels and so on. Large stockbroking houses can spend in the order of $30 to $35 million a year on research teams analysing the fundamentals of organisations. Clients of stockbrokers, in turn, predominantly assess the quality of the service provided by stockbrokers and how much brokerage they will pay them on the basis of this research. Both of these facts suggest that there is some value added by fundamental research and, consequently, that the market is not semi-strong efficient in an absolute sense.

It is normal in these studies to use the capital asset pricing model (CAPM) to estimate expected returns. Example 10.1 illustrates the calculation of expected returns and 'abnormal' returns using the CAPM.

In Chapter 7 the evidence relating to the CAPM was described and it was concluded that there was no strong evidence either way as to the validity of the model. Accordingly, many recent event studies have used alternative methods of estimating abnormal returns, and these are discussed below.

Do share prices on the ASX react rapidly to earnings announcements?

An example of an event study carried out on the ASX is Aitken, Brown, Frino and Walter (1995), which examined how quickly prices react to earnings releases.[11] The study looked at half-hourly abnormal share price returns around earnings announcements.[12]

EXAMPLE 10.1

Daily abnormal returns around an important information announcement

QUESTION

On 19 July 2011, Tabcorp Holdings Limited announced that it was to be awarded a Victorian wagering and betting licence. The daily stock price and S&P/ASX 200 Accumulation Index values around the announcement were as follows.

Date	Tabcorp price ($)	S&P/ASX 200 Accumulation Index
13 July	3.12	33511
14 July	3.06	33332
15 July	3.07	33204
18 July	3.10	33193
19 July	3.26	33164
20 July	3.28	33770
21 July	3.24	33817
22 July	3.28	34164

If the beta of Tabcorp Holdings Limited is 1.46 and 90-day bank-accepted bills were yielding approximately 4.87% p.a. (or 0.01% per day) around the time of the announcement, calculate the abnormal return of Tabcorp Holdings Limited on the days before and after the announcement.

ANSWER

	Tabcorp daily return	Accumulation Index daily return	Expected return	Abnormal return
Calculation	$\dfrac{P_t - P_{t-1}}{P_{t-1}}$	$\dfrac{I_t - I_{t-1}}{I_{t-1}}$	$R_f + \beta(R_m - R_f)$	$R_t - E(R_t)$
14 July	−1.92%	−0.53%	−0.78%	−1.14%
15 July	0.33%	−0.38%	−0.57%	0.89%
18 July	0.98%	−0.03%	−0.06%	1.03%
19 July	5.16%	−0.09%	−0.13%	5.29%
20 July	0.61%	1.83%	2.66%	−2.05%
21 July	−1.22%	0.14%	0.20%	−1.42%
22 July	1.23%	1.03%	1.49%	−0.26%

Hence, the abnormal return on the day prior to the announcement is 1.03%, on the day of the announcement 5.29% and on the day following the announcement −2.05%.

The study analysed 78 of the largest stocks and 78 of the smallest stocks trading on the ASX, and earnings announcements that occurred during the year ended 30 June 1992. The sample of stocks was divided into those announcing 'good news' (where the share price is expected to increase abnormally) and those announcing bad news (where the price should decrease abnormally). Specifically, an earnings release was categorised as good news if the earnings per share (EPS) announced was greater than the consensus EPS forecast published by a well-known bank, or bad news if the EPS was less than the consensus forecast.

Figure 10.4 reports the findings of the study for large stocks. For both good news and bad news announced by companies, there is a clear and sharp abnormal price movement during the first 30-minute interval after the actual earnings announcement. There is no obvious abnormal price movement in any other interval. This suggests that the information conveyed by the earnings announcement is fully impounded into share prices within 30 minutes of its release. These results imply that new information is impounded very rapidly in security prices and, hence, is consistent with the semi-strong version of the efficient markets hypothesis.

Figure 10.5 reports the findings of the study for small stocks. The results are similar to those for large companies in relation to bad news announcements. However, similar consistency is not observed for good news announcements, where there appears to be a second positive abnormal return at 12 intervals—or approximately six hours—after the initial announcement. This implies that it takes much longer for information announcements to be impounded into the price of small stocks, and suggests that the market is less semi-strong-form efficient for small stocks than for large stocks.

Do share prices on the ASX react rapidly to information contained in large trades?

Another event study carried out on the ASX is by Aitken and Frino (1996), which examines how quickly prices react to information conveyed by large trades.[13] It is often argued that large traders are 'better informed' than small traders. For example, large transactions may come from fund managers, who are provided with information advantages by analysts in return for large brokerage fees. (Smaller traders don't receive this privileged information since their trades don't generate large fees.) Hence, it is possible that when market participants learn that a large buyer is in the market they will infer that the price of a stock must be too low. Given that the size of transactions is publicly available (e.g. from a ASX Trade screen), any study examining how quickly a market reacts to large trades can be interpreted as a test of how quickly a market reacts to a public information release. That is, it can be considered a test of the semi-strong-form version of the efficient markets hypothesis.

The Aitken and Frino study examined abnormal share price returns from one transaction to the next around large trades—so-called 'block trades'—that occurred between 1 July 1991 and 30 June 1993.[14] To determine the block trades that were executed, the study ranked all transactions and then selected the largest 1% of trades for each stock. In total, the study examined 4544 block buys and 4554 block sales.[15] The average value of block buys examined was $339 637, and the average value of block sales was $355 423—all very large trades!

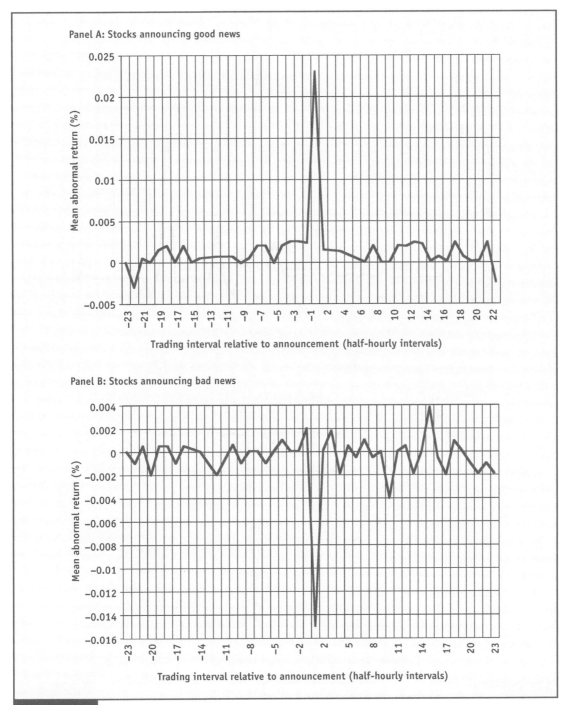

Panel A: Stocks announcing good news

Panel B: Stocks announcing bad news

Figure 10.4   Share price reaction around earnings releases made by large companies

Source: M. Aitken, P. Brown, A. Frino and T. Walter (1995), 'Price reaction and order imbalance surrounding earnings announcements', *ASX Perspective*. © Australian Stock Exchange Limited ABN 98 008 624 691 (ASX) 2002. All rights reserved. This material is reproduced with the permission of ASX. This material should not be reproduced, stored in a retrieval system or transmitted in any form whether in whole or in part without the prior written permission of ASX.

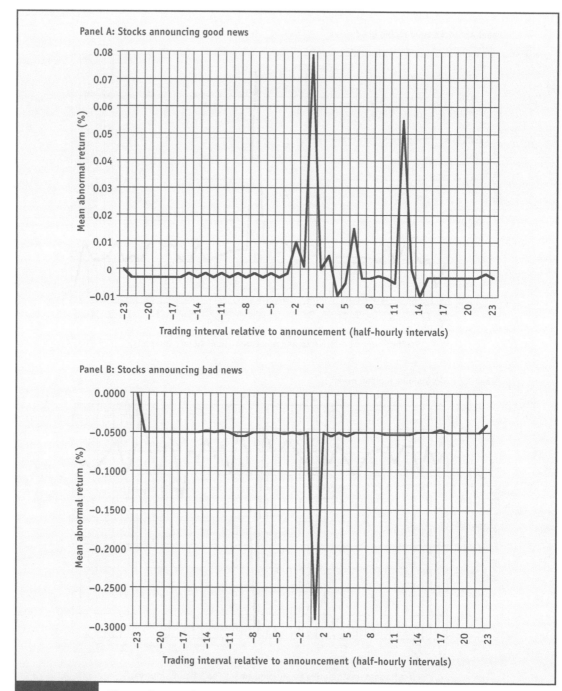

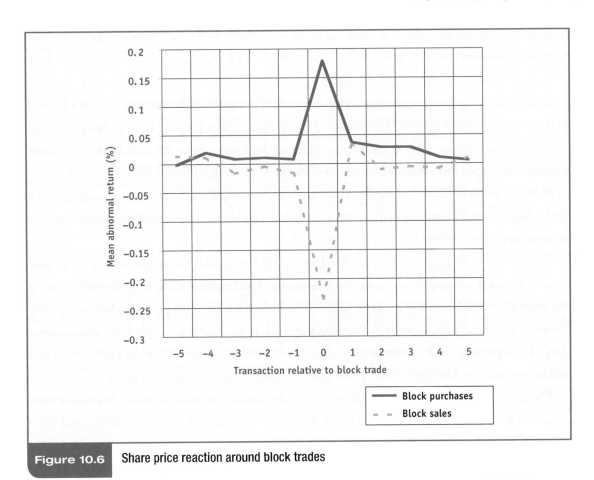

| Figure 10.6 | Share price reaction around block trades |

Source: Constructed from Table 2 in M. Aitken and A. Frino (1996), 'Asymmetry in stock returns following block trades on the Australian Stock Exchange', *ABACUS,* 54–61.

Figure 10.6 reports the findings of Aitken and Frino. The diagram illustrates that a large upward abnormal price movement occurs when a block purchase occurs (at point 0), and that the next three transactions (points 1, 2 and 3) are progressively executed at slightly higher prices. For block sales, there is a large abnormal downward movement in the share price at the time of the trade. As a whole, the evidence implies that it takes no more than three transactions for the information conveyed by block trades to be impounded in share prices (i.e. they react very rapidly). This evidence is again consistent with the semi-strong-form version of the efficient markets hypothesis.

Is the ASX strong-form efficient?

The previous section established that there is some evidence to suggest that the ASX is semi-strong-form efficient, which is one of the preconditions for strong-form efficiency. But is the market strong-form efficient? Recall that strong-form efficiency implies that prices should impound all available information—whether it is private or public. This implies that it should not be possible to trade on inside information, an illegal activity, and profit from it. However, there are documented instances of individuals profiting from insider trading—activities that have been subject to prosecution in Australian courts.

On 16 July 2010 Justice Fullerton of the Supreme Court of New South Wales made a finding in favour of the Crown against Mr Noel James Stephenson. The offender, Mr Stephenson, pleaded guilty and was convicted of a breach of s. 1043A of the *Corporations Act 2001* (Cth) for insider trading. Mr Stephenson held shares in Sam's Seafood Holdings (Sam's) Limited and disposed of 4514 shares upon obtaining inside information concerning Sam's. Mr Stephenson learnt that Sam's had obtained loans from Rabobank and that Rabobank was intending to demand the repayment of those loans.

The insider trading provisions contained in s. 1043A required Mr Stephenson to be in possession of inside information. Section 1042A defines inside information as information that is not generally available and, if it were available, would lead a reasonable person to believe that the information would have a material affect on the stock price. Section 1043A(1)(b) also required that Mr Stephenson had known or ought reasonably to have known that the information was inside information. Mr Stephenson plead guilty to breaching the provisions above.

On 26 April 2005 when Mr Stephenson disposed of his holdings in Sam's, his shares were priced at $1.00 at the close. On 3 May 2005 Sam's had received the letter of demand from Rabobank and on 4 May 2005 had requested a suspension of share trading following the receipt of the letter of demand and the appointment of a receiver. On 3 May 2005 Sam's had already requested a trading halt that was granted. On the previous day's trade (2 May 2005) Sam's closed at $0.50. Mr Stephenson had thus averted a loss of up to 50%.

Mr Stephenson had profited (minimised his loss) from the inside information that he traded on. In strong-form efficient markets it is not possible to profit from your trades because the market is able to impound private information. It was difficult to measure the precise loss incurred to shareholders as a result of the appointment of a receiver because Sam's shares were suspended when the information was released. Mr Stephenson was not required to repay the loss that he had averted which is estimated to be in the order of $2257. Instead he was required to pay a pecuniary penalty of $20 000 before 31 July 2010.

Convictions for insider trading illustrate that the ASX is not strong-form efficient, and it is worth considering the pervasiveness of this type of activity. That is, how often do individuals, or groups of individuals such as fund managers, profit from trading on private information?

A study by Sawicki (2000) examines the ability of fund managers in Australia to generate abnormal returns, presumably from access to better (or private) information that is eventually priced into stocks.[16] The study examines the performance of 124 superannuation funds over the period 1981 to 1995. Using monthly returns generated by the superannuation funds,

FINANCE EXTRA!

Prosecutions cut cost of capital

WITH a great deal of commotion and a very ambitious timetable, the federal government has announced the Australian Securities and Investments Commission will be increasing its enforcement role in the regulation of equity markets. It will be expanding its role from investigation and prosecution to detection of breaches of securities regulations.

But let's consider some hard data on the performance of ASIC in investigating and prosecuting referrals from the Australian Securities Exchange—a role it has played for many years in the enforcement process.

In a number of press releases over the past couple of years, ASIC has clearly expressed its appetite for pursuing breaches of insider trading legislation. This raises a question: how good is ASIC at enforcing insider trading laws?

Between 1999 and 2008, ASIC successfully prosecuted insider trading cases involving about 10 transactions. Over the same period, there were 320 million transactions executed on the Australian Stock Exchange. This implies that ASIC successfully prosecuted about one illegal insider transaction in every 30 million. Over the same period, the Securities and Exchange Commission prosecuted 2.7 and 2.9 illegal transactions in every 30 million trades executed on the New York Stock Exchange and NASDAQ stock markets, respectively.

This suggests the prosecution rate in Australia has been roughly one-third of the prosecution rate in the United States—a very poor report card indeed.

ASX annual reports provide sufficient information to estimate the number of suspected transgressions of insider trading laws detected by the exchange and referred to ASIC for investigation and prosecution over the 10 years to 2008. It seems that ASX has referred approximately 350 such matters to ASIC for investigation. Again, this suggests that only a minute portion of transactions referred to ASIC for investigation have resulted in successful prosecutions. Again, not the best report card.

Why the difference, and is ASIC really to blame for its poor showing? One of the key differences between how the SEC and ASIC prosecute insider trading is the type of proceeding they initiate.

In Australia, ASIC typically prosecutes insiders in criminal proceedings, in which the onus of proof is 'beyond reasonable doubt', and hence, it must be proved beyond reasonable doubt that the illegal insider trade took place. This means that ASIC must prove beyond reasonable doubt the insider actually had the information at the time they traded (a sufficient condition for proving a breach of insider trading laws). In the US, most of the cases are prosecuted in civil actions, in which the onus of proof is 'balance of probabilities'. That is, it need only be proved that the crime is more likely to have occurred than not have occurred. Hence, the SEC need prove only the insider is more likely to have had the information than not at the time they carried on the insider trading—it is much easier to prove, and is likely to account for the SEC's higher prosecution rate.

But what does it all mean for investor confidence and the cost of raising funds in Australian capital markets? In a seminal paper published a few years ago, Utpal Battacharya from the Kelley School of Business at Indiana University conducted a survey of insider trading laws in 103 countries, including Australia. He examined the impact of the introduction of insider trading laws, as well as their enforcement, on the cost of capital of companies.

Battacharya found that the cost of capital changes very little on the date that insider trading laws are first introduced. However, he finds the cost of capital falls significantly on the date that the first insider trading prosecution occurs. Apart from confirming the notion that clean markets promote cheaper capital raising, his results also suggest that it's the enforcement of insider trading and not simply the existence of laws that is important.

If we take Battacharya's findings and extrapolate them, it's prosecutions for transgressions of regulations that have the greatest impact on reducing the cost of capital. Further, there is no evidence to suggest the magnitude of the penalty makes a difference. Some food for thought as our regulator super-sizes its role in enforcement of securities regulations.

Alex Frino is chief executive of Capital Markets CRC and professor of finance at the University of Sydney.

Source: Alex Frino, *The Australian Financial Review*, 27 August 2009.

Sawicki estimates the abnormal returns systematically generated for different types of funds.[17] Table 10.1 lists her results for funds that invest in securities listed on the ASX alone. While the raw returns generated by the funds are between 10.35% and 12.98% p.a., abnormal returns are between −0.25% and 4.44%. Hence, after adjusting for broad market movements, there is little

Table 10.1	Are fund managers who invest in ASX securities able to generate abnormal returns?	
	AVERAGE RETURN (%)	AVERAGE ABNORMAL RETURN (%)
Superannuation pooled trust	12.98	4.44
Non-superannuation pooled trust	10.35	−0.25

Source: Constructed from Table 1 in J. Sawicki (2000), 'Investors' response to the performance of professional fund managers: Evidence from the Australian wholesale funds market', *Australian Journal of Management*, vol. 25(1), 47–66.

evidence that fund managers are in a privileged position (i.e. continually receiving private information) and are able to generate systematic abnormal returns. These results can be interpreted in either of two ways. First, this evidence is consistent with the strong-form version of the efficient markets hypothesis, and could be interpreted as suggesting that, while there may be isolated cases of evidence against the strong-form version of market efficiency, it is not pervasive. On the other hand, it might just be indicative of the fact that professional fund managers either do not receive privileged (insider) information or are unable to act on it sufficiently quickly to generate consistent abnormal returns.

Evidence against the efficient markets hypothesis: A final word

While the material discussed above suggests, roughly, that the ASX is at least semi-strong-form efficient, a substantial body of academic literature accumulated over the years intimates that perhaps the market is not as efficient as this evidence would suggest. These studies have centred on providing evidence of repeated patterns, or 'seasonal' behaviour, in share price movements. The existence of these patterns—commonly known as 'anomalies' or 'regularities' in the literature—is contrary to the weak-form version of the efficient markets hypothesis. The anomalies documented in research based on the Australian market include:

1. Prices tend to rise at the end of the day ('day-end effect').[18]
2. Prices tend to fall on Tuesdays ('day-of-the-week effect').[19]
3. Prices tend to rise in January ('January effect').[20]
4. Returns on small stocks tend to be larger than returns on large stocks (the 'size effect').[21]

Although there is an ongoing debate as to whether these anomalies really exist, or whether they are inconsistent with the notion of market efficiency, it is instructive to examine closely two examples of studies that have documented these effects.

Hodgson (1996) examined whether there are any intraday patterns in the Australian All Ordinaries Index.[22] Hence, rather than examine prices from one month to the next, or one day to the next, the study examined whether there are any patterns in share price movements from one 15-minute period to the next 15-minute period. The study calculated average returns on the All Ordinaries Index over 15-minute intervals during the period 1 April 1992 to 30 March 1993. Figure 10.7 illustrates the study's main findings.

The most striking finding from Hodgson is the large positive average return in the first 10 minutes of the trading day (in fact, the overnight return) and in the last 15 minutes of the trading day. While this finding appears to fly in the face of the weak-form version of the efficient markets hypothesis, have a closer look at the magnitude of the returns. They are between 0.03 and 0.04 of 1%—a very small return. It would be impossible for traders profitably to exploit these minuscule patterns in average returns after paying transaction costs, such as brokerage

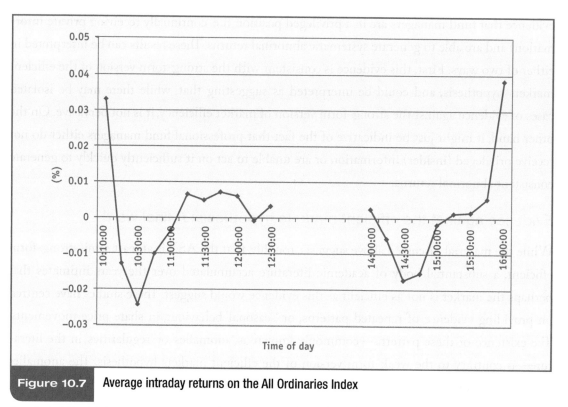

Figure 10.7   Average intraday returns on the All Ordinaries Index

Source: Constructed from A. Hodgson (1996), 'Information transfer, microstructure and intraday price return spikes', *Accounting and Finance*, vol. 36(2), 229–257.

commissions and bid–ask spreads.[23] If the efficient markets hypothesis is interpreted to imply that it is possible to profitably exploit any anomalies or share price patterns, as it sometimes is, then the findings in Hodgson are not necessarily inconsistent with the efficient markets hypothesis.

Aitken and Ferris (1991) examined the so-called size effect for stocks listed on the ASX.[24] They calculated abnormal monthly share price returns for 818 stocks over the period January 1980 to December 1985. Their study found that the average abnormal return on the decile of smaller stocks is higher than the abnormal return on the decile of larger stocks. (Unfortunately, they don't tell you what it is!) While this appears to be inconsistent with market efficiency, the study goes on to analyse whether it is possible to profitably exploit this apparent pattern in share prices after paying transaction costs (bid–ask spreads and brokerage).

Aitken and Ferris recognised that the fixed dollar cost of trading smaller stocks can be significantly greater than the costs of trading larger stocks. This is because the share price of small stocks is lower than that of large stocks. For example, a bid–ask spread of one cent on a small stock with a price of 10 cents represents a cost of 10%, while a bid–ask spread of one cent on a large stock priced at $10 represents 0.1 of 1%. Aitken and Ferris found that the average cost of trading the portfolio of smallest stocks is 13%, while the average cost for the largest stocks is 6%.

The study calculated abnormal returns after paying transaction costs, and found that an investor who turned over (bought and then sold) a portfolio of small stocks after two to three months would not earn a sufficient return on the smaller stocks to cover transaction costs. This implies that the small-firm effect cannot be profitably exploited by investors with an investment horizon of less than approximately two to three months. Their finding that the outperformance of small firms is difficult to exploit profitably after accounting for transaction costs suggests that the 'size' effect is not necessarily inconsistent with the efficient markets hypothesis.

In conclusion, while the existence of anomalies has been well documented in a number of financial markets around the world, the jury is still out on their impact on the theory of efficient markets. Overall, the better view appears to be that financial markets are generally efficient in the semi-strong form, anomalies notwithstanding, but markets do not appear to be efficient in the strong form.

CONCEPT CHECK

4. What evidence is there to support each of the levels of market efficiency?
5. What evidence is there to reject each of the levels of market efficiency?
6. Are investors able to make a profit by trading on the market anomalies? Explain your answer.

For the answers, go to MyFinanceLab

Student Learning Centre

My FinanceLab ■ To test your mastery of the content covered in this chapter and to create your own personalised study plan, go to MyFinanceLab: www.pearson.com.au/myfinancelab

CONCEPT CHECKLIST

In this chapter the following concepts were discussed:

➤ The nature of market efficiency and, in particular,
 – what keeps markets efficient
 – the different levels of market efficiency
➤ Evidence suggesting that the ASX is efficient, including:
 – weak-form tests based on filter rules
 – semi-strong-form tests based on event studies
 – strong-form tests based on examining the ability of fund managers to outperform the market
➤ Evidence questioning whether the ASX is semi-strong-form efficient, based on the existence of patterns or regularities in share prices

SELF-TEST QUESTIONS

1. Co Ltd announced its earnings results on 20 February. Using the following information, calculate the abnormal returns for Co Ltd around this event. Co Ltd has a beta of 0.9.

Date	Co Ltd price	13-week T-note	Accumulation Index
12 Feb	7.00	5.95	6000
13 Feb	7.10	5.85	6100
16 Feb	7.20	5.75	6125
17 Feb	7.05	5.65	6000
18 Feb	7.30	5.55	6250
19 Feb	7.00	5.55	6000
20 Feb	7.50	5.55	6050

2. Given the information in Question 1, was Co Ltd's earnings result good or bad news?

3. Is the pattern in abnormal returns in Co Ltd consistent with an efficient market?

Self-test answers

1. Abnormal returns for Co Ltd are as follows.

Date	Co Ltd daily return $\frac{P_t - P_{t-1}}{P_{t-1}}$	T-note daily return $\frac{R_f}{365}$	Accumulation Index daily return $\frac{I_t - I_{t-1}}{I_{t-1}}$	Expected return $R_f + \beta(R_m - R_f)$	Abnormal return $R_t - E(R_t)$
13 Feb	1.43%	0.02%	1.67%	1.50%	−0.07%
16 Feb	1.41%	0.02%	0.41%	0.37%	1.04%
17 Feb	−2.08%	0.02%	−2.04%	−1.84%	−0.25%
18 Feb	3.55%	0.02%	4.17%	3.75%	−0.21%
19 Feb	−4.11%	0.02%	−4.00%	−3.60%	−0.51%
20 Feb	7.14%	0.02%	0.83%	0.75%	6.39%

2. Co Ltd exhibited a large positive abnormal return of 6.39% on 20 February. This suggests that the earnings result was good news. The earnings figure must have been higher than the market had anticipated.

3. This result is consistent with semi-strong-form market efficiency. That is, new information was released to the market and the price responded quickly.

DISCUSSION QUESTIONS

1. (a) Discuss what is meant by the theory of market efficiency.

   (b) Explain what is meant by 'weak', 'semi-strong' and 'strong' forms of market efficiency.

   (c) Outline the empirical evidence on market efficiency. Does this mean that you cannot 'beat the market'? Explain.

2. Under the efficient markets hypothesis, what type of information is relevant in the efficient pricing of securities?

3. Describe the process by which the share price of National Australia Bank should be kept efficient in the following circumstances. An interim dividend of 70 cents per share has just been announced. This dividend is lower than the previous interim dividend and the market had been expecting an increased dividend.

4. 'Any test of market efficiency is necessarily also a test of the model that is used to estimate expected returns (e.g. CAPM).' Comment on this statement.

5. If the market was efficient in the weak form, would technical analysts (chartists) play any meaningful role? Why do most stockbrokers and other investment advisers have chartists in their research teams?

6. Do you think that the ASX is efficient? Give reasons for your answer.

7. Assume that the Australian stock market is weak-form efficient only. Which of the following situations should not provide an opportunity to earn excess (abnormal) returns? Explain your answers.

   (a) Your investment adviser calls to tell you that his company's technical analyst has been tracking the performance of Patrick Corporation Ltd stock for the past 12 months and is certain that its price is about to increase by 40–60% in the next two weeks. 'You should buy some quickly.'

   (b) BHP announces an earnings-per-share figure that is 20% higher than the majority consensus of market analysts.

   (c) A friend who works at a solicitor's office has advised you to buy shares in a company that is in confidential negotiations to be taken over.

   (d) You have discovered that each time the price of a gold-mining stock drops by 25% in any four-week period it falls by another 20% before the price increases again.

   (e) CBA pays a dividend that is 25% higher than the previous dividend.

8. Assume that the Australian stock market is semi-strong-form efficient. Which of the following situations could be expected to provide an opportunity to earn excess (abnormal) returns? Explain your answers.

   (a) BHP announces an earnings-per-share figure that is 20% higher than the average consensus of market analysts.

   (b) Your friend who works at BHP tells you that tomorrow the company will announce an earnings-per-share figure that is 20% higher than the average consensus of market analysts.

   (c) A listed Australian company, Large Ltd, announces a takeover bid for a company that you are thinking of investing in, Small Ltd.

(d) An analyst tells you that company ABC will announce an earnings-per-share figure that is double previous levels. However, the higher EPS will arise as a result of a change in the company's accounting practices.

(e) You have discovered that each time the price of a gold-mining stock drops by 25% in any four-week period it falls by another 20% before the price increases again.

(f) CBA pays a dividend that is 25% higher than the previous dividend.

9. Which of the following situations is inconsistent with the strong-form version of the efficient markets hypothesis? Explain your answers.

(a) Evidence indicates that, on average, investment fund managers do not consistently earn abnormal returns.

(b) You make consistent abnormal profits by trading shares after the announcement of an unexpected rise in earnings.

(c) You make consistent abnormal profits by trading shares before the announcement of an unexpected rise in earnings.

(d) In any given year, approximately half of all managed investment funds outperform the market.

(e) Through your work in a corporate advisory firm, you become aware of a takeover deal before it is officially announced. You make profits by purchasing shares in the company that is to be taken over.

(f) Your friend has been engaging in 'day-trading' on the Internet, and is showing a profit of 300% since he began trading four months ago.

10. 'It is about time that financial advisers reviewed their role, since there is ample evidence that markets are generally efficient. Therefore, instead of having investors believe that it is possible to earn superior returns by following their (the advisers') advice, they should concentrate on advising investors on the benefits of diversification and the like.' Do you agree or disagree with this statement? Explain your answer.

11. Is the existence of managed investment funds consistent or inconsistent with the belief that financial markets are generally efficient? Explain.

12. Comment on the following statements.

(a) The existence of seasonalities (i.e. calendar-based anomalies) means that share markets are not efficient.

(b) The stock market crash of October 1987 proves that financial markets are inefficient.

(c) The efficient markets hypothesis implies that securities are always priced correctly.

(d) The efficient markets hypothesis holds that markets are operationally and transactionally efficient.

13. You have been following an investment strategy that involves applying the following filter rule: (a) buy $10 000 worth of all shares that decline in price by more than 5% over the past week; and (b) sell (short) $10 000 worth of all shares that have risen in price by more than 5% over the past week. Over the past year, the return on this strategy has been 30%, while the return on the ASX 200 Index over the year was 12%. Does this demonstrate that the market is not weak-form efficient? Discuss.

14. The efficient markets hypothesis implies that investors do not possess 'superior' investment abilities, in the sense that consistent abnormal profits cannot be earned. Accordingly, what investment strategy might be advisable?

PRACTICAL QUESTIONS

1. Corporate Ltd announced that it had won a new contract in a sealed tendering bid process on 1 June. The share price of Corporate Ltd and other data are as follows.

BASIC

Date	Price	Market index
30 May	1.50	2182
31 May	1.52	2186
1 June	1.44	2187
2 June	1.42	2186
3 June	1.45	2188

The beta of Corporate Ltd is 1.2 and the 13-week Treasury note yield over the period was 8% p.a. Calculate the abnormal returns around the date that Corporate Ltd announced it had won the contract. Can you explain the abnormal returns?

2. I have observed that the price of Caught Out Ltd consistently ends the day 0.5% higher than the price observed at 3.30 pm.

BASIC

   (a) Can I profit from this information?

   (b) Is this consistent with market efficiency?

3. On 2 August, Caught Out Ltd announced that its earnings for the year ended 30 June had increased by 8% to $500 million. Given the following price and index data, calculate the abnormal returns of Caught Out Ltd, and discuss the effect of the announcement on its value. Yields on 10-year bonds in August were running at 4.80% p.a.

INTERMEDIATE

Date	Price	Market index
25 July	5.00	3000
26 July	5.05	3010
27 July	5.10	3015
28 July	5.08	3000
29 July	5.10	3015
1 August	5.07	3010
2 August	5.45	2950

4. Co Ltd announced that it had cut its dividend by 5 cents per share to 15 cents per share on 20 July. The share price, index data and other data around 20 July were as follows.

Date	Price	Index	Accumulation index	13-week T-notes
13 July	20.40	2000	10000	4.50
16 July	20.20	1900	9900	4.55
17 July	20.30	1930	9990	4.50
18 July	20.00	1925	9980	4.50
19 July	20.45	2025	10 090	4.45
20 July	20.40	2020	10 080	4.50

Using the data above, calculate the beta of Co Ltd. Use the CAPM to estimate the unexpected return for Co Ltd on the dividend announcement date. Can you explain these unexpected returns?

5. ABC Ltd and XYZ Ltd announced their earnings figures on 3 February. The pattern in their abnormal returns is provided below.

Date	ABC abnormal return	XYZ abnormal return
1 Feb	–0.34%	0.79%
2 Feb	0.12%	–0.23%
3 Feb	2.10%	2.79%
4 Feb	1.05%	0.78%
5 Feb	–0.21%	–0.53%

ABC Ltd is a large, highly liquid stock with an average bid–ask spread of 0.5%, while XYZ Ltd is small and infrequently traded with an average bid–ask spread of 3%. If I were able to predict accurately the earnings figures, could I earn an abnormal profit? Discuss.

6. Obtain a recent copy of *The Australian Financial Review*. Find an article that discusses the release of new information by a listed company (perhaps an earnings or dividend announcement). How did the price of the stock react to the new information? Was this information anticipated by the market? Is this behaviour consistent with the efficient markets hypothesis?

7. Below are some monthly data for the ASX 200 Index. Does the index appear to exhibit 'runs'? Is this evidence of market inefficiency? What are the practical problems with trading on any trading patterns exhibited in the ASX 200 Index?

INTERMEDIATE

Feb 2001	3327	−0.00456
Mar 2001	3147	−0.05541
Apr 2001	3329	0.056279
May 2001	3379	0.014817
Jun 2001	3490	0.032378
Jul 2001	3325	−0.04867
Aug 2001	3276	−0.01482
Sep 2001	3050	−0.07152
Oct 2001	3250	0.063554
Nov 2001	3338	0.02669
Dec 2001	3422	0.025091

8. An analyst examines the price behaviour around announcements for a sample of 30 small stocks and 30 large stocks (by market capitalisation), using the CAPM to calculate abnormal returns. Stocks are divided into 'good news' and 'bad news' announcements depending on whether the earnings per share reported was greater or less than consensus forecasts. The following intriguing abnormal returns (in per cent) are calculated in the three months including and following the earnings announcement date.

INTERMEDIATE

	Small stocks	Large stocks
Good news	32.1%	16.1%
Bad news	1.1%	−15.1%

Does this represent evidence of inefficiency?

9. On 22 August 2005, Toll Holdings Ltd (TOL) announced that it wished to acquire more than 50% of the shares of Patrick Corporation (PRK) (i.e. it launched a 'takeover bid'). Below is end-of-month share price data for TOL and PRK. Calculate a market model beta for TOL and PRK, and then estimate the abnormal returns on the announcement month and the month after.

CHALLENGING

	TOL	PRK	ASX Accumulation Index
Apr 2005	12.70	5.69	22 664
May 2005	12.50	5.69	23 413
Jun 2005	13.06	5.59	24 534
Jul 2005	13.52	5.81	25 173
Aug 2005	14.08	7.04	25 678
Sep 2005	13.90	6.89	25 678

Based on your calculations:

(a) Comment on the information that appears to be conveyed by the announcement.

(b) Is the price adjustment efficient, as far as you can tell?

(c) Is the data above sufficient for you to calculate a reliable beta?

(d) What kind of data would enable you to gauge more accurately the efficiency of the adjustment to the announcement?

CHALLENGING 10. Using the share price data below for BHP, explain whether a 1% filter rule would have made money (allow short-selling). Is this sufficient data to conclude that the market for BHP is inefficient?

1 Sep 2005	20.93
2 Sep 2005	20.83
5 Sep 2005	20.46
6 Sep 2005	20.25
7 Sep 2005	20.55
8 Sep 2005	20.03
9 Sep 2005	20.19
12 Sep 2005	20.2
13 Sep 2005	20.47
14 Sep 2005	20.59
15 Sep 2005	20.7
16 Sep 2005	20.99

CHALLENGING 11. The STX 200 is a fictitious stock which mimics price movements in the underlying stock index. A trader has executed the following trades and can hold a maximum position of one contract. Holding one position gives the trader a profit of $10 every time the index moves one point. The trader used a single simple 30-day moving average. When the STX 200 was above the 30-day average, the trader would buy and when it was below the average they would sell. The trader had to close out all positions

at the end of the day on the 15 June 2011. What do the results below imply about the efficiency of the stock index excluding transaction costs? Is the market efficient after factoring in brokerage? Is the market efficient after adjusting for risk where a buy-hold strategy is used to estimate the level of risk?

	STX 200	30 day SMA	Signal	Points	1 pt = $10 Gross profit	1 trade = $10 Commission	RISK Buy-hold
1 June 2011	5500	5403	BUY 1 contract			10	5500
2 June 2011	5510	5407					
3 June 2011	5600	5413					
6 June 2011	5700	5423					
7 June 2011	5400	5422	SELL 2 contracts	−100	−1000	10	
8 June 2011	5300	5418					
9 June 2011	5500	5421	BUY 2 contracts	−100	−1000	10	
10 June 2011	6000	5440					
13 June 2011	5900	5455					
14 June 2011	5800	5467					
15 June 2011	5900	5481	SELL 1 contract	400	4000	10	5900
					$2000	$40	400

Excel question

1. On 8 November, BCD Ltd announced that it wished to acquire XYZ Ltd at a price 25% higher than the current market value of the XYZ. The share price of BCD and XYZ and index data from 23 October to 9 November were as follows:

Date	BCD	XYZ	Market Index
23 Oct	45.66	106.45	6677.50
24 Oct	45.47	104.50	6652.10
25 Oct	44.41	104.43	6644.80
26 Oct	45.43	107.00	6716.40
29 Oct	46.95	112.59	6808.20
30 Oct	46.54	111.90	6772.50
31 Oct	45.76	110.00	6779.10
01 Nov	46.56	115.00	6853.60
02 Nov	44.67	110.96	6726.70
05 Nov	43.38	108.75	6620.10
06 Nov	43.83	108.50	6659.10
07 Nov	44.53	112.22	6728.10
08 Nov	41.00	125.50	6568.50
09 Nov	41.10	130.90	6607.40

Assuming the risk-free rate over the period is running at 6.8% p.a., calculate the betas of BCD and XYZ. Then use the CAPM to estimate the abnormal returns of both firms on the announcement date, before the day and after the day, and discuss whether the results are consistent with the market efficient hypothesis.

CASE STUDY

Henry Baskin has operated a family restaurant for more than 20 years, and he has invested his family superannuation in a retail superannuation fund. During the last several years, many of his friends have set up their own DIY super fund. One of his friends, David Watson, told Henry that the DIY super fund provides more flexibility and involves fewer fees relative to the conventional funds. During his conversation with Henry, David talked about lots of concepts with which Henry is not quite familiar, such as market efficiency, technical analysis, fundamental analysis and different trading strategies. David said he has used several invest-ment strategies to 'beat the market'. In order to clarify his understanding of the relevant financial concepts and decide whether he also needs to set up a DIY super fund for his family, Henry has invited you, a financial planner, to give a private seminar to him and his family members. As a financial planner, you plan to provide answers for the following questions to David and his family members during the private seminar.

CASE STUDY QUESTIONS

1. What is an efficient market? Illustrate your answer with an example.

2. What are the different levels of market efficiency?

3. What is technical analysis? What is the empirical evidence on market efficiency for technical analysis? What is the implication of this empirical evidence?

4. What is fundamental analysis? What is the empirical evidence on market efficiency for fundamental analysis? What is the implication of this empirical evidence?

5. Can investors 'beat the market'?

6. What investment strategy would you advise for David and his family members?

FURTHER READING

The original paper written by Professor Fama is still quite readable:

- Fama, E. (1970), 'Efficient capital markets: A review of theory and empirical work', *Journal of Finance*, vol. 25(2), 383–417.

The sequel is also worth looking at:

- Fama, E. (1991), 'Efficient capital markets: II', *Journal of Finance*, vol. 46(5), 1575–617.

Finally, the *Australian Journal of Management* and *Accounting and Finance* are Australian academic journals that contain numerous examples of event studies based on the Australian markets, which are usually quite readable.

NOTES

1. *Oxford English Dictionary*, vol. XVII, 902.
2. The original paper written by Fama is: E. Fama (1970), 'Efficient capital markets: A review of theory and empirical work', *Journal of Finance*, vol. 25(2), 383–417. A sequel was later published: E. Fama (1991), 'Efficient capital markets: II', *Journal of Finance*, vol. 46(5), 1575–617.
3. Fama (1991), 1575.
4. *Oxford English Dictionary*, vol. VII, 582.
5. Fama (1970), 404, n. 2.
6. Ibid., 409.
7. *Corporations Act 2001*, section 1043A.
8. R. Ball (1978), 'Filter rules: Interpretation of market efficiency, experimental problems and Australian evidence', *Accounting and Finance*, 1–17.
9. There is nothing special or illegal about short-selling shares. This activity essentially involves selling shares you do not own and promising to deliver them at a later date. Since you do not own the shares, you are obviously compelled to purchase them before you are required to make delivery (hopefully when the shares can be purchased at a lower price). If an investor believes that the price of a security is going to fall, they can short-sell the share (thus, 'selling high') and then at a later date 'buy low' and deliver

the shares originally sold in order to make a profit. The whole strategy tends to come unstuck if the price of the security rises instead of falls. When this occurs, short-sellers are forced to take a loss when they purchase the shares they promised to deliver.

10. See, for example, R. Sullivan, A. Timmerman and H. White (1999), 'Data snooping, technical trading rule performance and the bootstrap', *Journal of Finance*, vol. 54(5), 1647–91, and H. Bessembinder and K. Chan (1995), 'The profitability of technical trading rules in Asian stock markets', *Pacific Basin Finance Journal*, vol. 3, 257–84.

11. M. Aitken, P. Brown, A. Frino and T. Walter (1995), 'Price reaction and order imbalance surrounding earnings announcements', *ASX Perspectives*.

12. Rather than use a CAPM-based measure of abnormal returns, the study calculated the average 30-minute return at the same time of the day as each interval around each earnings announcement, for the whole year surrounding the earnings release, and used this as the expected return. The reason the authors did this is not important; what is important is to appreciate that they attempted to remove the effects of broad market movements to isolate the effects of the earnings releases by carrying out this calculation.

13. M. Aitken and A. Frino (1996), 'Asymmetry in stock returns following block trades on the Australian Stock Exchange', *ABACUS*, vol. 32(1), 54–61.

14. Again, rather than use a CAPM-based approach, the study calculated the expected returns using the average return for transactions around trades that occurred in the same minute as each block trade, for the whole year prior to the block trade. It is not important to understand why they did this for our purposes here, but it is important to understand that the study attempted to remove the effects of broad market movements and to isolate the effects of the information conveyed by the block trades themselves.

15. The study defined block buys as large trades initiated by a buyer (i.e. an order that is entered on ITS and executes against several sell orders displayed on the ITS screen), and block sales as large trades initiated by a seller (i.e. an order that is entered on ITS and executes against several buy orders displayed on the ITS screen).

16. J. Sawicki (2000), 'Investors' response to the performance of professional fund managers: Evidence from the Australian whole-sale funds market', *Australian Journal of Management*, vol. 25(1), 47–66.

17. The Superannuation pooled trust/Non-superannuation pooled trust classification reported in Table 10.1 is merely a tax status distinction and is not important.

18. A. Hodgson (1996), 'Information transfer, microstructure and intraday price return spikes', *Accounting and Finance*, vol. 36(2), 229–57.

19. R. Ball and J. Bowers (1988), 'Daily seasonals in equity and fixed interest returns—Australian tests of plausible hypotheses', in E. Dimson (ed.), *Stock Market Anomalies*, Cambridge University Press, Cambridge.

20. M. Gultekin and N. Gultekin (1983), 'Stock market seasonality: International evidence', *Journal of Financial Economics*, vol. 12(4), 469–81.

21. M. Aitken and G. Ferris (1991), 'A note on the effect of controlling for transaction costs on the small firm anomaly: Additional Australian evidence', *Journal of Banking and Finance*, vol. 15(6), 1195–202.

22. Hodgson (1996), op. cit.

23. During the period of Hodgson's study, stamp duty of 0.3 of 1% would also have been levied on all trades.

24. Aitken and Ferris (1991), op. cit.

11

Dividend policy

CHAPTER PREVIEW

The previous chapters were concerned with the valuation of companies and how they are priced in the marketplace. To this point, there has been little explanation of the financial policies undertaken by the management of a company and how these may affect its value or price. This chapter is concerned with one such important financial policy—dividend policy.

When a company generates free cash flow, it can retain all or part of this free cash flow for future use or, alternatively, it can pay a dividend to its shareholders. Dividend policy is concerned with the size and type of dividends paid by a company. The dividend policy decision is tied directly to the financing of a company. Any funds required by a company, and which cannot be covered by its retained funds, must be raised from capital markets. This chapter examines the nature of dividend policy.

KEY CONCEPTS

CONCEPT 11.1   What is dividend policy?

Practitioner's POV

Entities able to be admitted to the official list of the ASX include both companies, which issue shares, and trusts, which issue units through a responsible entity. Companies are able to distribute free cash flow by paying a dividend and trusts are able to distribute cash flow by paying a distribution. Entities may issue stapled securities, which comprise one share in a company and one unit in a trust stapled together to form a single stapled security. Free cash flow distributed from these entities normally comprises dividends from the company and distributions from the trust, together referred to as the entity's distribution policy. Dividends from the company may be franked to the extent that franking credits are available. Entities may be structured as stapled vehicles in order to distribute cash flow in a tax advantageous manner.

Companies typically pay dividends twice a year: an interim dividend halfway through their reporting year and a final dividend at the end of their reporting year.[1] A company with excess cash that it wishes to return to shareholders, without signalling an ongoing increase to its dividend policy, may choose to pay a 'special' dividend. This special dividend will be declared and paid at the same time as either the company's interim or final dividend. **Dividend policy** refers to the decision by companies to pay out net profit after tax or retained earnings to shareholders (as dividends) or alternatively to reinvest those profits (retained earnings). The dividend payout ratio defined in Chapter 3 quantifies the dividend policy decision. It measures the proportion of net profit after tax paid out as dividends. Table 11.1 sets out the earnings and dividends per share and dividend payout ratio of Telstra Corporation between 2007 and 2010.

Dividend policy
The decision by companies to pay out net profit after tax or retained earnings to shareholders as dividends.

> ## CONCEPT CHECK
>
> 1. What types of dividends are typically paid by Australian companies?
> 2. When are these dividends paid?
>
> For the answers, go to MyFinanceLab

In 2010, Telstra Corporation generated earnings per share (EPS) of 31.4 cents. It paid an interim dividend of 14 cents and a final dividend of 14 cents, bringing the total dividends per share (DPS) for 2010 to 28 cents, consistent with the previous year. The payout ratio for 2010 was 89.5%, compared with 85.3% in 2009 and 106.9% in 2007, clearly showing how companies like to maintain absolute dividend per share payments, even as earnings vary. This chapter is concerned with the decision-making processes which led Telstra to pay a total dividend of 28

Table 11.1	Earnings per share, dividend per share and dividend payout ratio of Telstra Corporation			
	2010	2009	2008	2007
Earnings per share (cents)	31.4	32.9	29.9	26.3
Ordinary dividend per share (cents)				
Interim	0.14	0.14	0.14	0.14
Final	0.14	0.14	0.14	0.14
Total	0.28	0.28	0.28	0.28
Dividend payout ratio	89.5%	85.3%	94.1%	106.9%

Source: Telstra Corporation Limited Annual Reports, 2007–2010. © Telstra. Reproduced by permission of Telstra.

cents per share or adopt a payout ratio of approximately 90%. The chapter also explores the implications for the wealth of Telstra's shareholders of paying this level of dividend rather than something higher, or possibly lower.

Practitioner's POV

Analysts typically find it easier to forecast dividends rather than earnings. While earnings are influenced by unpredictable developments in the economy and industry in which a company operates, dividends are set by directors, who usually like to pay a smooth and growing dividend stream. Companies are able to pay a smooth growing dividend because they typically avoid paying out 100% of their cash flows as dividends. This means they have a free cash flow buffer that they can use when earnings growth slows.

An appropriate dividend policy will depend on the structure of the company's share register, as different shareholders may have varying dividend preferences:

- retail investors tend to value progressive dividend policies (increasing dividends on a per-share basis)
- institutional investors generally recognise the capital efficiency of a proportional dividend policy (dividends paid as a percentage of earnings).

A progressive versus proportional dividend policy reflects the balance between paying increasing dividends to reward shareholders and retaining profits to finance growth opportunities or other capital expenditure.

CONCEPT 11.2   How companies pay dividends

Australian companies typically make two dividend payments a year: an interim dividend and a final dividend. Depending on the company's constitution, directors may need to have dividend payments ratified by the company's shareholders at its annual general meeting. If this is the case, at the meeting a motion is usually put forward by the directors to pay a particular level of final dividend. This motion is then voted on by shareholders and, if passed, determines the size of the dividend payment by the company to its shareholders. Once set and announced, the dividend is described as 'declared'. The interim dividend is usually set at the discretion of the directors.

Once declared, the shares of the company trade **cum-dividend**, which means that the shares trade with the right to the dividend payment attached to them. If the owner of the shares sells them to another investor, the new investor becomes entitled to the dividend payment. From a certain day known as the ex-dividend date, new purchasers of the shares are no longer entitled to the dividend payment.[2] In effect, the right to the payment detaches from the shares and the last person to own those shares prior to the **ex-dividend date** is entitled to the dividend. As a consequence, the price of the shares typically falls by the value of the dividend on the ex-dividend date. The actual dividend payment is then mailed out or paid into shareholders' bank accounts, generally within two months after the ex-dividend date.

Figure 11.1 depicts the significance of the ex-dividend date. The diagram sets out the price of Telstra Corporation (TLS) at the open and close of trading around 21 February 2011, which was the ex-dividend date relating to TLS's interim dividend. TLS announced an estimated interim dividend of 14 cents fully franked on 10 February 2011. The price of TLS at the close of 18 February was $2.96. In theory, this represented the value of one TLS share plus the dividend that holders were entitled to, had they purchased securities prior to the close. The very next

Cum-dividend
'Cum' means 'with'. When a share trades cum-dividend, it means that the dividend entitlements are attached to the share.

Ex-dividend date
The day when the dividend entitlement detaches from the share.

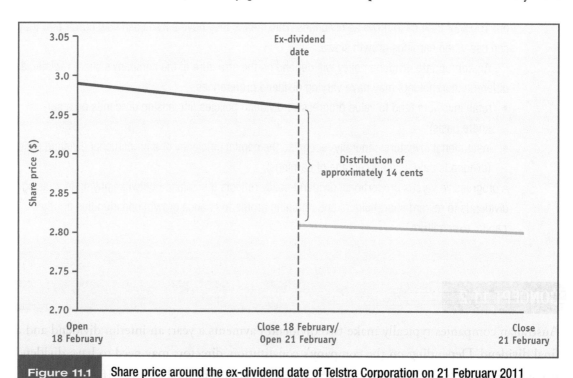

| **Figure 11.1** | Share price around the ex-dividend date of Telstra Corporation on 21 February 2011 |

Source: Based on data from IRESS.

trading day (on the company's ex-dividend date) TLS opened at a price of $2.81. Its price had fallen by roughly the same amount as the dividend.[3] The reason for the fall is simple—investors purchasing TLS securities on its ex-dividend date were no longer entitled to the dividend of 14 cents and were pricing shares accordingly.

> CONCEPT CHECK
>
> 3. What approval is required for companies to pay dividends?
> 4. What do the terms 'cum-dividend' and 'ex-dividend' mean?
>
> For the answers, go to MyFinanceLab

CONCEPT 11.3 Alternatives to dividends

The previous section described the payment of cash dividends. This section describes a number of alternatives to dividends that are available to companies. All of these alternatives can be considered part of dividend policy.

Share buy-backs

In a **share buy-back** (or share repurchase), a company buys back its own shares from its shareholders in return for cash. A company can conduct share buy-backs on-market or by way of an off-market tender. The shares participating in the buy-back are then typically cancelled. With an on-market buy-back, shares are purchased by the company in the ordinary course of trading on the ASX. Stock exchange rules require that the price paid is not more than 5% above the average of the last sale price over the previous five days to prevent manipulation of the share price. An off-market buy-back consists of a written offer to purchase shares being sent to all shareholders. A share buy-back is similar to a cash dividend because the ultimate effect is the same—the company takes some of its cash and places it in the hands of shareholders. The key difference between a cash dividend and a share buy-back is that with a cash dividend all shareholders obtain a portion of the cash, while with a share buy-back only shareholders offering part or all of their shares for sale will obtain the cash being offered by the company. In addition, with an off-market buy-back, a company is able to distribute franking credits as part of the buy-back consideration. For this reason, the after-tax return to some shareholders from selling their shares in a buy-back may be greater than a sale of their shares on the ASX and enables the company to optimise its buy-back price. A company may not buy back more than 10% of its capital in any 12-month period, except with shareholder approval.

> **Share buy-back**
> Occurs when a company buys back its own shares from its shareholders in return for cash.

Prior to 1989, share buy-backs were not permitted in Australia. Since then, they have grown in number and become quite common. Figure 11.2 illustrates the amount and method of capital

FINANCE EXTRA!

Woolworths Ltd announces $700 million off-market share buy-back

ON 26 August 2010, Woolworths Ltd (WOW) announced its intention to return $700 million to shareholders through an off-market share buy-back. The off-market share buy-back was the next step in WOW's ongoing capital management program, having bought back $325 million of capital in the first half of the calendar year in an on-market buy-back and declaring $1.3 billion in fully franked dividends in the financial year.

WOW's managing director and chief executive officer, Michael Luscombe, said 'Woolworths currently sets its capital structure with the objective of enhancing shareholder value through optimising its weighted average cost of capital while retaining flexibility to pursue growth opportunities. In pursuing this objective, Woolworths maintains strong credit ratings which underpin its debt profile. To the extent consistent with this objective and target credit ratings, Woolworths undertakes capital return strategies.' The announcement stated that shareholders who continued to hold shares in WOW were expected to benefit from the improved earnings per share, improved dividends per share and improved return on equity.

The buy-back was conducted as an off-market tender, with the proceeds received by participating shareholders treated in part as a capital component and in part as a fully franked dividend. Eligible shareholders were able to tender their shares as a final price tender or at seven specified discounts between 8% and 14% (at 1% intervals) to the market price of $29.7951 (determined as the volume weighted average price over the last five days of the tender period).

On 11 October, WOW announced that it had successfully completed the buy-back, with the final price set as $25.62, a 14% discount to the $29.7951 market price. The buy-back price comprised a $3.08 capital component and a fully franked dividend component of $22.54, being the excess of the buy-back price over the $3.08 capital component.

WOW confirmed with the Australian Taxation Office (ATO) that the market or 'tax value' of shares sold into the buy-back was $28.54, which was the base value of $26.36 adjusted for the movement in the S&P/ASX 200 Index from the opening of trading on the day the buy-back was announced, to the close of trading on the day the buy-back closed. The $2.92 difference between the tax value and buy-back price was added to the $3.08 capital component to give total deemed capital proceeds of $6.00 for Australian capital gains tax purposes. If the buy-back price had been above the 'tax value', the excess amount would have been deemed to be an unfranked dividend.

This example shows how off-market buy-backs can be structured so that shareholders who sell shares into the buy-back may receive certain tax benefits.

Source: Company announcements and IRESS.

returned by companies on an annual basis between 2006 and 2010. Total capital returned dropped significantly in 2008, as companies adopted conservative capital management policies to decrease leverage and in the face of an uncertain growth outlook. More recently, we have seen some companies with strong balance sheets announcing significant capital management policies. For example, in February 2011 BHP Billiton announced a US$5 billion off-market buy-back.

It is worth noting that, in theory, share buy-backs should have no effect on the share price of a company if its shares are bought back for their fair value. Take, for example, a company whose assets are worth $20 billion, that has 20 billion shares on issue and that undertakes to buy back one billion shares. The company spends $1 billion buying back one billion of its own shares. After the buy-back, the company will have $19 billion worth of assets (original assets less the cash used to repurchase shares) and 19 billion shares on issue. Hence, each share will be worth $1 both before and after the repurchase.

However, a study by JP Morgan found that the majority of companies announcing buy-backs outperform the market in the months following the announcement. They suggest that this is because management is signalling to the market that the equity is good value.[4] This is discussed in the chapter. Further, investors are often encouraged by the fact that the buy-back will provide a minimum or 'floor' price for the share, as any selling pressure in the market will be countered by the company's buying.

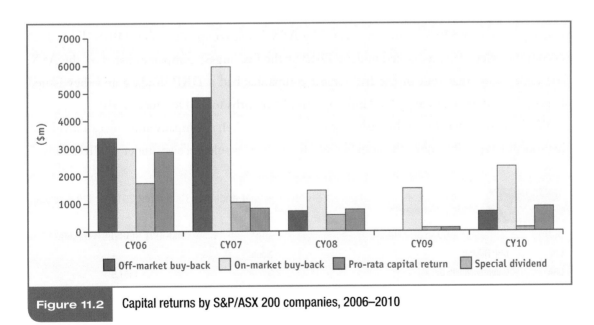

Figure 11.2   Capital returns by S&P/ASX 200 companies, 2006–2010

Source: IRESS, various reports.

Note: CY = Calendar year. Includes value of shares actually returned in each calendar year; excludes buy-backs, special dividends and capital returns not completed or paid.

Practitioner's POV

An analyst following a company that appears to be undervalued by the market (i.e. a buy) and which has a strong cash position, with no obvious large-scale capital expenditure or 'acquisition' on the horizon, will often predict that it is likely that the company will undertake a share buy-back. Buy-backs are typically viewed as positive, because the mere act of the company entering the market as a buyer usually has the effect of consolidating or strengthening a company's share price. A company entering the market and buying undervalued equity with its own cash through a buy-back is also adding value for existing shareholders.

Dividend reinvestment plans (DRPs)

Dividend reinvestment plan (DRPs)
A plan that gives shareholders the option of reinvesting their dividends in shares rather than receiving cash.

A **dividend reinvestment plan (DRP)** offers shareholders an alternative to receiving cash dividends. Under a DRP, shareholders are given the option of receiving new shares instead of dividends. The benefit of acquiring shares in this way is that shareholders do not need to pay brokerage or any other transaction cost in order to acquire the additional shares and the shares are generally offered at a discount of between 0% and 5% to the market price. Under a DRP, investors are deemed to have received the cash dividend and will be taxed on it; however, they also receive franking credits to offset all or part of their tax liability. DRP shares are exempt from the requirement to issue a prospectus.

DRPs are a popular way for companies to raise equity capital. During the 2009/10 financial year, approximately $10.3 billion was raised by ASX-listed companies using DRPs. Table 11.2 sets out the value of shares issued under a DRP by the five largest companies listed on the ASX. The table shows that four of the five largest companies had a DRP in place and they issued shares valued at approximately $4.2 billion in the 12 months to 31 December 2010.

While shareholders know the cash they are to be paid when a company announces a dividend, they do not typically know the number of shares they would receive under a DRP. This is

Table 11.2	Value of shares issued under a DRP for the year ended 31 December 2010 by the 5 largest listed companies*		
CODE	**COMPANY NAME**	**DRP**	**AMOUNT REINVESTED ($M)**
BHP	BHP Billiton	None	–
CBA	Commonwealth Bank	Active	1451.5
WBC	Westpac Banking Corporation	Active	568.1
ANZ	ANZ Banking Group	Active	1254.4
NAB	National Australia Bank	Active	908.3

*Five largest listed stocks as at December 2010.

FINANCE EXTRA!

Direct marketer Salmat beats all forecasts

SHARES in direct marketer Salmat rose yesterday after it beat its own and the market's forecast.

And the company handed a special dividend to shareholders.

Sydney-based Salmat reported a 42.5 per cent rise in full-year net profit to $49.1 million, up from $34.5m a year earlier, as cost control, new business wins and higher sales volumes at key units drove growth.

Key earnings before interest, tax and amortisation rose 17.3 per cent to $91.2m, eclipsing its forecast of between $85m and $90m, largely due to an 'outstanding performance' from its Targeted Media Solutions division.

Credit Suisse had predicted EBITA at the upper end of guidance.

Salmat's board declared a special dividend of 10c a share, fully franked, as a result of consistent growth in earnings, significant debt reduction and strong cash flow.

This brought the total dividend for the year to 33.5c a share, up 67.5 per cent on the year before, payable on September 28, after the group declared a final dividend of 12.5c, fully franked.

'We are extremely pleased to deliver double-digit growth in EBITA and net profit, and to pass on these earnings to our shareholders via an increased final dividend and special dividend,' chief executive Grant Harrod said.

'This result reflects the focus of the past 12 months on streamlining the Salmat business and aligning our suite of services under our One Salmat strategy to drive profitable growth.'

Salmat predicted market conditions to remain 'fairly consistent' over the next 12 months and said it would provide an update at its annual meeting in November.

'With our strong cash flow and solid new business pipeline, we are in a prime position to capitalise on opportunities within our client base, extend into new markets and pursue strategic acquisition targets,' Mr Harrod said.

Normalised revenue rose 1 per cent to $878.8m but reported sales revenue slipped 1.3 per cent because of a fall in revenues and unfavourable foreign exchange rates at its Asian businesses.

Salmat shares closed 14c higher at $4.04.

Source: The Australian, 28 August 2010.

> ## EXAMPLE 11.1

Calculation of shares issued to a shareholder under a DRP

QUESTION

Woolworths Limited (WOW) has a dividend reinvestment plan in place. Its 'Dividend Reinvestment Plan Rules' state the following:

> Shares are allocated at an amount equal to 100% (or such lesser percentage, not less than 90%, as the Directors determine in respect of a particular dividend) of the average of the daily volume weighted average market price of ordinary shares of the Company sold on the Stock Exchange Automated Trading System over the period of 10 trading days commencing on the second trading day after the record date for the dividend.

The final dividend per share paid out by WOW for 2010 was 62 cents and the final DRP price based on the daily weighted average market price for the 10 days commencing on the second trading day after the record date was $29.2317.

If an investor owns 2000 WOW shares, how many additional shares will they receive under the DRP?

ANSWER

The shareholder's total dividend received is:

Total dividend = 62 cents × 2000 shares = $1240

Since each share will be issued at a price of $29.2317, the shares issued to the shareholder will be:

Shares issued = 1240/$29.2317 = 42.4

Thus, each investor will be issued with an additional 42 shares and their shareholding will increase to 2042.

Source: Based on ASX releases.

determined by the way in which the company decides to calculate the issue price of the shares. The issue price is usually a weighted average share price based on transactions occurring over a pre-specified time period. Example 11.1 illustrates the calculation of shares received under a DRP by Woolworths Ltd (WOW).

Bonus issues

A company also has the power to issue bonus shares—shares for whose issue no consideration is payable and for which there need not be any increase in the company's share capital. No cost is attributable to the shareholders for the new bonus shares and the cost of the original shares will be spread across the original and bonus shares. A bonus issue is not strictly a dividend, as there is no cash payment. The effect of a bonus issue is to increase the number of shares on issue and is hence distributed on a per share basis. A share split is essentially the same as a bonus issue and may be undertaken by a company that wishes its shares to trade in a smaller price range.

5. There are a number of alternatives to a cash dividend available to companies. What are these alternatives?

For the answers, go to MyFinanceLab

CONCEPT 11.4 How companies decide on the amount of dividends paid

In a famous paper published in 1956, Professor John Lintner released the findings of his research into the dividend policy of US corporations.[5] Lintner's research involved interviews with a large number of executives in order to determine the way in which they set dividends. There were four so-called stylised facts that emerged from the study—namely, that in setting dividends, executives:

1. set long-run target payout ratios
2. focus on the change in dividends
3. base dividends on long-run forecast profits and are consequently reluctant to change dividends
4. are reluctant to cut dividends.

Some precision can be added to Lintner's ideas by using algebra, as follows. First, if the management of a company adopts long-run target payout ratios (defined as ρ), then the dividend in the current period set by management can be described by the following equation:

$$D_t = \rho EPS_t \tag{11.1}$$

where D_t is the dividend paid in period t and EPS_t is the earnings generated in period t. However, given that management focuses on the change in dividends $(D_t - D_{t-1})$, then subtracting D_{t-1} from both sides of Equation 11.1 gives the variable that management focus on:

$$D_t - D_{t-1} = \rho EPS_t - D_{t-1} \tag{11.2}$$

However, while Equation 11.2 gives the amount by which managers might 'desire' to change the dividend, their reluctance to change dividends implies that only a portion, say α, of the desired change will be implemented in any period. Hence, the following describes the actual change in dividends:

$$D_t - D_{t-1} = \alpha(\rho EPS_t - D_{t-1}) \tag{11.3}$$

The term α is a number less than 1 and in statistics is known as an 'adjustment coefficient'. Equation 11.3 can be rewritten as follows:

$$D_t - D_{t-1} = \alpha \rho EPS_t - \alpha D_{t-1} \tag{11.4}$$

Equation 11.4 is typically referred to as Lintner's model of dividend formulation. The equation can be expressed in a so-called empirical form as follows:

$$D_t - D_{t-1} = a + b\, EPS_t + c\, D_{t-1} + e_t \tag{11.5}$$

where a is a constant, b is $\alpha\rho$, c is $-\alpha$ and e_t is the well-known error term in statistics that accounts for any randomness in the variables examined that is not explained by the model. The coefficients a, b and c can be estimated using historical data for a company and a statistical technique known as regression analysis.[6] The empirical version of the model is typically used in academic studies of the Lintner model. Example 11.2 illustrates the use of Lintner's model to infer the long-run target payout ratio and adjustment rate for the Commonwealth Bank of Australia Limited (CBA).

The procedure in Example 11.2 has been used extensively in previous academic studies to test the Lintner model.[7] One Australian study examined data for 23 firms listed on the ASX between 1950 and 1978 and data for a further four firms between 1957 and 1978. The study found that the average value of b across firms was 0.28 and the average value of c was −0.51, implying an average target payout ratio of around 55% and an adjustment rate of around 51%.

In another study of the Lintner model in Australia, the researcher sent survey questionnaires to a number of Australian companies.[8] The study surveyed 93 firms listed on the ASX in 1980. Consistent with the Lintner model, it was found that 59% of companies in fact used a target payout ratio and 50% was the most common payout ratio. This finding was similar to that reported in the previous study. More importantly, the findings in both studies imply that the Lintner model is a valid representation of the way in which Australian companies set dividends.

EXAMPLE 11.2

Estimating the long-run target payout ratio and adjustment rate

QUESTION

The Commonwealth Bank of Australia generated the following earnings per share and paid the following dividends per share between 1994 and 2010.

Year	DPS	EPS
1994	60	77
1995	82	106
1996	90	115
1997	102	117
1998	104	117
1999	115	153

2000	130	291
2001	136	190
2002	150	210
2003	154	157
2004	183	196.9
2005	197	259.6
2006	224	308.2
2007	256	344.7
2008	266	363
2009	228	328.5
2010	290	367.9

Source: CBA 1994–2010 Annual Reports.

Using regression analysis and the data in the table above, an analyst estimates the following model:

$$D_t - D_{t-1} = 10.294 + 0.239EPS_t - 0.323D_{t-1}$$

Using the model above, calculate the estimated long-run target payout ratio of CBA and the rate at which dividends are adjusted towards this target.

ANSWER

Using Lintner's model and the parameters estimated in the equation above:

$a = 10.294$
$b = \alpha\rho = 0.239$
$c = -\alpha = -0.323$

where ρ is the long-run target payout ratio and α is the adjustment rate. Since

$-\alpha = -0.323$, then $\alpha = 0.323$

Substituting this value into b:

$b = \alpha\rho = 0.239$

and solving for ρ yields:

$\rho = 0.739$

Thus, the long-run target payout ratio of CBA is 73.9% but in any year the amount by which dividends are adjusted towards the target dividend is 32.3%.

CONCEPT CHECK

6. What factors influence the way managers set their dividend policy?

7. What is the typical target payout ratio for Australian companies?

For the answers, go to MyFinanceLab

CONCEPT 11.5   The impact of dividend policy on shareholder wealth

The conditions under which dividend policy is irrelevant

Professor Merton Miller and Professor Franco Modigliani (hereafter M&M), from the University of Chicago and MIT, respectively, published a now famous paper on the shareholder wealth effects of dividend policy in 1961.[9] For their efforts, including this paper, they received the Nobel Prize for Economics. Their paper mathematically proved that dividend policy has no impact on shareholder wealth, given a number of assumptions. The paper sets out what has become known as the 'dividend irrelevance' proposition. M&M's work should not be viewed as proving that dividend policy is irrelevant to shareholder wealth; rather, it should be seen as setting out the conditions (assumptions) under which it is irrelevant. In this way, by implication, their assumptions also suggest why dividend policy *may* be relevant to shareholder wealth—an issue taken up later in this chapter.

The main assumptions underlying the M&M dividend irrelevance proof are:

1. There are no costs of issuing shares.
2. There are no costs of trading shares.
3. All market participants (e.g. management and shareholders) have the same information.
4. There are no personal or corporate taxes.

Although the proof to M&M's dividend irrelevance proposition is somewhat mathematical, their intuition is straightforward and can be described as follows. Take a company that does not have any idle cash and that pays out all its free cash flows as dividends. If the company wants to increase dividends, then it has one of two options. First, it can cut back (i.e. sell off) its investment in current projects in order to generate the cash needed for the dividend. Second, it can issue new shares to finance current projects in order to free up the cash needed to pay a higher dividend. The effects of both these options are the same. Current shareholders will experience an increase in their cash wealth because of the increase in dividends; however, the price of their shares will decline. If the company cuts back on existing projects, its share price will decline because the future cash flows (and the value) of the company will fall. If the company issues new shares, the existing value of the company will be spread across a greater number of shares. Either way, the increase in dividends will be offset by a decline in the price of shares, leaving existing shareholders no better or worse off. A numerical example can be used to illustrate this intuition. Take a company with the following features.

1. The company operates two identical projects—*A* and *B*.
2. Projects *A* and *B* have cash inflows of $100 million and outflows of $50 million in perpetuity.
3. The company cost of capital is 5%.

4. The company has 1000 million shares on issue.

The breakdown of the wealth of a shareholder of such a company is depicted in Figure 11.3. The diagram illustrates that the total net cash flow produced by the two projects is $100 million, which spread across 1000 million shares results in a dividend of approximately 10 cents per share. In turn, the perpetual nature of the cash flows implies that their total value is collectively $2000 million. Since the value of the business will be spread across 1000 million shares, this implies a share price of $2.00. Quite clearly then, at the end of the period depicted in the diagram, the wealth of a shareholder is $2.10 per share.

Consider now the implications of the company deciding to increase its dividend level beyond 10 cents per share. One option available to it is to liquidate one of the projects and apply the proceeds from the sale to paying a dividend. The effect of this is depicted in Figure 11.4. The diagram implies that, if Project B was liquidated at a fair price of $1000 million, a total dividend of $1100 million could be paid to the shareholders of the company, or approximately $1.10 per share. Of course, under such a scenario the market value of the company would decline to the

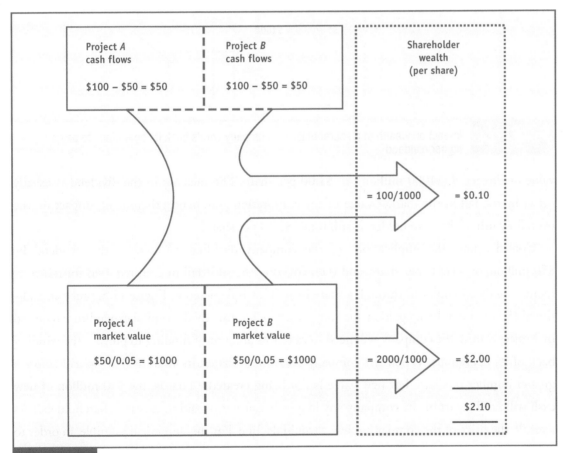

Figure 11.3   Wealth of a shareholder derived from a company with two projects with perpetual net cash flows of $50 million and a 100% dividend payout ratio

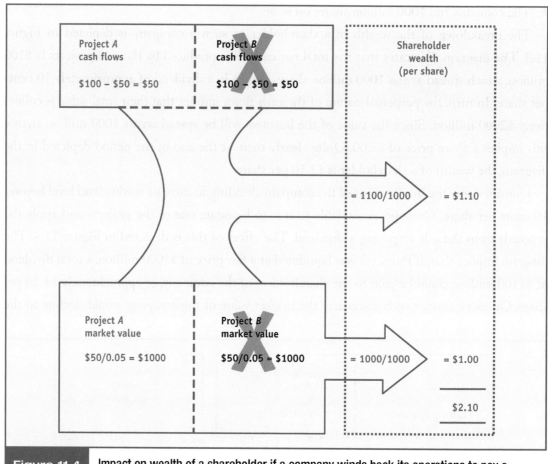

| **Figure 11.4** | Impact on wealth of a shareholder if a company winds back its operations to pay a higher dividend |

value of Project *A* ($1000 million), or $1.00 per share. The increase in the dividend is exactly offset by the fall in the market value of the corporation and, hence, there is no impact on the overall wealth of the shareholder. It still totals $2.10 per share!

Consider now the implications of the company deciding to increase the dividend by $50 million, or 5 cents per share, and then covering the shortfall in cash required for reinvestment (exactly $50 million) through a share issue. This is depicted in Figure 11.5. Since an additional $50 million is being paid by the company, which is exactly the capital expenditure required by Project *A* or *B*, the company will need to raise this amount of funding to prevent the winding back of its operations. When the company issues new shares, its value will be spread across a greater number of shares but new value is not being created. (That is, the $50 million of new cash will not be part of the company any longer, because it is paid to existing shareholders.) As a result, the price of the company's shares would decline. For the numerical example, in order to raise $50 million the company needs to issue approximately 25.6 million shares.[10] The net effect of this is that the value of the company would remain the same and its share price would fall to

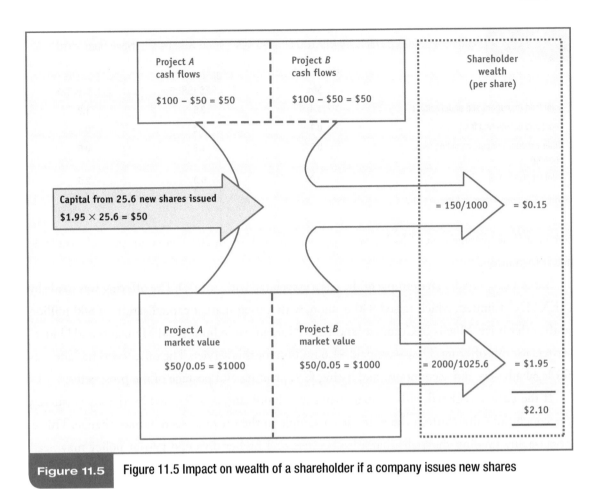

| **Figure 11.5** | Figure 11.5 Impact on wealth of a shareholder if a company issues new shares |

$1.95. The total wealth of the existing shareholders, nevertheless, remains at $2.10 per share.

Hence, regardless of whether the company winds back its operations or issues new shares to fund the higher dividend, the wealth of its shareholders remains at $2.10. The only difference is that a greater portion of their wealth becomes cash (dividends) and a smaller portion is tied up in the value of the shares. It is quite clear that a number of very significant and unrealistic assumptions are necessary in order for the two scenarios outlined above to work. These were stated earlier as (1) there are no costs of issuing shares, (2) there are no costs of trading shares, (3) all market participants have the same information about a company and (4) there are no personal and corporate taxes. The implications of relaxing these assumptions are discussed next.

Why dividend policy is relevant

COSTS OF ISSUING SHARES

Are the costs associated with issuing new shares significant? The nature of and costs associated with issuing shares is the topic of the next chapter. In general, the cost of issuing shares varies depending on the amount of capital raised, with smaller issues tending to have a higher percent-

Table 11.3	Estimate of fees payable by NEXTDC Limited associated with its IPO, November 2010		
	$M	% OF VALUE OF SHARES ISSUED	% OF VALUE OF ALL SHARES
Joint lead managers and underwriters	1.4	3.5	1.8
Legal and accounting fees	0.1	0.2	0.1
Other expenses (including listing fees, printing)	0.5	1.3	0.6
Total (approximate)	2.0	5.0	2.5

Source: NEXTDC Limited Prospectus, 9 November 2010.

age cost. The average cost of listing was approximately 4.3% in 2010 based on publicly available fee information.[11]

Table 11.3 provides an example of the costs associated with an IPO. The offering was made by NEXTDC Limited, which raised $40 million, with a total market capitalisation of $80 million at the offer price. Moelis & Company and RBS Morgans were Joint Lead Managers and Underwriters for this offering. They were paid $1.6 million for this service. The other costs include fees for legal advisers and accountants and listing fees, printing and postage of the prospectus.

If the costs associated with issuing shares are significant, as suggested by the above survey, the conclusions drawn from the numerical example in the previous section may change. This is because any funding shortfalls that arise because of a higher dividend payout policy may need to be met by a costly share issue.[12] The costly share issue, in turn, would result in a reduction in the market value of the firm by an amount equal to the costs of issuing shares. Another way of thinking about this is that an additional cash outflow needs to occur equal to the costs associated with the share issue. These costs would need to be deducted from the present value of the projects in order to arrive at the value of the firm, which would consequently be lower. Hence, the costs associated with a share issue can make a high dividend payout policy less attractive.

Costs of trading shares

The examples provided in support of M&M's 'dividend irrelevance' proposition also assume that, regardless of the payout ratio of a company, shareholders are unaffected because they are indifferent to holding wealth in the form of shares or cash. However, shareholders may prefer dividends to capital gains or vice versa. That is, there are 'dividend clientele' who are attracted to particular companies with high dividends. For example, retirees are likely to invest in low-risk shares and prefer a high dividend so that they can live off the dividend stream throughout their retirement. On the other hand, young high-income earners are likely to prefer capital gains to dividends that may be taxed at different rates, as described later in the chapter.

Practitioner's POV

Dividend clientele do exist! Some fund managers consider the prospective dividend yield (the forecast dividend divided by the current share price) predicted by analysts to be a very important number. These fund managers operate income funds that promise to pay a steady income stream. An example of such a fund is Colonial First State Investment 'Conservative Fund'. The stated objective of this fund, at the time of writing, was 'to provide a regular income stream while maintaining and potentially increasing the value of your capital over the medium term' <www.colonialfirststate.com.au>. While the existence of equity that is undervalued by an analyst's reckoning may not necessarily convince such funds that it is in fact worth buying, a company that appears to be undervalued and has a high prospective dividend yield may be a more convincing proposition!

In order for the dividend irrelevance theory to work in the face of such dividend clientele, shares must be able to be bought or sold at a very low cost. For example, if an investor who prefers a high dividend yield holds shares in a company with a low dividend yield, that investor can create a 'pseudo' dividend by selling small portions of their shareholding to generate cash.[13] Alternatively, an investor with a preference for a low dividend yield who holds shares in a company with a high dividend yield can purchase more shares with their dividends. In order for such investors to be indifferent to high-yield or low-yield equity, the cost of trading shares would need to be very small or insignificant. But is it?

There are at least three costs associated with trading shares in Australia: brokerage fees, goods and services tax (GST) on brokerage fees and bid–ask spreads. Broad information on brokerage fees charged by stockbrokers is difficult to obtain, because of its competitively sensitive nature. Table 11.4 describes the brokerage rates charged to a leading Australian fund manager (anonymous) on different-sized transactions between May 2001 and May 2002.[14] The table shows that there is little variation in the costs for different-sized parcels of shares. However, these costs are likely to vary across different fund managers. The table suggests that the average cost of transacting in the share market for large institutional traders is approximately 0.3%, or 0.6% for a round-trip transaction. Brokerage fees for retail clients are also competitive, with retail traders able to trade for as little as $20 per trade with some of the discount brokers. GST is levied on these brokerage fees at a rate of 10%.

The third component of costs is the *bid–ask spread*. The bid–ask spread was first defined in Chapter 1 and represents a round-trip transaction cost. Table 11.5 provides an indication of the average bid–ask spread for the 10 largest companies traded on the ASX.[15] These were the most heavily traded on the ASX and likely to have the smallest bid–ask spreads. The cost of trading these shares ranged from an average of 0.03% to 0.34%. Spreads for smaller, less actively traded companies are likely to be significantly higher.

Table 11.4	Average brokerage rates charged to a leading Australian fund manager for the year ended May 2002	
Trade size Category	Average Trade size	Average Brokerage rate (%)
1	1 790	0.29
2	7 145	0.29
3	15 404	0.29
4	28 028	0.28
5	46 637	0.28
6	76 545	0.28
7	123 821	0.28
8	211 599	0.27
9	400 223	0.27
10	1 387 367	0.25

Source: C. Comerton-Forde, A. Frino, C. Fernandez and T. Oetomo (2003), 'The impact of broker and industry on institutional execution costs', Working Paper, University of Sydney.

Table 11.5	Average bid–ask spread of the 10 largest ASX-listed companies for 2010
ASX code	Average spread (%)
ANZ	0.05
BHP	0.03
CBA	0.03
NAB	0.05
NCM	0.04
RIO	0.03
TLS	0.34
WBC	0.05
WES	0.05
WOW	0.05
	Average 0.07

Source: Thomson Reuters.

The estimates of the cost of trading provided above imply that the average total cost of trading shares for large institutional investors is in the order of 0.31% (0.25% + 0.025% + 0.03%) to 0.66% (0.29% + 0.029% + 0.34%). These figures imply that investors who trade shares in order to avoid any undesired consequences of corporate dividend policies can incur significant transaction costs. This can cause such investors to place a higher value on companies with dividend policies that they prefer. Hence, dividend policy can influence the value of a company.

Information asymmetry

It is reasonable to argue that the management of a company have more information relevant to assessing the company's future prospects than the shareholders. Consequently, dividend policy may act as an information 'signal' to investors. That is, intentionally or unintentionally, the dividend policy of a company may provide an information signal on the expected future cash flows and have an impact on the valuation of a company by its shareholders. For example, an increase in dividends by a company can signal to the market that the management of a company believes that the future prospects for cash flow growth are positive. This can cause investors to revise upwards their beliefs about the value of a company and cause its share price to rise. Alternatively, a cut in dividends by a company can signal that management is pessimistic about its future prospects, causing investors to revise downwards its value and price. Reporting obligations will generally result in an announcement by a company regarding a change in dividends being accompanied by guidance as to the company's outlook. For example, on 16 February 2011, The Reject Shop Limited announced an interim dividend of 23 cents per share, over 40% less than the previous comparable half-year period of 39 cents per share. The market traded to a low of $12.99 (versus a previous close of $13.50) as the market assimilated information associated with the dividend change along with the accompanying announcement where management declared they were 'unable to update' previous earnings guidance for the full year.

There is at least one Australian study that has examined the effects on share prices of changes in the dividends paid by companies.[16] The study examined whether companies that increased their dividends experienced positive unexpected share price returns and whether those that cut their dividends experienced negative unexpected share price returns.[17] The study examined 899 interim and final dividend announcements. The results of the study are illustrated in Figure 11.6.

Figure 11.6 illustrates the abnormal share price return in the announcement month for portfolios of shares that differ on the average size of the interim and final dividend change from one year to the next. Portfolio 1 contains companies and announcements with the largest average dividend change and Portfolio 5 contains companies and announcements with the smallest (including negative) average dividend change. As expected, companies that announced the largest positive change (average of around 35%) experienced positive abnormal returns in the month they announced the increase of approximately 1.5%. The size of the abnormal return decreases with the average size of the change in the dividend. At the opposite extreme, the portfolio that contains firms with the smallest change (or negative change) in dividends experienced average abnormal returns of around −1% in the announcement month. These findings are consistent with the idea that dividend policy can convey information to the market that causes investors to reassess the value of their shares. All in all, it implies that dividend policy can have an impact on the value of a company.

Personal and corporate taxes

The M&M dividend irrelevance proposition ignores the impact of personal and corporate taxes; however, both are likely to have an impact on dividend policy. In Australia, shareholders pay tax

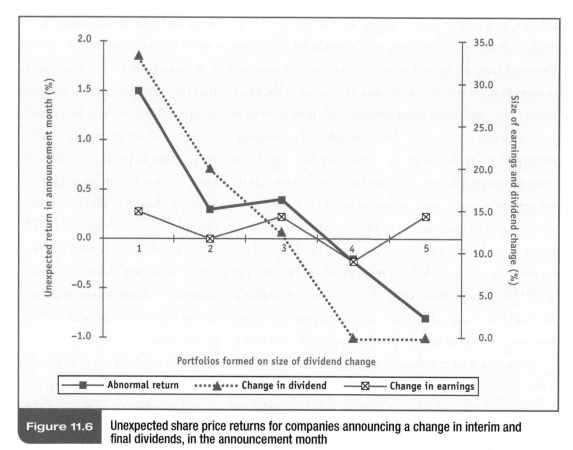

Figure 11.6 Unexpected share price returns for companies announcing a change in interim and final dividends, in the announcement month

Source: Constructed from Panel D in Table 5 of S. A. Easton and N. A. Sinclair (1989), 'The impact of unexpected earnings and dividends on abnormal returns to equity', *Accounting and Finance*, 1–19.

on the 'capital gain' on their shares in the year in which they are sold, under the provisions of the capital gains tax (CGT) legislation. The taxable capital gain is the difference between the sale price and the cost base of their shares comprising the amount paid to acquire the shares, including any brokerage fees and stamp duties. The CGT rate on the increase is an investor's marginal income tax rate, as set out in Chapter 8. If the shares are sold 12 months or more after the date of acquisition, then only half of the realised gain from the disposal of these shares is included as taxable income. On the other hand, dividends are subject to the imputation system of tax. Therefore capital gains may be taxed differently from dividends; dependent on the marginal tax rate of investors. Example 11.3 illustrates the net after-tax gain earned by an investor in a 45% marginal tax bracket. Such an investor would earn 38 cents for every dollar of free cash flow generated by the company if it retained earnings (assuming no CGT discount); alternatively, the investor would earn 55 cents for every dollar generated if the company paid out its earnings as fully franked dividends.

The example illustrates that an investor in a tax bracket of 45% benefits from a dividend policy that pays out a higher dividend.[18] It is worth noting, however, that the conclusion reached depends critically on the assumptions underlying the calculation. Different conclusions can be reached depending on the tax circumstances of the investor and the time period they hold their shares.

Practitioner's POV

Differing tax treatment of income and capital gains and the Australian imputation system will have an effect on investors' dividend preferences. While many investors prefer capital gains to dividends as they have control over where capital gains are made and because capital gains may be subject to tax concessions, some other classes of shareholders may be better off from an after-tax perspective if they receive a fully franked dividend (i.e. low marginal rate Australian shareholders who may receive a tax refund for franking credits). Non-resident companies do not receive the tax credit, however, they are generally not required to pay Australian withholding tax (up to 15%) to the extent dividends are franked. Superannuation funds are taxed at 15%.

EXAMPLE 11.3

Dividends earned by shareholders after personal and corporate tax

QUESTION

A company generated an unexpected net profit before tax of $1 per share in the financial year ended 30 June 2011. One of its shareholders has a marginal tax rate of 45% and the company tax rate is 30%. Calculate the net profit after personal and corporate tax earned by the shareholder if the company (1) retained the profit and consequently the investor made a capital gain, or (2) the company paid out the cash flow as a fully franked dividend.

ANSWER

	Capital gain of $1	Dividend of $1
Company level		
Net profit	1.00	1.00
Company tax	0.30[1]	0.30[1]
Capital gain/cash dividend	0.70	0.70
Shareholder level		
Taxable income	0.70[2]	1.00[3]
Personal tax	0.32[4]	0.45[4]
Franking credit	0	0.30
Tax paid	0.32	0.15
Profit after tax	0.38	0.55

Notes to calculations

1   Company tax = company tax rate × net profit = 30% × $1.
2   Taxable income under capital gains tax is the net increase in the share price, but this arises only if the shareholder realises the gain by selling the shares. The example assumes that the shareholder has held the shares for less than one year and hence pays tax on the total realised gain.
3   Taxable income under the imputation tax system is the sum of the dividend distributed by the company ($0.70) and the imputation (or franking) credit equal to the tax paid by the company ($0.30) [or $0.70/(1 − 0.30)].
4   Personal tax is the product of the shareholder's marginal tax rate (45%) and their taxable income.

CONCEPT CHECK

8. M&M's dividend irrelevance proposition is based on what four assumptions?
9. If dividend policy is irrelevant, why do prices fall on the ex-dividend date?
10. Why is dividend policy relevant?

For the answers, go to MyFinanceLab

Student Learning Centre

MyFinanceLab ■ To test your mastery of the content covered in this chapter and to create your own personalised study plan, go to MyFinanceLab: www.pearson.com.au/myfinancelab

CONCEPT CHECKLIST

In this chapter, the following concepts associated with dividend policy were discussed:

➤ How companies pay dividends
➤ The effect of dividend payout on share prices on the ex-dividend date
➤ Alternatives to dividends, including:
   — share buy-backs
   — dividend reinvestment plans
   — bonus issues
➤ Lintner's model of dividend formulation
➤ The assumptions underlying the Miller and Modigliani dividend irrelevance proposition, namely:
   — companies face no costs of issuing shares
   — investors face no costs of trading shares
   — all market participants have the same information
   — there are no personal or corporate taxes
➤ The intuition underlying the Miller and Modigliani dividend irrelevance proposition
➤ The impact on the Miller and Modigliani dividend irrelevance proposition of relaxing their four major assumptions

SELF-TEST QUESTIONS

1. Using the information provided in Example 11.3, recalculate the shareholder's profit after tax if their marginal tax rate was 20%.
2. Co Ltd has recently announced earnings per share of 22 cents. If the company has a dividend payout ratio of 20%, what was the company's dividend per share?

Self-test answers

1. If a shareholder has a marginal tax rate lower than the company tax rate, the shareholder is able to apply for a rebate from the Australian Taxation Office for the balance of the franking credit. Therefore, the shareholder's profit after tax is as follows:

	Capital gain of $1	Dividend of $1
Company level		
Net profit	1.00	1.00
Company tax	0.30[1]	0.30[1]
Capital gain/cash dividend	0.70	0.70
Shareholder level		
Taxable income	0.70[2]	1.00[3]
Personal tax	0.14[4]	0.20[4]
Franking credit	0	0.30
Tax paid	0.14	(0.10)
Profit after tax	0.56	0.80

Notes to calculations

1. Company tax = company tax rate × net profit = 30% × $1.
2. Taxable income under capital gains tax is the net increase in the share price, but this arises only if the shareholder realises the gain by selling the shares. This example assumes that the shareholder has held the shares for less than one year and hence pays tax on the total realised gain.
3. Taxable income under the imputation tax system is the sum of the dividend distributed by the company ($0.70) and the imputation credit equal to the tax paid by the company ($0.30) [or $0.70/(1 − 0.30)].
4. Personal tax liability is the product of the shareholder's marginal tax rate (20%) and their taxable income.

2. The payout ratio is DPS/EPS. Therefore, Co Ltd's dividend is 4.4 cents per share.

DISCUSSION QUESTIONS

1. Companies have become increasingly focused on capital management, including dividend policy, in recent years with some companies not declaring interim or final dividends. Explain some likely reasons for this.

2. Describe the key differences between an on-market and off-market share buy-back and why a company may choose one over the other.

3. Briefly outline the typical dividend payment process and define the following terms:
   (a) cum-dividend price
   (b) ex-dividend date
   (c) record date.

4. Explain the difference between a progressive and proportional dividend policy.

5. Explain imputation credits and franked dividends and how different shareholders may value these.

6. Discuss why a company may decide to issue bonus shares or undertake a share split.

7. Assuming restrictive (perfect capital markets) assumptions, explain why a company's market value is independent of its dividend policy.

8. Miller and Modigliani showed that, under a restrictive set of assumptions, the dividend policy of a company is irrelevant to the company's value.
   (a) Describe how dividend policy irrelevance is proved algebraically. (You do not need to present the algebraic proof.)
   (b) Choose any three market 'imperfections' and describe how their existence may result in dividend policy being relevant to company value.

9. (a) Describe the impact on a company's value of a variation in its dividend policy, assuming that the company operates in a perfect capital market. Be as specific as possible.
   (b) Now relax the perfect capital markets assumption. Does your answer to (a) change? Again, be as specific as possible, and use some examples (of capital market imperfections) to illustrate your answer.
   (c) If you were the chief financial officer of a large Australian public company, what type of dividend policy would you implement? Explain your answer.

10. Assume that companies operate in a perfect capital market with one exception—transactions costs apply to the buying and selling of new shares and to the issue of both dividends and new shares. Describe the impact of this 'imperfection' on a company's dividend policy.

11. Firms X and Y are two very similar companies. Yesterday, when firm X announced a 10% decrease in its dividend per share, the market reacted negatively, resulting in a decrease in X's share price. However, a similar announcement by firm Y resulted in a price increase. Explain the market's seemingly contradictory reactions to the same type of news.

12. 'Companies that have a high concentration of ownership held by owner-managers (insiders) will typically have a lower level of dividend payout than those with a high concentration of outside (external shareholders) ownership.' Do you agree with this statement? Explain your answer.

13. A company attracts investors in the top marginal tax bracket. If the company generates unexpected profits of $100 million, would the investors in the company prefer it to pay a dividend or to retain the profits?

14. Purchase the Monday edition of *The Australian Financial Review* this week. Estimate the minimum total cost that an institutional (large) investor would be likely to face in trading Commonwealth Bank and Sundance Resources shares. Which of these companies is less likely to change its dividend policy? Why?

15. Answer 'true' or 'false' to the following and explain your answers.

    (a) The benefit of DRPs is that investors can avoid paying tax on the income.

    (b) Companies set long-run target payout ratios.

    (c) Managers make dividend payout decisions based only on current earnings.

PRACTICAL QUESTIONS

1. An analyst has forecast the EPS of Industrial Ltd at 250 cents per share for next year. Further, Industrial Ltd has just paid a DPS of 125 cents per share. The analyst has used 10 years of historical EPS and DPS data and estimates the following model using regression analysis:

   $$DPS_t - DPS_{t-1} = 10 + 0.42\ EPS_t - 0.57\ DPS_{t-1}$$

   Calculate the estimated long-run target payout ratio and the rate at which dividends are adjusted towards this target by Industrial Ltd. Also use the model to forecast the dividend per share next year. **BASIC**

2. Company Beta Ltd does not pay dividends. As a shareholder in Beta Ltd you would like to earn a dividend stream. What can you do to achieve this objective? **BASIC**

3. Obtain a copy of the annual report for Telstra Corporation Limited (TLS) for the most recent financial year. Identify the dividend per share and dividend payout ratio as reported in this document. **BASIC**

4. On 15 February 2011 Primary Health Care Limited (PRY) announced it would cut its interim dividend per share 80% from 15 cents to 3 cents. The market responded by falling from about $3.57 the day prior to the announcement to $3.37 the day following the announcement. Explain the market reaction to this announcement. **BASIC**

5. Theta Ltd has recently paid a dividend of 50 cents per share. Under the company's DRP shares can be purchased at a price of $10.00. If I own 1000 shares, how many new shares can I purchase under the plan? Why would I choose to do this? **BASIC**

6. Mr Smith holds 150 000 stapled securities in Blue Group, which has just announced a final distribution of 20 cents per stapled security. The dividend component of 15 cents per share relating to Mr Smith's share in Blue Company is to be fully franked at the company tax rate of 30%. The distribution component of 5 cents per unit relating to Mr Smith's unit in Blue Trust is unfranked. What is the taxable amount of distribution to be included in Mr Smith's tax return? **INTERMEDIATE**

7. An investment bank has been advising listed company Digital Ltd, which has recently recorded an abnormal profit of $50 million. Digital Ltd has no foreseeable acquisition opportunities in the near term and the management and directors believe the shares in Digital Ltd are trading at a discount to intrinsic value. The shares have been trading within a range of $5.00 and $6.00, whereas the directors believe the intrinsic value is closer to $6.50. The investment bank has recommended an on-market buy-back to return the surplus capital. During the course of the on-market buy-back, Digital Ltd's share price rallied and is now trading over $7.00. Explain why the investment bank may have given this advice, what the alternatives were and whether you would recommend a different strategy to deal with the current market environment. **INTERMEDIATE**

INTERMEDIATE

8. John White holds 50 000 shares in XYZ Ltd, which has just announced a final dividend of 39 cents per share. The dividend is to be fully franked at the company tax rate of 30%. What is the taxable amount of dividend to be included in John's tax return, assuming he has the highest income tax rate? What is the taxable amount of dividend to be included in John's tax return, assuming his tax rate is actually 37%?

CHALLENGING

9. The Commonwealth Bank of Australia (CBA) completed a $532 million off-market share buy-back on 29 March 2004 with a buy-back price of $27.50 per share, comprising an $11.00 capital component and a $16.50 fully franked component. In March, the CBA also announced a DRP price of $31.61. In May 2004, the CBA announced a share purchase plan (SPP) under which shareholders could apply for shares at $31.36. The CBA's number of shares on issue prior to the buy-back was 1 261 255 152; 19 360 759 shares were bought back, 5 916 319 shares were issued under the DRP and 14 891 250 shares were issued pursuant to the share purchase plan. Show the theoretical impact on the share price of the off-market buy-back, DRP and SPP compared with a market price of $33.22 prior to the buy-back.

INTERMEDIATE

10. Consider the CBA buy-back where the ATO 'tax value' was set at $30.42. If the buy-back price was $27.50, comprising an $11.00 capital component and a $16.50 fully franked dividend, what would be the deemed disposal price for each share sold in the buy-back? Discuss how this would change if the 'tax value' was $25.00.

CHALLENGING

11. A listed company, Utility Ltd, has $250 million of surplus capital following the sale of one of its divisions. Assuming the facts set out below, prepare a short note for the chief financial officer of Utility Ltd recommending the most efficient mechanism(s) for Utility Ltd to return the $250 million of surplus capital to its shareholders. Give reasons for rejecting other possible mechanisms.

- Number of ordinary shares on issue—500 million
- Current market price—$10 per ordinary share
- Total current market capitalisation—$5000 million
- Share capital—$800 million
- Retained earnings—$2250 million
- Franking account balance—$400 million (on a tax basis)
- Ordinary dividends—$0.50 p.a.
- Shareholder base—20% foreign; 80% domestic comprising 20% retail and 60% institutions

CHALLENGING

12. ABC Pty Ltd is a small mail-order company run by Mr and Mrs Jones. In the year ended 30 June 2010, ABC had a taxable income of $15 000 on which tax at the corporate rate of 30% has been paid. The company has a 100% dividend payout policy and Mr and Mrs Jones are the only shareholders (each holding 50% of the issued capital). Mrs Jones is also a management consultant earning a salary of $150 000 a year, and she has allowable deductions of around $15 000 a year. Mr Jones performs home duties and has no other income.

(a) Assuming a dividend imputation system of taxation, calculate the effective tax rate on the dividend paid to (i) Mrs Jones and (ii) Mr Jones.

(b) What is the average rate of tax paid on ABC's net (taxable) income for the year ended 30 June 2010, after all distributions have been made?

(c) Recalculate (a), assuming a classical system of taxation.

Compare answers to (a) and (c) and explain any differences.

13. A company operates two factories, one of which generates an annual cash flow of $1000 million in perpetuity, and the other an annual cash flow of $200 million in perpetuity. The company has 10 000 million shares on issue and currently pays an annual dividend of 12 cents per share. The company believes that its share price is being depressed by the low dividend it pays. It would like to increase its dividend to 32 cents per share but has no desire to raise the cash from capital markets to fund the dividend. Under what conditions will the dividend not have an impact on the wealth of the company's shareholders? Illustrate this using the numbers provided, assuming the discount rate of the company is 10%.

CHALLENGING

14. A company operates two identical projects, each yielding annual cash flows of $75 million. The company has 100 million shares on issue and currently pays all its cash flows out as dividends. If the company decides to increase its dividend by 10 cents per share, and the cost of issuing new shares is 0.6%, calculate the impact on shareholder wealth of the company's strategy. Assume a discount rate of 10%.

CHALLENGING

15. Alpha Ltd paid an unfranked dividend of 10 cents, and went ex-dividend on 1 June. Share price and other data for Alpha Ltd are as follows.

CHALLENGING

	Price	Market index
30 May	1.50	2982
31 May	1.52	2986
1 June	1.44	2987
2 June	1.42	2986
3 June	1.45	2988

The beta of Alpha Ltd is 1.2 and the 13-week Treasury-note yield over the period was 8%. Calculate the daily abnormal returns (using the CAPM) of Alpha Ltd around its ex-dividend date. Explain the direction and magnitude of the abnormal returns. What seems to be the tax rate of the marginal investor?

WebEX

On 6 August 2010, ResMed Inc. announced that its Board of Directors had approved a 2 for 1 share split of its common stock, payable in the form of a 100% stock dividend. Use <www.asx.com.au> to review the announcement and describe the expected theoretical price change around the ex-date of 12 August 2010.

Excel Question

Using the data in Example 11.2, calculate the model from that example using the regression function in Excel.

CASE STUDY Background

- On 22 February 2011, BHP Billiton announced an off-market buy-back with a target size of A$5 billion, as part of its US$10 billion capital management program. On completion of the US$10 billion capital management initiative expected to be by the end of calendar year 2011, BHP Billiton will have repurchased a cumulative US$23 billion of BHP Billiton Limited and BHP Billiton Plc shares since 2004, representing 15% of the then issued capital.

- On 11 April 2011, BHP Billiton announced the successful completion of its A$6 billion off-market buy-back, representing a buy-back of 147 million shares or 4.4% of the issued share capital of BHP Billiton Limited.

- The final price of A$40.85 per share, which represented a discount of 14% to the market price of A$47.4985, allowed BHP Billiton to purchase a significant amount of shares at a material discount and was expected to have a positive impact on earnings per share, cash flow per share and return on equity

Key terms of the buy-back

Type of buy-back	Off-market tender
Final size	A$6 billion
Discount range	10% to 14% discount to A$47.4985 market price (adjusted volume weighted average price over last five days of tender period)
Discount range	Five specified discounts (at 1% intervals) and final price tenders
Buy-back price	A$40.85
Capital proceeds	A$9.31, being the A$0.28 capital component plus A$9.03, the excess of the tax value over the buy-back price
ATO 'tax value'	A$49.88

Key dates—2011

Buy-back announcement	22 February
Shares quoted ex-entitlement to participate in the buy-back	25 February
Buy-back record date	3 March
Buy-back tender period	21 March–8 April
Announcement of buy-back price and buy-back size	11 April

Source: Company announcements and IRESS.

CASE STUDY QUESTIONS

1. Explain why BHP Billiton might undertake an off-market buy-back as opposed to an on-market buy-back.

2. Using BHP Billiton's website <www.bhpbilliton.com> find BHP Billiton's current dividend dates.

3. If dividend policy is irrelevant, explain why BHP Billiton's share price reacted favourably to the announcement.

4. Describe the impact of a buy-back on a company's debt earnings per share and return on equity.

5. What is the last date investors may be able to purchase shares which are entitled to participate in the buy-back? Explain the difference between the ex-date and the record date.

6. What discount was the final buy-back price to the market price?

7. What is the deemed fully franked dividend?

8. Calculate the deemed disposal price.

9. BHP bought back 147 million shares. Explain the difference in cost to BHP vis à vis conducting an on-market buy-back based on the closing price of A$47.76 on 8 April 2011.

10. Show the theoretical impact on the share price of the off-market buy-back compared with a market price of $45.85 prior to the buy-back.

FURTHER READING

The original article on dividend policy by Professor Merton Miller and Professor Franco Modigliani is still worth a read:

- Miller, M. H. and Modigliani, F. (1961), 'Dividend policy, growth and the valuation of shares', *Journal of Business*, vol. 34, 411–33.

For a challenging, but not impossible, discussion of the behaviour of share prices on the ex-dividend day in Australia and an interpretation of the preference of capital gains over cash dividends see:

- Brown, P. and Clarke, A. (1993), 'The ex-dividend day behaviour of Australian share prices before and after dividend imputation', *Australian Journal of Management*, vol. 18, 1–40.

For a relatively readable but dated test of the Lintner model in Australia see:

- Shevlin, T. (1982), 'Australian corporate dividend policy: Empirical evidence', *Accounting and Finance*, 1–22.

For other articles discussing the impact of dividends in Australia, see:

- Walker, S. and Partington, G. (1999), 'The value of dividends: Evidence from cum-dividend trading in the ex-dividend period', *Accounting and Finance*, 39, 275–296.

- Balachandran, B. and Nguyen, T. (2004), 'Signalling power of special dividends in an imputation environment', *Accounting and Finance*, 44, 277–297.

NOTES

1. Although the reporting year-end of most companies coincides with the financial year-end (30 June) or the calendar year-end (31 December), this is not always the case. For example, some companies have a reporting year ending 31 March or 30 September.

2. Another date of legal significance is the record date. All shareholders on the share register as at the record date are theoretically entitled to the dividend payment. The ex-dividend date is determined by the ASX and currently falls four business days prior to the record date.

3. For the interested reader, the S&P/ASX 200 Index opened on the ex-dividend date at approximately the same level as the previous day's close. Hence, broad market movements do not explain the fall in price.

4. N. Burt, A. Harris and M. Hilan (2002), *Rules of Thumb Compendium: How to respond to events that affect share prices*, JP Morgan.

5. J. Lintner (1956), 'Distribution of incomes of corporations among dividends, retained earnings, and taxes', *American Economic Review*, vol. 46, 97–113.

6. The regression coefficients b and c are analogous to the beta coefficient in the CAPM and similar formulae can be used to calculate their value. Hence, parameter estimates of b and c in an equation which takes on the following form:

$$Y = a + bX_1 + cX_2 + e^t$$

can be found using the following (see D. Gujarati (1995), *Basic Econometrics*, 3rd edn, McGraw-Hill, New York, 198):

$$b = \frac{\sum_{t=1}^{n}(yx_1)\sum_{t=1}^{n}(x_2^2) - \sum_{t=1}^{n}(yx_2)\sum_{t=1}^{n}(x_1x_2)}{\sum_{t=1}^{n}(x_1^2)\sum_{t=1}^{n}(x_2^2) - \left(\sum_{t=1}^{n}(x_1x_2)\right)^2}$$

$$c = \frac{\sum_{t=1}^{n}(yx_2)\sum_{t=1}^{n}(x_1^2) - \sum_{t=1}^{n}(yx_1)\sum_{t=1}^{n}(x_1x_2)}{\sum_{t=1}^{n}(x_1^2)\sum_{t=1}^{n}(x_2^2) - \left(\sum_{t=1}^{n}(x_1x_2)\right)^2}$$

where $x_1 = X_1 - \bar{X}_1$, $x_2 = X_2 - \bar{X}_2$ and $y_1 = Y_1 - \bar{Y}_1$.

7. T. Shevlin (1982), 'Australian corporate dividend policy: Empirical evidence', *Accounting and Finance*, 1–22.

8. G. Partington (1984), 'Dividend policy and target payout ratios', *Accounting and Finance*, vol. 3, 63–74.

9. M. Miller and F. Modigliani (1961), 'Dividend policy, growth and the valuation of shares', *Journal of Business*, vol. 34, 411–33.

10. It is possible to calculate both the number of shares issued and the new share price by solving the following using simultaneous equations:

$xn = \$50$ and $\$2000/(1000 + n) = x$

where n is the number of new shares issued and x is the new share price.

Solution: $x = \$1.95$ and $n = 25.6$.

11. Company releases, CapitalIQ and IRESS.

12. It must be noted that costs associated with issuing shares as part of an IPO are likely to be higher than a follow-on offering once the company is listed. Furthermore, costs will vary significantly depending on whether the offer is underwritten.

13. This analysis ignores the impact of personal and corporate taxes on dividends and capital gains, which is discussed later.

14. C. Comerton-Forde, A. Frino, C. Fernandez and T. Oetomo (2003), 'The impact of broker and industry on institutional execution costs', Working Paper, University of Sydney.

15. The bid–ask spread in this table is a time-weighted average of the bid–ask spread divided by the average of the bid and ask prices over the period.

16. S. A. Easton and N. A. Sinclair (1989), 'The impact of unexpected earnings and dividends on abnormal returns to equity', *Accounting and Finance*, 1–19.

17. Unexpected returns were calculated by subtracting the expected return estimated from the market model (similar to the CAPM and defined in Chapter 6) from the actual return in a particular month.

18. Current tax laws allow investors with a personal tax rate that is below the corporate tax rate to apply to the ATO for a refund for their unused franking credits.

Capital structure policy

12

CHAPTER PREVIEW

The previous chapter was concerned with one very important corporate financial policy—dividend policy—and how it might affect the value or price of a company. This chapter is concerned with another important financial policy—capital structure policy.

When companies seek to raise the cash required to finance their operations, they must decide from what source they will obtain capital. Capital structure policy is concerned with the amount of debt versus equity used by a company to finance its operations and the segment(s) of the capital market from which companies source finance. At its most basic level, the capital market can be divided into debt and equity markets. This chapter examines the nature of capital structure policy.

KEY CONCEPTS

CONCEPT 12.1   What is capital structure policy?

Capital structure
The amount of debt relative to equity used by a company.

Capital structure relates to the mix of debt and equity used by a company, but the focus of capital structure policy is usually on debt. The distinguishing features of debt and equity were identified earlier, in Chapter 3. The amount of debt used by a company is also referred to as its 'leverage' or 'gearing'.

If the owner of a debt or equity security liquidated their holding, they would realise its market value. Hence, the market value of debt and equity securities provides an estimate of the value invested in the firm. For this reason, theoretically at least, the best way of measuring the leverage of a company is to take the market value of interest-bearing debt and divide it by the market value of equity. However, market participants will often look at the book value of debt and equity as well. The market value of equity is equivalent to the market capitalisation of issued shares, which for Australian listed companies can be estimated using the current traded price on the ASX. However, the market value of debt is not typically observable because the debt securities of Australian companies are not typically listed on the ASX. For this reason, net debt is often measured by taking the book value of the interest-bearing debt of a company and subtracting its cash and marketable securities. Hence the leverage or gearing of a company can be measured using a leverage or gearing ratio, as follows:

$$\text{Leverage ratio} = \frac{\text{net debt}}{\text{market capitalisation of equity}} \quad\quad \textbf{(12.1)}$$

Some measures of leverage of ASX-listed construction and engineering company, Leighton Holdings Limited, are set out in Table 12.1. On 11 April 2011, Leighton announced an equity raising of $757 million via an accelerated renounceable entitlement offer. The raising was under-taken by Leighton to strengthen its balance sheet, provide financial flexibility to pursue growth opportunities and support investment grade credit rating metrics. According to Leighton's investor presentation, without the raising, Leighton's gearing ratio would move beyond the high end of its internal target range of 35–45%. The gearing and leverage ratios of Leighton and the impact of the raising on the pro-forma financial information can be seen in Table 12.1. Prior to the equity raising, as can be seen in the December 2010 financial information, Leighton's headline gearing was in the upper end of its target range. It is evident that post the capital raising, on a pro-forma basis as at December 2010, gearing falls marginally below the bottom end of the internal target range.

This chapter is concerned with the types of securities that Leighton might use in order to manage its target debt or leverage ratios and how it can raise capital from the equity market. It is also concerned with the implications for the wealth of Leighton's shareholders from adopting a particular target leverage rate rather than something lower or possibly higher.

| Table 12.1 | The net debt to equity ratio of Leighton Holdings Limited |

BALANCE SHEET AS OF:	DEC 2010 PRO-FORMA[1]	DEC 2010	JUN 2010	JUN 2009
Total interest bearing liabilities ($m)	1414.0	1414.0	1347.2	1278.8
Capital leases ($m)	279.3	279.3	323.1	-
Total debt ($m)	1693.4	1693.4	1670.4	1278.8
Cash and equivalents ($m)	1924.5	1167.5	1313.7	665.8
Net debt ($m)	(231.1)	525.9	356.7	613.0
Total equity ($m)	3173.1	2416.1	2564.7	2339.3
Total capital ($m)	4866.4	4109.4	4235.0	3618.1
Market capitalisation[2] ($m)	7924.1[3]	9360.5	10 213.4	11 151.5
Headline gearing (total debt/total capital)	34.8%	41.2%	39.4%	35.3%
Leverage (net debt/market capitalisation)	(2.9%)	5.6%	3.5%	5.5%
Book leverage (net debt/equity)	(7.3%)	21.8%	13.9%	26.2%
Book leverage (net debt/(equity + net debt))	(7.9%)	17.9%	12.2%	20.8%

Notes
1. Pro-forma to show the impact on the historical balance sheet of the equity raising.
2. Market close price as at filing date.
3. Market capitalisation as at normal trading of all securities on 19 May 2011.

Source: Company releases, CapitalIQ and IRESS.

CONCEPT CHECK

1. What is capital structure?
2. What is leverage or gearing?
3. How is leverage measured?

For the answers, go to MyFinanceLab

CONCEPT 12.2   Methods of raising equity finance

Equity

In Australia, public companies listed on the ASX are legally known as limited liability companies and carry the extension 'Limited' (or 'Ltd') after their name. This means that the liability of shareholders is limited to the amount of capital they invest in the company. Almost without exception, equity (share capital) issued by companies listed on the ASX is in the form of ordinary shares (known as 'common stock' in the USA). The key characteristics of equity were discussed at length in Chapter 3. To recap and extend, ordinary shares can be characterised by the following features.

- They have an infinite life.
- They pay dividends, which are set annually.

- The owners of shares have a right to vote on resolutions put forward at annual general meetings or extraordinary general meetings.
- Shareholders are the last to be paid in the event of corporate failure, after all the other liabilities of a company have been paid.

When a firm is incorporated, one of the legal documents that must be prepared is its 'constitution'. Among other things, the constitution sets out the maximum number of shares that can be issued by a company. When a company desires to raise capital from the public, it undertakes what is known as an 'initial public offering' or 'float' in which it issues shares in return for cash from the public and is then 'listed', or commences trading, on the ASX. There are a certain number of conditions a company must meet before being able to be listed on the ASX and these conditions are set out in the ASX Listing Rules. At the date of writing, the most important of these were: (1) the company needs to have 500 shareholders, each with a parcel of issued shares exceeding $2000; and (2) the company must fulfil either the 'profit test' or the 'assets test'. Under the profit test, the company must have produced aggregated profits in the last three years exceeding $1 million, of which $400 000 must have been generated in the last year. Under the assets test, the company must have net tangible assets of at least $2 million after deducting the costs of fund raising or a market capitalisation of at least $10 million. After a company has been floated, it can seek further capital from the share market, in line with its constitution and the ASX and Australian Securities and Investments Commission (ASIC) requirements. The four most commonly used methods of raising additional capital are through (1) a rights issue, (2) a placement, (3) a share purchase plan, or (4) a dividend reinvestment plan. The first three methods will be discussed in this section; dividend reinvestment plans were discussed in Chapter 11.

Initial public offerings (IPOs)

Prospectus
A legal document required to be lodged with ASIC and ASX providing information on a new share issue when the issue is offered to the public, to provide a record of representations by the issuer to the prospective buyer.

When a company seeks to issue shares to the public for the first time, it must prepare and issue a **prospectus**. In most cases an IPO will involve a new issue of shares and may include a selldown of existing shares. The prospectus is a comprehensive document, which contains the formal invitation to subscribe for shares in the company and a number of important pieces of information, including:

- information about the issue, such as the number of shares to be issued and how the issue price will be set
- important dates, such as the last date for submissions of applications, the date the issue price will be determined and the date the shares will start trading on the ASX
- information about the company, its management structure and the risks it faces
- financial information, both historical and forecast, including earnings and dividends and any underlying assumptions.

FINANCE EXTRA!

Queensland raises $4.6bn from QR National IPO

THE Queensland government said today it raised $4.6 billion in gross proceeds from the initial public offering of its QR National railway.

The state government said $4.1bn worth of shares were issued.

The government was hoping to raise up to $5.05bn from the IPO of QR National, but concerns around pricing kept some investors at bay, forcing the government to retain a 40 per cent stake in the asset and to offer the shares at the low end of its targeted price range. The Queensland government is divesting QR as part of a broader asset sale program to raise money and improve its credit rating.

Dividends due to the government from the company and cash proceeds from a debt facility make up the difference between the $4.1bn worth of shares issued and the total revenue figure of $4.6bn.

Retail investors bought 34 per cent of the offering at a discounted price of $2.45 and institutional investors bought 66 per cent at $2.55 per share while just over 54 per cent of the stock will be held by domestic investors. The share pricing values the company at $6.7bn. The price range was $2.50 and $3.00.

'These proceeds will now be used to pay off debt and establish a stronger balance sheet,' Queensland State Premier Anna Bligh said. The state will retain its 40 per cent holding in the company until 2012.

The shares begin trading on Monday in a closely watched debut that could, if successful, help reignite the market for public offerings here.

That QR National priced at the low end of its price range isn't a surprise. Heading into the bookbuild, the pricing of the deal came under public scrutiny.

Domestic fund managers were openly critical of the float, in part because the railroad is planning a capital-intensive expansion plan on which it is pegging its earnings growth expectations. Also, Queensland was asking investors to pay 21.1 to 25.3 times forecast earnings in the year ending June 2011. The high end is almost twice the average valuation paid for Australian stocks these days.

The IPO received a warm reception from international investors, with the government coming out and making optimistic statements after the global road show.

QR National is a major test for the Australian IPO market. It is the first multi-billion dollar IPO to come to the domestic market since Myer Holdings late last year. Myer's disappointing performance post-IPO, followed by a handful of other IPOs that didn't trade well after listing, left the market for new floats essentially shut for much of this year.

As a result, Australia has been out of step with other markets in the region, where IPO activity has been picking up. Year-to-date, $US1.19bn of IPOs have priced in Australia compared to $US63.8bn in China, $US47.5bn in Hong Kong and $US11.3bn in Japan, according to Dealogic. Australia ranks 9th in the region for IPO activity with less than half of the volume of the 8th-ranked country, Indonesia.

A strong performance for the QR National IPO on Monday could set the stage for an active IPO market in 2011 in Australia with companies like the Hoyts Group, a cinema chain, potentially coming out of private equity hands and Valemus, the Australian construction arm of Bilfinger AG, possibly attempting a listing again after pulling its IPO due to adverse market conditions, to name a few.

Source: Cynthia Koons, *The Australian*, 20 November 2010.

It is important to note that there are a number of important 'prices' involved in the issue process. First, there is the issue price. The issue price is the price at which shares are actually issued to the public by the company. The issue price determines how much cash is raised by the company from the issue. Second, when the shares commence trading for the first time on the ASX, the market will determine a price at which the shares will trade, normally called the 'price on listing'.

Example 12.1 illustrates the significance of the prices and dates described above using the float of QR National Limited in November 2010. QR National was one of the largest IPOs in 2010 and 2011, issuing approximately $4.1 billion worth of shares. While there were a number of smaller IPOs in 2010 (around 90), excluding QR National these only raised around $3.7 billion.[1] This is compared to the $12 billion raised in 2005[2] prior to disruption of the equity and credit markets.

Practitioner's POV

Entities able to be admitted to the official list of the ASX include both companies, which issue shares, and trusts, which issue units through a responsible entity. It is also possible to issue stapled securities, which comprise one share in a company and one unit in a trust stapled together to form a single stapled security. When a group seeks to issue stapled securities to the public for the first time, it must prepare and issue a combined prospectus for the offering of shares and product disclosure statement for the offering of units.

EXAMPLE 12.1

QR National Limited IPO issue, listing prices and dates

QUESTION

QR National Limited (QRN) issued a prospectus in respect of its initial public offering, setting out the following dates:

Last day for applications (retail)	12 November 2010
Institutional bookbuild	18–19 November 2010
Listing date	22 November 2010

QRN's issue price for institutional investors was set at $2.55. QRN shares closed trading at $2.65 on the listing date. If a shareholder was able to purchase QRN shares on issue and then immediately sell them on the ASX by the close of trade on the listing day, what return would they earn over and above the return on the All Ordinaries Index if it stood at 4717.7 on Friday, 19 November 2010 and 4731.8 on Monday, 22 November 2010?

ANSWER

$$\text{Return on All Ordinaries Index} = \frac{4731.8 - 4717.7}{4717.7} = 0.299\%$$

$$\text{Return on QRN} = \frac{2.65 - 2.55}{2.55} = 3.922\%$$

Hence, the return on QRN shares over and above the return on the market was a gain of 3.623%.

The issue price is normally set by the company in conjunction with the investment bank (or underwriter; see below) involved in the IPO. The issue price is typically set in one of two ways. First, it can be a 'fixed-price offer', where the issue price is set prior to the IPO and appears in the prospectus. In a fixed-price offer, investors know the price of shares they are applying for at the time they complete their application. The second method is a 'book build'. In a typical book build, institutional investors submit their bids for shares (price and quantity) without knowing the issue price. The issue price is then determined by taking into account the number, pricing and nature of the bids submitted by institutional investors. Institutional investors are given a range and price increments at which to bid for.

An **underwriter** is commonly used in an IPO. In return for a fee, the underwriter contracts to purchase any shares not acquired by institutional or retail investors. The underwriter bears the risk that a company will not raise all the capital it requires from an IPO and draws a substantial fee for bearing this risk. Underwriters are employed so that a company will not fail to raise all the cash it needs. The underwriter also normally organises the IPO and generates additional fees in this way.

Typically, the smaller the capital raising, the higher the fees, because of the high level of fixed costs. In 2010, the average fee for IPOs was 4.3%.[3] It is worth noting that there are many parties involved in an IPO—lawyers, accountants, investment banks and so on. Consequently, the process of floating a company is not cheap. The main costs involved in an IPO include:

- underwriting fees/advisory fees
- legal fees

Underwriter
An underwriter is a broker or an investment bank that commits to arranging the sale of an issue of securities on behalf of a client and, if it does not sell all the shares to other institutions or investors, itself undertakes to purchase the unsold securities. By using an underwriter, the client is therefore assured of raising the full amount of money it is seeking.

- investigating accountant and other adviser fees
- prospectus design and printing costs
- ASX listing fees
- share registry
- printing and postage
- advertising.

Table 12.2 describes some of the largest IPOs since 1995. Many of the largest floats involved the sell-off of what were previously government businesses—for example, QR National, Telstra and Qantas. These are known as **privatisations** because ownership changes from public (i.e. government) to private ownership. In the case of privatisations, most of the proceeds from the sale of the businesses flow to government, with a portion flowing into the company for expansion and growth.

Table 12.2	Examples of IPOs					
Company	Date listed	Industry	Amount Raised ($m)	Issue price ($)	Listing price ($)	Gross fee (%)[1]
Westfield Retail Trust	2010	Property	2053	2.75	2.66	2.3
QR National Limited	2010	Transport	4052	2.55[2]	2.65	4.0
Myer Holdings Limited	2009	Retailing	2172	4.10	3.75	1.2
Boart Longyear	2007	Capital goods	2348	1.85	1.80	3.9
Goodman Fielder	2005	Food, beverage and tobacco	2649	2.00	2.04	3.2
SP Ausnet	2005	Utilities	1415	1.38	1.30	3.5

Notes
1. Gross fee includes any management, underwriting and selling fee, but excludes any incentive fee.
2. Institutional issue price.

Source: Prospectuses and IRESS.

Rights issues

A **rights issue** (also called an entitlement or pro-rata issue) is the most common method used by Australian companies to raise cash through the issue of new shares. A rights issue gives existing shareholders the right to purchase new shares in proportion to the number of existing shares held (i.e. pro rata to existing shareholdings) for a pre-specified price or price range. For example, a 1 for 8 rights issue is an offer to purchase up to one new share for each eight existing shares held. It is important to note that (1) a rights issue represents an offer or 'right' only, and not an obligation, and (2) the offer is made to existing shareholders only. Rights issues in Australia can be renounceable, which means that they can be sold to third parties by the recipient shareholder, or non-renounceable, which means that they cannot be sold and are forfeited if not taken up by the recipient shareholder. A company was traditionally required to prepare a prospectus to undertake a rights issue. In June 2007, changes were introduced to the Corporations Legislation allowing ASX-listed companies which satisfy certain conditions to raise additional equity via a 'rights issue cleansing notice' with the ASX without the need to lodge a prospectus. A rights issue cleansing notice must contain certain information, including information an investor would reasonably require for the purposes of making an assessment of the issue.

When a company announces a rights issue, the shares of the company trade 'cum-rights', which means that a buyer of the shares is automatically entitled to the rights. After a certain date, known as the 'ex-rights' date, the rights detach from the shares and the last shareholder to have held the shares owns them. A shareholder buying the shares after the ex-rights date is not entitled to the rights. However, if the rights are renounceable, these rights can be sold from the ex-rights date by the shareholder who ends up with them. Beyond the ex-rights date, there is usually a short time period (weeks) in which shareholders can decide to exercise the rights, in which case they must complete an application form indicating that they wish to take up the shares offered and pay for the new shares purchased. If the rights are not sold or exercised within this time period, they lapse.

What is the impact of a rights issue on a company's share price? Although a rights issue does not change the existing value of a company (value is not created from nothing), its value does increase by the amount of new cash raised through the issue. However, this new value is spread across a greater number of shares. Hence, a rights issue can 'dilute' the price of a share. Given the terms of a rights issue (the issue ratio and issue price), it is possible to calculate the expected (fall in the) share price under the theoretical scenario that the rights issue takes place immediately. This is known as the 'theoretical ex-rights price'. Example 12.2 illustrates the dilution effect of a rights issue.

Table 12.3 lists some examples of rights issues.

EXAMPLE 12.2

Impact of a rights issue on an entity's security price

QUESTION

On 15 March 2011, Origin Energy Limited announced a 1 for 5 pro-rata renounceable entitlement offer at an issue price of $13.00.

Its share price immediately before the announcement was $15.22. What is the theoretical ex-rights price?

ANSWER

Prior to the announcement, the value of five shares held by a shareholder was:

Value of five shares = 5 × 15.22 = 76.10

Each shareholder would be required to give Origin Energy $13.00 for each new share offered under the rights issue and, hence, the total value of the six shares held by the shareholder would become:

Value of six shares after right exercised = 76.10 + 13.00 = 89.10

Given that this value would be spread equally across the six shares, the price of each share is $14.85 (89.10/6) — its theoretical ex-rights price.

Table 12.3	Examples of rights issues					
Company	Date announced	Issue ratio	Amount raised ($m)	Issue price ($)	Share price[1] ($)	Under-writing fee (%)[2]
Macquarie Goodman	12 Apr 2005	1:10	458	3.64	3.80	2.00
Suncorp Metway	12 Mar 2007	2:15	1169	15.50	21.25	1.75
Wesfarmers	21 Apr 2008	1:8	2573	29.00	36.97	1.00
Woodside Petroleum	14 Dec 2009	1:12	2517	42.10	46.79	1.50
Boral	6 Jul 2010	1:5	490	4.10	4.74	2.10
Downer EDI	28 Feb 2011	1:4	279	3.25	3.78	2.25
Origin Energy	15 Mar 2011	1:5	2302	13.00	15.22	2.00
Leighton Holdings	11 Apr 2011	1:9	757	22.50	28.94	2.50

Notes
1. Prior to announcement.
2. Excludes any management fee.

Sources: Prospectuses and IRESS.

Placement

Placement
An issue of new shares to a small group of typically institutional investors, as opposed to a public offering.

Placements are a very common means by which companies raise cash by issuing new equity. Placements are issues of new shares to a small group of typically institutional investors. Placements normally involve less than 15% of a company's issued capital in any year, as the ASX listing rules allow this level of issuance to take place without the need for shareholder approval. The caveat is that they are offered exclusively to sophisticated investors, because companies issuing shares through a placement do not need to prepare and distribute a prospectus. Conditional placements can be used by companies that wish to raise greater than 15% of a company's issued capital through a placement; however, this is subject to shareholder approval at an extraordinary general meeting.

A company wishing to raise cash through a placement will normally mandate an investment bank or a broker as an arranger. The arranger typically seeks to place the new equity on a 'best endeavours' basis and may underwrite the placement at a particular price. This means that the arranger attempts to place the shares at the highest possible price. Placements can be executed within a number of hours and shares are usually placed at a discount to the existing share price in order to entice institutions to take up the shares.

For listed companies, issues that are not rights issues or authorised by shareholders, including placements as well as certain other issues, must not combine to exceed 15% of issued capital within a 12-month period.

A jumbo placement is a placement and non-renounceable rights issue offered to both institutional and retail shareholders. A jumbo placement commonly exceeds the maximum number of shares that can be issued for a normal placement without shareholder approval because, with ASX approval, the placement is allowed to be calculated on the enlarged capital base post the rights issue. The first jumbo placement was for Adsteam Marine in March 2001.

The key difference between a jumbo placement and an ordinary rights issue is that the institutional component is completed upfront through a book build, usually in the first 24 to 48 hours after announcement. The shorter timetable usually results in a smaller discount, reducing the cost of the equity, and reduces the period of risk exposure for underwriters hence reducing the required underwriting fee. The ability to complete a significant portion of the equity raising in a short timeframe, more easily secure underwriting commitments and raise more than 15% of ordinary capital through a placement without shareholder approval was developed to assist Australian companies making unconditional bids or acquisitions. However, in recent years, jumbo placements have also been associated with companies raising capital to reduce leverage. This is because jumbo placements are usually faster and more flexible compared with ordinary rights issues and can provide a greater degree of raising capacity than normal placements without shareholder approval.

An alternative to the jumbo placement is an accelerated renounceable rights issue, also known as an AREO (accelerated, renouncable entitlement offer). The key difference between a jumbo placement and an AREO is that, as the issue is renounceable, shareholders receive value for their rights even if they choose not to take them up. This is done through a dual book build structure, whereby a book build for renounced institutional rights is conducted at the beginning of the offer period and a book build for renounced retail rights is conducted at the end of the offer period.

Two further types of accelerated renounceable rights issues have been developed, with the objective of better aligning the participation of institutional and retail shareholders. In October 2009, CSR Limited raised $375 million through a new structure—the SAREO (simultaneous accelerated renounceable entitlement offer), whereby the bookbuild for the renounced institutional and retail rights was conducted at the same time at the end of the offer period. In March 2011, Origin Energy Limited raised $2.3 billion through a new structure—the PAITREO (pro-rata accelerated institutional, tradeable retail entitlement offer), whereby the institutional offer was accelerated but the retail entitlement offer enabled retail investors to trade their entitlements on the ASX throughout the retail offer period.

Table 12.4 provides examples of placements in major listed companies. The table illustrates that new shares are typically issued at a small discount, less than 10%, to the existing share price for the placements that have been illustrated.

Table 12.4	Examples of placements				
Company	Date announced	Amount raised ($m)[1]	Issue price ($)	Share price prior to announcement	Discount (%)
united Group	2 Jun 2005	140.0	8.40	8.68	3.2
IAG	6 Dec 2006	750.0	5.50	5.64	2.5
Mirvac Group	24 Jan 2008	300.0	5.20	4.84	(7.4)[1]
Nufarm	15 May 2009	300.0	11.25	12.49	9.9
Mirvac Group	7 Apr 2010	350.0	1.40	1.48	5.4
Macarthur Coal	24 Aug 2010	438.7	11.50	12.36	6.9
Sundance Resources	27 Apr 2011	60.0	0.405	0.435	6.9

Note
1.   Mirvac's placement was completed at a premium due to the introduction of a strategic shareholder through the placement.

Source: Prospectuses and IRESS.

Share purchase plans

As placements are offered exclusively to sophisticated shareholders, a company will often offer a share purchase plan (SPP) to all shareholders in conjunction with a placement. A listed company is able to issue up to $15 000 of ordinary shares to shareholders in any 12-month period through an SPP without the need for a prospectus. If done in conjunction with a placement, the SPP is usually done at the placement price. Any shares issued under an SPP are exempt from the 15% limit unless any shares have been underwritten by and are subsequently subscribed for by the underwriter.

Practitioner's POV

Rights issues and placements, which are fairly common, are examples of bread-and-butter 'deals' that investment banks are involved in. However, IPOs, especially for shares that are likely to involve companies in the top 100 on the ASX, are the deals that investment banks most often seek out. Mergers and acquisitions, especially of the large variety, are also very much sought after by investment banks.

CONCEPT CHECK

4. What is equity finance?
5. Name four ways of raising equity finance.
6. Are IPOs more suited for large capital raisings or small capital raisings?
7. What is a rights issue?
8. What restriction does the ASX have on placements?
9. Describe the differences between a jumbo placement and an accelerated renounceable entitlement offer (AREO).

For the answers, go to MyFinanceLab

CONCEPT 12.3   Sources of long-term debt finance

Accountants generally classify debt in reported financial statements according to its maturity. Short-term debt, which needs to be repaid within 12 months, is generally classified as a current liability, while long-term debt, which is to be fully repaid over a longer period, is generally classified as a non-current liability.

While there is a variety of debt instruments available, this section discusses the types of long-term debt that are most common in Australia and, hence, most likely to appear in the financial statements of Australian companies. Chapter 14 provides a discussion of types of short-term debt finance.

Unsecured notes

Unsecured notes or bonds are long-term debt securities issued by companies which specify that the creditor will receive regular interest payments during the term of the debt and the face value of the debt at the maturity date. Unsecured notes are so called because they are unsecured against any assets. Unsecured notes are typically issued with a term of between three months and 10 years. The yield at which the securities are issued depends on interest rates at the time of issue, the maturity date of the issue and the creditworthiness (credit risk measured by a credit rating) of a company. Unsecured notes, like the government bonds described in Chapter 3, will typically deliver a semi-annual coupon together with a lump sum (their face value) at the end of their term. They can be a fixed rate, floating rate or zero coupon.

Unsecured notes are generally issued in a similar way to new equity—that is, through (1) a private placement to a small number of institutional shareholders, or (2) a public issue via a prospectus. The contract underlying unsecured notes is known as a trust deed and determines the relationship between the company and the trustee, who represents the noteholders. The trust deed normally contains various 'debt covenants' that restrict the financial or operating activities of the company. For example, there may be restrictions on the ability of a company to issue further debt securities or pay dividends.

Australian companies that raise large levels of debt generally facilitate this through unsecured notes (bonds) as, up until recently, there has been an active market in Australia and internationally across a range of industry sectors, credit ratings, maturities (tenors) and sizes. The companies that issue these bonds are creditworthy entities, typically with strong credit ratings from rating agencies such as Standard & Poor's (S&P) and Moody's. However, in response to the US subprime crisis and credit crunch, this market activity has somewhat slowed. In particular, corporate debt tenors have been reined in to typically three to five-year terms, from up to 10 years, although companies may be able to raise a total amount of debt over different tranches with different maturities. Issues generally occur within the A$0.5 billion to A$1 billion range and the average raising is around A$250–300 million. The continuing difficulty of sourcing bank funding and expensiveness at tenors of more than three years has had an impact on debt issuance by companies. There is continued evidence of credit rationing within certain sectors, with investors demanding tighter covenants and reporting obligations.

Practitioner's POV

Reduced appetite for credit has also had an impact on mergers and acquisitions activity. Companies have had increased difficulty putting in place large debt facilities and securing debt underwritings. Combined with a volatile equity market, the difficulties associated with raising finance increases the risks associated with the success of hostile deals relative to consensual deals. More selective lending, with increased focus on core credit fundamentals, has also had an impact on private equity deals, with tighter leverage ratios, reduced tenors and increased pricing making it difficult for private equity players to be able to achieve the required returns for their investors.

When raising debt through international markets—for example, the US private placement market—money is generally raised in US dollars or euros and may be swapped into Australian currency. A company that is raising debt through international markets will rely on an investment bank or a syndicate of investment banks to arrange the issue. No prospectus is required to be lodged in relation to an offer to sophisticated investors; however, an information memorandum is prepared as part of the documentation. A global road show of one-on-one and group meetings will be organised and this may take representatives of senior management through Asia, Europe and/or the US. Institutions are then invited to bid into a book of demand for the raising and a book build will determine the pricing or spread of basis points over and above a particular rate. These rates include the Euro Interbank Offer Rate (Euribor) and the London Interbank Offer Rate (Libor) and are the rates of interest at which panel banks borrow funds from other panel banks, in marketable sizes, in the European Union interbank market or London interbank market, respectively. Domestic bonds are generally priced at a spread of basis points over and above the bank bill swap rate (BBSW), the Australian equivalent of the Euribor and Libor. The BBSW is the rate set daily by a group of banks by referencing rates for bank bills. The government bond market (i.e. the **risk-free rate**) is not the pricing reference although it is a trading reference benchmark. Floating rate notes are issues with a fixed margin to floating bank bills.

Risk-free rate
The rate of return on an asset with zero risk.

Secondary market activity outside the government sector tends to be concentrated in a range of benchmark corporate bonds. These are typically bonds issued by domestic financial institutions and key companies and also tend to be larger issues. A group of fixed interest dealers stand ready to make markets in these issues. Notes issued in Australia are lodged and traded on the Austraclear system. An issuer is not required to become a member of Austraclear but pays a fee for the securities lodged on the system. Links between Austraclear and Euroclear/Clearstream exist for the trading of securities in other domiciles.

Debentures

Debentures are very similar to unsecured notes, except that some form of security is normally offered by the issuing company. Debentures are sometimes listed on the ASX. There are two broad types of debentures: fixed-charge debentures and floating-charge debentures. The trust deed in a fixed-charge debenture identifies the specific corporate asset pledged as security. Hence, if a company is no longer financially viable, fixed-charge debenture holders are entitled to the proceeds from the sale of the specific asset. In contrast, floating-charge debenture holders are entitled to the proceeds from the sale of unpledged assets in the event of corporate failure ahead of unsecured creditors (e.g. unsecured noteholders) or the excess proceeds from the sale of pledged assets.

Debenture
Any unsecured long-term debt.

Financial leases

A company can borrow cash and purchase an asset. This would entitle it to the use of the asset and an obligation to make a series of loan repayments over a specified time period. A lease is a different form of financing and is essentially a contract in which one party pays another a series of cash flows for the use of an asset. The commercial outcomes of leasing an asset are identical to obtaining a loan and purchasing an asset, because (1) a company is locked into a series of future cash outlays and (2) it is entitled to use an asset. In this way, a lease can be thought of as a financing arrangement and, given that lease payments are fixed contractually, the arrangement takes on the characteristics of debt finance.

There are two broad types of leases: operating leases and financial (or capital) leases. The key distinguishing characteristic between the two is the duration of the lease. An operating lease is cancellable and has an indefinite duration. A good example of an operating lease is the renting out of an apartment or house. Such lease agreements can be cancelled by the lessee provided they give sufficient notice (usually 21 days). In contrast, a financial lease is a lease agreement that is non-cancellable and usually lasts for the entire life of the leased asset. A financial lease is more in the nature of a financial arrangement than an operating lease, as the use of the asset is acquired for its entire life.[4]

A special type of financial lease is a leveraged lease. Leveraged leases are complex (and costly) transactions to assemble and are used to acquire very large assets.

For example, Qantas uses a form of leveraged lease in order to acquire its jet aeroplanes. The current value of its leased fleet is just over three billion dollars (as at 30 June 2011). There are typically four parties to a leveraged lease: (1) the lessee, who wants the use of an asset; (2) the lease manager, typically a finance company that arranges the entire transaction and manages the lease; (3) equity investors, who form a partnership and borrow part of the funds to acquire an asset and lease it; and (4) debt investors, who loan funds to the partnership. The relationships between the parties involved in a leveraged lease are illustrated in Figure 12.1.

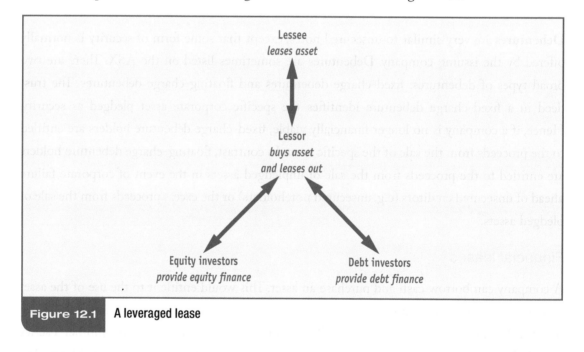

Figure 12.1   A leveraged lease

Term loans and mortgage loans

Australian companies can approach any bank, including the 'big four'—ANZ, Commonwealth, NAB and Westpac—and arrange a loan for a specified sum of cash to be repaid over a specified period. Companies can also approach overseas-based banks for term loans. The loans can be for any length of time negotiated between the bank and the company and loans generally extend from one to 10 years in the financial statements of Australian companies.

The rate of interest on a term loan can be fixed for the life of the loan or floating. The interest rate on floating-rate loans is typically linked to the BBSW and reset on a regular basis (e.g. quarterly or half-yearly). The interest rate on such loans is typically represented as BBSW + 1% or BBSW + 2% and so on. So, if the BBSW is 5%, the interest rate charged to the company under a BBSW + 1% is 6%; if the BBSW is 6%, the interest rate charged to the company under a BBSW + 1% is 7% and so on. The increment over and above the swap rate largely represents the risk premium charged by the bank to the corporate borrower given the creditworthiness of the company and the size and term of the loan being sought.

Term loans can be secured or unsecured, again depending on the creditworthiness of the company and the size and term of the loan being sought. Security can be in the form of a fixed or floating charge over the assets of the corporate borrower. If the security on the loan is a mortgage over property such as land and buildings, the loan is called a mortgage loan. The contract or deed between the bank and the company usually contains various restrictions on the financial or operating activities of the corporate borrower. These can include restrictions on the ability to pay dividends, raise additional equity or seek further loans.

US SUBPRIME CRISIS AND CREDIT CRUNCH OVERVIEW

In order to understand the current credit environment (or debt markets) it is relevant to understand the US subprime crisis and subsequent credit crunch.

Subprime mortgages in the US were high-risk housing loans extended to borrowers with a poor or limited credit history. Consequently they had higher interest rates attached to them. Subprime mortgages grew quickly in response to demand created by the marketing of real estate to risky borrowers in the early 2000s. Attracted by the higher interest rates, investor appetite increased for debt securities related to these subprime mortgages, which were packaged through securitised mortgage bonds and the use of credit derivatives. Mortgage originators, faced with growing demand for these products, began relaxing credit standards and marketing their products in order to increase the volume of these loans.

The increasing sophistication of credit markets throughout this period also resulted in rapid growth in structures such as Collateralised Debt Obligations (CDO) and Collateralised Loan Obligations (CLO). A CDO or CLO is essentially securitisation of a pool of underlying financial assets into a debt structure able to be rated via an assessment of credit risk determined by rating agencies. Highly rated credit structures were in some instances leveraged further to provide a higher return. As CDO or CLO structures had credit ratings, this allowed banks to sell their credit risk exposure to a broad base of investors, including hedge funds, middle markets (e.g. municipal councils) and retail investors.

The US housing market slumped in 2006 in response to increases in official US interest rates. Loan affordability dropped and many home owners were faced with the need to refinance short-term fixed-rate loans. As a result, mortgage defaults increased and recovery rates on defaulting loans dropped due to the low creditworthiness of the underlying borrowers, thus creating the so-called US subprime crisis. The surge in losses from US subprime mortgages caused a rapid unwinding of leverage (de-leveraging) and led to the liquidation of many CDO and CLO deals. Investor caution extended to companies, with investors having reduced confidence that risks had been fully disclosed.

Credit Default Swaps (CDS) are a credit derivative that allows the trading of default risk of a specific credit or company. A CDS is an over-the-counter contract which essentially allows the transfer of third party credit risk to a counterparty agreeing to insure this risk in exchange for regular periodic payments. The difference between an underlying bond and its CDS is called the basis and is a measure of the risk associated with the underlying bond. The credit market crisis saw a growth in this market.

In response to the US subprime crisis, major central banks around the world began actively managing money markets by undertaking a significant injection of short-term liquidity into the market to ensure there was sufficient liquidity in overnight money markets to meet the demand of banks and boost investor confidence. Global government intervention extended to 'bail out' packages, equity injections in major financial institutions, guarantees of investor deposits and global coordinated interest rate cuts. In addition to active monetary policy easing, governments also undertook major fiscal policy initiatives to provide support to economic growth.

From 2009, the focus of credit markets extended to fears of a sovereign debt crisis concerning some European states, in particular Greece, Ireland and Portugal. At the time of writing, the sovereign debt crisis in Europe remains a concern. Furthermore, in August 2011, Standard & Poor's took the unprecedented step of downgrading its long-term sovereign credit rating on the US from AAA, in part due to the rising public debt burden and perception of greater policymaking uncertainty.

With continuing global uncertainty there has been a 'flight to quality' in global debt markets, with supply (debt issuance) primarily from the banks and financials. Companies continue to rely on banks to support their short-term debt requirements. However, increased demand for bank lending, higher bank funding costs, shrinking balance sheets and restructuring of over-levered infrastructure and private equity assets were all continuing to impact on credit markets at the time of writing. This ongoing uncertainty continues to make capital structure decisions difficult for Australian companies.

CONCEPT 12.4   Sources of hybrid finance

Hybrid financing relates to instruments that combine characteristics of equity and debt. Hybrid capital instruments are a funding alternative that have some characteristics of equity but are not dilutive to existing shareholders. The equity characteristics include subordination to other instruments, the right to defer payments and the absence of a repayment obligation. The debt characteristics include no participation in profits above a fixed coupon, which is generally tax deductible. The different types of hybrid capital instruments have varying equity and debt characteristics and, hence, are subject to different balance sheet classifications and given different equity credit by ratings agencies. Furthermore, as the regulatory treatment of hybrid capital is constantly evolving, so too is the structuring involved in these instruments.

Financial institutions commonly raise hybrid capital for regulatory capital needs. Companies may also use hybrid capital as part of their capital structure to fund acquisitions or **share buy-backs**. Hybrid capital instruments generally have a covenant package consistent with, or less onerous than, other debt facilities, facilitate investor diversification, are straightforward to document and can be completed on a relatively short execution timetable. However, hybrid capital does complicate a company's capital structure and, hence, is generally appropriate for large companies only.

Share buy-back
Occurs when a company buys back its own shares from its shareholders in return for cash.

There is a variety of hybrid capital instruments and selection of the optimal instrument is driven by considerations including ratings agencies (the degree of equity credit required and impact on leverage ratios), taxation (efficient use of tax capacity and franking credits), accounting (statement of financial position classification and impact on diluted earnings per share) and share dilution (control, timing of potential conversion into ordinary equity and conversion premium). There are three main types of hybrid securities, which are discussed in this section.

Convertible bonds

A convertible bond is a bond that is convertible into equity. Convertible bonds may be mandatorily convertible or alternatively the investor may be able to choose whether they convert or the issuer repays the issue price. They may be denominated in any major currency and the target investor base is international and domestic institutional investors. The documentation required is an institutional offering circular. Depending on the converting mechanism, these are considered debt on the statement of financial position until converted and may be given no or minimal equity credit by ratings agencies. A mandatory convertible is more likely to be treated as equity and given higher equity credit. Convertible bonds typically have a maturity of three to five years and the coupon is cumulative. As convertible bonds convert into shares at a point in the future and typically at a premium to the current share price, they can be seen as an efficient funding mechanism for a company that believes its share price is undervalued. This is because it is less dilutive to current shareholders than issuing equity at a low price. Convertible bonds may also have a reset mechanism that resets the conversion price.

Reset preference shares

A reset preference share is a perpetual security with resettable terms and a conversion feature. These are generally denominated in Australian dollars and the target investor base is domestic retail and institutional investors. The documentation required is a short-form prospectus. Reset preference shares were originally qualified as equity on the statement of financial position and regulatory capital; however, under International Accounting Standards they are classified as debt. Reset preference shares are perpetual, with the first reset of terms typically at years three to five. At this point, an investor is able to require conversion into ordinary equity and the issuer is able to reset certain terms, require conversion into ordinary shares or redeem the securities for cash at face value. The coupon on reset preference shares may be cumulative or non-cumulative.

Step-up preference shares

A step-up preference share is a perpetual security with a step-up in coupon and issuer call right generally at years three to five. These are typically denominated in Australian dollars and the target investor base is domestic retail and institutional investors. The documentation required is a short-form prospectus. Step-up preference shares qualify as equity on the statement of financial position and regulatory capital. Ratings agencies generally allocate equity credit to these securities, with a longer-dated instrument—for example, 10 year—given more equity credit than a shorter-dated security—for example, five year. Step-up preference shares are perpetual, with investors unable to require conversion into ordinary equity at the call date. However, the issuer is able to require conversion into ordinary shares or redeem the securities for cash at face value. Furthermore, at the step-up date, the coupon steps up by a predetermined level. The coupon on step-up preference shares is non-cumulative.

CONCEPT 12.5 The impact of capital structure policy on the value of a company

The discussion in the previous sections outlined a number of different forms of debt and equity finance available to a company. The management team thus has a difficult decision to make in choosing between the different forms of debt and equity. However, even before deciding on which form of debt or equity to use, the management team needs to decide between debt and equity financing. Typically, the decision about the form of debt or equity used will be made after evaluating the costs, needs and risks associated with a particular form of finance. This section outlines an important theory that highlights the importance of the debt/equity decision. That is, does it really matter if the management team of a company decides to use debt rather than equity to raise cash or vice versa?

The conditions under which capital structure is irrelevant

Professor Merton Miller and Professor Franco Modigliani (M&M) published a paper in 1958 on the shareholder wealth effects of capital structure policy.[5] Analogously to their paper on dividend policy discussed in the previous chapter, this paper mathematically proved that capital structure policy has no impact on shareholder wealth, given a number of assumptions—the 'capital structure irrelevance' proposition. Again, their work should not be viewed as in fact proving that capital structure policy is irrelevant to shareholder wealth but, instead, as setting out the conditions (assumptions) under which it is irrelevant. These assumptions suggest why capital structure policy may be relevant to shareholder wealth, which is discussed in the next section.

To appreciate the meaning of capital structure irrelevance, consider the following scenario. A company has a debt to equity ratio of 1 and a total market value of $100 million, as follows:

Debt	$50 million
Equity	$50 million

Capital structure irrelevance implies that if the company borrows an additional $10 million and repurchases equity on-market, its value will remain at $100 million even though its debt to equity ratio has increased to 1.5, as follows:

Debt	$60 million
Equity	$40 million

Hence, capital structure irrelevance implies that the wealth of existing shareholders is unaffected because prior to the capital restructuring the shareholders held $50 million in shares and after the restructuring they end up with $10 million in cash and $40 million in shares—capital structure irrelevance. It is important to realise that, for the change in capital structure to have no effect on the market value of the firm, including both equity and net debt, the change must have no effect on the expected free cash flows of the business. That is, if the free cash flows were to change, the market value of the firm *would* change and the irrelevance proposition would break down.

The main assumptions underlying the M&M capital structure irrelevance proof are:

1. Investors can borrow at the same rate as the company.
2. There are no costs of trading shares.
3. All market participants (e.g. management and shareholders) have the same information.
4. There are no personal or corporate taxes.

The Miller and Modigliani proof

These assumptions are sufficient to prove that capital structure policy is irrelevant. While the proof to M&M's dividend irrelevance proposition is somewhat mathematical, their intuition is straightforward and is described using some simple algebra as follows. Imagine that there exist two firms, *A* and *B*, and they are identical in all respects except:

Firm *A* has debt

Firm *B* has no debt

Now, define the following simple terms:

V_D = the value of the firm with debt (firm *A*)

E_D = the value of the equity of the firm with debt (firm *A*)

D_D = the value of the debt of the firm with debt (firm *A*)

V_N = the value of the firm with no debt (firm *B*)

E_N = the value of the equity of the firm with no debt (firm *B*)

You should realise that the following are true by definition:

$$V_D = E_D + D_D \text{ or } E_D = V_D - D_D$$

That is the value of the firm with debt (firm *A*) is equal to the value of its equity and the value of its debt. Similarly:

$$V_N = E_N$$

That is the value of the firm with no debt (firm B) is equal to the value of its equity only.

Now consider an investment of 10% in firm A, which we will call 'strategy I'. The return from owning 10% of firm A is as follows:

$$0.10 \text{ (cash flows – interest)} \tag{12.2}$$

and the cost of purchasing 10% of firm A in order to achieve this return is as follows:

$$0.10\, E_D \text{ or } 0.10\, (V_D - D_D) \tag{12.3}$$

where cash flows are the free cash flows in dollars generated by firm A and interest is the interest expense of firm A.

Now consider an alternative investment strategy, 'strategy II', which involves purchasing firm B as follows:

1. Borrow an amount equal to 10% of the debt of firm A.
2. Buy 10% of the equity of firm B and finance the rest of the acquisition with your own cash.

The return from this investment strategy is as follows:

$$0.10 \text{ cash flows} - 0.10 \text{ interest or } 0.10 \text{ (cash flows – interest)} \tag{12.4}$$

The reasoning behind Equation 12.4 is as follows. First, if you own 10% of firm B you will be entitled to 10% of its cash flows. Since firm B is the same as firm A in all respects except capital structure, its free cash flow must be the same and, hence, the cash flow in Equation 12.3 which relates to firm A must be the same as the cash flow in Equation 12.4 which relates to firm B. Second, since assumption 1, provided earlier, underlying the M&M proof implies that the company and the investor borrow at the same rate, then the investor who has borrowed an amount equal to 10% of the debt of firm A must face the equivalent of 10% of the interest expense (which is equal to interest) of firm A on their own borrowings.

The dollar cost of the investment strategy (strategy II) is as follows:

$$0.10\, V_N - 0.10\, D_D \tag{12.5}$$

The first term in Equation 12.5 reflects that the investment strategy involves the purchase of 10% of the value of firm B. However, your actual cash outlay is reduced by the amount borrowed $(0.10\, D_D)$, which is the second term in Equation 12.5.

It has been shown that investment strategy II will yield a return (Equation 12.4) that is identical to the return on investment strategy I (Equation 12.2). Since two assets that have the same free cash flows must have the same value, the cost of purchasing strategy II must be equal to the cost of purchasing strategy I (i.e. Equation 12.5 must be equal to Equation 12.3):

$$0.10\, (V_D - D_D) = 0.10\, V_N - 0.10\, D_D$$

By simplifying this expression, for this to be true the following must also be true:

$$V_D = V_N$$

That is the value of the firm with debt must be equal to the value of the firm with no debt. The proof developed by M&M effectively boils down to the following: that individual investors can create their own 'home-made' debt risk by borrowing and investing in companies with no debt to replicate the returns on an investment in a leveraged company. Therefore, this implies that corporate debt policy does not matter to a shareholder, which in turn implies that the capital structure decision of a company is irrelevant. As in the previous chapter, again it needs to be noted that a number of very significant and unrealistic assumptions are necessary in order for the proof to work. The remainder of this chapter briefly considers the implications of relaxing these assumptions somewhat.

Practitioner's POV

How much should a company borrow? Theory aside, analysts will usually assess whether a company is under- or over-geared through a comparison with other companies in the same industry. It is not unusual for analysts who find that a company they are following is under-geared on this basis to suggest the possibility of that company proceeding with a suitable acquisition or undertaking an active capital management policy and returning cash to shareholders.

Why capital structure policy is relevant

The impact of relaxing the assumptions underlying the M&M theory is discussed by a very large body of academic literature and is hotly debated and researched to this day. It is beyond the scope of this book to discuss at length all the issues. Instead, the interested reader should refer to the further reading section at the end of the chapter. This section intuitively presents the key ideas.

One of the key assumptions underlying the M&M theory—that individual investors can borrow at the same rate as companies—is unlikely to be true. Companies should be able to borrow at much lower interest rates than individuals, for a number of reasons. Because companies generally seek large amounts of capital from banks, they will (1) be able to create significant economies of scale in borrowing cash and (2) have significant bargaining power. Combined with their greater creditworthiness, this means that it is likely that they will be able to negotiate significantly lower interest rates than individuals. This implies, for example, that such companies should lean towards a higher leverage ratio because they can borrow more effectively than individual investors in generating a leveraged investment.

Firms that borrow excessively face the possibility of 'financial distress' or, ultimately, liquidation. When in liquidation, the assets of a company are sold, the creditors of the firm are paid amounts owing to the extent available and the residual cash (if any) is paid out to equity holders. Firms that have high leverage ratios have a higher probability of experiencing financial distress because they have a fixed interest expense to pay regardless of market conditions (and the cash flows they generate). For example, firms that have high leverage may be unable to pay their interest expense during a small economic downturn that causes their earnings before interest to be lower than their interest expense or otherwise breach the financial or operating covenants associated with their debt. Such firms face the very real possibility of liquidation. Although in theory the assets of such companies should be liquidated at their market value and hence the residual cash flow paid to equity holders in a liquidation is a fair market value, this is unlikely to be the case. It is well known that in forced sales of assets, the assets are typically sold at substantial discounts to their market value. Second, there are other costs associated with bankruptcy and liquidation, including legal costs and the costs of hiring a liquidator. Such costs will be priced into the value of equity and lower its value. The upshot of this reasoning is that companies with high leverage, because of the risk of liquidation costs, may have a lower market value.

Another key assumption underlying the M&M theory is that all market participants have the same information. The previous chapter identified that information asymmetry exists between the management (and directors) of a company and its shareholders. That is, the management of a company have more information about the value of the company than its shareholders do. This idea is also relevant to explaining why capital structure is useful and is implicit in a theory that has become known as the 'pecking order theory'.[6] The pecking order theory can be explained as follows. The management of a company will not recommend issuing shares when they know that they are underpriced in the market (because they would be giving away corporate value and diluting existing shareholders). Hence, the management of a company will recommend issuing shares only when they are overpriced. However, the announcement of a share issue will immediately signal this to the market, cause its share price to fall and eliminate any advantage from issuing equity. As a result, the management of a company whose share price is either undervalued or overvalued are unlikely to use an equity issue to raise capital. This implies that there is a 'pecking order' in financing choice, with debt preferred to equity.

The final major assumption in the M&M theory is that there are no personal or corporate taxes. This is a difficult issue. Under a *classical tax* system, and focusing on corporate tax alone, it is typically argued that debt should be preferred to equity, because it is tax deductible at the corporate level and creates a tax shield which increases the total value of the firm (or the present value of the income stream flowing to debt holders and equity holders). This argument becomes less clear when *personal taxes* are included and especially in a dividend imputation environment. There would appear to be little impact on the value of the firm as a whole from issuing more debt than equity under a dividend imputation environment. The reason for this is that there is less benefit to paying a lower corporate tax bill under an imputation tax system because the total tax paid (personal plus corporate) on corporate income distributed as dividends is ultimately levied at an investor's personal tax rate. The imputation system of tax appears to equalise the total corporate and personal tax paid where investors can borrow at the same rate as a company. Therefore, tax considerations appear to be less relevant under the current imputation system of tax in Australia. But the argument is not perfect. For example, companies are not always able to distribute their imputation credits and investors are not always able to use them to their full extent.

CONCEPT CHECK

14. Is capital structure relevant in a world without taxes?

For the answers, go to MyFinanceLab

Student Learning Centre

My Finance Lab ■ To test your mastery of the content covered in this chapter and to create your own personalised study plan, go to MyFinanceLab: www.pearson.com.au/myfinancelab

CONCEPT CHECKLIST

In this chapter the following concepts associated with capital structure policy were discussed:

➤ The nature of capital structure policy
➤ The nature of equity and equity raising methods, including:
  - initial public offerings
  - rights issues
  - placements
➤ The main sources of long-term debt finance, including:
  - unsecured notes
  - debentures
  - financial leases
  - term loans and mortgages
➤ The main sources of hybrid finance, including:
  - convertible bonds
  - reset preference shares
  - step-up preference shares
➤ The intuition and assumptions underlying the Miller and Modigliani capital structure irrelevance proposition
➤ The effect on the Miller and Modigliani capital structure irrelevance proposition of relaxing the major assumptions

SELF-TEST QUESTIONS

Oscars Ltd has four million shares on issue and wishes to raise $4 million by a 1 for 4 rights issue.

(a) What is the theoretical value of one right if the share price immediately after the announcement (cum-rights) is $5?

(b) What is the theoretical ex-rights price?

(c) Does an investor gain through a rights issue?

Self-test answer

(a) The theoretical value of a right can be calculated as follows:

$$R = \frac{N(M - S)}{N + 1} = \frac{4(\$5 - \$4)}{4 + 1} = \$\frac{4}{5} = \$0.80$$

where N is the number of shares in a parcel of shares—that is, in a 1 for 4, $N = 4$, and M = cum-rights price and S = subscription price.

(b) The theoretical ex-rights price can be calculated as follows:

$$X = \frac{N M + S}{N + 1} = \frac{4(\$5) + \$4}{4 + 1} = \frac{\$24}{5} = \$4.80$$

(c) Generally, an investor should neither gain nor lose through a rights issue. However, announcement of a rights issue may be associated with share price changes, because of the information investors read into the announcement. For example, the share price may increase because investors believe that the project(s) being financed by the issue has a positive net present value (NPV) or the share price may fall because investors interpret the company's need for the funds as an indication of lower net cash flows.

DISCUSSION QUESTIONS

1. A company wants to raise $150 million by issuing shares over the next 12 months. Discuss the different methods available to the company for raising equity finance. Be sure to identify the possible risks and costs.

2. What are the advantages of a jumbo placement over a traditional rights issue?

3. What is the difference between a jumbo placement and an AREO?

4. What is the difference between an AREO, SAREO and a PAITREO?

5. What is the difference between an operating lease and a finance lease?

6. Why would a company choose to issue a hybrid capital instrument instead of a debt or equity instrument?

7. A large and well-known listed company wants to raise $200 million next month, which it wishes to apply to financing a project for a 36-month period. Identify the different options available to it and discuss the cheapest method.

8. Outline Miller and Modigliani's (M&M's) proof that capital structure is irrelevant to company value.

9. Outline the arguments against M&M's capital structure irrelevance proposition.

10. M&M's finding of capital structure irrelevance under a set of restrictive assumptions is of no importance to real-world finance, since most of these assumptions are violated in practice. Discuss.

11. Identify the costs of financial distress and discuss their impact on capital structure decisions.

12. Describe the potential impact of the global uncertainty regarding both economic outlook and credit markets on a corporate borrower.

13. Critically evaluate the following statements relating to corporate capital structure.

   (a) 'Australian companies should use as much debt as possible, for two reasons. First, debt is cheaper than equity capital, and, second, it is also tax deductible.'

   (b) 'The problem with M&M's capital structure analysis is that it totally ignores the fact that as you borrow more you have to pay higher rates of interest.'

   (c) 'The dividend imputation system has eliminated the advantages of debt financing.'

14. What is the fundamental proposition of M&M pertaining to a firm's capital structure in a world without taxes (and other frictions) and with perfect capital markets? Provide a brief intuitive explanation for the M&M proposition.

15. Indicate what is wrong with the following arguments.

   (a) 'As the firm borrows more and debt becomes risky, both shareholders and bondholders demand higher rates of return. Thus, by reducing the debt ratio we reduce the cost of debt and the cost of equity, making everybody better off.'

   (b) 'Moderate borrowing doesn't significantly affect the probability of financial distress or bankruptcy. Consequently, moderate borrowing won't increase the expected rate of return demanded by shareholders.'

PRACTICAL QUESTIONS

BASIC

1. The following information is available concerning XYZ Ltd.

Shares on issue	1 000 000
Shareholders' funds	$10 million
Debt on issue: perpetuity with interest rate of 5% p.a. and face value	$20 million
Net operating income	$5 million
Share price	$15
Market interest rate	10% p.a.

   (a) Calculate the market value of XYZ's outstanding debt.

   (b) What is the market value of XYZ's equity?

   (c) Calculate the debt to equity ratio.

INTERMEDIATE

2. Suppose that XYZ Ltd of Question 1 is subject to a company tax rate of 30%. There are no personal taxes and interest on debt is deducted from company income before company taxes are assessed. If XYZ Ltd were to adopt a capital structure that involved all equity and no debt, what would be the effect on its overall market value and capitalisation rate?

BASIC

3. Raising Ltd has just announced a 3 for 7 rights issue at $6 per share. If its share price is currently $7, what will be its theoretical ex-rights price?

4. On 11 April 2011, Leighton Holdings Limited announced a 1 for 9 pro-rata entitlement issue at $22.50 per new share. Calculate the theoretical ex-rights price for Leighton if the share price prior to announcement was $28.94 and the discount to the pre-announcement share price that the rights shares were issued at.

INTERMEDIATE

5. Revisit the above question, assuming that existing Leighton shares were trading cum dividend but that the new shares to be issued under the entitlement offer were not entitled to participate in the dividend of 60 cents per share.

INTERMEDIATE

6. In July 2011, each $100 ABC Ltd convertible preference share (CPS) converts into fully paid ordinary ABC Ltd shares at a 10% discount to the then market price of ABC Ltd ordinary shares. Complete the table below assuming the share prices in the table.

INTERMEDIATE

Ordinary share price	Ordinary share price less 10%	Number of ordinary shares per CPS on conversion	Value of ordinary shares per CPS
10.00			
11.00			
12.00			
13.00			
14.00			
15.00			

7. Tech Ltd operates an information technology business and needs 250 new computers which cost $1000 per unit. It is expected that the computers will have an eight-year life in total and zero scrap value. The computer equipment can be depreciated for tax purposes at a rate of 20% p.a. until fully depreciated. A computer leasing company offers a non-cancellable lease agreement for the computers requiring payment of $40 000 per year for the life of the computers. If Tech Ltd can borrow at a rate of 5%, is it better off leasing the computers or borrowing and buying them?

INTERMEDIATE

8. Modigliani Corporation and Miller Ltd are two remarkably similar companies. Each has the same asset base and both face identical future investment opportunities. Indeed, the only discernible difference between the two is that Miller Ltd is financed completely by equity capital, whereas Modigliani Corporation has some $500 000 of debt in its capital structure (at $k_d = 8\%$). The companies are also fortunate in that they operate in perfect capital markets, with no costs or taxes, in which all market participants have equal information access.

INTERMEDIATE

The earnings of the companies, and other relevant market information, are as follows.

	Miller	Modigliani
Net operating income	$100 000	$100 000
Interest on debt	–	40 000
Earnings available to shareholders	$100 000	$60 000
Equity cost of capital	0.10	0.10
Market value of equity	$1 000 000	$600 000
Market value of debt	–	500 000
Total value of firm	$1 000 000	$1 100 000
Implied cost of capital	0.10	0.091

(a) Describe how you would act to realise a risk-free profit if you held 5% of the shares in Modigliani Corporation and the situation outlined above was continuing. State the amount of profit you could make.

(b) Assuming that arbitrage activities occurred such that the market values of these companies became equal, what is Modigliani's correct cost of capital (k_o)?

(c) Why does k_o remain the same under the M&M scenario, when debt is clearly cheaper than equity and should therefore lower the overall cost of capital when added to a firm's capital structure?

INTERMEDIATE

9. Two firms, Unlevered Ltd and Levered Ltd, are identical in every respect apart from their capital structure. Both will earn $300 million if the market swings upwards and $100 million in a downward swing. There is an even chance of the market swinging upwards or downwards. Unlevered Ltd has no debt and its shares are valued at $1000. Levered Ltd has issued $800 million of its debt at an interest rate of 10% and, hence, $80 million of its income is paid out as interest. Assume that investors can borrow and lend at the same rate as the company.

(a) What is the value of Levered Ltd's shares?

(b) Suppose that you invest $40 million in Unlevered Ltd shares. Is there an alternative investment in Levered Ltd that would generate the same payoff? What is the expected payoff from such a strategy?

(c) Now suppose that you invest $40 million in Levered Ltd shares. Design an alternative strategy with identical payoffs.

INTERMEDIATE

10. Two companies, identical in every respect except capital structure, have a market value of $150 million. One company has debt and the other is all-equity financed. The company with debt has a leverage ratio of 1 and faces a debt cost of capital of 7%. The free cash flows generated by the companies are $15 million p.a. An investor with $1 million to invest desires to hold a portfolio with a leverage ratio of 1. If the assumptions underlying the M&M irrelevance proposition hold, which of the companies is the investor better off buying? Demonstrate.

INTERMEDIATE

11. Your firm has to raise new capital to finance a new product. You need to make a recommendation about whether to issue equity or bonds. The bond market is relatively good at the moment and you can probably issue the $100 million in bonds at 8% to raise the amount you need. Alternatively, you

could issue 50 million new shares and raise the capital in that way. The new project is worth doing to ensure you retain your market share, but it will give you a return on capital of only 12%. Your shareholders expect annual dividends of 15%. If you do not maintain those dividends, you can kiss goodbye to the holiday house at Palm Beach, the BMW and all your other essentials. What do you do?

12. The following information is available concerning ABC Ltd:

Ordinary shares on issue	1 500 000
Preference shares on issue: floating rate distribution of at least 7.85% p.a. and face value of $100	10 000
Debt on issue: perpetuity with interest rate of 5.5% p.a. and face value	$25 000 000
Ordinary share price	$18
Preference share price	$101
Market interest rate	8% p.a.

(a) Calculate the market value of ABC Ltd's outstanding debt.

(b) Calculate the market value of ABC Ltd's equity capital.

(c) Calculate the market value of ABC Ltd's hybrid capital.

(d) If ABC Ltd has a bank covenant which dictates that leverage should be no greater than 60%, show whether ABC Ltd is in breach assuming the hybrid security receives a 100% equity statement of financial position classification and using both market value and book value of debt.

(e) Repeat (d) assuming the hybrid security receives a 100% debt statement of financial position classification.

13. A boutique advisory firm is advising some entrepreneurs who are looking to establish StartUp Ltd. Their business plan illustrates that StartUp Ltd requires $50 million to purchase initial buildings and plant and equipment. The advisory firm is aware that the business that will be undertaken by StartUp Ltd has a given risk and the required return on that level of risk for an all-equity firm is 12%.

The expected annual cash flow of StartUp Ltd is $10 million p.a. in perpetuity. This cash flow will be paid out each year to the suppliers of capital. The advisory firm is considering three different financing scenarios.

Scenario 1: All equity (5 000 000 shares selling at $10 each).

Scenario 2: $25 million of debt capital with a return of 6% p.a. and $25 million of equity capital (2 500 000 shares at $10 each).

Scenario 3: $35 million of debt capital with a return of 6% p.a. and $15 million of equity capital (1 500 000 shares at $10 each).

Provide the advisory firm with some calculations to show that the returns to equity holders, assuming no tax, rise as gearing increases so as to leave the weighted average cost of capital (WACC) and total value of the company constant.

14. Revisit Example 12.1 on page 377. QR National shares closed trading at $2.70 on the first day of normal trading (7 December 2010). If an institutional shareholder was able to purchase QRN shares on issue and then sell them on the ASX by the close of trade on the first day of normal trading, what

return would they earn over and above the return on the All Ordinaries Index if it stood at 4717.7 on 19 November 2010 and 4781.6 on 7 December 2010?

CHALLENGING

15. John Black is planning to form a company. He has determined that $10 million will be required as an initial capital investment. Several financial backers have indicated that they would be willing to buy the debentures of the new company or personally lend John the capital he needs. John has delineated the following alternative financing plans.

    • Form the company with one million shares of $10 ordinary shares, borrowing the entire $10 million from his associates on a personal basis (paying 6% interest on his note).

    • Form the company with 500 000 shares of $10 ordinary shares, borrowing $5 million from his associates on a personal basis (6% note). Sell $5 million worth of 6% debentures to his associates.

    • Form the company with 250 000 shares of $10 ordinary shares, borrowing $2.5 million from his associates on a personal basis (6% note). Sell $7.5 million worth of 6% debentures to his associates.

    (a) Assuming no corporate or personal taxes, which of the three alternatives should John select if the firm is expected to earn $1 million p.a. before the payment of interest? Assume that all of the net earnings are paid out in dividends. Refer to the M&M thesis. Answer without making any calculations.

    (b) Confirm your answer with calculations. (Hint: Construct a *simple* statement of financial position and a *simple* profit and loss account.)

CHALLENGING

16. CapitalManagement Ltd announced a debt issue for $100 million, which would be used for a share buy-back on 30 September 2011. Share prices and other data for CapitalManagement Ltd are as follows.

	Price	Market index
28 September	1.50	2982
29 September	1.52	2986
30 September	1.58	2985
1 October	1.57	2987

The beta of CapitalManagement Ltd is 1.15 and the 13-week Treasury-note yield over the period was 8%.

(a) Calculate the daily abnormal returns using the capital asset pricing model (CAPM) around the time of CapitalManagement Ltd's announcement.

(b) Discuss the implications of the finding for capital structure irrelevance.

WebEx

Using the most recent annual report for Wesfarmers lodged on Wesfarmers' website calculate Wesfarmers' book leverage.

CASE STUDY

On 15 March 2011, Origin Energy announced an A$2.3 billion accelerated renounceable entitlement offer to refinance part of the debt used to fund the $3.26 billion acquisition of the Integral Energy and Country Energy retail businesses.

Offer details

Offer structure:	Pro-rata accelerated institutional, tradeable retail entitlement offer (PAITREO)
Offer size:	A$2.3 billion
Offer price:	A$13.00 per new share
Entitlement ratio:	1 new share for every 5 existing shares held
Closing price prior to announcement:	A$15.66 per new share
Number of existing shares:	855.2 million

Institutional entitlement offer

* Approximately 86.9 million new shares were issued under the Institutional Entitlement Offer and associated book build.
* The institutional book build clearing price was $15.00 per share.

Retail entitlement offer

* The Retail Entitlement Offer and associated book build raised a further $1.17 billion through the issue of approximately 90 million new shares.
* The retail book build clearing price was $15.80.

Rationale for transaction and use of proceeds

* The purpose of the entitlement offer was to refinance part of the debt used to fund the $3.26 billion acquisition of the Integral Energy and Country Energy retail businesses and the Eraring GenTrader arrangements, which completed on 1 March 2011, and to strengthen Origin's balance sheet for investment in other growth opportunities.
* The transaction was stated to be 'expected to be materially accretive to underlying earnings per share'.

Source: Company announcements and IRESS.

CASE STUDY QUESTIONS

1. Why would Origin undertake a PAITREO rather than
    (a) a traditional rights issue
    (b) a jumbo placement?

2. Calculate the number of new shares that will be issued.

3. Calculate the theoretical ex-rights price or TERP.

4. Calculate the discount to TERP of the offer price.

5. Calculate the value of each entitlement renounced (i.e. each new share not taken up) by institutional and retail shareholders who did not take up all of their entitlements.

6. Why did Origin want to raise equity?

7. Using the following data calculate Origin's gearing.

	31 Dec 10	Acquisition	Equity raising	Pro forma
Cash + equivalents	695			695
Current debt	362	1 800	−1 800	362
Non-current debt	3 164	1 539	−452	4 251
Total equity	10 968	−31	2 252	13 189

8. Why would existing holders want to 'follow their money' (take up their entitlement)?

9. Why would new investors want to purchase Origin shares through the PAITREO structure (either institutional or retail renounced entitlements)?

FURTHER READING

The original article on capital structure policy by Professor Merton Miller and Professor Franco Modigliani is still worth a read:

- Miller, M. H. and Modigliani, F. (1958), 'The cost of capital, corporation finance and the theory of investment', *American Economic Review*, vol. 48, 261–97.

For a relatively brief discussion of the very large body of literature that deals with why capital structure theory is relevant see:

- Copeland, T. E. and Weston, J. F. (1992), *Financial Theory and Corporate Policy*, Addison-Wesley Publishing Company, Melbourne, Chapter 14.

For another comprehensive discussion of capital structure see:

- Berk, J. and DeMarzo, P. (2007), *Corporate Finance, P & C Business*, Pearson Education, Upper Saddle River, New Jersey.

For a fairly comprehensive (although slightly out-of-date) account of the processes and mechanisms by which equity and debt are issued see:

- Bruce, R., McKern, B., Pollard, I. and Scully, M. (1997*), Handbook of Australian Corporate Finance*, Butterworths, Sydney.

NOTES

1. Company releases, CapitalIQ and IRESS.
2. *Survey of Sharemarket Floats,* February 2008, PriceWaterhouseCoopers.
3. Company releases, CapitalIQ and IRESS.
4. Under International Accounting Standards, the value of the debt obligation under financial leases needs to be calculated and appears as a liability in the financial statements of a company. IAS 17 requires companies to calculate the present value of financial lease payments and report this value as a liability in the statement of financial position. Prior to 1986, in Australia there was no such requirement, so financial leases were constructed by certain companies to avoid reporting a liability in their financial statements—so-called 'off-balance-sheet finance'.
5. M. H. Miller and F. Modigliani (1958), 'The cost of capital, corporation finance and the theory of investment', *American Economic Review,* vol. 48, 261–97.
6. See S. C. Myers (1984), 'The capital structure puzzle', *Journal of Finance,* vol. 39, 575–92.

13

Risk management

CHAPTER PREVIEW

This chapter deals with the management of *corporate risk*, and relies on a number of the concepts introduced in previous chapters. The main focus is on the identification of risks faced by an Australian company and the techniques that its financial manager might use to manage these risks.

KEY CONCEPTS

CONCEPT 13.1　What is corporate risk?

A basic idea, identified in Chapter 6, is that risk is present whenever there is uncertainty in relation to future outcomes. Since companies operate in an uncertain world, their operations are subject to risk from many sources. Two broad categories of corporate risk are generally recognised: business risk and financial risk.

Business risk can be thought of as the risk inherent in a company's operations. For example, the business risk of a gold-mining company includes the risk that is associated with gold-mining operations, such as determining prospective sites to mine, drilling mines, extracting the gold and finding a market for it. Business risk arises from a number of sources. These include the particular industry in which the company operates, the nature of the company's asset base, the number and quality of competitors in its industry, the susceptibility of the company's assets to technological change, the foreign exchange rate, the laws and regulations for companies with international transactions and so on.

Financial risk, on the other hand, is a function of a company's degree of leverage, and arises from the manner in which it is financed. As identified in the previous chapter, different sources of funds have different maturity dates, ranging from 'at call' to effectively infinite. The main source of financial risk is corporate debt and interest rate volatility. The possibility of increased interest rates related to debt charged at a variable or 'floating' interest rate, under which borrowers are subject to fluctuations in interest rates, creates financial risk. In this case, risk arises as a result of the obligation to make increased interest payments that are to be funded from uncertain future cash flows.

It is important to understand that the existence of risk is not in itself a problem and concern for financial managers. Rather, managers are more concerned with the *degree* to which a company is *exposed* to risk. A company's exposure to risk can be defined as the loss in economic value that can occur as a result of uncertain future outcomes.

Of all the risks faced by companies, the two faced by most Australian companies are **interest rate risk** and **foreign exchange risk**. Specifically, fluctuations in these factors can have a large impact on the cash flows of Australian companies, given the huge volume of banking/money market transactions (interest rate sensitive) and import/export transactions (exchange rate sensitive) that are undertaken each year. When a company has borrowings that are subject to a floating rate of interest, its net cash flows (and hence market value) will fall if interest rates increase. This decrease in value arises because an increase in interest rates results in a higher interest expense. Similarly, exchange rate fluctuations can lead to a reduction in cash flows and therefore a company's value.

Accordingly, much of the effort in managing corporate risk is devoted to the quantification of exposure, and the implementation of techniques for managing exposure. Figures 13.1 and 13.2

Interest rate risk
The variability in a bond's value (risk) caused by changing interest rates.

Foreign exchange risk
The risk that expenses and revenues which are contracted in foreign currency will vary in local currency terms when they are eventually paid and converted to local currency.

provide an illustration of the manner in which interest rates and exchange rates fluctuated over the past thirty-five years and two decades respectively.

Figure 13.1 charts short-term interest rates (represented by the yield on 90-day bank bills) on a monthly basis from 30 June 1976 to 30 June 2011. It is clear that interest rates were volatile, ranging from a high of 22% on 8 April 1982 to a low of 3% on 19 March 2009. However, in the last decade, the range between high and low interest rates was less than 2% except for financial year 2009 when the range was 4.79%. This has implications for how managers might approach managing interest rate risk, and is discussed later.

To clarify the effect of interest rate fluctuations, consider the impact on a company with net borrowings of $100 million. Assuming that these net borrowings are subject to a variable interest rate, if market interest rates increased by 1%, the company's cash flows would decrease by $1 million (i.e. $0.01 \times \$100m$).

Figure 13.2 charts the Australian dollar against the US dollar (i.e. the number of US dollars that can be bought for one Australian dollar) over the period 30 June 1991 to 30 June 2011. It illustrates that the Australian dollar has also been volatile over the years, ranging from a low of 48.33 US cents to one Australian dollar to a high of 110.6 US cents.

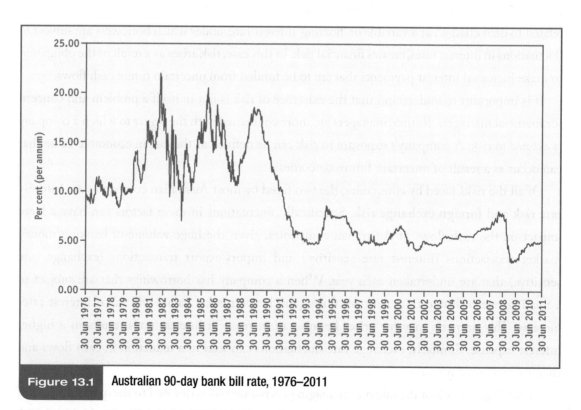

Figure 13.1   Australian 90-day bank bill rate, 1976–2011

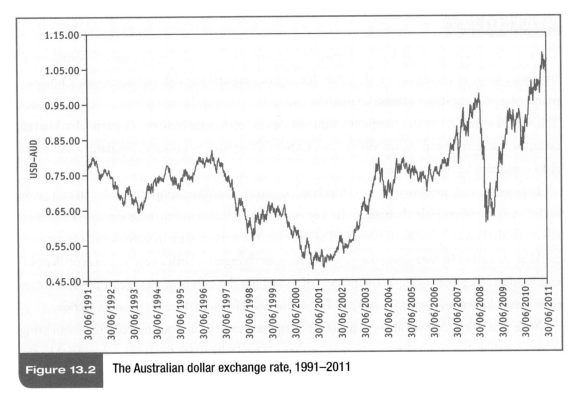

Figure 13.2   The Australian dollar exchange rate, 1991–2011

To illustrate the effect of exchange rate fluctuations, consider their impact on a gold-mining company that acquires some of its gold from the USA (in US dollars) from a US gold producer. Assume that it has agreed to purchase, in two months, 50 000 ounces of gold at USD1800 per ounce, and the exchange rate is currently AUD1 = USD1.02. This equates to a purchase price of AUD88.235 million (i.e. $1800/1.02 × 50 000). If the Australian dollar depreciated by one US cent (to USD1.01) in the two months, the purchase price would become AUD89.109 million. This represents an 'economic' loss (i.e. an additional payment) of almost $874 000 arising simply as a result of the purchase price being set in US dollars and the exchange rate fluctuating by one cent.

CONCEPT CHECK

1. What is risk?
2. Is risk a problem per se?
3. What are the two main types of risk faced by most Australian companies?

For the answers, go to MyFinanceLab

CONCEPT 13.2   How is risk managed?

The key aim of corporate risk management is *measurement* of a company's specific exposure to risk and *control* of its impact on its value. Ideally, in undertaking risk management, a financial manager would construct a financial model of the company and the markets in which it operates. This model would relate the company's value to various economic factors—in particular, interest rates, exchange rates and commodity prices. Other factors such as political, regulatory and credit risks could also be incorporated.

In practice, such models are very difficult to construct. However, simple models can still prove useful. A range of possible changes in the key economic factors could then be simulated and their effects on the company's value estimated. For example, the net exposure to short-term interest rates could be quantified by measuring the impact of forecast changes on both assets (e.g. cash on deposit) and liabilities (e.g. borrowings). The process of modelling the effects of a range of possible future outcomes is known as *sensitivity analysis*. This is discussed in more detail in the next section.

Note that risk as defined above—exposure to interest rate or currency movements—can bring gains as well as losses. However, risk management is typically more focused on potential losses, because such fluctuations can have a severe impact on corporate cash flows. In the extreme, the losses that could arise might ultimately result in the failure of a company. For this reason, the minimisation of a company's exposure to fluctuations in these economic factors may be essential to its long-term survival. Accordingly, it is important to identify a 'critical level' of price fluctuations at which the ongoing viability of the company would be seriously diminished. This 'critical level' will, of course, vary across companies. In general, however, a company's viability is considered to be diminished when losses are being realised, retrenchments become necessary, or where the company is unable to pay its debts as and when they fall due.

CONCEPT CHECK

4. What is risk management?
5. Why is it important to manage risk?

For the answers, go to MyFinanceLab

CONCEPT 13.3   Quantifying risk exposure

Exposure clock
A chart that illustrates the impact on the cash flows of a company from a change in a risk factor.

Sensitivity analysis can be used to assess a company's exposure to risk factors and the variability of its estimated cash flows. The critical level of fluctuation in risk factors can then be identified, and the likelihood of this level being reached can be estimated with reference to the estimated volatility of these factors. There are alternative methods of presenting the results of sensitivity analysis. One such method is a 'payoff diagram', which is also sometimes called an **exposure clock**.

Figure 13.3 is a payoff diagram for a gold-mining company's exposure to gold prices. The horizontal axis represents the range of possible gold prices over, say, the next 12 months, while the vertical axis represents the (dollar value) change in cash flows associated with the different gold prices. Assume the company's current stock of gold available for export is approximately 250 000 ounces. The financial manager can estimate the net impact of possible gold price changes. In this way, the manager can assess the extent of exposure to gold price fluctuations.

The starting point on Figure 13.3 (at the origin) is the current market price of gold, assumed to be $1290 per ounce for the purposes of the illustration. As an exporter, the impact of an increase in the market price of gold on the gold-mining company's cash flows is positive, as shown by the diagonal line. The reverse applies to gold price decreases. For example, if the price of gold were to fall to $1270 per ounce, the diagram shows that a loss (reduced cash flows) of $5 million would occur. It is this latter possibility—reduced cash flows if the gold price falls—that the manager is most concerned with and seeks to protect against by using risk management techniques.

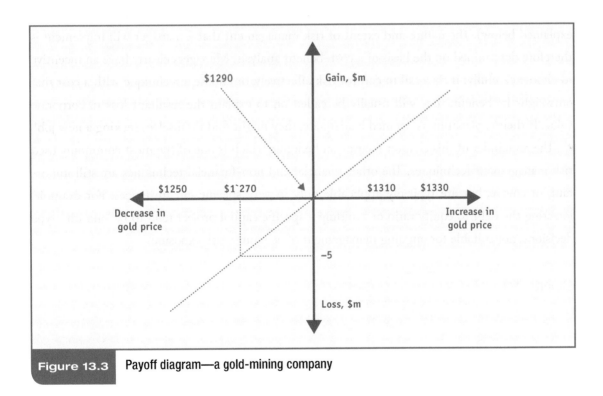

Figure 13.3   **Payoff diagram—a gold-mining company**

CONCEPT CHECK

6.   What is sensitivity analysis in a risk management context?

For the answers, go to MyFinanceLab

CONCEPT 13.4   Risk management techniques

Once the level of exposure to possible outcomes is determined, the next task is to manage that exposure. That is, the financial manager will implement particular risk management techniques to eliminate, or minimise as far as possible, the potential loss in corporate value from risk exposure. Risk management techniques that are available to the manager can be classified as either *financial* or *real*. Financial techniques include implementing so-called 'hedging' transactions (defined below), the purchase of insurance, and changing (lowering) the company's degree of leverage (i.e. debt reduction). Non-financial, or real, risk management techniques include avoiding or abandoning capital projects that carry high risk, or adopting less risky production processes.

One way of thinking about corporate risk management is that it is primarily concerned with the sharing of risk between a company and other parties. That is, the process of risk management does not involve diversification of risk in the context of portfolio theory (outlined in Chapter 6). Similarly, it does not reduce total risk—the risk is just shifted to another party. Accordingly, in one way or another, the company will bear a cost to have another party share the risk (this is explained below). The nature and extent of risk management that a manager will implement is therefore determined on the basis of a cost–benefit analysis. Managers clearly have an incentive to choose carefully: if they fail to control risk effectively, or choose a technique with a cost that outweighs its benefit, they will usually be called on to explain the resultant loss in corporate value. If their explanation is deemed inadequate, they might find themselves seeking a new job!

The remainder of this chapter focuses on hedging, which is one of the most commonly used risk management techniques. The other financial and non-financial techniques are still important, of course, but are typically applicable only in very specific circumstances. For example, lowering the debt to equity ratio or avoiding a specific capital project tend to be 'one-off'-type decisions, not suitable for ongoing management of economic risk exposure.

CONCEPT CHECK

7. What risk management techniques are available to a company?

For the answers, go to MyFinanceLab

CONCEPT 13.5   Risk management through hedging

The New Palgrave Dictionary of Money and Finance defines hedging as 'the purchasing of an asset or portfolio in order to insure against wealth fluctuations from other sources'.[1] In practice, the assets that companies purchase to hedge exposures are usually derivative securities, the most commonly used being forwards, futures, options and swaps. These are discussed in more detail in the next section.[2]

FINANCE EXTRA!

Sensible risk management is not an optional extra, in good times or bad

OIL shocks, credit crises, company collapses, possible US recessions—we are living in risky times, right? The truth is actually a little more prosaic: it has always been this risky.

Looking at economic activity through the years one can see the cyclical nature of shocks—be it the oil crisis of the 1970s, the 1987 stock market crash, the Asian financial crisis, the dotcom bust or the recent sub-prime problems.

Time intervals may vary, but the risks of economic shocks are always there.

Our situation in Australia is fairly unusual. Although the shocks are occurring internationally, we have been largely unaffected by the worst of these problems. However, our long stretch of robust economic activity and our healthy looking pipeline (driven by resources and the growth of China), does not mean that the spectre of risk is not real.

The recent global turmoil should remind us that effective risk management is not a luxury but a strategic necessity for all companies, in good times and in bad.

It is often the lament of businesses caught in a crisis (and this has been the case in the Australian companies that have recently faltered) that the situation was a 'perfect storm'. That is, all that could possibly go wrong did so—and all at the same time. This rings a bit hollow, as perfect storms can (and should) be planned for.

In many non-financial companies, risk management, only now beginning to emerge as a corporate priority, can help consumer goods companies think about matters such as whether they can pass along commodity price volatility or lock in long-term costs, assist energy companies in making climate change-related investments, or guide pharmaceutical companies on their research and development pipeline and which drugs they should licence.

Non-financial corporations often develop risk registers to identify and assess key risks, but few adequately value their risks based on quantitative models or traded risk markets. Globally, more than 80 percent of industrial corporations hedge using derivatives, but few go beyond generic currency and interest rate trades made by their treasury departments.

This must move beyond managers merely adding an arbitrary 2 percent to the cost of capital equation for 'risk', into more detailed evaluation of what the actual risks are, how they are triggered and how the impacts can be managed.

In the absence of strong risk processes, most non-financial companies gravitate towards one or two counterproductive and costly extremes. At one end are companies that overspend their risk capacity, leaving themselves vulnerable to internal and external shocks. When unexpected problems occur and credit sources dry up, they must slash important cash outflows.

At the opposite (and more common) end are

companies that over-insure by holding excess risk capacity, often driven by the desire to maintain a high credit rating.

These companies maintain capital structures with little or no debt and excess cash, a costly strategy that can raise the company's cost of capital by as much as 100 basis points and lower its value as materials or finished stock.

Boeing is an example of how this mindset can be changed with bottom-line benefits. With the goal of being the largest aircraft player, it maintained a huge amount of excess manufacturing capacity in case it had to manage a large order. Boeing subsequently kept less spare capacity, freeing up fixed and working capital and became much more profitable.

We have also found that companies lacking strong risk processes often struggle to make decisions informed by risk. At the core of many critical operational, financial, strategic and marketing choices lie risk-and-return trade-offs. Should we: manufacture or outsource, focus or diversify our supplier base, sell spot or contract, pursue this particular merger and acquisition deal?

These issues are not new, nor do they go away in good times. If companies put the correct controls in place, they can benefit from risk rather than merely protect themselves from it. Australian companies that have been successful here have understood their true economic exposures, stress-testing their business model for a variety of shocks and have been flexible enough to modify or reverse their strategy. As the saying goes: 'Make money while you sleep', rather than lying awake worrying whether an obscure event will wipe out your business.

Source: Adam Lewis, *The Australian*, 30 May 2008.

The payoff diagram in Figure 13.4 illustrates how hedging can be used to eliminate risk exposure, again using the example of the impact of gold price fluctuations on a gold-mining company's cash flows.

Specific transactions that could provide the payoff represented by the middle diagram (part (b)) in Figure 13.4 are discussed later. At this stage, it is important to realise that a range of possible transactions exists, enabling managers to implement a position with a payoff that offsets the identified exposure to risk. The reason that the hedging transaction is effective in eliminating the risk exposure is that it results in cash flows that offset the variability in cash flows associated with risk exposure.

It is also important to realise that some hedging techniques are more expensive than others. Accordingly, not all hedges are value adding. In the extreme, the financial manager could determine the company's exposure to every risk factor and undertake a hedging transaction for each exposure. However, this will often be sub-optimum, since there is likely to be a less costly approach available. To illustrate, consider the following (unlikely) example. A company has $5 million cash invested in a cash management account, maturing in six months' time. This company also has a bank loan of $5 million to be repaid in a year—that is, both an asset and a liability of the same value are exposed to fluctuations in interest rates. In this case, the company could hedge both transactions with different derivatives, but this would be costly and unnecessary. This is because a 'natural' hedge exists: any interest rate fluctuations will have opposite and offsetting effects on the asset and liability. This is an example of the so-called 'matching financial flows' hedging technique. Unlike other hedging transactions, it reduces risk exposure at no extra cost. In this case, the company would need to implement a (costly) hedging transaction only for the second six-month period of the loan.

As another example, again consider the case of a gold-mining company acquiring some of its gold stock from the USA (in US dollars). It could hedge both the gold price and the exchange rate risk in order to manage the exposure to fluctuations in both of these factors. However, it is well known that the price of gold tends to vary directly with the value of the US dollar on world markets.[3] In these circumstances, there is again a natural hedge where the two sources of risk are to some extent offset. That is, fluctuations in the cost of purchasing gold in US dollars would be offset to a large extent by fluctuations in the size of proceeds from sales of gold. It would there-fore be sub-optimum (excessively costly) to implement two separate hedging transactions—only the net exposure needs to be hedged.

There are also circumstances where the best risk management decision is to leave exposures unhedged. For example, consider an importer of coffee who has just contracted to buy 5000 kilo-grams of coffee from an Italian supplier at a price of 2 euros (EUR) per kilo, payable in 90 days. This importer can 'lock in' the dollar cost of this purchase by hedging—specifically, by buying EUR 'forward'.[4] If we assume an exchange rate of AUD1 = EUR0.80 the importer can lock in a purchase price of $2.50 per kilo. However, the act of hedging—locking in the purchase price—might be inappropriate if the majority of the importer's competitors do not hedge their purchase

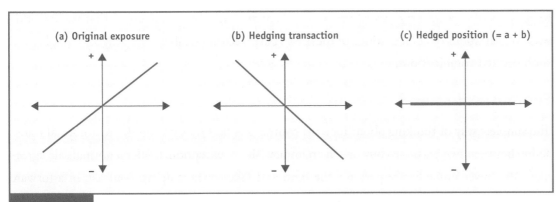

Figure 13.4   Payoff diagrams after hedging

costs, allowing their selling price to fluctuate with exchange rate fluctuations. For example, if the EUR were to depreciate against the AUD—say, to EUR1—all competitors who purchase in 90 days will have their AUD purchase price effectively reduced to around $2 per kilo. Hedging has ensured that the importer will pay $2.50 per kilo, meaning that they would not be able to compete effectively unless the coffee were sold at a loss. In this example, hedging has increased the importer's business risk, so the appropriate risk management decision was *not* to hedge.

The clear message from the foregoing is that managers need to be careful in determining 'true' exposure. Undertaking sensitivity analysis in respect of each of the risk factors to which a company is exposed is only the first step. The next step is to determine net exposure, and then determine the level of hedging that is most appropriate for managing this exposure.

Hedging with derivatives

Assuming that net exposure has been determined and hedging deemed appropriate, a decision must be made as to the specific hedging technique to adopt for management of the exposure. In practice, the majority of hedging transactions involve the use of derivative securities (hereafter, derivatives). These securities will be discussed briefly. The focus of this chapter is not on a detailed explanation and examination of the different types of derivatives that exist, but rather on the role that they can play in corporate risk management.[5]

Derivative contract
A contract whose value is based on the price of an underlying asset, including options, forwards and futures.

The starting point is to recognise that derivatives are so named because they *derive* their value from another (primary) asset. Specifically, **derivative contracts** are contracts that are written 'over' assets such as shares, interest rates and commodities. This will become clearer with an examination of specific derivatives. Derivatives markets are a highly significant segment of worldwide capital markets. They account for trillions of dollars of trading volume each month. There are over a hundred derivatives exchanges throughout the world, each facilitating trade in different types of derivatives.[6] It is also possible to trade derivatives 'over the counter' in many countries. There are literally thousands of derivatives in existence. Despite this, there are only two basic types of derivatives: *forward contracts* and *options*. All of the derivatives that trade worldwide are variations or combinations of these two basic securities, albeit often highly complex and sophisticated combinations.

Forward contract
A contract that gives a buyer and seller an obligation to trade a certain asset (underlying asset) at a given price (forward price) on a future date (maturity date). These are traded over the counter and all elements of the contract are negotiable between the parties.

Forward contracts

The simplest way of thinking about forward contracts is that they are similar to a normal transaction between two parties to buy or sell an item, with *one* exception. Under a normal sale agreement the buyer immediately pays for the item and takes ownership. In contrast, in a forward contract the buyer and seller agree to transfer ownership of the item and cash at *some future date*, but with the price fixed at the time the forward contract is written. Any fluctuation in the price of the item between the date the contract is written and the agreed future date of trade is irrelevant to the contract.

The sale of a house at auction is a good example of a forward contract. Once the buyer's bid is accepted by the vendor and the contracts signed, there is a delayed period until 'settlement'—that is, when the house is paid for and (ownership) title transferred to the buyer. This settlement period is subject to agreement between the buyer and the vendor, but the most common period is 90 days. Accordingly, this transaction is a forward contract, since both parties contract to transact at the price agreed on the auction date, irrespective of any changes in the market value of the house in the period until settlement.

In hedging, a forward contract is used to reduce or eliminate exposure to specific risks by effectively 'locking in' a buying or selling price or interest rate. Refer back to the example illustrated in Figure 13.4. In the example, the gold-mining company had identified an exposure related to fluctuations in the market price of gold and had quantified the impact of these fluctuations on its profitability. By taking a forward position in gold, a future selling price can be locked in and the exposure to fluctuations in the gold price eliminated. A specific example of this type of hedging transaction is given later in the chapter when gold futures are discussed. In the meantime, to illustrate how a forward contract works, consider the following example relating to US dollar to Australian dollar exchange rate exposure.

A key point to realise is that when hedging is implemented the overall position of the company is determined by the combination of the physical transaction (e.g. actual AUD cost in six months) and the hedging transaction. This is illustrated in Examples 13.1 and 13.2.

EXAMPLE 13.1

USD:AUD forward contracts

QUESTION

In June 2012 a gold-mining company agrees to purchase USD2 million of mining equipment in six months' time. Since it has a commitment to spend USD, the company will need to convert AUD to USD in six months. Its exposure therefore relates to the Australian dollar depreciating against the US dollar over that period. The Commonwealth Bank sells forward exchange contracts and has provided a six-month forward exchange buy/sell quote of 1.0010–1.0030. If no natural hedge or other offset exists for this exposure, how can the company effect a forward transaction to hedge its exposure?

ANSWER

The company can purchase US dollars forward at a rate of 1.0010. (Note that it will only get the lower amount when purchasing USD with AUD; if it wished to sell USD/buy AUD, it would be at the rate of 1.0030.) This means that in six months' time, the company will pay:

USD2m/1.0010 = AUD1 998 002

and receive USD2 million from the Commonwealth Bank, which it will use to purchase the equipment. The actual exchange rate in December 2012 is irrelevant to this transaction, since the forward contract fixes the rate at which the AUD will be converted.

The exposure to exchange rate fluctuations is fully hedged using a USD:AUD forward contract, as the exchange rate of 1.0010 has been 'locked in'.

EXAMPLE 13.2

USD:AUD forward contracts

QUESTION

Assume the same facts as in the previous example, except that we have now gone forward in time to December 2012 and the current (spot) USD:AUD exchange rate is 0.9824. How has the forward transaction with the Commonwealth Bank protected the company from its exposure to exchange rate fluctuations?

ANSWER

If the company did not purchase US dollars forward at 0.6010, to make the purchase in December it would have had to pay:

USD2m/0.9824 = AUD2 035 831

for the USD2 million. Remaining unhedged means that the actual exchange rate in December 2012 is the rate at which the AUD would be converted. The company would therefore have paid AUD37 829 more (2 035 831 – 1 998 002) for the equipment had it not entered into the forward transaction.

Accordingly, the exposure to exchange rate fluctuations is hedged using the USD:AUD forward contract, since the loss of $37 829 is avoided.

Although the traditional role of forward contracts is to provide for physical delivery of the agreed asset at the agreed date and time, it has become more common for traders not to deliver the underlying asset, but to reverse the contract at or prior to expiry and 'lock in' a profit or loss on the forward transaction. This is because companies that use forward contracts to hedge are not concerned with the party to whom they will sell, but rather are concerned with the possibility of adverse fluctuations in the market price of the item that they wish to sell in the future. Accordingly, for convenience,[7] they will generally prefer to reverse the forward position by taking an offsetting (opposite) forward contract, which will give the same end result as simply delivering the asset.

Futures contracts

Futures contract
Identical to a forward contract, except the contract is traded on an organised exchange. All elements of the contract are determined by the exchange except for the futures price, which is set by the parties entering into the contract.

A well-known and commonly used type of forward contract is a **futures contract**. This is simply a specialised form of forward contract traded on organised exchanges or futures markets. Futures contracts tend to be the most commonly used forwards in hedging interest rate and commodity price exposures.

In Australia, the official market for trading futures on Australian assets is the Sydney Futures Exchange (SFE) (which merged with the Australian Stock Exchange in 2006), although Australian traders also trade futures on overseas exchanges. The characteristic of futures contracts that distinguishes them from other forward contracts is that many of their features are standardised. These include contract amounts and settlement dates, the requirement to pay deposits and 'margins' to the exchange, and specific contract delivery or reversal procedures.

The SFE is the largest financial futures exchange in the Asia–Pacific region and ranks among the top 15 exchanges in the world. It trades futures contracts on financial instruments (e.g. equities, bank-accepted bills and Australian government bonds) and also on commodities (e.g. wheat, wool and electricity). Figure 13.5 depicts the different futures contracts traded on the SFE, and the volume in millions of trading for the 2010 calendar year.

Quite clearly, in terms of contract volume traded, the most significant contracts are the interest rate futures—those based on 90-day bank bills and government bonds. The volumes relating to other Australian futures are negligible, apart from SPI (Share Price Index) futures.

In 1995 the SFE formed a strategic trading alliance with a key US commodity futures exchange, the New York Mercantile Exchange (NYMEX). The practical effect of this alliance with NYMEX is that Australian investors can trade in NYMEX-listed futures contracts directly through the SFE's electronic link. Examples of futures contracts that can be traded through the link include crude oil, heating oil, gasoline, natural gas, electricity, gold, silver and copper.

Gold futures can be used, for example, by Australian gold producers to hedge exposure to gold price fluctuations. The specific standardised features of the NYMEX gold futures contract are:

- contract size: 100 ounces of gold
- contract months: current calendar month, plus next two calendar months, then quarterly over the next two years and six-monthly out to five years.

Example 13.3 and Table 13.1 illustrate the use of this futures contract.

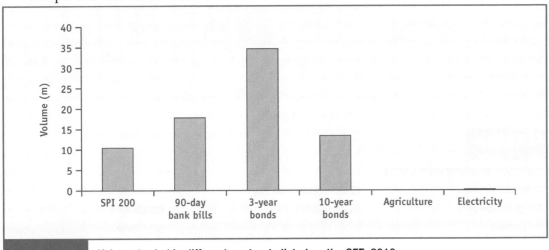

Figure 13.5   Volume traded in different contracts listed on the SFE, 2010

The outcomes of the hedge under the alternative scenarios and assuming reversal (not delivery) are summarised in Table 13.1. These outcomes confirm that the hedge has been effective, in that a net selling price of $1290 per ounce—as required—will be achieved irrespective of the direction or magnitude of gold price fluctuations over the year.

Table 13.1 illustrates that regardless of the gold price fluctuation over the hedging period (in this case, three months) the exposure is eliminated through hedging with gold futures. The com-

EXAMPLE 13.3

Hedging with gold futures

QUESTION

In late January 2012, a gold-mining company has 25 000 ounces of gold that it wishes to sell in April 2012. If it hedges the exposure to gold price fluctuations using NYMEX gold futures expiring in April 2012 and currently priced at $1290 per ounce, how effective is this hedge?

ANSWER

The gold-mining company can sell the gold three months forward by taking a short position in 250 gold futures contracts (i.e. each contract is for 100 ounces) at the current contract price of $1290 per ounce. (Entering into an agreement to sell in the future is known as 'opening a short position' in derivatives markets jargon.)[8] The effectiveness of this transaction as a hedge can be examined by rolling forward in time to the maturity date of the futures contracts. We evaluate two possible (alternative) scenarios in relation to the gold price in April 2012: (1) it rises to $1315 per ounce and (2) it falls to $1270 per ounce. It is assumed that at this time the futures price and the spot price will be the same.[9]

Under either scenario, the company could physically deliver 25 000 ounces of gold at $1290 per ounce pursuant to the futures contracts, thereby achieving that selling price. (This same effect would be achieved if the forward contract were reversed.) For example, in scenario (1), the company would reverse the contract at the price in one year, $1315, resulting in a loss of $25 per ounce ($1315 – $1290) on reversal. This loss would be offset with the gain from selling the gold at spot for $1315 per ounce. Conversely, should the price fall as in scenario (2), there is a gain (of $1290 – $1270 = $20 per ounce) on the futures position that offsets the loss associated with selling the gold at the lower market price of $1270 per ounce.

Hence, the exposure to gold price fluctuations is fully hedged using NYMEX gold futures.

Table 13.1	Hedging with a NYMEX gold futures contract	
SCENARIO 1: GOLD SPOT PRICE = $1315		
Settle futures contract	25 000 × ($1 290 – $1 315)	–$625 000
Sell gold at spot price	25 000 × $1 315	$32 875 000
Net proceeds		$32 250 000
SCENARIO 2: GOLD SPOT PRICE = $270		
Settle futures contract	25 000 × ($1 290 – $1 270)	$500 000
Sell gold at spot price	25 000 × $1 270	$31 750 000
Net proceeds		$32 250 000

bination of the futures trade and physical trade means that the net outcome will be equivalent to a sale of 25 000 ounces of gold at $1290 per ounce, yielding proceeds of $32.25 million.

The main reason that futures trading is so popular is that futures offer liquidity to the trader. That is, the role of an exchange (in Australia, the SFE) is to provide a trading environment that encourages a market in their futures contracts. In this way, parties wishing to trade in a futures contract will always be able to do so. This can be contrasted to forward contracts, where it is sometimes difficult to find a counterparty that is willing to enter into a forward agreement. In the example of a gold-mining company hedging the exposure represented by 25 000 ounces of gold, the liquid market in NYMEX gold futures (traded directly, via the SFE) means that it would be able to effect the required forward position without impediment. If, alternatively, a gold-mining company tried to implement such a position using a forward contract, it would need to locate a (creditworthy) counterparty willing to buy this quantity forward over the agreed time-frame (three months). In practice, this is a difficult transaction to execute—that is, such a counterparty could prove difficult to locate. An additional benefit of futures is that the risk of counterparty default is effectively eliminated in trading via a futures exchange, since all contracts are with the exchange. On the other hand, counterparty risk can be potentially significant when trading individually negotiated forward contracts.

Futures contracts can also be used to hedge interest rate and exchange rate exposure. For example, in Australia interest rate exposure is often hedged in the futures market using 90-day bank-accepted bill futures trading on the SFE (hereafter, BAB futures). As its name implies, the commodity underlying the BAB futures contract is a (physical) 90-day bank-accepted bill of exchange with a face value of $1 million.

The price of a BAB futures contract is quoted as 100 *less the yield* in per cent per annum, to two decimal places. For example, a price of 94.10 equates to a yield of 5.9%. This pricing convention is used so that the effect of interest rate movements on the BAB's price is reflected similarly in the price of a BAB future. For example, if the market yield increases from 5.9% to 6.25%, then the BAB price falls from 94.10 to 93.75. Similarly, the price of an actual bank bill will fall as interest rates rise, since the face value is being discounted by a larger factor.

To convert the quoted yield to the value of a BAB futures contract, the following standard bank bill pricing formula is used:

$$P = \$1\,000\,000/[1 + (f \times 90/365)] \tag{13.1}$$

where:

    f = futures yield $[= (100 - I)/100]$

    I = quoted BAB price

Example 13.4 illustrates the use of BAB futures to hedge interest rate risk, and the application of Equation 13.1. BAB futures are commonly used to reduce the exposure to interest rate risk on short-term borrowings (rather than on investments, as in Example 13.4). Example 13.5 illustrates this application.

Would this hedge still be effective if interest rate fluctuations were in the opposite direction? The answer is yes, as Example 13.6 shows.

Examples 13.4, 13.5 and 13.6 demonstrate how BAB futures contracts can be used for reducing exposure to interest rate fluctuations. Note that these examples represent a 'perfect' hedge, in that the risk is fully eliminated. The perfect hedge has arisen as a result of the specific assumptions of the example (e.g. the borrowing period was to be 90 days, corresponding to the life of the available BAB futures contract, and the rates implied by the futures price were equal to those available in the physical BAB market). In practice, these assumptions are unlikely to be applicable (especially the latter assumption in relation to equivalent rates),[10] so a perfect hedge will not usually be achieved. That is, futures hedging transactions will usually carry some small residual risk of losses, since the hedging instrument is unlikely to match exactly the exposure that is being hedged. However, the remaining risk is often quite negligible and therefore hedging with futures contracts is generally viewed as a very effective way of managing risk exposure.

EXAMPLE 13.4

Using BAB futures to 'lock in' an investment rate

QUESTION

An investor has $1 million on deposit maturing in a month, after which time he intends to invest in a bank bill. He is concerned about interest rates falling over the next month, and wishes to lock in a higher deposit rate. If BAB futures expiring in one month's time are currently priced at 94.10, how can the investor use these futures to lock in the deposit rate?

ANSWER

Since the investor wishes to buy a bank bill in the future, he should open a long position in one BAB contract, meaning that in one month he agrees to pay:

$$\$1\ 000\ 000/[1 + (0.059 \times 90/365)] = \$985\ 661$$

(This value is agreed now, based on the price of 94.1.)

If the investor were to take delivery of a BAB, rather than reverse the transaction, he would pay the $985 661 upon expiry of the BAB contract (in a month) and receive a 90-day bank bill. Ninety days later, he would receive the face value of the bill, $1 million.

The effect of this transaction is to lock in the investor's return on investing in a BAB (i.e. at 5.9%).

EXAMPLE 13.5

Using BAB futures to lock in a borrowing rate

QUESTION

On 10 June 2012 a company decides that it needs to lock in the cost of borrowing $20 million, which will be required for 90 days from mid-December 2012 (i.e. the borrowing period will be December 2012 to March 2013). How can December 2012 BAB futures trading on the SFE and priced at 93.70 be used for this purpose?

ANSWER

The company can hedge against a loss arising from an increase in interest rates by taking a short position in December BAB futures. Accordingly, a short position in 20 BAB futures contracts will be opened in June. The value of the position is:

$$(20 \times 1\,000\,000)/[1 + (0.063 \times 90/365)] = \$19\,694\,067$$

To show that this hedge is effective, we go forward in time to December, when the December 2012 contract is trading at 92.05 just prior to its maturity (i.e. interest rates have increased). The overall outcome is as follows.

Value of opening position in June (short):

$$(20 \times 1\,000\,000)/[1 + (0.063 \times 90/365)] = \$19\,694\,067$$

Value of closing position in December (reversal, so long):

$$(20 \times 1\,000\,000)/[1 + (0.0795 \times 90/365)] = (\$19\,615\,483)$$
Gain on futures position $78\,585$

Note that after reversal of the futures position the company still (mid-December) needs to enter the physical bank bill market to borrow. The hedge is completed only when the futures position is added to the physical position to obtain an overall (net) outcome. Assuming that the yield on physical 90-day bills corresponds to that implied by the futures contract (i.e. 7.95%), the company will draw down (sell) 20 BABs and generate the following cash inflow:

$$(20 \times 1\,000\,000)/[1 + (0.0795 \times 90/365)] = \$19\,615\,483 \text{ proceeds}$$

Of course, 90 days later the company is required to repay $20 million under the BAB arrangement, which implies that their borrowing rate is 7.95%.

Adding the gain on the futures position of $78 585 gives total proceeds from borrowing of $19 694 067. These total proceeds reduce the borrowing rate to 6.3% p.a. (over the borrowing period of 90 days), so the objective of the hedging transaction has been achieved. Specifically, the company opened the futures position in June 2012 with the objective of protecting against potential losses arising from interest rate increases. The effect of this futures transaction is to ensure a gain from this (increased interest rates) scenario should it eventuate, to offset the loss arising from the company's exposure to interest rate fluctuations.

EXAMPLE 13.6

Using BAB futures to lock in a borrowing rate

QUESTION

Assume the same facts as in Example 13.5, except that interest rates have fallen by December and the December 2012 contract is trading at 94.5 just prior to its maturity. Is this hedge still effective?

ANSWER

The hedge is equally effective. Note that the initial (opening) transaction is, of course, unchanged from the previous example.

Value of opening position in June (short):

$$(20 \times 1\,000\,000)/[1 + (0.063 \times 90/365)] = \$19\,694\,067$$

Value of closing position in December (reversal, so long):

$$(20 \times 1\,000\,000)/[1 + (0.055 \times 90/365)] = (\$19\,732\,396)$$
'Loss' on futures position $(38 329)

Again, the overall hedge is obtained by combining the hedging transaction with the physical market position. So, after the December reversal of the futures position, the gold-mining company enters the physical market to borrow (assuming the 90-day physical rate is also 5.5%) by drawing down bills as follows:

$$(20 \times 1\,000\,000)/[1 + (0.055 \times 90/365)] = \$19\,732\,396 \text{ proceeds}$$

Combined with the loss on the futures position ($38 329), total proceeds from borrowing are $19 694 067 — again confirming that the hedging transaction (short BAB futures) will be effective in eliminating the exposure to interest rate risk irrespective of interest rate movements over the hedging period.

Options

The other basic type of derivative, an option, is well named, since it is a contract that confers on its buyer a right, or option, to transact in the future. A technical definition of an option is 'a contract that gives the holder the right, but not the obligation, to buy (or sell) an asset at a specified price and date'. The key elements associated with an option are the underlying asset (as per forward contracts), the right but not obligation of the holder, the specified price at which the holder can transact and the date that the option expires.

There are two different types of options, distinguished by the nature of the right conferred on the buyer. If the buyer is given the right to *buy* an underlying asset, they are the holder (or taker) of a **call option**. Conversely, an option that gives the right to *sell* an underlying asset is a **put option**. Accordingly, the holder of a call option has the right to purchase the asset from the seller (or writer) at a specified price (known as the *exercise*, or strike, price). The holder of a put option has a similar right to sell to the writer. This right is obviously a valuable one, so the writer does not provide it for free—the buyer has to pay for an option contract. This payment is known as the option price, or premium. There is a huge volume of literature that addresses

Call option
A contract that gives the owner the right to buy a given asset (underlying asset) at a certain price (exercise price) up to or on a certain date (expiration date).

Put option
A contract that gives the owner the right to sell a given asset (underlying asset) at a certain price (exercise price) up to or on a certain date (expiration date).

issues associated with determining fair option prices, but such issues are beyond the scope of this book.[11]

Since the writer of an option will not wish the right to exist forever, there will also be a time limit on the option contract, known as the option's expiration, or maturity. A call or put option that allows the holder to exercise *at any time up to* and including the expiration date is known as an **American option**. In contrast, a **European option** allows for exercise only *on the date of* expiration. The profit diagrams associated with holding a call and a put option respectively are illustrated in Figure 13.6. The party that buys an option (the holder) has a *long* option position; conversely, the writer (or seller) of an option has a *short* position.

American option
A call or put option that can be exercised on any date up to and including the expiration date.

European option
A call or put option that can be exercised on the expiration date only.

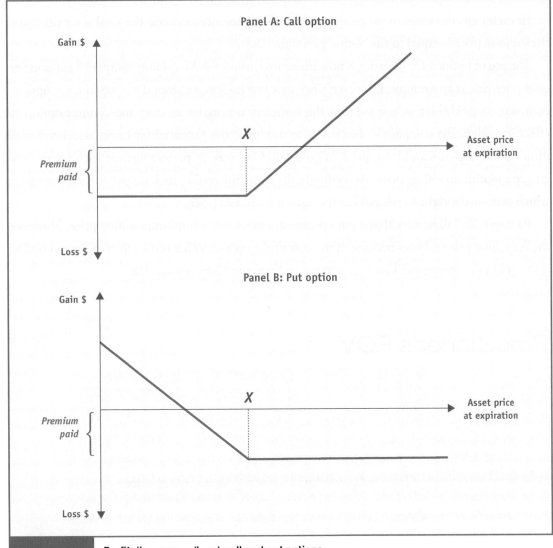

Figure 13.6   Profit diagrams—(long) call and put options

In both cases the holder makes an overall loss in the amount of the premium paid if the 'terminal asset price' (i.e. the price of the underlying asset at the date of the option's maturity) is below (for a call option) or above (put) the exercise price ($X). This is because in these circumstances the option is worthless. For example, who would exercise their right under a *call* option to buy an asset for $25 when it can be bought in the market for $20? On the other hand, there is a positive payoff for a *call* option if the market price of the asset is *above* the exercise price ($X). This is because the owner of the right could exercise it and purchase the underlying asset at a price of $X and then sell it at the higher market price.

Similarly, there is a positive payoff for a *put* option if the market price of the asset is *below* the exercise price ($X). This is because the owner of the right could purchase the underlying asset at the lower market price, then exercise the put option to sell at the (higher) price of $X.

In each case, the break-even point is where the difference between the final asset price and the exercise price is equal to the option premium paid.

The use of options for hedging is now illustrated, using a gold-mining company's exposure to gold price risk as an example. However, since very few exchanges around the world trade options contracts on gold,[12] let us assume that the company negotiates an over-the-counter option to effect its hedge. The company's objective is to minimise the potential for losses associated with future sales of gold should the price of gold fall. One way to protect against such losses is to ensure a minimum selling price. Accordingly, the company could purchase put options over gold, which gives it the right to sell gold at the agreed (exercise) price.

Example 13.7 illustrates that a put option effectively sets a minimum selling price. However, the *net* selling price is lower because of the cost of the option. What is the effect of the put option if the gold price increases? This is illustrated in Example 13.8 on page 428.

Practitioner's POV

Options and futures are not only used by companies for risk management but are frequently used by fund managers to obtain exposure to (i.e. invest in) particular stocks or protect their portfolios from price falls. This is in fact what these derivatives are more commonly used for. Call options on individual stocks can be bought by fund managers to profit from price movements in those stocks, or put options on stocks can be purchased to protect the value of stocks in a portfolio. One of the most heavily traded derivatives in Australia is the SPI, which is a futures contract on the All Ordinaries Index. The SPI is typically used by fund managers to protect a portfolio from broad market movements. The Australian Securities Exchange handles ASX's derivative market services, encompassing the ASX and ASX 24 (formally Sydney Futures Exchange).

EXAMPLE 13.7

Using options to hedge gold price exposures

QUESTION

A gold-mining company has negotiated a put option contract for 25 000 ounces of gold at an exercise price of $1290 per ounce. The seller of this put option charges an option premium of $20 per ounce,[13] so the total premium that the company pays is $500 000. Under the terms of the put option, the company is entitled to sell the gold to the option writer at any time up to maturity (i.e. the option is American), which is in three months' time. How does this strategy perform as a risk management technique, if in three months' time the price of gold is $1270 per ounce?

ANSWER

Since the exercise price exceeds the current market price of gold, the company will exercise the put option, thus selling the gold to the option writer at the exercise price of $290 per ounce. The net outcome is summarised in the table below.

Put option cost		−$500 000
Sell gold at exercise price	(25 000 × 1 290)	$32 250 000
Net proceeds		$31 750 000

The put option hedge has been effective, in that a minimum selling price of $1 290 per ounce (before costs) has been achieved.

The outcome of each of these examples is graphically depicted in Figure 13.7. Note that under the first scenario, where the gold price equals $1270 per ounce, the put option will be exercised. The overall option position is break-even, since the profit on the sale of gold at $1290 per ounce (relative to the current market price) just offsets the (premium) cost of the option of $20 per ounce. Under the second scenario, where the gold price is $1315 per ounce, the option will

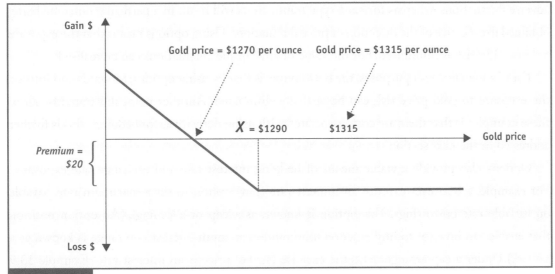

Figure 13.7   Put options payoff diagram—a gold-mining company

EXAMPLE 13.8

Using options to hedge gold price exposures

QUESTION

Assume the same circumstances as in Example 13.7, except that in three months' time the price of gold is $1315 per ounce.

ANSWER

Since the current market price of gold exceeds the exercise price, the company will not exercise the put option, allowing it to expire worthless. It will simply sell the gold in the market at the current price of $315 per ounce. The net outcome, again determined after subtracting the option premium paid, is summarised in the table below.

Put option cost		−$500 000
Sell gold at market price	(25 000 × 1315)	$26 300 000
Net proceeds		$25 800 000

The put option hedge has been effective, and has also enabled a higher price than $1290 per ounce to be achieved on the sale of the gold.

not be exercised, so a loss on the option position equivalent to the amount of premium paid is realised (but this is more than offset by the increased selling price, as calculated in the example).

These examples confirm that the put option hedge has been effective, in that the $1290 per ounce minimum selling price (before costs) will be achieved regardless of gold price fluctuations. However, they also illustrate that for option positions the direction and magnitude of gold price fluctuations will determine the net overall position. In particular, a key feature of options that distinguishes them from forward/futures contracts in hedging is that they allow the holder to retain the benefit of any favourable price fluctuations while still protecting against potential adverse fluctuations, whereas forward-type transactions will result in a particular outcome being obtained irrespective of the direction of price fluctuations. Using options means that the exposure to 'downside' risk is minimised, but the value of any 'upside' fluctuations can be realised.

For risk management purposes, the bottom line is that by using options, forwards and futures, the exposure to gold price risk can be virtually eliminated. Another point illustrated by all of these examples is that there are costs associated with using derivatives for hedging. This is further addressed in the next section.

Options also provide a viable means of hedging interest rate and exchange rate exposures. For example, a borrower can use an interest rate (put) option to set a maximum rate payable on variable rate borrowings. This option is known as a 'cap' or a 'ceiling'. (An option position that enables an investor to implement a minimum–maximum interest rate range is known as a 'collar'.) Under a cap arrangement, the exercise (strike) price is an interest rate. Example 13.9 illustrates how a cap can be used in managing exposure to interest rate increases.

Practitioner's POV

Stockbrokers do much more than simply broker stock. The largest stockbrokers, especially those forming part of global companies, also typically have a futures trading desk and an options trading desk. These desks trade options and futures on their own account (as principal), or for clients (as agents), on the Australian Securities Exchange. Most of the global stockbrokers also have access to foreign options and futures markets—for example, the Chicago Board of Trade, New York Mercantile Exchange, etc. They can assist local companies to obtain access to the overseas-based risk management tools discussed in this chapter. Many stockbrokers also facilitate trades in over-the-counter derivatives that they create themselves or in line with the demands of particular clients.

The transaction described in Example 13.9 is graphically illustrated in Figure 13.8.

EXAMPLE 13.9

Using a cap to set a maximum borrowing rate

QUESTION

Assume that a company's net borrowings of $144 million are subject to quarterly variable interest rate resets (i.e. the lender will reset the rate in line with market interest rates every three months). How can the company set an upper limit on the variable interest rate that it pays?

ANSWER

To hedge, the company would purchase a cap at a strike rate that represents the maximum interest rate that it will pay. Assume that the company can purchase a cap at (strike =) 9.0%, at a cost (premium) of 0.25% of the principal amount covered by the cap.[14] If interest rates rise above 9%, the put option will be exercised, so that the maximum rate that the company would pay is 9.25% in any quarter (i.e. 9% maximum + 0.25% cost of cap). If the rate is below 9% in any quarter, the put option lapses and the interest rate that the company will pay is the market (reset) rate plus 0.25%.

The effect of this cap is to ensure that the maximum interest rate payable is 9.25% (but it will be lower if the market interest rate falls below 9%).

Swaps

Swaps are another popular form of derivative used for hedging. It was pointed out earlier that there are only two basic forms of derivative, so introducing this third derivative might appear contradictory to the earlier statement. However, this is not so, since swaps are essentially a 'strip' of forward contracts, in that each swap payment relates to the equivalent of one forward contract.

There are two major types of swap transaction: *interest rate* swaps and *exchange rate* swaps. Since the same principles essentially relate to both types, the focus here will be on the former.

Swap

A contract that allows two parties to exchange future (uncertain) cash flows. The most common type of swap contract is an interest rate swap in which parties exchange variable interest rate payments for fixed interest rate payments.

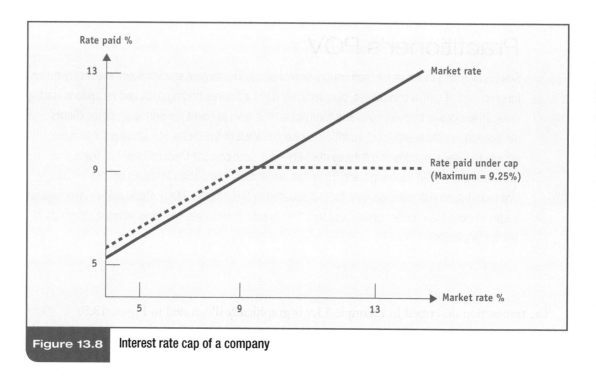

Figure 13.8   Interest rate cap of a company

The most common form of interest rate swap is a 'fixed for floating' swap. Put simply, in a swap transaction two parties agree to exchange their interest payment obligations over a given period (on the same principal amount) where one of the parties has a variable interest rate obligation and the other has a fixed interest rate obligation. This is based on the principle of 'comparative advantage', and is illustrated in Example 13.10.

Businesses that need to borrow funds typically have a choice between borrowing at a variable (floating) rate of interest or a fixed rate. For interest risk management purposes, often a business will have a preference for one form of borrowing (floating or fixed) over another. For example, a business might have a variable cash inflow that is a natural hedge against variable rate borrowings. However, there might be some advantage associated with borrowing at a fixed interest rate. In such circumstances, a company may borrow at the fixed rate and then undertake an interest rate swap. This is illustrated in Example 13.10.

Thus, interest rate swaps are also quite useful for managing exposure to interest rate fluctuations, and they can reduce the cost of borrowing. However, for the party that assumes the floating rate liability, the swap does not eliminate the exposure to interest rate fluctuations.

EXAMPLE 13.10

Using a swap to set a maximum borrowing rate

QUESTION

Assume that the borrowing rates relating to a semi-government body (SemiGov) and a listed public corporation (Corp) are as outlined in the following table. How can an interest rate swap improve the borrowing position of both parties?

	Floating rate	Fixed rate
SemiGov	BBSW + 1.0%	8.00%
Corp	BBSW + 1.5%	9.00%

ANSWER

Although SemiGov has the advantage in both markets in terms of lower borrowing cost, the fact that there is a net difference between the fixed and floating rates across the two borrowers suggests a swap can benefit both. This is where 'comparative advantage' applies—Corp is relatively better off borrowing in the floating market, since it pays only 0.5% more than SemiGov (it pays 1% more in the fixed market). The net difference in spreads (of 0.5%) can lead to a lower borrowing cost for both parties under a swap agreement. This is achieved by each borrowing in their 'comparatively best' market and transacting a fixed for floating swap (to their preferred market, assumed to be the one that is not the comparative best). Here, Corp will borrow at floating (BBSW + 1.5%); SemiGov will borrow fixed at 8%; and they will swap interest obligations.

The essence of the swap is that both can share the net difference of 50 basis points. For example, assume the following terms (which are subject to agreement between the two parties): Corp pays SemiGov 8.25% fixed in return for BBSW% +1% floating. This can be illustrated diagrammatically:

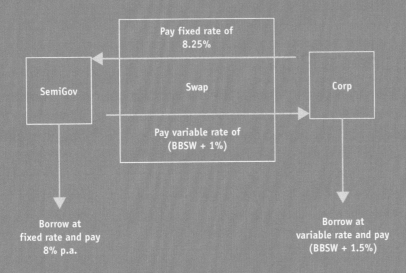

The net borrowing costs are:

Corp: (BBSW + 1.5)% + 8.25% – (BBSW +1)% = 8.75% net
SemiGov: 8% + (BBSW + 1)% – 8.25% = (BBSW + 0.75)%

Accordingly, each party is 25 basis points better off as a result of the swap agreement (relative to the rate that they would otherwise pay in each market).

CONCEPT CHECK

8. What is a 'hedge'?

9. What is a forward contract?

10. What is the difference between a forward and a futures contract?

11. What is an option?

12. What is a swap?

For the answers, go to MyFinanceLab

CONCEPT 13.6   A final word on the costs of hedging with derivatives

There are both explicit and implicit costs associated with using forward and futures contracts. Explicit costs are simply the expenses that are associated with executing the transaction—that is, exchange or vendors' fees and brokerage commissions. These costs are relatively minor, but the implicit costs can be significant. These include the bid–ask spread on the contract, a possible risk premium built into the price of the contract and, in particular, the elimination of the ability to profit from any favourable price fluctuations. That is, in setting up forward transactions to protect against adverse price fluctuations, the effect of favourable fluctuations is also eliminated. This is an opportunity cost, and was illustrated in the earlier examples relating to forward and futures contracts.

Practitioner's POV

Options and futures allow companies to protect only their short-term cash flows—at best. This is because the most active exchange-traded derivatives usually have a life of a few months. This means that a company can only use these derivatives to hedge cash flows it expects to receive or pay out over a few months. In valuing a company, however, free cash flows into perpetuity are relevant. As a consequence, the presence of derivatives in the balance sheet of a company is of marginal relevance to the task faced by an analyst in valuing it from a discounted cash flow perspective. However, it is relevant to forecasting earnings one year, and possibly two years, out.

Because options have a purchase price, the explicit cost of transacting in options is typically far greater than for forward contracts. In addition to the option premium, other fees and commissions are payable, as per forwards and futures. On the other hand, the implicit costs associated with options are minimal, in that there is no opportunity cost (options just lapse if price movements are favourable). Any 'risk' premium is explicitly priced into the option premium, so the only implicit cost of options is the bid–ask spread on contracts.

CONCEPT CHECK

13. What are the costs of hedging with an option?

For the answers, go to MyFinanceLab

Student Learning Centre

MyFinanceLab ■ To test your mastery of the content covered in this chapter and to create your own personalised study plan, go to MyFinanceLab: www.pearson.com.au/myfinancelab

CONCEPT CHECKLIST

In this chapter the following concepts were discussed:

➤ The risks faced by Australian companies—in particular,
  - the different sources of risk
  - the identification and measurement of exposure to risk
➤ The quantification of risk exposure
➤ Risk management techniques, particularly hedging with
  - forwards and futures
  - options
  - swaps
➤ The costs of risk management

SELF-TEST QUESTIONS

1. What is the payoff on a European call option on gold with an exercise price of $1300 per ounce if the contract size is 100 ounces and the gold price on the expiration date is $1400?

2. You sell 100 call options written on BHP. The percentage change in the option price to a movement in the share price is 0.50. (This percentage is known as the delta of the option and implies that a $1 move in the share price results in a 50 cents move in the option price.) How many shares in BHP must you buy or sell in order to hedge your position in the call options?

3. What is the payoff on a BAB futures contract purchased at a price of 95.10 and sold at a price of 96.10?

4. Given the following:

	Floating rate	Fixed rate
Company A	BBSW + 2%	5%
Company B	BBSW + 2.5%	6%

Explain how company B can benefit if it borrows at a floating rate, then swaps its floating rate for a fixed rate payment with company A.

5. Referring to Question 4, explain how company A benefits from engaging in the swap.

6. What are the costs involved in hedging using an option contract?

Self-test answers

1. The call option gives the buyer the right to buy gold for $1300. Hence, on expiration, the holder will exercise the right and buy gold for $1300 per ounce, then immediately sell the gold on market for $1400, realising a profit of $100 for each ounce of gold.

2. In writing call options, you have agreed to sell BHP shares to the writer if they exercise the options. Hence, you must buy shares in BHP in order to hedge. If the price of BHP increases by $1, then the delta of the options implies they will increase in price by 50 cents (and hence you have made a loss because you sold them at a lower price). In order to hedge this potential loss, you need to buy one BHP share for every two options sold. Hence, the price movement in the shares will perfectly offset the loss on the two options.

3. Since the price at which you have agreed to trade the BAB is:

    $$P = \$1\ 000\ 000/[1 + (f \times 90/365)]$$

    where f = futures yield [= (100 – futures price)/100]

    then you have agreed to buy the BAB for P = $1 000 000/[1 + (0.049 × 90/365)] = 988 062 and you have agreed to sell the BAB for P = $1 000 000/[1 + (0.039 × 90/365)] = 990 475. Hence, you have realised a profit of $2413 [990 475 – 988 062].

4. While A has an absolute borrowing advantage, it has a comparative advantage in borrowing at the fixed rate, while company B has a comparative advantage at borrowing at the floating rate. Hence, company B borrows at a floating rate, and engages in a swap which would result in a net borrowing cost as follows:

Borrowing cost	BBSW + 2.5%
Pays A	+ 5.25%
Receives from A	−BBSW + 2%
Net borrowing cost	5.75%

    Hence, it has reduced its net borrowing cost from 6% to 5.75%.

5. Company A borrows at a fixed rate, and engages in a swap which would have a net borrowing cost as follows:

Borrowing cost	5%
Receives from B	−5.25%
Pays B	+BBSW + 2%
Net borrowing cost	+BBSW + 1.75%

    Hence, it has reduced its net borrowing cost from BBSW + 2% to BBSW + 1.75%.

6. The explicit costs involved in engaging in a hedging transaction using options include (1) the option price, (2) the brokerage fee and (3) exchange fees.

DISCUSSION QUESTIONS

1. Describe the two broad categories of corporate risk. Identify the circumstances under which one of these broad categories would not apply to a company.

2. Define exposure to risk, and explain why exposure to risk is more important to a company than its mere existence.

3. Interest rate risk and exchange rate risk are the two most significant risks that Australian companies face. Explain why.

4. What is a natural hedge? Give three examples of natural hedges.

5. Under what circumstances would the most appropriate risk management decision be to do nothing (i.e. leave the exposure unhedged)? Give a specific example (other than that given in the chapter).

6. A financial manager was recently heard to comment: 'One of the important concepts I learned when studying finance at university was that an individual can diversify risk more effectively than a firm. Since both diversification and risk management are about reducing the risk of the firm, why then should I spend corporate resources on risk management if individual shareholders can do it more effectively anyway?' Address the manager's statement, explaining the role of corporate risk management and how it adds value to the firm.

7. You are the corporate financial manager of a medium-sized Australian-listed company in the industrial sector of the stock market. Your firm's capital structure is 60% debt, 40% equity. Explain what steps (if any) you would take to hedge the firm's interest rate risk. Justify your decision, giving reasons.

8. Given that there is always a cost (explicit or implicit) in managing corporate risk, how is it that interest rate swaps reduce the borrowing costs of all parties? Has the risk simply disappeared? If not, which party is bearing the cost?

9. A 50% debt-financed Australian gold-mining company sells its gold into the US market. Identify three risks faced by the company and specific instruments that can be used to control these risks.

10. Explain the costs associated with purchasing an option to manage risk.

PRACTICAL QUESTIONS

1. For the following hedging transactions, (i) indicate what the transaction could be used to hedge, and (ii) calculate the profit/loss on the hedge.

   (a) You are long a bank-accepted bill futures contract. The price of the futures contract rises from 95.2 to 97.3.

   (b) You pay $20 for a gold call option with an exercise price of $300. On expiration, the underlying gold price is $400.

   BASIC

2. A company enters into a $1 million five-year interest rate swap. The current five-year swap rate requires the company to pay a fixed rate of 5% and to receive BBS + 1%. When the bank enters into this swap, the BBS rate was 4%. Twelve months later interest rates rise and, consequently, the four-year swap rate requires payment of 5.5% fixed and to receive BBS + 1%. Has the bank made a profit or loss on its swap?

   BASIC

3. Sketch a payoff diagram for each of the following exposures of a company: (a) net borrowings over the next year subject to a variable interest rate (currently 8.5%) totalling $3 million; (b) a purchase

   BASIC

order amounting to 12 million Japanese Yen needs to be paid in three months (the current Yen:AUD exchange rate is 66.7); (c) a fixed-term investment denominated in US dollars—amounting to USD2 million—will mature in six months (the current AUD:USD exchange rate is 1.10); (d) the company is a large-scale importer of crude oil, and anticipates importing an average of one million barrels of oil per month over the next 12 months. (The current price of crude oil is $110 per barrel.)

BASIC

4. (a) Sketch the payoff diagrams for (long and short) futures and options contracts.

   (b) Use the diagrams to explain the similarities and differences between futures and options contracts.

   (c) Use the diagrams to demonstrate how a company whose value is directly related to changes in the AUD:USD can use futures and options to: (i) eliminate the risk; and/or (ii) minimise adverse outcomes.

INTERMEDIATE

5. XYZ Ltd is a company whose profitability is to a large degree influenced by market interest rates. When interest rates rise, XYZ's profits fall, and vice versa.

   (a) Describe a technique that XYZ could use to determine the extent of its exposure to potential future interest rate fluctuations. Use a diagram if appropriate.

   (b) XYZ would prefer to borrow funds at a fixed rate of interest, but finds it can borrow at a variable rate on more favourable terms (i.e. a smaller credit risk premium is charged on variable than on fixed). Describe how XYZ could use an interest rate swap to obtain a fixed rate on borrowings, while still retaining at least some of the favourable variable rate terms. Illustrate your answer by constructing a numerical example, assuming a semi-government borrower as swap counterparty.

   (c) Now assume that XYZ wishes to raise 90-day funds in six months' time. It has decided to purchase a 10% interest rate cap, which will cost 35 basis points. What will XYZ's nominal borrowing cost be (in % p.a. terms) if, in six months' time, 90-day interest rates end up at: (i) 9.5%; (ii) 10%; or (iii) 10.75%?

   (d) What will XYZ's maximum borrowing cost be under the cap in (c)?

INTERMEDIATE

6. In the four independent scenarios below, the use of one particular derivative instrument would be the most appropriate for achieving the stated objective. In each case, state the derivative transaction that would be appropriate in the circumstances. Briefly explain your answers.

   (a) Your company wants to borrow at a variable rate of interest but, given its credit rating, is subject to a margin of 2% above the variable benchmark rate. On the other hand, it can borrow at a margin of only 1% above the fixed benchmark rate.

   (b) You are the manager of an investment bank that has significant funds on term deposit maturing in two months. You intend to reinvest the funds for a further three months, and want to lock in your deposit rate now.

   (c) In 90 days, your company will need to borrow around $2 million for a period of 180 days, and want to lock in the borrowing rate.

   (d) A company has a rolling bank loan facility that is subject to variable interest rate resets every two months. It wants to take advantage of falling interest rates, but would like to reduce the cost effect of increasing interest rates.

INTERMEDIATE

7. State whether the following statements are true or false. Briefly explain your answers.

   (a) Two months ago, Sam Slick opened a long position in 10 BAB futures contracts when the price was 93.6. If he were to close out his position today at the current market price of 92.6, he would make a profit of almost $24 000.

(b) If a company wishes to hedge a borrowing requirement of $1 million which is anticipated for six months from now, an appropriate strategy to adopt is a short position in 90-day BAB futures.

(c) The risk associated with an option contract is shared equally between the writer and the holder of such a contract.

8. In late March, the owner of a small manufacturing business has decided to expand operations. It is decided that the business needs to borrow between $2.5 million and $3 million in late June to fund the initial expansion. It is further decided that this initial borrowing will be for a period of about three months, and will be in the form of a draw-down of bank-accepted bills. Given the risk associated with expansion, it is critical that borrowing costs are minimised. With this in mind, it is decided that the future borrowing should be hedged. Current market rates have been identified as: (physical) 90-day bank bills 7.5%; June BAB futures –92.2; September BAB futures –91.9.

What hedge transaction should be opened now (late March)? What is the overall borrowing cost (in % p.a.) if the hedge position is held until late June, when the draw-down of bills occurs? Assume that, in June, market rates are: (physical) 90-day bank bills 6.25%; June BAB futures 93.7; September BAB futures 93.3.

INTERMEDIATE

9. You are the corporate treasurer of a medium-sized Australian public company. Your main responsibility is to manage the exposure to financial risk. There is no formal hedging policy—the manner in which you manage risk is entirely at your discretion—but, of course, your performance is evaluated against how successful your risk management activities have been.

Currently, you are concentrating on managing the company's exposure to interest rate risk over the next year. You have the following information available to you, comprising a payoff diagram detailing interest rate risk exposure, and current yields.

The company's borrowings are on a variable rate basis, with a revision from the current rate of 8% due this week. All current hedge positions (including natural hedges) expire this week. The following are the available hedging transactions, including their current prices.

CHALLENGING

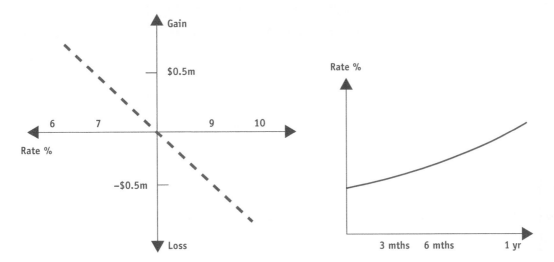

(a) BAB Sept trading at 91.8; Dec: 91.5; and Mar: 91.1

(b) Cap @ 8.4% costing 10 basis points quarterly

(c) Borrow fixed one year @ 8.75%

(d) Do nothing (i.e. remain unhedged).

Which hedging transaction would you implement? Why?

CHALLENGING

10. An Australian airline company has just entered into a contract to purchase a new fleet of airplanes for USD2 billion and the current exchange rate is approximately 1.050 (i.e. AUD1 buys USD1.050). The company must pay for the fleet in six months' time. The Australian/US dollar futures contract trading on the Sydney Futures Exchange and expiring in six months is currently priced at 1.010 How can the airline company hedge its exposure to foreign currency risk? If the actual exchange rate in six months' time is 0.950, explain how the hedge has protected the company from its exposure to exchange rate fluctuations.

CHALLENGING

11. An Australian transport company is concerned about the escalating price of oil and the impact on its business over the next 12 months because it finds it hard to pass on cost increases to its customers. The next batch of petrol and diesel the company expects to purchase in 12 months, based on current prices, is expected to cost USD27 million and the current AUD:USD exchange rate is approximately 1.050. The Australian/US dollar futures contract trading on the Sydney Futures Exchange and expiring in 12 months is currently priced at 1.060. The current price of light crude oil is $106 per barrel, and light crude oil call options with a strike price of $106 and expiring in 12 months are available from the New York Mercantile Exchange for a price of $3 each (per barrel). Note that one option contract covers 1000 barrels. The price of light crude oil closely tracks the market price of petrol and diesel that the transport company can obtain. How can the company hedge the price of petrol and diesel that it purchases? If the price increases 20% and the Australian dollar depreciates by 10%, demonstrate how the hedge works.

CASE STUDY

On Friday 4 July 2008 your company buys $500 million worth of 90-day bank-accepted bills (BABs). The intention of the company is to invest over the weekend, then sell the BABs on the open market on the following Monday (7 July 2008) afternoon. The average BAB rate on Friday 4 July 2008 was 7.77. On 4 July the following information is available for SFE BAB options and futures.

SFE CALL OPTIONS

	Exercise Price	Prev Price	Opening Trade	High	Low	SETTLEMENT Price	Change	$ Value of Change	Volume	Prev O/P
90-Day Bank Bills (100 minus yield % p.a.)										
Sep 08	92.000	0.225	-	-	-	0.235	+0.010	23.72	0	5852
Sep 08	92.125	0.155	-	-	-	0.160	+0.005	11.86	0	103
Sep 08	92.250	0.100	-	-	-	0.100	0	0.00	0	7250
Sep 08	92.375	0.060	-	-	-	0.060	0	0.00	0	4250
Sep 08	92.625	0.015	-	-	-	0.015	0	0.00	0	5440
Sep 08	92.750	0.005	-	-	-	0.010	+0.005	11.90	0	2240
Sep 08	93.000	-	-	-	-	-	0	0.00	0	9200
Sep 08	93.250	-	-	-	-	-	0	0.00	0	2000
Dec 08	92.000	0.270	-	-	-	0.285	+0.015	35.57	0	500
Dec 08	92.500	0.090	-	-	-	0.095	+0.005	11.88	0	100
Dec 08	93.000	0.020	-	-	-	0.020	0	0.00	0	750
Mar 09	92.500	0.115	-	-	-	0.125	+0.010	23.77	0	1000

SFE PUT OPTIONS

	Exercise Price	Prev Price	Opening Trade	High	Low	SETTLEMENT Price	Change	$ Value of Change	Volume	Prev O/P
90-Day Bank Bills (100 minus yield % p.a.)										
Sep 08	92.500	0.390	-	-	-	0.380	-0.010	-23.77	0	150
Sep 08	93.375	1.230	-	-	-	1.220	-0.010	-23.87	0	100
Dec 08	91.625	0.115	-	-	-	0.105	-0.010	-23.67	0	1166
Dec 08	91.750	0.155	-	-	-	0.145	-0.010	-23.69	0	1166
Dec 08	92.000	0.260	-	-	-	0.245	-0.015	-35.57	0	1566

SFE BENCHMARK FUTURES

	Prev Price	First Trade	High	Low	SETTLEMENT Price	Change	$ Value of Change	Volume	Prev O/P
90-Day Bank Bills (100 minus yield % p.a.)									
Sep 08	92.140	92.140	92.160	92.130	92.150	+0.010	23.73	11125	339790
Dec 08	92.010	92.020	92.060	92.000	92.040	+0.030	71.15	8985	206527
Mar 09	91.990	92.010	92.040	91.990	92.030	+0.040	94.86	3853	102684
Jun 09	92.010	92.030	92.060	92.030	92.050	+0.040	94.87	2003	73714
Sep 09	92.070	92.090	92.110	92.090	92.110	+0.040	94.89	964	49338
Dec 09	92.160	92.180	92.200	92.180	92.190	+0.030	71.20	784	29727
Mar 10	92.230	92.260	92.280	92.260	92.270	+0.040	94.97	725	18179
Jun 10	92.300	92.340	92.340	92.320	92.340	+0.040	95.00	125	6938
Sep 10	92.340	-	-	-	92.380	+0.040	95.02	0	1307
Dec 10	92.350	-	-	-	92.400	+0.050	118.78	0	1019
Mar 11	92.370	-	-	-	92.420	+0.050	118.79	50	1104
Jun 11	92.380	-	-	-	92.440	+0.060	142.56	50	230
Sep 11	92.360	-	-	-	92.420	+0.060	142.54	0	0
Dec 11	92.370	-	-	-	92.430	+0.060	142.55	0	0
Mar 12	92.360	-	-	-	92.420	+0.060	142.54	0	0
Jun 12	92.360	-	-	-	92.420	+0.060	142.54	0	0
Sep 12	92.360	-	-	-	92.420	+0.060	142.54	0	0
Dec 12	92.360	-	-	-	92.420	+0.060	142.54	0	0
Mar 13	92.360	-	-	-	92.420	+0.060	142.54	0	0
Jun 13	92.360	-	-	-	92.420	+0.060	142.54	0	0

Source: The Australian Financial Review, 4 and 7 July 2008. © AFR, Fairfax Media.

On Monday 7 July the SFE BAB options and futures are as follows:

SFE CALL OPTIONS

		Exercise Price	Prev Price	Opening Trade	High	Low	SETTLEMENT Price	Change	$ Value of Change	Volume	Prev O/P
90-Day Bank Bills (100 minus yield % p.a.)											
Sep	08	92.000	0.235	-	-	-	0.230	-0.005	-11.86	0	5852
Sep	08	92.125	0.160	-	-	-	0.155	-0.005	-11.86	0	103
Sep	08	92.250	0.100	-	-	-	0.095	-0.005	-11.87	0	7250
Sep	08	92.375	0.060	-	-	-	0.055	-0.005	-11.88	0	4250
Sep	08	92.625	0.015	-	-	-	0.015	0	0.00	0	5440
Sep	08	92.750	0.010	-	-	-	0.005	-0.005	-11.90	0	2240
Sep	08	93.000	-	-	-	-	-	0	0.00	0	9200
Sep	08	93.250	-	-	-	-	-	0	0.00	0	2000
Dec	08	92.000	0.285	-	-	-	0.290	+0.005	11.85	0	500
Dec	08	92.500	0.095	-	-	-	0.100	+0.005	11.89	0	100
Dec	08	93.000	0.020	-	-	-	0.020	0	0.00	0	750
Mar	09	92.500	0.125	-	-	-	0.135	+0.010	23.77	0	1000

SFE PUT OPTIONS

		Exercise Price	Prev Price	Opening Trade	High	Low	SETTLEMENT Price	Change	$ Value of Change	Volume	Prev O/P
90-Day Bank Bills (100 minus yield % p.a.)											
Sep	08	92.500	0.380	-	-	-	0.380	0	0.00	0	150
Sep	08	93.375	1.220	-	-	-	1.220	0	0.00	0	100
Dec	08	91.625	0.105	-	-	-	0.100	-0.005	-11.84	0	1166
Dec	08	91.750	0.145	-	-	-	0.135	-0.010	-23.68	0	1166
Dec	08	92.000	0.245	-	-	-	0.230	-0.015	-35.57	0	1566

SFE BENCHMARK FUTURES

		Prev Price	First Trade	High	Low	SETTLEMENT Price	Change	$ Value of Change	Volume	Prev O/P
90-Day Bank Bills (100 minus yield % p.a.)										
Sep	08	92.150	92.150	92.170	92.130	92.150	0	0.00	13422	334950
Dec	08	92.040	92.060	92.090	92.040	92.060	+0.020	47.44	12809	206990
Mar	09	92.030	92.040	92.090	92.040	92.070	+0.040	94.87	12219	99253
Jun	09	92.050	92.080	92.120	92.060	92.100	+0.050	118.61	5562	74224
Sep	09	92.110	92.130	92.170	92.130	92.150	+0.040	94.91	656	49523
Dec	09	92.190	92.240	92.250	92.230	92.240	+0.050	118.69	771	29435
Mar	10	92.270	92.320	92.330	92.310	92.320	+0.050	118.73	247	18725
Jun	10	92.340	92.390	92.390	92.380	92.390	+0.050	118.77	168	6943
Sep	10	92.380	92.420	92.420	92.420	92.430	+0.050	118.79	11	1307
Dec	10	92.400	92.440	92.440	92.440	92.450	+0.050	118.81	1	1019
Mar	11	92.420	-	-	-	92.460	+0.040	95.05	0	1104
Jun	11	92.440	92.470	92.470	92.470	92.480	+0.040	95.06	10	226
Sep	11	92.420	-	-	-	92.460	+0.040	95.05	0	0
Dec	11	92.430	-	-	-	92.470	+0.040	95.06	0	0
Mar	12	92.420	-	-	-	92.460	+0.040	95.05	0	0
Jun	12	92.420	-	-	-	92.460	+0.040	95.05	0	0
Sep	12	92.420	-	-	-	92.460	+0.040	95.05	0	0
Dec	12	92.420	-	-	-	92.460	+0.040	95.05	0	0
Mar	13	92.420	-	-	-	92.460	+0.040	95.05	0	0
Jun	13	92.420	-	-	-	92.460	+0.040	95.05	0	0

Source: The Australian Financial Review, 7 and 8 July 2008.

The BAB rate fell by 0.01 from Friday 4 July to Monday 7 July.

CASE STUDY QUESTIONS

1. On 4 July 2008 if you were worried about interest rates rising over the weekend and the value of your BABs falling:

   (a) Describe how you would hedge using an at-the-money option (be sure to identify which option you would trade)

   (b) Describe how you would hedge using the nearest to delivery futures contract.

2. Calculate the profit or loss on your BABs from Friday to Monday.

3. Calculate the profit or loss of your entire position in Question 1 above if you had:

   (a) hedged using the option you identify

   (b) hedged using the futures contract.

FURTHER READING

The following references provide a good introduction to derivative securities:

- Chance, D. M. (1998), *An Introduction to Derivatives*, 4th edn, The Dryden Press, Harcourt Brace College Publishers, USA.
- Hull, J. C. (2002), *Fundamentals of Futures and Options Markets*, 4th edn, Prentice-Hall Inc., USA.

An Australian text dealing specifically with risk management is:

- Daugaard, D. and Valentine, T. (1995), *Financial Risk Management: A Practical Approach to Derivatives*, HarperEducational Publishers, Sydney.

NOTES

1. *The New Palgrave Dictionary of Money and Finance*, vol. 1, 299.
2. Note that in addition to that covered in the above definition, hedging can encompass matching financial flows within the company, and adjusting the maturity of the company's assets and liabilities.
3. For example, the correlation coefficient between the quarterly change in the gold price and the quarterly change in the AUD:USD exchange rate over the five-year period to 31 December 2007 is 0.30. This correlation is calculated in the manner demonstrated in Chapter 6, using data from the *Reserve Bank of Australia Bulletin*.
4. Forward contracts are explained in more detail in the next section.
5. Many textbooks deal with derivatives in detail. There are two recommended texts in the 'Further reading' section.
6. For information on derivatives exchanges and the different types of derivatives that are traded on them see *The Handbook of World Stock, Derivative and Commodity Exchanges* (2005), Mondovisione, London.
7. Reversal is generally seen as more convenient since the parties don't have to meet to exchange the asset and payment and don't need to wait until the contract's (specified) maturity date to transact.
8. The side of the transaction going 'short' in a futures contract is agreeing to sell the underlying asset at a price agreed today. Hence, a fall in the price of the underlying asset (and future) will result in a profit for the shorter. The opposite is true for the side going 'long' which is agreeing to buy the underlying asset.
9. It is possible to prove that the spot price and futures price will be equal (within transactions costs bounds) at the date of maturity of a futures contract. Interested readers are referred to the 'Further reading' section.
10. The relationship that links futures prices with the spot price of the underlying asset is known as 'cost-of-carry'. Coverage of this relationship is beyond the scope of this text, but interested readers can obtain more information from the references listed in the 'Further reading' section.

11. Again, interested readers can obtain more information from the listed references.

12. The gold options contract on the COMEX division of NYMEX is an option on the gold futures contract. There is an option contract on gold that is traded on the Brazilian exchange, BM F, but this is denominated in Brazilian real ($B) and is not a very liquid contract.

13. Again we note that there is a significant body of literature that provides guidance as to how to set the appropriate option premium. Two of the variables relevant to the premium are the current spot price of the asset and the option's exercise price. If the gold company wished to set a higher minimum selling (exercise) price (say, $1425 per ounce), the option premium would cost more.

14. Accordingly, at each interest reset date, the explicit option premium cost is $144m × 0.0025 = $360 000. Note also that this is actually a 'strip' of caps, rather than a single cap, since it is effectively a series of discrete put options every three months.

14

Working capital policy

CHAPTER PREVIEW

The objective of this chapter is to provide an introduction to the management of working capital. After introducing the concept of working capital, this chapter identifies that the most important components of working capital of primary concern to the finance manager of an organisation are cash, short-term debt and accounts receivable. Consequently, the chapter begins with a discussion of cash management, identifying the determinants of the optimum cash balance that should be kept by a company. Different forms of long-term debt were discussed in Chapter 12, which dealt with capital structure. In this chapter, this discussion is extended to short-term debt instruments as mechanisms for raising cash. Finally, the chapter provides a discussion of accounts receivable (i.e. the granting of credit), specifically the methods by which the credit worthiness of a possible client can be assessed and optimum credit granting decisions.

KEY CONCEPTS

CONCEPT 14.1   What is working capital?

Net working capital is the difference between the current assets and current liabilities of a corporation. Current assets are those assets which are cash or expected to be converted into cash within the next 12 months, while current liabilities are those debts which are required to be paid within the next 12 months. A company which is not able to pay its debts as and when they fall due is insolvent. The board of directors of a company which knowingly allows the company to trade when it is insolvent is breaking the law, risks being taken to court by its creditors and facing possible gaol terms. Hence, working capital, which provides a primary indication of whether a company will 'naturally' be able to repay its immediate debts as and when they fall due is an important consideration for the management of a company.

A company which goes into liquidation because it is insolvent imposes costs on its shareholders—or impairs their wealth. If the value of a company reflects the fair value of its assets and liabilities, and in a liquidation the assets of the company could be sold at fair value, then the shareholders of a company would not suffer a wealth loss if a company went into liquidation. However, in an insolvency, there is typically an urgency in shutting down a business which is losing money. Consequently, the assets of a business may be sold quickly at significant discounts. Hence, a company which has sound working capital policy will avoid insolvency and preserve the wealth of its shareholders. For these reasons, sound working capital policy is an important consideration for shareholders as well as the directors of a company.

CONCEPT CHECK

1. What is working capital?
2. Why is working capital important?

For the answers, go to MyFinanceLab

CONCEPT 14.2   How is net working capital calculated?

Table 14.1 lists the current assets and current liabilities of a well-known building materials manufacturer in Australia—Boral Limited.

The current assets and current liabilities of Boral Limited are typical for an industrial company. The current assets of a corporation are typically cash and cash equivalents, accounts receivables and inventories. While cash is straightforward, the cash equivalents may require some explanation. Cash equivalents are anything which can be converted into cash quite rapidly. The notes to the accounts of Boral Limited reveal that their cash and cash equivalents are made up of cash at bank (most likely in an account where it can be obtained at call) and fixed-term deposits.

| Table 14.1 | Working capital of Boral Limited |

Boral balance sheet extract as at 30 June

	ALL FIGURES IN $ MILLION				
	2006	2007	2008	2009	2010
Current assets					
Cash and cash equivalents	76.2	35.7	47.4	100.5	157
Receivables	759.7	799.9	881.7	776.9	783.7
Inventories	528.5	584.0	600.1	632.6	548.5
Other	36.4	31.4	41.6	67.0	63.3
Assets classified as held for sale					59.5
Total current assets	1400.8	1451.0	1570.8	1577	1612.0
Current liabilities					
Payables	608.8	619.3	686.4	608.9	640.9
Interest-bearing loans and borrowings	1.0	25.6	47.2	6.7	8.9
Current tax liabilities	63.5	81.3	96.9	28.5	98.9
Provisions	189.9	195.6	194.8	200.2	246.0
Liabilities classified as held for sale					9.9
Total current liabilities	863.2	921.8	1025.3	844.3	1004.6
Net working capital	537.6	529.2	545.5	732.7	607.4

Source: Boral Limited 2006–2010 Annual Reports.

Other important current assets are marketable securities such as bank-accepted bills, which will be discussed later in this chapter.

The choice between holding cash and cash equivalents or securities is an important decision made by management. The next section discusses the important considerations in deciding on an optimum cash balance.

The notes to the accounts of Boral Limited reveal that most of the accounts receivables are trade receivables. When goods are sold by one company to another, the company does not always require immediate payment for those goods but supplies a bill which must be paid by a certain period. These unpaid bills are known as trade receivables or trade credit. This chapter also discusses the management of trade receivables, specifically how a company can determine if another company is a good or bad credit risk and therefore whether credit should or should not be granted.

Another important component of current assets includes inventories. The notes to the accounts of Boral Limited reveal that the inventories are comprised of raw materials, work in progress and finished goods. Raw materials are materials used by the company in making its goods and services which are yet to be utilised. Work in progress are goods currently being produced but which are partly finished. Finally, finished goods are goods produced and ready for sale, but yet to be sold. In the case of Boral, raw materials include sand and cement used in

FINANCE EXTRA!

ABC Learning sell-off begins

THE receivers for ABC Learning, acting on behalf of banks owed $1 billion following the childcare operator's collapse last year, have formally begun the sale of the 715 viable centres today.

'ABC Learning has been stabilised and its model restructured to place it on a sustainable footing for the future,' said the company's receiver, Chris Honey from McGrathNicol.

'The business is trading well and, notwithstanding the receivership, occupancy is rising steadily, in line with previous years . . . We therefore consider that the time is now right to begin the sale of the business to new owners,' he said.

The receivers have until March 31 to sell the remaining 715 childcare centres or face eviction.

Two of ABC Learning's biggest landlords challenged a court application by the company's administrators this month seeking to extend the second creditors' meeting until late next year. This would allow the receivers more time to sell the remaining centres.

But the receivers have now committed to the March deadline.

'The sale process will not impact the ongoing operation of the centres in any way. Our focus during the sale process will remain firmly on ensuring there is continued, stable provision of high quality childcare for ABC children and their families; and ultimately a smooth transition to the new owners,' Mr Honey said.

During the court proceedings this month, a barrister for the receiver, Fabian Gleeson, told the court Mr Honey had undertaken a 'market testing process designed to solicit expressions of interest from potential bidders'. He noted that UBS had been 'assisting' in the initial sales process but had yet to be formally engaged.

However, the centres are expected to sell for less than $1 billion, and even the banks are not expected to get their money back.

Source: Colin Kruger and Vanda Carson, *The Sydney Morning Herald*, 31 August 2009. © Fairfax Media Publications Pty Limited.

making bricks, roof tiles and pavers, etc. Work in progress include bricks, pavers and tiles which are drying and solidifying. Inventories are typically recorded in the financial statements at the cost incurred in producing or acquiring them.

The current liabilities of Boral Limited are also typical. The most significant current liabilities are accounts payable, interest-bearing loans and other borrowings, tax liabilities and provisions. The notes to the financial statements of Boral Limited reveals that the accounts payable are trade creditors. That is, amounts owing to other firms who have provided it with goods and services on credit. Another important current liability is interest-bearing loans. In the case of Boral Limited, the notes to the accounts reveal that this is primarily bank loans. However, it can also be commercial paper such as bank-accepted bills, or the other forms of short-term debt which will also be discussed later in this chapter.

CONCEPT CHECK

3. How do you calculate working capital?

4. What are the most important components of working capital for normal Australian industrial companies?

For the answers, go to MyFinanceLab

CONCEPT 14.3   The optimum cash balance of a company

One of the important decisions that needs to be made by the management of a company is how much cash to keep in its bank accounts to fund its expenses. Having sufficient cash is important for solvency. But cash balances held in cheque accounts typically earn interest close to 0%. The company could alternatively hold some kind of fixed income security, for example, short-term Treasury notes, and earn 5–6% interest. Hence, there is an opportunity cost to holding cash in cheque accounts. So what is the optimum cash balance that should be held by a company?

Baumol model

In a now famous paper, Professor William Baumol from Princeton University derived an equation that can be used to determine the optimum cash balance that should be kept by a company.[1] His model and the rationale underlying the model is as follows. Consider a company that has to pay total bills worth T dollars over a year, and which are spread evenly throughout the year. Also, imagine the company holds a fixed income security which earns interest of i%. Every time the company wants to raise cash, it must liquidate a part of the fixed income security, say C. Assume the company does so at equal time intervals during the year. Every time a part of the fixed income security needs to be liquidated, the company pays transaction costs of b dollars, for example a fee to a fixed income broker.

The total cost of liquidating the fixed income security repeatedly during the year is made up of two parts. First, when the company liquidates the fixed income security, it misses out on the interest that it was earning on the fixed income security for part of the year. If the amount withdrawn is C dollars, and the company allows the cash to deplete to 0 before making another similar draw on its fixed income security, then the average cash balance during the year is $\frac{C}{2}$, and hence the amount of interest lost on the cash is $i\frac{C}{2}$. For example, if the company has $1000 in fixed income securities, and it liquidates 2 lots of $50 to pay off $100 in bills spread evenly throughout the year, then the average cash balance is $25. If this average had remained invested in the fixed income securities earning 5% interest, then it is clear that the company has missed out on $1.25 (i.e. $25 × 0.05) in interest.

The second cost associated with repeatedly liquidating the fixed income security is the brokerage fee. If the company has to pay T dollars of bills over the year, and withdraws C dollars at a time, then it must make $\frac{T}{C}$ withdrawals during the year. For example, if the company has $100 in bills to pay and withdraws $25 at a time, it must make four withdrawals—one every quarter. Every time the company makes a withdrawal, it incurs b dollars in transaction costs. Hence, its total costs incurred will be $b\frac{T}{C}$.

Hence the total costs (TC) associated with liquidating part of the fixed income investment and converting it into cash are made up of the lost interest on the fixed income security and the transaction costs associated with selling fixed income securities as follows:

$$TC = i\frac{C}{2} + b\frac{T}{C} \qquad \text{(14.1)}$$

The objective of the company is to choose the portion of its fixed income investments to liquidate so as to minimise its total costs over the year. This can be found by finding C which minimises TC (i.e. C^*), which is as follows:[2]

$$C^* = \sqrt{\frac{2bT}{i}} \qquad \text{(14.2)}$$

Where C is the amount which the company withdraws every time its cash is depleted, b is the transaction cost in dollars incurred from liquidating C dollars worth of its fixed income investments, T are the total cash payments to be made by the company over the year and i is the interest rate earned by the company on its fixed income investment (the opportunity cost of holding cash).

EXAMPLE 14.1

Cash management using the Baumol model

A small company is expecting to make $500 000 in payments next year. It holds most of its cash in Treasury notes which yield 6% interest. Transaction costs associated with liquidating Treasury notes are $150 for each trade.

1. What is the optimum amount of its fixed income investment that the company should liquidate periodically?
2. How often will the company liquidate its fixed income investment?
3. What will be the cash balance of the company?

ANSWER

1. Using Equation 14.2:

$$C^* = \sqrt{\frac{2 \times 150 \times 500\,000}{0.06}}$$

$$C^* = 50\,000$$

Therefore, the company should liquidate $50 000 and soon let the balance run down to 0, and then liquidate another $50 000, and so on

2. The company needs to liquidate its Treasury notes 10 times during the year (500 000/50 000) and hence needs to make a trade every 1.2 months.

3. The cash balance carried by the company is $25 000 (50 000/2)

The Miller-Orr model

Professor Merton Miller from the University of Chicago together with Professor Daniel Orr from the University of California wrote a now famous paper in 1966 in which they built on the work of Baumol.[3] Rather than assuming that the cash flow of a firm runs down evenly every day until it hits a point after which the cash is replenished, they assume that the cash flows of a firm fluctuate randomly from one day to the next. They again examine the situation where the firm holds a cash balance which earns no interest or, alternatively, the firm holds fixed income securities which earn interest. They seek to determine the optimum cash balance of the firm.

The Miller and Orr model implies that a corporation should set an upper limit to the cash balance (say h). When the cash balance of the corporation hits the upper limit, the firm buys fixed income securities. In doing so, it incurs transaction costs but earns interest on the cash converted into a fixed income security. In contrast, when the cash balance of the firm hits 0, then the firm liquidates fixed income securities. In doing so, it incurs transaction costs, loses interest on the securities converted to cash but importantly has cash to pay its debts as and when they fall due.

Their paper determines the optimum upper limit to the cash balance (h^*) which minimises (1) the opportunity cost of holding cash (which is given by the interest rate on the fixed income security, say $i\%$ per annum), and (2) the need to frequently convert cash to securities or securities to cash which incur transaction costs of b dollars. They derive the following expression for the optimum upper cash balance:

$$h^* = 3\,z^* \tag{14.3}$$

In turn, z^* which is the return point for the cash balance (that is, the balance that should be restored by selling fixed income securities if the cash depletes to zero or the cash balance that should be restored by buying fixed income securities if the cash balance rises above h^*), is given by the following equation:

$$z^* = \left(\frac{3}{4} \times \frac{b\sigma^2}{i/365}\right)^{\frac{1}{3}}$$

Substituting z^* into (14.3) gives the following equation for the optimum upper cash balance:

$$h^* = 3\left(\frac{3}{4} \times \frac{b\sigma^2}{i/365}\right)^{\frac{1}{3}}$$ **(14.4)**

While the mathematics underlying the derivation of Equations 14.3 and 14.4 is beyond the scope of this book, the intuition underlying the equations is straightforward. An inspection of Equation 14.4 reveals that the higher is the variance of cash flows (σ^2) or cost per trade in fixed income securities (b), the greater will be the upper limit. The reason for this is straightforward. The higher the variance of cash flows, the more often the upper limit and 0 will be hit and the greater the transaction costs incurred in trading fixed income securities. Hence, the optimum upper limit needs to be higher to minimise this cost. An inspection of Equation 14.4 also confirms that the greater the cost of trading fixed income securities per trade, the greater the total transaction costs that will be incurred by the firm. By setting a greater upper limit in the face of high price volatility and transaction costs, the lower will be the total transaction costs paid by the firm. On the other hand, Equation 14.4 implies that the upper limit decreases with i. The reason for this is that the cost of holding idle cash balances becomes more expensive as i increases; hence, requiring cash to be converted to fixed income securities more often results in a lower opportunity cost. Hence, overall, the Miller and Orr model attempts to balance transaction costs from trading fixed income securities with the opportunity cost of holding idle cash. Example 14.2 illustrates the mechanics of applying the Miller and Orr model.

EXAMPLE 14.2

Cash management using the Miller and Orr model

QUESTION

A small company is expecting to make $500 000 in payments next year. It holds most of its cash in Treasury notes which yield 6% interest. Transaction costs associated with liquidating or buying Treasury notes are $150. The company has a standard deviation of daily cash balances of $250. What is the optimum cash balance (the return point for cash) and the optimum upper limit to the cash balance?

ANSWER

The optimum cash balance is as follows:

$$z^* = \left(\frac{3}{4} \times \left(\frac{b\sigma^2}{i/365}\right)\right)^{1/3}$$

$$z^* = \left(\frac{3}{4} \times \frac{150 \times 250^2}{0.06/365}\right)^{1/3}$$

$$z^* = 3\,497$$

The upper limit to the cash balance is as follows:

$h^* = 3 z^*$

$h^* = 3 \times 3497 = 10\,491$

Therefore, if the cash balance of a company (1) deteriorates to 0 or (2) increases above $10 491 then the company should sell or buy, respectively, fixed income securities to restore the cash balance to $3497.

CONCEPT CHECK

5. What are the costs of holding too much cash?
6. What are the costs associated with holding too little cash?
7. What is the economic rationale of the Baumol model?
8. What is the economic rationale underlying the Miller-Orr model?

For the answers, go to MyFinanceLab

CONCEPT 14.4   Cash management policy in large corporations

A final word on cash management policies. While the models discussed in the previous sections are widely discussed in classrooms around the world, they are not designed as definitive solutions to the cash management problems of a company—nor were they intended for that purpose. They are designed to clearly expose the important considerations involved in determining optimum corporate cash levels including the tradeoff between the opportunity cost of holding cash and the costs associated with holding insufficient cash (i.e. transaction costs from liquidating marketable securities to raise cash). The practical realities of cash management can be far more complex.

Consider Table 14.2, which lists the year end cash balances of the largest non-bank companies listed on the ASX in 2010. Banks are excluded because cash is actually inventory for banks, and hence their cash management strategy is complex. The table highlights that large companies hold significant amounts of cash relative to their total assets. Such cash holdings cannot be explained by models which balance the opportunity cost of holding cash against the small cost of converting marketable securities into cash. For example, the opportunity cost of holding $1 billion in cash implied by the bank-accepted bill rate on 1 August 2011 of 5% is $50 million per annum or more than $136 000 per day! This is likely to dramatically exceed the costs of liquidating any marketable securities to meet cash needs. Consequently, the models reviewed in the previous section would all conclude that such companies should hold trivial amounts of cash because the opportunity cost is so great relative to the cost of liquidating securities such as Treasury notes. So why then do large companies hold cash in such huge quantities?

Table 14.2		Cash balances of the largest companies listed on the Australian Securities Exchange for 2010		
		Cash or cash equivalents	Total assets	Total assets held as cash %
	Stock	**($M)**	**($M)**	
1	BHP Billiton	BHP	12 456	88 852	14.0%
2	News +	NWS	8 709	54 384	16.0%
3	Rio Tinto	RIO	9 948	112 402	8.9%
4	Telstra	TLS	1 936	39 282	4.9%
5	Wesfarmers	WES	1 640	39 236	4.2%
6	Woolworths	WOW	713	18 487	3.9%

+ in USD

Source: 2010 Annual Reports of BHP Billiton, News, Rio Tinto, Telstra, Wesfarmers, Woolworths.

The likely reason is that these companies have decentralised operations and are likely to have hundreds of bank accounts across different businesses they operate. Hence, a company with 100 bank accounts across different businesses it owns, each with $500 000 in their cash account to meet the business units' cash needs can hold an aggregate of $50 million in cash! That said, the cash management policy for each of the business units will be made taking into account the considerations discussed in the previous section.

CONCEPT CHECK

9. Why do you think industrial companies may not have cash balances that conform to the Baumol or Miller-Orr model?

For the answers, go to MyFinanceLab

CONCEPT 14.5   Forms of short-term debt

Companies can borrow money through issuing short-term debt securities or borrowing from banks. This section discusses types of short-term debt finance, building on the discussion from Chapter 12 on long-term debt finance instruments. The focus is on securities known as commercial bills, bank-accepted bills and promissory notes. While these securities form part of short-term debt or current liabilities, a corporation can also invest surplus cash in these securities, in which case they become current assets!

Commercial bill
An unconditional order in writing requiring the party to whom it is addressed to pay a certain sum on a fixed date in the future. Commercial bills are negotiable between 90 and 180 days and sold at a discount to face value.

Commercial bills

Commercial bills are debt securities, typically facilitated by banks, that allow companies to borrow cash for periods of between 90 and 180 days. A commercial bill generally involves three parties: (1) a drawer, (2) an acceptor, and (3) a discounter.

The **drawer** represents the company borrowing the cash and is the seller of the bill. On the day the bill is created, drawers receive cash from a discounter or purchaser of the bill. They undertake to repay an amount of cash equal to the face value of the bill on its maturity date.

The **acceptor** is the financial institution facilitating the entire transaction. On the maturity date of the bill, the acceptor takes cash from the borrower and passes it on to the owner of the bill at that time. The acceptor guarantees payment by taking responsibility for payment. In the event of default by the borrower, the acceptor must bear the cost of paying the owner of the bill. If the acceptor is a bank (typically ANZ, Commonwealth, NAB or Westpac), the commercial bill is called a **bank-accepted bill** or bank bill. The credit risk attached to these securities is that of the big banks and, hence, the security is virtually risk free. Of course, banks charge a fee for acting as acceptors, part of which covers them for the default risk associated with the drawer.

The **discounter** is usually another company that is lending or investing cash. A discounter initially provides cash to the drawer (i.e. borrower) under the bill arrangement by purchasing the bill. Discounters are entitled to a single lump sum repayment equal to the face value of the bill on the maturity date. It is important to note that the discounter can sell its right to this cash flow (the face value) and, hence, commercial bills are marketable securities. Anyone purchasing the bill is not concerned with the identity of the drawer, or the risk that the drawer will default because such bills are *accepted* by banks. For this reason, the yield on bank-accepted bills has a negligible risk-premium built into it. The standardised nature of the risk associated with all bank bills means that one bank bill is as good as any other and this makes bank bills very marketable.

Discounters are so named because they pay an amount equal to the discounted face value of the bill when it is created. The discounted face value of the bill is calculated using the following equation:

$$P = \frac{F}{1 + (i \times t/365)} \tag{14.5}$$

where:

> P = the value of the bill
>
> F = the face value of the bill
>
> i = the yield on the bill
>
> t = the time to maturity of the bill (in days)

Figure 14.1 depicts the creation of a bank bill and the flow of cash from the lender (the discounter) to the borrower (the drawer) when the bill is drawn down and sold. The acceptor is presented with the bill and owns a right to repayment from the drawer on the maturity date, as well as an obligation to pay the discounter.

Figure 14.2 describes what happens on the maturity date. The drawer pays the acceptor the face value of the bill and the acceptor pays the current owner of the bill the same amount.

Drawer
The party who issues a bill of exchange to raise money (the borrower). The drawer undertakes to repay the face value of the bill on its maturity date.

Acceptor
The party to whom a bill of exchange is addressed, and who assumes primary liability to pay on maturity the face value of the bill to its holder. Normally, the acceptor is a well-known bank which acts to increase the creditworthiness of the bill.

Bank-accepted bill
A bill of exchange of which the acceptor is a bank. See also *commercial* bill.

Discounter
The party who purchases the bill of exchange, usually at a discount to face value, and is lending the money to the issuer/ drawer.

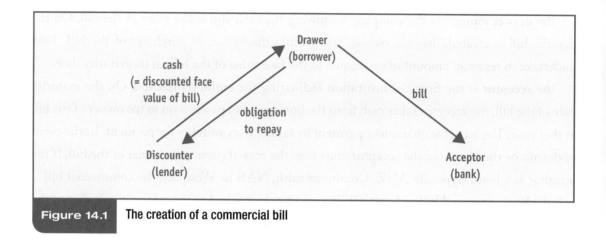

Figure 14.1   The creation of a commercial bill

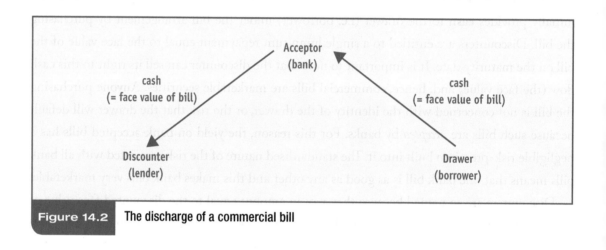

Figure 14.2   The discharge of a commercial bill

Promissory notes

Promissory note

A note issued by a debtor promising to pay a certain amount at some specified time in the future.
They are short term in nature, usually less than 180 days.

Promissory notes are debt securities that are issued by companies and that allow them to borrow cash for periods typically between 30 and 180 days. They each represent a written promise to pay a specified amount of cash (the face value) to the bearer on an agreed future date. They are unsecured. This means that, while the promise to repay cash has the force of law, a company does not pledge any of its assets in return for the promise to pay the face value. Promissory notes are otherwise known as commercial paper or one-name paper. Promissory notes are zero-coupon securities and are issued at a discount to face value. They are almost identical to commercial bills, except that there is no acceptor involved in their issue. For this reason, they are typically issued only by very large, well-known companies.

Practitioner's POV

The most famous credit ratings agencies in the world are Standard & Poor's (S&P) and Moody's. The highest credit rating awarded by the ratings agencies is Aaa in the case of Moody's and AAA in the case of S&P, while the lowest is C. Ratings agencies have come under considerable criticism following the global financial crisis, for rating securities Aaa and AAA which ex-post turned out to be 'junk' (i.e. turned out to have very poor credit worthiness).

CONCEPT 14.6   Credit management and credit analysis

When a firm sells its products, it can potentially extend credit to its customers. If the credit is granted to other firms, it's called trade credit, whereas credit granted to end consumers is called consumer credit. When credit is granted, the company recognises this by raising an accounts receivable in its balance sheet. The terms of sale include (1) the terms under which credit is granted, including whether credit will be granted at all (or whether the firm requires cash on delivery) and the credit period (how many days before an invoice for sale is paid), and (2) discounts, for example, for early payment. An important determinant of whether credit will be granted is an assessment of the credit risk of the firm or consumer purchasing the good. This is an attempt to determine whether its customers will or will not pay an invoice, or their credit worthiness.

There are a number of different ways that a corporation can determine the credit worthiness of its customers. For example, there are firms that specialise in determining the credit worthiness of firms and sell this information. One of the best known firms of this kind is Dun and Bradstreet, which provides subscribers with credit reports on firms right around the world. Banks may also be able to provide information on credit worthiness to its business customers. The bank can verify information provided to their client by customer firms seeking credit (with permission from the customer of course!).

In one of the most famous papers published in finance, Professor Ed Altman from New York University developed a model which can be used to estimate a customer's credit risk by providing a score indicating the probability of insolvency. This is known as Altman's Z-score.[4] Variations of Professor Altman's model are now widely used by banks and credit ratings firms to determine the credit worthiness of firms. Professor Ed Altman used a statistical tool known as multiple-discriminant analysis to determine which financial (accounting) ratios of companies in the USA predicts those that will later file for bankruptcy (i.e. 'fail'). He examined 66 companies in his study, 33 of which filed for bankruptcy, and a group of 33 in the same industry and of similar size which did not file for bankruptcy. He then used multiple-discriminant analysis to determine whether the financial ratios constructed from the annual reports of those firms could be used to predict which would file for bankruptcy and which would not.

He estimated a number of different models with different variables and found that the following model did the best job of predicting which firms would fail:

$$Z = 1.2X1 + 1.4X2 + 3.3X3 + 0.6X4 + 1.0X5$$

where:

$X1$ = working capital/total assets

$X2$ = retained earnings/total assets

$X3$ = earnings before interest and taxes/total assets

$X4$ = market value equity/book value of total liabilities

$X5$ = sales/total assets

and where Z is a score which predicts the probability of bankruptcy.

He found that this model could correctly classify firms as non-failing or failing with more than 95% accuracy. He also found that the model works best in predicting failure within two years. For example, if you take the financial statements for firms this year, the model can be used to successfully predict which firms will fail in the next two years, but not beyond. Finally, he found that a Z-score of 2.675 did the best job of discriminating between bankrupt and non-bankrupt firms, in that it minimised errors in classifying firms (i.e. did not classify firms as unlikely to fail when they later did fail, and classify firms as likely to fail when in fact they did not later fail).

The specific model above produced by Professor Altman may not be relevant in Australia today because of different accounting standards, legal conditions and operating environment for firms. Consequently, there have been a number of studies which have examined the ability of an approach like Professor Altman's to predict firms which would become insolvent in Australia. Such a paper was published in 2006 by Mark Uebergang, a director of the Australian firm Korda Mentha: a firm famous for liquidating failed Australian companies. He concludes, 'Our research supports the use of Altman's Z-score as a means of detecting financial distress in Australia, albeit the level of accuracy was well below that observed by Altman in his original study' [p. 11].[5]

As an example of the mechanics of applying Altman's model, consider Example 14.3 below.

EXAMPLE 14.3

Calculation of Altman's Z-score for an Australian company

QUESTION

On 31 January 2005, Henry Walker Eltin Group Limited announced that it had been placed into voluntary liquidation. This means that its directors assessed that it could not pay its debts as and when they fell due and the company was insolvent. The financial statements of Henry Walker Eltin Group Limited released in September 2003 for the reporting period ending 30 June 2003 were as follows (in $ millions):

Current assets	303.5
Current liabilities	233.8
Total assets	671.3
Retained earnings	33.1
Earnings before interest and taxes	−18.4
Total liabilities	467.6
Revenue	1071.6

Its share price around September of that year when its accounts were released were approximately 88 cents and its issued shares were 164.4 million.

What was the Z-score of Henry Walker Eltin Group Limited in 2003, and on the basis of the Z-score was the corporation likely to fail?

ANSWER

Since:

$X1$ = working capital/total assets = (303.5 − 233.8)/671.3 = 0.10
$X2$ = retained earnings/total assets = 33.1/671.3 = 0.05
$X3$ = earnings before interest and taxes/total assets = -18.4/671.3 = −0.03
$X4$ = market value equity/book value of total liabilities = (164.4 × 0.88)/467.6 = 0.31
$X5$ = sales/total assets = 1071.6/671.3 = 1.60

Therefore:

Since

$$Z = 1.2X1 + 1.4X2 + 3.3X3 + 0.6X4 + 1.0X5$$

Then

$$Z = 1.2 (0.10) + 1.4 (0.05) + 3.3(-0.03) + 0.6(0.31) + 1.0(1.60) = 1.9$$

Therefore Z = 1.9. Since this score is less than 2.675 on the basis of Altman's Z-score you would have (correctly) predicted that the company would fail.

Credit warning models should not be used as a definitive reading on the health of a potential customer. They serve as an indication, and the extent you should rely on them is a function of the costs of getting the decision wrong. The credit granting decision is discussed in the following section.

CONCEPT CHECK

13. What is Altman's Z-score?

14. How can Altman's Z-score be used in credit granting decisions?

15. How is Altman's Z-score calculated?

For the answers, go to MyFinanceLab

CONCEPT 14.7 Optimum credit granting decisions

The decision of when to grant credit has been examined by Professors Bierman and Hausman from Cornell University—the examples and analysis in this section are adapted directly from their original work.[6] Consider the simple one-period credit decision depicted in the probability tree in Figure 14.3. The logic underpinning the tree is as follows. Imagine that you are a company faced with a decision of whether to grant a customer credit, if that customer has just decided to purchase your goods. You carry out some analysis of the type in the previous section, and assess the probability that the customer will pay its debt at 3/5, and hence the probability that the customer will not repay their debt at 2/5. If you do not grant credit, the customer does not purchase your goods and hence your profit is 0—this is depicted in the lowest branch of the probability tree. If you do grant credit, then there are two possible outcomes. First, your customer does not pay their debt and the present value of the goods delivered to them cost $6200—which is your loss on the sale. Alternately, your customer does repay the debt, in which case the profit on

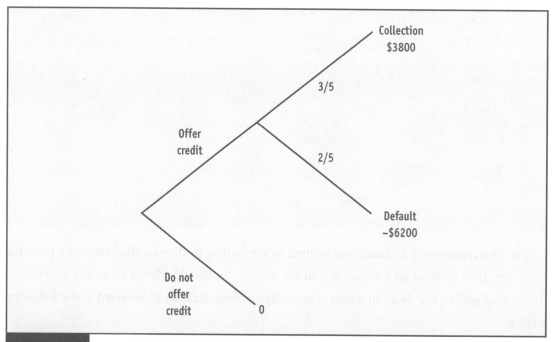

| **Figure 14.3** | Possible outcomes if you grant or do not grant a customer credit |

collection is $3800. The expected profit from granting credit is therefore −$200 [i.e. 3/5 × 3800 +2/5 × −6200]. Because this is less than 0 (the expected profit from not granting credit) then you should refuse credit in this instance.

In the previous example, the optimum decision was to not grant credit. This is the correct decision if repeat business from the same customer is unlikely. However, the purpose of credit is to build a good relationship with a customer so as to induce repeat business from them. Hence, granting credit to a customer this period can lead to another order being placed by your customer in the following period. Furthermore, if the customer does pay their debt in the first period, then the chances of them repaying their debt in the second period is likely to be higher. Let's extend the previous example to examine the possible outcomes in the second period. This is depicted in Figure 14.4.

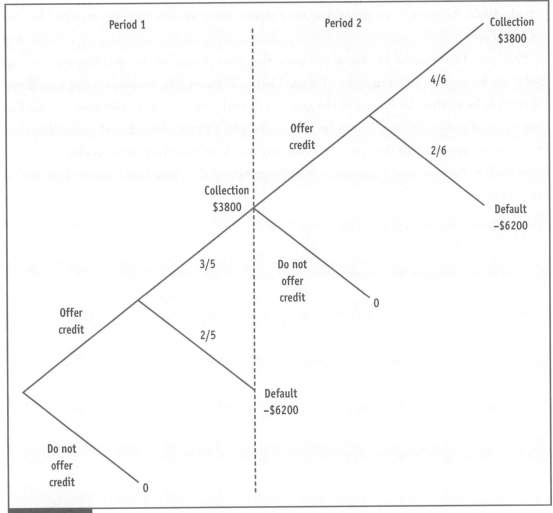

Figure 14.4   Possible outcomes if you grant or do not grant a customer credit where repeat business is possible

Figure 14.4 provides a probability tree that illustrates the possible outcomes in the second period. They are virtually identical to the first, however the probabilities have changed. If the customer did in fact pay in the first period, then let's assume that the probability that they will pay in the second period increases to 4/6. Examining purely the second period, the expected profit in the second period is $467 [4/6 × $3800 + 2/6 × −$6200]. Hence the (repeat) trade in the second period is very profitable. To assess whether credit should be granted in the first period, an assessment of the total expected profit over both periods from granting credit is required. This is equal to the expected profit in the first period (−$200) plus the product of (1) the probability that the customer pays at the end of the first period so that there is a repeat order (3/5), and (2) the expected profit in the second period (i.e. $467). Hence, the overall expected profit from granting credit in the first round is in fact $80 [−200 + 3/5 × $467]. This implies that, with the possibility of repeat business in a second period, it is indeed optimum to grant credit in the first period. Hence, the chance that you will secure a repeat customer outweighs the expected loss on the initial order.

Professors Bierman and Hausman recognise that their framework for deciding on granting credit can be improved in a number of ways. First, it is reasonable to discount the cash flows expected to be received at the end of the first and second periods so as to take into account the time value of money. Second, it may be wise to include a further branch and probability that the customer, even though they pay their bill, may decide to take their business elsewhere. The framework of Bierman and Hausman can easily be extended to take into account these useful extensions.

CONCEPT CHECK

16. What are the consequences and risks from granting credit or not granting credit?
17. What other considerations apart from the implications of granting credit or not for the present sale are important in the credit decision process?

For the answers, go to MyFinanceLab

Student Learning Centre

My FinanceLab ■ To test your mastery of the content covered in this chapter and to create your own personalised study plan, go to MyFinanceLab: www.pearson.com.au/myfinancelab

CONCEPT CHECKLIST

In this chapter the following concepts were discussed:

➤ Working capital and its components
➤ The optimum cash balance that a company should carry
➤ Forms of short-term debt that can be used (or indeed invested-in) by a company
➤ How the credit worthiness of a customer can be assessed
➤ How to make an optimum credit granting decision

SELF-TEST QUESTIONS

1. A company is expecting to make annual cash disbursements of $1.26 million per year. The interest rate on Treasury notes is 8%. The cost of a trade in Treasury notes is $20.
   (a) What is the optimum amount of its Treasury notes that the company should liquidate periodically?
   (b) How often will the company liquidate its Treasury notes?
   (c) What will be the average cash balance of the company?

2. A small company is expecting to make $500 000 in payments next year. It holds most of its cash in Treasury notes which yield 0.025% per day. Transaction costs associated with liquidating or buying Treasury notes are $20. The company has a standard deviation of daily cash balances of $2500. What is the optimum upper limit to the cash balance?

3. One of your customers is a slow payer, and there is only an 83.3% chance that they will pay their bill. The profit on an item sold is $200 and the cost of the item sold is $1000. Should you grant seven days of credit? Assume the opportunity cost is negligible.

Self-test answers

1. (a) Using Equation 14.2:

$$C^* = \sqrt{2 \times 20 \times \frac{1\,260\,000}{0.08}}$$

$$C^* \doteq 25\,099$$

Therefore, the company should liquidate $25 099 in Treasury notes periodically, letting the balance run down to 0.

   (a) The company needs to liquidate its Treasury notes approximately 50 times during the year (1 260 000/25 099) and hence needs to make a withdrawal approximately four times a month.

   (b) The cash balance carried by the company is $12 550 (25 099/2)

2. The optimum cash balance is as follows:

$$h^* = 3\left(\frac{3}{4} \times \frac{20 \times 2500^2}{0.00025}\right)^{\frac{1}{3}} = 7211$$

$$h^* = 3 \times 7211 = 21\,633$$

Therefore, if the cash balance of a company (1) deteriorates to 0 or (2) increases above \$21 633 then the company should sell or buy, respectively, fixed income securities.

3. The expected profit from the sale if p is the probability that they will pay their bill, *profit* is the profit from selling the item, and *cost* is the cost of the item, is as follows:

$$= p \times profit - (1 - p) \times cost$$

$$= 0.833 \times 200 - (1 - 0.833) \times - 1000$$

$$= 0$$

Therefore this is a break-even transaction. You should be indifferent to granting credit and making the sale, or letting the customer walk away and losing the sale.

DISCUSSION QUESTIONS

1. What is working capital? Why is working capital important?
2. What are the most important components of current assets and current liabilities for industrial companies? How would the components of current assets and liabilities differ for service companies?
3. What is cash and cash equivalents? What are the advantages and disadvantages of holding cash?
4. What is the economic argument that underpins the Baumol model of cash balances? How does the Miller and Orr model of cash balances differ?
5. Why do the cash balances of large companies differ markedly from those implied by the Baumol or Miller and Orr models?
6. A company wants to raise \$100 million by issuing short-term debt over the next 12 months. Discuss the different methods available to the company for raising debt finance. Be sure to identify the possible risks and costs.
7. What are the advantages of bank-accepted bills over commercial bills?
8. Discuss Altman's Z-score and what it can be used for. What are the limitations of the Z-score?

PRACTICAL QUESTIONS

BASIC

1. A big company is expecting to make \$10 million in payments next year. It holds most of its cash in bank-accepted bills which yield 5% interest. Transaction costs associated with liquidating bank-accepted bills are \$40 for each trade.
   (a) What is the optimum amount of its fixed income investment that the company should liquidate periodically?
   (b) How often will the company liquidate its fixed income investment?
   (c) What will be the cash balance of the company?

BASIC

2. A small company is expecting to make \$1 million in payments next year. It holds most of its cash in Treasury notes which yield 5% interest. Transaction costs associated with liquidating or buying

Treasury notes are $150. The company has a standard deviation of daily cash balances of $1000. What is the optimum cash balance (the return point for cash) and the optimum upper limit to the cash balance?

3. This question requires you to think a little laterally about one of the models in the chapter. A shoe store is expecting to sell 1000 pairs of shoes a year at $200 each. The cost of carrying a pair of shoes for 1 year in stock is $25. The fixed cost of placing an order for shoes from the manufacturer (irrespective of the size of the order) is approximately $20. What is the optimum average inventory that the shoe company should carry? What is the optimum order size? What is the assumption underlying the model you use in your calculations?

INTERMEDIATE

4. A small company is expecting to make $1 million in payments next year. It earns interest on cash at the overnight rate of 5%, or alternatively could invest its money in bank-accepted bills which yield 6% interest. Transaction costs associated with liquidating bank-accepted bills are $25 for each trade.

INTERMEDIATE

   (a) What is the optimum amount of its fixed income investment that the company should liquidate periodically?
   (b) How often will the company liquidate its fixed income investment?
   (c) What will be the cash balance of the company?

5. The financial statements of a company are as follows (in $ millions):

INTERMEDIATE

Current assets	400
Current liabilities	300
Total assets	800
Retained earnings	40
Earnings before interest and taxes	-20
Total liabilities	500
Revenue	1000

Its share price is approximately $1 and its issued shares are 200. What is the Z-score of the company and should the company be extended credit?

6. The probability that a customer will repay their debts is 50%. The customer wants one year of credit to purchase your goods, worth $2000 and your cost of capital is 8%. The cost of the goods sold is $700. Should you grant credit?

INTERMEDIATE

7. You run a car dealership. The probability that a customer will repay its debts are 66%. The customer wants one year of credit to purchase a car worth $30 000 and the cost of capital is 8%. The cost of the car to your business is $20 000. If you grant credit, the chance of the customer returning for a repeat sale in one year is 90%. Should you grant credit?

INTERMEDIATE

8. C is the amount which a company withdraws every time its cash is depleted, b is the cost of liquidating fixed income securities, T is the total cash payments to be made by a company over a year, and I is the interest earned on the fixed income security. Assume that $c = a + bC$ — that is, that the cost of liquidating fixed income securities is a linear function of the amount of securities liquidated (it is normal for the cost to increase at a decreasing rate). Derive an expression for the optimum cash balance of a company, and the amount of securities the company should liquidate periodically.

CHALLENGING

FURTHER READING

- Baumol, W. J., (1952), 'The transaction demand for cash: An inventory theoretic approach', *Quarterly Journal of Economics*, pp. 545–56.
- Miller, M. and D. Orr, (1966), 'A model of the demand for money by firms', *Quarterly Journal of Economics*, pp. 413–35.
- Altman, E. (1968), 'Financial ratios, discriminant analysis and the prediction of corporate bankruptcy', *Journal of Finance*, pp. 589–609.
- Uebergang, M. (2006) 'Predicting corporate failure', *JASSA*, Issue 4, Summer pp. 10–11.
- Bierman, H. and Hausman, W. H. (1970) 'The credit granting decision', *Management Science*, 16, pp. B519–B532.

NOTES

1. Baumol, W. J., (1952), 'The transaction demand for cash: An inventory theoretic approach', *Quarterly Journal of Economics*, pp. 545–56.
2. Equation 14.2 can be derived by differentiating Equation 14.1 with respect to C, setting the resulting expression to 0, and then solving for (the optimum) C.
3. Miller, M. and D. Orr, (1966), 'A model of the demand for money by firms', *Quarterly Journal of Economics*, pp. 413–35.
4. Altman, E. (1968), 'Financial ratios, discriminant analysis and the prediction of corporate bankruptcy', *Journal of Finance*, pp. 589–609.
5. Uebergang, M. (2006) 'Predicting corporate failure', *JASSA*, Issue 4, Summer pp. 10–11.
6. Bierman, H. and Hausman, W. H. (1970) 'The credit granting decision', *Management Science*, 16, pp. B519–B532.

Glossary

Abnormal return Excess of actual return over the expected return predicted by an asset pricing model.

Acceptor The party to whom a bill of exchange is addressed, and who assumes primary liability to pay on maturity the face value of the bill to its holder. Normally, the acceptor is a well-known bank which acts to increase the creditworthiness of the bill.

Accounting rate of return (ARR) A measure of profitability calculated by dividing the average annual net profit from an asset by the average amount invested in the asset.

Accumulation index Takes into account both capital appreciation and dividend income when measuring the market return.

Agency trading A trade which a broker executes on behalf of a client.

All Ordinaries Index An index of approximately 500 of the largest Australian companies. The companies are weighted in the index according to their size in terms of market capitalisation.

Allowable deductions Expenses that are incurred in gaining assessable income.

American option A call or put option that can be exercised on any date up to and including the expiration date.

Annuity due An annuity in which the first cash flow is to occur immediately—that is, on the valuation date.

ASIC The Australian Securities and Investments Commission enforces the company and financial services law. It regulates Australian companies, financial markets, financial services organisations and professionals who deal and advise in investments, superannuation, insurance, deposit taking and credit.

Assessable income Income according to ordinary concepts, such as salary and wages, rent dividends, interest and annuities.

ASX Australian Securities Exchange Limited.

Bank-accepted bill A bill of exchange (commercial bill) of which the acceptor is a bank. See also *commercial bill.*

Bid–ask spread The difference between the best selling price and the best buying price.

Call option A contract that gives the owner the right to buy a given asset (underlying asset) at a certain price (exercise price) up to or on a certain date (expiration date).

Capital asset pricing model (CAPM) A model for determining the risk premium on a security. The CAPM implies that the risk premium is a linear function of the market risk of a security. Also known as the Sharpe Lintner and Black model after the researchers who developed the model.

Capital market The medium for the issue and exchange of assets.

Capital market line (CML) The efficient portfolio in the presence of risky securities and a risk-free security. On a risk–return chart, it is represented by the line that goes through the coordinates representing the risk-free rate and the market portfolio.

Capital structure The amount of debt relative to equity used by a company.

Clearing House Electronic Subregister System (CHESS) Provides an electronic record of transfers of share ownership.

Commercial bill An unconditional order in writing requiring the party to whom it is addressed to pay a certain sum on a fixed date in the future. Commercial bills are negotiable between 90 and 180 days and sold at a discount to face value.

Company cost of capital The return required by the providers of capital. See also *weighted average cost of capital (WACC).*

Correlation coefficient A coefficient whose value lies between +1 and −1 which indicates the direction and strength of the relationship between two variables.

Counterparty The party taking the other side of a trade. For example, if the client is a buyer, the counterparty is a seller.

Coupon rate The interest paid on bonds as a percentage of the face value of the bonds.

Cum-dividend 'Cum' means 'with'. When a share trades cum-dividend, it means that the dividend entitlements are attached to the share.

Daily returns The return on a security measured over a trading day.

Debenture Any unsecured long-term debt.

Debt A security which typically (a) pays a contractually fixed rate of return (interest); (b) has a finite life; and (c) in the event of default on payment of interest, the owners have first call on the assets of the issuer.

Decision tree A diagram that illustrates the different possible outcomes that may result from a particular situation or decision.

Deferred annuity Annuity where the cash flows are deferred for one or more periods. That is, the first cash flow is to occur after a time period that exceeds the time period between each subsequent cash flow.

Derivative contract A contract whose value is based on the price of an underlying asset, including options, forwards and futures.

Discounter The party who purchases the bill of exchange, usually at a discount to face value, and is lending the money to the issuer/drawer.

Dividend policy The decision by companies to pay out net profit after tax or retained earnings to shareholders as dividends.

Dividend reinvestment plan (DRP) A plan that gives shareholders the option of reinvesting their dividends in shares rather than receiving cash.

Drawer The party who issues a bill of exchange to raise money (the borrower). The drawer undertakes to repay the face value of the bill on its maturity date.

Effective interest rate Interest rate that accounts for the true amount of interest that is earned on both reinvested interest and principal earned over a year. It is the interest rate which, compounded annually, is equivalent to a given nominal interest rate.

Efficient frontier The line on a chart mapping risk and return which maps out the efficient portfolios.

Efficient market A market is efficient when prices reflect all available information.

Efficient portfolios A subset of minimum variance portfolios. The set of minimum variance portfolios which maximise return at each level of risk.

Equity A security which typically (a) pays a variable rate of return (dividends); (b) has an indefinite life; and (c) in the event of insolvency of a company, entitles owners to the residual proceeds from sale of the assets of the business after all other creditors have been paid.

Equivalent annual cost Involves converting the net present value of a series of cash flows into an annual cash flow of an annuity that has the same life as the project.

European option A call or put option that can be exercised on the expiration date only.

Exchange-traded Fund (ETF) An open-ended listed investment fund that combines some of the characteristics of shares and managed funds.

Ex-dividend date The day when the dividend detaches from the share.

Exposure clock A chart that illustrates the impact on the cash flows of a company from a change in a risk factor.

Face value The lump sum paid by a bond to its owner at the end of the life of the bond.

Feasible portfolios (opportunity set) All the possible portfolios (which provide different risk and return outcomes) that can be constructed from a given set of securities.

Financing project A project that involves borrowing money from a financial institution like a bank, where the decision rule is to accept the lowest cost of finance.

Foreign exchange risk The risk that expenses and revenues which are contracted in foreign currency will vary in local currency terms when they are eventually paid and converted to local currency.

Forward contract A contract that gives a buyer and seller an obligation to trade a certain asset (underlying asset) at a given price (forward price) on a future date (maturity date). These are traded over the counter and all elements of the contract are negotiable between the parties.

Free cash flows The cash flows available for distribution to the owners of a company. They are equal to the operating cash flows after capital expenditure and taxes.

Future value The value at some point in the future of a present amount of money invested at some interest rate.

Futures contract Identical to a forward contract, except the contract is traded on an organised exchange. All elements of the contract are determined by the exchange except for the futures price, which is set by the parties entering into the contract.

Global minimum variance portfolio The portfolio among the feasible set which provides the lowest level of risk.

Interest rate risk The variability in a bond's value (risk) caused by changing interest rates.

Internal rate of return (IRR) The interest rate that sets the net present value of the cash flows equal to zero.

Internal yield The discount rate that equates the present value of a project's cash inflows with the present value of its cash outflows. The internal yield is also sometimes referred to as the internal rate of return (IRR).

Interpolation Method of solving by trial and error the internal yield of a project.

Intrinsic value The amount that you are willing to pay for an asset, as opposed to its market price.

Investing project A project involving a capital investment where the decision rule is to accept the project with the highest positive net present value.

Limit orders An order which specify the maximum price at which at which a client is willing to buy shares or the minimum price at which a client is willing to receive to sell shares.

Market orders An order where the client is prepared to buy or sell a given volume of shares at the current best market price. For a buy order the client is prepared to buy at the lowest ask price, and for a sell order the client is willing to receive the highest bid price.

Market portfolio A portfolio made up of every single security in the market held in proportion to its market capitalisation relative to the value of the market as a whole.

Market risk premium The extra expected return over the risk-free rate demanded by investors to compensate them for investing in the market portfolio because of the higher-risk assets.

Minimum variance portfolios A subset of feasible portfolios. The set of feasible portfolios which provide minimum risk for each level of return.

Net present value (NPV) The difference between the present value of a project or investment's benefits and the present value of its costs.

Net working capital Consists of all assets needed for a project to run smoothly, minus any current liabilities.

Nominal interest rate Quoted annual interest rate that is adjusted to match the frequency of payments or compounding by taking a proportion of the quoted nominal rate to obtain the actual interest rate per period. It does not take into account that interest is reinvested and that interest is earned on both principal and reinvested interest.

Opportunity cost The return an investment or resource could have provided in its best alternative use.

Ordinary annuity A series of cash flows of equal size which occur regularly with an equal time period between each subsequent cash flow extending into the future, with the first cash flow occurring at the end of the first period.

Perfectly positively (negatively) correlated Two variables with a correlation coefficient of +1 (−1). This implies that an increase in the value of one variable results in a certain increase (decrease) in the value of another variable.

Perpetual annuity An annuity that is expected to continue forever. Also known as a perpetuity.

Placement An issue of new shares to a small group of typically institutional investors, as opposed to a public offering.

Present value The current value of one or more future cash payments, discounted at some appropriate interest rate.

Price–earnings (P/E) ratio The price of a share divided by its earnings per share.

Principal trading A trade which a broker executes on their own behalf.

Privatisation The alteration of the legal and management structure of a government trading body (e.g. a statutory authority) to permit private equity or ownership (as opposed to corporatisation, under which ownership and control remain with the government).

Promissory note A note issued by a debtor promising to pay a certain amount at some specified time in the future. They are short term in nature, usually less than 180 days.

Prospective P/E ratio The price of shares divided by its forecast earnings per share.

Prospectus A legal document required to be lodged with the Australian Securities and Investment Commission (ASIC) providing information on a new security issue when the issue is offered to the public, to provide a record of representations by the issuer to the prospective buyer.

Put option A contract that gives the owner the right to sell a given asset (underlying asset) at a certain price (exercise price) up to or on a certain date (expiration date).

Residual value Disposal value of a project's assets, less any dismantling and removal costs associated with the project's termination.

Reward-to-risk ratio An estimate of the market price of risk. Also known as the ratio of price volatility to excess share returns.

Rights issue An issue of ordinary shares to existing ordinary shareholders, where each shareholder receives the right to an additional number of ordinary shares in a fixed proportion to their current holding.

Risk The extent to which the return of a security is expected to vary from its expected return.

Risk-free rate The rate of return on an asset with zero risk.

Risk premium The return over and above the risk-free rate that a security is expected to generate given its risk.

S&P/ASX 200 Index An index of approximately 200 of the largest Australian companies. The S&P/ASX 200 Index is recognised as the investable benchmark for the Australian equity market.

Scenario analysis Analysis that measures the impact on NPV by changing several variables of the project at the same time and normally includes a base case scenario, a best case scenario and a worst case scenario.

Security market line (SML) The capital asset pricing model (CAPM). Represented by a straight line which plots the expected return on a security against the beta of the security.

Semi-strong-form efficiency Theory that current prices of securities fully reflect all publicly available information.

Sensitivity analysis Analysis that measures the impact on NPV by changing only one variable of the project while holding all other variables constant.

Settlement The process by which payment is made by the buyer to the seller and shares (ownership) are transferred from the seller to the buyer.

Share buy-back Occurs when a company buys back its own shares from its shareholders in return for cash.

Short sale The sale of shares that are not currently owned by the investor. This typically requires that the investor borrows the shares.

Side effect A positive or negative cash flow that relates to other aspects of a company's business as a result of implementing a project.

Simulation analysis (also called Monte Carlo analysis) Analysis that the NPV distribution is simulated by randomly choosing the values of different variables of the projects based on the assumption of mathematical distribution of these variables.

Strong-form efficiency Theory that all available information is fully reflected in prices of securities.

Sunk costs Unavoidable cash flows, or cash flows that have been incurred in the past, which are irrelevant in project evaluation.

Swap A contract that allows two parties to exchange future (uncertain) cash flows. The most common type of swap contract is an interest rate swap in which parties exchange variable interest rate payments for fixed interest rate payments.

Systematic risk (or non-diversifiable risk) The movement in the price of a security which is driven by broad market-related factors. The systematic risk of a security is measured by beta, which measures the relationship between movements in the price of the security and movements in the market as a whole.

Taxable income Assessable income less deductible expenses.

Time value of money The simple concept that a dollar now is worth more than a dollar in the future, even after adjusting for inflation, because a dollar now can earn interest or other appreciation until the time the dollar in the future would be received.

Underwriter An underwriter is a broker or an investment bank that commits to arranging the sale of an issue of securities on behalf of a client and, if it does not sell all the shares to other institutions or investors, itself undertakes to purchase the unsold securities. By using an underwriter, the client is therefore assured of raising the full amount of money it is seeking.

Unsystematic risk (or diversifiable risk) The movement in the price of a security which results from an event specific to the security. Unsystematic risk can be eliminated by combining a security in a large portfolio.

Weak-form efficiency Theory that current prices of securities reflect all information that is contained in the record of past prices.

Weighted average cost of capital (WACC) A weighted average of the returns required by different classes of security holders—used as a required rate for capital investment.

Index

Note: Terms in **bold** have definitions in the margins at the page numbers in **bold**, see for example, **abnormal return 316**. Entries with an *n*, see for example asset price 86*n*1, refer to numbered notes.